Protracted Contest

Protracted Contest

*Sino-Indian Rivalry
in the Twentieth Century*

JOHN W. GARVER

UNIVERSITY OF WASHINGTON PRESS
Seattle and London

This publication was supported in part by the
Donald R. Ellegood International Publications Endowment.

Copyright © 2001 by the University of Washington Press
Printed in the United States of America

Library of Congress Cataloging-in-Publication Data

Garver, John W.
    Protracted contest : Sino-Indian rivalry in the twentieth century / John W. Garver.
        p.   cm.
    Includes index.
    ISBN 0-295-98073-7 (alk. paper)—ISBN 0-295-98074-5 (pbk. : alk. paper)
        1. China—Relations—India.   2. India—Relations—China.
    I. Title: Sino-Indian rivalry in the twentieth century.   II. Title.

DS740.5.15 G37   2001   00-064827
303.48'251054—DC21

The paper used in this publication is acid free and recycled from 10 percent post-consumer
and at least 50 percent pre-consumer waste. It meets the minimum requirements of the
American National Standard for Information Sciences—Permanence of Paper for Printed
Library Materials, ANSI Z39.48-1984. ♾♻

To the memory of my father and mother,
William Lincoln Garver Jr., 1911–1996,
and Lila Rowena Selzer Garver, 1908–1996

and with grateful acknowledgment of the financial support
of the Smith Richardson Foundation, the family-fortune origin of
which came from Vicks Vaporub,® which my mother sometimes
rubbed on my throat when, as a small boy, I had a cold

Contents

List of Illustrations

TABLES

Acknowledgments

This book has been long on the anvil. I began to reflect on the interaction of China and India in 1978 when, as a graduate student returning to the United States after two and a half years of studying the Chinese language and doing dissertation research in Taiwan and Hong Kong, I spent a month crisscrossing India. A profound respect for Indian civilization was therewith joined to an already established respect for that of China. I began to think about how these two energetic and creative peoples had related and would relate in the decades to come. Serious academic work on this problem began in 1986 when I spent a semester as a Georgia Tech exchange faculty member at the Indian Institute of Management (IIM) in Ahmedabad, Gujarat state, India. During that visit I utilized the library at the IIM's School of Public Planning and spent several weeks at libraries, research centers, and embassies in New Delhi, where many people opened doors for me. My 1986 visit also afforded me an opportunity to explore Indian Kashmir.

I continued my academic work in 1990, when fellowships from the Committee on Scholarly Communications with the People's Republic of China (CSCPRC) and from the American Institute of Pakistan Studies permitted me several months of study each in Beijing and Islamabad. People at universities, embassies, and research centers in both capitals generously helped me understand various problems. My 1990 visit to Pakistan took place just after the India-Pakistan nuclear confrontation of that year, a fact that made people rather willing to share their views with me and stimulated my own thinking. During my visit to Islamabad I was also able to explore

Pakistani Kashmir, traveling over the Sino-Pakistan Friendship Highway as far as the Khunjerab Pass. Later the University of Michigan provided a library travel grant, allowing me to utilize that university's magnificent research library.

Stints of several months each in 1993, 1995, and 1997 with Carleton College's China Program in Beijing allowed me further opportunity to talk with people and collect documentary materials. In Beijing people at various research centers were invariably cordial and frequently frank and candid. These visits also afforded an opportunity to travel the "Burma road" and visit the Yunnan-Myanmar border areas. Georgia Institute of Technology was most supportive of my research efforts throughout, adjusting teaching schedules and providing financial support at critical junctures. Special thanks in this regard go to our provost, Michael E. Thomas, who made matching funds available at a crucial point. Most of all, the Smith Richardson Foundation provided generous support, permitting me the full 1998–99 academic year without teaching obligations. The Smith Richardson Foundation also supported research visits to India, Myanmar, and Bangladesh.

In Beijing the Institute of South Asian Studies of Beijing University served as host of my 1990 research visit, during which time I established my initial, invaluable set of contacts. Individual thanks are due to Zhang Minqiu and Han Hua of Beijing University, who helped make my initial research arrangements. Others who helped at various points along the way include Wang Hongwei of the Asia-Pacific Institute of the Chinese Academy of Social Sciences, Yan Xuetong of the Chinese Institute for Contemporary International Relations, Song Xinning of People's University, and Xu Yan, Xia Liping, Ye Zhengjia, Sun Peijun, Lin Liangguang, and Yu Qiyu. Among the many retired and active Chinese diplomats who assisted me were Li Guanghui, Li Lianqing, Cheng Ruisheng, Lin Shanglin, and Zhang Wenjin. Thanks are due especially to Ambassador Yang Gongsu, who shared with me a manuscript on China's diplomacy. Those in the U.S. Embassy in Beijing who shared their time and ideas with me include Colonel Michael T. Byrnes, Lieutenant Colonel John Caldwell, Captain John M. Holmes, Captain John W. Reddinger, David S. Sedney, and Major Larry Wortzel. Indian scholars who shared ideas with me during my 1986 visit to New Delhi include G. D. Deshingkar and Bhabani Sen Gupta. India's ambassador to China in 1990, C. V. Ranganathan, was a gracious and candid host during my visit that year.

At the American Institute of Pakistan Studies thanks are due to Afak Hadar and Charles H. Kennedy. In Islamabad Peter C. Dodd and Ali Imran Afaqi at the United States Educational Foundation in Pakistan made local arrangements for me. Others who helped me at the Institute of Strategic Studies,

Quaid-I-Azam University, and the Institute of Regional Studies, all in Islamabad, include Bashir Ahmad, Imtiaz H. Bokhari, Pervaiz Iqbal Cheema, Tariq Fatemi, Tariq A. Hussain, and Saeed Shafqat.

In February–March 1999 I returned to India with the support of the Smith Richardson Foundation after an absence of thirteen years to talk with officials, scholars, and diplomats. India's consul general in Houston, Rinxing Wangdi, and T. P. Sreenivasan at India's Washington Embassy helped with introductions, while Surjit Mansingh at Jawaharlal Nehru University and Air Commodore Jasjit Singh and Commodore Uday Bhaskar at the Institute of Defense Studies and Analyses helped with local arrangements. Those who shared time and ideas with me in India include Sujit Dutta, Akshay Joshi, Colonel Gurmeet Kanwal, Srikanth Kondapalli, Amitabh Matoo, Dawa Norbu, K. N. Ramachandran, Ambassador C. V. Ranganathan, Shreedhar, M. V. Rappai, Swaran Singh, and Joint Secretaries at the Ministry of External Affairs Raminder Singh Jassal, Alok Prasad, and Sudhir Vyas. Ambassadors Arundhati Ghose and Kamalesh Sharma also helped with ideas and documents. Among the Tibetan exile community in India, thanks are due to Tensin P. Alisha, Tsegyam Ngawa, Tashi Norbu, Tseten Norbu, Tsering Tsomo of the Tibetan Parliamentary and Research Institute, and Tashi Wangdi in Dharmsala. In New Delhi, Apita Anant and Satyanarayan Pattanayak, both at Jawaharlal Nehru University, served as invaluable research assistants. Barry Levely of the University of Waterloo produced the maps and graphics for the volume. At Georgia Tech Lakshmi Rajagopal served as my valuable graduate research assistant, while Linda Brady, Kenneth Knoespel, and William Long helped with budgetary and course scheduling matters.

In Washington, D.C., people who deserve thanks include Bruce Dickson and David Shambaugh at the Sigur Center of George Washington University, Walter Anderson and Tom Fingar at the State Department, Robert Sutter at the Library of Congress, David I. Steinberg of Georgetown University, and Janice T. Pilch of the National Security Archives. Stephen P. Cohen of the Brookings Institution most generously opened his personal library and research archives to me. Kenneth Lieberthal and Weiying Wan helped arrange the library travel grant at the University of Michigan. Thanks are also due to Michael Oksenberg, Andrew Selth, Sumit Ganguly, Probyn Thompson III of the U.S. Embassy in Yangon, and Donald Lu of the U.S. Embassy in New Delhi.

A number of people read and critiqued various rough drafts of chapters. They include Melvyn C. Goldstein, Eric A. Hyer, Steven I. Levine, Surjit Mansingh, Leo E. Rose, Allen S. Whiting, and Robert W.Wirsing. Admirals (both ret.) Eric A. McVadon of the U.S. Navy and Sumihiko Kawamura of the Japanese Maritime Self-Defense Force graciously helped me understand the intricacies of the Sino-Indian naval balance. Roy Grow of Carleton College provided comradely support during our stays in Beijing. Professor of Economics Penelope B. Prime, my beloved wife, served throughout as my computer consultant and counterpart in an ongoing dialogue on the course of Chinese and Indian development. Finally, Samantha Ravich and Marin J. Strmecki at the Smith Richardson Foundation provided the support that brought this long project to final fruition.

Protracted Contest

1 / Sino-Indian Relations

The Protracted Contest

THE SINO-INDIAN CONFLICT

Two of the most brilliant civilizations yet produced by humanity, those of China and India, lie side by side on the continent of Eurasia. The peoples that have produced these civilizations are both rightly proud of their histories and achievements, and determined that their nations will play a major role in the modern world. These two ancient nations emerged from long periods of foreign domination and established new states at about the same time—independent India in 1947, which became the Republic of India (ROI) in 1950, and the People's Republic of China (PRC) in 1949. The power and ambition of these states dwarfed the capabilities of the other states lying along their common flanks. For the next five decades the two powerful states struggled to reach a mutually acceptable accommodation. This was a difficult process, producing one limited but intense war, a half-dozen militarized confrontations, dozens of instances of sharp political-diplomatic struggle, chronic conflict over national policy, and layer upon layer of mutual suspicion. This book is about that conflict. It analyzes the protracted conflict between the foreign policies of India and China in the vast arc of land and water lying between and alongside those two great nations.

By *conflict* is meant the clash of foreign policies pursued by the national governments of the two states. Deliberate efforts by the central authorities of China and India to apply their states' capabilities to effect developments in the South Asian region frequently had mutually exclusive objectives. This conflict has only occasionally entailed the application of military force, and on only one occasion, in 1962, did the conflict culminate in war. In the last

3

two decades it has culminated in a direct, militarized confrontation only once, in 1986–87. There have also been several occasions on which the domestic use of military force (to suppress internal challenges to state authority) was linked to the conflicting policy objectives of the Chinese and Indian states. Far more common and significant than military conflict has been political conflict—that is, disagreements over diplomatic policies and differing objectives pursued through the application of other, nonmilitary, forms of national power. This study is largely a chronicle of such conflicting policies.

Yet, while military instruments have not been the main form in which Sino-Indian conflict has been manifest, security does seem to have been the primary basis of that conflict. The thinking of both sides seems to have been subtly but profoundly influenced by the possibility that the other side might use military force or might be tempted to use military force. While war has not been a frequent occurrence, that possibility, and the even graver possibility of national defeat in war, has very frequently underlaid the ROI's and PRC's perceptions of each other. Although typically unspoken, deterring the use of military force against oneself and creating conditions for defeating that hostile use of military force in the event that deterrence fails have been central elements of the Chinese-Indian conflict. This has meant that creating conditions advantageous for the *possible* application of military power has been important. Often, indeed typically, this has been done through nonmilitary means: building roads, establishing legal regimes permitting or denying certain activities, and creating political alignments that make up the political context in which military force is used or not used.

This study isolates and analyzes the conflictual element of ROI-PRC relations during the second half of the twentieth century. By doing so, it presents an interpretation of the broad pattern of interaction between these two great states, focusing on the deep and enduring geopolitical rivalry between them. My focus isolates one aspect of a far more complex reality. A balanced, comprehensive account of the overall evolution of ROI-PRC relations and of the shifting weight of conflictual and cooperative elements in that relationship is beyond the scope of this study.

Isolating PRC-ROI conflict permits an interpretative and analytical approach to that relationship. The danger of such an approach, however, is simplification. The major focus of both Indian and Chinese leaders throughout the period under consideration was not foreign affairs at all but their states' internal development. Alleviating widespread and deep poverty, promoting economic development and industrialization, and strengthening internal national unification were the primary concerns of the leaders of both countries. When they turned to foreign affairs, they thought first, longest, and hardest not about the other but, rather, about the United States and the Union of Soviet Socialist Republics and the alliance systems that the two superpowers led in global conflict against each other. It was the Soviet-American conflict, the so-called East-West conflict, which dominated Chinese and Indian thinking about foreign affairs, and it was this conflict that exercised the greatest influence on the international environment in which India and China operated.

An extremely valuable approach would be to explore the ways in which the Soviet-American conflict interacted with China-India relations. It would also be extremely useful to compare the ways in which the internal development processes of India and China interacted with their mutual rivalry and with the East-West conflict. These would be valuable approaches, but they are not what this book undertakes. Rather, because it focuses on Sino-Indian geopolitical conflict in the arc of land and waters lying between and alongside China and India, this study considers the Soviet-American conflict and internal development goals of the two countries only to the extent that they impinge on their geopolitical rivalry.

THE DOMINANCE OF GEOPOLITICAL CONFLICT IN ROI-PRC RELATIONS

Thus far geopolitical conflict has dominated relations between India and China. Sharp conflict between national policies erupted over Tibet in 1949 as the Chinese People's Liberation Army (PLA) was preparing to occupy that region. Conflicting policies over Tibet contributed substantially to war in 1962 and have plagued Sino-Indian relations ever since. Disagreements over Tibet are linked to others dealing with the entire Himalayan region. From 1949 through 1999 India and China have viewed the status of Nepal, Bhutan, and Sikkim very differently. India has insisted on establishing a special relation with those regions, one that guarantees India's security interests regarding China. Beijing, on the other hand, has insisted on its right to conduct the full range of regular state-to-state relations with those entities and has viewed Indian assertions to the contrary as acts of hegemonism. In the mid-1950s China reached a strategic understanding with Pakistan founded on their convergent interests vis-à-vis India. Successive Chinese and Pakistani regimes have maintained and deepened this strategic entente, much to India's dismay. The Sino-Pakistan entente evolved from very nearly a joint Pakistan-Chinese war against India in 1965 to covert Chinese assistance to Pakistan's nuclear weapons program after India's first nuclear test in 1974.

Across the Indian Ocean and South Asian region, India watches warily as

China expands its military and political roles, fearing that it is sliding into a state of "strategic encirclement" by China. Fundamental uncertainty is introduced into the Sino-Indian relationship by an unresolved territorial dispute, with China claiming virtually an entire Indian state and India claiming a strategically important western route into Tibet. That territorial dispute triggered a month-long intense war in 1962 in which powerful Chinese forces smashed ill-prepared Indian forces, advancing to the northern fringes of the Assam plain before halting and pulling back. Since 1962 the territorial dispute has slid several times into tense confrontation. The resolution of the territorial dispute also touches on the security of India's northeastern states and that of China's Tibet.

Relations between any two states cannot be reduced entirely to conflict. One can always find elements of policy cooperation as well. Even among states waging total war against each other, one can find areas of positive cooperation— regarding the humane treatment of prisoners of war, for example, or the mutual nonuse of poison gas. Certainly, in the relationship between India and China the two nations have sometimes cooperated, at times significantly. Yet, in reflecting on ROI-PRC relations over the last five decades, it seems fair to say that conflict has been the dominant characteristic of that relationship and thus requires analysis, explanation, and elucidation.

The centrality of conflict does not lessen the importance of diplomacy. Indeed, it places a premium on skillful diplomacy. In conflictual relations among states, diplomacy may regulate that rivalry and keep it from intensifying, perhaps leading to war. Solutions to some problems may even be found. Areas of cooperation may be deliberately sought out and emphasized, altering somewhat the overall balance of conflict and cooperation in the relationship. Confidence-building measures may be devised and implemented. But at bottom lies a deep and wide conflict of interests and perceptions. Periods of cooperation in Indian-Chinese relations have been brief and problematic. Repeated efforts at rapprochement have collapsed amid eruptions of renewed geopolitical rivalry, have had very limited success, or, at best, have reduced somewhat the level of tension and danger of miscalculation associated with Indian-Chinese conflict. Over the decades Chinese and Indian leaders and the analysts who advise them have also learned the rules of their rivalry. This greater understanding has facilitated diplomatic efforts to moderate tension. But the same processes that have educated leaders have also created lingering perceptions about the negative policies and intentions of the other side.

ROI-PRC rapprochement advanced steadily in the decade after 1988. In December Prime Minister Rajiv Gandhi made a pathbreaking visit to China, signaling an important reorientation of India's China policy.[1] Premier Li Peng made visits to Pakistan, Nepal, and Bangladesh a year later, conveying Beijing's desire for more cordial Sino-Indian ties. Then, in December 1991, Li Peng reciprocated Gandhi's 1988 visit by going to New Delhi. High-level Sino-Indian exchanges became routine during the 1990s. During Prime Minister Narashima Rao's visit to China in September 1993, agreements were signed on maintaining peace and tranquillity along the line of actual control on the border. In November 1996, while PRC President Jiang Zemin was in India, the two countries agreed to a set of confidence-building measures to be implemented along the border. Many other agreements were signed to increase bilateral trade, foster cultural and technology exchanges and military-to-military links, and promote other cooperative ventures. Yet deep tensions remained. Shortly after Jiang Zemin's 1996 visit, one of China's most authoritative analysts of China–South Asia relations found that, in spite of the progress in bilateral relations over the previous decade, "mutual understanding and trust between the two countries is still far from adequate, especially because in India a considerable group of people (*xiangdang yibufen ren*) have been influenced by the 'China threat theory' disseminated with ulterior motives by the West, and still have suspicions about China. Added to which is the fact that the negative influence of the 1962 war has not been entirely eliminated. This creates a certain market for rumors [about China] disseminated with ulterior purposes."[2]

The annual defense reports of the Government of India during the period of post-1988 ROI-PRC rapprochement show a deep undertone of concern about China's military power and links with India's neighbors. The 1993–94 report, for instance, noted that "China has embarked on an ambitious programme of modernization of its armed forces. China was supplying weapons to Sri Lanka and developing close ties with Myanmar especially economic-commercial and in the field of military cooperation." The 1994–95 report noted that "Beijing is engaged in building strategic roads from . . . border towns to rail-heads and seaports of Myanmar. . . . China has also been rapidly modernizing its armed forces and is equipping them with sophisticated aircraft, air defense weapons, and enhancing its blue water capabilities." China's transfer of M-11 missiles and allied technology to Pakistan was also a "cause of concern," according to the report. The report for 1995–96 noted China's continuing "extensive defense collaboration with Pakistan," including assistance to Pakistan's nuclear and missile program, and concluded that this arrangement "has a direct bearing on India's security environment." The 1996–97 report repeated earlier statements of concern about Sino-Pakistan links and Chinese military modernization and added that "upgradation of China's logistic capabilities all along the India-China border [and] for strengthened air operations has to be noted. China's posture in the South China Sea has implications for the region." China's "strengthening defense relations with Myanmar need to be carefully watched in view of the geostrategic location of Myanmar," the report said. Finally, the 1997–98 report, the last one issued before India's May 1998 nuclear tests and before the Bharatiya Janata Party (BJP) government took power on March 3, 1998, said:

> India is conscious of the fact that China is a nuclear weapon state and continues to maintain one of the largest standing armies in the world. Its military modernization programme is rapidly transforming the technological quality and force projection capabilities of its armed forces in all aspects. China's assistance to Pakistan's nuclear weapons programme and the sale of missiles and missile technology to Pakistan also directly affect India's security. India is aware of military collaboration between China and Myanmar, including the development of strategic lines of communication. India will continue to engage China through bilateral discussions in a spirit of good neighborly relations to address all outstanding differences with a view to enhancing mutual understanding and building a relationship of constructive cooperation based on a recognition of India's legitimate security concerns.[3]

India's May 1998 nuclear tests and declaration of India's nuclear weapons status surprised many American observers who had not been tracking Indian concern over China's growing power. Many analysts attributed India's nuclear decision to the BJP's idiosyncratic views and domestic political imperatives. While these factors played a role, as this book will demonstrate, India's nuclear decision had much deeper geostrategic roots. It was rooted in the decades-long, multilayered, and frequently sharp conflict with China over the two states' relations with the lands and peoples lying around and between them. Possession of nuclear weapons is linked in amorphous but important ways to international balances of power. Just as the Soviet-American nuclear balance during the Cold War had to do with calculations by both sides about situations arising in a half-dozen regions of the globe, so the nuclear balance between India and China could enter into the relative confidence and assertiveness of those two countries in dealing with issues related to the overall balance of power in South Asia. Stated bluntly, China's unilateral possession of nuclear weapons would make India less confident in countering Chinese efforts to move the South Asian balance along lines favorable to China and unfavorable to India. Indian possession of a credible nuclear deterrent vis-à-vis China could give India greater confidence, and thus greater assertiveness, in dealing with such Chinese efforts.

This stress on the conflictual aspect of Sino-Indian relations contrasts with the rhetoric of Chinese-Indian friendship which often decorates bilateral interactions between the two countries. Such rhetoric is, to a considerable extent (except for during the mid-1950s), an exercise in wish fulfillment. Political leaders may hope to alter negative stereotypes by using the rhetoric of friendship, helping to create a positive atmosphere conducive to better relations. By making statements about Sino-Indian friendship, well-intentioned people—including, naturally enough, people with responsibility for charting the course of Sino-Indian relations—hope it will become so. By creating a positive climate, they hope that the cooperative aspect of PRC-ROI relations will become greater and conflict lessened. The goal is to change the way things are, to find a way beyond the conflict that has thus far dominated the relationship, and thus become "friends."

At other times declarations of Sino-Indian friendship are used to cover up deeper tensions. Interactions surrounding India's nuclear tests in May 1998 provide an excellent and important example of the instrumental nature of the rhetoric of Sino-Indian friendship. In a letter of May 12, 1998, to United States President William Clinton, Indian President Atal Bihari Vajpayee justified India's nuclear tests and weaponization by referring elliptically but clearly enough to China's multiple challenges to India (this letter will be discussed in detail in chap. 11). Beijing reacted very strongly and negatively to Vajpayee's letter, with its open talk of the Chinese threat to India. Ever since 1989 Beijing had suspected Washington of trying to cobble together a new system of anti-China containment and had spent considerable energy refuting notions of a "China threat" that might underpin such a system. In this context Vajpayee's letter not only gave powerful credence to the "China threat theory" but suggested that India might be moving toward strategic alignment with Washington to deal with that threat. Beijing took a series of moves expressing Chinese displeasure with India's talk of a China threat. Beijing also insisted that, since Indian actions had precipitated the deterioration of Sino-Indian relations, it was up to New Delhi to take the lead in mending relations. China's ambassador to India, Zhou Gang, told the *Times of India* in September, for example, that, since the recent "abnormal developments" in Sino-Indian relations were the responsibility of India, New Delhi should make a "bold initiative" to unfreeze those ties.[4] It soon became apparent that what Beijing wanted was for India to retract the assertions about the China threat made in Vajpayee's letter.

Domestic and international pressure quickly mounted on Vajpayee's Bharatiya Janata Party government. Indian critics faulted Vajpayee for his ineptitude in having spoken so plainly and in writing, rather than using purely

oral or oblique statements, which are more normal diplomatic fare. Others
suggested that Vajpayee had been duped by the Americans, who for sinister
purposes had leaked a letter that the Indian side had expected to remain
confidential. As for Washington, rather than being sympathetic to Vaypayee's
appeal, it levied economic sanctions against India. As pressure mounted, the
BJP government began to assuage Chinese anger. In late October 1998
Vajpayee's principal secretary, Mr. Brajesh Mishra, issued a statement declaring, inter alia, that India did not view China as "a potential enemy." As Indian-
Pakistan tension mounted over Kargil on the Kashmir border in the spring
of 1999, Indian Foreign Minister Jaswant Singh further satisfied Beijing, reiterating that India did not see China as a security threat. Beijing was finally
placated, and movement toward Sino-Indian friendship was resumed. A member of the Chinese Foreign Ministry made the point that "the prerequisite of
the development of Sino-Indian relations is that the two sides do not consider themselves threatened by each other."[5]

In a sense this entire book is an elucidation of the Indian worldview embodied in Vajpayee's letter to Clinton. It is unlikely that leaders of the BJP government altered their views about China as a result of pressure from Beijing.
It is more likely that China's harsh reaction confirmed the wisdom of India's
securing a nuclear guarantee in the face of possible future Chinese pressure—
though not necessarily the wisdom of talking frankly with American leaders
about such matters. For reasons of diplomatic expediency BJP leaders
reverted to more benign-sounding formulations. The underlying Indian perceptions, embodied in Vajpayee's letter, remained unaltered but once again
safely camouflaged within the rhetoric of friendship.

Having stated these skeptical propositions, I must immediately qualify
them and clarify that they apply only to relations between the Chinese and
Indian states—not to bonds between individual Chinese and Indians.
Between individuals there may be, and often is, genuine and warm friendship. An objective analyst must also recognize that few enmities among states
are permanent. Almost always, conflictual relations among states eventually
give way to more cooperative relations. After examining in depth the nature
of Sino-Indian conflict, in the final section of this book I will speculate about
the conditions under which a qualitatively different Sino-Indian relation
might arise.

The phenomenal growth of China's national power in the period after
1978, plus Indian apprehensions about that growth, suggests that genuine
Sino-Indian rapprochement may come later rather than sooner. If the
conflict between Indian and Chinese aspirations and interests is as deeply
rooted as it seems, it may well increase further before eventually undergo-

ing a qualitative transformation into a cooperative relationship. The growth of Chinese capabilities may lead to the further expansion of ties between China and India's neighbors. India may feel increasingly vulnerable and seek ways of countering China's advances. China no doubt would take a negative view of these Indian counter-measures. Unless India is willing to become a junior partner of China in the emerging world order, Asia and the world may well see further Sino-Indian rivalry in the first part of the twenty-first century.

CONFLICTING SPHERES OF PERCEIVED NATIONAL GREATNESS

There are two taproots of PRC-ROI conflict. One is conflicting nationalist narratives that lead patriots of the two sides to look to the same arenas in attempting to realize their nation's modern greatness. The second, and more substantial, root is a conflict of fundamental national security concepts resembling a classic security dilemma.

Regarding the first, modern nationalism typically involves narratives—stories—about a country's past which are widely shared by the people constituting the national community. These stories are conveyed in various ways to the individuals constituting a nation. If the nationalism is successful, these stories are accepted by the individuals, become part of their belief system, and are associated with the individual's own concept of self-identity. These shared narratives thereby become an important part of the "imaginary community" that makes up the nation. Such narratives provide emotional fuel that powers the quest for international position and may be manipulated by states to rally popular support. Key symbols are embedded in narratives and used to evoke positive and negative sentiments. A successful nationalist doctrine achieves affective identification of living individuals with the postulated symbols of "the nation." This encourages individuals to obey and sacrifice on behalf of the state's nationalist efforts. The nationalist narratives of both India and China conceive of these countries as great nations that have historically exercised substantial influence over large areas beyond their boundaries. There is also substantial overlap between the perceived traditional spheres of influence of these two nations.

At the core of modern India's nationalist narrative is the notion that India is a great nation whose radiant influence molded a wide swath of the world beyond its boundaries. The creators of modern Indian nationalism looked in the late nineteenth and early twentieth centuries for a story of Indian national greatness comparable to those told by European nationalists. Indian thinkers found in their national history only brief periods of great empires and far longer periods of fragmentation and internecine war. This did not discourage them, however, for they turned to the religious, linguistic, and other cultural influences that emanated from the subcontinent, flowing over and deeply influencing other lands. The historic stage on which India had played out this great, creative role extended from the Himalayan Mountains in the north to the seas in the south, into Southeast Asia on the east, to Persia in the West, and into Central Asia in the northwest.[6]

The geographic scope of India's traditional sphere of influence was neatly presented by a series of exhibitions set up at the First Asian Relations Conference in New Delhi in March–April 1947. This conference was one of India's first major ventures into international politics. Although carefully nonofficial, it was a high-profile affair, attended by over two hundred representatives from twenty-eight countries, and organized and hosted by the proud leaders of soon-to-be-independent India. This pride was expressed in a series of exhibitions organized by several museums in association with the conference, illustrating India's influence on neighboring areas. The worldview presented through these exhibitions is especially valuable because it can be taken as an unalloyed expression of nationalist pride. Soon after they assumed responsibility for the nation's foreign relations, India's post-independence leaders discovered that declarations about India's historic influence on neighboring countries roused suspicions about its current motives. Indian representatives quickly learned to be more circumspect in their public expression of nationalist pride. Yet, while India's leaders became more restrained in publicly extolling India's greatness, the underlying vision remained.

The exhibition at the 1947 Asian Relations Conference identified Burma, Siam (Thailand), Malaya, Cambodia, Champa, Sumatra, Java, and Bali as regions of Southeast Asia which had received "strong influences from India in the domain of religion, language, art and architecture . . . The orbit of India's cultural empire once embraced these distant lands for several centuries."[7] According to the narrative describing the display, "Burma owes to India her script, religion and its sacred literature." Champa, a kingdom encompassing what later became southern Vietnam and eastern Cambodia, "was for a thousand years (ca. 3d to 12th c.) a land of mixed Indo-Cham culture." During much of that period "Champa was virtually a province of India in respect to its art, its Sanskrit language and Brahmanical religion." On Java and Sumatra, Hindu and Buddhist rulers looked to India for religious instruction and political support. "Indonesian contacts with India seem to have continued right up to the 15th century," that is, until they were disrupted by the arrival of the European imperialists. Ceylon was specified as another area historically within the ambit of Indian influence. "Ceylon owes to India its religion, sacred language, and some of the inspiration of its art and architecture." The son and daughter of India's great emperor Asoka were themselves missionaries "responsible for converting Ceylon to Buddhism." To India's north Nepal was shaped by interaction with India. "The Nepalese language and script, religion and art, have all been deeply influenced from India." Beyond Nepal, Tibet came within India's sphere of influence. Tibet in the seventh century "borrowed from India Buddhism and also the Indian script preserved with little change since that time." A series of Indian teachers also deeply influenced the development of Tibetan Buddhism, "serving as lights to people both in India and Tibet." Finally, in Central Asia "four civilizations, Greco-Bactrian, Iranian, Indian, and Chinese, met and mingled with one another round the central theme of Buddhism." "India's share in this [Central Asian] cultural inter-mixture predominated over the rest mainly through the influence of Buddhism and both the artistic and literary remains furnish important material for reconstructing substantial chapters in the history of Greater India."

China's nationalist narrative also postulates that throughout most of its history China was a great nation and, unlike India, a powerful state whose influence extended over wide regions of Asia. The Chinese nationalist view of China's historical sphere of influence can be deduced from its inventory of tributary states. The tributary system created a highly ritualized relationship between the Chinese emperor and a foreign ruler through which the foreign ruler symbolically demonstrated his complete submission and obedience to the emperor of China—at least that was the Chinese view of things. A tributary relationship existed between the Chinese emperor, the Son of Heaven, and a foreign king or potentate, when the latter acknowledged the emperor as a superior and pledged to obey and learn from him. In return, the emperor bestowed benevolent protection and instruction on his loyal vassal. Representatives of the foreign ruler, and occasionally that ruler himself, traveled to China, bringing tribute for the Chinese emperor. In doing this, and by performing certain carefully prescribed rituals along the way, the tribute bearer demonstrated his ruler's humble subordination to China's emperor. After completing the prescribed rites, including presenting the vassal's tribute to the emperor, the tribute bearer would receive from the emperor gifts usually worth substantially more than the tribute given to the emperor. Thus was the benevolence of the emperor demonstrated and a very practical incentive established for the tributary state's submission to China. A tributary relation with China's emperor was not necessarily onerous and was often quite profitable for foreign rulers. A tributary relation with China also opened chan-

nels for acquiring useful Chinese knowledge and techniques—calendars, manufacturing crafts, and so on. It also provided an imperial writ of office, which
helped warn off domestic and foreign rivals. Nor did a tributary relationship
necessarily mean a Chinese military presence or civil administration. Yet in
theory it meant that the ruler was subordinate to the emperor, and in fact it
meant that the country was open to a degree of influence by China's powerful culture.

In the modern Chinese nationalist view of the situation, China's traditional tributary system encompassed wide portions of Inner Asia, Southeast
Asia, and South Asia. Maps are often important nationalist symbols that can
be used to establish emotionally laden pictures in the minds of modern men.
A map produced in Chinese textbooks in 1954 neatly illustrated the geographic
scope of China's lost tributary system.[8] This particular map—showing
China's territorial losses at the hands of Western and Japanese imperialists
during the century between the Opium War in 1839 and China's "Liberation"
in 1949 and selected for classroom use by PRC educational authorities—was
intended to create a sense of bitterness, wounded pride, and thereby popu-
lar support for the PRC's efforts to wipe out the "humiliation" of the past.
According to the map, China's traditional sphere of influence included both
Inner and Outer Mongolia, Xinjiang, Tibet, parts of Central Asia, the entire
Himalayan-Karakoram region including Hunza and Gilgit in northern
Kashmir, Nepal, Bhutan, Sikkim in the central Himalayan region, the small
kingdoms of what later became India's northeastern states, Burma, Bengal,
Vietnam, Thailand, and Sulu Island.

When the 1954 Chinese map and another constructed on the basis of dis-
plays at the 1947 Asian Relations Conference are superimposed—as in map
1.1—the overlap between perceived Indian and Chinese historic spheres of
influence becomes clear. This is one key base of the chronic Sino-Indian
conflict. Chinese and Indian nationalists both perceive the same areas as rightfully falling under their influence. A corollary of this is that they see the
influence of the other country as a challenge to their own.

A sense of urgency exacerbated this clash. In the second half of the twentieth century India and China reemerged with a strong sense of lost time and
grievance against a world order that had denied them their rightful place for
too long. Both countries wanted to put things right as quickly as possible.
Nationalists in both the ROI and the PRC believed that the time had finally
come for them to reestablish their nations in their long-lost, but rightfully
deserved, place of eminence in the world. Nationalist architects of Indian independence in 1947 and those who established the PRC in 1949 viewed these
events as decisive turning points. A century or more of Western (and, in the

MAP 1.1 Overlap of Perceived Indian and Chinese Historic Spheres of Influence.
SOURCES: For India, *Asian Relations, Being Report of the Proceedings and Documentation of the First Asian Relations Conference, New Delhi, March–April 1947* (New Delhi: Asian Relations Organization, 1948), 302–10; for China, "A Brief History of Modern China" (Peking, 1954), reproduced in United States Central Intelligence Agency, *People's Republic of China, Atlas* (Washington, D.C.: United States Central Intelligence Agency, 1971), 75.

case of China, Japanese) domination had crucially weakened these great nations, damaging their international influence and stature—or so nationalists believed. The once great nations would now reestablish their international preeminence. These common anti-imperialist and anti-Western sentiments were a key basis of the period of Chinese-Indian "solidarity" in the mid-1950s and emerged occasionally in the 1980s and 1990s as the proposed basis for another period of Indian-Chinese cooperation. Shared Chinese and Indian anti-Westernism has not, however, proven to be a very viable basis for cooperation, mainly because rivalries between China and India have been too great. Their common desire to reestablish lost greatness has created ambitions, but historical patterns and perceptions have often led those ambitions into conflict. In this way shared resentment at imperialist oppression, rather than facilitating anti-Western cooperation, may in fact have encouraged Sino-Indian rivalry.

The second taproot of ROI-PRC conflict is a security dilemma. To guarantee its national security, the ROI wants to keep China (and other extra-regional powers) out of the South Asian–Indian Ocean region or at least limit its presence there. Doing this, however, necessarily poses challenges to the security of the PRC. A South Asia organized and led by India would pose a far greater potential threat to China than a fragmented South Asia. Moreover, without strong links to countries of South Asia, China would be less able to defend its southern territories should that need arise.

Analysts of Indian foreign policy generally agree that India has not had a clearly defined and explicitly enunciated regional security doctrine. Raju Thomas, for example, found in the mid-1980s that "changes in the Indian strategic environment over the last thirty years have produced significant shifts in Indian defense policies. However, these changes have rarely, if ever, been officially assessed and communicated through strategic doctrines. There have been, for instance, no Nehru, Gandhi, or Desai doctrines similar to an Eisenhower, Nixon, or Brezhnev doctrine. Instead Indian defense policy has usually been characterized by flexibility and ambivalence."[9] Analysts have found, however, that Indian policy behavior has largely conformed to an *implicit* doctrine of regional security. In other words, even though India's leaders did not explicitly formulate such a doctrine, they *acted as though they had.* Looking at the cases of Sri Lanka from 1983–90, the Maldives in 1988, and Nepal from 1989–90, one analyst found that India's leaders acted to exclude foreign powers from the region and to maintain regional stability there.[10] George Tanham concluded that there were two "core perceptions of Indian regional strategy" which could be deduced from India's foreign policy behavior. First, no neighboring state could undertake any action in foreign affairs or defense policy that India deemed potentially inimical to its security. Second, India would not permit an extra-regional power to establish an "unfriendly" presence in or influence over a neighboring state. India saw itself as a benevolent protector of the South Asian region, the guarantor of peace and stability. It vehemently denied that this constituted some sort of hegemony or a threat to the security of other South Asian nations. Because the security of its neighbors was integral to its own, India's security efforts simply could not be construed as a threat to its neighbors.[11]

Britain had a very clear view of South Asia and the Indian Ocean as a single strategic region, stretching from the passes of Afghanistan through the Tibetan buffer to northern Burma and from the Red Sea to the Strait of Malacca, with India at the center. Independent India inherited this strategic view, but it withered under Nehru's globalistic nonalignment in the 1950s. For its first fifteen years the ROI also felt comfortable with a slowly decaying and benign British presence in the Indian Ocean, though not, of course, with the U.S. link to Pakistan. The intensification of ROI-PRC conflict in the 1960s and the beginning of China's push to build relations with the countries of South Asia revived India's regional strategic perspective. With various degrees of vigor and through various means, India contested China's advances into the region. Under Indira and Rajiv Gandhi India developed a stronger sense of its own regional security zone and of the need to minimize or exclude extra-regional powers from that region. New Delhi objected to both the U.S. and Soviet presence in India's South Asian region, but China was, and remained, India's top extra-regional concern.

India has not, of course, opposed any and all Chinese links to South Asian countries. A wide range of commercial, diplomatic, and cultural intercourse between China and South Asia has taken place without causing Indian concern. But when that intercourse shades into close political alignments or when security issues enter the picture, Indian concerns mount.

Jaswant Singh, a leader of the BJP and minister for external affairs in the government headed by that party in 1998–99, has lamented India's lack of an explicit, carefully thought through, long-term, and consistent doctrine of regional security. Producing such a doctrine was a central purpose of his 1999 manifesto *Defending India.*[12] In that tract Singh traces India's lack of an explicit policy to deep cultural and historic barriers to strategic thinking generally. This may be, but one should also note that explicit enunciation of an Indian regional security doctrine would not necessarily be advantageous to the very end sought by the doctrine (exclusion of hostile extra-regional powers). As we shall see, a major factor pulling China into South Asia is the resentment of the smaller countries of that region at perceived Indian domination. Links with China are often attractive to India's South Asian neighbors precisely because of perceived Indian efforts at domination. Thus, while proclamation of an "Indian Monroe Doctrine" might forewarn China or other extra-regional powers, it would also make links with those powers even more attractive for countries of the region. India could then prevent these "anti-Indian, pro-Chinese" impulses from being realized only by the exercise of superior power. This is not necessarily the more efficient way to approach India's regional security problem. And, if superior power is still India's ultimate barrier, why not develop and quietly use that power without promulgating offensive doctrines?

This tension between asserting Indian power and encouraging South Asian resentment of Indian domination has given rise to an oscillating cycle in India's de facto regional policy. Periods of Indian assertiveness toward India's smaller neighbors, assertiveness partially inspired by a desire to exclude China and other extra-regional powers, have been followed by periods focused on building good-neighborliness and friendship. After a while that relaxed approach is again replaced by another period of defensive assertiveness. Thus, Nehru's 1949–50 efforts to block the PRC's military occupation of Tibet, to impose prophylactic treaties on Nepal, Bhutan, and Sikkim, and military intervention in Nepal and Burma to prevent instability that might be exploited by China , were followed in the mid-1950s by an effort to assuage fears of Indian domination. These good-neighborly efforts included toleration of expanding links between China and India's neighbors. By the early 1960s Indian policy entered another assertive phase, inspired by China's efforts to build closer ties with Nepal, Burma, Afghanistan, and Pakistan as Sino-Indian relations deteriorated. This assertive phase lasted until the late 1970s.

The Janata Party's displacement of Congress in 1977 marked a pendulum swing toward another period of good-neighborliness. Indira Gandhi attacked these policies during her 1979 election campaign as weak and indecisive, and her return to power in 1980 marked the start of another assertive period. These policies were continued by Rajiv Gandhi. The inauguration in 1990 of V. P. Singh as prime minister, with Inder K. Gujral as foreign minister, marked another period of good-neighborliness. Gujral sought to ease India's "big brother" image in the region by substantially satisfying the demands of its neighbors on a number of issues.[13] Gujral's initial term as foreign minister was brief, but he returned to that position under H. D. Deve Gowda in mid-1996 and then became prime minister himself in April 1997. Throughout this time Gujral continued his policies of what his critics called "unilateral goodwill and generosity" and what he called making India's power a benefit rather than a threat to its neighbors.[14]

Excluding a Chinese or other extra-regional presence from South Asia has thus been a long-standing Indian concern. Like a perennial plant, it is not always in bloom or apparent but its roots are always there, ready to push to the surface when rising temperature rouses it to activity.

PRC policy toward India's links with other South Asian nations has also varied over time. The core Chinese perception has been that India is an aspiring hegemonic power seeking to dominate the entire South Asian–Indian Ocean region and all the countries in it. India has been prevented from achieving·this by the resistance of China, Pakistan, and other countries of the region. An authoritative, classified 1990s Chinese study of the 1962 war traced that conflict to Nehru's assimilation of the British imperialist mentality and strategy. Nehru's core ambition was to establish a "greater Indian empire" (*da yindu diguo*) within the realm of the old British Empire and stretching from Southeast Asia to the Middle East. Afghanistan, Burma, and Tibet were to be "buffers" (*huan chong guo*) within this imperial framework. The countries around India were to become subservient to Indian power. Indian security strategy under Nehru was premised on achieving this empire.[15] A second authoritative 1990s Chinese study of the 1962 war also traced the root of the problem to Nehru's embrace of British imperialist thinking, leading to Indian policies of expansion and attempts to dominate neighboring countries. The ideological glue of the Indian independence movement had been "pure nationalism"; India had sought to become leader of the smaller countries in the region. Nehru's "regional expansionist policies" (*dichu kuozhang zhuyi zhengse*), plus his "nationalist" ideology, led the nation to want to establish its leadership across the Indian Ocean region.[16] From the Chinese perspective the root cause of the 1962 war and the chronic tension that has plagued the PRC-ROI relationship is India's desire for imperial dominion. The link between this underlying Chinese perception and PRC policy has not always been direct or simple. The limits, form, and content of this support varied depending on circumstances, but the broad policy direction was there.

During the period between 1962 and 1979 Beijing encouraged and supported virtually all anti-Indian struggles in South Asia. Under Deng Xiaoping, China's policy became more complex. Deng understood something of India's fears of Chinese activities in South Asia and moved to assuage those fears to open the way for improved PRC-ROI relations that would serve both China's development and its security objectives. During the twenty years between 1979 and 1999 the leaders of the ROI and the PRC both desired better bilateral relations and worked toward that goal. China's links with South Asia and India's policies toward other South Asian countries were major obstacles in this regard. Neither country was willing to give the other carte blanche. India insisted there were limits beyond which China could not and should not go. China denied the right of India to specify such limits and frequently denied that it had, in any case, transgressed the limits stipulated by India.

In contrast to India, China *has* an explicit, enunciated (indeed a frequently enunciated) doctrine detailing relations between China and the nations of South Asia and relations between India and the other South Asian countries. First enunciated in a Sino-Indian agreement of 1954, the Five Principles of Peaceful Coexistence are mutual respect for sovereignty and territorial integrity; mutual nonaggression; mutual noninterference in each other's internal affairs; equality and mutual benefit; and coexistence. According to Beijing, the Five Principles should govern relations between all countries in the world, including China and those countries that happen to be located in South Asia or on the Indian Ocean. All countries big or small are equal in terms of their sovereignty and have an absolute right to regulate their internal affairs and their relations with other countries. No country should attempt to dictate to another country regarding internal or external policies. To do so is completely unacceptable power politics, or hegemonism. For India to attempt to dictate or limit relations between China and China's neighbors is tantamount to an Indian attempt to exercise hegemony over the South Asian region. So long as relations between any two sovereign countries are peaceful and do not involve aggression against some third party—as is the case with China's links with the South Asian countries, as Beijing sees it—the governments of those two countries are entirely within their rights to undertake those relations. India may not fairly interfere. For it to do so is a violation of the sovereignty of China and other smaller nations and, therefore, a violation of the Five Principles of Peaceful Coexistence.

To this day the Five Principles remain China's standard rhetorical stock-in-trade. In a high-profile speech in Pakistan in December 1996, for example, President Jiang Zemin said: "We sincerely hope that . . . South Asian countries will treat one another as equal and live harmoniously, thus becoming exemplary of the Five Principles of Peaceful Coexistence in practice; and that they will settle their differences and disputes peacefully in the spirit of seeking common ground while reserving differences, mutual understanding, and mutual accommodation." These words were a two-edged sword. On the one hand, they signaled Islamabad that it would not have China's support for conflict with India over Kashmir. On the other hand, they signaled New Delhi that China expected India not to coerce its neighbors. Jiang also underlined in his talk the PRC's determination to continue expanding its "multi-dimensional exchanges and cooperation" with South Asian nations: "To solidify our friendly and good-neighborly ties with the surrounding countries is our sincere wish and unswerving policy . . . the multi-dimensional exchanges and cooperation between China and the various South Asian countries in many fields have grown steadily from strength to strength. We are ready to join hands with the South Asian countries in building a friendly and good-neighborly relationship that is long-term, stable, and oriented towards the 21st century."[17]

There is a tendency among international affairs analysts steeped in the realpolitik tradition to smile when they hear the frequent Chinese references

to the Five Principles of Peaceful Coexistence, seeing Beijing's fondness for
the Five Principles as reflecting the Chinese notion that, while foreigners have
interests, China has principles. This conclusion is understandable but not
entirely well founded. Emphasis on the Five Principles of Peaceful Coexistence
accords well with China's interests in South Asia. The exercise of power is
almost always linked to values. Those exercising power typically need to believe
that their exercise of power is, in some basic sense, fair and that the actions
of the people being coerced are, in some basic sense, unfair. Values deriving
from existing moral codes combine with beliefs about the behavior of others to justify one's own exercise of power. If those ideas are persuasive to others, the exercise of power will be easier and more effective. There is good reason
to take seriously the moral code underpinning the exercise of power. In China
the symbols associated with the Five Principles are linked to extremely powerful emotions—China's own "century of humiliation." These beliefs can
evoke deep and bitter sentiments among modern Chinese. If those sentiments
can be roused and associated with Indian actions through the use of certain
verbal symbols, such as the Five Principles of Peaceful Coexistence, this may
provide an effective justification of power, at least in Chinese minds. The extent
to which the justification would be effective with those living in South Asian
countries is another matter. Given that public opinion in South Asian countries is shaped by resentment at Indian "bullying," the symbolism of the Five
Principles of Peaceful Coexistence may be effective in generating support for
Chinese policies.

Beijing combines the Five Principles with its "friendly neighbor policy"
(*mulin zhengce*) especially to foster friendly, cooperative ties with countries
neighboring China. Such relationships, including cooperative security relationships, reduce the danger posed to China by hostile powers. The rub in
the case of ROI-PRC relations is that, in strengthening its own security by
developing military or security relations with its neighbors, China ipso facto
diminishes India's security situation. In pursuing policies premised on the
Five Principles, China has repeatedly come into conflict with India's South
Asian security zone and chipped away at the stage on which the drama of
Indian national greatness is to be enacted.

In concluding these introductory remarks, a final caveat is necessary. The
following pages and chapters will focus on Indian fear of China and especially
of China's links to South Asia. China, of course, has not been India's only
extra-regional concern. Arguably, India has sought since the mid-1960s to
exclude *all* extra-regional powers. Following the deployment of the Enterprise
battle group to the Bay of Bengal during the December 1971 war, when Indian
forces intervened in East Pakistan to detach that region from Pakistan and

create the new state of Bangladesh, India's fears regarding the growing U.S. presence in South Asia may, for a period, have exceeded its concerns with the Chinese presence. China took a relatively low-key approach to this Indian dismemberment of Pakistan, in contrast to the United States, which undertook the act of naval diplomacy on Pakistan's behalf. Once again, this study will leave to others the task of balancing the weight of Indian concerns with Chinese "encirclement" against India's concern with the "American threat" at various points. (In fact, New Delhi saw these threats as tied together in the "Beijing-Washington-Islamabad axis" during the 1970s and early 1980s.) Assessing the balance of various Indian concerns over time and as reflected in Indian foreign policy is not the task set for this book. Rather, it seeks to isolate and analyze PRC-ROI conflict per se. Intellectual honesty requires, however, that I reiterate at the outset my belief that, if this is done, the analyst will find that among the extra-regional powers that have played a role in post-1947 South Asia—including the United Kingdom, the United States, the USSR, the Russian Federation, France, Portugal, the Netherlands—concern with China's looming presence weighed most heavily with Indian leaders even if it was not always at the top of their explicit foreign policy agendas.

THE GEOGRAPHIC STAGE

The conflict between Chinese and Indian concepts of national greatness and security has been played out in well-defined geographic circumstances of location, terrain, climate, and ethnic demography. These circumstances deeply influenced the pattern of interaction, and it is for this reason that we refer to it as "geopolitical conflict."

The geophysical processes that produced the absolutely unique ruggedness of this terrain have happened only once in our planet's history, as far as geophysicists currently know. With the breakup of earth's primordial single supercontinent Pangaea about 180 million years ago, the Indian tectonic plate split off and traveled northeast across what eventually became the Pacific and Indian Oceans. About 65 million years ago that tectonic plate began approaching the Laurasian plate, made up of both Eurasia and what later became North America. One of the most immense collisions in earth's history resulted, with the hard rock of the Indian plate thrusting under the softer Laurasian plate. The earth's crust rapidly thickened and rose, creating the world's highest mountains and plateaus and some of its most rugged terrain.

This rugged terrain made it difficult for ancient and modern Indian and Chinese states to assert their power in these areas effectively, heightening their

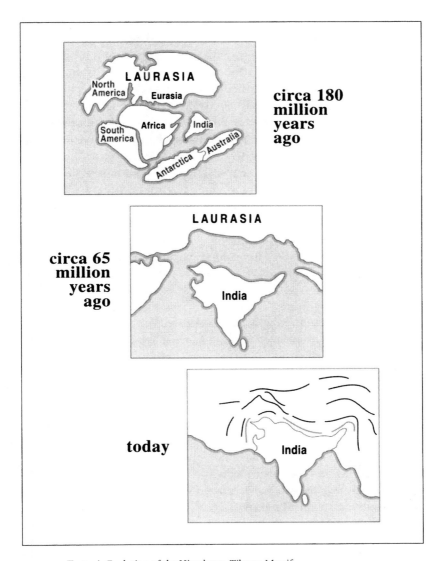

MAP 1.2   Tectonic Evolution of the Himalayan-Tibetan Massif

sense of vulnerability to the efforts of the other state to assert its influence. This was further conditioned by the relatively limited financial, industrial, and technological resources available to the two states at various points. The costs of even penetrating, let alone effectively administering, many of these regions was very high, while the economic resources available to the two states were tightly constrained. Additionally, sometimes the indigenous populations of these remote areas did not identify with the newly established Chinese and Indian states. Occasionally, they, or at least significant portions of them, were inspired by the desire for autonomy and independence from the ROI and PRC. These difficulties of national integration were greatly compounded by difficult terrain and location and by the ability of the rival state on the other side of the Eurasian continent to magnify them.

The vast belt of territory stretching from the mountainous jungles of northern Burma westward to the Karakoram Range of northern Kashmir and northward to the edge of the great Tibetan plateau—what I will call the "Himalayan-Tibetan massif"—can be seen as a single geopolitical system whose basis is the extreme ruggedness and remoteness of its land. This rugged terrain makes the movement of men and material, for either civilian or military purposes, very difficult, and it has made the modern economic development of the region unusually slow and difficult. Even as we enter the new millennium these lands remain "remote," with transportation grids far less developed than those of surrounding areas that are lower and flatter. Because of terrain, the modern economic development of this region has been unusually slow and difficult. The significance of these basic topological facts is, of course, conditioned by technology. The transportation technologies of the late twentieth century—airplanes, railways, but especially hard-surfaced, all-weather roads with modest grades, frequent bridges, and cargoes moved by efficient internal combustion engines—have rendered these regions far more passable, far less of a barrier to civilian or military intercourse, than was the case in earlier centuries. Yet, while technology has modified the impact of geography, it has not eliminated it. Movement in and through the Himalayan-Tibetan massif remains relatively slow, difficult, and expensive.

The Tibetan plateau, ranging 800 miles north to south, is mainly above an elevation of 6,500 feet (2,000 m) with the central plateau at an elevation of 13,000–15,000 feet (4,000–5,000 m). On the southern fringe of the central plateau lie the Himalayan Mountains. These emerged as three gigantic, highly folded, parallel ranges of which the central range is the highest, with many peaks over 25,000 feet as well as, of course, the world's highest peak at just below 30,000 feet.[18] The north to south width of the Himalayan system is about 300 miles. This high ground can be depicted by contour lines, as shown in map 1.3.

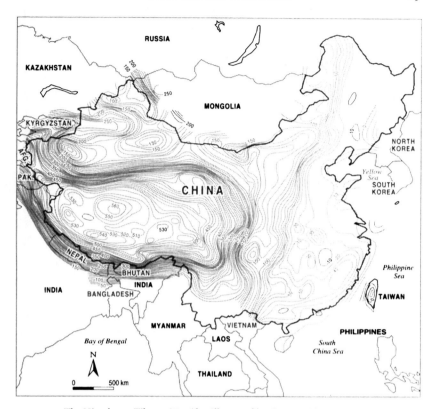

MAP 1.3   The Himalayan-Tibetan Massif as Illustrated by Contour Lines.
SOURCE: Huang Jiqing et al., *Geotectonic Evolution of China* (Beijing: Sciences Press, 1987).

The Himalayan-Tibetan massif separates the densely populated, economically developed heartlands of Indian and Chinese civilization. In other
words, if the rulers of Indian and Chinese states decided, as they occasionally did, to mobilize their resources for war against the other, their forces would
have to go over or around that massif, as the armies of the expansionist Mongol
Khanate did. Those extremely powerful armies swept outward in all directions in the thirteenth and fourteenth centuries—over the seas to Japan and
Southeast Asia, across China and into Burma and Vietnam, across the steppes
of Inner Asia to central Europe and Persia. Eventually, an offshoot of the
Khanate conquered India, advancing through Afghanistan. Mongol armies
went everywhere but through Tibet, which they went around. In the seventeenth century the Dogra rulers of Kashmir sent armies into western Tibet—
thereby laying the basis for the subsequent Indian claim to Askai Chin. In

the early eighteenth century a Dzungar Mongol army marched from the Ili Valley via Hetian in today's southern Xinjiang to atop the Tibetan plateau and thence to Lhasa. In the late eighteenth century the first genuine trans-Himalayan military expedition occurred when a Chinese-Tibetan force responded to a Nepalese seizure of Shigatze by marching on Kathmandu. The expedition of British captain Francis Younghusband to Shigatze in 1904 should perhaps be counted as a trans-Himalayan expedition. But it was not until 1962 that modern technology was used to apply large-scale trans-Himalayan military force. That year was the first time that armies commanded by the Chinese and Indian states fought each other. This fact was a testament both to the ability of the Tibet-Himalayan massif to separate the two states throughout most of history and to the modification of these geographic facts by modern technology.

Another key element making up the Himalayan-Tibetan system is the configuration of political regimes administering parts of it. Have the PRC and/or the ROI exercised adequate administrative control over one or another component of this region to prepare or deny transit through the territory? An actor who controls a territory politically can prepare lines of swift advance or deliberately not prepare them while readying fortifications to obstruct movement. It can position men and material beyond the roughest zones or prevent such forward deployment. Factors that touch on such political control include: (1) the administrative status of Tibet relative to the PRC and the ROI; (2) the location of the Chinese-Indian boundary; (3) the status of Nepal, Bhutan, and Sikkim; and (4) the status of the north Burma flank of the Himalayan-Tibet massif.

Taken together, the regions of Nepal, Sikkim, and Bhutan occupy about half the total distance from the line of actual control separating Indian and Pakistani-occupied Kashmir in the west to the Indian-Burmese-Chinese border trijuncture in the east. Nepal and Bhutan are kingdoms, as was Sikkim until its annexation by India in 1975. Nepal is a sovereign state seated in the United Nations and conducting diplomatic ties with many countries. Bhutan was a semi-sovereign state in the 1950s but gradually expanded its range of international activity while still respecting India's key interests as regards China. Sikkim held a status roughly comparable to Bhutan's from 1950 until 1975. The status and role of Nepal, Bhutan, and Sikkim relative to India and China has been profoundly influenced by their location on the fringe of the Tibetan plateau and wedged between those two powerful states. Their status has been a chronic source of conflict between Beijing and New Delhi.

The ethnicity of the indigenous populations of these highland regions is another factor influencing the interactions of the massif system. To a substantial degree these peoples are ethnically distinct from both Han Chinese and Hindi-speaking north Indians. These non-Chinese, non-Hindi people of the massif regions are less numerous, less wealthy, and less powerful than neighboring Hindi and Han centers of power—this was not always the case historically but seems to have become a constant by the nineteenth century. The differences in size, wealth, and power have meant that, more often than not, these smaller groups have been subjected to the force of Indian or Chinese states. Viewed from a long historical perspective we can conclude that what is probably happening is that these smaller, weaker nations are gradually being assimilated into the larger, more powerful amalgamated nations of India and China. This is not always a conflict-free process; it often creates grievances among the people being assimilated, which in turn can create internal instability that may be exploited by the other powers. The PRC has exploited such ethnic divisions within India's northeast, while the ROI has exploited China's ethnic vulnerabilities in Tibet. Parallel with this process of mutual exploitation of ethnic vulnerabilities is a longer-term but more effective process of assimilation, driven, it seems to me, by modern technology, which makes possible the swift and easy movement of people, goods, ideas, and information, and by state security, which encourages the use of modern technology to integrate these vulnerable areas.

Which brings us to the final element of the Himalayan-Tibetan system: the level of development of the transportation network within this zone and between these highlands and Chinese and Indian centers of power and wealth. The speed and ease with which Indian and Chinese military resources could be moved into and across these lands, supported, and effectively coordinated, is directly linked to the structure of the political regimes of these territories. Developed transportation technologies also link the economies of these regions more closely to the economies of India and China or, if such technologies are not well developed, keep economies from being tied together.

The key elements of the Himalayan-Tibetan system are thus: the lay of particularly rugged terrain, political administrations, ethnicity, and the level of development of transportation networks. These elements must be understood in relationship to one another. A now-classic Indian realistic view of the Himalayan-Tibetan system was presented by Sardar Vallabhai Patel in a letter of November 7, 1950, to Jawaharlal Nehru. Patel had been the organizational mainstay of the Congress Party during the 1930s and 1940s. While inspired by Mahatma Gandhi's saintliness, Patel tended toward a hardheaded view of politics. As home minister and deputy prime minister in the period after independence, Patel presided over the integration of the 562 Princely States into the Indian union (except for Kashmir, which Nehru insisted, against Patel's objection, on submitting to the United Nations) and the suppression of a communist revolt in southern India.[19] Patel's letter to Nehru came shortly after the Chinese People's Liberation Army (PLA) defeated Tibetan forces at Qamdo on the eastern gateway to Tibet, thereby positioning itself to carry out the previously proclaimed mission of military "liberation" of Tibet. The imminent Chinese occupation of Tibet, together with a number of other factors, posed new and fundamental challenges to Indian security, according to Patel.

Throughout its history, Patel told Nehru, India had not faced Chinese armies stationed in Tibet on India's northern borders: "Throughout history we have seldom been worried about our northeast frontier. The Himalayans have been regarded as an impenetrable barrier against any threat from the north. We had friendly Tibet which gave us no trouble." This was about to change with the PLA occupation of Tibet. The "disappearance of Tibet, as we know it, and the expansion of China almost up to our gates" presented India with a new and dangerous situation. The broader power equation had also changed. Previously, "the Chinese were divided. They had their own domestic problems and never bothered us about frontiers." Now China was unified under an effective and centralized regime. This regime also rejected the old notion of suzerainty under which Tibet had been an entity able to enter into treaty relations with other countries. This crucial shift threw "into the melting pot" the various frontier settlements India had previously reached with the Tibetan government and rendered the entire Indian-Tibetan/Chinese-Indian border undefined. "Our northern and northeastern approaches consist of Nepal, Bhutan, Sikkim, the Darjeeling (areas) and tribal areas in Assam" and "The undefined state of the frontier and the existence on our side of a population with its affinities to the Tibetans or Chinese have all the elements of a potential trouble between China and ourselves." Communication with and Indian administrative authority within these areas were weak. The border was extremely porous, and "there [was] almost an unlimited scope for infiltration" of "spies, fifth columnists and communists." Ethnic factors also created opportunities for Chinese exploitation. "All along the Himalayans in the north and northeast we have on our side of the frontier a population ethnographically and culturally not different from Tibetans and Mongoloids . . . The people inhabiting these portions have no established loyalty or devotion to India . . . [and] are not free from pro-Mongoloid prejudices." All of these factors created many Indian "weak spots" that China could exploit. Patel also raised the possibility of a link-up between China and Pakistan which could put India in a "perpetually weak" position in which it "would not be able to stand up to the double threat of difficulties both from the west and north and northeast."[20] Patel concluded his letter with a list of measures designed to meet these new challenges.

Patel's views did not become policy—at least not for another decade. In 1950–51, while Nehru pushed through prophylactic treaties with Sikkim, Bhutan, and Nepal, more broadly he rejected Patel's realpolitik approach in favor of a policy that can perhaps fairly be termed "appeasement." (Patel himself died shortly after he wrote his letter to Nehru.) Nehru sought to persuade China of India's friendship by vigorously promoting China's cause on international issues such as United Nations representation and a Korean War truce while eschewing actions potentially objectionable to China in the frontier regions. On the crucial issue of Tibet, after a brief period of using diplomatic means to uphold Tibet's autonomy, Nehru conceded China's core demands. In sum, Nehru attempted to deal with China's challenges by actively befriending China and sidestepping efforts it might otherwise have taken to construct a position of strength favorable to India.

Bitter experience can be an effective teacher. In 1950 Patel's realpolitik view was a distinct minority perspective. In the aftermath of the 1962 war it became representative of mainstream Indian thinking *on China*, if not of India's view of the world generally. While Gandhian-Nehruvian idealism still played an important role in Indian diplomacy in the 1960s and 1970s, in terms of dealing with China, after 1962 Indian policy rested squarely on realist premises. The 1962 war produced a sea change in Indian public opinion about China as fundamental as the rejection of isolationism among Americans following the 1941 attack on Pearl Harbor. While much diplomatic water has flowed under the bridge of Sino-Indian diplomatic relations since then, the realpolitik lessons of 1962 remain at the core of mainstream Indian thinking about China.

"INDIAN HEGEMONY" VERSUS "CHINESE STRATEGIC ENCIRCLEMENT"

Chinese and Indian security interests have clashed in terms of the relations of each with the countries and areas of the South Asian region. Beijing's objective has been to prevent the emergence on the PRC's vulnerable southwestern borders of a threatening or potentially threatening power or combination of powers. Beijing's primary security concerns have been elsewhere: along the eastern coast from the United States, Japan, and Nationalist China; and along China's northern and northwestern borders from the USSR. Yet, because of factors of ethnicity and terrain outlined earlier, Beijing has also felt vulnerable along its southern borders. One of Beijing's overriding strategic objectives has been to prevent the greater threat emanating from the east or the north from linking up with a threat to the PRC's southern borders. As a result, two at times inconsistent policy directions have emerged. On the one hand, China has sought to cultivate friendly, cooperative ties with the smaller countries of South Asia. By developing friendly ties with these countries, China might support their struggles against Indian "hegemonism." On the other hand, Beijing courted, or confronted, India.

China's long-term security interests and the long-term growth of Chinese prominence in Asia would be best served by having more, smaller states rather than one larger state on China's southern border. The only realistic possibility of such a single large state came from India. Thus, Chinese policy has sought to prevent the possibility of Indian domination or unification of the South Asian region. An Indian-led South Asian bloc would be far more dangerous (because it would be more powerful) if it pursued policies antithetical to Chinese interests. The greater power of such a state might also serve to encourage it to pursue policies antithetical to China's interests. An Indian bloc would also be better able to restrict the development of China's friendly ties with South Asian countries. Indeed, such restriction would be the virtual definition of Indian domination.

Indian leaders and analysts take a skeptical view of China's relations with India's South Asian neighbors, especially concerning security relations. One senior Indian analyst, Sujit Dutta, wrote in 1998 that Beijing "has over the years . . . developed some of its closest external relationships in the [South Asian] region built on defense and intelligence ties, military transfers, and political support. Unlike China's ties in East Asia, where they are essentially economic, in South Asia [China's] ties are primarily political-military in content."[21] Dutta found several types of reactions to China's role in South Asia among the countries there. The most common response—represented by Pakistan, Iran, Bangladesh, Myanmar, and Sri Lanka—is to see China as "a benign state whose power and independent role enhance their security by balancing other major states such as India or the United States or Russia that are their pivotal concern." These countries do not feel threatened by China's growing military power and have "close, friendly ties with China and welcome the growth of China's overall power and role" in South Asia. A second type of response—represented by Nepal and Bhutan—comes from landlocked countries dependent on India and with economic and security policies that "revolve around" India. India's views are sui generis in South Asia, according to Dutta. Being the dominant power there, India views China's South Asian activities with suspicion. While Sino-Indian relations have improved since 1988, "there has been little movement on resolving outstanding disputes, settling the issue of [Tibet], or removing Indian insecurities regarding China's strategic postures and defense ties in the region." Another Indian analyst, Colonel Gurmeet Kanwal, writing in 1999, perceived a Chinese policy of "strategic encirclement": "While China professes a policy of peace and friendliness toward India, its deeds clearly indicate that concentrated efforts are under way aimed at strategic encirclement of India. For the last several decades, China has been engaged in efforts to create a string of anti-Indian influence around India through military and economic assistance programs to neighborly countries, combined with complementary diplomacy. Pakistan, Bangladesh, Nepal, and Sri Lanka have been assiduously and cleverly culti-vated toward this end."[22] According to Kanwal, "China's foreign and defense policies are quite obviously designed to marginalize India in the long term and reduce India to the status of a sub-regional power by increasing Chinese influence and leverage in the South Asian region." While we should not nec-essarily accept the proposition that China is indeed motivated by the strate-gic calculations attributed to it here, we can accept this view as representing Indian perceptions.

What Indian leaders perceive as well-justified concern for India's secu-rity, Chinese leaders perceive as Indian hegemony. Since the mid-1970s (when Chinese concern for Soviet hegemonism became acute) Chinese sources have usually not spoken openly about Indian "hegemony"—although there is a tendency toward frankness in internal documents or in public polemics when Beijing wishes to express displeasure, as, for example, following India's annexation of Sikkim in 1975 and its nuclear tests in May 1998. Nor is Chinese policy necessarily predicated on opposing what China perceives as Indian hegemony. Other goals often rank higher for Beijing in its order-ing of priorities (e.g., thwarting Soviet or U.S. domination), and these higher-ranking objectives frequently lead China to downplay its opposition to Indian hegemony and its support for India's neighbors against Indian pres-sure. But, while political and diplomatic exigencies may moderate Beijing's response to India's efforts to restrict relations between China and India's South Asian neighbors, the underlying perception remains essentially unaltered: to China India is a regional hegemonist that presumes to block the natural and rightful expansion of China's relations with its neighbors.

2 / The Tibetan Factor in Sino-Indian Relations

The essence of the Tibetan factor in Indian-Chinese relations is that this large, ethnically distinct, and strategically located region, which historically was not subject to direct Chinese administration and ongoing military occupation, has since 1951 been brought under precisely such Chinese control. This fundamental change in the long-established status of Tibet was viewed very differently by the governments of the People's Republic of China and the Republic of India. Beijing viewed Tibet as an integral part of the Chinese state, was determined to bring it under direct administrative and military control, and saw Indian expressions of concern regarding Tibet as manifestations of Indian interference in China's internal affairs. New Delhi saw the permanent stationing of Chinese armies on India's northern borders for the first time as constituting a major adverse change in India's national security situation. Where India had previously faced no danger of military attack, it now confronted large, modern, and battle-hardened Chinese armies. Many Indians, although initially not Nehru and his closest advisors, also lamented Beijing's destruction of Tibet's unique and deeply Indian-influenced culture. By 1959 preservation of Tibet's unique cultural heritage had become a mainstream Indian concern.

India has resisted but gradually been forced to accommodate China's creation of a new political reality in Tibet—that is, the creation of a Tibet under direct Chinese administration and Chinese military occupation. New Delhi had, by the end of the twentieth century, largely adjusted to the irrevocable loss of its long-extant Tibetan buffer. It did so with considerable reluctance, resentment, and a deep awareness of what it had lost in terms of national security. China, for its part, while able to impose its will in Tibet, faces serious vulnerabilities there. Within Tibet there is deep hostility to Beijing's rule. Beijing rules over a sullen Tibetan populace deeply resentful of China's takeover of their ancestral homeland. Rebellion is an ever-present danger. Internationally, Beijing's claim to Tibet enjoys low acceptance. No foreign government openly challenges its claim, but public opinion in many countries, including the Western democracies, Buddhist countries, and India, has been appalled by what has befallen the Tibetan people and their culture under Chinese rule. Beijing's objective is to prevent these factors from coming together in such a way as to undermine the PRC's control of Tibet, possibly leading to its loss from China. The essence of Beijing's policy toward India regarding Tibet has been to apply pressure to compel India to desist from policies and actions that work counter to China's control over Tibet. The modalities of pressure have run the gamut from low-level diplomatic protests to full-scale war in 1962.

Marxism-Leninism deeply colored Chinese Communist Party (CCP) thinking about the China-Tibet relation. Party leaders viewed all of their country as "semifeudal" and in dire need of revolutionary social change—and if this were true of Han-populated regions of China, it was even more true of "China's Tibet," with its titled aristocracy, theocratic government, pervasive "superstition" (as the CCP deemed all religion), and near complete absence of industry. When the CCP "liberated" Tibet in 1951, it hoped to unite with "progressive Tibetans," mobilize the oppressed laboring classes, and gradually bring Tibet into the modern age in ever closer association with the other "nationalities" of the PRC. Through this ideological prism New Delhi's opposition to the PLA's occupation of Tibet and support for Tibetan autonomy were seen as an effort to uphold a backward way of life and, according to China, reflected the "reactionary class nature" of India's rulers. By keeping Tibet weak and the PLA out of Tibet, New Delhi hoped to keep Tibet open to Indian penetration and exploitation in ways established by and inherited from the British imperialists. This line of CCP thought rested on the premise that Tibet is a part of China, a proposition that takes us to a second level of Chinese thinking about Tibet.

Contemporary Chinese thinking about Tibet is part of what Chinese nationalists refer to as China's "national humiliation." As constructed by modern Chinese nationalism, during the period between 1839 and 1949 China was bullied, oppressed, and exploited by foreign imperialism. One dimension of this humiliation was the seizure of Chinese territory by aggressive imperialist powers. These territories included lands populated by ethnic Chinese, the Han (e.g., Taiwan, Hong Kong, Macao), but also those populated by non-

Han people which had owed allegiance to China's imperial government for centuries (e.g., Vietnam, Mongolia, Korea, and Tibet). China's administrative and military presence in the latter areas had been weak, and Chinese nationalists concluded that weakness was a key reason that they had been seized by foreign powers and lost to China. It followed that reversing these losses, where that was still possible, or preventing further losses required strengthening China's control. As nationalist thinking developed in China during the early twentieth century, Chinese leaders—imperial, republican, and then communist—struggled to enhance China's administrative and military presence in Tibet, although Tibet—with the help of Britain—strenuously resisted. From China's perspective this was simply part of a pattern of British imperialist aggression against China and "China's Tibet."

The relation between Tibet and China's pre–twentieth century imperial governments was sui generis. The Tibetans, like the Koreans and the Vietnamese, were indisputably not ethnically Chinese. They did not speak Chinese. Tibet's basic beliefs and institutions were very different from those of Confucian China. In this regard the gulf between Tibet and China was far greater than that between Korea or Vietnam and China; Korea and Vietnam drew deeply from Chinese art, institutions, and philosophy. Tibet also interacted with China, but its civilization was sharply distinct from that of China.[1] The relationship between China's imperial government and Tibet's Lamaist government, headed by the Dalai Lama, was also unique—both more intimate and more equal than the relation between the emperor and the rulers of, say, Korea and Vietnam. Largely for reasons of state, both China's Yuan (1279–1368) and Qing (1644–1911) dynasties adopted Lamaist Buddhism as dynastic religions and established a close relationship with Tibetan Lamaist sects. Tibetan lamas served as tutors and advisors to the Qing and, especially, the Yuan courts, while Beijing patronized the Lamaist church. This unique religious link made Mongol rule over Tibet less intrusive and coercive than in other areas. Mongol armies entered Tibet proper on only one occasion, in 1239, to punish a rebellious principality.[2]

A second, perhaps even more important difference between the China-Tibet relation and the China-Vietnam, China-Korea, or China-Mongol relation was that China was never compelled to formally relinquish sovereignty over Tibet, as was the case with Vietnam, Korea, and Mongolia. The key point of the Sino-French war of 1885 was Chinese recognition of Vietnam's "independence" and renunciation of the traditional tributary relation with Vietnam. Recognition of Korean independence was similarly the core issue of the Sino-Japanese war of 1984–95. In the case of Mongolia, the USSR, with the assistance of the United States, exerted great pressure on China in 1945, compelling it to recognize Mongolia's full independence. In the case of Tibet the pattern of great power rivalry worked to uphold rather than destroy China's legal claim to paramountcy, which Chinese nationalism would translate into the more absolute concept of "sovereignty."

Throughout the nineteenth century British imperial strategists perceived Russia as the major threat to British rule in India. They also feared that an end to Chinese authority over Tibet would facilitate the growth of Russian influence there. Consequently, Britain upheld Chinese authority over Tibet as a way of keeping the Russians out. British strategists preferred the term *suzerainty* to describe that authority, and this term was embodied in various Anglo-Chinese treaties regarding Tibet. *Suzerainty* implied a low level of Chinese administrative and military presence and a high level of both Tibetan autonomy and British-Indian influence in Tibet. United States strategic calculations also led to support for China's authority over Tibet. Initially, this approach was founded on commercial interests and the Open Door policy. Then, as Japanese-American rivalry intensified, U.S. strategists concluded that a stronger, bigger China would better counter Japan. Chiang Kai-shek made American support for China's authority over Tibet part of the price for China's support of the United States in world affairs. As the Cold War spread to the Far East in 1949–50, U.S. strategists recalculated but once more concluded that U.S. interests would not be served by recognizing Tibetan independence. The USSR was deemed the major threat in the new global contest, and drawing Communist China away from the USSR was judged to be the paramount U.S. interest. Recognizing Tibetan independence would have worked counter to driving a wedge between the PRC and the USSR. In the early 1950s India could conceivably have altered U.S. policy but, as we shall see, did not attempt to do this.

The CCP came to power in 1949 determined to end the period of national humiliation in China's history. In terms of Tibet this meant asserting full administrative and military control. This would be done flexibly, influenced by the exigencies of terrain plus domestic and international politics, but the general direction was clear. The concept of "suzerainty," with its implied limitation of China's presence in Tibet, was rejected as an instrument of imperialist aggression against China. China's government would now exercise absolute and unlimited—that is, sovereign—authority over Tibet. It would use that authority to promote cooperation between the "fraternal" Han and the Tibetan "nationalities" of New China, delivering wealth and international power for both—or so the leaders of the CCP imagined.

There were two main ways in which the exercise of PRC sovereignty over Tibet was linked to making China strong: (1) greater security against foreign military threat or attack; and (2) the exploitation of Tibet's rich mineral resources. From the standpoint of national security, if domestic or foreign enemies of the PRC established themselves in Tibet, interior regions of China such as Sichuan and Yunnan would become insecure. China's grip on Xinjiang would also become much more tenuous, given that the former region was linked to China only by the narrow Gansu corridor. As Mao Zedong explained to the Dalai Lama in 1954, if Tibet were not under firm Chinese control and Britain and other "imperialist" powers were allowed to continue their presence there, Tibet would become a base from which the imperialists could menace China's west. Counterrevolutionary forces based in Tibet might join with similar forces elsewhere, possibly leading to a counterrevolutionary victory on a nationwide scale. And, Mao explained, in the event of war between China, India, or the Soviet Union, Tibet's location would make it extremely important.[3]

In terms of economic development, the contemporary Chinese view of Tibet must be placed in the context of an extremely numerous people, the Chinese, trying to sustain and better themselves on a relatively limited piece of land. In a seminal April 1956 talk Mao Zedong stressed opposition to "Han chauvinism" toward the national minorities but paired that with the need for Han migration into minority areas to exploit the natural resources there. "The national minority areas are extensive and rich in resources. While the Han nationality has a large population, the national minority areas have riches under the soil that are needed for building socialism," Mao said. "The Han nationality must actively assist the national minorities to carry out socialist economic and cultural construction, and, by improving relations between the nationalities, mobilize all elements, both human and material, which are beneficial to socialist construction."[4]

Twenty-three years after Mao's comments his successor, Deng Xiaoping, expressed similar views in an important March 1979 talk on "building socialism with Chinese characteristics." The two dominant characteristics of China, Deng said, were poverty and a large population relative to cultivated land. Deng fundamentally differed from Mao regarding the question of controlling the growth of China's large population. Regarding the underlying demographic problem, however, Deng shared Mao's view:

> We must vigorously intensify planned birth work; however, even if population no longer increases . . . the problem of a large population will continue to exist for some time. *Our vast territory and abundant resources are favorable conditions.* However, numerous resources have not been completely surveyed, developed and used . . . As a small amount of cultivated land with a large population . . . is a situation that cannot be readily changed, this becomes a fea-

ture of China's modernization we must take into consideration. Chinese-style modernization must proceed from China's characteristics.[5]

China's demographic problems are indeed severe. In terms of arable land per capita, China ranks twelfth from the bottom among all nations of the world. With .08 hectares per capita compared to a world average of .24, China falls just above Bangladesh and Egypt and on the same level with Haiti, the Philippines, and Vietnam.[6] The Tibet Autonomous Region is vast—1,228,000 square kilometers—constituting 12.8 percent of the PRC's total land area.[7] While most of Tibet is not suitable for farming, it can be exploited economically in other ways. Without Tibet, China's demographic problems would be much worse. Over the years the CCP has adopted a number of measures to address China's basic demographic problem, including bringing additional land under cultivation, increasing land productivity, limiting population growth and/or urban sprawl that takes agricultural land out of production, developing maritime resources, and expanding international trade. The full integration and exploitation of Tibet and its resources is another measure.

Tibet and other Tibetan-populated regions of the PRC (areas still claimed by the Dalai Lama as part of Tibet) are rich in minerals. An official Chinese study in the early 1980s found that the Tibet Autonomous Region contained 40 percent of all PRC mineral resources.[8] By 1992 seventy types of minerals and nearly one hundred deposits that could be exploited for industrial use had been discovered in Tibet, including copper, boron, magnesium, iron, gold, uranium, cobalt, lead, arsenic, barite, gypsum, graphite, sulfur, lithium, antimony, tungsten, silver, porphyry, and chromium. Tibet's copper deposits are potentially the largest in Asia, its lithium deposits potentially the world's largest. The gold deposits are China's richest; the Pengnazangbo mine in northern Tibet produced one ton of gold in 1997 alone.[9] Most of China's chromium deposits are in Tibet; these, too, are among the world's largest. High-grade uranium is found near Lhasa, while rich deposits occur in Tibetan regions of western Sichuan, Gansu, and Qinghai. Northeastern Tibet, along with Qinghai, contains large coal-bearing formations. Qinghai also has deposits of asbestos, lead, zinc, chromium, iron, potash, and salt. Petroleum is also found at Qaidam in north central Qinghai, and mica, copper, phosphate, asbestos, and iron in ethnically Tibetan western Sichuan.

Having a large and diverse mineral base is one of the PRC's major advantages in its struggle for wealth and power. Developing these resources is important to meeting the demands created by China's rapid industrialization. According to a study by the U.S. Bureau of Mines, "China is one of the few countries that possesses a vast as well as diverse mineral resource base, and

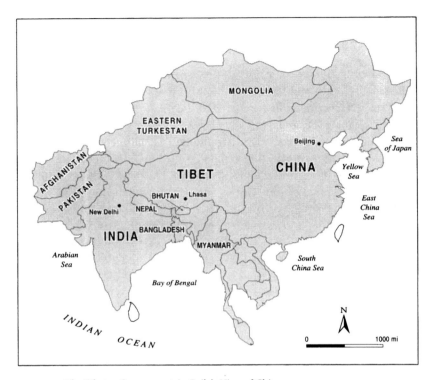

MAP 2.1   The Tibetan Government-in-Exile's View of China.
SOURCE: *Indian Leaders on Tibet* (Dharamsala: Department of Information
and International Relations, Central Tibetan Administration, 1998).

the Government has stressed the development of the mining industry to foster economic growth."[10] By 1992 mining was a mainstay of Tibet's economy:
there were then thirty-eight mines contributing a third of the region's total
industrial output—up from 7 percent in 1986.[11]

The stakes involved in the Tibetan issue are suggested by a map distributed by the Tibetan Government-in-Exile in Dharmsala (the town in India's
Himachal Pradesh state where the Dalai Lama and his exile government
reside), showing the vast region of the Tibetan plateau as separate from China.
The extent of China depicted on this map is about the same as what existed
under the Ming dynasty. In Chinese nationalist eyes the Ming was one of
China's weaker dynasties.

From a Chinese nationalist perspective, if the Chinese people are to raise
themselves to prosperity and international prominence, they must exploit
Tibet and its resources. This is a powerful, though typically unspoken, incentive for Chinese to conclude that Tibetans are Chinese and that the ancestral

land of the Tibetans is rightfully part of China. Tibet is still thinly populated and its resources relatively undeveloped. As the PRC develops economically, however, it will be able to open that region more fully. More and better roads, railways, airports, and pipelines will be built. New means of transportation and communication which we cannot now imagine will be invented. Tibet will be developed and its resources will contribute to the rise of the Chinese people and nation. Conversely, if China were to lose Tibet, its situation would be much worse.

INDIAN THINKING ABOUT TIBET

Indian thinking about Tibet can also be derived from a nationalist narrative and state security. The modern Indian nationalist narrative sees Tibet as part of India's historic sphere of cultural influence. Buddhism was carried to Tibet by a series of missionaries from India. In the seventh and eighth centuries these gurus (teachers) worked under Tibet's two great founding kings, Songtsen Gampo and Trisong Detsen, to help lay the foundations of Tibetan civilization. Later, after Buddhism had withered under a revival of aristocratic-supported Bon shamanism, it was rekindled by a second wave of Indian Buddhist masters, who brought the strong Tantric component that gave Tibetan civilization much of its distinctive flavor. The monastic system, in which specialized institutions train young men for lives of spiritual and social service (under an essentially nonaristocratic chain of command), came to Tibet from India—at least in the Indian view. Eventually, these monasteries became the base of Tibet's political and cultural systems, providing the officials who staffed the Dalai Lama's agencies and maintaining and promoting Tibetan arts, literature, and religion. The Tibetan script is derived from Sanskrit, and ancient Indian Sanskrit literature had a deep influence on Tibet. Indian classics were translated into Tibetan at a very early date and shaped subsequent Tibetan literature. Tibetan arts were also deeply influenced by Indian styles and techniques.

Most important, again in the Indian view, the fundamental Tibetan approach to life reflected Indian inspiration. In Tibetan thought, as in Hinduism and its Buddhist derivative—but unlike either Confucianism or Western rationalism—man is *not* the measure of all things. Rather, man is a "humble creature" with his share of karma. What is "titanic" in man is not his vanity or reason but "the effort to emerge out of it through suffering and sacrifice, meditation and prayer, compassion and congregation." Life, in short, is a spiritual endeavor. What makes life meaningful is progress in that endeavor. "Thus the culture of Tibet, is a glowing example of how the stream of Indian consciousness crossed the Himalayan frontier and flowed into far-off lands, transforming them body, mind, and soul into an eternity of love, peace, and compassion through a community of ideals and institutions."[12] The deepest offense to Indian nationalist opinion regarding China in Tibet derives from the perception that an India-derived Tibetan civilization is rapidly being destroyed by superior brute force. The Chinese perpetrating this destruction pretend it is not happening while proclaiming that Chinese-Indian friendship could flourish if only India would ignore what is happening in Tibet.

Indian policy *was not* initially dominated by this perceived affinity between Indian and Tibetan culture. Nehru was deeply secular and saw much of Tibetan culture as out-of-date and in urgent need of reform. He also sympathized with the "progressive" mission of the CCP in leading the process of social reform in Tibet. Yet even in the early 1950s, when Nehru's disdain for Tibetan medievalism dominated Indian policy, there was a strong counter-current of identification with Tibet. As Indian president Rajendra Prasad explained to parliament in November 1950: "It was a matter of deep regret to us, therefore, that the Chinese Government should have undertaken a military operation in Tibet, when the way of peaceful negotiations was open to them. Tibet is not only a neighbor of India, *but has had close cultural and other ties with us for ages past.* India must, therefore, necessarily concern herself with what happens in Tibet and hope that the autonomy of this peaceful country will be preserved."[13]

Even in the early 1950s Prasad's views were probably representative of nonelite Indian opinion. In any case, once China launched a systematic campaign against Tibet's traditional culture in 1959, there was an eruption of strong popular Indian sympathy for Tibet which swept all up in it, compelling Nehru to shift policy course. In the aftermath of China's imposition of direct rule in Tibet in 1959, Nehru also explained to the Lok Sahba his newly discovered understanding of India's "cultural interest" in Tibet:

> The major things that we have to consider are [that] the contacts of India with Tibet are very old, geographical, of course, [and involving] trade, but much more so, cultural and religious. . . . So . . . this contact, this relationship is something deeper than the changing political scene. Naturally we are affected by it. . . . Because of these contacts our reaction to everything that happens in Tibet is bound to be very deep. . . . There is this feeling of a certain kinship, if I may use that word, cultural kinship between the people of India and the people of Tibet.
>
> We have no desire . . . to interfere in the slightest degree in Tibetan affairs. But we could not give up our interest, call it if you like sentimental interest . . . and

you can observe for yourself the enormous feeling that has been roused in India by these recent developments in Tibet. . . . Tibet, culturally speaking, is an off-shoot of India. That is to say of Buddhism not of India politically. . . . Buddha is the greatest Indian that ever lived and we still in India are under the umbrella of this feeling for the Buddha.[14]

At the end of the 1990s there was widespread, and frequently passionate, Indian interest in Tibet—strong sympathy with Tibet and a desire not to see its unique, Indian-influenced culture obliterated. Since India is a democracy in which such sentiments are freely expressed and pressed on those elected to office, these views influence policy. A significant number of Indian voters are concerned with and pay attention to Tibet. They are outraged by Chinese suppression of that Indian-influenced way of life. Tibet has thus become an issue in Indian domestic politics.

For India's government, concerns having to do with Indian national security have far outweighed India's cultural interests in Tibet. India's national security interests require it to exclude, eliminate, or at least minimize a Chinese military presence in Tibet. Historically, China was a great military power in East and parts of inner Asia, but not until modern times, except for a brief period in the 1790s, did China deploy a significant part of that military power to Tibet. Only in the 1950s, for the first time in the long interaction between China and India, was a permanent and large Chinese military presence established on India's northern borders in Tibet. Maintaining genuine Tibetan autonomy would work, India hopes, to limit China's military presence in Tibet.

A modest Chinese administrative and military presence was first established in Tibet in the early eighteenth century. Beijing's chief concern then was with the growing power of the Dzungar kingdom based in the Ili Valley and contesting Qing control over what later became known as Xinjiang. The Dzungars were a Lamaistic Mongol people. The loyalty of various Mongol tribes was important in this Qing-Dzungar struggle, and those tribes were greatly influenced by the Lamaist Holy See in Lhasa. Thus, when the Dzungars began to assert themselves in Lhasa, Qing emperor Kang Xi felt compelled to respond. A Dzungar invasion of Tibet in 1717 led to a counter-invasion in 1719 by a Qing force of Manchu Bannermen, Mongols, and ethnic Chinese soldiers raised in Sichuan. This was the first ethnic Chinese military force to enter Tibet proper. With Qing military occupation came the clearer institutionalization of Tibet's subordination to the court in Beijing. An imperial representative, know as the Amban and guarded by a small military contingent, was established in Lhasa for the first time. The Amban played no role in the

government or administration of Tibet; those powers lay with Tibet's Lamaist theocracy.[15]

Three more times in the eighteenth century turmoil in Tibet led to
Chinese military intervention. Each intervention was followed by reorganization of the Lhasa government and then withdrawal of Chinese military
forces. Substantial Chinese forces entered Tibet in 1793 to wage a punitive
war against Nepal. (This war will be discussed in chap. 5, on Nepal.) After
those forces were withdrawn, Chinese military forces did not reenter Tibet
for over a century. Growing Chinese nationalist sentiment in the first years
of the twentieth century combined with mounting British interest in Tibet
to produce growing Chinese pressure on the region. In the aftermath of
Britain's Younghusband military expedition to Tibet in 1904, the Amban's
garrison was increased to over six thousand. Forces of the Sichuan military
leader Chao Erfeng also moved into central Tibet, with two thousand soldiers reaching Lhasa by 1910. China then deposed the Dalai Lama and began
setting up direct administration over Tibet. This produced a strong coun-
terreaction from both the Tibetan government and Britain. The Dalai Lama
fled to India, where he sought British diplomatic intervention. The British
minister in Beijing protested China's moves in Tibet. Meanwhile, the Qing
dynasty collapsed, to be replaced by a weak republic. Fighting between
Tibetan and Chinese forces escalated. Confronted by pressing needs elsewhere,
Chinese military forces and officials were withdrawn from Tibet in 1913.[16] They
would not return until 1951.

In 1951 twenty thousand veteran troops of the PLA entered Tibet from the
east, north, and west, quickly occupying urban centers and lines of communications and building new roads. By 1959, for the first time, there was a large
and permanent Chinese military presence in Tibet. The PLA infrastructure
in Tibet was steadily expanded and improved over the course of the next five
decades. By the mid-1990s between 40,000 (Beijing's figure) and 250,000
(Dharmsala's figure) PLA soldiers were stationed in Tibet.[17] New and large
compounds were built to accommodate the troops and are today visible from
nearby highways. According to U.S. information, nine airfields have been constructed. In the late 1990s several of them were lengthened to accommodate
advanced aircraft being acquired from Russia. The entire PLA complex in
Tibet is supported by ever-improving road, rail, and air links to industrial
and population centers in China proper. In short, China's military presence
in Tibet is large, powerful, and apparently permanent. India now faces
Chinese military power for the first time in the long history of interaction
between the two nations.

INDIA AND THE TRANSFORMATION OF THE TIBET-CHINA RELATIONSHIP

India's policy reaction to the transformation of the traditional Tibet-China relation shifted over time, though its support for Tibetan "autonomy" remained a constant. Four distinct periods of policy can be identified:

1. From 1947 to 1951 New Delhi boosted the international status of the Tibetan government and pressured Beijing not to move militarily into Tibet.
2. From 1954 to 1959 New Delhi attempted to persuade Beijing to grant Tibet a substantial degree of continued autonomy and to minimize its military presence in Tibet by convincing Beijing that there was no need to do otherwise and that Indian-Chinese friendship would thereby prosper.
3. From 1962 to 1977 New Delhi supported Tibetan resistance and mobilized international pressure on China in Tibet.
4. From 1986 to 1999 New Delhi balanced accommodating Beijing's demands to restrict Tibetan exile activities with condoning exile efforts to mobilize international pressure on Beijing to reach a political settlement of the Tibet issue.

All phases of Indian policy were predicated on the notion that the basic change in Tibet's traditional status which occurred circa 1951 was antithetical to India's interests, yet the policy reaction to this proposition varied greatly from period to period. All phases also seem to have been inspired by a sense of weakness, by a judgment that there was not really very much that India could do to alter the basic direction of developments regarding Tibet, and that the costs of trying to do so were likely to be unacceptably high. This was precisely the lesson that Mao Zedong hoped to teach when he decided in favor of war with India in October 1962. China has consistently sought to compel India to accept the fait accompli of unlimited Chinese sovereignty over Tibet in place since 1951, alternately using pressure and positive inducements to gain India's acceptance.

Upon independence India's leaders inherited the British policy of upholding the Tibetan buffer while recognizing China's suzerainty over Tibet. For British India, Tibet had served as a buffer lying north of the main defensive escarpment of the Himalayas and Karakoram Mountains. In August 1947 Indian leaders reconsidered and decided to continue British policy. At the same time, they hoped this would not be incompatible with maintaining

friendly relations with China. As a report by the British high commissioner
to India at the time stated:

> To prejudice her relation with so important a power as China by aggressive
> support of *unqualified* Tibetan independence is therefore a policy with few
> attractions [for Indian leaders]. It follows that while the Government of India
> are *glad to recognize and wish to see Tibetan autonomy maintained,* they are not
> prepared to do more than encourage this in a friendly manner and are cer-
> tainly not disposed to take any initiatives which might bring India into conflict
> with China on this issue.[18]

K. P. S. Menon, deputy foreign minister in charge of relations with China
and Tibet in the late 1940s, wrote that independent India had inherited and
continued the two-pronged British policy of "support[ing] the independence
of Tibet, subject to the suzerainty of China." In 1950 Nehru also spoke of
India's inheriting the two components of British Indian policy toward Tibet:
"We have accepted that policy. We take the two positions together."[19]

In March 1947 India's new leaders moved to strengthen Tibet's ability to
resist Chinese efforts to reduce its autonomy. That month the interim Indian
government signed off on a British cabinet decision to supply covertly a modest amount of arms and ammunition to the Tibetan government.[20] The
Tibetan government had belatedly begun trying to assemble a military force
capable of resisting the PLA and had looked to Britain for material support.
The decision of India's Congress leaders was taken under British tutelage but
also reflected the conclusion of India's new leaders that this policy would serve
their nation's interests. Parallel with these efforts to strengthen Tibet's military capabilities were Indian moves to raise Tibet's international profile. The
leaders of emerging independent India were effectively the organizers of the
Asian Relations Conference of March 1947. They invited the Tibetan government to participate along with representatives of other Asian nations. China
(then still the Republic of China) strongly protested Tibet's invitation, but
India refused to disinvite the Tibetans.[21] At the conference Tibet was accorded
treatment comparable to other national participants—the newly adopted
Tibetan flag was displayed, Tibet's representatives were seated with those of
other nations or soon-to-be-independent nations, and a map was posted
showing Tibet as a separate country independent from China. Again, China's
representative strongly protested this treatment of Tibet. In response, the
Tibetan flag was removed, the map revised, and a statement was issued saying that various delegates had been invited by Nehru in a personal capacity.
Mahatma Gandhi, however, told the Tibetan delegation in a private meeting

that India planned to circulate a document about the conference which would serve as documentary proof to the world of Tibet's independence.[22] Fifty years later the Tibetan exile government still lauded the 1947 conference as "the last occasion when Tibet registered herself a free and equal nation on the world stage."[23] It may be that India's leaders did not give proper forethought and deliberation to the question of inviting Tibet to the Asian Relations Conference, and that their actions were premised on a naive belief that China's leaders, whether Nationalist or Communist, would accept a continuation of Tibet's traditional status. Be that as it may, this effort to usher Tibet onto the international stage pointed in the same direction as New Delhi's other Tibetan policies at this juncture.

As the PLA swept across China and toward Tibet, the government of India approved three more covert shipments of arms, in June and August 1949 and in March 1950.[24] According to Chinese sources, the Indian representative in Lhasa encouraged Tibetan authorities to undertake military deployments to block the Chinese advance.[25] In November 1949 the secretary-general of India's Foreign Ministry briefed the British ambassador on Nehru's views on Tibet. The Britisher reported to his government that "the present Government of India were as anxious as any past government to retain Tibet as a buffer between them and China and they certainly did not want to see any increase in Chinese . . . influence there. On the other hand [they believe that] the present regime in Tibet was completely out of date and [could not] in the long run resist Chinese infiltration if this were skillfully carried out on the basis of Communist propaganda and if an attempt [were made] to improve economic and social conditions of the Tibetan population."[26]

A final element of India's early effort to uphold Tibetan autonomy was diplomatic pressure on Beijing to suspend a military push into Tibet. The PLA began preparing to move into Tibet as soon as it advanced into adjacent regions in Sichuan and Xinjiang in 1949. On January 1, 1950 Beijing announced its determination to "liberate" Tibet, thereby informing India of its intention and of the stakes involved in the situation it now confronted. The very next day Mao Zedong ordered military forces under Deng Xiaoping and Liu Bocheng to prepare the military occupation of Tibet, entering the territory from Sichuan and focusing on the seizure of Qamdo.[27] The battle for Qamdo began on October 6 and continued for eighteen days. Fighting was heavy, and there were over 5,700 Tibetan casualties. In the CCP's estimate, the PLA victory at Qamdo "laid the basis for the peaceful liberation of Tibet."[28] Once the PLA assault on Qamdo began, the Tibetan government requested help from India along the lines of the British mediation of 1904 and 1931, when China's central government had attempted to send troops into Tibet.[29] In this context India sent three notes to China protesting the PLA's resort to military force against Tibet and urging China to use peaceful means to solve problems relating to its ties with Tibet. The first Indian note, sent on October 21 while the battle for Qamdo was still under way, maintained that China's occupation of Tibet would "give powerful support to those who are opposed to the admission of the People's government [of China] to the United Nations and the Security Council." Beijing interpreted this as a hint that India would oppose the PRC's entry into the United Nations unless China halted its military move into Tibet. The second Indian note, on October 28, argued that Beijing's move would impede talks between Beijing and the Tibetan authorities under the Dalai Lama.

Beijing viewed these notes as interference in China's internal affairs, and Mao Zedong ordered the Foreign Ministry to "adopt a harder approach" (*taidu hai ying qiangying yidian*) toward Indian "interference."[30] On October 30 China replied to India's two notes, saying that Tibet was "an integral part of Chinese territory" and "the problem of Tibet is entirely a domestic problem of China." If countries used China's actions in "its Tibetan territory" as a pretext for "obstructing" the PRC's participation in the United Nations, China's reply warned, "it is then but another demonstration of the unfriendly and hostile attitude of such countries towards China. Therefore, with regard to the viewpoint of the Government of India on what it regards as deplorable, [China] cannot but consider it as having been affected by foreign influences hostile to China in Tibet and hence expresses its deep regret."[31]

The third Indian note, dated November 1, 1950, directly raised the question of Tibet's status. India hoped that "the Tibetan problem" could be resolved by "adjusting [the] legitimate Tibetan claims to autonomy within the framework of Chinese suzerainty." Tibetan autonomy was "a fact," the note said, that the Indian ambassador to China had led the Indian government to believe that "the Chinese Government were themselves willing to recognize and foster." The note also enumerated "certain rights" enjoyed by India in Tibet and stated that "the Government of India are anxious that these establishments, which are to the mutual interest of India and Tibet, and do not in any way detract from Chinese suzerainty over Tibet, should continue."

Beijing replied on November 16, demanding, in effect, that India choose between accepting Beijing's unlimited sovereignty over Tibet or confrontation with China. Beijing's note warned that China "has repeatedly made it clear that Tibet is an integral part of Chinese territory" and that "the problem of Tibet is entirely a domestic problem of China." The question of Tibetan autonomy would be determined on the basis of Chinese law and "within the confines of Chinese sovereignty." Beijing was "greatly surprised" that India was attempting to "influence and obstruct the exercise of its sovereign rights in Tibet by the Chinese government" and "deeply regretted" that India "has regarded a domestic problem of the Chinese government—the exercise of its sovereign rights in Tibet—as an international dispute calculated to increase the present deplorable tension in the world." The Indian government had repeatedly professed its desire for Sino-Indian friendship and for "preventing the world from going to war." Now "the forces of the imperialist aggressors" were threatening "the independence of nations and world peace." For this reason PLA entry into Tibet was necessary and would proceed. Implicit in the Chinese note was the message that Beijing was willing to go to war with India over Tibet. Beijing's message to New Delhi was this: if you challenge our rule of Tibet, you will come face to face with China, and such a confrontation could lead to war.

Beijing's tough response precipitated a policy debate within India and ultimately forced a reorientation of Indian policy. Deputy Prime Minister and Home Minister Vallabhai Patel advocated a series of practical measures designed to strengthen India's position: accelerated road building in the frontier areas, strengthening of India's military capabilities, moves to better integrate the northeastern territories into India. Many of these measures were eventually adopted but only halfheartedly or very belatedly. Patel also saw clearly the linkage between Tibet and what would become the crux of the border/territorial issue: if, as Beijing insisted, China's sovereignty over Tibet precluded Tibet from independently entering into treaty relations with other countries, then agreements between Tibet and various Indian states upon which India believed the border to be founded were invalid. This being the case, the entire boundary between India and Tibet/China was undefined. If a completely new boundary were to be drawn, that process would be greatly influenced by the balance of power (though Patel did not use that phrase) between China and India, and India should act accordingly. Patel went so far as to suggest that India reconsider its relations with the West. This was a key point. United States policy toward the PRC had shifted sharply with the beginning of the Korean War in June 1950. Up to that point Washington had sought to disengage from "the Chinese civil war," maintain official ties with China's new government, minimize conflict with the PRC, allow Soviet-PRC contradictions to develop, and, when the time was right, draw a "Titoist" Communist China away from the USSR, which U.S. leaders believed presented the major challenge to the United States. But once the United States was at war with China-backed North Korea, and even more so after large-scale Chinese intervention in the Korean War in late November, U.S. leaders began to seek ways to punish the PRC. Support for various insurgencies within the PRC was one such measure.[32] At this juncture (in October–November 1950) the United States apparently approached India about the possibility of cooperating to support Tibetan resistance to the Chinese advance,[33] but New Delhi was not interested in the American proposal. Nehru realized such a course would lead India into alignment with the United States and confrontation with China, and neither consequence was acceptable.

Had India adopted Patel's recommendations in early 1951, history might have been very different. The PLA had still not entered Tibet or constructed the roads that by the mid-1950s allowed it to sustain a robust military presence and intense pace of operations in that region. The PLA had not yet undergone a decade of Soviet-assisted modernization that transformed the PLA into a motorized force able to grind down the Tibetan resistance in 1959–61. Most important, after China's entry into the Korean War, the United States stood ready and able to provide very large-scale military assistance to Tibetan forces. On the other hand, the Tibetan people had yet to experience the cataclysm of CCP misrule which eventually pushed them to revolt in the late 1950s. In any case, once New Delhi indicated it was not interested in the U.S. proposal, Washington concluded that operations in Tibet were not feasible and dropped the idea—at least for a while.

Indian-American cooperation along these lines would have required, of course, a very different Indian strategy than the "nonaligned" approach that emerged in the early 1950s under Nehru and his ambassador to the United Nations, Krishna Menon. This was the main reason why it was rejected. Nehru's overriding objective in the 1950s was to avoid entangling India in the Cold War, which was rapidly being extended to Asia. He understood that a confrontation with China over Tibet would align India with the United States, thereby destroying its hopes for partnership with China in constructing a new Asian order. Both elements of this proposition were unacceptable to Nehru. He made his views clear in his reply to Patel. If China and India fell out, Nehru said, "the advantage will go to other countries. It is interesting to note that both the UK and the USA appear to be anxious to add to the unfriendliness of India and China towards each other." If India and China could cooperate, on the other hand, this "would make a vast difference to the whole set-up and balance of the world." Nehru believed, in effect, that preferences regarding global alignments should determine preferences regarding local geopolitical issues, while Patel argued that the linkage should work the other way around. For these reasons Nehru desired to demonstrate India's friendship for the PRC by such means as advocating its entry into the United Nations, favoring Beijing's position on a Korean truce, and, to come back to the Tibetan issue, by dropping the diplomatic effort to block the PLA's entry into Tibet and disassociating itself from American proposals for joint support of Tibet.

Until China's harsh response to India's notes of October–November 1950 Nehru seems to have imagined that China would forgo full military occupation of Tibet and more or less accept continuation of Tibetan autonomy for the sake of good relations with India. Following Beijing's tough reply, it was clear that this was not the case and that Indian opposition to the full "integration" of Tibet into the PRC would lead to hostility between the two nations. Nehru then shifted course. This is not to say that Nehru became unconcerned with the destruction of Tibet's traditional buffer status. His views in this regard were not remarkably different from Patel's. Nehru, like Patel, believed that India's security would be diminished by the establishment of a large and permanent Chinese military presence in Tibet and by Tibet's political integration into a centralized Chinese state system. In his reply to Patel, Nehru acknowledged that China seemed determined to overturn the traditional status quo of Tibet vis-à-vis China and India: "I think it may be taken for granted that China will take possession, in a political sense at least, of the whole of Tibet. There is no likelihood whatever of Tibet being able to resist this or stop it. It is equally unlikely that any foreign power can prevent it. We cannot do so. If so, what can we do to help in the maintenance of Tibetan autonomy and at the same time avoiding continuous tensions and apprehensions on our frontiers?"[34]

Nehru felt that the best way of minimizing China's military presence in Tibet was by refraining from taking hostile actions toward China. By not provoking China, by not giving it reason to crush Tibet, India might, Nehru felt, preserve a substantial part of Tibetan autonomy. Nehru ruled out Patel's proposal that India consider supporting Tibet's appeal to the United Nations, saying: "There may be some moral basis for [the Tibetan] argument. But it will not take us or Tibet very far. It will only hasten the downfall of Tibet. No outsider will be able to help her, and China, suspicious and apprehensive of these tactics, will make sure of much speedier and fuller possession of Tibet than she might otherwise have done. We shall not only fail in our endeavor but at the same time have really a hostile China on our doorstep."

Nehru concluded that the best way to prevent China from establishing a large military presence in or direct political rule over Tibet was by convincing Beijing that there was no need for such measures. The logistic difficulties and costs of keeping Chinese military forces in Tibet were so great that Beijing would assume these burdens only if it saw a pressing need to do so. If there were no reason for Beijing to bear these costs, why should it? If New Delhi

demonstrated its friendship with the PRC and the practical diplomatic value
of that friendship to China, Beijing would have an incentive to strengthen
the relationship by adopting an understanding attitude toward India's friendly
interests in Tibet. India's core interests vis-à-vis the Tibetan buffer would thus
be protected by accepting Beijing's claim to Tibet, avoiding confrontation,
and befriending the PRC.

Nehru's post-1951 approach to Tibet was based on an overestimation of
the impact of Tibet's terrain, or, more precisely, on an underestimation of
the impact of modern technology on movement into and through Tibet.
Nehru was convinced that the immense logistical and financial difficulties
confronting a major and permanent Chinese military occupation of Tibet
would incline Beijing toward a relatively low military presence in the region.
"It is reasonable to assume that given the very nature of Tibetan geography,
terrain and climate, a large measure of autonomy is almost inevitable," he
explained. Terrain also led Nehru to rule out a major attack by China: "There
is, in my opinion, practically no chance of a major attack on India by
China."[35]

Following the PLA seizure of Qamdo, the Dalai Lama fled to Yadong in
the Chumbi Valley, only a few miles from the Indian border, where he could
escape into India if need be. In line with Nehru's emerging policy of appeasement, Indian officials urged the Dalai Lama to return to Lhasa and seek a peaceful settlement with Beijing which safeguarded Tibetan autonomy.[36] At the
United Nations India helped shelve Tibet's appeal for help. Urging by India
that he reach a settlement with Beijing, together with the lack of American
and British support, persuaded the Dalai Lama to order his representatives
to Beijing to negotiate an agreement with the CCP.[37] A seventeen-point agreement between "the Central Government and the Local Government of Tibet"
was signed in Beijing in May 1951. The very first sentence of the agreement
enshrined the new Chinese nationalist view of Tibet's relation with China:
"The Tibetan nationality is one of the nationalities with a long history living
within the boundaries of China." Point 1 reiterated the same theme: "The
Tibetan people shall return to the family of the motherland—the People's
Republic of China." The earlier nonpresence of Chinese civil and military
authority in Tibet was attributed to "imperialist forces" and to an "unpatri-
otic attitude" by the "local government of Tibet." Multiple provisions of the
agreement made it clear that whatever "autonomy" Tibet might henceforth
enjoy was to be exercised "under the unified leadership of the central People's
Government and the direct leadership of higher levels of the People's
Government." The May 1951 agreement provided a legal basis for the PRC's
takeover of Tibet.[38]

Nehru eventually came to see the seventeen-point agreement as accommodating substantial Indian interests. While a Chinese military presence in Tibet was established under the agreement, Tibet nonetheless maintained a degree of real autonomy. For several years after the seventeen-point agreement was signed, India continued its efforts to befriend the PRC, serving in the United Nations as the major noncommunist advocate of PRC admission to that body and tilting toward Beijing's side on Korean War issues.[39] Cordial, cooperative relations with China were essential to Nehru's nonaligned approach to the world. Tibet was an irritant that could not be allowed to spoil ROI-PRC relations and thus India's nonaligned approach.[40]

This led to a desire to minimize friction over Tibet and thus to a decision to relinquish the rights in Tibet inherited by India from Britain. The CCP viewed these rights as part of the imperialist aggression that had humiliated China and was therefore determined to terminate them. On the other hand, the economic consequences associated with the PLA's entry into Tibet were greater than anticipated. PLA purchases of food led to considerable inflation, causing hardship for Tibet's poorest, whom the CCP hoped to win over. New roads to bring food and other goods into Tibet from China had not yet been completed, and most of those goods still came from or through India. Therefore, according to Yang Gongsu, the young foreign affairs assistant of the central government team dispatched to Lhasa in 1951, continued trade with India served China's interests, and Beijing was willing to offer relatively lenient treatment for India's old rights in Tibet.[41] This led to an agreement in April 1954. By abandoning its special rights in Tibet, India reduced the incentives for China to suppress Tibetan autonomy, or so Nehru hoped. Responding to strong criticism of the 1954 agreement, Nehru explained to the head of India's Intelligence Bureau, B. N. Mullik, that, once the "last vestiges" of suspicion between China and India were removed, China's leaders would be more inclined to adopt a reasonable attitude toward Tibetan autonomy, thus preserving its substance and safeguarding India's broader interests.[42]

The 1954 agreement substantially pared down the size of India's missions in Tibet while providing for continuing Indian-Tibet trade and Indian pilgrimages to Tibetan holy sites.[43] More fundamentally, by referring repeatedly to "the Tibet region of China," the agreement embodied implicit ROI recognition of PRC sovereignty over Tibet. The agreement also spoke in its preamble of what subsequently became known as the Five Principles of Peaceful Coexistence, or, as India prefers, Panchsheel. These principles specified "mutual respect for each other's territorial integrity and sovereignty" and "mutual non-interference in internal affairs." In Beijing's eyes this meant that New Delhi had no standing to comment, let alone attempt to influence, affairs inside PRC boundaries—that is, inside the Tibet region of China. Beijing saw the 1954 agreement as an Indian promise to follow a hands-off policy toward Tibet. Subsequent Indian efforts to maintain Tibetan autonomy thus became evidence of Indian "duplicity" in Chinese eyes. From New Delhi's perspective, however, an essential if unspoken premise of the 1954 agreement was substantial de facto Tibetan autonomy. The agreement said nothing about Tibet's "autonomy"; that word appeared nowhere in the agreement or the associated notes. Yet, at the time the agreement was signed, Tibet enjoyed a real and high degree of self-rule. A few years later, when Beijing fundamentally changed this situation and pointed to the 1954 agreement as proof of Indian acceptance of China's ownership of Tibet, India saw China as reneging on its half of a bargain while insisting on keeping the half it had received. In Indian eyes this was "betrayal."

There was much Indian criticism of Nehru's concessions on Tibet, both in 1954 and in subsequent years. Retired foreign secretary J. N. Dixit in a 1998 book, for instance, maintains that India got very little in exchange for conceding the main point to Beijing:

> The first occasion when we could have negotiated a realistic deal with China was when Nehru acquiesced with the Chinese resuming their suzerainty and jurisdiction over Tibet. We could have told the Chinese that, in return for our accepting their resumption of authority over Tibet, they should confirm the delineation of the Sino-Indian boundary as inherited by them and us from the British period. We could have and should have demanded the quid pro quo of their not questioning the delineated boundary of British times and asked them not to revive any of their tenuous claims on what was Indian territory. We did not utilize the opportunity of our agreeing to China resuming authority in Tibet to safeguard our territorial interests.[44]

Part of the problem with the 1954 ROI-PRC deal was that what India gave (recognition of PRC ownership of Tibet) was virtually impossible to withdraw, while what India received, friendship, was as changeable as government policy. Once recognition is given, it is very difficult to revoke. Under international law the principle of estoppel requires states to act consistently, blocking moves that contradict earlier official actions. Politically, once one state recognizes a piece of territory to be part of another state, altering that recognition almost always comes in the context of civil war or regime breakdown and is considered to be an extremely hostile act. Until it has secured such recognition, however, the state claiming the relevant piece of territory is the suitor and must cajole or pressure other states to secure recognition of its sovereignty. Recognition of territorial sovereignty is virtually impossible to withdraw. Chinese goodwill, on the other hand, would vanish swiftly in 1959, leaving India with nothing in exchange for its major concession regarding the status of Tibet. Nonrecognition of China's overturn of the status quo in Tibet might have served India's interests better. The principle of nonrecognition was well established by the 1950s. The United States, for example, had applied it to Japan's creation of Manchukuo in 1932 and the Soviet seizure of the three Baltic republics in 1940. China itself would later apply the doctrine to India's 1975 annexation of Sikkim.

SINO-INDIAN FRIENDSHIP AND TIBETAN AUTONOMY

The brief period of Sino-Indian friendship from 1954 to 1958 coincided with a limited but genuine degree of Tibetan autonomy exercised under the agreement of May 1951. Throughout the four years of Sino-Indian friendship Nehru continued to value Tibetan autonomy and imagined that objective was being promoted by friendly relations with China. Simultaneously, Indian policy encouraged Tibetans to uphold their autonomy in the face of possible encroachment by Beijing. Nehru explained his mid-1950s Tibetan policy in an interview given as that policy was collapsing:

> We have not interfered in Tibet.... All that we have done is to use our influence in a friendly way to persuade the Chinese to go slow in the matter of reforms and avoid repression. We tried to convince them that it is impossible to make good Communists of the Tibetans, and that even reforms, necessary as they be, work better when they come from persuasion and education rather than coercion or imposition.... Tibet, of course, is part of China, but Mr. Chou [Enlai] himself told me that it was not a province of China , and would not be treated as such, that Tibetans were not Chinese but [non-]Han people different from the Chinese people and that, therefore, the Peking government would consider Tibet as an autonomous region of China and treat it as such.[45]

In the aftermath of the 1954 agreement Tibetan refugees in Kalimpong, Sikkim, were "shocked and anguished" by what they took to be Indian abandonment, B. N. Mullik reported to Nehru. Tibetans were "anxious to maintain their opposition to the Chinese" and "knew that they could not get any material help from India," but Mullik felt that "even moral support would sustain them in the fight." Nehru agreed to a series of moves to boost Tibetan morale. Tibetan refugees were to be assured that India would not deport them to China even if Beijing demanded this. Tibetans were to be allowed to bring gold, silver, and money freely into India, and these valuables were to be exempt from customs, plus currency and income taxes. Regarding the "spirit of resistance" in Tibet, Nehru told Mullik that, even if Tibetan refugees in India helped their brethren inside Tibet, the Indian government would not take any notice and would not entertain Chinese protests unless the refugees compromised themselves by acting too openly. As to the form of Tibetan "resistance," Nehru was of the opinion that nonviolent struggle to protect Tibetan culture and religious autonomy was best. Taking up arms, Nehru felt, would only give China an excuse to use military might to crush Tibet. In such an event India was too weak to do anything militarily.[46]

When the Dalai Lama visited India in 1956–57 to participate in the celebration of the 2,500th anniversary of the birth of Lord Buddha, Nehru encouraged him to use nonviolent struggle to uphold Tibetan autonomy. Beijing had initially opposed the Dalai Lama's personal participation in the celebration. Eventually, Beijing relented, in part because of lobbying by Nehru. While the Dalai Lama was in India, there was great debate among Tibetan leaders about the question of openly declaring independence from China. Many Tibetan leaders pressed the Dalai Lama to stay in India and reopen negotiations with Beijing through the Indian government. Nehru, however, advised him to return to Tibet and work peacefully with the Chinese, relying on the provisions of the May 1951 agreement to uphold Tibet's autonomy. Nehru took a copy of the 1951 agreement and tutored the young Tibetan leader on the implications of its clauses for Tibetan autonomy.

Concerned by the possibility that the Dalai Lama might stay in India, Zhou Enlai flew to India in November 1956 and again in January 1957 to persuade the Tibetan leader to return to China. Nehru used the occasion of Zhou's visits to discuss Tibetan autonomy. He left those talks with the belief that he had a secured commitment from Zhou to respect Tibetan autonomy. Nehru thought he heard Zhou stress Tibetan autonomy and China's intention to give "full autonomy." China was willing, Nehru heard Zhou say, to uphold Tibetan autonomy with the Dalai Lama as leader but also warned that "foreign subversive activities directed against Tibet" would compel China to increase its control there.[47] When Nehru encouraged the Dalai Lama to return to Tibet, he urged him to struggle to uphold Tibetan autonomy. From China's perspective Nehru's actions associated with the Dalai Lama's 1956–57 visit to India was a further demonstration of India's duplicitous policy. Beijing's decision allowing the Dalai Lama to visit India had been a demonstration of friendship and trust toward India. India had abused that trust, Chinese leaders felt, by encouraging him to resist Beijing's "legitimate assertions of authority" in Tibet.

THE TIBETAN INSURGENCY AND THE END OF TIBETAN AUTONOMY

From the late 1950s through the early 1970s Tibet experienced a series of linked processes which fundamentally altered its relation with China and with India, destroying the autonomy that underlay the brief period of Sino-Indian amity. One process was a systematic CCP totalitarian effort to remake Tibetan society according to the dictates of Maoist ideology. A second was the eruption of a deep-rooted and tenacious armed Tibetan resistance to Chinese rule. A third process was covert American and Chinese Nationalist (Taiwanese) support of the Tibetan resistance.

Tibetan resistance to Chinese rule erupted into armed rebellion in ethnically Tibetan regions of Sichuan in 1954. Not considered part of Tibet by Beijing, those regions were subject to collectivist reforms that precipitated rebellion among the Tibetan populace. The United States Central Intelligence Agency (CIA) and nationalist Chinese intelligence agencies had established contact with anticommunist Tibetans in 1950, and the eruption of armed rebellion opened interesting possibilities. In mid-1957 the CIA began covert parachute drops into Tibet of U.S.-trained Tibetan guerrilla fighters along with guns, ammunition, and supplies. These drops increased in frequency, reaching their peak in early 1960 and numbering "more than thirty," with 250 tons of supplies being dropped between 1957 and 1961. Tibetans were sent for training to Saipan in the South Pacific and later to Camp Hale in the Colorado Rocky Mountains. CIA support for the Tibetan insurgency peaked about 1960 but continued until 1969.[48] American support was probably marginal to the course of the Tibetan rebellion. (Fifty tons of supplies per year was a tiny amount.) It did, however, significantly influence the course of Indian-Chinese interactions.

Spreading resistance in Tibet accelerated the CCP's destruction of Tibetan autonomy. As the insurgency spread, CCP cadre assumed administrative authority and used it to the fullest to deal with any challenge to Beijing's authority. Those living in rebel areas were registered and interrogated. Lamaist monasteries and monks were divested of administrative authority. After the rebellion spread to Lhasa in March 1959, the CCP decided to move forward with the "reform" of Tibetan society, which would destroy the power of Tibet's old "reactionary upper classes" and, so the CCP hoped, win the support of Tibet's oppressed laboring classes. Monasteries were shut down and lamas and monks forced to undertake manual labor. Religion was ruthlessly suppressed. All significant economic and large-scale social activity was brought under the control of the CCP cadre. The Party made efforts to recruit an ethnically Tibetan cadre from the lower classes, but most high-ranking cadre, and those who held sensitive and influential positions, were Han. More important than ethnicity of cadres was the fact that all cadres, whether Tibetan or Han, were now part of a centralized administrative system taking orders from Beijing and judged carefully on the basis of obedience to those orders. The Tibetan autonomy that India perceived as the quid pro quo for its recognition of China's ownership of Tibet in 1954, and which it believed China had promised to respect in 1954–57, was destroyed.

The so-called reforms of the late 1950s exacerbated an already large ethnic gulf between Han and Tibetan. During the early and mid-1950s a significant portion of Tibet's lower classes had, in fact, welcomed the CCP's enlightened influence, hoping it would alleviate their poverty and oppression by Tibet's traditional upper classes. But the CCP progressively squandered this popular support. Repression of Lamaist monasteries, plus forced collectivization of lands and herds in the ethnically Tibetan regions of western Sichuan province, sparked rebellion in 1956. PLA pacification efforts generated refugees and hatred of China. A growing tide of refugees carried this resentment into Tibet proper, where it mixed with apprehension about the growing Chinese military presence. The mixture exploded into a general uprising in Lhasa in March 1959, following which the Chinese campaign of repression extended across Tibet. Monasteries and other religious monuments were closed down, the Tibetan government disbanded, and the CCP/PLA apparatus assumed direct administrative authority. The PLA unleashed a systematic pacification campaign. As in most such campaigns, large numbers of heavily armed alien troops (Han in this case) struggled to find and destroy guerrillas enjoying substantial popular support. The sheer brutality of CCP repression was appalling. Interrogation by torture, summary executions, reprisals, and forced relocation of population were common.[49] Even after the insurgency was suppressed, the fanaticism and Han chauvinism of the Maoist era led to continued administrative reliance on brutal means. The nadir was reached during the Cultural Revolution, when even private practice of religion was prohibited and severely punished. Thousands of Tibet's monasteries were also destroyed. Nor did CCP rule of Tibet improve the standard of living there. Indeed, it may have fallen as agriculture was collectivized and oriented along lines dictated by Beijing but inappropriate to Tibetan conditions, as foreign trade withered, and as the region was forced to support a large military presence.

By the 1970s the CCP ruled in Tibet over a bitter and sullen population. Obedience was achieved almost exclusively by provoking fear. This was a situation that tempted foreign exploitation. In a way a new, more modern Tibetan nation had been created by the holocaust of Maoist misrule. There was now a much more coherent Tibetan people, united by their experience of Chinese oppression. Under such circumstances a hostile foreign power might calculate that an expeditionary force could precipitate and take advantage of widespread popular revolt.

A sea change in Indian opinion toward China also resulted from the confluence of events in Tibet in the late 1950s. Indian public opinion was repulsed by the repressive and antireligious Chinese policies in Tibet.[50] Thus, when the Dalai Lama fled to India following the Lhasa revolt of March 1959, he was welcomed as an honored guest by the Indian government. When tens of thousands of Tibetan refugees followed him, New Delhi accorded them refugee status, provided material relief, and permitted them a wide range of activities. These Indian actions were primarily inspired by the overwhelming groundswell of sympathy for Tibet among ordinary Indians. Nehru, or any other elected leader, simply could not ignore it. Beijing's Communist leaders, however, viewed Indian references to such political pressures as mere pretexts advanced to cover deeper geostrategic calculations. China's leaders viewed Indian criticism of Chinese actions in Tibet as incitement and India's sympathetic reception of Tibetan refugees as support for the armed resistance inside Tibet.

Following Nehru's rejection in April 1960 of Zhou Enlai's proposal for a comprehensive compromise settlement of the boundary issue, Chinese leaders concluded that India was colluding with U.S. covert operations to support the Tibetan insurgents. Mao became convinced that the United States and India, along with (increasingly) China's erstwhile ally the USSR, were all working together against China. India was inciting Tibetan resistance and supporting it via its tolerant policies toward the Dalai Lama's "government-in-exile" and Tibetan refugees. New Delhi was turning a blind eye to U.S. covert anti-China activities on and over Indian territory. India also rejected a reasonable, compromise solution to the boundary issue and demanded Chinese withdrawal from critical territory so as to further weaken China's position in Tibet. The United States was covertly supporting the Tibetan insurgents, while the USSR, for its part, had declared its neutrality in the Indian-Chinese territorial dispute in September 1959, thus announcing to New Delhi that China would not have Soviet support. Soviet leaders were also pressuring Mao to concede to India's demands on the border. The goal of this anti-China conspiracy, Mao concluded, was nothing less than to split Tibet from the People's Republic of China. Splitting Tibet from China and denying China nuclear weapons were two key ways in which the American-Indian-Soviet anti-China coalition sought to keep New China weak.[51] Forceful blows were necessary to foil this anti-China conspiracy, Mao concluded.

Because of India's continued refusal to declassify documents relating to Nehru's handling of Tibetan affairs, it is impossible to determine the accuracy of Chinese views regarding Nehru's collusion with U.S. covert support for Tibetan rebels. Scholars can still only guess. Steven Hoffman, in his close study of Indian decision making, found that in the mid-1950s Nehru had directed Mullik to overlook Tibetan refugee activity in India. About January 1958, however, as the insurgency in Tibet flared and the boundary issue erupted following China's announcement of the construction of the Aksai Chin road, Nehru shifted course and began curbing many previously tolerated Tibetan activities—although not to a degree adequate to satisfy Beijing. Regarding CIA operations, Hoffman concludes that we still cannot know to what extent the highest levels of the Indian government knew of, tolerated, and cooperated with these efforts.[52]

The small circle of U.S. officials familiar with CIA covert operations prior to the 1962 war was itself divided about whether Nehru condoned those operations. Advocates of the CIA's operations pointed to various Indian actions as signaling tacit approval. In November 1960, for example, the Indian foreign secretary informed U.S. Ambassador Ellsworth Bunker of Chinese charges that U.S. airplanes were violating Chinese boundaries via Indian airspace. India had no way of knowing whether the Chinese charges were true, the Indian official said, but India hoped that if the U.S. were planning any future airdrops in Tibet, it would avoid Indian airspace, since India was planning to take vigorous actions to shoot down any foreign aircraft violating its airspace. Bunker took this message—and told the Indian official as much—as an indication that the Indian government was "not averse to aid being rendered to the Tibetans." U.S. officials opposed to CIA operations in Tibet argued against this interpretation.[53] Beijing's view was far less equivocal. Chinese leaders believed Nehru had knowingly turned a blind eye to CIA activities while coordinating his "forward policy" on the border with Soviet and American pressure on China.

TIBET AND THE 1962 SINO-INDIAN WAR

Trans-Himalayan wars are extremely difficult and costly to wage. Yet China has twice undertaken such wars: in 1793 and in 1962. In both cases China went to war because it feared losing control over Tibet. The 1793 case will be discussed in a subsequent chapter on Nepal (see chap. 5), but it is appropriate to summarize here Leo Rose's conclusion about Beijing's calculations at that point. Geography created close links between Tibet and the Himalayas, and when a regime based in the Nepali Himalayas attempted to assert its own control in central Tibet, thereby challenging China's suzerainty, China quashed that threat. A powerful Chinese-Tibetan army marched through the Himalayas to the outskirts of Kathmandu.[54]

Regarding the 1962 war, "The major problem [in Indian-Chinese relations] is not the problem of the McMahon line, but the Tibet question," Mao Zedong told a visiting Nepali delegation in 1964. "In the opinion of the Indian government," he told them, "Tibet is theirs."[55] Contemporary Chinese studies of the 1962 war are in line with Mao's analysis; they too perceive an Indian effort to turn Tibet into a buffer as a major cause of the 1962 war. A synopsis of the war by China's foremost South Asian specialist, Wang Hongwei, places Indian aspirations toward Tibet at the center of the process leading to war. Imperial Britain long tried to bring Tibet into its realm. This imperialist mentality was assimilated by Nehru and other Congress Party leaders, who had been educated in England and peacefully took over state power from the British. From 1949 through 1953 Indian leaders struggled to maintain the imperialist position in Tibet which they had inherited from Britain. Chinese firmness foiled this effort, and in 1954 New Delhi was forced to come to terms. In 1959, however, Nehru concluded that the time was right for action. According to Wang, the "slave owners' rebellion" in Tibet, the deterioration of the Sino-Soviet alliance, and China's domestic crisis convinced Nehru that the situation was advantageous to India. Thus, New Delhi supported the Tibetan rebellion, allowed the rebels to conduct anti-China activities in India, gave military training to some Tibetan refugees, and sent them to the border area, and so on. Nehru then rejected Zhou Enlai's "entirely objective and fair" proposal for a border settlement and adopted his forward policy embodying India's "peremptory attitude." This Indian approach was predicated on the assumption that China "would not dare to contest it" (*bu gan yu ta jinxing jiaoliang*). China's devastating blow created greater realism and caution in India and "produced a situation of long-term security and stability on the Sino-Indian border."[56]

Other authoritative Chinese studies of the 1962 war go even further, seeing Indian policy as a manifestation of a strategy calculated to restore Tibet to its pre-1949 status. The most authoritative Chinese history of the 1962 war to date, published by China's Academy of Military Sciences, maintains that Nehru adopted a deliberate imperialist strategy from Britain. Nehru's aim was establishment of Tibet as a buffer zone (*huan chong guo*), guarding the northern flank of India's "great Asian empire." The Indian leader understood that whoever controlled Tibet, whether by direct or indirect means, would occupy a position of absolute superiority, and he was determined to secure that advantage for India.[57] Another authoritative Chinese scholar, Xu Yan of

China's National Defense University, reaches essentially the same conclusion. Throughout the 1950s, according to Xu, Nehru secretly pursued a policy designed to detach Tibet from China to serve as a northern defense zone of India's realm. The encouragement of the Dalai Lama's resistance to Beijing, New Delhi's toleration of U.S. covert links to the Tibetan splittists, and the nonnegotiable demand for Chinese evacuation of "all Indian territory," plus the forward policy, were all elements of this strategy. Nehru's support for the Tibetan splittists was the "decisive factor" on the road to the 1962 war.[58]

The Tibetan issue was central to the deterioration of Sino-Indian relations which culminated in the 1962 war. Chinese leaders noted with suspicion that, following the Dalai Lama's return to Tibet from India in early 1957, Tibetan insurgent attacks increased and the CIA began supporting the Tibetan rebellion. Tibetan insurgent activities in Kalimpong also increased. In July 1958 China sent a note to India detailing U.S., Nationalist Chinese, and Tibetan insurgent activities in Kalimpong and asking India to prohibit them. India did nothing, at least in China's view.[59] Chinese officials also believed that India played a role in encouraging the Lhasa uprising of 1959. During the early days of the uprising a large group of Tibetans had gone to the Indian consulate to ask for Indian support. According to Yang Gongsu, the Indian consul told the group that a verbal statement regarding such a request was inadequate and asked the Tibetans to put their request in writing—which could be construed as an invitation to make a formal declaration of independence. Several days later a procession of Tibetans returned to the Indian consulate to present a copy of their now-written declaration of Tibetan independence and to ask that it be transmitted to New Delhi. The Indian consul again met with the procession, accepted a copy of their declaration, and said he would transmit it to his government to "let the issue be decided between the Chinese and Indian governments"—words that could be construed as promising Indian government intervention on Tibet's behalf.[60] Beijing construed these actions as Indian encouragement of the pro-independence Tibetan rebels.

Once the Dalai Lama arrived at India's borders in April 1959, he and his party were immediately granted permission to enter Indian territory and provided with comfortable accommodations at Mussoorie. High officials of India's Foreign Ministry, and on April 24 Nehru himself, met with the Dalai Lama. Nehru told him that, although Tibet was a part of China, Beijing had violated its 1951 guarantee of autonomy by resorting to armed suppression. The Indian media was highly critical of Chinese actions in Tibet. Between the end of February and early April 1959 Indian newspapers carried over three hundred articles attacking China for "exercising sovereignty in Tibet," by Beijing's count. The Nehru government permitted these activities, Chinese leaders believed, as a way of increasing pressure on China. To further pressure China—again, so Chinese leaders believed—New Delhi began implementing economic sanctions designed to increase hardship in Tibet. In April 1959 India forbade the export of grain to Tibet. In September it forbade the export to Tibet of various steel products without special licenses. In October fuel oil, auto parts, clothing, tools, sugar, and tea were added to the list. In April 1960 wood (a scarce and crucial construction material in central Tibet) was embargoed. Meanwhile, various high officials of the Congress Party helped organize a committee to assist the Tibetan rebels and called for UN intervention and for the convocation of a tripartite Sino-Indian-Tibetan conference to resolve the issue. According to Chinese leaders, India hoped that, as China faced mounting difficulties in Tibet, it would ask India to mediate the dispute.[61]

Whatever the actual extent of Indian complicity with U.S. covert operations may have been, Beijing *believed* that Nehru knew of and cooperated with CIA efforts. Zhou Enlai explained China's view of the situation in a briefing to the Soviet and East European ambassadors in May 1959, just after the suppression of the Lhasa revolt and as PLA troops were pouring into Tibet to crush the insurrection. India was strongly protesting Chinese actions in Tibet, including its introduction of large numbers of troops. Zhou began his explanation of China's policy to his Soviet bloc allies by outlining the role of foreign support for the "counterrevolutionary rebellion" in Tibet: "Tibetan rebels have continually been going to Kalimpong to conduct activities with Chiang Kai-shek, United States and British special agents. . . . For several years Kalimpong has been the center of activity for Tibetan rebels outside of China. The desire of the Tibetan upper class to uphold the system of exploitation and oppose reform is the main reason for the rebellion in Tibet. But without foreign support and instigation, it could not have started a rebellion like this."[62] Regarding India, Zhou explained that it was following a duplicitous (*liang-mian xing*) policy. New Delhi professed to respect China's sovereignty, but covertly it colluded with Washington to violate it:

> India's ambition of setting up a "buffer" (*huan chong guo*), of preventing reform in Tibet, of forcing the PLA to withdraw, and so on, are not easy to make public. It's better to work from behind the scenes. While publicly saying they are not interfering in China's internal politics, have no territorial ambitions towards Tibet, uphold the five principles of peaceful coexistence, want to consolidate Sino-Indian friendship, and so on. . . . [In fact Nehru] wants to use Cold War and political pressure to bring about a Sino-Indian-Tibetan tripartite meeting to interfere in China's internal politics.

According to Zhou, Nehru and other "upper-class elements" in India objected to the CCP's initiation of reforms in Tibet because "they hope to keep Tibet in a backward state for a long time so it can serve as a 'buffer state' between China and India." "This is the center of the China-India dispute," Zhou told his Soviet-bloc comrades. He dismissed Nehru's argument that Indian actions were motivated by sympathy for Buddhism in Tibet. This was a mere pretext for India's interfering in the internal affairs of China. Nehru's true motive was to prevent progress in Tibet, keeping it poor and backward so it could "serve as a 'buffer' under the Indian sphere of influence, and become their protectorate." This policy, Zhou explained, was tied to Nehru's class nature.

INDIA'S OPTION OF EXPLOITING CHINA'S TIBETAN VULNERABILITY

The 1962 war led to a radical reorientation of India's Tibet policy. New Delhi adopted a policy of "benign tolerance" toward previously prohibited Tibetan refugee activity. In 1963 the Indian government did not prohibit the Dalai Lama from promulgating a new constitution for Tibet. It also allowed the Dalai Lama to open Tibetan offices in New York and Geneva. It agreed, without any official announcement, to U.S. efforts to train a cadre of young Tibetans to staff Tibet's new overseas offices. India also began supporting efforts to raise the Tibetan issue in the United Nations. In the fall of 1965 the Indian government went so far as to hint it was prepared to withdraw India's recognition of China's suzerainty over Tibet. Speaking at the opening of a Tibetan office and cultural center in downtown New Delhi, Home Minister M. C. Chagla said that India had recognized China's suzerainty on the condition that Tibet's autonomy be maintained. Now it was clear that this autonomy no longer existed. Tibet's "culture has been driven out," and "the conditions under which we recognized China's suzerainty no longer exist."[63] This hint that India might withdraw its recognition of China's suzerainty was quickly dropped and not subsequently revived.

India also began cooperating with the CIA and Tibetan insurgent organizations to support Tibetan armed resistance to Chinese rule in Tibet. The Research and Analysis Wing (RAW) of India's Intelligence Board set up a special communications base in a radio signal–sparse area of Orissa state. There two large receivers and transmitters were hooked up to special antennas to maintain regular, encrypted radio contact with Tibetan insurgent forces operating in even the most remote regions of the country. Transmissions were encoded and decoded by a staff of ten. RAW, CIA, and Tibetan rebel officers met weekly to review activities inside Tibet and issue directives for future operations.[64] A group of "private individuals," who happened to be mostly former Indian air force pilots headed by former Indian army commander General K. S. Thimayya, were also organized to fly clandestine air missions into Tibet. Throughout the 1960s RAW pilots dropped supplies and arms to insurgents inside Tibet.[65]

India also established a substantial Tibetan military force. Founded in November 1962 after negotiations between Mullik and leaders of the Tibetan resistance movement, the force was formally named the Special Frontier Force (SFF). Informally, it was known as Establishment 22, after the Twenty-second Mountain Regiment commanded in World War II by the SFF's Indian commander, Major General Urban. Except for a few top-level officers, the SFF was entirely Tibetan. Within a few years it had grown to over ten thousand men, recruited on the basis of a hope of someday fighting to free Tibet from Chinese rule. Mullik believed that Nehru was "preparing for the day when it would be possible for India to restore Tibet to a semi-independent if not independent status."[66] It is impossible to determine the extent to which the promise that the SFF would eventually fight for Tibet's independence represented Indian contingency planning for a future Sino-Indian war, as opposed to an illusion cultivated by India to maintain Tibetan morale. In any case the SFF became a very competent, dedicated, and disciplined military force. Unlike the Tibetan resistance, which operated as lightly armed guerrillas, the SFF were professionally trained, high-altitude commandos. The SFF operated effectively in the Chittagong Hills during the 1971 India-Pakistan war and again during the India-Pakistan fighting over the Saichen Glacier in Kashmir in the 1990s. The SFF was, and remains, a highly potent force inspired by the hope of someday liberating Tibet.[67]

The creation of the SFF became more significant against the background of the Indian military buildup that followed the 1962 war. The catastrophic defeat of 1962 ushered in a revolution in Indian defense thinking and preparedness. Within a decade the regular army had doubled in size, to 750,000, with total armed strength of over a million. Ten new mountain divisions were created—the first such units in the Indian army. The officer corps was reorganized and incompetent generals removed. Modern arms of all types were purchased. Defense spending grew rapidly until by the early 1970s it accounted for 40 percent of the central government budget and over 3 percent of GNP.[68] Within a few years of India's 1962 debacle, the Indian forces that faced the PLA were a far more modern and potent force. Some of the leaders of that force also looked forward to the day when they could revenge the humiliation of 1962.

According to John Avedon, who enjoyed close contacts with the Tibetan community in India, Indian contingency planning in the 1970s called for a bold move to wrest Tibet from China in the event of another Sino-Indian war. The SFF was to be parachuted behind Chinese lines throughout Tibet, where they would sever PLA transportation and communications links, rally the populace, and disrupt the PLA's flank and rear areas. Meanwhile, the Indian army would advance into Tibet, meeting the PLA head-on. India's planned objective in the event of a war, according to Avedon, was nothing less than the independence of Tibet.[69] It is possible that such visions were (and are) wishful thinking by the Tibetan exile community. India has an interest in keeping alive among that community hope of an eventual fighting return to Tibet, for such a hope is vital to sustaining the morale of any Tibetan fighting force. Be that as it may, the preparation of the appropriate Tibetan exile and Indian military capabilities, plus percolation of such ideas and plans among India's strategic elite, creates a standing threat to Beijing's control over Tibet, albeit one that would materialize only under the extreme conditions of war.

An offensive thrust by Indian-Tibetan forces into Tibet in the context of a China-India war, whether in the 1970s or in the 2000s, would be a risky but potentially high-pay-off move. It would have the advantage of allowing Indian forces to seize the initiative, forcing the PLA to respond to Indian offensive moves rather than the other way around. It would also carry the war to enemy territory, rather than allowing China to devastate Indian lands again. And it would offer the possibility of a strategic victory for India in a war with China— a victory that might significantly shift the balance of power between the two countries for a long period of time. A bold, offensive thrust into Tibet would offer India the possibility of fundamentally eliminating, on a long-term basis, the Chinese threat to northern India. The objective of such an offensive would be nothing less than the restoration of Tibet as a buffer state.

One of the great dangers China has perceived from close Indian association with either the United States or the Soviet Union was, and remains, that such an association may lead India to "play the Tibetan card." By itself New Delhi would be most unlikely to opt for a high-risk offensive strategy in Tibet. With American or Soviet encouragement, however, it becomes more likely. Following Indian-U.S. estrangement in the mid-1960s and the formation in 1971 of an Indian-Soviet strategic partnership, Chinese concern shifted from possible American to possible Soviet sponsorship of an Indian thrust into Tibet. Perhaps in conjunction with a Soviet-Chinese conflict arising elsewhere, Moscow might have persuaded India to open a second front in Tibet. In such an eventuality the PLA's situation would have been dire. Indian forces, with advantages of shorter distances, superior lines of logistic support, and greater mobility, could quickly seize Lhasa. An independent Tibetan government could then be formed which would organize Tibetan resistance to a Chinese effort to retake Tibet. Large numbers of Tibetans could quickly be rallied to the anti-PRC cause. Adequately armed by the USSR, those forces could multiply the strength of the SFF and/or Indian-Tibetan expeditionary force. The Tibetan populace might welcome invading Indian forces as liberators. Once inside Tibet, Indian forces would benefit from intelligence, willing laborers, and partisan support. Chinese forces, on the other hand, would be hobbled by sabotage and withholding of intelligence by the Tibetan populace. If Soviet forces interdicted PLA logistic lines into Tibet running south of Kashgar or Lanzhou, the PLA would be confronted with fighting a campaign with logistical lines across the rugged mountains of western Sichuan. South of Kashgar the road to Tibet runs only 135 miles east of the PRC-USSR boundary. Xining, at the head of the Qinghai road to Lhasa, is only 400 miles from the Mongolian border.

The conjunction of the Cultural Revolution in Tibet with the Sino-Soviet confrontation of 1969 created propitious conditions for a Soviet-supported Indian move to "liberate" Tibet. Soviet propaganda began to express support for Tibetan "self-determination."[70] Chinese fear of a Soviet-supported Indian move into Tibet apparently reached its peak about 1971, when Sino-Soviet relations were extremely tense. Only the year before, Moscow had proposed to American representatives at the Strategic Arms Limitation Treaty (SALT) negotiations in Helsinki joint action to preempt China's burgeoning nuclear program. India was then preparing to deliver a death blow to Pakistan as a united country by intervening to support the Bengalis of East Pakistan. (This crisis is discussed in chap. 7.) Beijing feared that India, after dealing successfully with its Pakistan threat by supporting "Bangladeshi national liberation," might turn north to deal with its northern nemesis in a similar fashion in Tibet, while China was still weak from the chaos of the Cultural Revolution and Lin Biao's attempted coup d'état. It is virtually certain the Tibetans would have welcomed Indian-Tibetan forces as liberators from the terror of the Red Guard. It was in this context that Foreign Minister Huang Hua addressed the United Nations Security Council on December 4, 1971. Regarding India's justification for invading East Pakistan, to facilitate the return of refugees from India to East Pakistan, Huang said: "This is utterly untenable. At present, there are in India large numbers of so-called 'refugees' from Tibet, China; the Indian government is also grooming [the] Dalai Lama, the chieftain of the Tibetan counterrevolutionary rebellion. According to the Indian government's assertion, are you going to use this also as a basis for aggression against China?"[71]

Again in the late 1970s, as Sino-Soviet relations deteriorated, Moscow hinted that it might adopt a more assertive approach toward Tibet. In a United Nations debate over the China-Vietnam war of February 1979, the Soviet representative raised the question of Tibet and implicitly condemned its occu-

pation by China in 1950 by comparing that move to China's 1979 attack on
Vietnam. Then in June the Dalai Lama made his first visit to the USSR, followed by a visit to the Mongolian People's Republic.[72] The psychological purposes served by Soviet support for Tibet were outlined in *The Coming Decline
of the Chinese Empire,* a book by the well-known KGB operative Victor Louis,
published in 1979. Louis's book portrayed Manchuria, Inner Mongolia,
Xinjiang, and Tibet as seething with anti-Chinese nationalism and passionate desires for independence. The book elliptically raised the possibility that
the Soviet Union might support the secession of these nationalities from China
in order to create a cordon sanitaire between the USSR and the PRC. As
Harrison Salisbury stated in his "dissenting introduction" to Louis's work,
the significance of such speculation was that Louis, "as a KGB man, is presenting a rationale intended to justify a Soviet 'war of liberation'—God help
us—against the People's Republic of China."[73] Louis's book was certainly part
of Moscow's psychological war against China. The point, however, is that
Moscow was playing on Chinese fears.

Into the late 1980s Indian defense analysts continued to pay close attention
to Tibetan history and developments and were well aware of China's vulnerabilities there. Some analysts who have studied the protracted Tibetan guerrilla war against the PLA in the 1960s see the victory of the Afghan Mujahadeen
over the Soviet army as a sign that such low-intensity war can win. They pointed
also to U.S. support for wars of anticommunist liberation under the Reagan
Administration as a possible model for India's future policy toward Tibet.[74]

Both Beijing and New Delhi are aware of the possibility that India could
exploit China's Tibetan vulnerability. For Chinese leaders this awareness
increases apprehension about the development of Indian military power. It
also contributes to their suspiciousness about the true intent of Indian policy toward the Tibetan refugees. Perhaps India's leaders want to keep the Dalai
Lama and his supporters in India, Chinese leaders suspect, because they want
to keep alive the option of an active policy toward Tibet. From the Indian
perspective the fact that India has not supported a Tibetan war of national
liberation (at least not since the 1970s) is proof of India's circumspection. It
is proof, from New Delhi's perspective, of India's fundamentally nonthreatening policy toward China and China's autonomous region of Tibet.

POST-MAO "OPENING" AND THE NEXT
CRISIS OF CHINESE AUTHORITY IN TIBET

The reform-minded leaders who came to power in Beijing in 1978 hoped to
use social, economic, and political reform to ease the chasm between PRC

authority and Tibetans created by two decades of Maoist misrule. These reforms moved Tibet in a much more humane direction. Collectivized agriculture was abandoned and land handed over to families. Individuals were again allowed to pursue herding and sideline occupations. Rural trade fairs were reopened. Border trade with Nepal, Bhutan, and Burma resumed. Private religious activity was no longer grounds for punishment. A number of monasteries were allowed to reopen and to recruit young monks again. Many monks previously forced to do other types of work were allowed to return to monasteries and resume their religious practice. Literally truckloads of religious idols shipped to China proper during the Cultural Revolution were returned to Tibet. A large number of political prisoners were released, and "counterrevolutionary" labels removed from 80 percent of participants in the 1959 rebellion. Status and property were restored to many people punished during the Maoist years. Many Han functionaries were withdrawn in the early 1980s—some twenty thousand during 1980–82. Foreign tourism was allowed and encouraged as an engine of economic development for the impoverished region.[75]

While the post-1978 relaxation was welcomed by Tibetans, there remained a deep cleavage between them and Chinese state authority. Generally speaking, revolts against dictatorial regimes do not occur when conditions are most dire and repression most severe but, rather, during periods of relaxation and relative prosperity following periods of deeper repression. This was the case in Tibet. The decade of relative relaxation and opening which began in 1978 culminated in the most widespread open opposition to Chinese rule since the 1959 rebellion. In some ways opposition to state authority was encouraged by China's post-1978 reforms. Political liberalization and increased foreign contact encouraged Tibetans to express openly their anti-Beijing sentiments.

An important element of Beijing's new approach to Tibet was to work toward a settlement with the Dalai Lama and his return to China. Contacts between Beijing and the Dalai Lama were established late in 1978. Discussions ensued, and eventually the Dalai Lama agreed to send delegations to Tibet for talks and to see the changes taking place there. The first delegation came in August 1979, a second group in mid-1980, and two more in 1982. A tremendous, spontaneous outpouring of popular welcome greeted these representatives of the Dalai Lama. It quickly became apparent that, in spite of decades of antireligious indoctrination, ordinary Tibetans still venerated the Dalai Lama, and many looked to him for deliverance from Chinese rule. This overwhelming popular reaction apparently surprised both Beijing and Dharmsala. As a result, Beijing apparently concluded that return of the Dalai Lama to Tibet under any conditions would undermine Beijing's authority. Although this conclusion was not translated into a more hard-line integrationist policy toward Tibet until 1989, by the mid-1980s the Chinese government was no longer enthusiastic about reaching an accommodation with the Dalai Lama. Given the still-fervent popular support of ordinary Tibetans for the Dalai Lama, were he allowed to return to Tibet, he would instantly become an alternate focus of authority, challenging that of the CCP. Beijing and Dharmsala also remained far apart. The Dalai Lama demanded that China give Tibet genuine autonomy, with Tibet equal to China within a federal system and holding United Nations membership, as did the Ukraine or Belorussia in the USSR. Beijing rejected these terms.

Tibetan discontent began to coalesce in September 1987 when the Dalai Lama was scheduled to visit the United States and speak to the United States Congress. Pro-independence demonstrations erupted in Lhasa that month, followed by riots culminating in bloodshed in October. Further demonstrations and riots occurred in 1988 and 1989. Early March 1989 saw the most widespread resistance to Chinese rule since 1959, with anti-Chinese mobs in Lhasa looting Han-run businesses and attacking CCP and government offices for several days. On March 8, two days before the fortieth anniversary of the 1959 uprising, martial law was imposed in Lhasa for the first time since 1959. Large numbers of soldiers moved in to restore order.

Internationalization of the Tibetan issue paralleled the 1987–89 eruption of Tibetan resistance to Beijing's rule. It began with the Dalai Lama's September 1987 visit to the United States and the European Union—the same month the protests in Lhasa began. The next month the European Parliament issued a resolution "urging the Chinese government to respect the rights of the Tibetans to religious freedom and cultural autonomy" and endorsing the Dalai Lama's plan for a settlement with Beijing. A year later the U.S. Congress issued a more elaborate resolution supporting the Dalai Lama. Thereafter, resolutions from the United States and European nations followed regularly for the next decade.[76] The most dramatic demonstration of growing international sympathy for Tibet was the award of a Nobel Peace Prize to the Dalai Lama in October 1989 for his "consistent resistance to the use of violence in his people's struggle to regain their liberty." Beijing denounced the award as part of a "western plot to destroy China's unity." Beijing's position deteriorated further in April 1991, when U.S. President George Bush, under mounting criticism for his conciliatory policies toward China, became the first sitting U.S. president to meet with the Dalai Lama. White House officials stressed that the Dalai Lama was received purely as a religious leader, not as a political one, and that their meeting did not signal a change in the U.S. policy of not recognizing Tibet as an independent entity. Nonetheless, the Bush–Dalai Lama meeting was an ominous sign for Beijing.

Afterward, meetings between the Dalai Lama and Western leaders became fairly routine.

Foreign criticism of China's rule in Tibet mounted during the 1990s, eventually equaling or surpassing the wave of international condemnation that met Beijing's repressive policies of 1959–61. This was in spite of the fact that Chinese rule in Tibet in the 1990s was far more benign than it had been thirty years earlier. Times had changed; the events associated with the end of the Cold War sharpened international concern with Tibet. There was too glaring a contrast between the peaceful ways the Communist government of Eastern Europe and the USSR dealt with popular protests and the way the CCP dealt with them. The CCP's decision to use military force to crush protest movements in Tibet, and then against the student movement in Beijing in June 1989, reinforced international criticism. By the 1990s Beijing faced a vicious cycle between repression of opposition in Tibet and mounting international criticism. The greater international attention to events in Tibet, the more dissidents there were encouraged to make the sacrifices associated with openly protesting Beijing's policies. Resistance was met with repression by Beijing, which in turn attracted greater international attention.

The eruption of opposition within Tibet, the deadlock in talks with the Dalai Lama, growing international criticism of Chinese rule in Tibet, and, by no means least, the disintegration of several former Communist states along ethnic lines led Beijing to shift directions in Tibet. Efforts to move the CCP apparatus in Tibet toward less repressive and integrationist policies were abandoned in the fall of 1989, and priority was henceforth placed on maintaining tight control over Tibet. Antireligious education was stepped up and tighter scrutiny paid to loyal members of the ethnic Tibetan cadre. Most important, earlier limits on Han migration to Tibet were dropped and efforts intensified to integrate Tibet's economy more closely with that of the rest of China. Accelerated economic development encouraged Han migration to Tibet.

THE FINAL SOLUTION: DEMOGRAPHIC INUNDATION OF TIBET?

China's history has seen a process of gradual expansion in which more numerous, richer, and better-organized Han settlers have assimilated lesser non-Han peoples.[77] This process has continued during the twentieth century in Manchuria, Inner Mongolia, and Xinjiang. In Inner Mongolia, for example, Han as a segment of the total population grew from 25 percent in 1949 to 84 percent in 1982. In Xinjiang the number grew from 6 percent in 1949 to 40 percent in 1982. Beijing hotly denies that a similar process is under way in Tibet. According to Beijing's 1992 White Paper on Tibet:

> Another lie [of the Dalai Lama clique] is the claim that a large number of Hans
> have migrated to Tibet, turning the ethnic Tibetans into a minority. It is very
> easy to confuse and poison the minds of people who are not aware of the truth.
> In Tibet, the natural conditions are harsh, the air is oxygen-poor and the cli-
> mate is bitterly cold. . . . Customs there are so different from those in the heart-
> land of the country that people from the interior can hardly adapt to them. . . .
> The figures from various national censuses have thoroughly exploded the lie
> that the Han population of Tibet has already surpassed that of the Tibetans.[78]

According to China's 1990 census, 2.096 million of 2.196 million people in
Tibet, or about 95 percent, were ethnic Tibetan. Han and other ethnic groups
constituted only about 5 percent. Most foreign observers, including this one,
simply do not find these figures credible. Travel in Tibet's major cities makes
clear that Han constitute a far more substantial portion of the population
there. Independent observers who have visited these cities repeatedly over
the course of decades, remark on the rapid increase in the Han population
which has turned wide areas of these cities into "new Chinese cities," virtually indistinguishable from small cities in China proper. Even though Tibet
is overwhelmingly rural, the Tibetan population is so sparse that an urban
population of perhaps several hundred thousand Han would constitute a far
larger portion of Tibet's population than 5 percent.

Han migration to Tibet has long been associated with economic development. In 1987 Deng Xiaoping explained the logic of this relationship to
visiting former President Jimmy Carter. Tibet needed Han immigrants
because the region's population of about two million was inadequate to
develop its resources. There were then about 200,000 Han in Tibet, Deng told
Carter.[79] That would have been just under 10 percent of the official Tibetan
population. Deng's statement to Carter dovetails with a careful study entailing ten weeks of clandestine field research in Tibet by a social anthropolo-
gist. On the basis of field surveys conducted in the summer of 1994, this study
set the Han component of Tibet's population at about 12–15 percent.[80] By
the end of the 1990s it was probably higher still.

Current trends make it likely that the Han component of Tibet's population will increase rapidly over the next several decades. Beijing's plans for Tibet
at the beginning of the twentieth-first century focus on accelerated economic
development, which will speed the economic integration of Tibet into the
PRC economy, the migration of Han into Tibet, and the assimilation of
Tibetans into mainstream (Han) Chinese culture. In mid-1998 ambitious
development plans for Tibet were unveiled whose objectives include a dou-
bling of Tibet's per capita GNP by the year 2015 to place the region in line

with the PRC national average. According to the plan, this will be achieved by accelerated development of mining, timber, and tourist industries. Tibet's rich mineral deposits will be exploited, with more advanced stages of processing and refining being done in Tibet to increase the value added there. Tibet's rich forests, ranking second in size among China's provinces, will be exploited to produce wood, furniture, and other forestry products. The productivity of agriculture and animal husbandry will be improved and related light industries developed. Expanded export of Tibet's products to the rest of China and the world will require further development of infrastructure. Highways, telecommunications, and electricity will be emphasized. All of these efforts will require skilled human talent. "We are desperately short of talent," said the vice chairman of the Tibet Autonomous Region (TAR). "We are extremely short of well educated persons and experts in economic management, law, and many other important social sciences."[81]

Rapid development objectives will require that this need for well-educated persons and experts be met mainly by hiring in other regions of China. While education of ethnic Tibetans might provide some of the needed human talent, relying on local talent is incompatible with accelerated development. China proper, on the other hand, has a fairly large pool of skilled talent. Unemployment is also a major problem in Chinese cities. The Asian economic crisis that began in late 1997, combined with market-oriented reform of state-owned enterprises, has created dangerously high levels of unemployment, exacerbating fears about social instability. Many unemployed or potentially unemployed Chinese possess the skills currently needed in Tibet. Their immigration to Tibet would ease a key developmental bottleneck while strengthening social stability in two ways: it would ease the discontent caused by reform in Han-populated regions of China, and it would shift the demographic balance in Tibet in favor of a more politically loyal ethnic group, the Han.

Given present trends, it appears likely that the population living in Tibet will rapidly become more Han. Ethnic Tibetans will constitute a steadily smaller proportion, eventually becoming a minority. Han will dominate Tibet's large-scale economy, while Tibetans remain in a lower economic stratum. Beijing's denials of these trends is, in all probability, a strategy of calculated deception. Beijing will probably continue to deny these processes until the Chinese nature of Tibet is so overwhelming and indisputable that there is no longer any need to do so—Tibet will have truly become a part of China. For India this will nullify its hope that Tibet be "an autonomous region" of China in any meaningful sense, and it will mean the final obliteration of India's cultural interests in Tibet. It will also mean that Tibet will forever be a military platform with logistical links ever more thickly tied to the Chinese heartland.

INDIAN POLICY TOWARD TIBET DURING
THE PERIOD OF ROI-PRC RAPPROCHEMENT

There is deep resentment in India over the course of Beijing's Tibet policy. China is widely seen as destroying Tibet's traditional Indian-influenced civilization. It does this in ways that violate basic human rights, which are at the core of India's own political culture: denying free expression of political views and discriminating against religion. China's denial of genuine autonomy to Tibet is seen as a negation of the 1954 Indian-Chinese understanding over Tibet. There is also resentment that China apparently expects India to ignore its own liberal values in dealing with the Tibetan refugees in India. In the background is knowledge that India's long-term national security environment has been diminished by the transformation of Tibet into a permanent base for Chinese military operations.

Throughout the process of ROI-PRC rapprochement Beijing has tried to persuade New Delhi to reduce, or better yet suspend, its tacit support for the Dalai Lama and the Tibetan exile community. New Delhi has responded marginally to Beijing's demand but has been unwilling to accede to Beijing's core demands regarding the Tibetan exile community in India. When Minister of External Affairs Atal Bihari Vajpayee visited Beijing in February 1979 (the first such visit by an Indian foreign minister to China), the issue of the Tibetan refugees in India was on the agenda. Vajpayee explained that the Dalai Lama was given refuge in India purely in deference to his spiritual position. Ordinary Tibetans were granted refugee status on strictly humanitarian grounds. If individual Tibetans wished to return to China, India would not stand in their way, but India also would not pressure them to leave India or return to Tibet. During Rajiv Gandhi's landmark visit to Beijing in December 1988 the question of Indian policy toward Tibetans living in India ranked high on the agenda. According to the joint communiqué signed at the conclusion of the visit, "The Chinese side expressed concern over anti-China activities by some Tibetan elements in India. The Indian side reiterated the long-standing and consistent policy of the government of India that Tibet is *an autonomous region of China* and that *anti-Chinese political activities* by Tibetan elements are not permitted *on Indian soil.*"[82] The use of the phrase *autonomous region* reminded Beijing of the promise it had made (as New Delhi understands it) in 1954–57, when India endorsed China's ownership of Tibet. The Chinese side replied to Gandhi's December 1988 formulation by announcing it had taken note of India's "principled position" and promise not to interfere in China's domestic affairs. By the time of Li Peng's December 1991 visit to India, the Chinese expression of "concern" in the final communiqué had expanded from the fourteen words of the 1988 communiqué to forty-nine words: "The Chinese side expressed concern about the continued activities in India by some Tibetans against their motherland and reiterated that Tibet was an inalienable part of Chinese territory and that it was firmly opposed to any attempt and actions aimed at splitting China and bringing about 'independence of Tibet.'"[83] By linking Tibetan activities in India to "splitting China," Beijing intensified pressure on New Delhi.

India's ability to regulate the activities of the 110,000 Tibetan exiles living in India gives it important ways of pressuring China on Tibet. India has felt compelled to respond to Beijing's demands to restrict these activities but only very reluctantly and to a limited degree. India's core political values are, after all, liberal, holding such things as free expression and travel to be intrinsic human rights. By upholding these values in the face of Chinese condemnation and pressure, India not only wins considerable support from the Indian public and media but also a degree of recognition and respect from Western countries. India's leaders ask why they should help Beijing consolidate its control over Tibet when Beijing has ignored its own 1954 implicit promises to uphold Tibetan autonomy. Indians also ask what they will get from China in return for helping Beijing break Tibetan resistance. Nor is the fact that China's Tibetan policies are subject to international criticism as a result of some activities of the Tibetan exiles contrary to India's interests.

India's position has been that, while it welcomes Tibetan refugees within its borders, and while it sympathizes with their efforts to maintain their cultural traditions, it does not allow them to engage in anti-Chinese political activities on Indian soil. The words contain important caveats. Representatives of the Dalai Lama's group undertake extensive international travel to mobilize support for their cause. All such travel is undertaken on the basis of an identity certificate and associated travel document issued by the government of India. The travel document must specify each country to be visited. Because it is issued by the Indian government, these documents are accepted by most foreign governments for purposes of visa issuance. In addition, to reenter India a Tibetan refugee traveler must secure an ROI Home Ministry certificate of "non-objection to reentry."[84] Without these official ROI documents Tibetan representatives could not travel abroad and return to India. A good portion of this international travel is for purposes objectionable to Beijing: to lobby foreign legislatures or executive agencies, to build nonofficial popular support networks, to publicize the Dalai Lama's responses to Beijing's moves, to participate in various activities keeping the Tibet issue on the international agenda, and for the Dalai Lama to accept such laurels as the Nobel Peace Prize. These Tibetan exile efforts to build international support expanded greatly beginning in the late 1980s and throughout the 1990s. The point here is that this travel required the active cooperation and tacit approval of the Indian government. Stated differently, Dharmsala's fairly successful efforts to internationalize the Tibetan issue from the mid-1980s onward were predicated on quiet but vital tacit support from New Delhi.

The definition of "impermissible political activities" is also vague and shifting. In Beijing's view the self-styled "Tibetan government-in-exile," headed by the Dalai Lama and based in Dharmsala, is quintessentially "political" and "anti-China." Established in the early 1960s, the Tibetan government-in-exile has evolved into a complex organization of representative, executive, economic, educational, cultural, and social relief organs, with offices in ten major cities around the world.[85] Those organs collect "voluntary contributions" of 2 percent of the income of Tibetan refugees in India and use the monies to conduct various activities designed to improve the lives and maintain the Tibetan culture of the exile community. Many of the activities require cooperation with organs of India's central or state governments. The Tibetan government-in-exile, in other words, looks and acts very much like what it claims to be. That, in Beijing's view, makes it "political" in essence. Other activities have also been a perennial source of conflict—for example, where, when, and in what fashion protests by these refugees will be permitted; the organization of conferences around certain slogans (e.g., "Tibetan independence"); and the participation of certain prominent or official individuals, Indian or foreign, in Tibetan activities. In the view of Tibetan representatives in India, restrictions imposed by the Indian government increased as Beijing and New Delhi maneuvered to improve ties in the 1980s and 1990s. As a result, there has been considerable public criticism in India over these creeping restrictions of Tibetan refugees' freedoms under pressure from Beijing.

From New Delhi's perspective, helping to keep the Tibetan exile community intact and facilitating the Dalai Lama's effort to mobilize international support for the Tibetan cause are ways of keeping the Tibet issue alive. This in turn pressures China. Chinese representatives tend to dismiss explanations of Indian policy based on democratic pressures and public opinion in India and to conclude that India is following a secret, long-range strategy designed to dilute Chinese authority fundamentally in Tibet, as was the case there prior to 1951. These suspicions may or may not be correct.

China maintains that, since India recognizes Tibet as part of China, the Indian government should not allow demonstrations, or any other actions "hostile to China," by Tibetans in India. By "hostile to China," Beijing means not only openly pro-independence activities but also any open criticisms of Chinese policy or authority in Tibet. When Chinese representatives raise these issues with Indian officials, the Indians reiterate their formal position on Tibet and promise to prohibit political activities. Such activities nonetheless continue, at least in the Chinese view.[86] The official Indian position is that aliens resident in India enjoy certain rights under Indian law which are not easily restricted by the Indian government. Moreover, there is great popular sympathy within India for the plight of the Tibetans. A democratically elected government simply cannot ignore this pressure. Any hospitality India grants to Tibetan refugees is purely on humanitarian grounds and in deference to the humanitarian sentiments of the Indian electorate. Indian diplomats frequently make these points to Chinese officials, but Chinese tend to be very skeptical about such disclaimers, often seeing them as further evidence of Indian duplicity.

TIBET IN THE POST–COLD WAR ERA

Tibet is virtually the only effective mechanism of leverage India has against Beijing. China's vulnerability in Tibet is to India what India's vulnerability vis-à-vis Pakistan is to China. The extremely deep ethnic cleavage between Han and Tibetan is similar to the Indian-Pakistani gulf. Repeated efforts to bridge both gulfs have had limited success, and hard-minded strategists recognize the leverage offered by these deep and durable cleavages. The closeness of Pakistan to Indian industrial and political centers, combined with the proven martial competence of Pakistan, increases the Pakistani threat to India. Similarly, the immense logistical difficulties associated with Tibet's terrain and remoteness increase the threat to Beijing created by a possible Indian-Tibetan link. Just as China has never played its Pakistan card to the extent of actually entering an India-Pakistan war, so India has never played its Tibet card by using its military forces to support a Tibetan rebellion against China. But both sides are well aware of these options, which figure into their calculations. Just as New Delhi has pondered the possibility of Chinese entry into an India-Pakistan war, Beijing has considered the possibility of Indian support for a Tibetan rebellion.

Indian views of Beijing's continuing repression in Tibet are colored by India's own experience in dealing with ethnic insurgencies. Over its history the ROI has faced many secessionist movements, which on occasion have taken up arms. When this has happened, New Delhi often used military force to thwart the insurgency. But military repression was usually combined with political compromise. At some point, once it became clear that Indian military power would prevent the seizure of power by secessionists and make the costs of continuing the struggle for independence very high, New Delhi would offer acceptable terms to the rebels. Often, in exchange for abandoning armed struggle and dropping the demand for secession from the Indian union, former insurgents became the leaders of state governments. In contrast, the PRC has been unwilling or unable to come to terms with the Dalai Lama and his exile government. Since the mid-1980s Beijing has not shown real interest in having a dialogue with the Dalai Lama. The CCP regime in Beijing seems congenitally unable to share power, as would be required by a deal with the Dalai Lama. Instead, Beijing has relied on repression and, since the 1990s, on a demographic "final solution" to Beijing's Tibetan problem while demanding that New Delhi deny political rights to Tibetan exiles in India. New Delhi maintains that India cannot settle the Tibetan problem for China. That is something Beijing must do for itself. India has recognized Tibet as an autonomous region of China and has prohibited explicitly anti-China political activities by Tibetans in India. Now it is necessary for Beijing to reach an accommodation with the Tibetan émigrés which will allow them to return to their homeland. This can be done only via discussions with the Dalai Lama and through guarantees of genuine political and cultural autonomy in Tibet. From New Delhi's perspective Beijing blames India for problems that really stem from the CCP's own refusal to share power.[87]

Tibet policy is contested in India. Some commentators bridle at the continual reiteration by Indian officials, at China's request, of the mantra "Tibet is a part of China." India gains nothing, they argue, by such rhetorical genuflection.[88] If such declarations are to be made, according to these commentators, they should be paired with Chinese declarations that Sikkim or Kashmir are parts of India. For decision makers in New Delhi, resolving the border issue probably ranks higher than the status of Tibet. Although during the 1980s New Delhi decided to stop insisting on a solution to the border issue as a precondition for improvement of bilateral relations, that issue remains very high on the Indian agenda. If we assume that Tibet ranks lower, various trade-offs become possible. Some Indian analysts have suggested that China might be willing to make concessions on the border issue in exchange for Indian help in securing the return of the Tibetan émigrés to China. One analyst has suggested, for example, that China might be willing to recognize Bhutan's status as an Indian protectorate and make territorial concessions in the Chumbi Valley as a quid pro quo for expulsion of the Tibetan refugees from India.[89] Such swaps may have been discussed during the Sino-Indian talks of the 1980s.

India may also play the Tibet card in a more forceful fashion. The explicitly nationalist BJP government that came to power in March 1998, for example, responded to criticisms of the weak Tibetan policy of earlier governments by adopting a marginally tougher approach. During an April 1998 visit to India by PLA chief of staff Fu Quanyou, the government tolerated a hunger strike by six young Tibetans protesting Chinese "aggression against Tibet." This was a departure from the practice of Indian governments over the preceding decade. Under strong Chinese pressure and in hopes of fostering better Indian-Chinese relations, Indian governments had taken a steadily stricter, more narrow approach to protest activities by Tibetan exiles during visits by high-ranking Chinese officials.[90] As former foreign secretary J. N. Dixit pointed out, prior to earlier Chinese visits someone from the Indian foreign ministry would ask the Dalai Lama to use his influence to insure that the Chinese guest would not be embarrassed. With the early 1998 hunger strike, however, this apparently was not done. Indian police finally intervened only when several protesters were on the verge of death and after Defense Minister George Fernandes had visited the strikers' compound.[91]

Five months later, in the midst of the deterioration of Sino-Indian relations following the nuclear tests of May 1998, Vajpayee met with the Dalai Lama. Virtually every previous sitting Indian prime minister had done likewise, but, in the context of post-test deterioration of Sino-Indian relations, Vajpayee's meeting with the Dalai Lama signaled a determination not to collapse before Beijing's anger. Beijing condemned the meeting as "interference in China's domestic affairs" which violated the Indian commitment not to allow the Dalai Lama to engage in "anti-China activities in India" and caused "deep resentment" among the Chinese people.[92] The BJP government did not reply to China's criticism with the previously standard recognition of Tibet as a part of China. In fact, during its first thirteen months in power BJP spokesmen refrained from uttering these previously de rigueur words.[93] Three days after Vajpayee's meeting with the Dalai Lama, and after strong Chinese protests that the meeting violated India's pledge not to allow the Dalai Lama to conduct anti-China activities on Indian soil, the prime minister's private secretary, Brajesh Mishra, issued a statement on India-China relations declaring, inter alia, that India "welcomed" the prospect of negotiations between Beijing and the Dalai Lama.[94] Chinese ambassador Zhou Gang replied to Mishra two months later, saying that talks between China's government and the Dalai Lama "are entirely China's internal affairs; there is no need for a third party to intervene." The "channel of communication" between the Dalai Lama and China's government was "open," Zhou said, but it was clear that the Dalai Lama was insincere. He was playing "deceptive tricks on the international stage" in an attempt to influence international opinion to pressure Beijing. Ambassador Zhou continued: "Any government leader, including those of India, who meet the Dalai Lama under any name and in any form . . .

will be interfering in China's internal affairs and will seriously hurt the Chinese
people's feelings. China expresses deep regrets and dissatisfaction over this
as a matter of course. China asks India to earnestly honor its promise of not
allowing the Dalai Lama to engage in anti-Chinese activities in India."[95]

In response to the BJP's slightly tougher approach to Tibet and to China
(an approach that included the May 1998 nuclear tests with China as their
explicit justification) Beijing uncorked salvos blasting India's desire to "split
Tibet from China." As one article said: "According to India's hegemonic logic,
the most thorough way to remove this so-called 'threat' [to India's north] is
to facilitate Tibet's separation from China. Tibetan independence will create
a buffer zone between China and India and enable India to take bolder action
on the South Asian continent and, subsequently, in the Indian Ocean region,
without fear of being attacked front and rear."[96] From this perspective, the
article continued, it was not hard to understand Indian defense minister
George Fernandes's statement that the "latent threat" to India from China
exceeded that from Pakistan. What Fernandes really meant was that "China's
capability to resist Indian hegemonism in South Asia is greater than
Pakistan's." India was pursuing its hegemonist goals with the support of the
Western powers:

> [In] the next century, to split China's western part, or, more specifically, to
> split China's Tibetan region in actuality, regardless of the form (such as "a high
> degree of autonomy" as termed by the Dalai Lama), is probably the target of
> the Western world's geopolitical strategy. This dovetails with India's political
> plot to create a Tibetan buffer zone between China and India. Currently India
> is pulling out all stops to convince the West that it is willing to play the van-
> guard for the West's effort to achieve this goal, under the prerequisite that the
> West will adopt an appeasement policy toward its nuclear option. . . . India's
> spearhead is now aimed at China. India's strategic objective to split Tibet from
> China is consistent with that of the West.

By unleashing such rhetoric, Beijing was in effect saying to New Delhi: if you
want to resort to public talk based on your worst-case scenario, we will do
likewise. China's darkest fears concerned India, Tibet, and Western-Indian
collusion to undermine Chinese rule in Tibet.

3 / The Territorial Dispute

China and India dispute ownership of two rather large blocs of territory. On the southern slope of the eastern wing of the Himalayan range is an area of about 90,000 square kilometers, or 36,000 square miles, roughly corresponding to the Indian state of Arunachal Pradesh. India has administered this region since the 1940s and continues to do so today. In the west, on the border between China's Tibet and Xinjiang provinces, lies the high, dry, and desolate Aksai Chin plateau. This region is about 38,000 square kilometers, or 15,200 square miles, was brought under PRC control when the People's Liberation Army "liberated" Tibet in 1951, and continues today under Chinese administration. There is a robust literature on the historic evolution and legal claims and counterclaims in the Sino-Indian territorial dispute. Only a brief summary of that literature is necessary here.

China claims that the traditional, customary limit of Tibetan administration in the eastern sector ran along the southern foothills of the Himalayas, and that as successor to the traditional Tibetan state, the PRC inherited a right to that boundary. Beijing nonetheless conceded that the boundary between India and Tibet/China had never been formally delineated, and in 1960 began calling for negotiations to achieve such a delineation. India countered that a well-defined boundary did in fact exist, running along the crest line of the eastern Himalayas, and that this had been agreed to by the Tibetan government in 1914. China rejected the validity of that 1914 agreement because China's central government of the time had rejected it. Since it maintained that the boundary was already defined, New Delhi refused "negotiations," although it eventually agreed to "talks." The precondition of such talks, New Delhi insisted, was Chinese evacuation of Aksai Chin, across which the Chinese built a road in the mid-1950s. Beijing rejected this and insisted on unconditional negotiations. Nehru, acting from a position of incredible military weakness and oblivious to the logistic realities of operations in the Himalayas, then ordered Indian forces to advance into disputed areas and clear Chinese forces, though without firing first. India ignored Chinese warnings to halt this "forward policy," and the PLA struck suddenly with overwhelming force. During a month-long war of October–November 1962 Indian defenses crumbled ignominiously and Chinese armies advanced to the limits of China's claim line. There they unilaterally halted and pulled back northward behind what China said was the line of control prior to the beginning of India's policy of pushing into contested forward areas. Negotiations finally began in the 1980s, but little progress was made in resolving the substance of the dispute.

From a geopolitical perspective, establishment and maintenance of Chinese authority over Tibet required, and continues to require, transport from the population and industrial centers of China into Tibet of substantial numbers of military and civilian personnel along with large quantities of materiel. Given the extreme remoteness and ruggedness of Tibet, this has always been a difficult task for China's government. The very few roads linking Tibet to the rest of China have thus been vital to every Chinese central government concerned about asserting its authority in Tibet.[1]

There have been, and in the early part of the twenty-first century continue to be, three main routes into Tibet from the rest of China: from the north via Xining in Qinghai province and proceeding south over the Qinghai plateau (this plateau is actually part of the Tibetan plateau); from the Sichuan basin in the east and proceeding westward; and from the west via Kashgar southeasterly onto the Tibetan plateau crossing Aksai Chin, a cold desert lying on the westernmost edge of the Tibetan plateau.

A major problem with the northern Qinghai route has been the extreme desolation of the vast distance it traverses. The northern route is 2,100 kilometers (1,300 miles) and crosses fifteen mountain ranges with much of the road at an elevation of 4,500 to 5,000 meters (14,000–16,400 ft.). Only a very few nomads inhabit the sparse grasslands of this region. This means that there were, and are, few local people and resources that can be mobilized to build or repair the road. All resources and manpower to build, operate, and maintain the road must be trucked in.

The eastern route sets out from Yaan on the western edge of the Sichuan basin and proceeds west more or less along 30 degrees north latitude, cross-

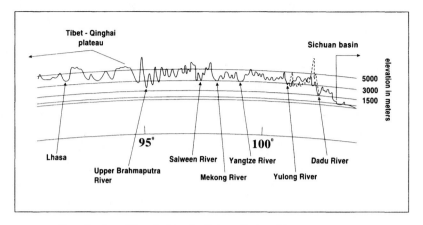

MAP 3.1   Cross-Section of Terrain from the Sichuan Basin to Lhasa.
SOURCE: *Zhonghua Renmin Gongheguo putong dituji* (Collection of ordinary maps of the People's Republic of China) (Beijing: Ditu chubanshe, 1995).

ing fourteen mountain ranges and covering a distance of 2,400 kilometers (1,500 mi.). This route traverses more populated areas than does the northern route. Local authorities governing Sichuan are much more able to mobilize the large numbers of laborers, machines, and materials necessary to build and maintain roads to Tibet. In western Sichuan and eastern Tibet there is abundant timber for fuel and construction. There is also enough human settlement with agriculture and animal husbandry to provide some succor for road and transport crews. In terms of its proximity to China's major population and economic centers, the Sichuan route is also best. The drawback of the eastern route is the extreme ruggedness of the terrain. The roads through this region snake their way up and down a series of deep canyons defined by the rivers they carry—the Yangtze, the Mekong, the Salween, plus many other less well-known rivers—making this some of the most rugged terrain in the world. A cross-section of the terrain along this route is depicted by map 3.1.

The western route into Tibet begins at Kashgar in southwestern Xinjiang and proceeds southeast along the edge of the Taklamakan basin of Xinjiang to the town of Yecheng, where it begins the climb atop the Tibetan plateau. From Yecheng for a distance of about 460 kilometers the road penetrates one of the canyons radiating northward from the Karakoram Range. It then follows several water courses, climbing up from the Karakorams to the Tibetan plateau.[2] Following either route is not an easy task for man or machine, but the western route has a much more continuous rise in elevation than either the northern or the eastern route. On the western route, once you have climbed up to 4,600 meters (14,000 feet) or so, you more or less stay there and in any case do not have to descend back down to 2,400 meters (8,000 feet) elevation to start over, as with the Sichuan route.

There are also important differences in precipitation between the northern, eastern, and western routes. Rain and snowfall on the Qinghai-Tibetan plateau generally decline moving from the southeast to the northwest. Warm moist winds from the southern oceans blow across the Southeast Asian peninsula and move up the canyons of western Sichuan, western Yunnan, and eastern Tibet—canyons that generally run southeast to northwest, serving as excellent conduits for moist maritime winds. Mountain areas in western Sichuan thus receive 750–1,000 millimeters of precipitation per year, while still farther to the west, in eastern Tibet, the annual average is 500–750 millimeters. Many valleys in the southeast part of the Tibetan plateau average over 1,000 millimeters per year. The western and northern reaches of the Qinghai-Tibetan plateau are far less influenced by moisture-bearing southern winds. The average annual precipitation for the entire Qinghai-Tibetan plateau is a mere 100–150 millimeters per year, with most of that falling in the eastern region. The Aksai Chin area, for instance, receives only 100–125 millimeters per year. Winters, although bitterly cold in the west, have little snow.[3] Heavy rain and snowfall in western Sichuan and eastern Tibet mean snow-blocked roads and frequent avalanches in winter and flooded rivers, plus mud and rock slides, during the rainy season. When heavy precipitation is combined with the extremely rugged terrain of the eastern route into Tibet, the result are roads that are very difficult to keep open. The northern route does not receive much snowfall for most of its length, but in the Tangula range there is extremely heavy snowfall.

The Sino-Indian border dispute became entangled with the stability of China's control over Tibet via these factors of terrain and weather. To assert and uphold its authority over Tibet, Beijing needed multiple and good roads into Tibet. In 1950–51, when the PLA began the process of asserting PRC authority over Tibet, there were in fact no motor roads into the region at all. Of the three traditional ways into Tibet, Mongol armies had favored the northern Qinghai route. China's central governments found that road building is labor-intensive work and that the shortage of manpower along the sparsely populated Qinghai route was a major constraint on developing that road. Keeping a road operating also required substantial personnel stationed along the way, and these people had to be fed. Again, this was difficult in a desolate region like Qinghai. In 1950 a motor road along the northern route extended only as far as Xining. From there only very primitive trails crossed two major mountain ranges, not much different in 1950 than when the

Mongols had used them centuries earlier. The terrain of the first mountain range was not too difficult, but the altitude was very high, making construction work difficult. When the PLA crossed this route in early 1951, the men had to disassemble vehicles and carry them over the mountains by mule.[4]

The route from Sichuan had been Qing China's main way to and from Tibet. Chinese armies had passed this way in 1720 to counter the Dzungarian Mongol intervention. Along this route the Qing state had built trails passable by horse or donkey, with occasional way-stations, but they were impassable to motor vehicles. The main force of the PLA advanced over this route in 1951, in spite of great difficulty.

The westerly route via Aksai Chin was an old caravan route and in many ways the best. It was the only route that was open year-round, throughout both the winter and the monsoon season. The Dzungar army that had reached Lhasa in 1717, precipitating the Qing counter-intervention mentioned in the previous chapter, had followed this route. A detachment of PLA cavalry also followed this route in 1951 to participate in the occupation of Tibet. The western route also provided the only logistically effective supply line into western Tibet. Had Beijing been forced to transport men and material all the way to western Tibet via Qinghai or western Sichuan, the cost would have been ruinously expensive. Control of Aksai Chin was thus essential to Chinese control of *western* Tibet and very important to its control over *all* of Tibet.

Building motor roads into Tibet was a top order of business for the PRC. Mao's 1950 orders to the PLA as it prepared to "liberate" Tibet was to "advance while building roads." Work on a line through western Sichuan began in April 1950 and on the road south from Xining in June 1950. "Several thousand" workers died building the roads, but the work went forward regardless of casualties. The road via Qinghai was declared open by the end of 1950. The Sichuan route took longer and was not opened until December 1954.[5] The western route via Aksai Chin was formally opened in mid-1957. Beijing also began laying out new routes into Tibet via western Sichuan. Three routes were considered in 1951. The middle one was the old imperial courier route and was initially selected as the chief route. Very soon, however, a more southerly route was selected because the climate was milder, forests provided fuel and building material, and the population was greater, providing labor power and food. Maximum resources were concentrated on the southern road, but progress was difficult and slow. Rock slides and avalanches were frequent. Rainfall and snowfall exacerbated these problems. Modern earth-moving and construction equipment was scarce, so most of the work was done by sheer muscle. Conditions were dangerous, and casualties from accidents were high. Again, thousands of men died from accidents and harsh conditions. Still work continued at a breakneck pace. Road construction was treated as combat. Once the Sichuan route was completed, keeping it open required great effort. Each winter ice and heavy snow blocked the road, and long sections of it were completely destroyed. In spite of these immense difficulties, work pressed ahead simultaneously on the three new Sichuan roads. All of them were opened about the same time, in 1956–57.[6]

As work on the Sichuan roads into Tibet proceeded, the roads and PLA trucks moving over them came under increasing attack by insurgents from the Kham tribes of eastern Tibet and western Sichuan. Unlike the sedentary farming populations of central Tibet, the nomadic Kham tribesmen had substantial martial skills, which they traditionally used for raiding and banditry. The Kham tribesmen were also fiercely proud of their independence and deeply suspicious of outside authority, whether that was represented by lamas from Lhasa's monasteries or officials and soldiers of the Chinese state. As the PLA pushed roads through Kham lands in 1949–50, it came to face the classic problem of being an occupying power defending its lines of communication in the midst of a hostile population. The possibilities inherent in this situation soon came to the attention of U.S. and Nationalist Chinese clandestine agencies, and by the late 1950s the agencies were cooperating to strengthen the anticommunist guerrilla activities of Kham rebels. PLA convoys, bridges, and roads as well as construction crews were prime targets for Kham attacks.

The PLA's western road into Tibet was significantly more secure than the eastern route in the 1950s. There was nothing comparable to the Kham insurgents in that region. Indeed, there was hardly anyone in that region at all. The PLA's improvement of the western route in the mid-1950s proceeded unperturbed by the sort of uncertainties that plagued its road-building efforts along the eastern routes. From the PLA's standpoint the westerly route into Tibet provided an important backup in the event the eastern route was severed by hostile action or bad weather.

The importance of these roads must be seen in the context of the demands created by the entry of tens of thousands of Chinese soldiers and officials into Tibet. The PLA's occupation of Tibet created heavy demands for food, fuel, supplies, and equipment. All manufactured goods had to be shipped in. As for food, the low productivity of Tibetan agriculture and animal husbandry meant that Tibet produced a relatively small surplus. When Chinese authorities in Tibet purchased significant quantities of this surplus to feed PLA troops and road crews, the result was a strong inflationary push on prices paid by Tibetans. In 1954–55 in Lhasa, for instance, the price of meat increased by 50 percent and salt by 800 percent. The opening of the new roads from China in 1956–57 helped alleviate inflationary pressure by bringing in more goods, but it also increased pressure on the primitive roads. Convoys had to carry their own fuel and supplies. For every ten trucks, three had to carry fuel for the rest.[7]

Chinese authorities in Tibet clashed repeatedly with the Tibetan local government over the question of the building of roads. The Tibetan government feared the disruption and economic burden imposed by road building. The Chinese believed that the Tibetan government hoped that primitive transportation would make it impossible for the Chinese government to provision the PLA and therefore force its withdrawal from Tibet.[8] China therefore pushed forward with road construction in spite of Tibetan opposition. The PLA was in a dilemma. To assert Chinese authority in Tibet, it had to establish a substantial presence there—at least, so the leaders of the Chinese Communist Party concluded. Yet feeding Chinese cadres and troops imposed a heavy economic burden on an already poor and suspicious Tibetan population. More troops and road-building crews led to more inflation, which led to more resentment, which led to the need for more troops. A key base of this vicious cycle was the great cost and difficulties of transportation into Tibet. More numerous and better roads into Tibet meant that the PLA presence fell less heavily on Tibet's farmers and herders, whom the CCP hoped to win over. Conversely, severing those roads by one means or another would intensify PLA food levies on Tibet's populace, which would create more fertile ground for anti-Chinese guerrilla activity.

Mao was cognizant of this danger. Early in 1950, while planning the PLA's advance into Tibet, he ordered the PLA, "Don't eat locally" (*bu chi difang*), meaning that the PLA should import all the food it needed. PLA commander Zhu De later "supplemented" (and fundamentally altered) Mao's directive with an order providing that all local purchases should be paid for with silver coinage.[9] Local purchases with silver eased the demand on the PLA's overburdened logistic lines. They also pushed up prices for ordinary Tibetans.

Transport between India and central Tibet was substantially more convenient than between China and that region of Tibet. In fact, after the signature of the May 1951 Seventeen-Point Agreement between the Dalai Lama and Beijing, central personnel dispatched to Lhasa traveled via India and thence up the Chumbi Valley. Food for central government personnel in Lhasa also had to be imported from India. Prior to 1956, when the new roads via Qinghai and western Sichuan were finally opened, most of the rice, fuel, and supplies used by PLA forces in Tibet came via the Indian port of Calcutta. Off-loaded from ships in that harbor, supplies for Chinese personnel moved northward by rail and road to Gangtok in Sikkim. From there a two-day journey by mule, yak, horse, or donkey carried the cargo to Yadong inside Tibet in the Chumbi Valley. The Lhasa-Yadong road was one of the first renovated by China after its 1951 occupation, but, because of Indian sensibilities, the road from Yadong was not pushed up to the Sikkim border. Most of Tibet's foreign exports also went to India. Tibetan salt, wool, and yak tails were exchanged for Indian grain, cloth, and daily necessities. The absolute need for continued trade with India made it "extremely important to develop good neighborly cooperative relations" with India, in the words of Yang Gongsu, and it was an important reason why Zhou Enlai was willing to accommodate Indian interests in Tibet in 1954. Abruptly extirpating India's special trading facilities in Tibet would have severely damaged the Tibetan economy. Continuing the pre-1949 Indian representative offices, on the other hand, facilitated vital Indian-Tibet trade.[10]

The opening of the new roads via Qinghai, western Sichuan, and Aksai Chin greatly reduced the importance of the Chumbi route. Once India began implementing economic sanctions against China in 1959, trade via the Chumbi fell rapidly. Indo-Tibetan trade, the greater part of it via the Chumbi, fell by 90 percent during the first quarter of 1960 compared to the same quarter of the previous year. According to Yang Gongsu, the economic sanctions implemented by India in 1959–60 were intended to create economic crisis in Tibet. Because of China's vigorous road-building efforts during the preceding several years, however, India's efforts to destabilize Tibet came several years too late.

During the 1950s and 1960s the road via Aksai Chin was extremely important to China's control over Tibet, linked in a direct way to China's ability to assert and maintain its authority in that region. Opposition and even open rebellion against Beijing's authority was growing by the late 1950s, requiring ever more troops in Tibet, which further increased popular discontent. Feeding Tibet's PLA garrison was vulnerable to Indian control over the Chumbi corridor, and, once that corridor was closed, Beijing's problems deepened. The eastern routes into Tibet were costly and vulnerable to weather and to CIA-supported raiders. It was in this context that the Indian government in 1959–62 insisted on Chinese evacuation of Aksai Chin. From India's perspective this was Indian territory that was illegally occupied by China. From Beijing's perspective India's demand for Chinese withdrawal from Aksai Chin was linked to U.S. activities in support of the Tibetan insurgency. Both were designed to undermine China's control over Tibet.

The security environment in which Tibet's logistic lifeline functioned steadily improved. In 1959 the PLA began asserting its control in forward areas along the border, patrolling, building roads, and setting up outposts and surveillance positions there. Within a few years China had secured effective control over previously porous borders. A decade-long counterinsurgency war waged by the PLA against Tibetan insurgents was also successful. The grinding down of that insurgency by the mid-1960s reduced the level of PLA activity in Tibet, thereby reducing the weight of the PLA's logistical demands. The crushing of the rebellion also reduced road and convoy losses to ambush and sabotage. Finally, the PLA's dramatic defeat of Indian forces in 1962 led to greater caution in Indian policy. While there were costs to the PLA's victory over India (including a major buildup of Indian military capabilities vis-à-vis Tibet), the chastising of New Delhi did lead to a suspension of India's earlier "forward policy" and greater Indian respect for Chinese warnings. Cumulatively, these factors meant that by the 1980s and 1990s Aksai Chin and its road were far less important to Beijing than had been the case in the 1950s.

The geopolitical significance of the Aksai Chin highway was also reduced by decades of investment in the construction of a fairly robust transport network into Tibet. In the early 1970s it took thirty-two days and nearly two tons of gasoline for a truck to make a round-trip between Xining and Lhasa. That gasoline had to be trucked in. To alleviate this, in 1972 the PLA began building a petroleum pipeline from Xining via Golmud to Lhasa. Completed by 1977, this thousand-kilometer-long pipeline delivered fuel to truck stops and other essential facilities along the route as well as to Lhasa. The PLA also began work in the early 1970s on the construction of a rail line along the same route. By September 1979 the rail line was opened as far as Golmud, where work was suspended because of costs.[11] Improving the Xining-Lhasa road was designated a national construction project in the mid-1970s. Ten thousand workers toiled for over ten years on the project. Between 1974 and 1985 the most difficult portion of the Qinghai road between Golmud and the Tangula Mountains was paved with asphalt, and by 1984 the road had been entirely hard-surfaced, which helped improve efficiency. Trucks frequently broke down under the extremely harsh and rugged conditions of the Qinghai plateau. Tires also wore out quickly on the largely crushed-rock surface of the road. Repairs required spare parts, which also had to be trucked in. During the early 1990s the Qinghai road was again renovated at a cost of $130 million. By 1992 it carried 85 percent of all goods into and out of Tibet.[12] The fleet of trucks working the road was steadily improved. "Hotel-style quarters" and "restaurant-standard mess halls" plus facilities for a "diversified cultural life," along with hospitals, clinics, and "oxygenating stations," were built along the Xining-Lhasa road to make life better for the men assigned to this desolate route. The route was also paralleled by a hard-wired PLA communication line running between Beijing and Lhasa.[13] China's ability to provide its construction crews with modern road-building equipment also improved with economic development, especially with China's post-1978 opening. Air transport also played an increasing role. Tibet's first airport was opened at Lhasa in 1956, and more were built in the following years. The PLA's airlift capability and the size of China's civilian air fleet also expanded, again especially in the post-1978 period, which further reduced the significance of ground transport. In 1987 the PLA began rotating troops into and out of Tibet by air rather than by road. In the event of an emergency China's civilian air fleet could be mobilized to ferry reinforcements and supplies into Tibet.

Transport was a key component of a long-term development plan for Tibet adopted in mid-1998, and further expanding Tibet's links with China proper and the outside world remains at the core of Beijing's plan for Tibet in the twenty-first century. The objective is to facilitate export of Tibet's mineral resources, timber, and other products to the world and moving tourists into Tibet. The construction of a rail line to Lhasa is also being studied. A railroad from Dali in Yunnan to Lhasa would cost 4.5 times as much as completion of the Golmud-Lhasa line but would have the advantage of linking Tibet to the sea via planned rail links between Yunnan and Myanmar. It would also further strengthen the PLA's operational capabilities in Tibet.

INDIA AND AKSAI CHIN

Plumbing the geopolitical significance of Aksai Chin from the Indian perspective is more difficult than from the Chinese. Aksai Chin's significance for India must have been substantial, for it was largely to secure that region that Nehru first rejected China's proposal of a compromise solution and then pursued his forward policy of asserting military control over territory claimed by India. China's occupation of Aksai Chin was Nehru's—and to this day remains India's—major grievance against China, at least as regards the territorial issue. Nehru insisted that China withdraw from Aksai Chin, relinquishing that region to India. Until Beijing indicated its willingness to do this, there was nothing to discuss. Chinese withdrawal from Aksai Chin was a precondition for India's agreeing to initiate negotiations. To secure Chinese evacuation of Aksai Chin, Nehru lobbied with the USSR and within the Afro-Asian movement. In short, India's firm demand for Aksai Chin was the crux of the boundary dispute. Why, then, was Aksai Chin so important to India?

Shortly after independence India's government reviewed the matter of the location of the border in Ladakh—the northeastern section of Indian Kashmir of which Aksai Chin is an extension. According to Steve Hoffmann's detailed investigation of the Indian policy process, a definitive decision about the location of the boundary in this section was not made until 1953, when New Delhi decided to reject an earlier British policy of 1899 which had placed the boundary in the Aksai Chin region along the northern edge of the Karakoram Range. This 1899 line had placed most of Aksai Chin outside India. In 1953 New Delhi decided to draw the boundary along the northern edge of Aksai Chin. According to Hoffmann, this move was based on a determination that Aksai Chin had been included within the jurisdiction of the pre-British Dogra government of Kashmir—which was the view of Indian specialists and of the Kashmir government of the time. Nehru deeply believed that, prior to the British arrival in South Asia, India's traditional boundaries had been fairly well defined by customary administration—a perception colored by his core beliefs about India's traditional greatness. Part of the mythology of British rule over India, Nehru believed, was that India had never been a true nation until the British arrived to cobble it together. As part of his nationalist self-enlightenment in the early part of the century, Nehru had come to reject this imperialist mythology—as he concluded it was. Since ancient times India had been a well-defined, and great, nation. Thus, the belief in a fairly clearly defined Indian nation with far-flung boundaries was linked to Nehru's concept of India as a great and ancient nation. Britain, not being governed by Indian nationalism, had occasionally compromised India's traditional boundaries for the sake of strategic expediency. This, Nehru believed, had been the case in Ladakh. Independent India, now acting in its own interests, should reassert its traditional boundary.[14]

The Indian government was aware of Chinese activity in Aksai Chin as early as 1951. It decided not to protest these activities because the area was so remote as to make enforcement of Indian jurisdiction extremely difficult and because the area was judged to hold few natural resources. Moreover, developing friendly relations with China was deemed more important than possessing Aksai Chin. Beijing's 1957 announcement of its road-building activities in Aksai Chin made it impossible to continue ignoring China's presence there. India protested and then started sending patrols into the area. The Sino-Indian boundary conflict had begun. According to Hoffmann's reconstruction, geopolitical factors of the sort that clearly governed China's calculations played little role in Indian deliberations. Rather, nationalist ideology and legalistic considerations dominated.

Yet it is also *likely* that Nehru understood the vital importance of the Aksai Chin road for effective Chinese control over Tibet. During the early 1950s, when Nehru acquiesced to China's use of Aksai Chin, his recognition of China's suzerainty over Tibet was combined with a belief that China's actual military and administrative presence there would remain limited because of

Tibet's difficult terrain and Beijing's desire for friendship with India. As the Chinese presence in Tibet grew in the mid-1950s, perhaps exceeding what Nehru had anticipated, he may have concluded that additional constraints on the development of China's presence in Tibet should be erected. If this speculation is correct, Nehru may have concluded that, if China had fewer roads into Tibet, it would be more likely to grant Tibet the higher level of autonomy India desired. As we saw in the previous chapter, maintaining Tibetan autonomy and minimizing Chinese military presence in Tibet had been a key Indian goal since 1950. Again as we have seen, Nehru also understood something of the logistical difficulties faced by the PLA in Tibet and hoped that those difficulties would limit the Chinese presence there. In the several years prior to mid-1957 when India first protested China's activities in Aksai Chin, Nehru had lobbied Zhou Enlai to secure what he thought was a firm commitment to uphold Tibet's autonomy. Nehru may have hoped that pressure on Aksai Chin, or better yet complete Chinese evacuation of that region, would increase economic and logistical difficulties that would help Beijing see the wisdom of continued Tibetan autonomy. It may have been precisely in order to cut this PLA supply line and increase the army's difficulties that Nehru pushed to oust China from Aksai Chin. This *may* have been one reason why Nehru turned a blind eye (if, indeed, he did) to CIA–Chinese Nationalist covert operations toward Tibet, expecting (again perhaps) that this activity would help pressure Beijing to accede to India's demand for Tibetan autonomy and Aksai Chin.

Nehru may have been operating at two levels. For public consumption he may have stressed morality and principle, which was understandable to Indian public and parliamentary opinion. In private, perhaps in still-classified meetings, he may have concluded that the greater were PLA logistic-political difficulties in Tibet, the more likely Beijing would be to agree to a high level of autonomy for Tibet. By mobilizing international and bilateral pressure on China to evacuate Aksai China, while allowing PLA logistical-political difficulties in Tibet to mount, Nehru may have hoped to create conditions leading Beijing to agree to a far lower, perhaps nominal, Chinese military presence in Tibet. Cognitively, Nehru may have squared this dual moralistic-realpolitik approach through his perception of Chinese versus Indian policy. Nehru deeply believed that India's own policy was based on firm, higher principles of law, history, and simple justice. China, however, seemed to be pursuing its policies oblivious to those principles. India acted on the basis of high moral principle, while China acted on the basis of mere power and expedient advantage. Any law-upholding power, confronted by a flagrant violation of law, must resort to force to achieve compliance with norms. China was violating recognized legal norms for the sake of its own power, and counterpower must be used to constrain it for the sake of upholding those norms. This reconstruction of Nehru's calculations is purely speculative. When Indian records are finally opened, scholars may be able to answer the question authoritatively, but it is also possible that even this will not settle the issue. Many leaders never reveal or record their innermost calculations on such issues. Franklin Roosevelt's understanding of Japan's probable course in the weeks before Pearl Harbor, for instance, will probably forever remain unclear.

Chinese analysts of India's policy view the situation more simply. In their view it is clear that Nehru sought to cut the Aksai Chin road as part of an effort to force the PLA out of Tibet. The Indian government, they believe, was encouraging and supporting Tibetan "splittist" opposition to Beijing's authority while colluding with U.S. efforts to supply arms to Tibetan rebels and at the same time advancing an uncompromising demand that China turn Aksai Chin over to India. Without the Aksai Chin road the PLA would have been much less able to repress the Tibetan splittist rebellion.[15]

THE EASTERN SECTOR: THE SOUTHERN SLOPE AND INDIA'S NORTHEAST

The first thing to note about the geopolitical significance of the southern slope of the eastern Himalayas (which I will refer to as the "southern slope") constituting the eastern sector of the Chinese-Indian territorial dispute is that this region is a rather large piece of land. As Zhou Enlai pointed out in a September 1959 letter to Nehru, the 90,000 square kilometers of the eastern slope are roughly equivalent to China's Zhejiang province.[16] The southern slope is *not* a treasure house of valuable minerals like Tibet. There are some significant deposits of dolomite, limestone, graphite, quartzite, kyanite, colbaltiferous and sulphide-containing iron ore, marble, and copper. The region also has modest coal reserves estimated at 90 million tons and oil reserves estimated at 1.5 million tons.[17] The mountain slopes are also verdantly forested, creating rich timber resources. Perhaps the most important of the southern slope's natural resources is falling water for generating electricity. Electricity production is one of India's critical developmental bottlenecks. Unlike China, India does not have extensive reserves of coal or petroleum. It does have large deposits of thorium, which can be processed for use in nuclear generation of electricity. Nuclear power and hydropower are India's best long-term prospects for meeting its growing demands for electricity. In terms of water power, however, India also faces limitations. Most of the subcontinent is flat, with low elevation, typically creating meandering rivers that are not easily dammed. The store of water is also greatly dependent on rainfall. Low rainfall leads to power brown-outs.[18] Among the best prospects for hydropower are the rivers flowing out of the Himalayas fed by the melting snows of southeastern Tibet. There is considerable potential for generating hydroelectric power by harnessing the rivers of the southern slope.

India, with its 968 million people, and China, with its 1.2 billion (in 1997), together constitute one-third of humanity. Both are densely populated and rapidly industrializing countries. Both have voracious and rapidly growing demands for resources and energy. Leaders on both sides are loath to abandon a large piece of resource-rich land which their nation needs and which they believe is rightfully theirs.

National security concerns outweigh considerations of natural resources in India's thinking about its ownership of the southern slope. Simply stated, control of the southern slope is linked to the defensibility of India's entire northeast, including the Indian states of Tripura, Mizoram, Manipur, Nagaland, Meghalaya, and Assam, as well as Arunachal Pradesh. In its northeast India confronts complex problems of vulnerability similar in some ways to the problems China faces in Tibet. To begin with, the peoples of that region are ethnically distinct from the largely Hindi-speaking, Hindu-faith, and "Aryan"-race peoples that populate the Indian heartland and dominate India's central government. A large majority of the people indigenous to India's northeast fall into one of over two hundred tribes, most of whom are of mongoloid racial stock and speak languages derived from the Tibeto-Burman linguistic family. These people are closer to the hill tribes of Burma, Laos, and Thailand than they are to the Aryans and Dravadians who constitute the mainstream of India. The processes of "Sanskritization" and "Islamization" which shaped the culture of the subcontinent stopped when they came to the hills and mountains that physically define India's northeast.

Seventy percent of that region is hilly. Much of it is densely forested. Until very recent times there were very few roads into the region. Modern state boundaries frequently cut across ethnic communities, facilitating movement across these state boundaries. The assertion of modern state authority is also a recent phenomenon. Prior to the British no Indian kingdom was able to assert its authority over the primitive but warlike tribes of the northeast. Some of these tribes had formed powerful kingdoms in antiquity and remained proud of those accomplishments. British authority was also lightly asserted and the northeastern peoples became accustomed to being left alone. Western missionaries during the nineteenth and twentieth centuries found willing converts to Christianity, and large numbers converted to this religion, further differentiating them from the mainstream of India. The region also became a major theater of combat operations during World War II, with its residents acquiring arms, combat experience, and new expectations about life in the process. Opium production became a mainstay of the region in the nineteenth century, and this continued throughout the next century. Cash generated by the narcotics trade was frequently converted into munitions to challenge state authority in one way or another. Finally, the close proximity of international boundaries made it easy for rebels to find refuge in neighboring countries or support from the sympathetic government of a neighboring country. In sum, India has confronted major difficulties in asserting its authority in the northeast.[19]

Ruling the peoples of the northeast has been a continual challenge for New Delhi, with many episodes of outright rebellion. The Naga tribes were the first of the northeastern peoples to rise up against New Delhi. The Nagas are a martial people whose fierce warriors held off British encroachment until the 1860s, when continual Naga headhunting raids into the commercially important Assam Valley prompted British Indian leaders to order the "pacification" of the Naga hills. That project took ten years. Under British rule American Baptist missionaries mounted a large-scale missionary effort in the region with immense success. When India was approaching independence after World War II, Naga leaders pushed for independence of Nagaland and actually declared such independence one day prior to India's own declaration of independence in August 1947. They were ignored. Naga independence advocates continued to agitate and in 1951 organized a plebiscite in which 99 percent reportedly endorsed independence. Then in 1956 a "Federal Republic of Nagaland" was declared. This move prompted New Delhi to send in the Indian army. Fierce repression and resistance followed, with Indian forces unable to pin down and crush the core of the rebellion. A flimsy cease-fire was in place from 1964 to 1972, when it collapsed and sharp fighting resumed.[20] Alongside military repression New Delhi tried political co-optation and economic incentives. In December 1962 the state of Nagaland was carved out of Assam, establishing a precedent that would be followed on several subsequent occasions. In exchange for greater autonomy within the Indian union, moderates in the Naga cause abandoned their fight for independence. New Delhi also undertook heavy financing of Naga development efforts. Yet the fighting continued. A further "peace agreement" was signed in 1975. More moderates laid down their arms, but a radical wing carried on the armed struggle for Naga independence.

A pro-independence rebellion among the Mizo people began in 1966 and continued until 1986, when a peace agreement led to the abandonment of armed struggle in exchange for establishment of the state of Mizoram and

moves to limit immigration into the state.²¹ In 1978 urban insurgency began
in the Impal Valley of Manipur. A "Manipur People's Liberation Army"
emerged to carry out a campaign of political assassination, robbery, and attacks
on Indian security forces. In the early 1980s armed resistance to Indian authority began in the Tripura region. Once again the key issue was illegal immigration, and once again a deal was concluded, in 1986, whereby rebels laid
down their arms in exchange for establishment of a new state, Tripura. In
the early 1990s violent agitation began in Assam against illegal immigration
into the region. A group of perhaps eight hundred guerrillas carried out ninety
assassinations and scores of kidnappings. It continued until August 1985, when
a peace agreement limiting illegal immigration was signed.

The chronic political instability of India's northeast created opportunities for China to exploit. Between 1962 and 1979 China supported and encouraged insurgencies in India's northeast. About 1967 China began training
groups of Naga guerrillas at a camp near Tanzhong in southwestern Yunnan
Province. Groups of Naga fighters trekked to Yunnan via the Kachin state
in north Burma. In China they were given training and modern arms and
then returned to India's northeast. Nearly eight hundred Naga rebels were
trained in China through the mid-1970s. Several hundred more attempted
to reach China but were turned back by the Burmese government or Kachin
state military forces. China also broadcast radio programs to Naga insurgents, conveying encouragement, political education, and instruction in techniques of guerrilla warfare. Chinese training substantially increased the
combat effectiveness of the Naga insurgents. Indian causalities rose whenever they engaged Chinese-trained Nagas.²² The Indian army struggle against
the Naga insurgency dragged on for twenty years, from 1954 to 1974.²³

In 1969 China began supplying arms to the Mizo insurgency. Training in
China followed several years later. A first group of 38 Mizo fighters arrived
in Yunnan for training in 1973, and a second group of 108 followed in 1975.
In 1976, 18 or so Manipuri militants were trained in Yunnan, returning to
India in 1979 to launch a campaign of urban warfare. Chinese assistance peaked
in the early 1970s. In May 1969 China and Pakistan set up a Coordination
Bureau to oversee the supply of arms, training, and funding to Indian north-
eastern insurgencies.

As Deng Xiaoping consolidated power, he ended this support. In mid-1978
the Nagas were told no more Chinese assistance would be forthcoming. Two
years later, when another group of Nagas showed up at the Yunnan border,
they were refused entry. China refused to discuss further Naga requests for
support, and Deng Xiaoping insured that India's leaders were aware of this
shift in Chinese policy. During Foreign Minister Vajaypee's February 1979

visit to Beijing, Deng told him that such aid as China might have given to the Nagas, Mizoris, and Manipur rebels was a thing of the past.[24] Beijing also began denouncing reports to the contrary as Soviet "social imperialist" disinformation, as indeed they may have been.[25]

Beijing's support for these Indian insurgencies during the 1960s and 1970s is probably best understood as an attempt to punish India for its supportive attitude toward the Dalai Lama, his exile government, and the Tibetan insurgency. Implicit in this repayment-in-kind was a proposed deal: if New Delhi would drop its support for Tibetan anti-Chinese activities, Beijing would drop its support for anti-Indian rebels in the northeast. It is interesting to note that Beijing stopped aiding northeastern insurgencies several years after the Tibetan insurgency ended. Subir Bhaumik has also pointed out that India's large-scale support for Bengali insurgents in East Pakistan in 1971 can be seen as retaliation for Chinese-Pakistan support for insurgencies in the northeast. (Pakistan's role is discussed in chap. 7.) Chinese leaders may have concluded that continuing support for northeastern insurgencies would encourage India to step up its support for the Tibetan insurgency, perhaps even applying the Bangladesh model to Tibet. Bhaumik suggests that a sort of deterrence developed between China and India regarding support for insurgencies in the other country. Both sides gradually concluded it was best to abstain in this regard because they feared that the other side would follow suit if they did not.[26]

Indian security planners feared during the 1960s and 1970s that, in the event of a second Sino-Indian war, China would seek to detach the northeast from India. If one of several of the insurgencies had been successful enough to defend a large liberated base area against the Indian military, a logical extrapolation of Beijing's policy would have been for Beijing to extend material and political support to that new state. The pressing need for support against India would almost certainly have insured strong links between that new state and China. Once Indian military power was driven from the northeast, Chinese power would serve as the protector of the newly independent states. Because of continuing Chinese reticence to talk frankly about its support for foreign insurgencies during the Maoist era, we can only speculate about China's real policy objectives. It is suggestive, however, that China gave substantial assistance to revolutionary movements all along its southern borders, from Vietnam, to Laos and Cambodia, to Burma, and to India's northeast. It seems likely that the CCP's objective was to create a belt of pro-PRC socialist states guarding the PRC's soft southern borders.

Since 1978 China has not supported insurgencies in India's northeast. Other countries (Pakistan and Bangladesh) have, however, and China has

enjoyed very cordial relations with these countries while they were extending such support. This has made Indian observers very suspicious. Was China
tacitly or covertly supporting northeastern insurgencies through third
countries? Indian intelligence has watched closely for evidence of this but
thus far has found none. India has also remained apprehensive that at some
future date China might again begin supporting northeastern separatist movements. More ominously, Chinese strategists might integrate utilization of the
deep ethnic cleavages of India's northeast into Chinese military strategy in
the event of a future Sino-Indian war. Under such conditions Chinese military forces might attempt to ally with anti-Indian forces in the northeast.
India's main counter to this possibility has been to accelerate northeastern
development.

THE SILIGURI CORRIDOR

Indian security perceptions regarding defense of the northeast are influenced
by the fact that the region is connected to the rest of India by only a very narrow strip of land lying between Nepal and Bangladesh. The West Bengali city
of Siliguri sits in the middle of that corridor, which measures only twenty-
five kilometers at the narrowest point. Through that narrow corridor run the
roads and rail lines between India's northeastern states and the Indian heartland. The Chumbi Valley points south toward the Siliguri corridor. The distance from Yadong to Siliguri is only a bit over one hundred kilometers. The
Chumbi Valley is full of strong PLA bases, and the road between Yadong and
Lhasa is one of two funnels through which could be poured the PLA strength
normally concentrated between Shigatze and Zedang. In the event of collusive military operations between China and Pakistan (prior to 1972) or
between China and Bangladesh (after 1972), Indian planners believe that the
Siliguri corridor would be the most profitable objective for Chinese attack.
Chinese forces would have to drive south only a very short distance before
they reached friendly Pakistani or Bangladeshi territory, where they would
find their supply problems greatly alleviated. Indian contingency planning
in the months prior to the December 1971 war with Pakistan assumed that
the most likely form of Chinese entry would be joint actions with Pakistani
forces against the Siliguri corridor. Such an eventuality was deemed to
present a serious threat to Indian security. A PLA offensive against the
Siliguri corridor could serve as the "anvil" for a hammer blow by the PLA
once again through Bomdila, with the objective of shattering Indian defenses
along the entire northeast.

India's situation in the Siliguri region was greatly improved by the detachment of East Pakistan from New Delhi's traditional nemeses. Once that region became Bangladesh, in December 1971, the territory would no longer automatically become available to India's enemies in Islamabad and Beijing. Unfortunately for India, after several years of close Indian-Bangladeshi relations under Sheik Mujibur Rahman, following Rahman's assassination in August 1975 Bangladesh drifted away from India and back toward alignment with Pakistan, Sri Lanka, and Nepal—India's other neighbors, who looked somewhat favorably on China as a counterbalance to India. We will return to the problem of Bangladesh's link with China later. Here it will suffice to note that, in the event of looming or actual war with China, a prime objective of Indian diplomacy will be to keep Bangladesh from aligning with China while securing transit rights across Bangladesh territory for itself.

Developments during 1987, when India and China slid into military confrontation, illustrate this situation. A conflict began developing in mid-1986 in the Sumdurong Chu Valley in the vicinity of Thagla Ridge north of Tawang, just east of the Indian-China-Bhutan trijuncture. The confrontation escalated further in March 1987, when India launched Operation Chequerboard, a large-scale mobilization based on a hypothetical war with China. Large Indian forces were deployed for war with China. Beijing expressed "extreme concern" with Indian deployments and accelerated its own counterdeployments.[27] By May the PLA was shifting twenty-two thousand soldiers, fighter-bombers, and U.S.-made Blackhawk high-altitude helicopters from the Chengdu and Lanzhou military districts into Tibet. The confrontation carried the danger of war, which U.S. and Soviet diplomats worked hard to prevent. In this context CCP Politburo member Qiao Shi traveled to Burma, Nepal, and Bangladesh to discuss "international issues of mutual concern." According to press reports, Qiao delivered to Dhaka a request that, in the event of a Sino-Indian war, Bangladesh not allow India to move men and materiel across its territory. When Bangladeshi President Hussain Mohammad Ershad visited Beijing the following month, he reportedly gave China the required assurances.[28] Regardless of the accuracy of these press reports, they indicate the nature of Indian interests and concerns.

Bangladeshi neutrality would be India's minimal requirement in the event of a Chinese-Indian conflict. New Delhi would insist on guarantees that Bangladesh would not consent to, and presumably would protest against, the movement of Chinese men or materiel across its territory. Nor would China be allowed to have goods off-loaded in Dacca or Chittagong for shipment northward to Chinese forces. Strict Bangladeshi neutrality might not be enough, however. India could also require the right to itself move men and materiel across Bangladesh territory. Such movement would be vital to the defense of India's eastern states in the event of a PLA "anvil and hammer" offensive at Siliguri and down the Assam plain.

Indian fears were reflected in a popular book published in India in 1997. Written by a colonel in the Indian army who had retired after twenty-eight years of distinguished service, the book speculates about a Pakistan-inspired war to detach India's northeast. Northeastern insurgent groups and a Pakistani proxy war in Kashmir figure prominently in the anti-India scheme. As those insurgencies reach a crescendo, according to the author, Bangladesh throws its army and air force into the struggle against Indian hegemonism. Swift blows by Bangladesh cut the Siliguri corridor isolating that city and Sikkim. A multidivision Chinese force then pushes through western Bhutan toward Siliguri. God intervenes to save India, however, and heavy rains create floods and landslides that isolate Bangladeshi and Chinese forces, enabling their defeat by India.[29]

Many imponderable factors would influence Bangladesh's response to Indian requests in such an eventuality, and there is probably no way of knowing in advance how Bangladesh's government would respond to India's wartime diplomacy. Such uncertainties enhance Indian apprehensions about their ability to defend the Siliguri corridor and the entire Indian northeast. In the worst-case scenario Indian forces might be isolated in the northeast, while other Indian forces would have to force their way through Bangladesh, bringing on India the onus of having first violated the neutrality of a small, weak country.

THE SOUTHERN SLOPE AS INDIA'S DEFENSE ZONE

The southern slope of the eastern Himalayas plays an important role in India's defense of the northeast. Indian security planners conceive of this region as a defensive buffer that will absorb and hopefully halt the PLA offensives that are anticipated in the opening phase of another Sino-Indian war. Chinese conduct of war—from Korea in 1950, to India in 1962, to Vietnam in 1979— suggests a proclivity for offensive operations in the opening stages. The doctrine of "active defense" embraced by the PLA since the strategic reorientation of the mid-1980s also calls for boldly striking at an enemy in the opening stages of a conflict, seizing the initiative, and swiftly defeating him, rather than "passively" waiting for the enemy to strike. Indian security planners believe that at least some of these offensive operations will involve thrusts through the southern slope—a belief based on the 1962 experience, India's vulnerabilities in the northeast, China's long attention to insurgencies in India's northeast, and the configuration of PLA deployments in Tibet. This begs the question, of course, of whether an opponent in war would do what he is expected to do.

The PLA would enjoy certain important tactical advantages in an offensive drive through the southern slope. Most obvious, but also most important, it is far easier to move men and materials downhill than up. PLA forces would be moving from the Tibetan plateau down to the Assam plain. That would be considerably easier and faster than moving in the opposite, uphill direction. The PLA would also presumably have the tactical advantage of surprise and selection of point of attack. India's ability to shift forces to the point of Chinese attack would be hindered by the fact that the canyons extending south off the Tibetan plateau run generally north-south, making it necessary for Indian units to move back nearly to the Assam plain before shifting laterally and then moving up to meet the Chinese advance. The PLA would thus be able to muster considerable local superiority in the opening stage of a conflict, while India would be kept guessing where the main PLA attack would come.

China's considerable tactical advantages would be offset by India's ability carefully to prepare defensive positions in the extremely rugged terrain of the southern slope. Indian military engineers have laid out multiple defensive lines of resistance along all anticipated lines of PLA attack and are free to select the best defensive terrain on which to force the PLA to fight and to design and construct supporting positions, interlocking fields of fire, mine fields, and obstacles. The most forward areas closest to the line of actual control are without roads or bridges. Under a decision adopted in August 1959, shortly after the army assumed responsibility for coordinating road construction in the North East Frontier Agency (NEFA), as the southern slope was then known in India, roads and airfields were not to be constructed within thirty miles of the border. Connecting the forward border areas with the interior of India, and assuming that attacking Chinese forces would enjoy tactical surprise, could well serve Chinese offensive purposes more than Indian defensive purposes.[30] Fighting through a well-defended but roadless thirty-mile-wide zone would slow the Chinese advance enough to give Indian defenders time to concentrate and respond. Beginning thirty miles south of the border, roads and other logistic and communications lines supporting Indian positions have been carefully prepared for the swift movement of reinforcements. During the Fourth Five Year Plan (1966–71) a highway was constructed running east-west along the foothills of the southern slope to speed the lateral shift of Indian forces from one sector to another. This road offset to some degree China's ability to choose the point of attack and advance downhill. Indian support bases have been built and supplies pre-positioned, and careful preparations have been made to demolish bridges, vulnerable sections of roads, and other facilities before they are reached by advancing PLA forces. If all goes well for India, PLA offensives will be halted long before they reach the Assam plain. Should Chinese forces succeed in reaching the plain in spite of Indian defensive preparations, the tactical advantages in the subsequent stage of combat on the southern slope could be reversed. If the PLA then switched to strategic defense, Chinese soldiers would enjoy the tactical benefits of having carefully prepared future battlefields. Indian forces would be advancing uphill through prepared defensive lines.

India's enjoyment of these tactical advantages in the southern slope is premised on its administrative control of that region. Hence, if it were to lose that control through one means or another, it would also lose those advantages. Chinese forces would then stand, ceteris paribus, on the Assam plain, where there are fewer natural obstacles, other than the Brahmaputra River, of course. Open-field maneuver is possible here, and the transportation grid is far more developed. If the PLA were able to choose when and where to move onto this plain, India's northeast would be virtually indefensible.

THE TWOFOLD PROPOSAL AND FAILURE OF AN EAST-WEST SWAP

As the preceding discussion has shown, Chinese control of Aksai Chin was, and to some extent still is, important to China's control of Tibet. Indian control of the southern slope is important to its defense of the northeast. This was the geopolitical logic underlying the proposal of an east-west trade-off between Chinese and Indian claims. China would abandon its claim to the southern slope, recognizing Indian sovereignty over that tract. In exchange India would abandon its claim to Aksai Chin, recognizing Chinese sovereignty over that area. Through such mutual compromise each side would protect its own vital security interests while conceding a similar right to the other. The Gordian knot of complex legal and historical arguments would be cut. Most important, the threat to each side's territorial security posed by the claims of the other side would be eliminated.

China has twice proposed such an east-west swap. The first time was in 1960. In April of that year Zhou Enlai, during his talks in New Delhi with Nehru, proposed "reciprocal acceptance of present realities in both sectors." There would be mutual compromise, and neither side would have to undertake major withdrawals. At a press conference at the conclusion of the talks, Zhou said that, regarding Aksai Chin, "there exists a relatively bigger dispute," thereby implying that China did not dispute India's claim in the east. Zhou summarized China's position for the assembled reporters by saying that he had asked India to adopt toward the western sector an attitude similar to China's attitude toward the eastern sector.[31] The cautious and elliptical way in which Zhou broached his offer was meant to indicate, as Steve Hoffmannn has pointed out, that it was unofficial and might therefore be withdrawn.[32]

In 1980 Deng Xiaoping revived Zhou's 1960 proposal. Speaking with the editor of an Indian defense journal—as in 1960 in an unofficial venue—Deng explicitly suggested that the border issue could be solved via a package deal. China would recognize the McMahon Line in the east, while India would recognize the status quo in the western sector.[33] The calculated nature of Deng's remarks was confirmed by a Xinhua commentary two days after the leader's interview. The commentary asserted that the development of good neighborly relations between China and India accorded with the fundamental interests of both peoples. The key problem between the two countries was the boundary question, which could be solved by "mutual understanding and concessions." The commentary quoted Deng's interview, in which he said that the boundary issue could be solved if both sides would "respect the present state of the border." It concluded that "China has never asked for the return of all the territory illegally incorporated into India by the old colonialists."[34] In 1980, as in 1960, Chinese proposals of an east-west swap were carefully unofficial and elliptical. Yet the essence of Deng's 1980 proposal was the same as Zhou's in 1960: "reciprocal acceptance of present realities in both sectors." China would accept India's ownership of the southern slope, and India would accept China's ownership of Aksai Chin.

Both the 1960 and 1980 proposals seem, to this author in any case, to have been sincere Chinese efforts to improve Indian-Chinese relations fundamentally. The authoritative Chinese analyst of the 1962 war, Xu Yan, outlined the strategic rationale underlying Mao's approval of the 1960 swap offer. China at that juncture faced multiple grave security concerns along its eastern frontier—with the United States in Korea, the Taiwan Strait, and Laos. Each of these regions was tense and required substantial deployments of Chinese forces. An easing of U.S. pressure on China was not in sight; instead, the situation with the United States along China's southeastern borders was highly unstable. Chiang Kai-shek's forces on Taiwan were becoming increasingly active in an attempt to exploit China's internal difficulties, which were also increasingly desperate. The Great Leap Forward had gone awry. Hunger and economic depression were spreading across the land. China's alliance with the USSR was unraveling, further compounding Beijing's economic, diplomatic, and military problems. In this situation Mao did not want to add hostility with India to the list of problems confronting China. Thus, he ordered Zhou to propose concessions, the prime one being the swap proposal, to stanch the deterioration of Sino-Indian relations. Although the McMahon Line was a product of imperialist aggression against China, Mao ardently believed, China would nonetheless accept it as a basis for settlement in the east.[35]

Deng's 1980 revival of the swap offer also seems to have been sincere. Deng was then engineering a fundamental reorientation of China's foreign relations premised on the notion that the country's international conflicts should be reduced to create a more propitious environment for economic development. Trade and other mutually beneficial economic exchanges could thus expand. Reduced tension would also allow China to shift resources from national defense to economic modernization. At a second level Deng viewed Soviet expansionism in such places as Cambodia and Afghanistan as posing the greatest threat to China. He recognized India's substantial international influence and realized that it could play an important role in thwarting or facilitating Soviet moves. All factors pointed toward improving relations with India. Settlement of the boundary issue on the basis of an east-west swap was a way of doing this.

India was not interested in an east-west swap either in 1960 or 1980. In neither case did India explore with Chinese negotiators the question of Chinese sincerity or the modalities of the proposed swap. In 1960 Nehru unequivocally and forcefully rejected the proposal. He and most of his advisors felt deeply aggrieved by what they perceived as Chinese seizure of Indian land in Ladakh (i.e., Aksai Chin) and believed that to accept that seizure in any way was wrong. Indian popular and parliamentary opinion strongly shared these beliefs, and Nehru was fully aware of that domestic sentiment. There had even been strong public and parliamentary criticism of Nehru's meeting with Zhou in April 1960. As he told a governmental meeting at the time: "If I give them [Aksai Chin] I shall no longer be Prime Minister of India—I will not do it."[36] There was also a fear that acceptance of the principle of an east-west swap was tantamount to conceding that the entire Sino-Indian boundary was undefined, rather than being clearly defined by treaty, geography, and custom, as India had been arguing. If India conceded the principle that China was to be rewarded in the western sector, for example, who knew how high a price Beijing might demand?[37]

Again in 1980 India's leaders rejected Beijing's swap proposal. Speaking to the Lok Sabah in July 1980 Minister of External Affairs P. V. Narasimha Rao explained why: "The government of India has never accepted the premise on which it is based, namely, that the Chinese side is making a concession in the eastern sector by the giving up of territory which they allege is illegally incorporated into India. Nevertheless, we welcome the prospect of the eastern sector being settled without any particular difficulty."[38] According to this view,

India would be making a major concession by relinquishing land in the western sector which rightfully belonged to it but which had been stolen by China. China would gain that land and give up nothing, since it had never administered the southern slope, while India's claim and de facto administration of that region was incontrovertible. India had not occupied any Chinese territory, nor did it claim any Chinese territory. It did not make sense to suggest that India relinquish some of its own territory to China in order to get China to drop its claim to other pieces of Indian territory. A more earthy way of saying this was formulated by one of India's leading legal experts on the Indian-Chinese border dispute: If a thief breaks into your house and steals your coat and your wallet, you don't say to him that he can have the coat if he returns the wallet. You expect him to return all that he has stolen from you.[39]

It is difficult to overstate the impact on informed Chinese opinion of India's twofold rejection of China's east-west swap proposal. Such Chinese strongly believe that China's proposal of an east-west swap was fair and reasonable. It would have involved compromises by both sides accommodating the most important security interests of each. China would have accepted the line drawn by the imperialist McMahon, leaving India in secure possession of the southern slope. India would have dropped its claim to Aksai Chin—which it never actually administered—leaving China with secure access into western Tibet. By rejecting China's reasonable proposal, India demonstrated, once again, its arrogant attitude: what's mine is mine, and what's yours is mine too. And, of course, there is no question of China's genuine sincerity. Why, then, did Indian leaders reject such a fair and reasonable solution? Perhaps because of arrogance, China's India hands conclude—the same sort of arrogance India demonstrates repeatedly toward its other neighbors, Nepal, Sri Lanka, Bangladesh, when India attempts to dictate to those countries what sort of foreign relations they should have. The Indian leaders were students and heirs of the British imperialists. Their policies and attitudes are deeply influenced by that heritage—their embrace of the McMahon Line, for instance. Their policy toward Tibet, too, has been influenced by British imperial policy. They aspire to maintain a special status in the Tibet region of China. The link between China's control in Tibet and the Aksai Chin road has long been clear. Could the real reason Indian leaders demand Aksai Chin be that this would further their schemes in Tibet?[40] The perceptual gulf between India and China on the issue of rejection of the east-west swap remains huge.

Both the 1960 and the 1980 swap proposals were stated in unofficial terms, which meant they could be easily withdrawn. That withdrawal came in 1985. The two sides finally began talks on the border issue in December 1981. It soon became clear that New Delhi was still not prepared to adopt the "comprehensive package deal" approach favored by Beijing but continued to insist on Chinese withdrawal from Aksai Chin. The only progress was made at the fourth round of talks in October 1983, when Beijing agreed to India's proposal to discuss the border dispute sector by sector.[41] When the sixth round of talks began in October 1985, Chinese negotiators pressed China's claims in the *eastern* sector—that is, south of the McMahon Line. The Indian side was stunned. They had assumed that China implicitly accepted that line and that there would be little disagreement about it.[42]

With the 1985 shift in policy China for the first time began actively asserting its claim to the southern slope. Early the next year a long article in the authoritative Chinese journal *Guoji wenti yanjiu* (International studies) made public China's position. Regarding India's claim that the crest line of mountain ranges and natural watersheds should determine boundaries, the journal author said, this was only one possible criterion and "cannot provide the only or the decisive factor in determining the boundary." "It is unreasonable to maintain that the boundary has already been determined by a special characteristic of nature" (i.e., the watershed or crest line principle). In fact, the McMahon Line based on that supposed "special characteristic of nature" was "illegal and without any binding effect on China." The traditional, customary line of jurisdiction in the east ran along the southern foothills of the Himalayas, not the crest line, and there were all sorts of records—tax ledgers, records of administrative acts, etc.—to prove this. The "vast area" between the illegal McMahon Line and the traditional, customary line had historically been part of China. The people there were ethnically related to China. China could never agree to an action as "humiliating and injurious to its national sovereignty as selling . . . so large a piece of land." "The main area of conflict is in the eastern sector," and it was there that India would have to make concessions.[43]

Again during the seventh round of talks, in July 1986, China pressed its demands south of the McMahon Line. In an interview shortly before those talks began, China's vice foreign minister Liu Shuqing said that "the eastern sector is the biggest dispute and key to the overall solution." He also stressed that a settlement had to involve concessions by both sides. Implicitly, he was calling for Indian concessions in the eastern sector, not in the west as in the 1960 and 1980 proposals. During the talks Liu Shuqing asserted that the line of actual control could not serve as a basis for settlement. India had aggressively occupied Chinese territory on the southern slope, and that land had to be returned to China. While some irregularities in the western sector had been solved during the 1962 war, problems in the middle and eastern sectors remained unresolved. If India were willing to make concessions *in the east,*

China would certainly consider making a gesture *in the west*. Liu thereby explicitly reversed the geopolitical logic of the 1960 swap by asserting that Indian accommodate China in the east. When asked whether this did not involve a reversal of Zhou Enlai's 1960 proposal, Liu replied that "Premier Zhou was only talking about ideas, not specific proposals."[44] Later, when the Indian side queried China more directly about whether the 1960 proposal still stood, the Chinese reply was, quite correctly, that the record of previous negotiations showed no trace of such a proposal as mentioned by the Indian side.[45]

This shift in Chinese position coincided with the confrontation in Sumdurong Chu, mentioned earlier, to produce a very serious confrontation between the two countries. Seen from the Indian perspective, China's actions at Sumdurong Chu in 1986 were intended to underline its new, active claim in the east. Shortly after Beijing began asserting its claim in the east, the Indian parliament moved, in December 1986, to upgrade the administrative level of the southern slope from a union territory to a full state of the Indian union named Arunachal Pradesh. (The NEFA had been renamed Arunachal Pradesh in 1971, when it became a union territory.) The establishment of Arunachal Pradesh as a state was only indirectly related to ROI-PRC interactions. It grew directly out of India's federal process in which New Delhi accommodated major northeastern ethnic groups by granting them statehood. As we have seen, Nagaland led the way in 1962. Mizoram was moving toward statehood in 1986. The Naga and Mizo claims to statehood had been fueled, again as we have seen, by violent struggle. NEFA / Arunachal Pradesh, on the other hand, had consistently been tranquil and obedient to the center. Statehood was popular in Arunachal Pradesh. Were the more loyal people of that region to be penalized and denied statehood because they had been loyal? A desire to reward rather than penalize loyalty was a major impulse underlying the establishment of Arunachal Pradesh as a state.[46] Of course, everyone was aware that establishing Arunachal Pradesh in the context of late 1986 was also a way of rebuffing China. It would also make it constitutionally more difficult for New Delhi to abandon that territory.

China strongly protested the "establishment of an Indian state on Chinese territory" which Indian had "illegally occupied" and which was "the major [territorial] dispute" between the two countries. Such an action "seriously violated China's territorial sovereignty, gravely injured the feelings of the Chinese people," "created obstacles for the resolution of the boundary issue, and made that problem more complex." According to a *Renmin ribao* editorial, China "absolutely will not recognize" (*jue bu cheng ren*) India's establishment of Arunachal Pradesh.[47] When the state of Arunachal Pradesh was formally established, in February 1987, China's Foreign Ministry again protested in similar terms.[48] As is often the case, the CCP-controlled Hong Kong newspaper *Wen wei bao* was more threatening. India, the paper said, was "occupying another country's territory, and legalizing it through domestic legislation." Did India believe that it could "force the invaded country to submissively obey and hand over its territory by this means? Even a weak country will resist, let alone a strong and independent China!" The Indian government was "lifting a rock only to drop it on its own feet [and] will certainly eat its own bitter fruit." Referring to tension in the Sumdurong Chu region near the Thagla Ridge about the same time, the paper warned: "History has proved that it is unwise to try to solve border disputes by force of arms. The border conflict of 1962 may serve as a lesson." "We would like to remind the Indian government that it should not mistakenly take China's sincerity as a sign of weakness and act according to its wishful thinking."[49]

Why did Beijing withdraw the east-west swap proposal that had, apparently, been on the table for two decades? There seem to be three related explanations. The first is that, ever since the talks began in 1981, India rejected the concept of a "package deal" and insisted on a "section by section" approach. China finally agreed to India's demand for independent, nonlinked treatment of each sector. The logic of bargaining may have been that, if concessions in one area were no longer to be linked to gains in some other area, it made the most sense to push for the maximum in all sectors. A second factor, also having to do with enhancing China's bargaining leverage, was that it was necessary to disabuse India of the idea that China had no serious claim in the eastern sector and was therefore giving up nothing by dropping that claim. As Foreign Minister Narasimha Rao's 1980 comments to the Lok Sabah indicated, India simply did not believe China was making a significant concession by abandoning its claims to the southern slope. China seemed to have tacitly accepted the crest line principle in the east. These Indian beliefs put China at a disadvantage. Vigorously asserting China's claims to the southern slope would undercut both beliefs, increasing China's leverage. In this fashion the Indians might be disabused of their belief that China "was giving up nothing" by accepting the line of actual control in the east. The third explanation of China's dropping of the swap concept and asserting its claim in the east is that some influential people in China felt that the country needed to pursue a tougher approach to settling the territorial problem with India.

CHINESE VIEWS ON THE TERRITORIAL DISPUTE

Different prominent and influential Chinese had different views about how to deal with India in the late 1980s. Labels are always problematic, but perhaps we can use the old standbys "moderates" and "hard-liners." The moderate viewpoint was elaborated in early 1989 by Wang Hongwei, longtime director of the South Asian Institute of the Chinese Academy of Social Sciences. The publication of Zhou Enlai's correspondence with Nehru circa 1959–60 had created real political constraints in China.[50] Zhou's letter of September 8, 1959, for example, stated that China would never accept the McMahon Line and that to do so would be to "relinquish its rights and disgrace the country by selling out national territory" (*cang quan wu guo, chumai guotu*).[51] These were strong words, Wang explained, and nationalist sentiments were strong in China: "A significant number of comrades believe" (*you xiangdang yi xie tongzhi renwei*), Wang continued, that China's territory south of the illegal McMahon Line must be recovered. If not peacefully, then through the use of force. If China's strength was not adequate at present, then long-term preparations should be made. Wang marshaled many arguments against a war to recover the southern slope: casualties were certain to be heavy, possibly heavy enough to "injure national morale"; China would lose international sympathy; the use of military force to settle territorial disputes was less and less acceptable to the world; transportation would be very difficult, as would construction of roads; costs would be huge. Also, once China had occupied the southern slope, there would be a basic shift in the situation advantageous to India. A large, proud country like India would not accept defeat but would organize a large-scale counterattack. Even if such an attack did not materialize, Wang explained, China would face a long-term danger of surprise attack, bombing, or encirclement.

Nonrecovery of the entire southern slope could not really be considered "disgrace by selling out territory," Wang continued, because China's case for ownership of all that region was actually rather weak. Some areas of the southern slope had been inhabited historically by very primitive tribes who were never administered by either China or India. In other areas there was not a single, clear, traditional, customary boundary (as China's legal position insisted). Nor was there uniform and convincing evidence that China, or its Tibetan predecessor, had actually administered all areas of the southern slope. In some areas India could also claim sovereignty on the basis of the right of discovery and administration for several decades at least. In sum, China's legal claim to the southern slope was not ironclad. Nor was it worth going to war over. China should be willing to drop its claim to most of the southern slope and settle for Indian concessions in the Dawang area (just east of Bhutan), where evidence of a history of actual administration by the Tibetan government is strongest.

A more hard-line view was expressed by a retired PLA general interviewed

in early 1990. According to him, Zhou Enlai's 1960 swap proposal had been
made when China was poor, weak, and isolated. In that situation China had
been willing to make significant concessions, giving up more than it received.
It made similar offers to other countries—Burma, Afghanistan, Pakistan,
etc.—and those countries accepted, to their advantage. India did not, and
now it had lost its chance. China was no longer poor, weak, or isolated. Now
it was developed, strong, and with a firm international situation, and its offer
to recognize Indian possession of the southern slope no longer stood.
According to the general, China could not afford to give up its rich territory
on the southern slope. That region contained one-third of the timber, hydroelectric, and mineral resources of all of Tibet. It was also a region appropriate to agriculture. China, with its large population, could not afford to abandon
this rich territory. If there were to be an east-west swap, why shouldn't China
make concessions in the west and India give up the east? Aksai Chin was far
poorer and less useful than the southern slope. Besides, the road there was
far less critical now than it had been in the 1950s. Possession of the eastern
slope would have a significant impact on the future national power of China
or India, whichever possessed it. China must control that region if it is to be
a great power. A high-ranking Indian diplomat in Beijing, whom I interviewed
about the same time as the PLA general, said that Indian diplomats had
received contradictory signals from different Chinese regarding the "return"
of the southern slope to China. The Indian side had concluded, according to
this Indian diplomat, that the Chinese side was not unified on this issue.

The debate between moderate and hard-line views on the territorial
conflict with India was subsumed by the tidal wave of international condemnation in the aftermath of the Beijing massacre of June 1989. More cordial relations with India quickly became an important part of Beijing's
diplomatic effort to escape international isolation. Under such circumstances there could be no consideration of a hard-line approach to solving
the territorial problem with India, and the whole question was shelved. What
conditions would lead to a revival of that debate in China remains unclear.

A key problem in solving the territorial conflict along the moderate lines
proposed by Wang Hongwei is that the Dawang area he specifies as the region
having the strongest historic evidence of actual administration by Tibetan
authorities happens to be the most sensitive geopolitically. Other authoritative Chinese writers, such as former ambassador Yang Gongsu, also found
the evidentiary basis of Chinese claims regarding customary administration
to be strongest, and evidence of British administration to be weakest, in the
Dawang area.[52] While the triangle of territory, with its lower point south of
Dawang, would be quite small, Chinese possession of such a tract would cre-

ate a second salient of Chinese territory bracketing Bhutan. This area was the PLA's main line of advance in 1962 and lies at the end of some of its shortest logistic lines extending from the Lhasa area. Moving the boundary south of Dawang would move the PLA's jump-off point for any future offensive about halfway to the edge of the Assam plain. It would also put some of the most rugged terrain behind the PLA's front. This would be difficult for Indian security planners to accept. It is important to keep in mind that this is the *moderate* Chinese approach to solving the territorial issue.

If the Sino-Indian territorial issue is to be solved peacefully through negotiations, the solution must come from the very highest level. The top leaders of China and India will have to decide that, simply in order to reduce the possibility of war between the two countries, they must reach an agreement and then impose it on their respective countries. When they agree to do this and proceed to draw a line on a map, they will probably need to keep their specialists on the border issue out of the room—their soldiers and strategists too.

4 / Sino-Indian Rivalry for Influence and Status among Developing Countries

One of the major characteristics of post-1945 global politics was the breakup of empires whose growth had been one of the principal global trends of the previous several centuries. After 1945, within an amazingly brief period, these empires largely disappeared. In their place emerged scores of newly independent African and Asian countries. As diverse as these new countries were, they shared certain common characteristics. First was the experience of Western domination. Second, they were mostly poor, preindustrial countries and were weak relative to both their old colonial masters and to the new post–World War II superpowers, the United States and the USSR. It must also be said that, although both of the superpowers had broken sharply with Western colonialism (America in 1776, Russia in 1917) and though they both supported the dismantling of the European colonial empires, they were nonetheless largely of European derivation racially and culturally, and this fact subtly influenced the attitude of the developing African and Asian countries toward them. These common interests inspired a variety of movements that helped define post-1945 politics. I will refer to these newly independent countries that emerged from the post-1945 process of decolonization as the "developing countries."

There have been five stages of Indian-Chinese rivalry for status and influence among the developing countries since 1949.

1. 1949–59: China sought to enhance its standing in Asia through an alliance with the USSR, while India sought to engineer a developing countries movement led by itself. This stage ended when Moscow refused to support China against India.

2. 1959–65: China fostered Afro-Asian radicalism directed against India's "third way," while India supported a nonalignment that excluded China.

3. 1966–72: The CCP fostered Marxist-Leninist Communist Parties as alternatives to the Soviet-American-supported Indian path of development.

4. 1976–82: China and India tried to move the nonaligned movement (NAM) in contrary directions regarding its stance toward the USSR and Moscow's friends in Asia and Africa.

5. Post-1989: The policies of the two countries clash over reorganization of the UN Security Council and recognition of India as a nuclear weapons state.

During their early days both the ROI and the PRC felt a strong sense of mission toward the developing countries. Both felt, with considerable justice, that their own national struggles had played an extremely important role in bringing about the collapse of colonialism, Western and Japanese. Exercising leadership among the developing countries also gave China and India a way to compete with the Western countries, and with the superpowers, for influence. The European countries, in spite of their far greater economic and military power, seemed excluded from leadership among the developing countries by their recent histories as colonial masters. The two new superpowers seemed too similar to the old Western powers—at least in the eyes of many of the new leaders of the developing countries. The superpowers' advocacy of their respective ideologies struck many in the developing countries as ideological justification for new types of imperialism.

In the early days of both the ROI and the PRC, the leaders of those respective states were occasionally open about their aspirations. Speaking to India's Constituent Assembly in December 1946, shortly before independence, Nehru proclaimed that "the new constitution for India will lead India to real freedom ... [It] will lead also to the freedom of other countries of Asia because, however unworthy, we have become—let us recognize it—leaders of the freedom movement of Asia, and whatever we do, we should think of ourselves in these larger terms."[1] During its early months in power the CCP issued proclamations about the applicability of China's revolutionary experience to other Asian countries. Simultaneously, it began assisting revolutionary movements in countries around China's periphery. These actions were rooted in the Marxist-Leninist ideology of the CCP and in the decades-long revolutionary struggle it had waged in its rise to power. Mao Zedong and his comrades were determined that the "New China," the PRC, should no longer be a weak, passive country but should vigorously throw its substantial weight into the struggle of the world's "progressive" forces against the "imperialist" forces led by the United States. The success of revolutionary movements in countries neighboring China would enhance the security of New China against U.S. imperialism, fulfill China's ideologically derived "proletarian internationalist duty," and allow China to play a prominent international role.[2]

The leaders of both the PRC and the ROI soon learned that too open an expression of their aspiration of leading Asia roused suspicions among smaller countries, which feared that Indian or Chinese imperialism might replace European colonialism. To avoid rousing these suspicions, Chinese and Indian representatives soon learned the best way to exercise leadership was to renounce the desire for leadership. In 1959, for example, just as he was engineering what eventually became the nonaligned movement, Nehru explicitly eschewed a leadership role. Asked by a sympathetic journalist whether India's membership in the Commonwealth "might obstruct our leadership of newly liberated Asia and Africa," Nehru replied, "We desire no leadership or domination over any country." He went on to explain: "We cannot remain unaffected by the highest single fact of contemporary history—that is, the reemergence of Asia and Africa. We are affected by the tremendous event because we are part of it, part of the movement and the revolution as well as part of the geography, at the very heart of these two continents, placed as we are in the center of the Indian Ocean."[3]

Leaders of countries that looked to India for leadership could be and were more frank. In 1964 the distinguished Philippine diplomat Carlos Romulo characterized India's role in this way:

What is happening in the "under-developed" or emergent societies in Afro-Asia and in Latin America is a complex of revolutionary movement. . . . India is the conscience of this revolutionary movement. For in this revolution it was India that renounced violence and, instead, insisted on asserting moral, philosophical, and intellectual force. In the nationalist movement of our times, it was India's exemplary role to assert a revolutionary force essentially with the power of reason and ethical conduct and to make this action a cogent political alternative in the rigid balance of power of our time. It was India that first called attention to the ethical problems in modern politics. . . . Indeed, it was India, through the example of Mahatma Gandhi and the intelligence of Nehru, that has provided Asian nationalism with its conscience.[4]

In unguarded moments Chinese and Indian leaders revealed glimpses of their inner thinking. A 1974 poem by Mao Zedong, for example, gave a clear, if poetic, description of the scorn with which he viewed India's aspirations of greatness:

> The tiger averts its head,
> The tattered lion grieves.
> The bear flaunts its claws,
> Riding the back of the cow.
> The moon torments the sun.
> The pagoda gives forth light.
> Disaster comes to birth.
> The olive is seen waving.[5]

In this quintessential expression of Mao's weltanschauung, the tiger was the United States, the lion Britain, the bear the Soviet Union, the moon the Islamic countries of the Middle East, the sun the rich countries of the West, the pagoda the Vietnamese revolutionary struggle, and its light the prospect of imminent victory. A pagoda giving forth light is a common Chinese literary simile indicating good fortune. The phrase *disaster comes to birth* referred to Mao's dictum that either revolution would prevent war or war would lead to revolution, while the olive branch referred to the people's desire for peace. The cow was India. As a Maoist exposition of the poem, from which the several explanations presented here derived, explained, "Chairman Mao's use of the cow as a metaphor for India could not be more appropriate. It is no better than a cow . . . it is only food or for people to ride and for pulling carts; it has no particular talents. The cow would starve to death if its master did not give it grass to eat. . . . Even though this cow may have great ambitions, they are futile."

INDIA'S EARLY ANTICOLONIALIST EFFORTS

Interest in and sympathy for independence movements elsewhere in Asia were an important strand of Indian nationalist thinking from the very beginning. The young Rabindranath Tagore, for example, wrote an article condemning the Western import of opium into China, while the very first session of the India National Congress in 1885 protested Britain's annexation of Upper Burma and dissolution of the Burmese monarchy. Later Congress sessions passed resolutions supporting nationalist struggles from Afghanistan and Iran to Tibet's resistance to the Younghusband expedition of 1903–4, and disassociating Congress from Britain's use of Indian troops for colonial repression. By 1928 Congress saw India's independence struggle as part of a worldwide anti-imperialist struggle. Throughout the 1920s and 1930s it issued frequent statements of solidarity and moral support for Asian anticolonial struggles.[6] Alongside this strong sense of pan-Asian solidarity was a conviction that India, as the largest and wealthiest colony of the greatest European empire, was destined to play a special role in the rise of the Asian peoples. When India won its freedom, the entire colonialist system would come crashing down, freeing all the peoples of Asia. The brilliant achievements of traditional Indian civilization also qualified it for greatness. Shortly before his death, Bal Gandadhar Tilak foresaw India as "a leading power within Asia" in a letter to the head of the Versailles Peace Conference in 1919, French President Clemenceau. Tilak was leader of the militant wing of the Indian independence movement in the early twentieth century, who unabashedly advocated the superiority of Hindu civilization.[7]

India's Congress Party leaders emerged from British detention at the end of World War II determined that India would play an important role in shaping the future of Asia. They strongly believed that India should help bring about the end of Western colonialism and guide the development of independent Asia. The first order of business for the Congress Working Committee, formed after its members' release from British prisons, was issuance of a declaration demanding freedom for India, Burma, Malaysia, Indochina, and Indonesia. India's new leaders also quickly attempted to give organizational form to growing pan-Asian sentiment by convening in March 1947 (five months prior to full independence) a First Conference on Asian Relations. Sino-Indian rivalry erupted at the March 1947 conference, even though China was represented by the moribund Nationalist-led Republic of China (ROC) regime. As weak as that regime was, it challenged India's exercise of Asian leadership. India had hoped the conference would establish a permanent organization based in India, and, indeed, it did establish a provisional council headed by Jawaharlal Nehru, but, when the question of forming a permanent organization came up, it floundered on the question of whether it should be based in India or China. Neither country would agree to the other acting as permanent host. In deference to Chinese pride the ROC representative was elected vice president of the provisional council, and it was decided that the next session of the conference, at least, would be held in China.

Indonesia quickly emerged as an early focus of Indian efforts to influence Asian developments. In December 1946, when Dutch forces in Java and

Sumatra began military action against Indonesian Republican forces, the Indian government (not yet fully independent but already with substantial operational autonomy) dispatched a Dakota C-47 aircraft to Java to pick up independence leader Sultan Sjahror and deliver him to Singapore. Sjahror visited Delhi a short while later to hear Nehru condemn Dutch repression in Indonesia. As fighting in Indonesia escalated, India acted to further influence events. In July 1947 all Dutch aircraft were banned from landing in India. Six months later India, joined by Pakistan and Ceylon (as Sri Lanka was named prior to 1972), extended the embargo to all Dutch ships as well as aircraft. In January 1949 a conference of eighteen Asian countries convened in New Delhi at the invitation of the government of India and under the chairmanship of Nehru to discuss the Indonesian situation. The conference concluded by calling on the United Nations Security Council to take early action to end Dutch imperialism. Nehru transmitted the resolution to the Security Council on behalf of the conference.[8]

The CCP, whose armies were marshaling to cross the Yangtze River at the time of the January 1949 conference, scorned Indian efforts on behalf of Indonesia. *China Digest,* then the CCP's main English-language organ and printed in Hong Kong, reported that the conference "decided nothing in favor of immediate action to support the Indonesian people, nor to condemn the Dutch." The conference's communications to the Security Council "leave the Indonesian people to the aggression of the Dutch imperialists . . . no immediate practical step has been proposed. Even as a protest, the resolution was weak and misleading." The CCP organ insinuated that the conference was in fact an imperialist plot to stifle Indonesia's struggle:

> By now, Western imperialists have learned their lessons of failure and have resorted to more subtle ways by which they hope to soften the feeling of the colonial people. A "Third Force" in Asia is very much contemplated by the colonial powers who seek to appease the seething national emancipation movement in Asia. It is natural that the Western imperialists will pour down their hope on the Asian conference in whose resolution they find "there is nothing to which the Western world can take exception."[9]

India was emerging as leader of this "third force" among developing countries. The CCP had more radical ideals about the direction in which the emerging nations should march. Mao was then lining up Soviet support for Chinese leadership to guide those nations along a more "correct" revolutionary path.

CHINA'S SPECIAL ROLE IN THE ASIAN REVOLUTION
AND THE SINO-SOVIET ALLIANCE

Between 1949 and early 1950 Chinese and Soviet leaders reached a series of understandings underpinning a projected global strategic partnership. There was deep suspicion between leaders of the two sides, but those suspicions were overridden by convergent global perspectives about the struggle against imperialism. Chinese leaders persuaded Stalin that the situation in Asia offered great opportunities for revolutionary advance—that is, for expanding the socialist camp. Colonialism and neocolonialism in Asia were in deep crisis. The victory of the Chinese revolution had shaken the whole imperialist system in Asia. China's revolutionary experience—encircling the cities with expanding base areas in the countryside, combining illegal armed struggle with legal struggle— were applicable in many Asian countries. If this were done, prospects were good for further revolutionary gains in Asia. In the words of one close study of these interactions, "By focusing on this unique [revolutionary] history, the Chinese were demonstrating their aspiration to act independently in world affairs and their hope, if not determination, to become the leader of the colonial and semi-colonial states."[10] Talks about a division of labor in the world revolutionary movement constituted a focal point of the Stalin-Liu Shaoqi talks of January–August 1949. Stalin appreciated the size and effectiveness of the resources at the command of the CCP and concluded that, if those resources could be used to win regions in Asia from the imperialist camp, the global balance would be shifted further in favor of the socialist camp.

China exercised its leadership of the Asian revolutionary movement in two theaters: Korea and Vietnam. Both were traditional Chinese tributaries, both had strong indigenous revolutionary movements, and in both cases the CCP endorsed wars of national liberation and went as far as necessary to insure the victory of those wars. In Korea Mao gave his critical approval to Kim Il Sung's war plan, supplied crucial manpower for that offensive, and then undertook a very costly three-year war with the United States once U.S. intervention defeated Kim's initial plan. In Vietnam, China supplied what was necessary to Ho Chi Minh's successful war to force the French out of Vietnam.[11]

During the first period of the PRC-USSR alliance Beijing directly contested India's efforts to influence the developing countries. India's attempts to build a third, nonaligned force in world affairs prevented developing countries from allying with the anti-imperialist socialist camp. The "bourgeois-nationalist" Nehru regime stifled "progressive" class struggle within India and encouraged other regimes to do the same, according to the CCP line of the early 1950s. This militant approach, combined with the communist offensives in

Korea and Indochina in the early 1950s served to facilitate U.S. efforts to recruit participants in its efforts to contain the Sino-Soviet bloc. Mao and Zhou Enlai recognized this and in 1953, shortly after the end of the Korean War and Stalin's death, shifted policy gears. China would, they decided, begin to court the governments of the newly independent and "noncommitted" countries. A key objective was to create a "zone of peace" along China's southern borders encompassing Burma, Cambodia, Ceylon, India, Indonesia, and Nepal. This zone of peace would exclude U.S.-engineered positions hostile to China.[12]

INDIA'S EFFORTS TO BRING CHINA ONTO THE INTERNATIONAL STAGE

During the 1950s a key dimension of India's effort at Asian leadership was toward the PRC itself. As the perceptive Pakistani diplomat Mohammed Yunus pointed out, Nehru's desire to establish Indian leadership during these years enhanced the value of friendship with China. For Nehru, bringing the PRC into the international system in spite of American objections was a key component of his effort at Asian leadership.[13]

Solidarity with China figured prominently in the pan-Asianism of Indian nationalism in the early twentieth century. China's sharp anti-imperialist struggles of the 1910s and 1920s evoked frequent declarations of Congress Party support. The brutality of Japan's attack on China in the 1930s produced an important shift in Indian perceptions. Previously, many Indians had seen Japan as the leading power in Asia. Now Japan's brutality seemed to exclude it from the Asian community, while Indian sympathy for China grew. Congress sent a medical unit to the CCP base at Yan'an, and Nehru himself visited China as a guest of the government. Wherever Nehru went in China, he received a rousing welcome. He talked with both Nationalist and Communist Chinese leaders about the future. The growing sense of Sino-Indian friendship further intensified when Generalissimo Chiang Kai-shek outfoxed his British hosts during his February 1942 visit to India and succeeded in meeting with Congress leaders. By the end of World War II Nehru had developed a clear vision of cooperation between India and China.[14]

India became a major crusader for PRC interests. At the United Nations it opposed efforts to condemn the PRC for "aggression" in Korea. It advocated and lobbied for the PRC to assume China's seat at the United Nations. During the 1950–51 negotiations regarding a peace treaty with Japan, New Delhi pushed to include the PRC as a signatory. When it became apparent that this would not occur, India still pushed to have the PRC invited to express its views on the terms of the treaty and tried to insure that the treaty's terms were acceptable to China. Regarding Formosa, for example, India felt that the treaty should specifically cede that island to China, not merely have Japan renounce ownership of it. When it was clear that India would not be satisfied on these and other points, it decided not to participate in the multilateral peace conference and treaty with Japan. Nehru then briefly considered organizing an independent Asian peace conference with Japan, which would certainly have included the PRC, but dropped the plan under strong U.S. pressure.[15] In 1954–55 India pressed for PRC participation in the 1954 Geneva conference on Indochina and in UN discussions of the tense Taiwan Strait situation.

Indian lobbying on China's behalf was based in part on Nehru's belief that China's international isolation made it more dependent on the USSR and increased the likelihood of belligerent Chinese behavior toward other Asian countries. China's leaders had seriously distorted views of noncommunist Asian countries, Nehru believed, leading them both to underrate those countries' dislike for China's close association with the USSR and to overestimate noncommunist Asian countries' support for U.S. policies. Broader contacts outside the communist camp, especially with noncommunist Asian countries, would educate China's leaders, dispelling these misperceptions, and make China less likely to undertake aggressive moves and more likely to act independently of the USSR.[16] Nehru hoped that, as China became more independent of the USSR, it would look increasingly to partnership with India. His induction of the PRC into the conference of twenty-nine Asian and African countries in Bandung, Indonesia, in April 1955 was part of Nehru's effort to broaden China's international contacts. The proposal for the conference came originally from Indonesia and would have involved only African and Asian members of the United Nations, a formulation that would have excluded China. Nehru proposed inviting communist China, and, once this was agreed to, became an enthusiastic proponent of the conference.[17]

The Bandung conference was an important milestone for the developing countries movement. The conference itself was a stage for a remarkable display of Sino-Indian cooperation, but there were undertones of the rivalry that would soon shake that relationship. According to the Philippine representative to the conference Carlos Romulo, Nehru "deftly played 'mother hen'" to China's representative, Premier and Foreign Minister Zhou Enlai. Nehru arranged a number of private gatherings calculated to bring Zhou into closer contact with other delegates.[18] Zhou Enlai came to the conference determined to impress upon the assembled delegates China's peace-loving and reasonable attitude, which he did with considerable skill. Nehru supported Zhou's efforts. Following Zhou's major address, Nehru urged the delegates to accord it the "highest consideration." Zhou and Nehru actively supported each other at the conference. When Zhou was thrown onto the defensive by a broad-based push to include a reference to "Soviet colonialism" in Eastern Europe in a resolution condemning colonialism, Nehru undertook a lengthy intervention against that effort. When the Indian leader found himself heading toward confrontation with U.S. allies over the question of alliance versus nonalignment, Zhou came to Nehru's assistance. China did not feel particularly threatened by such alliances as Pakistan's tie with the United States, he explained. Zhou's comments helped to "bridge a widening gap between the positions of India and the Western-aligned states," in George Kahin's words.[19]

India succeeded at Bandung in substantially expanding China's international stature. There is no doubt that the primary credit for China's greater international prominence belongs to Zhou Enlai's diplomatic skill and to China's growing national power. But India did what it could to help this process, and its assistance probably accelerated the expansion of PRC contacts. In any case, China's standing among the African and Asian nations grew considerably following Bandung. In only a few instances did this greater respectability translate into de jure recognition for the PRC, but China's de facto relations with the developing countries expanded. Nehru was also satisfied that at Bandung Asian and African attention had been focused on China's repeated promises of nonbelligerent behavior. This, Nehru believed, would create political constraints on China which would help keep it peaceful for at least the immediate future. Seven years later, after the 1962 war, Indian opinion would reflect again on the results of Bandung. It was then apparent that organized moral stricture was not a particularly effective deterrent. The fact that India enjoyed relatively little support among the Afro-Asian nations at the time of the 1962 war (only Cyprus and Malaysia openly supported India) was also due in part to China's ability to build ties with those countries in the late 1950s—thanks, in part, to India's assistance. This reinterpretation of India's mid-1950s diplomacy was another element of the reorientation of Indian thinking toward China after the 1962 war.

There were also undertones of personal rivalry between Nehru and Zhou at Bandung. In the astute appraisal of Carlos Romulo, most delegates had come to the conference expecting it to be dominated by Nehru. Many, however, were "jolted by his pedantry. His pronounced propensity to be dogmatic, impatient, irascible, and unyielding, especially in the face of opposition, alienated the good will of many delegates." Nehru's attitude seemed to typify "the affectation of cultural superiority induced by a conscious identification with an ancient civilization." Zhou Enlai's apparent humility and reasonableness was in sharp contrast to the characteristics perceived in Nehru. It was Zhou rather than Nehru who dominated the proceedings and impressed the delegates. Nehru could not help but notice. Nehru's preference for nonalignment as opposed to Afro-Asianism in the years after Bandung may have had a personal element: it would keep him from sharing the stage with Zhou.

Nehru's main speech to the Political Committee of the Bandung conference foreshadowed the differences between India and China that would erupt in 1959. In that speech Nehru argued forcefully that the prime problem facing the developing countries, and indeed the human race, was avoiding war. In the modern era war would inevitably become nuclear war, which would "lead to the total destruction of mankind." "Therefore, the first thing we have to settle is that war must be avoided," Nehru argued. The second thing was for the developing countries to disassociate themselves deliberately from the two camps of the Cold War—to adopt nonalignment—thereby reducing the likelihood of war. The "realistic" policy of trying to maintain peace by forming alliances had failed, Nehru maintained, and had "led us to the brink of war, a Third World war." "If all the world were divided up between these two big blocs," the "inevitable result would be war." Every step that reduced the nonaligned area was a "dangerous step and leads to war" by reducing "that balance, that outlook which countries without military might can perhaps exercise." The more countries that refused to align with either bloc, the greater the moral and political force working for peace.

Point by point Nehru's speech at Bandung tracked Beijing's post-1957 objections to Soviet and Indian policies. Whereas Nehru argued against global polarization, Beijing would argue for such polarization. From Mao's post-1957 perspective *all* progressive forces in the world, including the socialist camp led by the USSR, should join together to struggle against imperialism. Such polarization would not lead to war but, rather, increase the chances for peace. The main cause of war was the aggressive policies of U.S. imperialism. The stronger the global anti-imperialist struggle, the less bold and reckless U.S. imperialism would be. Nor would all war lead to nuclear war. Wars of national liberation would help restrain the aggressive propensities of imperialism and were unlikely to lead to nuclear war. Finally, if world war occurred, even nuclear war, it would not be a catastrophe. Anti-imperialist wars of national liberation in developing countries led to great historic progress for the country involved. And, even if U.S. imperialism launched a nuclear world war, such a war would lead not to the destruction of human civilization but to the end of imperialism and the construction of a global, socialist civilization.

NONALIGNMENT VERSUS AFRO-ASIANISM

Following the Bandung conference Nehru began to make explicit non-alignment the fundamental principle of the developing country movement. Since China was firmly allied with the USSR, nonalignment had the effect of excluding China from the new movement. In July 1956 Yugoslav leader Josip Broz Tito, Egyptian leader Gamal Abdel Nasser, and Nehru met at the Adriatic island of Brioni to issue a communiqué condemning the division of the world into two hostile camps and affirming the interests of the nations that chose to abstain from participating in that division. Cambodian leader Prince Norodom Sihanouk and Indonesia's Sukarno later joined the communiqué. The Brioni communiqué marked the beginning of the nonaligned movement.

India's role in the nonaligned movement was unique. As Peter Willetts has pointed out, aside from India, the adherents of nonalignment were weak, vulnerable countries, beset by internal division and external enemies, and apprehensive about the possible loss of sovereignty. For them nonalignment was a defensive strategy to avoid giving offense, seek protection in numbers, and strengthen international norms providing some protection for the weak. India was different. Its independence was never seriously threatened after 1947. For India nonalignment provided a way to give expression to its strong sense of national greatness. It provided a high-minded, moralistic formulation for Indian foreign policy, differentiating India's morality-based leadership from the supposedly amoral power politics of the two Cold War camps, while giving India an arena within which it could play an independent, major role in the world.[20]

As noted earlier, by late 1953 Beijing welcomed Indian nonalignment as a way of countering U.S. containment. The political ground began to shift in December 1957, when Mao began an effort to set the international revolutionary movement on a more militant path. Mao pointed to such things as the rapid industrialization of the USSR, the PRC, and Eastern Europe, the breakup of European empires, and the growing military power of the Sino-Soviet bloc exemplified by the Soviet development of intercontinental missiles and thermonuclear bombs to argue that a fundamental shift in the global correlation of forces had occurred. This shift gave the revolutionary camp a clear advantage over the imperialist camp. The time was right, Mao began to argue, for swift revolutionary advance. The focus of militant, anti-imperialist struggle would be in the vast intermediate zone lying between the imperialist and the socialist camp—for example, in the developing countries of Asia and Africa

(Latin America was later added after Castro's rise to power). Political lines had to be drawn with increased clarity and rigor in this intermediate zone, with strong support going to progressive forces willing to challenge imperialism. A key target of struggle were intermediate-zone bourgeois-nationalist regimes linked with and subservient to imperialism. Intensifying struggle against these traitor regimes would polarize the situation in the intermediate zone, pushing the anti-imperialist struggle forward to victory in country after country. The socialist countries should support militant anti-imperialist struggles raging in the intermediate zone, Mao argued, not fearing the intimidation and threats of aggrieved imperialists.[21]

Mao's militant line soon brought China into conflict with India. In terms of policy prescriptions for the developing countries, the most fundamental difference between India and China had to do with drawing political class lines within the developing countries. From the CCP's perspective this was essential because the transition from colonialism to political independence in much of the intermediate zone had been an empty sham—actually a type of imperialist trick. Confronted by a rising revolutionary tide in the developing countries, the U.S. imperialists had responded by contriving a new form of colonialism, "neocolonialism," in which their local agents exercised political power on behalf of the imperialists. The imperialists no longer ruled directly as colonialists, but the substance of imperialist domination and exploitation remained unchanged. National emancipation, true national independence and liberation, required overthrowing the local lackeys of imperialism. Failure to draw such class lines and wage intense struggle against local lackeys would leave nations enslaved to imperialism.[22]

For Nehru and his Congress Party followers such political polarization within and among the developing countries was unnecessary and counterproductive. From Nehru's perspective achieving independence by the African and Asian nations invariably marked a fundamental transformation—the transfer of sovereignty from foreign colonialists to local peoples and leaders. The citizens of these new nations were now masters of their own destinies. While various reforms might still be necessary, encouraging domestic division and strife would only weaken the government and divert energies from that task. Nor would internal division and strife be conducive to economic development. It was also impermissible for the governments of some developing countries to pass judgment and work to alter the internal political arrangements of other developing countries. That was the sort of thing imperialists did. The developing countries should adhere to a higher standard of strict noninterference in the internal affairs of other countries, especially other developing countries.

A "SECOND BANDUNG" OR A NONALIGNED CONFERENCE?

Conflicting approaches to the developing countries movement began to take specific focus in 1960, when Indonesia leader Surkarno started pushing for a second meeting of African and Asian countries. The first had been the 1955 meeting at Bandung. The Bandung conference had envisioned a second assembly and scheduled it for Cairo, but that meeting was indefinitely postponed because of Egypt's 1956 Suez War. Sukarno favored a "second Bandung" throughout the late 1950s but met a cool response from Nehru. Then in 1960 Beijing began to support Sukarno's proposal. A joint communiqué signed during Foreign Minister Chen Yi's April 1961 visit, for example, called for the convocation of such a conference at the earliest possible time.[23]

Nehru remained unenthusiastic about a second Bandung. He increasingly saw Afro-Asianism as a forum that allowed China to advance its radical and anti-Indian views. As Asian countries, both China and Pakistan had participated in the 1955 conference and would certainly participate in a second Bandung. An assembly of nonaligned nations, on the other hand, would automatically exclude both China and Pakistan, which were allied with the USSR and the United States, respectively. A convocation of nonaligned nations would thus deny an international forum to India's new and old nemeses. Without Chinese or Pakistani obstruction, India's sober views about the developing countries movement could more easily prevail. A nonaligned conference would also include Yugoslavia. Tito was a close supporter of Nehru and had served between 1958 and 1960 as the chief target of Chinese "antirevisionist" polemics within the international communist movement. While Sukarno pushed with Chinese support for a second Bandung, Nehru and Tito pushed for a nonaligned meeting.

The first formal conference of nonaligned nations met at Belgrade in September 1961. Sukarno attended, and considerable tension quickly developed between him and Nehru. The two men also laid out divergent lines for the developing countries. Nehru downplayed the issue of Western colonialism and stressed the importance of peaceful coexistence, while Sukarno took a far more militant approach. Representatives from radical countries like Cuba, Algeria, and Ghana added their voices to the anti-imperialist chorus of the first nonaligned conference. China, of course, did not attend the September 1961 conference. From the sidelines, however, it strongly cheered for the radical forces in attendance and condemned India's opposition to them. An editorial in *Renmin ribao* lauded the conference for strengthening "the struggle against colonialism and imperialism, the fight to win and uphold national independence and defend world peace." The editorial referred elliptically to

Nehru, saying that "somebody at the conference" advanced the argument that
"'the old era of classic colonialism is gone and is dead' and anti-colonialist,
anti-imperialist and anti-racial discrimination problems were secondary."
"Obviously," the editorial declared, "such arguments are totally contrary to
the facts." U.S. imperialism was alive and active. In this regard it would be
"necessary to hold a second Afro-Asian conference in the near future." *Renmin
ribao* rebutted Nehru's stress on peaceful coexistence at considerable length.
While the declaration of the conference calling for general disarmament, total
prohibition of nuclear weapons, and settlement of outstanding questions via
negotiations reflected "the aspirations of the people of the world for peace,"
a realistic view had to acknowledge that "world peace can be defended only
by constantly intensifying the struggle against imperialism." Militant struggle against U.S. imperialism was the only way to peace.[24]

The 1962 war came in the context of this sharp rivalry between New Delhi
and Beijing over the direction of the developing countries movement. New
Delhi saw Beijing's decision for war as, in part, a function of a desire to punc-
ture India's prestige with the developing countries. In an article in the
American journal *Foreign Affairs* shortly after the 1962 war Nehru explained
that "the conflict provoked by Chinese aggression raises wider issues than
the simple demarcation of a remote border." Beijing sought global polarization, and "the nonaligned nations must, in this context, seem to be occupying an unstable, anomalous position for which, if they could de dislodged,
either by cajolery or coercion, the result would be to accentuate the polarization of world forces." "China's multiple campaigns against India," Nehru
continued, "were an exercise in realpolitik on these lines. India is such an outstanding member of the nonaligned community that her defection, whether
voluntary or enforced, cannot fail to bring grave and far-reaching consequences in its train." China was attempting "to demonstrate, by her attack
on India, that nonalignment has no reality and that the Soviet policy toward
the nonaligned countries is wrong; the only right course is to work for a polarization of forces in the world."[25] The thesis that a desire to diminish India's
influence with the developing countries inspired China's 1962 decision for
war became a common theme of orthodox Indian analyses of that conflict.

China's dramatic victory over India apparently did influence some
developing-country leaders, such as those of Indonesia and Pakistan. For
Sukarno India's dramatic defeat demonstrated that India was a decadent country dependent on the imperialist West, while China reflected the strength of
Asia's "new emerging forces." Sukarno determined to move closer into alignment with China, confident that Beijing could effectively support Indonesia's
efforts to eliminate Western influence from the region. For Pakistan, China's

1962 victory demonstrated the utility of China as a counter to India. During 1963, as China and Pakistan consolidated their anti-Indian entente, one dimension of their partnership was common encouragement of Indonesia's efforts to bring about a second Bandung. The joint communiqué issued at the end of PRC president Liu Shaoqi's visit to Indonesia in April 1963, for example, declared China's "full support" for a second Asian-African conference.[26]

China's criticism of India's role in the developing countries movement became far more direct after the 1962 war. Chinese polemicists no longer minced their words. A *Renmin ribao* editorial appearing two months after the war, for instance, asserted that India's nonalignment was merely "camouflage" that allowed it to peddle to Asian and African countries its anti-anti-imperialist "absurdities," thus serving India's masters in Washington and Moscow. India's actions in the Congo proved that it was "serving in fact as U.S. imperialism's mercenaries, helping it to strangle the national liberation movement" of the Congo. This showed that, "far from being a representative of the 'newly developing forces' of Asia or Africa, [India] is becoming more and more an accomplice of U.S. imperialism, acting behind a camouflage of 'non-alignment.'"[27]

India intensified its efforts to block a second Bandung and worked, instead, to organize a second conference of nonaligned nations. Its efforts were inspired by a desire to counter the efforts of a coalition of powers hostile to India—Pakistan, China, and increasingly Indonesia—to advance their anti-Indian purposes among the developing countries. Nehru suspected that the objective of Karachi, Beijing, and Jakarta was to create a third global bloc, thereby diminishing the importance of nonalignment and peaceful coexistence. It would be far better, Nehru concluded, to convene a second nonaligned conference. Nehru believed that, if he could secure support for a second nonaligned conference from Yugoslavia and Ceylon (as Sri Lanka was named prior to 1972), Indonesia would be compelled to go along with the proposal. Indian efforts in this regard succeeded. In October 1963 an Indian, Egyptian, and Ceylonese communiqué called for the convocation of a second nonaligned conference within the next year. In February 1964 Egypt issued invitations to twenty-six nonaligned countries to attend a preparatory meeting.[28]

China and Indonesia countered by intensifying their efforts for a second Afro-Asian conference. Zhou Enlai undertook a tour of thirteen African and Asian nations between December 1963 and February 1964 in an effort to mobilize support for the proposed Afro-Asian conference. The major theme of Zhou's visits was the need for increased Afro-Asian solidarity against imperialism, colonialism, and neocolonialism, and he argued that such a conference was necessary to achieve this aim. According to a *Renmin ribao* editorial at the conclusion of Zhou's tour: "Many leaders of African and Asian countries expressed the opinion that the time is ripe for the convocation of a second Afro-Asian conference and that active preparations should be made to this end. We believe that the holding of such a conference will undoubtedly contribute to the unity of the Asian and African people in their struggle against imperialism and in defense of peace."[29] In fact, only seven of the thirteen joint communiqués issued after Zhou's visits endorsed the convocation of such a conference. Moreover, a month after his tour ended, ten of the thirteen countries he visited attended the Indian-sponsored nonaligned preparatory meeting in Colombo in March 1964. Sharp conflict between India and Indonesia occurred at the Colombo preparatory meeting, and Beijing cheered on Indonesia from the sidelines.

In April 1964, the month after the Colombo nonaligned preparatory meeting, a preparatory meeting for the proposed Afro-Asian conference convened in Djakarta with the PRC in attendance. India submitted a series of proposals carefully designed to sabotage the radical Indonesian-Chinese forces. India proposed that the upcoming conference should be held in Africa in April 1965, on the tenth anniversary of the Bandung conference. An April 1965 date meant that the Afro-Asian conference would meet after the nonaligned conference scheduled for October 1964. Indonesia and Pakistan wanted to convene the Afro-Asian conference in August 1964, that is, just *prior* to the nonaligned conference. An African venue would keep the conference out of Pakistan, China, or Indonesia and in an area where the diplomatic influence of those countries was not particularly strong. An African venue was also politically difficult for India's opponents to oppose. Eventually, Beijing and Djakarta accepted Africa as the venue, although a precise location was not specified.

India also proposed that the conference invite the USSR and Malaysia. The proposal to invite the USSR was made with full awareness of the rapidly deepening Sino-Soviet schism and was designed to force Indonesia to make a clear choice between Beijing and Moscow. Inviting Malaysia was equally embarrassing. That newly independent state was a member of the United Nations and was recognized by over a hundred countries. It also had fairly good standing with other noncommunist developing countries, and its invitation, once that invitation had been proposed, would make clear the extent to which the radical agendas of Indonesia and China dominated the conference. Yet, given Indonesia's policy of denying the legitimacy of Malaysia's very existence, Sukarno was reluctant to countenance its participation. China took the lead in opposing participation by the USSR and gave "resolute support" to Indonesia's opposition to Malaysia's participation. "Just like Israel," Foreign Minister Chen Yi explained, Malaysia had been set up "with the purpose of splitting Asian-African unity." It was a product of neocolonialism, which had been established to encircle Indonesia and China.[30] The preparatory meeting eventually referred the proposal to invite Malaysia and the USSR to a subcommittee, which in turn referred the matter to a meeting of foreign ministers who would assemble immediately prior to the main conference. These critical issues were thus left pending. Over the next year India continued to insist on inviting both countries.

The nonaligned conference met as planned at Cairo in October 1964, and forty-seven counties attended. Indonesia and India were represented by Sukarno and Lal Bahadur Shastri, who had replaced Nehru as prime minister after his death in May 1964. A central dynamic of the conference quickly became debate between radicals from Indonesia, Ghana, and Algeria, on the one hand, and more moderate Indian viewpoints, on the other hand. In his speech Shastri maintained that peace was the highest objective, ranking above all else. Abolishing war, particularly nuclear war, was a top-ranking objective. In this regard, Shastri announced, China's plans to test nuclear weapons (then being widely reported by the media) were very disturbing. He proposed that the conference dispatch a special mission to Beijing to persuade it to desist from developing nuclear weapons. In terms of relations between the nonaligned nations and the Western nations, as long as Western nations complied with the principles of peaceful coexistence, there was plenty of room for cooperation. Moreover, such cooperation could play an important role in the economic development of the nonaligned nations.[31]

Sukarno's address to the Cairo conference stressed the increasing irrelevance of peaceful coexistence. Colonialism, neocolonialism, and imperialism still existed, Sukarno insisted, and the primary need for developing countries was to struggle against the power and domination of the "Old Established Forces." Sukarno criticized "those countries" that put priority on economic development through cooperation with the Old Established Forces, rather than uniting and struggling against them. Only an end to domination by the Old Established Forces would create the necessary preconditions for development.[32] In a six-hour session the political committee debated these sharply divergent views about peaceful coexistence. The radical countries—Algeria, Guinea, Mali, Tanganyika, and Indonesia—opposed giving priority to "peace" or "peaceful coexistence." Eventually, this radical viewpoint was outvoted and India's perspective endorsed in the final communiqué.

From the sidelines of the Cairo conference Beijing cheered the radicals' views and damned India's moderate line. Commenting on Shastri's speech, *Peking Review* noted that he had "made no mention at all of fighting imperialism, the common enemy of the people of Asia, Africa, and Latin America."

Shastri tried, rather, to "turn the discussion in another direction" by advocating "a brand of 'peaceful coexistence' which would in effect vitiate the struggle against imperialism and colonialism."[33] The conference had become a struggle "between two different lines," according to another commentary.[34] India and Yugoslavia were engaged in a "conspiracy against the people's cause of fighting imperialism." "India tried to scare the people with a gruesome picture of the destructive effect of atomic weapons. But it did not say a single word for the national independence movement, which is sweeping Asia, Africa, and Latin America." India urged oppressed peoples "to subordinate everything to . . . 'peaceful coexistence,' even at the expense of the independence and liberation movements."

Conflicts multiplied in the months following the April 1964 Afro-Asian preparatory meeting. India continued to insist on inviting the Soviet Union and Malaysia. The USSR was a major supplier of economic aid to a number of African and Asian countries, and those countries were reluctant to offend Moscow by voting against its participation. Regarding Malaysia, many nations saw little reason to fault it and felt that taking sides in a dispute between two developing countries was a dangerous precedent for the Afro-Asian movement. Even Beijing was apparently willing to drop its opposition to Malaysia's participation if that were necessary to secure the requisite votes to keep Moscow out of the conference. Mounting conflicts made it apparent that the conference, were it convened, would be a display of Afro-Asian disunity rather than unity. India took the lead in mobilizing a group of moderate nations to call for postponing the conference. China lobbied against this, but the conference was nonetheless delayed. Conflict between China and India continued right up to the end. When drafting the announcement of the postponement, China proposed blaming "imperialist intrigues." India opposed this suggestion. Eventually, a blandly worded compromise was adopted. All in all, the abortion of the anti-imperialist-inspired second Afro-Asian conference was an impressive reassertion of Indian leadership among the developing countries after a lapse of several years. It also involved a joint Soviet-Indian attempt to block China's political efforts toward the developing countries.[35]

ROUND TWO: INDIA AND CHINA REENTER THE ARENA

A series of major setbacks for the global revolutionary movement in 1964 and 1965 led to a reorientation of Beijing's approach. Throughout the rest of the 1960s Chinese energies were focused—with the highly significant exception of Pakistan—on ideologically pure "genuine Marxist-Leninist" parties and states. In a sense China's efforts to foster genuine Marxist-Leninist communist parties in Asia and Africa was a form of rivalry with India (and, of course, with the Communist Party of the Soviet Union). China's Maoist leaders believed that India, with Soviet and American support, was misleading the Third World. By stressing economic development and economic cooperation with imperialism rather than militant class struggle, India and the development model it was peddling via the nonaligned movement were helping to keep the oppressed countries of Africa and Asia open to exploitation. From a Leninist point of view, communist parties armed with correct doctrine might foil these erroneous ideas, alter the course of history, and lead these countries along a more progressive path. But, while the policy objectives advanced by Beijing and New Delhi were most stark in the 1960s, China's Maoist enthusiasm for revolution served to diminish direct Indo-Chinese rivalry. The two powers were then playing to different constituencies—Beijing to revolutionary movements and parties, New Delhi to established governments.

India's own interest in the developing countries also fell off in the mid-1960s, due partly to Nehru's death in May 1964 and the political turmoil that followed. Neither Shastri nor the young Indira Gandhi, who succeeded him in January 1966, had the interest or the stature Nehru had held in the developing countries movement. It was only after Indira Gandhi consolidated her position in 1969 that Indian interest in the nonaligned movement revived.

During the 1970s there was a second period of PRC-ROI rivalry to influence the developing countries. This round of rivalry was less direct than the first. India deliberately assumed a lower profile within the nonaligned movement (which became known by its initials, NAM, in the 1970s) and tried to act as mediator between pro- and anti-Chinese/Soviet positions that emerged within NAM. China, for its part, chose to remain outside NAM and refrained from attacking India, choosing instead to concentrate its polemics against countries it perceived as being Moscow's Trojan horses within NAM, Vietnam and Cuba. Yet, while less direct and intense than the first round of competition, the fact remains that during the 1970s Beijing and New Delhi were attempting to move the developing countries in substantially different directions.

In 1970 Indira Gandhi outlined a new direction for the nonaligned movement as part of an effort to raise India's international profile. From primarily political objectives the nonaligned movement should shift to an economic orientation. "The biggest danger" to nonalignment, Gandhi told the Yugoslav news agency in August 1970, "is the economic pressure of large countries." Increased economic cooperation among nonaligned countries was the way to thwart such pressure. Over the following decade, under Gandhi, India played a leading role in refocusing the nonaligned movement on international economic issues. New Delhi exercised its influence in a far more circumspect, low-profile approach than had been the case two decades earlier. As conflicts developed between ideologically inspired pro-Soviet and pro-Western members of NAM during the 1970s and early 1980s, India generally abstained from those debates and tried to moderate them for the sake of nonaligned unity. India also tried to direct NAM attentions away from divisive "political" issues toward economic issues on which they enjoyed a broader community of interests vis-à-vis the wealthy, industrialized countries.[36]

China's interest in the developing countries and the nonaligned movement also began to revive in the early 1970s. Following a major expansion of PRC diplomatic relations with Sino-American rapprochement, Beijing enunciated the Three Worlds theory in 1974. This move marked a major shift away from infatuation with "genuine Marxist-Leninist parties" toward cooperation with established governments regardless of ideology. According to the Three Worlds theory, the central dynamic of contemporary world politics was the clash between Soviet and American efforts to achieve hegemony, on the one hand, and the efforts of the developing countries to achieve full independence and sovereignty, on the other. The developing countries bore the brunt of superpower domination, bullying, and exploitation. The Third World was the great driving force of history and should unite to struggle against the superpowers.[37] China's Three World theory abstractly targeted both superpowers, the United States and the Soviet Union, but, as the 1970s progressed, it increasingly assumed an anti-Soviet cast.

The nonaligned movement for a variety of reasons had traditionally been directed primarily against the West, rather than against the Soviet Union. Indeed, there was considerable sympathy within NAM for the Soviet Union as an ally in challenging the West, a position advanced most forcefully by Cuba and Vietnam.[38] Beijing, on the other hand, had concluded that the USSR— or "Soviet social imperialism," in Beijing's nomenclature—posed the gravest danger to China. As China's concern over Soviet expansionism grew in the 1970s, it became increasingly apprehensive that NAM's traditional anti-Western sentiment might make the nonaligned countries vulnerable to Moscow's traps. China used diplomatic lobbying and rhetorical exhortation to direct NAM along anti-Soviet lines. All possible forces should be mobilized to check Soviet expansionism, Beijing concluded, and NAM had an important role to play in this regard.

From New Delhi's perspective China's prescription of anti–Soviet hegemony was unacceptable. Anti–Soviet hegemony policies pursued by India's neighbors could easily result in expanded Chinese or American influence in those countries, an outcome that was not in India's interest. The USSR also happened to be India's major backer against China under the August 1971 treaty.

In the event of another ROI-PRC confrontation, a stronger Soviet position vis-à-vis China would serve Indian interests better than a weaker one. It was better to have stronger friends, and one should be wary when one's enemies begin trying to weaken one's friends. Reducing Soviet influence was not, therefore, necessarily in New Delhi's interest and might result in weakening India's position vis-à-vis China. Reestablishing a Khmer Rouge Chinese client-state in Cambodia by securing a Vietnamese withdrawal from that country or forcing Vietnam to dissolve its security treaty with the USSR on "antihegemony" grounds, for example, did not serve Indian interests. Endorsing antihegemony was also potentially risky to India's relations with its South Asian neighbors. New Delhi understood that China viewed India's efforts to restrict links between its neighbors and China for the sake of Indian security as "regional hegemonism." If the term *hegemony* gained wide credence in international discourse and if Beijing became recognized as an authority on what was and was not considered hegemonism, India could easily find itself a target of antihegemony criticism, perhaps even from within the nonaligned movement.

The key division within NAM in the 1970s and early 1980s had to do with the relation of that movement to the Soviet Union. Beginning with the September 1973 fourth NAM summit in Algiers, Cuba began pushing for more favorable NAM treatment for the USSR than for the United States. The Soviet Union supported anticolonial and national liberation movements, Castro argued, while the United States attempted to crush them. Following Vietnam's unification in 1976, Hanoi joined Cuba as a vigorous advocate of the idea that the USSR was the "natural ally" of the nonaligned movement. India did not play a leading role in opposing this natural ally theory. As noted earlier, it preferred, rather, to moderate between the pro-Soviet and anti-Soviet camps within NAM. When a NAM foreign ministers conference in July 1978 became divided over the use of the term *hegemony* in a resolution, for example, India introduced verbiage that would allow the term to be interpreted as a reference to either Soviet or Western hegemonism. Chinese injection of *antihegemony* into NAM proceedings allowed New Delhi to win a few kudos from Moscow by gently foiling the efforts of nonaligned members who shared Beijing's antihegemonist views.

With the first nonaligned summit after the promulgation of the Three World's doctrine (the fifth NAM summit held in Colombo, Sri Lanka, in August 1976), Beijing began to align itself with the nonaligned movement and offer it advice. Premier Hua Guofeng's message to the fifth NAM summit declared that, "like the numerous nonaligned countries, China belongs to the Third World." China would "firmly support" the nonaligned countries in combating "imperialism, colonialism, neo-colonialism, racism, Zionism, and big power hegemonism."[39] A Xinhua article on NAM endorsed the "new development" of the nonaligned countries "in the economic field." It showed special concern, however, with the machinations of Soviet social imperialism to use NAM for its own purposes.[40]

By 1978 Beijing's anti-Soviet exhortations to NAM were direct and strident. "The numerous non-aligned countries constitute an important part of the Third World," read a *Renmin ribao* commentary in August 1978.[41] "That superpower which dons the guise of 'socialism' in particular has for a long time been engaged in frenzied aggression, intervention and subversive activities in Africa, the Red Sea area, and some parts of Asia. It has gravely jeopardized the independence, sovereignty, and security of the nonaligned nations and the countries of the Third World." Countries like Cuba that tried to justify Soviet actions were "surrogates" of Soviet social imperialism, which tried to undermine NAM's unity and deflect it from its proper course of opposing "all forms of foreign exploitation and domination." According to a *Beijing Review* article, NAM should reject the argument that the USSR was a natural ally of the nonaligned countries in their struggle against imperialism, colonialism, and neocolonialism—as was being advocated by Cuba and Vietnam. Introducing such ideas into NAM proceedings was "sabotage from outside and interference from within." In fact, countries that allied themselves with the USSR, like Cuba and Vietnam, were not qualified for membership in the nonaligned movement. The nonaligned countries, individually and collectively, should explicitly condemn the hegemonist actions of the USSR and its puppets, Cuba and Vietnam. They should offer material support and moral assistance to countries fighting Soviet or Soviet-backed hegemonism. NAM should support resolutions in the United Nations General Assembly and in other fora condemning Soviet social imperialism and its hegemonist actions. NAM should overcome its "inertia" and convene an "emergency non-aligned foreign minister meeting at the earliest possible moment" to deal with Soviet moves.[42]

India was deeply suspicious of Beijing's efforts to move the nonaligned movement in antihegemonist directions. In an address to a meeting of the NAM Coordinating Bureau in May 1976, for example, Minister of External Affairs Y. B. Chavan argued against inclusion in NAM of "several non-member countries [that] have expressed desire to join it in some capacity or the other." "The hard core of non-alignment still remains the commitment not to get involved in the rivalries of Great Powers, not to subserve the interest of their blocs and not to join their multilateral military alliances," Chavan said.[43] While directed partly at Moscow—which since 1973 had sought some sort of association with NAM—Chavan's warning applied also to Beijing's newfound friendship with NAM.

Chinese attention to the nonaligned movement waned along with China's concern for Soviet expansionism in the mid-1980s. China still routinely endorsed NAM resolutions when they were directed against the superpowers or the developed countries. But the urgency apparent in Chinese exhortations of NAM in the 1970s disappeared. By the 1990s appeals to NAM had become merely one element of China's broader appeal to the Third World. In May 1992 China finally joined the nonaligned movement as an observer. This move was part of an effort by both Beijing and New Delhi to improve bilateral relations. By joining the nonaligned movement that India had mid-wifed against Chinese opposition thirty years before, Beijing was agreeing to close the door on that source of conflict. China would lend its prestige to India's efforts to mobilize the developing countries. Nehru's hope of the early 1950s was finally realized, in the early 1990s. But, just as one arena of Sino-Indian rivalry was fading in importance, another was emerging: the United Nations Security Council.

CHINA'S AND INDIA'S BIDS FOR PERMANENT UN SECURITY COUNCIL SEATS

During the post–Cold War era the contest for status between China and India was manifest in two ways—first in India's effort to enter the Security Council as a permanent member and China's tacit opposition to that effort; and, second, India's effort to secure recognition as a nuclear weapons state and China's opposition to that effort. The nuclear factor will be discussed in chapter 12. Here I will focus on the United Nations issue.

China's high international status is institutionalized and symbolized by its permanent seat on the United Nations Security Council. As one of five permanent members, the "Perm Five," China stands at the institutionalized center of global politics on equal status with the United States, the USSR (or now the Russian Federation), Britain, and France. In that elite club China is the only non-Western, nonwhite, developing, and Asian country. This gives China considerable status. It also gives China a prominent arena in which to act as spokesman and advocate of Asia and the developing countries. As the only non-Western, developing country holding veto power in the Security Council, other developing countries looking for an advocate on the Security Council or seeking to block UN action engineered by the Western nations look to China. While China has not frequently utilized its veto power, it has threatened to do so. China's permanent seat on the Security Council also gives it a relatively cheap way to maintain significant influence with the developing countries. Beijing contributes far less money to development assistance or to support of United Nation operations than do the other four permanent members of the Security Council. Yet, as a permanent member with veto power, China nonetheless enjoys considerable leverage. Entry of additional Asian, African, and Latin American powers as permanent Security Council members would be a loss for China's relative status. Indian and/or Japanese membership would be an even more serious setback for China. China would no longer be the clear, senior power in Asia—the only, recognized, and legitimate great power in Asia. It would, instead, be one of two or three such powers. The veto China holds as a permanent member also gives it leverage over core issues of particular interest to it. First and foremost among these has been Taiwan. Various new aspirants to UN membership or states seeking Security Council action such as dispatch of a peacekeeping or election observer mission must first satisfy Beijing by recognizing PRC claims to Taiwan.[44]

China's exclusive position on the Security Council came under challenge with the push for reform of that body which began in the 1990s. As old East-West tensions eased, cooperation increased among the Perm Five, and especially between the West and the USSR / Russian Federation. This led to a great increase in United Nations activity. During the thirty-one months between March 1991 and October 1993, for example, the United Nations dispatched fifteen peacekeeping and observer missions, compared to seventeen during the entire forty-six years of the United Nations history up to that point. This great increase in activity led to a sense that a reform of the UN system was necessary to make it more efficient and more capable of bearing the increased burdens being put on it during the post–Cold War era.[45]

In January 1992 the Security Council held its first summit to consider whether changes in UN organization were necessary as a result of recent developments. At that summit the Perm Five declared they were not opposed in principle to reform of the Security Council system, and an Open-Ended Working Group (OEWG) on Security Council reform was established.

While UN reform was a multifaceted problem, the aspect of concern here is India's inclusion among the permanent members of the Security Council. The push for expansion of permanent membership came from newly reunified Germany and from Japan, both of which felt that their economic power and political role entitled them to a permanent Security Council seat. In September 1992 the German foreign minister laid before the General Assembly Germany's desire for a permanent seat on the Security Council. Soon after Japan did likewise. Both Berlin and Tokyo made their bids with U.S. backing and with the backing of each other. Non-Western and developing countries quickly noted that adding Germany and Japan would further strengthen the rich countries' already great dominance of world politics and began to make counterproposals. India was among the leaders of this process.

In September 1992 a NAM summit at Jakarta called for democratizing the UN system, including a review of Security Council membership with an eye to more equitable and balanced representation. In December 1992 India introduced a resolution in the General Assembly calling on the secretary-general to ascertain the views of members regarding the composition of the Security Council. This was agreed to. India then submitted its views to the OEWG, calling for inclusion of at least five new permanent Security Council members to be selected on the basis of their population, size of the economy, contribution to the United Nations system and to peacekeeping operations in particular, global role, and future potential.[46] India did not immediately make explicit its claim to a permanent seat under these criteria, but it did make clear that it believed it met these standards. From the earliest days of the UN, Prime Minister I. K. Gujral later explained to the General Assembly, India had been instrumental in placing on the UN agenda issues that had experienced the most success, including decolonization, the struggle against apartheid in South Africa, and human rights. India had long-standing and prominent participation in UN peacekeeping operations, with a clear record of dedication and professionalism, plus strong political will on the part of the Indian government in this regard. India had in fact sustained a fairly high level of casualties in these operations over the years, demonstrating that it was one of the few countries willing to bear this burden for the United Nations.[47]

India's working paper to the OEWG did not specify who the new permanent Security Council members should be, but the most commonly discussed candidates were Germany, Japan, Brazil, Nigeria, and India. The argument for Germany and Japan was based on their economic strength and financial contribution to the UN and its related organs. The argument for Brazil, Nigeria, and India was largely geographic. Each major region of the world should be represented by at least one country. Regional rivals quickly challenged this particular slate of nominees. Egypt wondered why Nigeria rather than itself should represent Africa. Mexico and Argentina questioned Brazil's candidacy. Pakistan opposed India's nomination.[48]

In October 1994 India formally laid before the General Assembly a claim to permanent Security Council membership. Indian UN representative Pranab Mukherjee told the assembly in a speech that, "given any criteria," "India deserves to be a permanent member of the Security Council."[49] The UN reform process did not move quickly. In March 1997 General Assembly president Razali Ismail of Malaysia submitted a paper to the OEWG on Security Council reform. The "Razali Framework," as it quickly came to be known, proposed that two new permanent Security Council seats be given to industrialized countries (e.g., Germany and Japan), and three to the developing countries of Africa, Asia, Latin America, and the Caribbean. The means by which the latter countries would be selected were not specified. In July 1997 the United Sates endorsed the Razali Framework, thereby going beyond its earlier endorsement of permanent seats for only its allies, Germany and Japan, to endorse permanent seats for three developing countries.[50] India, which had lobbied for U.S. support, lauded this shift in American policy.

India mobilized its political influence behind its Security Council bid. It argued that any change in council composition should be "broad-based rather than piece-meal expansion."[51] This put Berlin and Tokyo on notice that, if they wanted the support of India and its friends for their own entry into the Security Council, they would have to accept the inclusion of the developing countries. India also mobilized the nonaligned movement. A NAM foreign ministers meeting convened in New Delhi in April 1997 and passed on to General Assembly president Razali its views about the need for increased developing country representation in the council. A NAM heads-of-state meeting at Durban, South Africa, in September 1998 called for decisions about council composition to be made under Article 108 of the UN Charter, requiring a two-thirds majority of all UN member states.[52] This would have meant the existing Perm Five would not be able to veto the establishment of new permanent members. Not the least aspect of India's diplomatic push was an effort to secure Chinese support. During President Jiang Zemin's November 1996 visit to India, the Indian side explained its view on "the reform of the U.N. system, including the question of giving adequate representation to nonaligned and other developing countries in the U.N. organs." "We pointed out," the Indian foreign minister reported to parliament, "that any objective criteria for the restructuring of the U.N. Security Council would provide for Indian inclusion in the expanded Security Council as a permanent member."[53]

Until India's nuclear tests of May 1998 China's position on enlarging the Security Council was a combination of rhetorical support for increased Third World representation and insistence on a consensus decision-making process, which made any change in existing arrangements unlikely.[54] In a speech to the General Assembly on September 23, 1998, for example, Foreign Minister Tang Jiaxuan "reiterated the basic stand of China." China thought it necessary, Tang said, "to carry out appropriate reform of the U.N. so that it [can] keep abreast of the changing situation," but "there are still differences among member states" about how this should be done. Security Council reform required "extensive and full consultations" so that "reasonable proposals" of all member states are "reflected to the full in the final decisions." Moreover, said the foreign minister, "it is essential to adhere to the principle of consensus."[55] Left unsaid was the reality that, if the views of no state could be overridden by a strong majority, full agreement and therefore any change was unlikely. It was absolutely certain, for example, that Pakistan would not agree to India's becoming a permanent member of the Security Council.

The question of expanding the Security Council is far more complex than rivalry between China and India. Japan's bid, in fact, is probably perceived as a greater challenge to China than is India's bid. A close reading of Chinese statements suggests greater opposition to a Japanese permanent Security Council seat than to one for India.[56] The point is, however, that India pushed vigorously for a permanent Security Council seat to raise its international status, and China helped block that bid in a subtle but effective way. When the dispute over Security Council reform is joined together with the Sino-Indian dispute over nuclear or non–nuclear weapons state status, it becomes apparent that Sino-Indian rivalry for status at the close of the twentieth century was nearly as sharp as that in the period just after the PRC and ROI were formed.

5 / Indian-Chinese Rivalry in Nepal

Nepal is the only one of the three Himalayan kingdoms with enough power to play an autonomous role between China and India. Since the seventh century, when a central political authority first emerged in Tibet, Nepal served as a major conduit for trade between India and Tibet. That trade was a lucrative source of income for Nepali rulers, and control over it was a major element of their hold on power. Nepali rulers soon developed a fairly acute sense of the balance of power between the states ruling in India to their south and over Tibet to their north. By the late seventeenth century, Nepali statesmen turned this balancing act into a sophisticated diplomatic art, and the tradition of diplomatic maneuver and balance has continued into the early twenty-first century. Its precondition is the conflicting policy objectives between Nepal's powerful neighbors.[1]

In the Chinese view of things Nepal was a Chinese tributary for many hundreds of years. Nepal and China first exchanged emissaries during the seventh century, and, as was China's wont, those exchanges were conducted under the modalities of the tributary system, or at least so China's rulers thought and so Chinese official historians recorded. The Mongol Yuan dynasty (A.D. 1279–1368) established China's suzerainty over Tibet but did not attempt to extend its influence into the Himalayas.[2] During China's Ming dynasty (1368–1644) the vigorous founding emperor, Hong Wu, dispatched a mission to one of the Nepali rulers then contending for mastery of the Kathmandu Valley. A tributary relationship was thus reestablished (yet again, in the Chinese view), and between 1384 and 1427 seven Nepali missions traveled to

Beijing to demonstrate obeisance to the Chinese emperor, the Son of Heaven. Those missions were suspended after 1427, when Nepal was unified under different rulers.

While we are primarily concerned here with the Chinese view of the world, it is important to note that China's understanding of its tributary relations with foreign rulers often differed substantially from the understanding of those foreign rulers themselves. Various subterfuges were used by Chinese imperial officials to make it appear that interactions between the imperial government and foreign rulers conformed to the model of Chinese superiority, when, in fact, that was often not the case. In the case of Nepal, Chinese records refer to "tribute" from Nepali rulers, but Nepali records never use that term, speaking instead of "gifts" of equivalent value exchanged by the two courts. Letters from the king of Nepal sent with each mission to Beijing made it clear that this was a relationship of equals. Such a letter went to a Chinese official, who translated it into Chinese to suit Chinese purposes, and it was these translated letters that went into Chinese archives and which were used by subsequent generations of Chinese scholars as proof of Nepal's "tributary" status.[3]

Be this as it may, from the Chinese perspective a tributary relation with Nepal was reestablished in the late eighteenth century. In the 1780s ambitious rulers in Kathmandu sought to establish Nepali economic dominance over at least the western regions of Tibet, in the process displacing China as suzerain in that region. To this end Nepali invasions of Tibet were launched in 1788 and 1791. The latter invasion advanced as far as Shigatze, where the Tashlihumpo monastery was plundered and a Nepali-supported claimant established as Panchen Lama (the second-highest-ranking lama in Tibet's theocratic system). China's emperor Qian Long saw Nepal's moves as a major challenge to China's control over Tibet, which was, in turn, an integral component of China's frontier defense system. He resolved to teach Nepal a lesson it would "remember for all time." An army of twenty-six thousand (mostly) Tibetans and (some) Chinese commanded by one of China's top generals, Fu Kang-an, was ordered to march on Kathmandu to seize and punish the Nepali officials responsible for challenging China's authority in Tibet. The Chinese-led army overcame strong Nepali resistance, disease, and immense logistical difficulties to march to within twenty miles of Kathmandu, where it shattered Nepali defenses before it was halted by severe weather. A settlement was then arranged whereby Chinese forces withdrew in exchange for Nepali agreement to resume the old practice of sending missions to Beijing every five years. Such "tributary missions" were faithfully dispatched until 1852. Thereafter they became more irregular, the last arriving in Beijing in 1908.[4]

The political influence derived from China's powerful 1792 demonstration of its capabilities south of the Himalayas lasted for about thirty years. For several decades British Indian authorities were carefully respectful of Beijing's rights in Nepal lest they provoke another expedition, while Nepal used China's influence to check the British advance. China's failure to support Burma (another of China's tributaries) during the Anglo-Burma war of 1824–26 convinced Nepal's rulers that China was now too weak to support Nepal against Britain. They adjusted Nepal's policy accordingly. Yet until the 1840s—and to a lesser extent all the way to 1911—British authority in India moved carefully regarding Nepal, to avoid provoking China, although by the end of the nineteenth century London's greater fear was that China might align with Russia. From Kathmandu's perspective China's weakness was a diplomatic liability for Nepal. A stronger neighbor better able to balance the power to Nepal's south was preferable. China's long period of relative powerlessness limited Kathmandu's ability to balance its southern neighbor. In 1950, when Chinese power finally returned to the region north of the Himalayas, Nepal's leaders reverted to their country's traditional diplomatic strategy of balancing.

INDIA'S AND CHINA'S RETURN TO THE NORTHERN HIMALAYAN REGION

As we saw in chapter 2, Beijing's early 1950 declaration of its determination to "liberate Tibet" and expel the influence of "American-British imperialists" from the region caused consternation in New Delhi. China's occupation of Tibet completely changed Nepal's status for India. Since the middle of the nineteenth century Tibet rather than Nepal had served as India's buffer with China. If the Tibetan buffer disappeared through direct Chinese administration and occupation, the role of buffer would pass to Nepal, which was far less ideal than Tibet as a buffer because of its much smaller size. But, because it held a thousand kilometers of the central Himalayan range, pierced by many passes, and shielded the central Indo-Gangetic plain, denying control of that area to the PRC and upholding the preeminence of Indian security concerns in that region was deemed vital.

Indian concerns led to a Treaty of Peace and Friendship concluded between Nepal and India on July 31, 1950, which forms the basis of Indian policy toward Chinese-Nepal relations today. Article 1 of the treaty provided that "there shall be everlasting peace and friendship between the Government of India and the Government of Nepal. The two Governments agree mutually to acknowledge and respect the complete sovereignty, territorial integrity and independence of each other."[5] India thereby renounced the annexation of Nepal, but this was paired with "friendship" between the two countries.

Article 2 of the treaty touched on security, providing that "the two Governments hereby undertake to inform each other of any serious friction or misunderstanding with any neighboring state likely to cause any breach in the friendly relations subsisting between the two governments." A letter ancillary to the treaty further provided that "neither Government shall tolerate any threat to the security of the other by a foreign aggressor. To deal with any such threat, the two Governments shall consult with each other and devise effective counter-measures." A secret codicil of the treaty not made public until 1959 went still further, providing that any aggression against Nepal would be considered as aggression against India and would be dealt with accordingly.[6]

Article 5 of the treaty regulated Nepal's foreign acquisitions of military equipment, saying: "The Government of Nepal shall be free to import from or through the territory of India, arms, ammunition, or warlike materials and equipment for the security of Nepal." An ancillary letter further specified that any military material "necessary for the security of Nepal and that the Government of Nepal may import through the territory of India shall be so imported with the assistance and agreement of the Government of India." The 1950 treaty and ancillary letters did not stipulate that Nepal would import weapons *only* with India's consent. India would argue forty years later, however, that this was implicit in the spirit of the 1950 treaty. The treaty was written to remain in force indefinitely until terminated by either party upon one year's notice.

Maintaining the 1950 treaty has been the cornerstone of Indian policy toward Nepal and Nepali-Chinese relations. Forty years after the treaty was signed, when New Delhi concluded that the Nepali government was in effect seeking to nullify the agreement, India resorted to extreme measures against its neighbor to prevent this. A few months after the conclusion of the 1950 treaty Nehru explained to India's parliament the significance of the treaty: "Apart from our sympathetic interest in Nepal, we are also interested in the security of our own country. From time immemorial, the Himalayas have provided us with a magnificent frontier. Of course, they are no longer as impassable as they used to be, but they are still fairly effective. We cannot allow that barrier to be penetrated because it is also the principal barrier to India."[7]

Nepali resentment of Indian domination impinged directly on India's effort to uphold its special security relation with that country. Indian economic, political, and cultural influence on Nepal was pervasive. The greater size, wealth, level of development, and dynamism of India's economy compared to that of Nepal inevitably meant that Indian businesses could, more often than not, and assuming the absence of protective measures by the Nepali gov-

TABLE 5.1 Nepal's Foreign Aid, 1951–1978 (in millions of Nepali rupees)

Year	China	India	Soviet Union	United States	Others
1951–56	—	70.018	—	24.951	—
1956–57	—	14.570	—	12.753	—
1957–58	—	9.605	—	48.473	—
1958–59	—	17.102	—	17.951	—
1959–60	32.135	18.450	—	56.225	18.530
1960–61	—	22.355	8.456	86.997	19.291
1961–62	N.A.	N.A	N.A	N.A	N.A
1962–63	3.200	13.600	15.000	46.800	5.100
1963–64	14.700	34.000	33.400	74.400	9.400
1964–65	12.140	62.736	0.463	65.530	0.174
1965–66	16.200	93.000	5.000	57.000	3.200
1966–67	24.583	77.633	4.875	34.926	0.219
1967–68	26.160	95.867	3.069	32.226	0.537
1967–69	46.870	126.185	3.800	86.949	0.432
1969–70	76.670	160.301	4.500	66.747	15.156
1970–71	47.170	125.362	21.750	59.734	35.666
1971–72	53.100	109.270	5.000	45.202	47.546
1972–73	34.200	94.800	2.500	38.600	34.200
1973–74	34.300	112.700		31.850	18.770
1974–75	49.200	103.900		84.700	112.700
1976–77	105.900	117.600		42.800	99.200
1977–78	67.000	113.200		58.800	326.200

Sources of foreign aid include grants and loans but not technical aid.
SOURCE: T. R. Ghoble, *China-Nepal Relations and India* (New Delhi: Deep and Deep, 1991), 108.

ernment, out-compete those of Nepal. Politically, Nepali political leaders, in government and in the opposition, looked to India for advice and financial assistance. For Nepal's government, India was the ultimate guarantor of law and order. Culturally, India's fine universities, religious and artistic institutions, media, and scientific-technological institutions also exercised a strong influence on Nepal. While this influence could be viewed benignly, it could also cause resentment. Indian statesmen understood this quite well and knew that India would have to tread lightly. They were quite willing to make concessions when confronted with Nepali nationalist sentiment. As soon as the 1950 treaty was signed, it was modified by a letter recognizing that "for some time to come" it would be necessary to afford Nepali businesses protection against competition from Indian industry. The nature and extent of such protection was to be determined by the two governments. The original treaty had provided for nondiscriminatory "national" treatment of both sides' citizens in economic and commercial affairs. Over the years India agreed to a whole set of preferential arrangements for Nepal, giving Nepal's products highly preferential treatment in Indian markets on a nonreciprocal basis. Nepali nationals faced no restrictions in terms of property ownership, business operation, and so on, while India acquiesced to the imposition of such restrictions on its own nationals in Nepal.[8] Indian economic aid to Nepal was also generous, as indicated by table 5.1. Nor did India object to development assistance to Nepal from the United States, the Soviet Union, European countries, or Japan. Even in the security area India was willing to compromise. In 1969, for instance, in response to Nepali demands, India withdrew its military liaison group from Nepal and the military checkpoints it had established along Nepal's border with China.[9] India was prepared to be generous with Nepal. All it asked in return, in the words of an editorial in an Indian newspaper after Indian-Nepali comity finally broke down, was "genuine appreciation of our concerns and an open and candid friendship on a par with our own [toward Nepal]."[10]

Because China is much farther away from Nepal, because its influence in Nepal is far less than India's yet it is great enough to serve as a potential source of support for Nepal against Indian aggrandizement, Nepali nationalists naturally look northward for solace in dealing with their resentment toward India. China has responded to this situation by following a policy designed to court Nepali friendship. Aside from a few rhetorical statements in the early years of the PRC and again during the Cultural Revolution, China did not support Nepali communist or other dissident movements, as it did, for example, in Burma. Nor was Chinese propaganda critical of the Nepali monarchy. The usual thrust of Chinese propaganda toward Nepal between 1959 and about 1979 was to praise and encourage "brave little Nepal" for its resistance to Indian domination. China was scrupulous in avoiding making demands on Nepal's government. As table 5.1 indicates, Chinese economic aid to Nepal was substantially less than India's, but it was extended on more generous terms, and Chinese propaganda toward Nepal strove to insure that the Nepali people knew this. Beijing generally endorsed Nepali diplomatic initiatives and lauded the Nepali role in international affairs whenever it could. In short, China tried to be Nepal's good friend.[11]

Geography fundamentally conditions the India-Nepal-China triangle. Nepal is landlocked between China and India, with access to major industrial-commercial centers and to world markets far easier through Indian than through Chinese territory. The difficulties of transport over the Tibetan plateau have already been discussed. Roads running southward from Nepal's cities to the relatively well-developed road and rail network of India travel through far easier terrain and for far shorter distances than is the case with roads running through Tibet. Indian roads and rails then connect with numerous commercial-manufacturing centers and seaports. A modest amount of Nepali goods can be, and are, sold commercially in Tibet, and some Chinese goods are sold in Nepal, but in 1995 trade with China constituted 0.7 percent of Nepal's total foreign trade. The rest, 99.3 percent, was with or went through India. This meant that, if India closed or restricted Nepal's lines of communication, Nepal would be in dire straits. If China undertook to supply through its own territory the manufactured goods and foodstuffs that Nepal must import, the transportation costs would be very high. If those costs were passed on to Nepali consumers, most goods would become unaffordable. If Beijing undertook to finance the subsidy, that cost would also be very heavy. Assuming that Nepal could have survived during an Indian blockade on half its normal level of imports, the cost of such an amount represented about 2.6 percent of China's total foreign exchange holdings in 1990, when such a blockade finally occurred. (I will discuss the 1990 blockade more fully later.) Even this assumes that the cost of delivering such a volume of trade would remain constant, which would not be the case. The costs of delivering volumes of goods to points in Nepal by truck over the Tibetan plateau would have been extremely heavy—even assuming that this logistical difficulty could be overcome. Moreover, once such a burden was assumed, it would also be difficult to put down. India might let such a situation continue for some time so as to teach Nepal a lesson and drain Beijing financially. Chinese financial underwriting of Nepal's resistance to India could also lead India to intervene to topple the "pro-Chinese" Nepali regime, whose actions had created such a situation. This would confront China with a Hobson's choice of either acquiescing to complete loss of its influence in Nepal or countering Indian action at a very high cost.

Just as New Delhi understands the logic of Nepali nationalist resentment of India, Beijing understands the logic of Nepal's geography. Until 1988 Beijing was careful not to overplay its hand. Chinese leaders have understood that Chinese interests are best served by encouraging and supporting Nepali independence from Indian domination but not pushing so hard as to either rouse Nepali suspicions of China or prompt vigorous Indian countermeasures. Only in 1988, when China attempted to initiate a military relation with Nepal, did Chinese leaders miscalculate the threshold required to prompt New Delhi to play its geographic trump card.

EVOLUTION OF CHINESE-INDIAN RIVALRY OVER NEPAL

During the period of Sino-Indian amity between 1954 and 1958 Beijing was careful not to challenge India's preeminent position in Nepal.[12] China's objective during this period was to expand relations with the Asian and African countries as a way of countering U.S. containment. For the sake of expanding China's ties with these countries, Beijing followed India's lead on Nepal.

In the early 1950s New Delhi advised Kathmandu to defer links with China until India had itself reached an understanding with Beijing. In the process of negotiating the April 1954 Chinese-Indian agreement on Tibet, New Delhi believed it had secured implicit Chinese recognition of India's primacy in Nepal, Sikkim, and Bhutan. During his October visit to China Nehru discussed the matter further with Zhou Enlai and, upon his return to New Delhi, announced that China recognized Nepal as an exclusive Indian sphere of influence. At the same time, New Delhi presented Kathmandu with an aide-mémoire providing for close and continuous consultation regarding Nepal's foreign relations, "in particular in matters relating to the relations of Nepal with Tibet and China."[13] Nepal's leaders politely declined. To have accepted would have severely limited Nepal's ability to reduce its dependence on India through leverage with China. Kathmandu's hesitation notwithstanding, Nehru felt confident enough about having secured Chinese recognition of India's position in Nepal, or so Nehru thought, that the Indian leader gave the green light for the establishment of Sino-Nepali diplomatic relations.

With India's approval Nepal-China relations began to move forward swiftly. Diplomatic relations at the ambassadorial level were formally established on August 1, 1955. India advised Kathmandu, however, against establishing Nepali and Chinese resident embassies in each other's capitals. Again out of deference to Indian wishes, China and Nepal agreed that their relations would be handled by their embassies in New Delhi. Not until 1958, after the United States set up an embassy in Kathmandu, did China itself open an embassy in that city.[14] Handling Nepali-Chinese relations in New Delhi made it easier for Indian intelligence to keep tabs on developments. The year after Sino-Nepali diplomatic relations were established, China began giving foreign aid to Nepal. In 1956 Beijing *gave* Nepal 60 million Indian rupees to support its first five-year plan. Indian economic aid to Nepal had begun the year before. Between 1956 and 1964 Nepal was the eighth-ranking recipient of Chinese aid among noncommunist countries, coming after Indonesia, Egypt, Burma, Pakistan, Cambodia, Algeria, and Tanzania.[15] Four of the eight top-ranking recipients of Chinese aid were in the overlapping zone of Indian and Chinese influence outlined earlier, in map 1.1.

The death of King Tribhuvan in March 1955 and the coronation of his son, King Mahendra, as monarch also encouraged Nepal to maneuver more boldly between its two neighbors. Mahendra began moving away from the tight alignment with India which characterized his father's approach and toward a policy of improving relations with China. King Mahendra had a far more jaundiced view of India than had his father and was more willing to exploit Chinese leverage to diminish Nepal's dependence on India. His objective was to move Nepal toward a more equidistant position vis-à-vis its two giant neighbors. "Equal friendship" and "friendship with all" were Mahendra's new slogans. India apparently approved of the early stages of this developing Nepal-China friendship, assuming that its evolution would continue to be limited by India's security concerns. Only after Sino-Nepali friendship continued to wax while Sino-Indian relations soured in 1959 did New Delhi realize that it had miscalculated and could not control Sino-Nepali relations.[16] China no longer felt compelled to respect Indian sensibilities and began to compete openly with India for influence in Nepal. Chinese propaganda became openly critical of Indian policies toward Nepal, condemning them as manifestations of Indian expansionism. China's willingness to disregard Indian sensibilities regarding Nepal created new opportunities for Nepali diplomatic maneuvering. Nepal responded positively to China's overtures. Kathmandu, like Beijing, would no longer allow New Delhi to hold an absolute veto over Sino-Nepali relations.

King Mahendra's dismissal of pro-Indian prime minister B. P. Koirala in December 1960 troubled New Delhi. During his nineteen-month tenure as Nepal's first elected head of government, Prime Minister Koirala had presided over a process of democratic reform which New Delhi hoped would more favorably incline Nepal toward India. New Delhi correctly perceived Mahendra and his advisors as the source of policies seeking to balance China and India and believed that greater democratic checks on royal power would limit this impulse. Koirala also followed a distinctly pro-Indian tilt while in office. He consulted closely with Indian leaders in the process of negotiating the Sino-Nepal boundary agreement of 1960, making statements and insisting on treaty provisions supportive of India's position in its territorial conflict with China. Koirala also concluded a trade and transit agreement with India which, had it been implemented, would have created a common market between the two countries. He also rejected a number of Chinese proposals including a non-aggression pact and the proposal for constructing a road linking Kathmandu and Lhasa. Only after Koirala's dismissal did Nepal accept a Chinese proposal to build the highway.

The Kathmandu-Tibet highway agreement concluded by Nepal and China in October 1961 roused grave concern in India. Under the agreement China *gave* Nepal 3.5 million pounds sterling for use in constructing the highway within Nepali territory. China was to construct a road on its side of the border, creating a new highway linking Lhasa and Kathmandu and creating for the first time a highway through the Himalayas passable by motor vehicles. The Chinese initially proposed building the road over the same route via Kerong Pass followed by the Chinese army in 1792, but King Mahendra insisted on a somewhat longer route via Kuti Pass northeast of Kathmandu. The Nepal government dubbed the road the "Kathmandu-Kodari road" to minimize the fact that it pierced the Himalayas. Kodari was the Nepali town where the road crossed into Tibet. Such symbolism notwithstanding, New Delhi took a dim view of the Kathmandu-Lhasa highway. As Nehru told the Lok Sabha the month after the road-building agreement was announced: "India's security interests would be adversely affected by the road," and "Nepal's failure to consult with India on the matter was a flagrant violation of the treaty of 1950, both in letter and spirit." The Indian government conveyed its concerns to Nepal. King Mahendra dismissed those concerns, saying, "Communism will not arrive in Nepal via a taxi cab." In fact, as Leo Rose pointed out, New Delhi was more concerned about the possibility of the People's Liberation Army arriving in Nepal via tanks.

A sophisticated map created by joining satellite-generated topographic data with computer graphics and published by the National Geographic Society in 1988 depicts the stretch of the central Himalayas containing the Kathmandu-Lhasa road.[17] It shows the valley below Kuti pass along which the road passed, descending more or less gradually and without blockage by transverse mountains, from the high Tibetan plateau to the cultivated tableland where Kathmandu is situated. This passageway is second only to the Chumbi as a route from the Tibetan plateau through the Himalayas. The new trans-Himalayan highway considerably shortened the time it would take Chinese military forces to reach Kathmandu. Once the road was completed, in 1967, the driving time between the border and Kathmandu was reportedly cut to three hours.[18] The new road also opened a supply line for trade with Tibet. As noted, India began embargoing trade with China in 1960. But, while India was squeezing the PLA in Tibet, Kathmandu was opening new supply lines that India could not control. And in the event that New Delhi ever decided to levy economic or military sanctions against Nepal, the new road would improve Nepal's situation. Mao Zedong summarized the situation very succinctly a few years later, when receiving a visiting Nepali delegation and discussing the possibility of building more roads between Nepal and its rear door to China: "Once these roads are open, India may be a bit more respectful towards you," Mao told his Nepali guests. "The members of the [Nepali] delegation nodded in agreement with this," according to the Chinese transcript of the meeting.[19]

Almost as troubling to New Delhi as the Kathmandu-Lhasa road was the beginning of secret military cooperation between China and Nepal. As rebellion spread across Tibet in 1959, many refugees fled into Nepal. Several of the camps where those refugees assembled became centers of support activity for the insurgents inside Tibet. Men were recruited and trained, supplies and food assembled, and operations planned from these camps. One of the largest refugee camps was in the Bu Ba La (transliterated from Chinese) area of western Nepal, a region not effectively administered by the Kathmandu government but controlled by a local tribe in cooperation with the Tibetan refugees. In 1960 the Chinese government explained to Nepal's leaders the serious, hostile nature of the activities emanating from this camp, and the Nepali government invited China to send PLA forces into Nepal to expel the insurgents cum refugees. In a highly secret operation about a thousand PLA soldiers advanced quickly on the rebel base / refugee camp. No artillery was used so as to lessen chances of outside detection. Nepali liaison officers accompanied Chinese forces, and the Chinese advance was coordinated with deployments of Nepali police. The Chinese advance pushed the Tibetans into a Nepali police net, where they were detained for deportation. The entire operation lasted only a week or so and from the Chinese point of view was highly successful. It was a highly secret operation so as not to disturb India. Indian intelligence assets within Nepal nonetheless learned of the operation and informed New Delhi.[20]

Indian leaders were dismayed by Koirala's dismissal, the secret Nepal-PLA cooperation against Tibetan refugees, and the building of the Kathmandu-Lhasa road. In order to pressure Mahendra to shift course, New Delhi began supporting (or perhaps stepped up its support for) the pro-democratic reform movement led by the Nepali Congress Party operating out of bases in India. As Indian pressure mounted, Mahendra turned even more to China for support. A vicious cycle began which would be broken only by China's 1962 assault on India. As Chinese-Indian relations were sliding toward war in 1962, Beijing issued direct statements of support for Nepal in the face of mounting Indian pressure. Speaking in Kathmandu on the first anniversary of the signing of the Kathmandu-Lhasa road agreement, in October 1962, Chinese foreign minister Marshal Chen Yi lauded Nepal's history of resistance to foreign invasion and warned: "I assure His Majesty, King Mahendra, His Majesty's government and the Nepalese people, that in case any foreign forces attack Nepal, we Chinese people will stand on your side."[21] The nuances of

Chen's carefully considered phraseology was not as strong as it might have been. The "Chinese people," rather than the "Chinese government" and/or the "Chinese army," would stand beside Nepal. Still, taken in context, Chen's statement must be viewed as a warning to New Delhi not to intervene in Nepal.

During the 1962 war Nepal followed a carefully neutral line. Afterward, Mahendra was well aware that Indian defeat had heightened its security concerns and, therefore, the risks Nepal would run if it tilted toward China. But India's defeat in October 1962 also greatly diminished its prestige in Nepal. If India could not defend even its own borders, how could it defend Nepal against China? This awareness cut both ways, however, and was not entirely comforting to Kathmandu. The stakes were now higher for all three parties in the China-Nepal-India triangle. India felt an increased need to limit China's position in Nepal. As a result, Indian aid and concessions to Nepal increased substantially, and New Delhi ordered all anti-royal Nepali exiles in India to cease their activities. Nepal welcomed India's more solicitous post-1962 attitude and maneuvered very cautiously to balance its relations between India and China.

India was unable to reverse the Nepal-Tibet road and witnessed several hundred Chinese road-building experts enter Nepal to assist with that project. With components trucked in from China, they built five major bridges with load-bearing capacity of up to sixty tons rather than the fifteen to seventeen tons stipulated in the construction agreement.[22] As the road neared completion, India proposed an agreement under which India and Nepal would undertake joint defense against China. Kathmandu declined, yet India was able to prevent Chinese arms sales to Nepal. In letters exchanged in January 1965, India agreed to provide military material to Nepal on a gratis basis.[23] The letters also provided that "the Government of Nepal shall be free to import from or through the territory of India arms, ammunition or warlike materials necessary for the security of Nepal." Procedures for this were to be "worked out by the two governments acting in consultation." Any "shortfalls" in supply were to be met by the United States or Britain, with details to be "coordinated at a suitable time." In 1969 Nepal called for major changes in the Nepali-Indian security relation and asserted that both the 1965 letters and the 1950 treaty were no longer binding on Nepal. New Delhi refused to assent to this declaration.[24]

When King Birendra—or, to use his full name, Birendra Bir Birkram Shah Dev—became Nepal's king after his father's death in 1972, he continued his father's policy of balancing China and India. One of his major vehicles for doing this was to propose an international agreement to declare Nepal a "Zone of Peace." Promulgated officially at the time of Birendra's coronation in 1975,

Nepal pushed the Zone of Peace plan vigorously for the next fifteen years. The Nepali government repeatedly denied there was any conflict between the Zone of Peace plan and Nepal's 1950 treaty with India, though New Delhi did not believe this. Indian leaders thought that the real purpose of the plan was to extricate Nepal from the security obligations to India under the 1950 treaty by placing its relations with India on a par with its relations with China. As Indian analysts noted, in Birendra's very first major statement on Nepal's strategic doctrine he revived the concept of balanced neutrality first enunciated by Nepal's king in 1769. Birendra avoided a direct challenge to the 1950 treaty because he knew that this would provoke a strong Indian reaction. Instead, he adopted an indirect attack via the Zone of Peace proposal. New Delhi refused to endorse the Zone of Peace plan and unofficially told Nepali officials that it felt the proposal was in conflict with the 1950 treaty. Kathmandu persisted in pushing the plan in various international fora. By 1990, 112 countries had endorsed the Zone of Peace plan.[25] China was an early supporter of the plan.

China openly exhorted Nepali assertions of independence vis-à-vis India throughout the period up to 1978. Intense anti-Indian propaganda was directed by China toward Nepal. When India annexed Sikkim in 1974, Chinese propagandists had a heyday, stressing that Nepal might be India's next target. In 1976–77 Chinese aid to Nepal reached a record high of 106 million Indian rupees (about U.S.$2 million at 1976 exchange rates), nearly equaling for the first time Indian aid to Nepal. This stage of intense, direct rivalry continued until after the death of Mao Zedong. It ended with Deng Xiaoping's consolidation of control over China's foreign policy.

DENG XIAOPING AND CHINESE POLICY TOWARD NEPAL

Deng Xiaoping initially shifted the course of China's policy toward Sino-Nepal-Indian relations back toward the India-deferring approach of the mid-1950s. The reasons inspiring this late 1970s shift were similar to those that had prompted the original mid-1950s policy. India was an important neighbor of China, and reducing tension with India would enable China to focus energies on more pressing developmental problems. India also had significant influence among the developing countries, and lessening Indian hostility would make China more able to influence those countries in ways that would diminish a hostile superpower's threat to China. In the late 1970s the hostile superpower was, of course, no longer the United States, as had been the case in the 1950s, but the Soviet Union. Deng's revival of the long-dormant proposal for an east-west swap solution to the territorial question was discussed earlier. Another element of Deng's effort to improve relations with India was a move to reduce rivalry with India over Nepal.

Under Deng the anti-Indian content of Chinese propaganda toward Nepal declined rapidly. Chinese aid to Nepal continued under Deng Xiaoping but in a less contentious fashion. During Deng's February 1978 visit to Kathmandu, China quietly shelved a road-building project previously discussed by Chinese and Nepali officials.[26] Deng also dropped hints, unofficially of course, that China would respect India's position in Nepal. Speaking to a member of India's parliament in May 1981, Deng referred to India as the "elder brother" of South Asia—at least this is what Deng's Indian interlocutor heard and reported.[27]

Chinese willingness to placate India did not go too far or last very long, however. In the mid-1980s China resumed its highway construction activities in Nepal, and in June 1984 it agreed to build a second trans-Himalayan highway, this one cutting through the Mustang region of western Nepal and linking the city of Pokhara with the Xinjiang-Tibet highway. Work was still under way on this road in 1989 when India imposed its blockade. In 1987 Beijing decided to construct a road from Lhasa to Dazhu on the border with Nepal, further strengthening Tibet-Nepal transportation links. The Tibetan government allocated $23 million for the project, which was expected to open in October 1990. Beijing's reversion to a less India-deferring policy toward Nepal circa 1984 may have been related to India's failure to accept the east-west swap settlement of the boundary issue revived by Deng in 1980.

In 1988 a series of Chinese-Nepali moves ignoring India's security interests finally prompted New Delhi to play its geographic trump card. The first of two especially egregious Sino-Nepali moves was the conclusion of a secret agreement in the fall of 1988 providing for the exchange of intelligence between the two governments.[28] India quickly learned of the agreement through its numerous sources in the Nepali government. A second, equally egregious move was Nepal's purchase, and Beijing's sale, of Chinese munitions. As noted earlier, Nepali arms purchases had been regulated by letters exchanged in 1965. New Delhi viewed Kathmandu's 1988 purchase of Chinese arms as a violation of those earlier agreements. A final move that India might have shrugged off had it occurred in isolation was Kathmandu's decision to award contracts for a major project near the Indian border to a Chinese company. Ever since the 1962 war India had sought to exclude Chinese personnel from regions of Nepal close to India on grounds that the personnel involved in those projects might be Chinese spies. In March 1965 letters were exchanged between India and Nepal excluding Chinese involvement in construction or development activities in the Terai (the low-lying plain along the southern fringe of the Himalayan foothills and constituting a narrow belt of Nepali territory along the border with India).[29]

Any single move would have created friction in Indian-Nepali relations. Taken together, they led to an Indian conclusion that Birendra's government was trying to dissolve Nepal's long-standing security relation with India and initiate a military-security relation with China. According to diplomatic sources in Beijing interviewed by this author in 1990, China had offered for many years to sell arms to Nepal. Kathmandu had declined, preferring instead to continue relying on India as its primary armorer. New Delhi, however, did not always meet Kathmandu's requests. In 1972 and 1976 Nepal requested the purchase of antiaircraft guns, but New Delhi declined on the grounds that Nepal did not need them.[30] Again in the early 1980s, Kathmandu approached India regarding the purchase of antiaircraft guns, but India did not reply for several years. Indian diplomats in Beijing in 1990 explained this lapse as the result of simple bureaucratic sluggishness.

King Birendra reportedly ordered negotiations for the arms deal to begin in March 1988. A Nepali delegation visited China in that month to be received by CCP Politburo members Qiao Shi and Peng Zhen, both of whom reiterated China's "sincere support" for Nepal's Zone of Peace proposal.[31] The Nepali arms purchase negotiators *may* have been included in this delegation. In any case, the first consignment of arms, five hundred truckloads worth $20 million, began arriving in Nepal in June 1988 over the Kathmandu-Lhasa highway. The convoys reportedly moved under heavy security, the trucks covered with canvas and civilian traffic along the highway restricted to facilitate rapid movement of the convoys. Included in the shipment were light arms and ammunition, uniforms and boots, and sixteen antiaircraft guns. The total sale consisted of about three thousand truckloads.[32]

The sale did not take India by surprise. New Delhi got wind of Kathmandu's intentions and in December 1987 warned Nepal of the consequences of purchasing antiaircraft guns from China.[33] Once Kathmandu went ahead with the purchase, over Indian objections, India's minister of external affairs, Natwar Singh, flew to Kathmandu as Rajiv Gandhi's special envoy on July 22, 1988. Singh carried with him a letter from Gandhi for King Birendra asking for assurances that Nepal would not again purchase arms from China and that the weapons already purchased would not be used against India.[34] Birendra refused to give such assurances, insisting that it was Nepal's sovereign right to purchase weapons it considered necessary for its defense and that the weapons were intended for internal security and antiterrorism and did not constitute a threat to India. When Singh argued that the Himalayas were India's vital defense barrier, which it could not allow China to breach,

Birendra argued that such thinking was out-of-date.[35] According to some reports, Birendra also told Singh that Nepal planned to increase the size of its army by two divisions over the next decade. That would roughly double the size of Nepal's military.[36]

New Delhi argued that the arms purchase violated the spirit of Article 5 of the 1950 treaty, the ancillary letters exchanged at the time of that treaty, and the 1965 letters on arms sales. Kathmandu maintained that all of these documents had to do only with munitions imports via India and not with imports *not coming via India* (i.e., those coming via China). New Delhi insisted that the provision of the 1965 letters that any "shortfalls" be made up by the United States or Britain, "coordinated" by New Delhi and Kathmandu, clearly ruled out Nepal's acquisition of munitions from China without Indian approval. New Delhi argued that, since there was no other route to Nepal than via India when the various agreements were signed (the Kathmandu-Kodari highway was not opened to regular traffic until May 1967), their spirit was clearly intended to regulate all of Nepal's foreign arms acquisition. In response to New Delhi's charge that Nepal was obligated by Article 2 of the 1950 treaty to consult India over any "misunderstanding" that might "cause any breach" in friendly relations between Nepal and India, Kathmandu replied that New Delhi had not consulted with Nepal before going to war with China in 1962 or with Pakistan in 1965 and 1971. King Birendra and Rajiv Gandhi discussed these issues at the ninth nonaligned summit in Belgrade in September 1989. Birendra urged Gandhi not to link security to the trade and transit issues. Gandhi insisted on such a linkage and on the necessity of reviewing the entire gamut of relations, including security perceptions and the 1950 treaty.[37]

The precise reasons why China sold these weapons to Nepal are unclear. The Chinese principal in the arms transaction was apparently the North China Industries Corporation (NORINCO). NORINCO is one of China's major arms exporters, and presumably its motives were purely commercial. Munitions have become one of China's major manufactured goods exports since 1978, and China's leaders clearly place a high priority on generating foreign currency via exports. The weapons were apparently sold to Nepal at "friendship prices," but this does not necessarily vitiate possible commercial motives. In many such cases China earns the real money in follow-on sales of replacements and spare parts. China has several important arms customers in South Asia—Pakistan and Bangladesh—and presumably would be happy to add another. Thus, there is no reason to believe that commercial motives were not an important consideration on the Chinese side, both from the standpoint of NORINCO and the higher-ups, who may or may not have cleared NORINCO's export contract. On the other hand, initiating a China-Nepal military relation where none had existed before almost certainly required clearance by high levels. The military confrontation over the Sumdurong Chu situation the previous year, together with the continuing nonsettlement of the boundary dispute, probably persuaded China's top leaders that China's situation vis-à-vis India would be improved by a military relation with Nepal. I suspect, though frankly speaking I have no hard proof, that the cluster of Chinese moves toward Nepal in 1988 was approved at the highest levels in Beijing.

Once the arms sales issue erupted in 1989, Beijing justified it on the basis that military relations are part of the normal gamut of state-to-state relations. A sovereign, independent country such as Nepal has the right to acquire such materials as it deems necessary for its defense, and China, as a sovereign country, equally has the right to sell such materials. Moreover, the materials sold to Nepal could not be construed as in any way constituting a threat to India. During a visit to Kathmandu in November 1989 Premier Li Peng specifically addressed the question of China's arms sales to Nepal. Such weapons as China had sold, Li said, were intended purely to increase the defensive capability and insure the security of friendly countries. Such sales were not directed against any country and were entirely legitimate. "In fact," said Li, "Pakistan, Bangladesh and Nepal not only obtain weapons from China but from other countries as well."

New Delhi was very concerned by the initiation of a Sino-Nepali military relationship. Would Nepal evolve toward a Pakistan-like security relation with China? Even excluding this, Nepal would no longer be within India's security zone. If Beijing's 1988 moves stood, the 1950 treaty, already much frayed, would become a dead letter. The fact that antiaircraft guns and ammunition constituted a substantial portion of the sale was highly troubling to New Delhi. Such weapons were obviously of no use for internal security or antiterrorism. India was the only country with a significant air force that might conceivably threaten Nepal. Moreover, air superiority was one major advantage India enjoyed vis-à-vis China in the Himalayan region. New Delhi thus saw the sale of antiaircraft weapons as degrading India's military position in the central Himalayas.[38] From New Delhi's perspective the sale represented a change in the military status quo in the Himalayan Mountains and the initiation of a substantive military relation between China and Nepal where none had existed before. If allowed to continue, the ultimate consequences of this process were incalculable. Training by the PLA in the use, maintenance, and repair of the equipment supplied was virtually certain—and, according to Indian diplomatic sources, was part of the March 1988 deal. The secret agree-

ment between Nepal and China providing for the exchange of intelligence
was even more troubling to New Delhi. While arms purchases could be
explained in terms of essentially commercial considerations, an intelligence
exchange agreement suggested that Kathmandu and Beijing were deliberately
moving toward some sort of security understanding.

INDIA'S ECONOMIC BLOCKADE OF NEPAL

From New Delhi's perspective the 1988 actions of the Nepal government indicated that it did not wish to continue a friendly, special *security* relation with
India. Yet that relation was linked, inevitably, to the friendly, special *economic*
relation between Indian and Nepal. Having indicated its intent to dissolve
the special security relation, Kathmandu could not expect to continue enjoying a friendly, special economic relation with India. In the diplomatic words
of a Ministry of External Affairs spokesman: "India has always valued the
special relationship with Nepal as embodied in the 1950 Treaty of Peace and
Friendship . . . For the last four decades India has done everything possible
to live up to the letter and spirit of the treaty. Good neighborliness implies
a degree of mutual sensitivity and concern for the interests of both countries. This is particularly necessary if the special relationship between India
and Nepal is to be maintained."[39]

Indo-Nepalese trade and transit through India for Nepal's trade with third
countries had been regulated by a series of treaties signed successively in 1950,
1960, 1971, and 1978. The last in the series expired in March 1988 but was
extended twice by six months each time, finally expiring on March 23, 1989.[40]
Agreement on a draft trade treaty had been reached in October 1988, but disagreement over a series of problems prevented consensus on a transit treaty.
There were a number of economic issues in dispute between India and Nepal
at this juncture. Analysts differ over the importance they assign to the economic and security disputes between the two countries. Many feel that the
economic issues were merely a pretext seized upon by India. The real issue,
they believe, was the Chinese arms sale. Others, including myself, believe that
the economic issues were genuinely important but that they have to be seen
within the context of a broad effort by Birendra to reduce Nepal's economic
dependence on India. Security issues, however, were clearly uppermost in
Indian minds.

Kathmandu's failure to satisfy Indian demands led New Delhi to adopt a
tough approach. In February 1989 it began insisting that trade and transit issues
be incorporated into a single treaty. This had been the case prior to 1978, much
to the displeasure of Kathmandu, which believed that transit was a funda-

mental and permanent right of landlocked countries, while trade was purely a bilateral and constantly changing matter that could be rearranged periodically at mutual convenience. From Kathmandu's perspective trade and transit should be dealt with in separate treaties. The Janata government of Morarji Desai had conceded this point to Kathmandu in 1978, and, according to the Nepali government, New Delhi's 1989 demand for a single treaty was an attempt to turn the clock back eleven years. Kathmandu also tried to play hardball. Under the draft trade treaty signed in October 1988, Nepal was to lift additional customs duties recently imposed on Indian goods and not extend such exemptions to any third country. Nepal said it would lift these duties only after treaties of trade and transit were signed. Kathmandu then proceeded, according to Indian press reports, to ease customs duties on Chinese goods. Even after the Indian embassy gave notice in February that unless agreement on outstanding issues were reached by March 1 the old treaties would expire, Kathmandu refused to back down, asking India to reconsider its proposal for a single treaty and offering to send a team to New Delhi to negotiate *two separate* treaties.

With the expiration of the 1978 treaties on March 23, 1989, there was, according to New Delhi, no legal basis for continuing trade and transit relations between India and Nepal. Nor was India a signatory to the 1965 International Convention on Transit Trade of Landlocked Countries or to the United Nations Convention on the Law of the Sea—both of which guaranteed certain transit rights to landlocked countries. Nor was Nepal a member of the General Agreement on Tariffs and Trade and entitled to nondiscriminatory treatment by India under that agreement. Thus, India closed down thirteen of fifteen transit points on the Indo-Nepali border. The two major crossing points at Raxaul and Jogbani were left open, New Delhi said, in order that essential goods such as medicines, baby foods, and cement might continue to reach the Nepali people, against whom India held no animus. Under international law a landlocked country has a right to only one transit route to the sea. Thus, leaving two routes open was a gesture of Indian magnanimity.[41] It also allowed New Delhi to deny that it was implementing an economic blockade of Nepal. Nonetheless, the message, according to an Indian government spokesman, was "Be prepared to reciprocate if you want special privileges."[42]

Indian pressure tightened rapidly. On March 31, 1989, a separate agreement expired under which Nepal had purchased oil from third countries and had it delivered to the Indian oil corporation, which, in turn, provided Nepal with a mix of petroleum products of comparable value at various points along the Nepali border. The nonrenewal of this agreement was a severe blow to Nepal's fuel supply. On June 23 still another agreement under which Nepal was allotted warehouse space in the Calcutta port expired and was not renewed. Additional checkpoints were also established along the Indo-Nepali border to prevent smuggling, which might circumvent the closure of regular transit points. (These measures had limited effect, however, and smuggling shot up drastically.) Indian authorities also became particularly stringent about monitoring transit movement via the two crossing points that remained open. India also refused to supply railway wagons for the movement of goods between Nepal and Bangladesh.[43]

CHINESE SUPPORT FOR NEPAL

According to diplomatic sources in Beijing, during late 1988 China quietly advised Kathmandu not to expect China to provide an alternative to Nepal's economic connection with India. The difficulties of transportation between Nepal and China and the serious financial constraints China then faced precluded such a possibility. Once India imposed economic sanctions, China gave Nepal modest assistance. Chinese transport aircraft ferried three hundred tons of petroleum products into Kathmandu during the first months of the crisis. Three hundred tons would be about fifteen standard-size 5,000-gallon trailer-tank trucks—not a large amount. By April an agreement for Chinese supply of fuel and food had been signed. Chinese tank trucks began to deliver supplies to Kathmandu by early May. During April and May another three hundred tons of petroleum products were imported from China via road.[44] Greatly increased transport costs meant that Nepal paid above–world market prices for its Chinese oil. On the other hand, China gave a considerable amount of salt—of which Tibet has a surplus—to Nepal free of cost. Moves were also taken to increase trade between Tibet and Nepal. Trade promotion delegations traveled back and forth between Kathmandu and Beijing. More passes on the Nepal-Tibet border were opened to local trade, although most of these routes were nothing more than mule tracks. China also pressed forward with its aid projects in Nepal. One of these, a sugar mill in Lumbini district, was inaugurated in January 1990. (Lumbini is adjacent to India in central Nepal. From New Delhi's perspective, Kathmandu's consent to permit Chinese activities in such regions was another manifestation of Nepal's insensitivity to India's security concerns.) Finally, China extended a $13.6 million grant to Nepal in November 1989 for the construction of new projects and the consolidation of existing ones.

These were modest moves. Nor did China employ the monetarily costless forms of political support available to it—in the United Nations, for example. China's public criticism of India's actions was indirect and opaque, so much so that it was unclear whether or not it was actually criticizing India. China's advice to Nepal was not to expect China to bail it out and to come to the best terms possible with India. When China raised the issue with India, its tone was one of pleading, calling on India to be magnanimous as befitted its large size. There was no intimation of threat or pressure. Nor did Sino-Indian relations suffer as a result of the Indian blockade of Nepal. When Vice Premier Wu Xueqian and Foreign Minister Qian Qichen visited India (in October 1989 and March 1990, respectively), the Chinese commentary issuing from these visits was glowingly optimistic about the good prospects for Indo-Chinese relations.

China gave low-keyed political support to Nepal. A *Beijing Review* article of July 1989, for example, said that "India wants its security interests to take priority in its relations with Nepal, while Nepal persists in keeping friendly relations with India on the basis of mutual respect for sovereignty, equality, and mutual benefit."[45] The clear implication was that Nepal's position was just, while India's derived from unjust power politics. When Vice Premier Wu Xueqian stopped in New Delhi in October 1989, he said that "China sincerely hopes that the South Asian countries will handle their mutual relations in accordance with the Five Principles of Peaceful Coexistence and strengthen their cooperation in a spirit of equality and mutual benefit."[46] These comments were implicit criticism of India's violation of the Five Principles of Peaceful Coexistence in its relations with Nepal. Declarations of support were another way China could assist Nepal politically. During his November 1989 visit to Kathmandu, Li Peng said that China felt happy about the achievements of the Nepali people under the leadership of King Birendra and his government and praised the "unremitting efforts" of the Nepali people in the "safeguarding of their national independence and state sovereignty."[47] Li also promised that, with Nepal facing "difficulties," China would offer moral support and support in other fields according to its own strength.

China's support did not extend to action in the United Nations. On October 5, 1989, Nepali foreign minister Shailendra Kumar Upadhyaya commented at some length in the General Assembly on Nepal's situation. Upadhyaya did not directly mention India, but his inferences were clear enough—for example, when he referred to the difficulties faced by landlocked countries "especially if actions taken by transit countries result in the denial or delay of unrestricted transit to such countries."[48] China's representatives spoke in the General Assembly in September, October, and November 1989 but said nothing about Nepal's plight. A *tour de horizon* by Foreign Minister Qian Qichen on September 29, for example, made no mention of the Indo-Nepali conflict, although it did mention Afghanistan, the Iran-Iraq war, Central

America, Namibia, Angola, South Africa, and numerous other topics. Qian called for the creation of a "new international political order" and noted that "facts show that hegemonic practices and power politics still exist. Cases of big countries bullying the small and strong countries domineering the weak still occur, Qian said."⁴⁹ There was no intimation, however, that this applied to India-Nepal relations.

China's highest-profile support for Nepal came during Li Peng's visit to Kathmandu as part of his three-nation South Asian tour. Li's visit served multiple domestic and diplomatic purposes. In terms of South Asia, it was intended to demonstrate China's continuing interest and involvement in that region, especially in the context of Sino-Indian rapprochement. This required some expression of support for Nepal. Thus, at his press conference in Kathmandu, Li said that China was "concerned" about the situation in South Asia. There were still "some factors" giving rise to "instability" in the region, Li said. In this regard China believed that "all countries, big or small, should be treated equally. Problems and disputes should be handled according to the Five Principles of Peaceful Coexistence without resorting to force or other means."⁵⁰ Li also gently chided India when he said he hoped that India, as a major country in South Asia, could be "more generous" in handling issues with Nepal. Li reassured his Nepali hosts that China would not bow to Indian pressure and disengage from South Asia when he said: "It has always been China's steadfast policy to develop good neighborly and friendly relations with every country in South Asia. No matter what happens in the international situation [this was primarily an allusion to Sino-Indian rapprochement] China will always support Nepal and other South Asian countries in their efforts to safeguard independence and sovereignty."⁵¹

The issue of Sino-Indian relations was apparently on the agenda of Li Peng's talks with Nepal's leaders. It makes sense to assume that Kathmandu was somewhat dissatisfied with the level of China's support. Beijing also wanted to assure Kathmandu that the limits on Chinese assistance were due to geographic and financial constraints rather than to a desire to placate New Delhi for the sake of better Sino-Indian relations. It is hard to say whether a genuine meeting of the minds occurred, but the Nepali prime minister implicitly accepted Beijing's explanations when he said that Nepal "appreciated China's role in maintaining international peace and security" and welcomed its initiatives and efforts to normalize, develop, and improve relations with all its neighbors." We can also infer from this statement one of Beijing's arguments: the greater the investment India had in cordial ties with China, the more cautiously it would act toward its small neighbors that were China's friends. To Kathmandu, Beijing's advice was apparently to come to the best terms it could with India. Commenting in November 1989 on Li Peng's South Asian tour, Beijing's *Liaowang* magazine said that China "sincerely hopes that through fair talks and consultations the historical discrepancies and disputes between Nepal and India . . . can be resolved."[52]

One elemental reason for the modest character of Beijing's support was the difficulties of transportation between China and Nepal. The Kathmandu-Lhasa road was in pretty bad shape. In June 1982 a protocol had been signed providing for Chinese assistance in rebuilding the border bridge and repairing the road. Work commenced in April 1983 on a twenty-seven-kilometer stretch near the border on the Nepali side. Road construction in that part of the world is immensely difficult, dangerous, and expensive, and thus the work proceeded slowly. In 1987 an eighty-kilometer section of the road was washed away by heavy rains. In August 1988 a strong earthquake covered long sections with many tons of rock and earth.[53] In May 1989 Kathmandu announced that it intended to reconstruct the entire Kathmandu-Kodari road. China sent a surveying team to study the problem of repairing and maintaining critical portions of the road. During the visit by Li Peng in November 1989, China agreed to improve transport conditions on the highway. Embargo-induced shortages of fuel and construction materials hampered road construction and maintenance efforts. Those materials had to be diverted from Nepal's tight civilian markets or trucked in from Xinjiang or Sichuan. In mid-1989 the Chinese government began to study the possibility of constructing a third Tibet-Nepal road, this one via Tinkar Pass in northwestern Nepal. This road would then run many hundreds of miles via Tibet and the famous Aksai Chin road to link up with the Karakoram highway and then run many more hundreds of miles through Pakistan to Karachi and the sea. Once the road was completed, India's stranglehold on Nepal would be somewhat eased. This was a very long-term project, however, and would take many years to complete.

An equally elemental reason was China's own weaknesses at this juncture. It was Nepal's bad luck that it violated India's anti-China taboos just as China was entering the political upheaval of 1989 associated with the massacre in Beijing in June. In those circumstances China's leaders, and even working-level bureaucrats in the ministries, had very little time to focus on events in Nepal. If they did think of Nepal, China's own dire needs disinclined them to assume any new, major foreign commitments. The rapid deterioration of China's relations with the Western democracies in 1989 dissuaded Beijing from running the risk of confrontation with India at that point. One of Beijing's diplomatic responses to the decline of its ties with the West was to push to improve relations with the Third World and with China's neighbors. Had

China's international position been better, its response to Indian coercion of Nepal could well have been stronger.

Many Indian analysts believed that the "anti-India, pro-China" tendencies of the Nepali monarchy arose out of a fundamental insecurity of royal institutions confronted by democratic ideas and forces. The Nepali monarchy eschewed parliamentary democracy, relying instead on a partyless advisory body called the Panchayat. In an age when democratic ideas were pervasive, Indian analysts believed, the Nepali monarchy was an "anachronism" seeking to cling to royal prerogatives. Since Nepali democrats naturally looked to India for inspiration, sympathy, and sometimes support, Nepali monarchists were just as naturally fearful of Indian influence. China was nondemocratic and had demonstrated it would not support anti-royal Nepali movements. Moreover, communist China, unlike democratic India, had little attraction for the Nepali middle-class. Securely preserving Nepali royalism thus required taking Nepal out of the Indian sphere of influence and bringing it under the protection of China, according to this Indian interpretation of Nepali thinking.[54] Close links with communist China were less threatening to Nepal's autocratic monarchy than were links with democratic India. Moreover, by stirring up anti-Indian sentiments, the Nepali monarch could divert the attentions and disgruntlements of his impoverished and powerless subjects. It followed from this analysis that the way for India to deal with Nepal's "anti-Indian, pro-Chinese" monarchy was to bring about a basic democratization of Nepal's political system. For proof, advocates of this viewpoint pointed to the period of Nepali Congress rule in 1959–60. That liberal parliamentary government had vetoed the proposal to build the Kathmandu-Lhasa road on the grounds that it would strain Nepal's relations with India. It also concluded the common market agreement between the two countries. Once Mahendra dismissed the Congress government and banned political parties in December 1960, however, Nepal returned to its policy of playing the China card against India.

India's sanctions devastated Nepal. Scarce goods led to shortages and spiraling inflation. Enterprises shut down because of lost markets, rising costs, and inadequate inputs. As economic hardship increased, popular discontent with King Birendra's government mounted. It may be that India's leaders under Rajiv Gandhi were pursuing a deliberate, long-range plan first to destabilize Nepal via economic pressure and then to support anti-monarchy forces to bring about a radical restructuring of Nepal's political system. This is, I think, a plausible explanation and a hypothesis that merits further examination. Yet there is no evidence to support it directly. Regardless of Indian intentions, however, the problems that destabilized Nepal's traditional monarchical system seem to have been the result of Indian policy.

A pro-democracy movement surfaced in Nepal in February 1990 calling for full legalization of political parties and constitution of a multiparty transitional government to guide Nepal to parliamentary democracy. Negotiations between the royal government and the democratic movement quickly deadlocked. King Birendra ordered a government reshuffling, but this failed to placate the opposition. Protest demonstrations swelled in size, only to be met with police gunfire and a curfew. Bloody but incomplete repression only fueled further protest. Tensions peaked on April 15, when a large crowd besieged a building where negotiations were under way between the royal government and the opposition. A confrontation seemed imminent. Tension began to dissipate only when Birendra capitulated to the basic demands of the opposition. The next day the incumbent royalist government resigned, while Birendra dissolved Nepal's undemocratic representative assembly, the Panchayat, lifted the thirty-year ban on political parties, and asked opposition leaders to form a multiparty coalition transitional government. The revolution had won. On April 19 the Congress Party's acting president, Krishna Prasad Bhattarai, was sworn in as prime minister.

Indian leaders and political parties quickly gave support as Nepal's democratic movement confronted the government. The royal government's attempts at repression outraged the democratic sympathies of many Indians. Both Rajiv Gandhi and V. P. Singh (who replaced Gandhi as prime minister in December 1989) condemned the crackdown and described the repression as state violence. Indian political parties also gave encouragement and financial support to the Nepali Congress and Nepali Communist Parties. (The Nepali Communist Party was, along with the Nepali Congress, a leading force in the pro-democracy movement.) It should perhaps be noted that India was not alone in condemning the repression in Nepal. Strong criticism also came from the United States, Japan, and West Germany.

King Birendra apparently sought assurances of Chinese support as he maneuvered toward confrontation with the pro-parliament movement. Hong Kong's *Zheng ming* magazine reported that shortly before the crackdown Birendra had secretly sent a representative to Beijing to solicit Beijing's support. The emissary was received by Yang Shangkun, who expressed China's complete support for the king's efforts to prevent "chaos" in Nepal. The Hong Kong magazine also reported that China had quietly deployed military forces to its border with Nepal.[55] Beijing also gave Birendra low-keyed public support. On April 9, three days after police fired on a massive demonstration in Kathmandu, China's Foreign Ministry issued a statement saying that the events in Nepal were entirely an internal affair of Nepal. But, as a neighboring country, China hoped to see peace and stability maintained there. Several days later *Renmin ribao* reported on developments in Nepal. Regarding the confrontation between the government and the opposition, the paper said, it was unfortunate that Nepal had encountered these difficulties while it still had not recovered from the "economic difficulties" of the past year.[56] These comments constituted justification of the government's repression, and opposition to criticism or sanctions in response to that repression. Well-connected Chinese South Asian analysts with whom I spoke were very concerned about events in Nepal and about whether or not King Birendra would be able to consolidate his power. *Sankao ziliao*, the internal publication made up of translations from the foreign press, also carried many articles regarding developments in Nepal during April. On April 18, by which point Birendra had dissolved the Panchayat and lifted the ban on political parties, another article in *Renmin ribao* analyzed recent developments in Nepal. The reason for the disturbances, bloodshed, and destruction of property in Nepal, according to the article, was the nationwide movement for a multiparty parliamentary system. This explanation resonated with analogies to China's own post–June 4, 1989, situation and was a strong, if implicit, condemnation of Nepal's pro-democracy movement.

On April 17, the day after Birendra dissolved the Panchayat and asked the opposition to form a government, Prime Minister designate K. P. Bhattarai told Japanese reporters that the most important task of his new government would be the restoration of relations with India. Regarding relations with China, Bhattarai said he was satisfied with the attitude of China thus far. It had remained neutral and had not interfered in the pro-democracy movement. Bhattarai moved quickly to come to terms with New Delhi. Among his first moves was to send a letter to V. P. Singh conveying his personal desire to find ways of resolving outstanding issues between India and Nepal. Bhattarai's letter also proposed restoration of the pre–March 23, 1989, status quo ante and prompt conclusion of new transit and trade *agreements*.[57] Bhattarai also asked Beijing to "delay" delivery of the last consignment of arms "in view of the possible reaction of our southern neighbor with whom we have to finalize a trade and transit treaty." The final consignment of Chinese munitions, scheduled for May 1990, constituted 10 percent of the total purchase.[58] More important than the size of the final shipment, however, was the symbolic import of its cancellation.

When Bhattarai visited New Delhi from June 8 to 11, 1990, he accepted India's demands on a broad range of issues. Regarding security issues,

Bhattarai told a press conference that Nepal "recognizes India's security concerns": "We tried to assure them that our own views would show and prove that we shall take care of their security perceptions and shall not allow Nepal to be used as a base by anyone—China or any other country." Regarding weapons purchases, Nepal would definitely prefer to buy Indian weapons if they were as cheap and as good as Chinese weapons.[59] The communiqué signed by Bhattarai and Singh provided that "the two countries shall have prior consultations with a view to reaching mutual agreement on such defense-related matters which in the view of either country could pose a threat to its security."[60] Singh, for his part, stressed that Indian-Nepali friendship should be viewed in a positive spirit in light of the special relationship between the two countries and not as directed against any third country.

Throughout the Indo-Nepalese confrontation New Delhi sought to minimize the adverse effect that confrontation might have on Sino-Indian relations. At a press conference on April 17, 1989, for example, Prime Minister Gandhi was careful not to identify China as a factor in the Indo-Nepali dispute. He explained that China was not behind the recent trouble with Nepal, nor was it inciting Nepal in order to create a "tense situation" in South Asia.[61] While Gandhi's characterization of China's noninflammatory approach was quite accurate, his assertion that China's relations with Nepal were not a factor in precipitating the India-Nepal confrontation was obviously based on diplomatic considerations. A year later, at his joint press conference with Bhattarai in June 1990, V. P. Singh also sought to minimize the "China factor." India was not opposed to close Sino-Nepali relations, Singh explained. Indian ties with Nepal were "special," but that did not make them "against" China or anyone else.[62]

From New Delhi's perspective the disagreements it might have with Nepal (or Sri Lanka or Pakistan or Bangladesh) are questions to be settled bilaterally between it and its South Asian neighbor. To state this too forcefully or directly, however, could provoke China to challenge the proposition. Thus, New Delhi seeks to uncouple Indian-Chinese relations from the question of India's relations with its South Asian neighbors.

CHINA AND INDIAN HEGEMONY OVER NEPAL

In private conversations with this author in Beijing during 1990, authoritative Chinese analysts of South Asian affairs were bitter about what they saw as India's bludgeoning of Nepal. What was involved, they felt, was an Indian effort to exert its hegemony in South Asia, to dictate to Nepal what sort of foreign relations and even internal political system it should have. It is safe to assume that these views reflect those of China's top leaders. But in no case that I know of were such critical views expressed publicly. Indian diplomats in Beijing were generally satisfied with China's approach to the Indo-Nepali confrontation and did not feel that China was playing an inflammatory role. Nor were accusations of inciting Nepal leveled against China by the Indian press, which usually loses no opportunity to expose China's nefarious plots.

In my opinion it would be wrong to conclude that Beijing's modest level of support for Nepal during the 1989–90 confrontation and Beijing's urging of Kathmandu to come to terms with India represented some sort of implicit Chinese acceptance of India's domination of Nepal. More likely, it represented an attempt to sustain a modicum of Nepalese independence given the realities of the currently existing situation. As a more detached observer, Beijing was perhaps in a better position than Kathmandu to see that the advantages of the situation were overwhelmingly with India. It also understood, again perhaps better than Kathmandu, that China was simply not in a position to provide assistance adequate to Nepal's needs. Thus, Beijing probably understood that the longer the confrontation lasted, the weaker King Birendra's position would become. Chinese intelligence may also have made Beijing aware that there was mounting danger of Nepal being thrown into turmoil by the deepening economic collapse, thus giving India a pretext for direct military intervention or leading to the overthrow of Birendra's regime. Given these realities, it made sense to conclude the lost battle as soon as possible and survive to fight another day. And, as noted earlier, the Nepal imbroglio occurred just as Beijing faced a most serious deterioration of its relations with the Western countries following the Beijing massacre of June 1989. Facing strained relations with the West, Beijing did not want to risk trouble with India, possibly inducing India to associate itself with Western anti-China efforts.

China's policies during the 1989–90 confrontation do not suggest that China's foreign policy planners had decided to concede Nepal to an Indian South Asian sphere of influence for the sake of a stable modus vivendi with India. A more plausible explanation is that China's response was molded by the overwhelming impact of terrain and the crisis of China's relations with the West. One may plausibly argue that Beijing is moving toward acceptance of Indian hegemony over Nepal as a result of ad hoc, incremental decision making. The long-term result may be the same, but the process of getting there will be substantially different. If Beijing has *not* made a conscious decision to recognize Indian paramountcy in South Asia beginning with Nepal, one can expect continuing Chinese rivalry with India for influence in South Asia when circumstances are more propitious for Beijing.

Resentment toward India's overwhelming presence is a constant of Nepali politics. The opposition parties that formed after the dismantling of the party-less Panchayet system perennially appeal to this anti-Indian sentiment to mobilize support. Once in power, however, Nepal's parties become much more cautious in their criticism of India and want to settle problems with it via bilateral talks.[63] China can nonetheless appeal to this widespread Nepali anti-Indian sentiment. It can claim that, unlike other big countries in the region, it does not bully or interfere in Nepal's internal affairs. This appeal may have considerable potency, although China's ability to exploit it will remain limited by hard geographic constraints.

India's disciplining of Nepal via an economic blockade had a deep impact across South Asia. Other countries that are deeply dependent on Indian markets or on transit via Indian territory—Bangladesh, Sri Lanka, Bhutan, the Maldives—took note that New Delhi was willing and politically able to shut its markets if India's concerns about China were ignored. The economic sanctions of 1989–90 were the first time New Delhi had used such means against regional countries. This made very clear the costs of violating India's security taboos about China. India also made it clear that it has effective, extreme means other than military ones.

China's handicap in Nepal is unique. The cost of shipping material over Tibet is prohibitively high. Most South Asian countries (other than Bhutan) have seaports where Chinese vessels can cheaply deliver or pick up cargoes. China's ability to provide an alternative for Nepal will also increase somewhat with the future completion of the projected rail lines from Golmud to Lhasa and Kunming to Lhasa, along with the projected accelerated economic development of Tibet. Nepal will become far more able to balance economically between China and India if, as Beijing anticipates, Tibet approaches average Chinese levels of economic development two or three decades into the twenty-first century and is tied more robustly to the transportation grid of China proper.

6 / Sikkim and Bhutan

SPECIAL RELATIONS WITH INDIA OR EQUAL
RELATIONS WITH CHINA AND INDIA?

The essence of Sino-Indian rivalry regarding Sikkim and Bhutan has been that India believes it rightfully enjoys special relationships with these two entities, while China rejects this position and insists that China's links with these entities should be on a par with India's. This clash of policy is conditioned by the fact that between Sikkim and Bhutan lies the single most strategically important piece of real estate in the entire Himalayan region—the Chumbi Pass.

The modern Chinese image of these two areas lying on the southern fringe of the Tibetan plateau is suggested by a compendium of maps compiled by Tan Qixiang, China's foremost contemporary cartographer.[1] This atlas contains authoritative depictions of China's boundaries throughout various dynasties, with the area that became the PRC shown in several colors to distinguish it from the surrounding gray areas of non-China. Beginning with the Western Han in the second century B.C., Bhutan and Sikkim are shown as part of Tibet. This situation is depicted as continuing throughout all subsequent dynasties—a period of some 1,400 years—until the Yuan dynasty in the thirteenth century, when Bhutan and Sikkim are depicted as an integral part of China itself. This situation continues during the Ming dynasty. Only beginning with the Qing dynasty in the mid-seventeenth century are Bhutan and Sikkim depicted as separate from China. If one throws in the modern Chinese nationalist propositions that the People's Republic of China is the successor to the traditional Tibetan state and that Tibet is part of the family

of nationalities making up the modern Chinese state, this means that Sikkim
and Bhutan were virtually part of "China" for over 1,800 years. At least this
is the message conveyed by the powerful symbolic images of these maps. This
is not to say that contemporary Chinese nationalists aspire to incorporate
Sikkim and/or Bhutan into China. The point, rather, is that, from the Chinese
perspective, this long history makes it entirely unreasonable for China to
accede to India's demands that it have no, or minimal, relations with these
areas.

There is a wide gap between this Chinese view of China's premodern relations with Sikkim and Bhutan and the views of most non-Chinese scholars
regarding these matters. As is the case of putative "tributary relations"
between China's imperial court and foreign rulers, independent scholars see
modern Chinese historiography as deeply biased by nearly exclusive reliance
on Chinese sources and a nationalist urge to demonstrate China's ancient
influence over as wide-ranging an area as possible. Leo Rose's response to
these Chinese views was that "Sikkim and Bhutan were never under any form
of control by the Chinese government, or, for that matter, of Tibet except
for a short period in the nineteenth century."[2] Since we are concerned most
with Chinese perceptions, we may largely set aside the question of the *accuracy* of those perceptions. Whether or not contemporary Chinese views of
China's historic relation with Sikkim and Bhutan are accurate, those views
underpin PRC policy.

India's starting point in looking at and dealing with these two areas is geography and the perceived role that geography plays in maintaining the integrity
of India's defensive barrier in the Himalayan massif. Between Sikkim and
Bhutan lies the Chumbi Valley, a salient of Chinese territory thrusting south
toward the narrow Siliguri corridor and including the best passage through
the entire Himalayan range. Historically, this was the main trade and transportation route between India and the central Yarlong Zangbo (upper
Brahmaputra River) Valley region of Tibet. It was also the route followed by
the Anglo-Indian expeditionary force that seized Shigatze, Tibet, under the
command of Francis Younghusband in 1904. Were Sikkim and or Bhutan
cleared of Indian influence and military forces, the PLA's ability to move
swiftly through the Chumbi Valley would be greatly enhanced. Conversely,
Indian control and defense of Sikkim and Bhutan means that a PLA advance
through the Chumbi Valley would be subject to Indian observation, artillery
bombardment, and flank attack. Instead of advancing swiftly on Siliguri,
Chinese columns might be stacked up in a narrow corridor and subjected to
devastating Indian air and artillery bombardment.

Regarding Bhutan, India seeks to exclude under any conditions a Chinese military presence in that region and to maintain conditions favorable to swift establishment of an effective Indian military presence there in an emergency. As Indian-Chinese relations deteriorated in the early 1960s and again during the lead-up to the 1971 war with Pakistan, Indian leaders considered deploying Indian forces to Bhutan. That move was ultimately rejected as provocative to China by rubbing salt in the wound of China's refusal to recognize the "special relation" between India and Bhutan. It was also unnecessary since Indian forces could rush into Bhutan to meet any Chinese advance in the high mountains in Bhutan's far north—at least they could once adequate roads were built.

In 1960 India's road network was far from adequate to permit such movement. There was only a low-grade, single-lane road running to Gangtok, Sikkim's capital at the southern end of the Chumbi Valley. Between Gangtok and the main pass into the Chumbi, Natu La, there was only a narrow, steep road passable by jeep in good weather. Into the northern reaches of Sikkim there were only a few mule and foot tracks. The situation in Bhutan was even worse. That region then had *no* motor roads. When Nehru and his daughter Indira visited Bhutan's capital, Thimpu, in September 1954, they traveled first to Gangtok and then eastward, by horse, through the Chumbi Valley and on to Thimphu. This was the traditional way of reaching Thimphu, a route brought under Chinese control by the PLA's occupation of the Chumbi Valley early in its process of "liberating" Tibet.

With the establishment of the Border Roads Organization (BRO) in 1960, India began building roads into Sikkim and Bhutan. By 1996 the BRO had built fifteen hundred kilometers of roads in Bhutan, linking Thimpu with an east-west trunk line in India just south of Bhutan's borders as well as with all other cities in Bhutan. When the BRO began work in 1960, Sikkim was given the second-highest priority, coming only after work on the Leh-Kargil sector of Indian Kashmir south of Aksai Chin. As with the southern slope of what became Arunachal Pradesh, none of these roads were pushed into the northernmost border areas, the logic being that Chinese forces would thus have to fight their way slowly across this roadless zone, giving Indian forces time to deploy into carefully picked and prepared blocking positions farther south. Following the 1962 war, highly trained mountain units of the Indian army were earmarked for deployment into Bhutan and positioned accordingly. A small Bhutanese army of about five thousand was also trained and armed by India. On Indian advice Bhutan's army established observation and control points at forward positions. The purpose of the Bhutanese army, from the Indian perspective, was to detect and give early warning of any Chinese advance into Bhutan. The sine qua non of Indian policy toward both Sikkim and Bhutan has been to uphold political conditions that make possible these defensive strategies.

During British rule Sikkim was not considered part of British India, either as an allied princely state or as a colonial territory. Relations between Sikkim and British India were handled, instead, under a separate set of treaties. Those agreements did, however, establish direct British administrative control over Sikkim.[3] Following Indian independence, India's role increased, when an Indian official was "loaned" to Sikkim to serve as prime minister and reorganize the region's administrative system. Thereafter, all Sikkim's prime ministers were Indian civil servants, appointed by Sikkim's *chogyal* (king) in consensus with the Indian government. The Sikkim-India relation became closer still in 1950, as the PLA occupation of Tibet destroyed India's Tibetan buffer. China's move prompted India's leaders to debate the proper approach to Sikkim. Sadar Patel favored the outright annexation and incorporation of Sikkim into the Indian union at that point. Eventually, annexation was rejected in favor of a protectorate.[4]

Sikkim became an Indian protectorate under a treaty of December 12, 1950, which outlined relations between the "two countries" of Sikkim and India and granted Sikkim "autonomy in regard to its internal affairs." Sikkim recognized its status as a "protectorate of India," with its external relations and security matters "to be conducted and regulated solely by the Government of India." The treaty also specified that the government of Sikkim "shall have no dealings with any foreign power." An Indian political officer was stationed in Sikkim under the treaty to insure that its provisions were carried out. Disputes arising under the treaty were to be settled through mutual consultation or, failing that, by a decision of the chief justice *of India*.[5]

Indian leaders fretted about possible Chinese subversive activities toward Sikkim and Bhutan during the early 1950s. Securing Chinese guarantees against this possibility, and creating political constraints that would inhibit Chinese violation of these guarantees, was one of Nehru's objectives in involving China in the April 1955 Afro-Asian conference at Bandung.[6] Indian influence within Sikkim also grew, in spite of the 1950s treaty's provision for Sikkim's internal autonomy. Many of Sikkim's civil servants were Indians; adequately educated Sikkimese were simply not available to fill these positions. New Delhi also provided the bulk of Sikkim's revenues, both for government operations and for economic development efforts.

By the mid-1960s a new Sikkimese *choygal* began pushing for revision of the 1950 treaty so as to recognize Sikkim's sovereignty and independence. Indian officials attributed these moves to machinations of the United States via the *choygal*'s American wife, the former Hope Cooke, whom the *choygal* had married in 1964.[7] Early that year China sent a message directly to Sikkim's new *choygal* expressing condolences about the death of his father. When the Sikkim government answered directly to Beijing, there was considerable consternation in New Delhi. India protested this "improper procedure" to Beijing, pointing out that, since India was responsible for Sikkim's external relations, all communications should be sent to India and then forwarded to Sikkim. China ignored the Indian protest.[8]

The bloodiest Sino-Indian clashes since the 1962 war occurred on Sikkim's borders in 1967, rousing Indian concerns about China's intentions regarding Sikkim. The clashes occurred at Natu La Pass. There had apparently existed a thirty-yard-wide no-man's-land on some of the hills near the pass, and the two sides began contesting construction of various structures there. Intense fighting flared for several days in mid-September, leaving several hundred dead on both sides.[9] Indian and Western opinion attributed the initiative for the clashes to the Chinese side and noted that the beginning of Chinese construction activities in the region had coincided with the start of a highly publicized two-week visit to India by the *choygal* and his American wife.[10] The Indian side was quite pleased with the combat performance of its forces during the Natu La clashes, seeing it as signaling dramatic improvement since the 1962 debacle.

By the early 1970s New Delhi was receiving reports that the *choygal* was contacting U.S. and Chinese emissaries during his visits to foreign countries. On a visit to London, for instance, he reportedly visited a Chinese restaurant, where he met with officials of the Chinese embassy. In Sikkim he was reportedly in touch with a man jailed for supplying rations to the Chinese army during the 1962 conflict. These reports deepened Indian suspicion about the *chogyal*. Indian opinion began to shift toward the conclusion that Nehru's rejection of Patel's 1950 advice to incorporate Sikkim into India had been a blunder that might endanger India's security.[11]

There were also strong demands within Sikkim for a democratization of the territory's political system. Sikkim's *chogyal* ruled autocratically, and many of Sikkim's democrats looked to India for inspiration and support. Some even advocated Sikkim's accession into the Indian union.[12] Sikkim was also ethnically divided. About 20 percent of the population were Bhutia Lepchas, deriving racially and culturally from Tibet, while over 70 percent were of Nepalese origin. Each of these communities was further divided by tribe and caste.[13] The eruption of serious ethnic rioting and anti-*chogyal* demonstrations in early 1973 provided India with an opportunity to act. According to B. S. Das, the Indian political officer in Gangtok at the time, Indian policy was inspired by a belief that India must act or China would take advantage of the situation. Units of the Indian army and the paramilitary Central Reserve Police Force were deployed to Sikkim to reestablish order. Das then undertook to mediate a settlement among the Sikkimese parties.[14]

China, along with Pakistan, condemned India's intervention in Sikkim in the strongest terms. Coming barely two years after India's intervention in East Pakistan, a pattern of Indian intervention seemed to be emerging. According to Das, the strongly negative international reaction to India's early 1973 intervention led India to modify its policy, which became more gradual. Rather than remove the *chogyal*, in May 1974 India negotiated an interim agreement with him which left Sikkim a monarchy but provided for the popular election of a representative assembly. When the agreement was signed, Das told the *chogyal* that Sikkim's strategic location meant that India's interests would necessarily be dominant there and that, consequently, Sikkim could never hope to be a sovereign, independent country. India, Das stated, was committed to establishing a democratic political system in Sikkim. When the assembly established under the May 1974 agreement met, it passed a resolution calling for "further strengthening of the Indo-Sikkim relationship and Sikkim's participation in the political and economic institutions of India." New Delhi responded by proposing that Sikkim assume a status equivalent to India's centrally ruled territories. Sikkim accepted. In September 1974 the Indian parliament adopted a constitutional amendment making Sikkim an "associate state" of the ROI.

China's Ministry of Foreign Affairs "strongly condemned" India's declaration of Sikkim as an "associate state." The move was seen as "outright expansionism" and "colonialism," which roused "great indignation" among the Chinese government and people. India had "sent troops to invade and occupy Sikkim" in a "provocation to the justice-upholding peoples of the world and a challenge to the historical trend of national independence." "The Chinese Government solemnly states that it absolutely does not recognize India's illegal annexation of Sikkim and that it firmly supports the people of Sikkim in their just struggle for national independence and sovereignty and against Indian expansionism." The statement continued:

Expansionists never come to a good end. The Indian Government . . . must not think that it can enslave a nation and annex a state without getting due punishment. The crime of the Indian government's annexation of Sikkim is bound to arouse the Sikkimese people and the people of the whole world, including the Indian people, to even stronger resistance. It can be said with certainty that the Indian Government, which starts with injuring others, will end up by ruining itself.[15]

In Das's view this "foreign support" encouraged the *chogyal* to attempt to use foreign influence to limit India's embrace of Sikkim. In March 1975, against Das's advice, the *chogyal* attended the coronation of Nepal's King Birendra in Kathmandu. While there, he met with Chinese and Pakistani representatives, seeking their support. He also gave a press conference in Kathmandu criticizing India's moves and challenging the legality of Sikkim's new status as an Indian territory. The meeting with Chinese and Pakistani representatives sealed the *chogyal*'s fate and provided the pretext India had been waiting for to move ahead with the full incorporation of Sikkim.[16] On April 10, 1975, Sikkim's assembly called for the *chogyal*'s removal and full merger with India. A referendum was quickly organized, resulting in overwhelming support for both moves. On April 29, 1975, Sikkim was incorporated into the Republic of India as a full state. Sikkim's monarchy was abolished, and the region became a state of India operating under the administrative and constitutional rules applicable to other Indian states. India's objective now became securing PRC recognition of this fait accompli.

CHINA'S VIEW OF SIKKIM

From China's perspective it enjoyed a long-standing, friendly, and indeed protective relation with Sikkim until that relation was destroyed by British colonialism in the nineteenth century. From China's perspective friendly relations between Sikkim and "China's Tibet" trace back to the eighth century A.D. During the mid-seventeenth century relations became much closer, when Sikkim's king adopted Tibetan-style Lamaist Buddhism and political institutions. Responding to a request by Sikkim's king, Tibetan authorities dispatched a group of aristocrats to settle in Sikkim, who eventually became an important part of Sikkim's ruling class. Sikkim's administrative system was reorganized along the lines of Tibet's, with monasteries being established. Relations between "China's Tibet" and Sikkim became still closer about 1700, when Sikkim became a tributary of Tibet. This took place under the pressure of Bhutanese aggression, indicating a geopolitical logic that brought Sikkim into alignment with "China's Tibet" for over a hundred years. Weak and wedged between more powerful Nepal and Bhutan, Sikkim looked to Lhasa, and behind Lhasa to Beijing, for support—at least in the modern Chinese view of history. Bhutanese conquest of Sikkim shortly after 1700 prompted Sikkim's King

Chakdor to flee to Lhasa. There he became a secretary in the Potala palace and undertook study of the Dalai Lama's teachings. After a while the Tibetan government dispatched troops to return Chakdor to Sikkim. Bhutanese forces were expelled from Sikkim, although they later retook some Sikkimese territory. Following his recovery of Sikkim with Tibetan help, King Chakdor established Sikkim as a tributary of Tibet, with the appropriate rituals being performed.

After a Chinese administrative and military presence was established in Tibet in 1720, imperial China became Sikkim's protector. In 1770 Bhutanese forces again conquered Sikkim, forcing its king to flee once more to Lhasa. China's Emperor Qian Long sent an army to clear Bhutanese forces from Sikkim and force the release of Sikkimese imprisoned by Bhutan. Eighteen years later a similar action was again undertaken when Nepali forces occupied Sikkim. Once again, Sikkim's ruler fled to Tibet, where the Eighth Dalai Lama gave him an appanage to support himself. Qian Long again dispatched an army to assist Sikkim, this time as part of a broader effort to punish Nepal for its aggression against Tibet itself. Sikkimese forces attempted to cooperate with Qing armies but were too weak and were defeated by the Nepalese. In 1792, when Qing forces undertook their punitive expedition against Kathmandu, the Chinese commander, Fu Kangan, ordered Sikkimese forces to cooperate with the Chinese campaign. This time the Sikkimese king declined on grounds that his forces were too weak. This refusal reportedly angered Fu Kangan, who then refused a Sikkimese request to liberate Sikkimese territory. This refusal led to the alienation of Sikkim from China, laying the basis for imperial Britain's later relation with Sikkim.[17]

The PRC denounced India's 1949 and 1950 treaties establishing special relations with Sikkim and Bhutan, but more pressing problems soon diverted Beijing's attentions elsewhere. Latent disagreements over the status of Sikkim and Bhutan remained dormant during the mid-1950s but reemerged with the Sino-Indian boundary dispute. In his 1959 correspondence with Zhou Enlai over the boundary issue, Nehru had advanced propositions regarding the location of the boundary between Tibet and Sikkim. In his September 8, 1959, reply to Nehru, Zhou Enlai rejected them, saying: "In your Excellency's letter, you also referred to the boundary between China and Sikkim. Like the boundary between China and Bhutan, this question does not fall within the scope of our present discussions."[18] In other words, Beijing would not talk to New Delhi about China's borders with Sikkim and Bhutan but only with the governments of those two countries. Since 1959 China has insisted that Sikkim and Bhutan are fully independent, sovereign countries and that Indian actions to the contrary, limiting or even abolishing their sovereignty, are unjust, hegemonist actions that China will not recognize.

Beijing has consistently followed a policy of nonrecognition regarding India's annexation of Sikkim. An annual almanac published by China's Foreign Ministry long carried the same one-line entry under the heading "China's relations with Sikkim": "The Chinese government does not recognize India's illegal annexation of Sikkim."[19] At the time of this writing, maps published in China continue to show the line between Sikkim and India as an international boundary. India for its part periodically protests Chinese assertions that Sikkim is an independent country. Beijing typically rejects these protests, saying that China's position on Sikkim is well-known.

While insisting on keeping its position on Sikkim on the record, Beijing has tried to otherwise minimize that issue as a source of discord in Indian-Chinese relations. In a discussion with an Indian member of parliament in April 1981, Deng Xiaoping said that, while China was "thoroughly disappointed" by India's annexation of Sikkim, it would not make an issue of it in bilateral relations.[20] Deng's statement came during a push to improve relations with India; in the same talk Deng revived the idea of a "package deal" solution to the territorial question and referred to India as the "big brother" of the subcontinent. Deng's pairing of Sikkim with a package deal territorial settlement may not be coincidental. One authoritative Chinese analyst suggested to me in 1993 that China might be willing to recognize Sikkim as part of India and conclude a boundary treaty *with India* specifying the Sikkim-Tibet border as part of a general territorial settlement. Sikkim, in other words, would be a bargaining chip. Periodic Chinese assertions of its nonrecognition of India's annexation keep the value of that chip somewhat higher.

As India and China worked to find a way of improving relations in the late 1990s, India insisted that Beijing accept that Sikkim is part of India. In his parliamentary briefing on Jiang Zemin's November 1996 visit to India, for instance, India's minister of external affairs said he told Jiang that Sikkim is an integral part of India and that India would expect "early Chinese recognition of this reality."[21] In his introduction to a 1996 volume of proceedings of a high-level Chinese and Indian conference on bilateral relations, the director of India's Institute for Defense Studies and Analysis, Jasjit Singh, noted that "India treats Tibet and Taiwan as parts of China. China is, however, yet to fully reconcile to the fact that Sikkim is an integral part of India."[22]

THE EVOLUTION OF INDIA'S SPECIAL RELATION WITH BHUTAN

The treaty establishing Bhutan as a protectorate of India was signed on August 8, 1949, based on an earlier Anglo-Bhutanese treaty of 1910. Article 2 of the English-language text of the 1949 treaty provided that "Bhutan agrees to be guided by the advice of India" in the conduct of its foreign relations, while India undertook not to interfere in any way in Bhutan's conduct of its internal affairs.[23] There were discrepancies between the English and Bhutanese texts of the treaty, however, and the treaty did not specify which version was the authoritative one. Thus, the two sides disputed whether under Article 2 Bhutan had obligated itself to *be guided by* Indian advice (as New Delhi insisted) or merely to *seek and consider* Indian advice (as Thimpu insisted). After several decades of disagreement over this core issue, in the mid-1980s India finally agreed to accept Thimpu's interpretation.[24]

A second foundation of Indian policy toward Bhutan—and the major factor distinguishing it from India's approach to Sikkim—was support for Bhutanese independence. This principle was laid down in 1958, when Nehru made the first official Indian reference to Bhutan's "independence." The Indian leader carefully linked that affirmation with Indian-Bhutanese security cooperation: "Our only wish is that you should remain an independent country, choosing your own way of life and taking the path of progress, according to your will. At the same time, we two should live with mutual goodwill. We are members of the same Himalayan family and should live as friendly neighbors, helping each other. Freedom of both Bhutan and India should be safeguarded so that none from outside can do harm to it."[25]

Nehru's statement, and Indian policy, were carefully balanced. His country's support for Bhutan's independence was linked to Bhutan's cooperation with India in dealing with security challenges. India wanted Bhutan to remain an independent country but felt that India and Bhutan should also "help each other" and "safeguard" the freedom of both countries. There was an implicit quid pro quo between Indian respect for Bhutan's independence and Bhutan's sincere security cooperation with India.

Bhutan has felt more comfortable in its special relation with India than have either Nepal or Sikkim. Unlike Nepal, Bhutan has never attempted to play its two giant neighbors against each other. Ethnic factors and fear that China might someday claim Bhutan on the basis of common ethnicity also play a role. Being ethnically and culturally very close to Tibet, the Bhutanese were shocked by China's brutal war against Tibet's Lamaist institutions. A wave of anti-Chinese sentiment swept across Bhutan as Chinese repression and destruction of Tibetan Buddhist institutions began to unfold in 1959. Word of Chinese atrocities was carried to Bhutan by Tibetan refugees. The presence of these refugees became a major problem for Bhutan's government and a significant factor drawing Bhutan into the Sino-Indian rivalry.[26] Because of Bhutan's small size, Thimpu has recognized the futility and great danger of trampling on India's fears of China. Bhutan's leaders watched closely

Nepal's and Sikkim's efforts to "play the Chinese card." In the case of Nepal that policy led to a devastating embargo. In the case of Sikkim it led to Indian annexation. Bhutan's rulers concluded that they could do no better. India also gave Bhutan a fairly loose rein, granting it substantial economic assistance plus gradual, carefully limited, participation in international politics.

Beijing's objective has been to draw Bhutan away from its special relation with India, and it has pursued this goal with remarkable consistency from 1959 to the present day. Several policies have served this objective. One was its refusal to accept India's right to handle Bhutan's external relations. Another was its creation of incentives for Thimpu to deal directly and bilaterally with Beijing. A third was persuading New Delhi that PRC-ROI rapprochement would be served by opening the way to Sino-Bhutanese relations. Challenging India's special relation with Bhutan was part of this. By denouncing the 1949 treaty as an "unequal treaty" and Indian efforts to restrict Bhutan's foreign contacts as examples of "expansionism" and "hegemonism," China appealed to Bhutanese nationalism and world opinion. India was thus pressured to prove that it was not a hegemonist, while some Indians were convinced that, if India wanted friendship with China, it should not block normal state-to-state relations between China and Bhutan. The counterpart of these denunciations of Indian policy was a carefully proper Chinese approach to Bhutan. China never called for revolution in Bhutan, supported Bhutanese dissidents, or attempted to manipulate the Tibetan refugee community in Bhutan to create disorder. In their interactions with Bhutanese leaders Chinese officials constantly reiterated China's policy of noninterference in Bhutan's internal affairs and respect for its existing monarchical institutions. The point was to contrast India's big-power "bullying" and "interference" with China's scrupulous adherence to the Five Principles of Peaceful Coexistence.

From 1959 to 1984 New Delhi blocked direct contacts between Beijing and Thimpu. In 1959, shortly after the Sino-Bhutan border issue first arose, Bhutan had communicated directly to Beijing a protest regarding boundary alignments shown on Chinese maps. India swiftly intervened and charged Bhutan with thereby violating the 1949 treaty. India, New Delhi said, would henceforth make representations to Beijing on Bhutan's behalf.[27] As Nehru explained, "The Government of India is the only competent authority to take up with other governments matters concerning Bhutan's external relations. As such, if any rectification was to be made regarding their boundary it must be discussed along with the boundary of India."[28] Indian representatives subsequently made representations to Beijing on Bhutan's behalf regarding the Sino-Bhutanese border, citing Article 2 of the 1949 treaty as the basis for doing this. As noted in the earlier discussion of Sikkim, Zhou explicitly rejected

India's right to speak on behalf of either Bhutan or Sikkim. China was quite
willing to negotiate an equitable solution to the boundary problem directly
with the Bhutanese government itself but would not do so with the Indian
government. When the Indian Foreign Ministry tried to protest Chinese maps
showing wide areas of what New Delhi and Thimpu believed was Bhutanese
soil as Chinese, the Chinese chargé in New Delhi refused to listen to the protest.
India had no right to make representations on Bhutan's behalf.[29] Beijing also
indicated in 1959 its willingness to establish diplomatic relations and extend
economic assistance to Bhutan.

Confronted by Beijing's explicit rejection of India's claims to speak for
Bhutan, New Delhi moved to strengthen India's position in and over
Bhutan. In August 1959 Nehru informed the Lok Sabha that India was committed to safeguarding the territorial integrity of Bhutan. The 1949 treaty
had contained no such undertaking. The Indian Planning Commission also
drafted a long-term development plan for Bhutan which was translated into
Bhutan's First Five-Year Plan in 1960. India financed its entire cost, as it did
again with Bhutan's Second Five-Year Plan. An Indian Army Training
Team began advising and training the small Bhutanese army. Senior Indian
administrators were assigned to advise higher organs of the Bhutanese government and to perform critical tasks at lower and mid-levels. In the late
1960s there were, according to B. S. Das, about twenty senior Indian advisors and perhaps two hundred Indians serving at the mid- and lower levels
of Bhutanese administration.[30]

As noted earlier, the bloody Chinese repression in Tibet after March 1959
made the royal court and the people of Bhutan more comfortable with Indian
protection. At the same time, however, the rapid expansion of Indian
influence in Bhutan led to fears that India might swallow up the small state.
Bhutan saw membership in international organizations as a way of preventing this from happening. Bhutan's only foreign mission was then in New Delhi.

In 1960 Thimpu informed India of its desire to join the United Nations,
but New Delhi evaded the request for a decade. New Delhi advised Bhutan
against entering into diplomatic relations with other foreign powers, as the
costs would be too great.[31] Nehru did agree, however, to facilitate a slow expansion of Bhutan's international ties. India's support for Bhutan's entry into
the society of independent states was implicit in the India-Bhutan understanding worked out in 1958. Yet, given Beijing's desire for "normal" diplomatic relations with Bhutan, allowing Bhutan to progress down this path
carried dangers for India. Normal political and economic ties between China
and Bhutan would erode India's special relation with Bhutan. Yet to reject

Thimpu's request risked fostering Bhutanese resentment of India. The result of these contradictory impulses was an Indian policy of a very slow, deliberate, and, it was hoped, Indian-controlled process of expansion of Bhutan's international status as a sovereign state. As of the early twenty-first century, that expansion did not encompass Bhutanese diplomatic ties with China or with India's other nemesis, Pakistan.

In 1961 India sponsored Bhutan's first membership in an intergovernmental organization, the Colombo Plan. By 1964 some Bhutanese leaders believed that more forceful assertions of independence were necessary to prevent their country from being swallowed up by India. Membership in the United Nations, an assembly of recognized independent, sovereign states, would be the best guarantee against Indian absorption. Moreover, links with China, some disgruntled officers and courtiers felt, might prevent overdependence on India. These sentiments apparently proceeded to discussions of a coup d'état. When New Delhi learned of the discussions, it informed King Jigme Dorji Wangchuk that he would have India's support if he needed it to suppress a revolt. No coup d'état attempt materialized.[32]

Indian leaders were divided about how to best secure India's crucial interests in Bhutan. Outspoken voices in the Ministry of External Affairs believed that India should treat Bhutan more or less as it did Sikkim and insist on controlling all aspects of Bhutan's foreign relations. Others believed that Bhutan should be granted far greater autonomy and allowed to conduct a range of foreign relations—except where Indian security interests were affected. Supporters of this latter position, such as Das, believed that India had many instruments it could use to protect its vital interests in Bhutan regardless of UN membership. UN membership would not block India from using those instruments, if necessary. Conversely, if India failed to use its power to defend its vital interests in Bhutan, it would not be because of Bhutan's membership in the United Nations. Excluding China was New Delhi's top, but not only, concern regarding Bhutan. Indian officials were suspicious of virtually any third country presence there. They suspected, for example, that the U.S. Central Intelligence Agency wanted to use Bhutan as a base of operations against Tibet and that West European and Japanese diplomats sought to undermine Indian influence in Bhutan.[33]

In 1966 a formal Bhutanese request for UN admission was placed before Indian prime minister Indira Gandhi. King Jigme urged her to accept the proposal by alluding to the possibility of a Chinese role in Bhutan if the request was refused. Indira Gandhi traveled to Thimpu in 1968 to discuss the UN issue with King Jigme. While there, she reaffirmed her father's 1958 commitment to Bhutan's independence and agreed to eventual Bhutanese entry into the United Nations while also being careful to state that she considered the 1949 treaty to remain the basis of the Indian-Bhutanese relation. She also believed that considerable India-assisted preparatory work was necessary before Bhutan could actually enter the United Nations. King Jigme agreed with Gandhi's proposals and was delighted to have secured Indian support for Bhutan's entry into the United Nations. When Bhutan finally entered the General Assembly in February 1971, India sponsored its petition for membership, and its representative welcomed Bhutan's entry as "a final manifestation of Bhutan's independent stature and nationhood."[34]

With entry into the United Nations, Thimpu persuaded New Delhi that the two states should transform each other's representatives and offices in their respective capitals into "ambassadors" and "embassies." Bhutan's relations with India thus took a further step toward normalcy. Bhutan's first diplomatic relations with a country other than India were with Bangladesh. This was done in a carefully engineered fashion without India's prior consent but under conditions in which India found it hard to object. As India moved toward confrontation and ultimately war with Pakistan in 1971, King Jigme gave India extremely enthusiastic support. The very day the war began, the king sent a message to Indira Gandhi declaring that, "till the threat to India is removed, I consider India and Bhutan as one country and one nation having common ends and interests." The day after India recognized the new state of Bangladesh, Bhutan did the same—without prior consultation with India. In the view of B. S. Das, India's ambassador to Bhutan at the time, Thimpu had maneuvered carefully to be able to accomplish this precedent successfully: "By lending full support to India at a crucial time, Bhutan precluded a possibility of Indian resistance to closer links with Bangladesh."[35]

India's assimilation of Sikkim in 1973–75 coincided with the coronation of a new monarch in Bhutan, Jigme Singye Wangchuk, who was interested in more vigorous Bhutanese assertions of independence. Bhutan requested a gradual phase-out of Indian advisors. Its national assembly, the Tsongdu, called for revision of the 1949 treaty with India.[36] Bhutan also moved to open its first public links with China. This came in the form of an invitation to the chargé d'affaires of the PRC embassy in New Delhi to attend the June 2, 1974, coronation of King Jigme Singye Wangchuck. Beijing quickly agreed and even expressed a willingness to send a higher-ranking representative, Dong Biwu, the acting president of the PRC. India was dismayed by the invitation, fearing that Bhutan would follow Nepal's lead in using China to dilute its "special relation" with India. New Delhi conveyed its concerns to Thimpu. King Jigme refused to disinvite his Chinese guest, though he did decline the offer of more prominent Chinese representation. The PRC was represented at the coronation by the chargé d'affaires of its embassy in New Delhi. This was the first Bhutanese public reception of a Chinese official since 1908.[37] China now had a foot in Bhutan's door.

Beijing underlined the importance it placed on Sino-Bhutanese relations by sending a message from Premier Zhou Enlai and Dong Biwu congratulating Singye Wangchuk on his coronation, expressing the hope that "the traditional friendship between the peoples of China and Bhutan develop daily," and wishing Bhutan "new successes in safeguarding national independence and her national construction." At a press conference shortly after his coronation King Jigme Singye said that what Bhutan needed most was "self-reliance and preservation of sovereignty and independence." Regarding Sino-Bhutanese relations, the king said that, while some problems existed regarding the boundary, relations had "always been peaceful."[38] According to Xinhua's account, Bhutan's foreign minister said that the Bhutanese people were very happy that China's representative could attend the coronation ceremony and would have been quite disappointed had he not come. With his coronation King Jigme Singye clearly signaled his intention of developing ties with China, perhaps even in spite of Indian objections. New Delhi was dismayed about the directions Bhutanese policy was taking.

China's participation in the Bhutanese coronation was followed by India's annexation of Sikkim. This move created considerable apprehension in Thimpu, and King Jigme Singye traveled to New Delhi for talks with Indira Gandhi. A meeting of minds was reached, the 1958 compromise was reaffirmed, and each side emerged with its chief goals secured. India would respect Bhutan's independence, and Bhutan would respect India's security concerns.[39] The leaders of the Janata government, who had ousted Indira Gandhi in March 1977 and held power until January 1980, lacked the "rapport" with Bhutan's new king which Mrs. Gandhi had enjoyed. Thimpu soon resumed asserting its independence in ways contrary to India's wishes. The issues involved were minor, but they established the principle that Bhutan could act internationally independent of India's guidance. In 1978 Bhutan opened its first diplomatic mission outside of India—in Bangladesh. The fact that Thimpu did not feel obliged to consult with India in advance caused concern in New Delhi.[40] The next year Bhutan began to openly differ with India in international fora. At the sixth NAM conference in Havana in September 1979, Bhutan's representative strongly condemned Vietnam's intervention in Cambodia, while India took a much more benign approach to the action. When the Cambodian issue came before the UN General Assembly, Bhutan voted in favor of seating the China/U.S.-supported Democratic Kampuchea regime and against an Indian-proposed amendment that would have left vacant Cambodia's UN seat. The later action went too far, and an Indian representative conveyed to King Jigme Singye that India believed Bhutan's action represented a violation of the 1949 treaty. The Bhutanese monarch rejected the charge, insisting that India's role under the 1949 treaty was merely advisory. He also wondered aloud whether the 1949 treaty might need "updating."

During Indira Gandhi's election campaign to return to power in January 1980, she attacked the Janata Party's handling of relations with Bhutan as a demonstration of the party's weakness. A firmer Indian approach prevailed after Gandhi returned to power. In February 1980 King Jigme Singye traveled to New Delhi to reassure India's new prime minister, Mrs. Gandhi, disavowing any intention by Bhutan of seeking a revision of the 1949 treaty but also asserting that, on matters affecting Bhutan's interests, Bhutan must make the final decision. "One can have sincere and good relations if both countries support each other's aspirations and feelings," Jigme told Gandhi.[41] The two leaders also discussed Bhutan's relations with China.

Throughout the 1960s and 1970s Beijing used pressure on Bhutan's borders as a way of giving Thimpu and New Delhi reason to desire a settlement, or even merely clarification, of the Sino-Bhutanese border dispute. There was considerable disagreement between Chinese and Bhutanese/Indian maps regarding the location of the Sino-Bhutanese border. Chinese intrusions into these disputed areas began in 1962 and continued off and on until the mid-1980s, when bilateral PRC-Bhutan talks began. Sometimes the intrusions came in the form of PLA patrols. More often, they took the form of armed Tibetan herdsmen driving their animals into areas of Bhutan and refusing to leave when challenged. Sometimes they set up permanent or semi-permanent camps. Occasionally, these "grazer intrusions" were fairly extensive—those, for example, in 1967, 1979, and 1983.[42] Beijing also stationed several divisions of the PLA on Bhutan's borders. The continuing tension generated by these intrusions led Thimpu to fear that Bhutan would be dragged into any Sino-Indian clash and to desire talks with Beijing which might prevent such an outcome. New Delhi shared Thimpu's interest in reducing border tension. Given Beijing's refusal to discuss the issue with New Delhi, the only solution seemed to be direct, bilateral talks between Beijing and Thimpu.

During the 1970s India and Bhutan jointly and fully prepared for talks with China. In 1971 New Delhi and Thimpu undertook a joint documentary study of the PRC-Bhutan border. The next year a joint survey of the border was conducted. This preparatory work led to the formation of a Bhutan Boundary Commission and clarification of a Bhutanese position on the border. On the basis of this—plus a common Indian-Bhutanese understanding about

Indian-Bhutanese-Chinese relations—Indira Gandhi approved Bhutanese acceptance of Beijing's long-standing offer for direct, bilateral Sino-Bhutanese border talks. In 1979 an especially large-scale grazer intrusion occurred. Jigme Singye and Gandhi discussed their response during their 1980 meeting. Mrs. Gandhi was also interested in improving relations with Beijing—a desire that would lead to resumption of high-level Sino-Indian exchanges the next year. The Bhutanese embassy in New Delhi delivered a note to the Chinese chargé in 1981 proposing bilateral talks. Beijing quickly agreed,[43] though it would be three years before the first meeting took place. Early in 1982 *Renmin ribao* condemned India's efforts to continue its special relation with Bhutan under the 1949 treaty. According to the CCP newspaper, it was an "unequal treaty" that violated Bhutan's sovereignty. Bhutan wished to talk directly with China, and for New Delhi to prevent it from doing so would cast India into a "self-contradictory situation."[44] Apparently, Beijing was pressing India at their bilateral talks to permit the scheduled Sino-Bhutanese talks to move forward. Beijing's message was that permitting direct Sino-Bhutanese talks would allow Sino-Indian friendship to develop, while preventing them represented an act of Indian hostility toward China.

Chinese lobbying eventually overcame Indian resistance to direct Bhutan-Chinese talks. The first round of Bhutan-Chinese talks took place in Beijing in April 1984. This was the first Bhutanese delegation to visit China in a very long time, perhaps ever. A second round of talks was held a year later in Thimpu. Several months before the Chinese delegation arrived, King Jigme Singye reassured Indian leaders on Bhutan-China relations, saying, "At no point . . . in history has the relationship between India and Bhutan been as good as it is today." "There is complete understanding and trust on all issues of mutual concern and interest." The king also again disclaimed any quarrel with the 1949 treaty. That treaty, he said, had never been a constraint on Bhutan nor had it ever been invoked by India.[45] At a press conference three months later Bhutan's foreign minister affirmed that friendship with India was the cornerstone of Bhutan's foreign policy and that Bhutan was fully satisfied with the 1949 treaty, since it had never stood in the way of fulfilling Bhutan's national aspirations. Moreover, Bhutan had no plans to establish diplomatic relations with China. Be that as it may, Sino-Bhutan relations gradually expanded through the new venue of the border talks.

The Sino-Bhutan border talks continued for the next fifteen years. At the turn of the century there had been twelve rounds of talks, the last in 1998. The talks succeeded in substantially reducing the area in dispute along the border. They also became a regular venue for the conduct of bilateral PRC-Bhutan relations. They provided a mechanism for regular exchange of visits by fairly high-level officials and for the exchange of views on issues of common concern.[46] As such, the talks provide a mechanism for conduct of de facto relations, one that has been approved by New Delhi and to which, therefore, India cannot reasonably object. Slow, incremental development of relations with China have thus been paralleled by reassurances to India.

Prior to the beginning of talks in 1984, comments by Beijing suggested that the Sino-Bhutanese border problem would be relatively easy to settle. As the talks dragged on year after year without result, Indians began to suspect that Beijing would agree to such a settlement only in the context of the establishment of Sino-Bhutanese diplomatic relations. When the talks began, in 1984, Beijing proposed they be conducted on the basis of full diplomatic and trade relations. Bhutan declined, but Beijing repeatedly raised this proposal at subsequent meetings.[47] As of mid-1999, Bhutan had diplomatic ties with twenty-three countries and maintained embassies in five of those countries. China was not among them.

Beijing's obstinate refusal to accept New Delhi's right to speak for Bhutan and its constant pressure on Bhutan's border eventually paid off. New Delhi was finally compelled to accept direct Bhutan-PRC talks. The Sino-Bhutanese border issue was also delinked from the Bhutan-Indian border problem, and India was denied a direct voice (though not, of course, an important indirect voice) in the Beijing-Thimpu talks. Thimpu has gradually established its right to deal with international relations independent of Indian advice. Bhutan has thus far exercised this autonomy only on issues relatively unimportant to India and not on core issues touching on Bhutan's links with China. Still, the precedent has been established. If the future sees small moves to expand PRC-Bhutan relations against or without India's advice, New Delhi faces a dilemma. If New Delhi vetoes such moves, it risks rousing Bhutanese resentment. If it accedes, each increment will lessen the taboo on Sino-Bhutanese ties and put that relationship on a par with the Indian-Bhutanese relationship.

Diplomatic ties could well lead to establishment of a permanent Chinese presence in Thimpu. Chinese economic assistance and advisory missions might follow. Definitively settling the Sino-Bhutanese border issue combined with normalizing PRC-Bhutan relations and the growth of Sino-Bhutanese amity could also create pressure to withdraw the Indian military advisory and training mission from Bhutan. If trade links were reopened and roads linking Bhutan and Tibet built, Chinese economic influence could grow. Prior to Thimpu's sealing of the border in 1960, Bhutan's economy was oriented toward Tibet. Normalization of diplomatic relations and trade agreements and expanding the transportation infrastructure between Bhutan and Tibet could well move Bhutan toward that traditional economic orientation. As these trends progress, India's special relation would Bhutan would evaporate. Indian fears were given voice in the mid-1990s by one of its most prominent analysts of India-China relations:

> For the moment, China plays no role in Bhutan and disclaims any aspiration to do more than establish a diplomatic mission and "have good relations with an important, though small neighbor." Should China succeed or even attempt to create a relationship with Bhutan analogous to the one it has projected in Bangladesh, Nepal, Sri Lanka over the years . . . it will be the result of failures in the Indian polity and economy too hideous to contemplate.[48]

New Delhi's problem is that Sino-Indian friendship can evaporate as easily as decisions are made in Beijing. China's presence in Bhutan would be much more difficult to roll back and could probably be accomplished only by exercise of substantial Indian power. Once China is permitted to establish an embassy in Thimpu, dispatch aid teams, or open trade routes, those things can be reversed only at great cost to India. China would almost certainly defend its gains, though the extent to which it would do so would depend on many contingent factors. Thimpu would be reluctant to be crushed by its two giant neighbors and could well urge New Delhi to acquiesce to China's gains.

It is worth reiterating that China's objective is not to bring Bhutan into its own sphere of influence or to establish some sort of Chinese special or security relation with Bhutan. It is enough, rather, to bring about the dissolution of India's special relation with Bhutan, slowly and cautiously. India holds the same geographic trump card with Bhutan that it holds with Nepal. By cutting or restricting lines of communication through Indian territory, New Delhi can cripple the economy of Bhutan.

Before leaving the topic of Bhutan, there is a final point that needs to be made regarding the geopolitical connections between that region and - Arunachal Pradesh. If India were to cede even a small slice of territory in the direction of Dawang, it would place Bhutan between two Chinese salients—the Chumbi Valley on one side and a "Dawang salient" on the other—rendering any Indian forces assigned to Bhutan's defense in danger of being outflanked and isolated. This would diminish the defensibility of Bhutan and further complicate the problem India faces in defending its northeast.

THE HIMALAYAN KINGDOMS REVISITED

Taken together, and placed in the context of their particular location and terrain, the status of Nepal, Sikkim, and Bhutan are highly significant. The political-military regime regulating the three areas is a significant component in the overall correlation of forces between India and China. The existing political-military regime was largely established by India, serves India's basic security objectives, and has been upheld by the regular exercise of Indian power and influence. China has never accepted, and still does not accept, the existing regime regulating these areas and has regularly used its influence to challenge the existing status quo. The only instances in which China used or seems to have been ready to use coercive military force to alter this established regime were in October 1962, when, Chen Yi's comments suggest, Beijing was ready to use Nepal as a casus belli for its upcoming war with India, and in the 1967 clashes on the Sikkim border. The circumstances surrounding Chinese calculations in these two instances (especially the 1967 clashes) are far too murky to reach conclusions in this regard, however, and we must conclude that China has generally confined itself to using noncoercive influence to alter the established regime. Yet, while China has confined its challenges to the Indian-upheld regime to purely political means, it is also clear that Beijing is deeply unhappy with that regime. It feels that it is unjust, hegemonist, and fundamentally unfair to China and to the nations and peoples of Nepal, Sikkim, and Bhutan. It has consistently sought to alter that regime fundamentally.

From the Indian perspective China's approach is difficult to understand. China has taken for itself the largest buffer, the vast area of Tibet, destroying Tibet's culture in the process and over persistent Indian protests. India desires for itself a much smaller buffer in the three Himalayan kingdoms and does not seek to alter the traditional cultures of those areas. Yet Beijing denounces this as unacceptable hegemonism. Having consolidated its hold over Tibet, China now seeks to erode India's special position in the Himalayas. This, in any case, is the Indian perspective.

7 / The Sino-Pakistani Entente Cordiale

THE BASIS OF THE ENTENTE

There is a consensus among analysts who have studied the Sino-Pakistani relation that this partnership has consistently been of a truly special character.[1] Since almost the earliest days of the PRC, Chinese policy toward Pakistan has been based upon realistic power calculations deriving from extant or potential conflicts between China and India. Because of its understanding of the utility of a partnership with Pakistan in dealing with India, Beijing has been consistently willing to set aside ideological considerations, minimize or ignore clashes between Chinese and Pakistani policies in many secondary areas, provide Pakistan with a relatively high level and wide array of support, and restrain in truly exceptional ways the passions arising from Chinese domestic political strife. In the words of S. M. Burke, China's policy toward Pakistan is "an object lesson in how to attain long-term national goals by calm calculation, forbearance, and diplomatic skill."[2]

China's cooperative relation with Pakistan is arguably *the most* stable and durable element of China's foreign relations. China's partnerships with other countries, both large (the USSR and the United States) and small (Albania, Vietnam, Algeria, and North Korea) have waxed and then waned into coldly proper relations at best. China's partnership with Pakistan, however, emerged during the mid-1950s, when China was trying to make friends with all developing countries, deepened during the radical anti-imperialist phase of Chinese foreign policy in the early 1960s, persisted unmolested under the direct protection of Mao Zedong during the upheaval of the Cultural Revolution, proved useful during the anti–Soviet hegemony phase of Chinese

policy in the 1970s and 1980s, and continued with vitality after the dissolution of the USSR and the end of the Cold War. The Sino-Pakistani entente
can be traced back to the heyday of Sino-Indian amity in the mid-1950s; it
deepened during the long period of Sino-Indian hostility and has continued
as China and India restored a level of comity during the 1990s. It is, indeed,
a remarkably durable relationship.

At the foundation of the stable Sino-Pakistani entente is the utility of that
association to both its principals in dealing with India. Militarily, a strategic
partnership between China and Pakistan presents India with a two-front threat
in the event of a confrontation with either. A strong Pakistan, independent
of and hostile to India, severely constrains India's ability to concentrate its
forces against China in the event of a China-India war. Conversely, a militarily potent China aligned with Pakistan constrains India's ability to concentrate its forces against Pakistan in the event of war. Indian security
planners must assume that China may enter a major Indian-Pakistani war,
especially one in which India appears likely to win a decisive victory over
Pakistan. Similarly, they must assume that, should a major war develop
between China and India, Pakistan would seize the opportunity to (at a minimum) solve definitively the Kashmir problem. Even if China or Pakistan does
not actually enter the conflict, their strength, proximity to India, and close
partnership, supplemented perhaps by ominous wartime signals and maneuvers, require India to commit a substantial portion of its strength to stand
guard against potential entry.

China derives a second, far more amorphous but perhaps even more important, *political* advantage from the existence of India-Pakistan enmity. As long
as those two countries remain at loggerheads, foreign audiences automatically compare them with each other. China is left apart, in a separate category, either on a higher moral plane or in the category of a greater power.[3]
India's internecine feud with Pakistan pulls it down to Pakistan's level, to
China's benefit. Two cases nicely demonstrate the operation of this principle: the Bandung conference of 1955 and the international reaction to India's
nuclear tests of 1998.

At Bandung, Nehru and Menon went to that conference expecting to play
prominent, leading roles. A key reason why that did not occur was because
of repeated conflicts between Indian and Pakistani representatives. China was
then allowed to mediate—from a higher, uninvolved level. When India, China,
and Burma proposed agreement on the Five Principles of Peaceful Coexistence, for example, Pakistan's prime minister, Muhammad Ali Bogra,
immediately proposed adding two more principles that implicitly affirmed
Pakistan's alliances with the West and India's obligation to negotiate the

Kashmir issue with Pakistan. Nehru objected vehemently and argument ensued, leaving it to Zhou Enlai to propose a compromise between the two sides. This greatly facilitated China's effort to demonstrate its moderation and reasonableness. India was reduced from the level of high principle to intramural squabbles with its neighbor.

Regarding the 1998 nuclear tests, India's nuclearization was immediately placed in the context of its rivalry with Pakistan. The immediate concern of the international community was that Pakistan would follow suit leading to a nuclear arms race or, possibly, to an Indian-Pakistani "fourth round" of war with nuclear weapons being used. Had it not been for Pakistan, the response of the international community would probably have been quite different. In that case foreign opinion would probably have looked to China in the aftermath of India's 1998 tests. Indian statements about the Chinese threat, the PLA presence in Tibet, and so forth would have received far more attention and credence. That they did not is testament to Indian-Pakistani enmity. That enmity is India's albatross in its struggle for global eminence and equivalence with China.

Having boldly stated this geopolitical logic, I must immediately qualify it. First of all, there is far more to the Pakistan-China relationship than common hostility toward India. There are distinct Muslim and Middle Eastern aspects of that relationship. Karachi airport, for example, was in the early 1960s the first airport outside the Soviet bloc opened to PRC aircraft and in the early twenty-first century is the foreign airport most frequented by Chinese aircraft, serving as a transit point for Chinese air traffic to the Middle East, Africa, and Europe. China also benefits by having Pakistan host Chinese Muslims making the Haj to Mecca. Pakistan is an important customer for Chinese goods. In 1996 China-Pakistan trade totaled U.S.$964 million. This placed Pakistan in the mid-range of China's trading partners, far below the countries of East and Southeast Asia or the industrialized countries of the world but well above China's trade with a tier of small or poor countries.[4] But, while the Sino-Pakistan relation cannot accurately be reduced to common hostility vis-à-vis India, these common interests of the two countries are indeed the basis of the entente and key to understanding its remarkable durability. A second caveat is that one should not imagine that China is the cause of India-Pakistan enmity. That hostility arises out of far more fundamental and intractable causes. China merely recognizes this reality and profits from it in terms of policy. Chinese strategists and statesmen have recognized that they have an interest in keeping Pakistan strong and confident enough to remain independent of Indian domination and willing to challenge Indian moves in the South Asian region.

FORMATION OF THE SINO-PAKISTANI ENTENTE

Pakistan recognized the PRC on January 4, 1950, within a few days of India's doing so. From the very beginning Indian-Pakistan rivalry was a driving factor in Pakistan's relations with China. India and Pakistan were then locked in political conflict over Kashmir. During 1948 and 1949 the United Nations Security Council had adopted six resolutions dealing with Kashmir. The most important of these, from Pakistan's perspective, was Resolution 47, adopted in April 1948 and calling for resolution of the issue through a "free and impartial plebiscite" among the people of that disputed region. Pakistan's strategy for securing Kashmir then focused on the United Nations. If, as then seemed likely, the PRC was going to assume China's seat on the Security Council, Pakistan did not want that to happen with Beijing more favorably inclined toward India than toward Pakistan. Thus, once India decided to recognize the PRC, Pakistan quickly followed suit.

India established full ambassadorial relations with the PRC in April 1950, more than a year before Pakistan did so in May 1951. (Establishing ambassadorial relations is an act distinct from declaring recognition of a state.) The substantive issues conducted via ambassadorial links between New Delhi and Beijing were not particularly amicable, however, but fraught with conflicting interests and perspectives toward Tibet. During this time Beijing could not help but note Pakistan's complete disinterest in Tibet.[5] The deep hostility between India and Pakistan rooted in the event of Partition and its aftermath was, of course, well understood by all statesmen of the day, including those of China.

In 1954 Pakistan entered a military alliance with the United States, becoming a key link in the chain of containment around the Sino-Soviet bloc. Large-scale U.S. military assistance to Pakistan followed. Pakistan also inaugurated security links with Turkey, Iran, and Iraq, and joined with those countries to form the Western-supported Baghdad Pact. When the Southeast Asian Treaty Organization was formed to guarantee the Southeast Asian nations against communism after the 1954 Geneva conference, Pakistan joined it too. Pakistan thereby abandoned its earlier policies of nonalignment and became one of the major military partners of the United States. It also began voting in the United Nations in support of U.S. moves to keep the PRC out of that body. Chinese propaganda denounced Pakistan's moves toward alliance with the United States, but in terms that, in Anwar Syed's words, were "remarkable for their moderation."[6] The PRC, unlike the USSR, did not diplomatically protest Pakistan's acceptance of U.S. military aid under its various treaties.

An understanding between Chinese and Pakistani leaders was reached at the Bandung conference of April 1955. In two private meetings, Bogra assured Zhou Enlai that, although Pakistan was party to various military treaties, it was not against China and would not take part in any aggressive action launched by the United States against China. Bogra explained Pakistan's fear of India plus Pakistan's state of military unpreparedness and the consequent need to strengthen its defenses even if this was done via U.S. assistance. If the United States launched a war against China, Pakistan would not be involved in it, just as she was not involved in the Korean War. Three days later Zhou made Bogra's words public by reporting them to the Political Committee of the Bandung conference. Bogra's explanation, Zhou said, created "mutual understanding," "agreement and harmony amongst us in understanding each other on collective peace and cooperation." "I am sure the prime minister of Pakistan will have no objection to these views of mine," Zhou said. By making public Bogra's private statements to him, Zhou was testing the sincerity of those undertakings. The Pakistani leader rose to the test and publicly repeated his assurances to Zhou.[7]

The frank meeting of minds between Bogra and Zhou opened the way to broader relations over the next several years. Pakistan's prime minister, Huseyn Shaheed Suhrawardy, first visited China in October 1956 and Zhou Enlai reciprocated with a visit to Pakistan in December. The communiqué issued at the conclusion of the December visit announced that "divergences of views on many problems should not prevent the strengthening of friendship between the two countries" and "happily" noted that "there is no real conflict of interests between the two countries." Prime Minister Suhrawardy later told the parliament: "I feel perfectly certain that when the crucial time comes China will come to our assistance."[8] PRC Major General Geng Biao and Marshall He Long visited Pakistan in mid-1956 and returned to explain to Zhou Enlai the pivotal role of Kashmir in Indian-Pakistani relations. It would be best, Geng proposed, for China not to take sides in the Kashmir dispute, but to make friends with both India and Pakistan. Zhou agreed.[9] Again, this in spite of Pakistan's close military alliance with the United States. (Geng served as China's ambassador from 1956 to 1960.)

The deterioration of Chinese-Indian relations in 1959 prompted Pakistan's new leadership (led by president and former general Ayub Khan, who had come to power in a military coup d'état the previous year) to try a new tack toward solving the Kashmir question. Pakistan now began proposing that India and Pakistan jointly defend the subcontinent against external powers. The precondition of this "joint defense" was settlement of the Kashmir issue. China sent a note to Pakistan inquiring against whom Pakistan was proposing joint defense, but there was no propaganda condemning Pakistan's proposal. Nehru quickly (and perhaps unwisely) rejected it. Following this rejection, Ayub began working to improve ties with China. In October 1959 he proposed border negotiations with China. China did not reply until January 1961, however, and even then negotiations did not begin until February 1962.[10] In other words, China held off consolidating an entente with Pakistan until it became clear that India was unwilling to settle the territorial issue on terms acceptable to Beijing. China signaled this implicit warning to New Delhi, but Nehru was not dissuaded by this threat to "play the Pakistan card" from his policy of mobilizing increased pressure on China.[11] Once Chinese-Pakistan negotiations finally began, India protested China's willingness to negotiate regarding what India deemed Indian territory in Pakistan-occupied Kashmir. Beijing replied in May 1962 that it had never accepted the position that Kashmir was under Indian sovereignty.

THE 1962 HUMILIATION OF INDIA AND THE 1965 INDIAN-PAKISTANI WAR

There were links between the 1962 Sino-Indian war and the 1965 Indian-Pakistani war. By revealing India as weak and blundering, as militarily unprepared and incompetent, the 1962 war encouraged some Pakistani leaders to believe that India might respond indecisively to strong diplomatic or military pressure to liberate Kashmir.[12] It also encouraged some Pakistani leaders to believe that China, whose strength was obvious after its November 1962 victory, would support Pakistan in a conflict with India. Foreign Minister Ali Zulfiqar Bhutto, who was one of Pakistan's more ardent advocates of using the China card, told the National Assembly on July 17, 1963, for example:

> [If] India were in her frustration to turn her guns against Pakistan the international situation is such today that Pakistan would not be alone in that conflict. A conflict does not involve Pakistan alone. Attack from India on Pakistan today is no longer confined to the security and territorial integrity of Pakistan. An attack by India on Pakistan involves the territorial integrity and security of the largest state in Asia and, therefore this new element and this new factor which has been brought into the situation is a very important element and a very important factor.[13]

When Bhutto visited Washington a few months after making the above statement, he denied there was any definite understanding with China, but observed that "in case of another conflict the area's geopolitics might come into play." About the same time President Ayub said, "If we are attacked by

India, then that means India is on the move and wants to expand. We assume that other Asiatic powers, especially China, would take notice of that."[14] China apparently did nothing to discourage Pakistan's belief that it would assist Pakistan against India. In fact, Chinese leaders frequently stated China's support for Pakistan against India, while carefully qualifying and limiting the obligations assumed by China through such statements. On the critical issue of Kashmir, at the conclusion of a visit by Zhou Enlai to Pakistan in February 1964, the joint communiqué "expressed the hope that the Kashmir dispute would be resolved in accordance with the wishes of the people of Kashmir as pledged to them by India and Pakistan." China thereby aligned behind Pakistan on the critical Kashmir issue.

The initiation of American and British military aid programs to India within weeks of the 1962 war also had a substantial impact. Western military aid began just as India was discarding the antimilitary ethos that had dominated Congress Party thinking during the 1950s and was starting a substantial armaments program.[15] Pakistan resented and was alarmed by the prospect that Indian military power might grow substantially, nurtured by American technology and money. Pakistan felt that it was being penalized for being a loyal American ally. It had been Pakistan, not India, which had supported the American anticommunist effort since the mid-1950s, and yet now its objections were being ignored and India strengthened. Pakistani leaders were also certain that India's enhanced strength would be directed against Pakistan rather than against China. India was using the "China threat" to secure American military assistance against Pakistan. Indian diplomacy did very little to reassure Pakistan or alter Pakistani perceptions.

The establishment of an Indian-American military relation also expanded the parallel interests of China and Pakistan. China had a long-standing policy interest in reducing or eliminating the U.S. military presence along its periphery. Indeed, China was then involved in a protracted militarized confrontation with the United States over precisely such a presence in Indochina. A primary benefit of Indian nonalignment in the 1950s had been the exclusion of a U.S. military presence from India, and the establishment of such a presence after 1962 was a setback for China. From Beijing's perspective Pakistan's strength became a way to check and constrain a U.S.-linked India.

These new parallel Pakistani and Chinese interests were made clear during President Ayub's discussions with Zhou Enlai and PRC president Liu Shaoqi in Beijing in March 1965. Ayub reviewed for Zhou and Liu Pakistan's relations with the United States, expressing gratitude for American assistance but also his concern for U.S., and Soviet, military assistance to India. The United States, Ayub said, wanted "to make India into a counterforce to China, both economically and militarily." The United States was also trying to pressure Pakistan to drop its opposition to this policy, but Pakistan would stand up to U.S. pressure and remain true to its friendship with China. Zhou replied by assuring Ayub that, "if India commits aggression into Pakistan territory, China would definitely support Pakistan." The next day Ayub met with Mao Zedong in an atmosphere of extreme cordiality. "China and Pakistan could trust each other," Mao said, "as neither has the intention of pulling the rug [out from] under the feet of the other." The two leaders then discussed the road connections between Pakistan and China, and between Nepal and China. Mao left Ayub with these parting words: "We agree with you and we are not with [Indian prime minister] Shastri."[16]

While China and Pakistan had parallel interests regarding the Indian-American military link, Beijing did not pressure Pakistan to disassociate itself from Washington. The communiqué issued at the conclusion of Ayub's March 1965 state visit to China, for instance, said nothing about Vietnam—then the major foreign policy issue facing China. Beijing also suspended for the duration of Ayub's visit the huge public demonstrations against the U.S. bombing of North Vietnam so as not to embarrass China's Pakistani guests with their American friends. China was tolerant of Pakistan's need to retain U.S.—and later Soviet—support. This flexibility was testament to the importance of Pakistan to China's strategy for dealing with India.

The 1962 war also revived the Kashmir issue. Pakistan was dismayed that the United States was arming India without insisting on the settlement of the Kashmir issue as a precondition. A well-armed India was less likely to come to terms over the Kashmir issue, Pakistani leaders believed. In response to Pakistani pressure, U.S.-encouraged Indian-Pakistani talks over Kashmir began in December 1962. By the middle of the next year, however, it was apparent that no agreement would be reached in those talks. As it became apparent to Pakistan that Washington intended to arm India regardless of progress on Kashmir, Pakistan's desire to forge closer ties with China grew stronger. Pakistan's movement toward China increased the incentive for Washington to nudge India toward a settlement on Kashmir. In the event that this tack failed, closer Sino-Pakistan ties would create conditions for a different approach to the Kashmir problem, one which relied on combined Pakistan-China pressure.

CHINA AND THE 1965 INDIAN-PAKISTANI WAR

A cycle of escalating pressures between 1962 and 1964 carried Pakistan and India to the brink of their second war over Kashmir.[17] An arms race with both sides acquiring new, sophisticated weapons fed mutual fears and uncertainties. On the Pakistan side, U.S.-supplied Patton tanks were grouped into spearheads, which both Pakistani and Indian leaders believed might be able to smash through Indian defenses and race down the mere two hundred miles of the Grand Trunk road separating New Delhi from the Indian-Pakistani border. On the Indian side, an August 1962 deal with the Soviet Union led to production of supersonic MiG-21s. After the 1962 war American and British arms flowed into India. Again, both Indian and Pakistani leaders anticipated that these new weapons would have a significant impact on the military balance between the two countries. Indian and Pakistani passions on Kashmir also rose. India's 1962 debacle led to strong nationalist sentiments that typically translated into demands for tougher policies. Toward Kashmir that meant firm Indian rejection of Pakistani or American demands regarding that region, plus measures to integrate Indian-occupied Kashmir more fully into the Indian union. Those Indian moves created anger in both Pakistan and Indian Kashmir. This came on top of Pakistan's resentment at the American failure to insist on resolution of the Kashmir question as a precondition for arming India following the 1962 war. Finally, popular discontent within Indian Kashmir began to rise. It erupted into open, spontaneous revolt against Indian authorities in December 1963, when a sacred hair of the Prophet Mohammed was stolen from a shrine near Srinagar. In January 1964 Pakistan requested the Security Council reopen the Kashmir issue. The resulting diplomacy went nowhere.

In the early months of 1965 Pakistan's leaders considered and then in May adopted a plan to foment an anti-Indian uprising in Kashmir. Code-named Operation Gibraltar, the plan provided for training, arming, and equipping large numbers of Pakistanis, and infiltrating them into Indian Kashmir under the leadership of officers of the regular Pakistani army. Once in Indian Kashmir these "Kashmiri freedom fighters" were to attack communication and transportation infrastructure plus Indian administrative authority. When conditions were ripe, an urban insurrection would be staged in Srinagar and an interim Kashmiri authority independent of India established.[18]

While Pakistan's leaders were deliberating about Operation Gibraltar, they consulted extensively with Chinese leaders. While the content of these prewar discussions remains classified in both China and Pakistan, available evidence strongly suggests that they included discussions of Operation Gibraltar. As noted earlier, President Ayub visited China in March 1965 for talks with Zhou Enlai and President Liu Shaoqi. Foreign Minister and Vice Premier Chen Yi visited Pakistan in early April and again in early June for talks with Ayub and Foreign Minister Z. A. Bhutto. Zhou Enlai visited Pakistan briefly in April and again in June. During Ayub's March 1965 visit to China the two sides discussed Kashmir, and China strengthened its support for Pakistan's position by agreeing, in the communiqué issued at the conclusion of Ayub's visit, that the Kashmir issue *should* be resolved in accordance with the wishes of the Kashmiri people. The Chinese declaration of February 1964 had merely expressed the *hope* that the Kashmir dispute would be resolved in this fashion. Other Chinese rhetoric associated with Ayub's visit also indicated a firmer level of Chinese support. Speaking to Pakistani newsmen during Ayub's visit, Chen Yi said that "China would fight aggressors" because "if our friends are wiped out, how can we exist?" While such hints of support were carefully ambiguous, the emotional impact of Chinese support for Pakistan on the minds of Pakistan's leaders was considerable.[19] According to Pakistan's army commander General Mohammed Musa, during Zhou Enlai's early 1965 visit the Chinese premier discussed with President Ayub issues related to the operational conduct of the upcoming Operation Gibraltar.

A key assumption of Operation Gibraltar was that India would not respond to the insurgency in Kashmir with a conventional attack on Pakistan. Chinese support for Pakistan was understood to be an important factor deterring such an India response. In May 1965 Pakistan's foreign secretary informed a U.S. diplomat in a "private conversation" that, in the event India attacked East Pakistan in response to a conflict over Kashmir, "China would attack India."[20] According to G. W. Choudhury, during the March 1965 talks in Beijing, Zhou Enlai promised Ayub, "If India commits aggression into Pakistan territory, China would definitely support Pakistan." Zhou went on to explain how fear of Chinese involvement would lead the United States and Great Britain to prevent, or end quickly, an Indian-Pakistani war.[21] A written statement distributed by Zhou at the beginning of his two-day June visit to Pakistan called "the strengthening of friendship and cooperation" between China and Pakistan "a positive factor in the present international situation," while a *Renmin ribao* editorial marking Chen Yi's visit several days earlier declared that "the Government and people of China . . . have resolutely supported the just struggle of Pakistan to uphold its national dignity and oppose foreign pressure. . . . Increased friendship and cooperation between the two big Asian nations of China and Pakistan is of tremendous significance for . . . the defense of world peace."[22] China was apparently using its national strength to deter India from attacking Pakistan for supporting the "liberation" struggle in Kashmir. It is also interesting to note that China was then doing essentially the same thing for North Vietnam vis-à-vis the United States over Hanoi's support for the national liberation war in South Vietnam. Both North Vietnam and Pakistan were smaller countries and were bravely supporting "wars of national liberation" in neighboring areas. China was attempting to use its power to deter retaliation by the United States or India.

China also assisted Pakistan's implementation of Operation Gibraltar. According to Indian sources, Chinese instructors taught guerrilla warfare tactics in the training camps in Pakistani Kashmir. Chinese advisors also urged Pakistan to discard the British model of army organization and adopt a leaner, more flexible organizational structure—although it is unclear whether this advice was given before or during the war.[23] Chinese-manufactured non-military equipment (matches, flashlight batteries, incendiary materials, etc.) was found by Indian forces on infiltrators from Pakistani Kashmir.[24]

Striking similarities between Pakistan's Operation Gibraltar and the strategy Hanoi was then implementing in Vietnam raise important, if still unanswerable, questions about China's role in the conceptualization of Pakistan's war strategy. Infiltrators into Indian-occupied Kashmir were Kashmiris from Pakistani Kashmir, just as most of Hanoi's infiltrators into South Vietnam were (at least up to mid-1964) southerners "regrouped" to the north after the 1954 Geneva Convention. What was thus involved was a struggle of the Kashmiri and South Vietnamese people for national liberation. The Pakistani press often used the nomenclature of a "national liberation war" to analyze developments in Kashmir in 1965. Pakistan stood in support of the Kashmiri national liberation struggle, just as North Vietnam stood behind the national liberation struggle of the people of South Vietnam. In both cases, however, organizational and material aspects of that support was kept carefully clandestine. The regular military forces of both Pakistan and North Vietnam were to be kept largely in reserve, although elements of them were used to strengthen the "insurgency." And in both Kashmir and South Vietnam the political objective was the same: bringing to power an "independent" but pro-unification interim government. China was Hanoi's and Pakistan's intimate ally, providing substantial material plus political and military support to both. It thus seems likely that Mao Zedong saw both Kashmir and South Vietnam as areas in which China's revolutionary doctrine could be applied. The success of this application would refute the Soviet "revisionist" line in the international communist movement. And, once these wars of national liberation succeeded, China's southern borders would be more secure.

At the level of Indian perceptions there is little doubt that China played such a role. Indians were then and today generally remain fully convinced that China played an important role in developing Pakistan's war strategy. In the Indian view China not only gave general political sympathy and material aid to Rawalpindi's war plan but actively assisted in developing that plan.

Recent Chinese sources are remarkably quiet about China's diplomacy

before and during the 1965 war. The authoritative diplomatic history published by the Chinese Academy of Social Sciences in 1987, for example, says
nothing about the 1965 war.[25] Nor has this author been able to locate more
than the barest references in recent Chinese scholarly and autobiographical
literature to Chinese assistance to Pakistan before and during the 1965 war.
One of the few Chinese sources that touches, very briefly, on China's role in
the 1965 war states that China's support for Pakistan served two purposes. First,
it demonstrated China's position on the national liberation question by supporting the Kashmiri people's struggle for "national self-determination."
Second, it showed that China was working with Pakistan to oppose Indian
regional expansionism.[26] The reluctance of China's censors to permit discussion of China's 1965 support for Pakistan is in sharp contrast to the robust
Chinese literature that has emerged on China's aid to North Vietnam during the same period. All of this suggests that China's relations with Pakistan
in 1965 remain taboo and potentially embarrassing. The point seems to be
that China can be proud of its help to Third World countries fighting the
United States but had best not talk about helping Pakistan fight India.

China's view of the South Asian situation in 1965 was probably linked to
its analysis of the global anti-imperialist struggle, embodied in the September
1965 essay "Long Live the Victory of People's War," which offered a vision
of armed wars of national liberation proliferating throughout the Third World.
Those revolutionary wars would tie down and sap the military, economic,
and psychological strength of U.S. imperialism, thereby preventing it from
attacking the socialist countries, weakening the repressive onslaught that imperialism could launch against any one war of national liberation, and preparing conditions for the ultimate global collapse of imperialism. China's role
in this process was to provide support and encouragement. It could not substitute its own armed forces for those of another nation. Each nation had to
bear the burden of its own liberation. The primary war of national liberation supported by China in 1965 was in Vietnam. Another was in Kashmir
and was directed against the Indian "neocolonialist" regime.[27]

CCP editorials associated with Zhou's June 1965 visit to Pakistan squarely
placed the Sino-Pakistan entente and Pakistan's struggle in the context of the
global revolutionary struggle against imperialism. Pakistan had won many
victories "in the past few years in their tireless struggle to safeguard national
independence and sovereignty and oppose foreign pressure and threats." The
"situation is most favorable to revolutions in Asia and Africa." "The struggle against imperialist intervention and aggression and in defense of independence and sovereignty is being waged heroically and resolutely by the newly
emerging countries" and was "a mighty force combating imperialism and

defending world peace." U.S. aggression against "the people of South Vietnam" and North Vietnam was intensifying. But imperialism would be defeated. "The anti-imperialist struggle of the Asian and African peoples . . . remains indivisible. They continue to encourage and support each other," to tie down and deplete the strength of U.S. imperialism. "We are convinced that if Asian and African peoples remain united, support each other and persist in struggle, the defeat of the imperialist aggression headed by the United States is inevitable."[28] The CCP-controlled Hong Kong paper *Da gong bao* was more direct. Zhou's visit to Pakistan came, the paper said, while "the crest of the anti-imperialist revolutionary struggles in Asia, Africa, and Latin America is rising to a new high. . . . U.S. imperialism is being battered everywhere." This "unprecedented upsurge of the national liberation movement in Asia and Africa" made it imperative that the countries of the two continents "strengthen their unity, and support and help each other in their common struggle against imperialism, colonialism, and neo-colonialism."[29]

The logic of China's policy was this: India was a neocolonialist regime being built up by U.S. imperialism and the Soviet revisionists as a way of encircling China. The Indian reactionaries also refused to acknowledge the will of the Kashmiri people and tried to bully other countries in the region, including both China and Pakistan. Now the Pakistani "government and people" had resolved to "struggle" against Indian neocolonialism by supporting the Kashmiri people. China would render what support it could.

By August 1965 it became increasingly apparent that China's deterrent support for Pakistan might fail and that India would respond to Pakistan's support for the Kashmir uprising with a direct, conventional attack on Pakistan. On August 15 Indian forces seized strategic mountain positions near Kargil. Pakistan responded on September 1 with a limited thrust by an armored force to seize a position threatening India's main supply lines into the Vale of Kashmir. As the confrontation escalated toward conventional war, China weighed in to try to deter India. Foreign Minister Chen Yi stopped briefly in Karachi on his way to Africa on September 4 and warned that China "resolutely condemns" India for "violating the [Kashmir] cease-fire line and kindling and aggravating the conflict." China "firmly supports Pakistan's just action in hitting back at armed Indian provocations," Chen said. The next day a *Renmin ribao* "observer" unequivocally elaborated Pakistan's line that what was occurring in Kashmir was a spontaneous uprising of the people of Indian-occupied Kashmir against "the brutal rule and communal persecution by the Indian reactionaries." India was engaged in "wanton slaughter of the people of Kashmir," who, "pressed beyond the limits of endurance . . . have risen in revolt." The "root cause" of tension in "this part of Asia," the observer said, was India's "domineering attitude" toward all its neighbors. India's "chauvinist and expansionist" policies would never gain India anything good. "We would like to advise the Indian government to stop its domineering and . . . bullying its neighbor . . . and return to the Indian-Pakistan agreement to settle the Kashmir issue in accordance with the aspirations of the people of Kashmir."[30]

India was not deterred by Chinese warnings. On September 6 it unleashed major offensives toward Lahore and Sialkot in the Pakistan Punjab. With this the war became an all-out conventional conflict. The very next day the PRC government issued a statement condemning the Indian offensive as "naked aggression" constituting "a grave threat to peace in this part of Asia." The statement gave "firm support" to Pakistan in its "just struggle against aggression" and "solemnly warn[ed] the Indian government that it must bear responsibility for all the consequences of its criminal and extended aggression." "India's aggression against any one of its neighbors concerns all of its neighbors," the statement warned. In fact, ever since India's defeat in October 1962, it had never stopped "making intrusions and provocations along the Sino-Indian border." Indian forces were entrenched on Chinese territory on the Sino-Sikkim border in spite of "repeated warnings" by China. China was "now closely following the development of Indian acts of aggression and strengthening its defenses and heightening its alertness along its borders."[31]

The same day as China's statement, September 7, Zhou Enlai met with Pakistan's ambassador N. A. M. Raza to discuss the "question of India's expansion of its aggression against Pakistan."[32] Zhou promised Raza that "China would await further developments and would consider further steps as and when necessary." Zhou sought two assurances from Pakistan: that it would not submit to any Kashmiri solution favorable to India and that it would not submit to American, Soviet, or UN pressure for such a solution. Ayub cabled these assurances to Zhou, and the next day (September 8) Liu Shaoqi sent a letter to Ayub stating that China would respond to an Indian attack on East Pakistan not only in that area but also in the Himalayas.[33] The same day Ayub cabled these assurances to China, Pakistan launched a major counteroffensive against India's earlier attacks, throwing columns of Patton tanks down the Grand Trunk Road toward New Delhi. The main Pakistani armored forces went into action on September 10. Fighting was fierce. The intensification of fighting led the U.S. to suspend military assistance to both Pakistan and India, thus removing a major disincentive for Pakistan to want more help from China. Continued U.S. assistance was no longer at stake if China and Pakistan undertook closer military cooperation.

On September 9 Zhou ratcheted Chinese rhetoric up another notch. A "struggle between aggression and anti-aggression is unfolding beside China," he warned. The Indian aggressors had attacked first the people of Kashmir and then the people of Pakistan. "If peace is to be safeguarded, aggression must be opposed. . . . India's acts of aggression pose a threat to peace in this part of Asia, and China cannot but closely follow the development of the situation." Zhou concluded by reiterating the "stern warning" that "the Indian government must bear full responsibility for all the consequences arising from its extended aggression."[34] After the Indian offensives on Lahore and Sialkot and the Pakistani counterattacks (which developed into the biggest tank battles since World War II up to that point), the two sides regrouped for a further round of battle between September 14 and 17. As the new battle opened, China's Foreign Ministry took the occasion to protest India's November 1962 seizure of the assets of the Bank of China branches in Bombay and Calcutta. China's note demanded compensation and "a speedy and clear-cut reply on this matter."[35] Threatening statements were also disseminated by PRC embassies. The first secretary of the Chinese embassy in Damascus told the editor of a major Syrian daily on September 9 that China was ready to provide arms *and troops* to Pakistan if and when required.[36]

Adequate numbers of Chinese troops were positioned to carry out Beijing's threats. China had sixty thousand soldiers stationed in the Tibet Military Region and another eighteen thousand in western Xinjiang—compared to one hundred thousand during the 1962 war. CIA analysts thought China's 1965 deployments were adequate for "small-scale frontier clashes like those which preceded the 1962 war." Such actions "would probably create near-panic in New Delhi—where the Chinese maneuvers would in all likelihood be seen as a precursor to heavier attack on the scale of the 1962 incursions."[37] CIA analysts believed Chinese military action was likely:

Peking knows that the Indians are nervous and fearful of another Chinese attack. It almost certainly calculates that even very small military probes would cause the Indians great consternation and divert Indian effort and supplies away from the fighting with the Pakistanis. Indeed, the Chinese threat already ties down a significant portion of India's military forces in the northeast [where] India has some six divisions and about 90 combat aircraft positioned to defend against the possibility of Chinese attack. [PLA preparations] make it clear that Peking's warnings are something more that a piece of psychological warfare bluster [section deleted by CIA censor]. The pattern of Chinese activity [deletion] strongly suggests that at the time when the ultimatum was delivered Peking intended to launch diversionary probes along the Sino-Indian border when the three-day deadline expired. . . . Military force required for sharp, limited objective attacks were already in place and had been brought to a high state of alert under direct control of [Beijing]. There was, however, no indication that the Chinese were preparing for a full-scale attack on India.[38]

On September 15 the United States acted to deter direct Chinese support for Pakistan. At the U.S.-PRC ambassadorial talks in Warsaw, Ambassador Cabot informed Ambassador Wang Bingnan that recent Chinese notes to India "appeared to be designed to convey a threat of Chinese military action." The United States government deplored "even the making of such threats, which if pursued, could create a most dangerous situation, which it would be difficult to confine to the areas of parties initially affected."[39] This was a threat to strike against China in East Asia if China intervened in support of Pakistan.

On September 17, as the fighting in the Punjab was reaching its climax and two days after the U.S. demarche at Warsaw, China presented India with an ultimatum carrying a three-day deadline. Presented to the Indian chargé d'affaires in Beijing "sometime after one o'clock" in the morning, the Chinese note said: "The Chinese government now demands that the Indian government dismantle all its military works for aggression on the Chinese side of the China-Sikkim boundary . . . within three days of the delivery of the present note. . . . Otherwise, the Indian government must bear full responsibility for all the grave consequences arising therefrom."[40] When it issued its ultimatum, China had approximately fifty-five hundred soldiers positioned for quick commitment to combat in Sikkim. In the estimate of the CIA, by thus "focusing attention on the Sikkim frontier," Beijing "underscores the potential threat of a Chinese thrust down the Chumbi Valley which, if successful, would cut the main Indian communication line with Assam."[41] At 4 P.M. on September 19 China's Foreign Ministry delivered another note extending the deadline until midnight on September 22. The MFA draft of this note had initially given India only one day in which to comply. Mao Zedong had personally intervened, extending the deadline in order, he said, "to gain the sympathy of international opinion and of the Indian people."[42]

The Chinese note of September 19 was China's final demarche of the 1965 war. It was filled with strident rhetoric. China's policy of trying to live with India in peace had failed as "gradually [it] came to discover that peace is only a smoke screen used by the Indian government to cover up its prosecution of an expansionist policy" against its neighbors. India was "nibbling away, intruding into and making harassing raids on Chinese territory . . . and even launching a massive armed attack on China along the entire Sino-Indian boundary." Using words that evoked the 1962 war, the message continued:

"It was only when the Chinese government used stern language on talking to the Indian government and put its words into practice by repulsing India's massive armed attack in self-defense that the Indian government slightly restrained itself." Regarding the ongoing Pakistan-Indian war, the statement said: "The Chinese people can deeply understand how Pakistan has been bullied by the Indian government. The Indian government's expansionism has linked China with all the other neighboring countries which India has been bullying." The statement concluded by reiterating the demand that India dismantle "all its military works for aggression" on the Sikkim border before midnight on September 22. "Otherwise the Indian government must bear full responsibility for all the grave consequences arising therefrom."[43] About the same time the note of September 19 was delivered, PLA forces in Tibet were ordered into front-line positions.[44]

Xu Yan of China's National Defense University sees the September 19 note and the military demonstrations behind it as a success. India feared a two-front war and promptly accepted U.S. and Soviet mediation leading to a cease-fire with Pakistan.[45] The sequence of events leading up to the cease-fire fits with Xu Yan's interpretation. On September 20 the United Nations Security Council voted unanimously to demand that Pakistan and India accept a cease-fire by the morning of September 22, that is, before Beijing's extended deadline expired. The resolution also warned third parties (i.e., China) to do nothing that would further aggravate the situation. India accepted the next day. Pakistan delayed until, quite literally, the last minute. Foreign Minister Bhutto traveled to the United Nations in New York to deliver Pakistan's response. He delivered an impassioned speech telling the assembled delegates that Pakistan "will wage a war for a thousand years." Then, at the precise moment the UN deadline was to expire, Bhutto read out a telegram from President Ayub reporting that a cease-fire had been ordered "in the interest of international peace."[46] Clearly, the fear of Chinese involvement catalyzed international concern and helped precipitate a cease-fire.

It was Pakistan who made the decision to accept the cease-fire. China was apparently ready to render more direct assistance had Pakistan chosen to protract the war. G. W. Choudhury, director of research for Pakistan's foreign office from 1967 to 1969 and minister of communications from 1969 to 1971, said that his examination of classified documents in the Pakistan foreign office, plus his talks with President Ayub, led him to conclude that China was prepared in September 1965 to initiate military operations in the Himalayas designed to reduce Indian military pressure on Pakistan—if Pakistan requested this aid. Pakistan's military chiefs favored protraction of the war with Chinese assistance, according to Choudhury. According to him, Pakistan's military leaders drew up a plan in which China would seize a large chunk of the NEFA, drawing off Indian forces and allowing Pakistan to launch a successful offensive on India's western front. By the time the Americans and the Soviets could deploy significant forces to the subcontinent, Pakistan and China would have already established a new status quo there. President Ayub decided against extending the war and aligning with China against both the United States and the Soviet Union, and concluded that Pakistan would have to accept the UN cease-fire. Ayub was concerned, however, lest this move anger Beijing. He therefore traveled secretly to China for intensive discussions with Mao and Zhou. China's leaders told Ayub that the decision was his and that China would support him, whatever he decided. Even though the cost to China might be high, it would stand by Pakistan if it decided to continue the war. "Mr. President," Mao reportedly told Ayub, according to a Pakistani aide, "if there is nuclear war, it is Peking and not Rawalpindi that will be a target." China did not attempt to pressure Ayub but gave him full freedom of action with guarantee of Chinese support.[47] When announcing Pakistan's acceptance of the cease-fire to the Pakistani people on September 22, President Ayub lauded the role of China: "The moral support which the Chinese government extended to us so willingly and so generously will forever remain enshrined in our hearts. We are grateful for this."[48] China's role in the 1965 war made it immensely popular in Pakistan and had a deep and lasting effect on Pakistani opinion toward China. Popular "histories" of the war often greatly exaggerated China's role.[49]

Multiple objectives underlay China's wartime support for Pakistan. We must take seriously Beijing's stated objective of "liberating" Indian Kashmir from Indian control. Pakistan's absorption of Kashmir would have substantially strengthened the Pakistan-China position vis-à-vis India. At a minimum Beijing sought an ongoing war of national liberation in Kashmir. China also sought to deter India from attacking Pakistan for supporting that insurgency. Once China's deterrent support failed, Beijing sought to help Pakistan militarily by tying down Indian forces. Beijing also sought to generate goodwill in Pakistan by demonstrating that it was a reliable ally that, unlike India, did not throw its weight around. By doing this, Beijing also demonstrated to other South Asian countries that China could provide reliable support against India. China's actions made the Soviets pay a cost for their policy of supporting India against China. Likewise, the Americans learned that China's interests could be ignored only at great risk and that China could not be bullied into sacrificing its critical interests. China's firm support of Pakistan was a rebuff to the superpowers, which it saw as colluding to use India to contain China.[50]

THE SIX-YEAR INTERWAR PERIOD

Sino-Pakistani relations did not become noticeably closer during the immediate postwar period. On the other hand, neither did the strategic partnership deteriorate even though Pakistan sought to repair relations with the United States and the Soviet Union. As part of its effort to rebuild ties with Washington, Rawalpindi limited the development of Sino-Pakistani friendship and maintained a deliberate distance from China on such issues as Vietnam. Rawalpindi also expanded ties with the Soviet Union, with President Ayub visiting Moscow in 1967 and 1968. Beijing sought, and received, Pakistani assurances that these moves did not signify a weakening of Pakistan's entente with China. Pakistan received, in turn, Chinese pledges of support on Kashmir and in the event of an Indian attack.[51] In spite of Pakistan's effort to diversify its foreign relations, China emerged as Pakistan's major armorer in the post-1965 period. With the U.S. arms embargo still in place, Pakistan tried to buy U.S. weapons from third countries but was frequently thwarted in doing so by Indian pressure. The Soviet Union was also reluctant to sell very much to Pakistan for fear of alienating India. Under these circumstances Rawalpindi looked to China. In June 1966 Zhou and Ayub reached agreement on a military aid program. Pakistan received gratis arms for two infantry divisions, 200 T-59 tanks, 120 MiG-19 fighters, and other equipment.[52] China also expanded its aid to Pakistan's military industrial base, agreeing to establish an ordnance factory in Dacca, East Pakistan, and a heavy machinery complex at Taxila northwest of Rawalpindi.

China's relations with Pakistan were carefully guarded from disruption during the Cultural Revolution. Pakistan was the only Asian country not criticized by China's otherwise freewheeling Red Guards. Nor were Red Guards allowed to organize in China's embassy in Islamabad, unlike in China's other overseas embassies. Pakistan ranked with "genuine Marxist-Leninist" Albania and North Vietnam as the only countries to continue to enjoy fairly normal government-to-government relations with China during the Cultural Revolution. High-ranking Pakistani officials continued to visit China for discussions with its leaders throughout the halcyon radical days of 1967–68. Pakistani officials were among the very few noncommunist leaders to make such visits during those years. Mao had directly ordered this special exemption of China's links with Pakistan, and Zhou Enlai watched vigilantly to insure it was respected.[53]

Of greatest concern to India during this period was Chinese-Pakistani agreement to build a road linking Pakistani Kashmir with the highways of western Xinjiang. Pakistan drew up plans for such a highway in 1959 and sub-

Indian Jammu and Kashmir
Pakistani Azad Kashmir
Chinese occupied territory claimed by India
Road
Country boundary

KYRGYZSTAN
Kashgar
CHINA
TAJIKISTAN
Mintaka Pass
Morkund
Khunjerab Pass
AFGHANISTAN
Karakoram Pass
Gilgit
PAKISTAN
Aksai Chin
Srinagar
INDIA
Rawalpindi
Jammu
N
0   100 mi

MAP 7.1   The Sino-Pakistani Friendship Highway

sequently built sections of that road with its own resources. China agreed in 1964 to assist with construction of the road, and work on it began in 1966. Thousands of PLA soldiers and engineers then entered the Gilgit and Hunza regions of northern Pakistan to push the road through the high mountains and steep valleys of the Karakoram Range. Construction was extremely difficult and costly in both financial and human terms. By 1968 the Chinese had completed 97 miles of the road inside Pakistan. Two passes over the high Karakoram were also developed. Mintaka pass provided the first route. Later a second route branching off at Morkund and crossing the Khunjerab Pass was opened in 1969 because it was farther from Soviet territory and had less snowfall in winter. Truck passage was possible by 1969, and the road was declared opened in February 1971.[54] Map 7.1 depicts the alignment of what was named the "Sino-Pakistan Friendship Highway" upon its opening to travel by third-country nationals in 1978. The Kashmir-Xinjiang road followed the Kathmandu-Lhasa road as the second Chinese-built highway breaching the Himalayan barrier.

Indian leaders were dismayed by the road. In a statement to the Lok Sabha in July 1969, India's minister of external affairs pointed out that "the entire alignment of the road runs in Indian territory which is presently under the illegal and forcible occupation of Pakistan." The road would "give easier access to Chinese troops . . . into the Gilgit area in Pakistan-occupied Kashmir. . . . The military significance of this road is, therefore, self evident." Construction of the road was "a threat to the peace and tranquillity of the region" and showed "that Pakistan's intentions and ambitions in Kashmir equally serve Chinese designs in the area." "Emphatic protests" to this effect had been delivered to Pakistan and China. The Indian government was "fully alive to the danger posed to our security" by these roads and was "taking necessary steps to safeguard our interests," the foreign minister told parliament.[55] Construction of the Kashmir-Xinjiang highway was seen by India as another step in China's advance into the subcontinent, another element of China's effort to encircle India via cooperation with Pakistan.

THE INDIAN DISMEMBERMENT OF PAKISTAN

In 1971 India adopted a strategy toward East Pakistan similar in many ways to Pakistan's Operation Gibraltar of 1965. India's objectives were complex, having to do with preventing the destabilization of India's West Bengal and northeastern states by continuing upheaval in East Pakistan, plus bringing about a fundamental shift in the South Asian balance of power to its advantage and to Pakistan's and China's disadvantage.[56] In both regards New Delhi was successful. China's response to this bold Indian move was somewhat paradoxical. Although the geopolitical stakes were considerably higher in 1971 than they had been in 1965, China's response was far weaker. Whereas China in 1965 was apparently prepared for some level of military activity against India, China's support in 1971 never approached that level.

The constitutional crisis into which Pakistan dissolved in 1971 was rooted in ethnic and economic disparities between the eastern and western wings of Pakistan and in the inability of the political leaders of those two wings to reach agreement on the nature of the relationship between center and province within Pakistan's political system. Differences between the regions of Pakistan intensified in the second half of 1970, as the nation moved toward the country's first direct elections on the basis of full adult suffrage in December as a prelude to framing a new constitution. The December 1970 elections led to Pakistan's polarization. Regionally based parties won strong majorities in both east, where Sheik Mujibur Rahman led the Awami League, and west, where Zulfiqar Ali Bhutto led the Pakistan People's Party. Neither of these parties held a single seat in the other wing of the country, and the pro-autonomy Awami League held an absolute majority in the National Assembly. President Yahya Khan tried to arrange talks between these two parties in March 1971, but before they began, the Awami League launched a noncooperation movement in East Pakistan and then proceeded to set up a parallel government there. Unfortunately, the Awami League lost control of the situation, and law and order began to break down. Mob rule became common. In late March President Yahya ordered the arrest of Mujibur Rehman, banned the Awami League, and ordered Pakistan's armed forces to restore law and order in the east. Over the next several months ruthless and very bloody military repression was directed at the people of East Pakistan.

China's leaders apparently realized early on that Pakistan faced grave problems endangering its national unity and that efforts to solve those problems by military means could be disastrous. During a visit to China by President Yahya Khan (who replaced Ayub Khan by military coup in March 1969) shortly before the December 1970 election, Zhou Enlai urged the Pakistani leader to find a fair answer to the problems facing Pakistan. Shortly after the election Zhou wrote to the leaders of both wings of Pakistan urging them to come to a satisfactory political settlement.[57]

India quietly lent its support to the Awami League's resistance to Pakistan's authority. At the end of March 1971 India's parliament passed a resolution expressing "profound sympathy and solidarity with the people of East Bengal for a democratic way of life." Indian leaders apparently assured the Awami League of Indian support before it launched its insurgency against Pakistan. In April ethnic Bengali units of the Pakistan army stationed in East Pakistan defected to India, where they were given sanctuary and reorganized into Awami League "freedom fighters." Training camps were established in northeastern India, where young men recruited among the refugees streaming from East Pakistan into India were given military training. Weapons, ammunition, and explosives were supplied to the emerging Mukti Bahini—the armed force of the Provisional Government of Bangladesh established in Calcutta in April 1971. By July India had decided to wage a "quiet war" to "liberate" Bangladesh within a reasonable time frame by bringing the Awami League to power there. Indian soldiers first trained and advised, and then began accompanying Mukti Bahini insurgents on raids deep into East Pakistan. Additional Indian forces were assembled along East Pakistan's borders in order to deter Pakistani action against Mukti Bahini sanctuaries inside India and to provide occasional covering fire for insurgent operations inside East Pakistan. By mid-November Indian army units were conducting operations in East Bangladesh in cooperation with the Mukti Bahini. Most of these activities were covert. To maintain secrecy foreign relief workers were ordered out of the refugee camps, and movement by foreign journalists was restricted.

The analysis underlying India's covert support for the Awami League was presented by K. Subrahmanyam shortly after that program began. India's national interests would be served, he wrote in April 1971, by an end to a united Pakistan achieved by a "bold initiative" "to help the freedom struggle in Bangla Desh to end quickly and victoriously." Lacking such bold action, insurgency and counter-insurgency would drag on in East Pakistan for a considerable time. The result would be devastation of the area, thereby reducing its significance once it was free of Pakistan. Protracted war and devastation would also lead to political radicalization, providing an opportunity for Bengali Maoists. Lacking an Indian bold initiative, East Pakistan might become a Beijing-aligned People's Republic of Bangladesh. Regarding international norms proscribing interference in other states, other contemporary great powers—the United States, the Soviet Union, or China—had never proven to be bound by those norms when their vital interests were at stake.[58]

Beijing concluded early on that it had nothing to gain and much to lose by developments in East Pakistan. Pakistani repression was directed not only against a national liberation movement with deep roots and a good chance for success but against pro-Chinese elements as well. It also gave India justification for intervening. Chinese policy balanced between inactivity that would alienate China's ally Pakistan and activity that would encourage Indian intervention and endanger China's future ties to a Bangladeshi state.[59] Beijing did not respond quickly to the developing crisis in East Pakistan. On April 6, 1971, China delivered a protest to India, charging it with "gross interference" in the internal affairs of Pakistan and warning that Pakistan would have China's "firm support" if the Indian expansionists dared to launch aggression against Pakistan."[60] This note was not made public until some time later, however. China's first public comment came in a *Renmin ribao* commentary on April 11. This piece neither defended nor criticized either the Pakistan government or the Bengali rebels in East Pakistan. Instead, it concentrated on attacking Indian and Soviet "open interference in the internal matters of Pakistan." The commentary also stated that "the Chinese government and people will, as always, firmly support the Pakistan government and people in their just struggle to safeguard state sovereignty and national independence." Notably absent from this formulation was the phrase *territorial integrity*. This omission avoided Chinese opposition to the future independence of Bangladesh.

In private communications with Pakistan's leaders China was critical of the bloody methods being used to deal with the Awami League. About the time of the *Renmin ribao* commentary of April 11, Zhou Enlai frankly conveyed China's concerns to Pakistan's foreign secretary. A top-ranking member of Pakistan's military junta was sent secretly by Yahya to Beijing to secure Chinese support. Zhou conveyed China's concern at the use of military force against East Pakistan's civilian populace and warned of the grave consequences for Pakistan if a political solution were not quickly found.[61] Later Zhou warned Yahya that the large flow of refugees into India could give India an excuse to become openly involved.[62] China's ambassador to Islamabad also conveyed China's distress and perception of a mounting disaster in East Pakistan.[63] Leftist circles in East Pakistan believed that Beijing was trying to protect them against Pakistani army repression.[64] Most important, during April the Chinese government informed Pakistan's ambassador in Beijing that China would not intervene militarily in hostilities on the subcontinent, even *international* hostilities. By early June, at the latest, Indian intelligence had learned of China's message to Pakistan. Indian decision making henceforth proceeded on the assumption that China would not intervene militarily in an India-Pakistan war.[65]

China did extend considerable economic and military aid to Pakistan. At a time when Western nations had suspended aid to Pakistan because of its repression in East Pakistan, Beijing pledged $100 million in economic assistance in addition to $200 million it had already committed to in November 1970. Beijing also agreed to equip and train two additional divisions of the Pakistani army. Coming at a time when Islamabad was under strong international pressure, this support was greatly appreciated. Pakistan's foreign secretary, Sultan Khan, concluded that China looked upon a divided Pakistan or an independent Bangladesh under Indo-Soviet influence as being against its own national interest.[66] Beijing also gave political support to Pakistan. For seven months after the publication of the April 11 commentary the Chinese government remained silent about developments in East Pakistan. China's media continued to publicize Pakistan's charges of Indian subversion and infiltration but did not endorse Pakistan's actions in the east. Not until after the Indian-Soviet mutual assistance treaty was signed on August 9, 1971, did Beijing subordinate its distaste for Pakistan's methods in East Pakistan and begin to support Islamabad forcefully. Linkage between the Sino-Soviet-American triangle and the Indo-Pakistan conflict became increasingly intimate in mid-1971. China's support for Pakistan grew stronger as that happened. But Beijing's support was still equivocal and far short of credible threats to intervene which characterized the 1965 war.

Some analysts have explained Beijing's reticence during mid-1971 in terms of its reluctance to violate the principle of sympathy for a national liberation struggle.[67] While not disagreeing with this view, I would frame the issue somewhat differently. China's advice to Pakistan's leaders beginning in November 1970 indicates that China's leaders saw fairly clearly and early on the nature of the catastrophe being created by brutal repression in East Pakistan. Beijing apparently foresaw that resort to brute military repression in East Pakistan would not work but would lead instead to further rebellion, international antipathy to Pakistan, and ultimately Indian intervention. When Pakistan's leaders ignored China's advice to seek a political settlement averting civil war, China apparently concluded that the secession of East Pakistan was likely and posited two new major objectives for Chinese policy in South Asia (as opposed to globally). These were: (1) to uphold the independence and greatest possible strength of the rump Pakistan state in the west, along with China's strategic partnership with that state; and (2) to court popular and elite opinion in emerging Bangladesh by carefully avoiding words and actions associating China too closely with the bloody repression under way in the east or by indicating Chinese opposition to Bangladesh's independence.

In November 1971 Bhutto led a high-level mission to Beijing to ask it to reverse its April decision against intervention. Bhutto sought assurances that in the event of war China would be willing to undertake, as it had been in 1965, diversionary actions in the Himalayas to hold down Indian forces. China refused to alter its earlier position; it would not intervene militarily but would continue to provide material and political assistance. China also advised, even at this late date, a political settlement achieved via negotiations with the Awami League.[68] Acting Foreign Minister Ji Pengfei publicly issued a broad statement supporting Pakistan and charging that India had crudely interfered in Pakistan's internal affairs [and] carried out subversive activities and military threats against Pakistan." China was "greatly concerned over the present tension in the Subcontinent." "The East Pakistan question is the internal affair of Pakistan," and any interference in those affairs constituted a violation of the Five Principles of Peaceful Coexistence. Finally, "Our Pakistan friends may rest assured that should Pakistan be subjected to foreign aggression, the Chinese government and people will, as always, resolutely support the Pakistan Government and people in their just struggle to defend their state sovereignty and national independence."[69] The themes of Ji's speech were reiterated by Chinese representatives on subsequent occasions such as Tanzanian National Day and Albanian Independence Day celebrations.

India followed very closely China's signals during 1971. Detailed studies of China's actions in comparison with those of 1965 were prepared and debated.[70] Beijing's rhetoric was found to be less threatening and ominous than in 1965. Indian intelligence also detected no increased Chinese military activity along India's northern borders. This information dovetailed with Indian intelligence about Beijing's April 1971 communication to Pakistan. Chinese military assistance to Pakistan during the crisis was also rather modest. India's August 9, 1971, mutual security treaty with the Soviet Union provided an additional guarantee against the possibility of Chinese involvement. When the third war between India and Pakistan began, on December 3, Indian leaders were confident that China would limit its "firm support" to Pakistan to verbal and moral support.[71]

Several public statements by Pakistan's leaders in November 1971 gave the impression that China would enter the looming Pakistan-Indian war. Analysts have disagreed about whether these statements were a result of Pakistani confusion and miscommunication between Beijing and Islamabad, or deliberate deception by Pakistan. The repeated and apparently clear nature of China's rejection of belligerency, plus the fact that both Yahya Khan and Z. A. Bhutto made inaccurate statements about China's intentions, indicates to this author that Richard Sisson and Leo Rose are correct in concluding that Pakistan's leaders were deliberately trying to create apprehensions in the minds of Indian leaders.[72] Beijing was reportedly not pleased with this Pakistani ploy but did not publicly contradict it. China shared with Pakistan an interest in deterring Indian intervention.

Once war began and Indian forces drove rapidly into Bangladesh to bring the Awami League to power and accomplish the independence of Bangladesh, China launched a blistering polemic against India and its Soviet supporter. Those two had, Beijing charged, established through their aggression a new puppet state, Bangladesh, equivalent to Manchukuo established by Japan in China's northeast in 1932.[73] China used its then newly won UN seat to lend Pakistan vigorous diplomatic support. China's representatives countered Soviet support for India by condemning Indian aggression and demanding the immediate, unconditional withdrawal of Indian forces from Pakistan's territory. Political support aside, China did very little to tie down Indian forces along the Himalayan borders. On December 16, the day Pakistani forces in East Pakistan surrendered, China issued a weak statement protesting Indian violations of China's territory. Significant action in the Himalayas was unlikely, however, because the roads and passes there were blocked with snow—a fact well understood by Indian leaders.

Several factors explain China's nonmilitary response in 1971 as compared to 1965. China's relative position was much weaker in 1971. In 1965 the PLA was perhaps at its peak capability, having undergone a decade-long assimilation of Soviet military technology and fought successful wars in Korea, Tibet, and India. India's military was also much more powerful in 1971 than a decade earlier. In 1971 the PLA was deeply enmeshed in China's internal politics, as the Cultural Revolution drew to a close. Military action would have risked embarrassing defeats. The political costs of military action on Pakistan's behalf in 1971 would have been far higher than six years earlier. In 1965 China stood for liberation for the Kashmiri people; in 1971 intervention would have placed it squarely against the liberation of the people of Bangladesh. China also had a high-profile but nonmilitary way to demonstrate its "support" for Pakistan in 1971—in the Security Council. Lacking such prominence in 1965, there was greater incentive to make its point via military action. Military action on Pakistan's behalf also risked tempting a Soviet strike against China, the results of which were incalculable. Interestingly, however, in 1965 when China was apparently ready for military action, it stood in opposition to both superpowers, while in 1971, when it decided against such action, it enjoyed the support of the United States.

The dismemberment of Pakistan substantially shifted the correlation of forces in South Asia in India's favor. As explained by K. Subrahmanyam, Pakistan's economy had been reduced to about one-eighth and its population one-tenth the size of India's. The large volume of foreign exchange which previously flowed to West Pakistan from the sale of East Pakistan's cotton, jute, and tea—previously the largest source of Pakistan's foreign exchange— would no longer be available to underwrite Pakistan's military budget. That meant Pakistan would be far less able to maintain its disproportionately large military forces. By substantially diminishing the power of Pakistan in this way, the 1971 war meant that Pakistan would be less able to be "used as a countervailing power against India, thereby hampering India's due role as a major power in the international scene." Pakistan had always been a "proxy" for "external powers," Subrahmanyam explained, and by cutting it "down to

size . . . its future capability to play the role of proxy has been severely curtailed." "External powers will find it more difficult to fish in troubled waters
of the subcontinent." Separating Bangladesh from Pakistan also meant that
Assam would be at less risk of being cut off in the event of war with China.
Indian political and economic influence would also be enhanced. Expanding
the Indian institutions of adult suffrage, a viable democratic system, checks
and balances, and commitment to advancement of minority interests, which
Subrahmanyam assumed would occur in Bangladesh, would appeal to other
countries in South and Southeast Asia. Economically, goods would flow more
freely between all the areas around the Ganges delta, drawing those countries closer together and into closer cooperation with India's powerful and
dynamic economy.

In terms of India's broader relation with China, Subrahmanyam postulated that Indian domination of the subcontinent would not pose an insu-
perable obstacle to an eventual Sino-Indian reconciliation. If, as China was
proclaiming by 1971, its main interest in that region was to keep the two superpowers out, that objective could be achieved in either of two ways: via Chinese
domination or via Indian domination. If Indian strength and firmness made
the former impossible, China's own interests could lead it to accept the latter, Subrahmanyam observed.[74] This was an optimistic, if realistic, view. Other
analysts argued that in West Pakistan the core of Pakistan's power was preserved and could still serve to balance India.[75] Over the next three decades
the latter observation would prove to be more accurate.

There is one other aspect of the 1971 war which must be considered: the
Soviet-supported Indian intervention in Bangladesh as a precedent for possible intervention in Tibet. As Henry Kissinger sensed in his discussion with
China's UN ambassador Huang Hua during their talks in the midst of the
1971 war, China was deeply fearful that the precedent established by Bangladesh
might be applied to "other countries." Huang did not mention Tibet in his
discussions with Kissinger, but, since the discussion was about Soviet-Indian
collusion to partition other countries, the implication was obvious.[76] If
India, with Soviet support, could intervene to help the people of East Bengal
achieve national liberation, might it not next apply this to Tibet? And, if the
international community accepted the principle of foreign intervention in
the case of Bangladesh, might it not accept it in such a case as Tibet?[77] PRC
ambassador to the UN Qiao Guanghua was explicit in his December 7 speech
to the Security Council: "The Indian ruling circle had some time ago forcibly
coerced several tens of thousands of the inhabitants of China's Tibet into going
to India and set up a so-called government-in-exile headed by the Chinese
traitor Dalai Lama. To agree that the Indian Government is justified to use

the so-called refugee question as a pretext for invading Pakistan is tantamount to agreeing that the Indian Government will be justified to use the question of the so-called 'Tibetan refugees' as a pretext for invading China."[78] Perhaps the next "Manchukuo" might be an independent Kingdom of Tibet set up via Indian action, perhaps with "collusive" support from the Soviet Union and the United States. Of course, such a development had just been made far less likely by the then recently achieved Sino-U.S. rapprochement.

8 / Managing the Contradiction between Maintaining the Sino-Pakistani Entente and Furthering Sino-Indian Rapprochement

During the 1970s Beijing's view of the world became less revolutionary. Underlying this shift was the conclusion that the USSR now surpassed the United States as a source of potential attack and encirclement of China. This conclusion made less useful anti-imperialist wars of national liberation which Beijing had previously seen as a way of tying down U.S. forces and sapping U.S. will. Instead, Beijing began to look on U.S. strength as a way of checking the Soviet Union. Beijing also became increasingly desirous of drawing *all possible countries* into a global anti–Soviet hegemony united front. This led by the late 1970s to a desire for better relations with India. Chinese leaders understood that whether India gave or withheld support to Moscow's endeavors would be a significant factor determining the success or failure of those Soviet endeavors. Better relations between China and India would help limit India's support for Moscow.[1]

When Deng Xiaoping succeeded Mao in 1978, another rationale was added to the push for better relations with India: a drive to quadruple China's standard of living by the end of the twentieth century. This was Deng's stated objective. To achieve it, he sought to hold down defense expenditures, expand China's international economic contacts to the greatest extent possible, and reduce the chance of wars that would disrupt the development drive. All of these objectives pointed toward better relations with India. These development-oriented motivations continued into the post–Cold War period,

but the epochal shifts associated with that transition added an additional rationale for better Chinese relations with India: strengthening China's position
in the face of U.S. "unipolar" pressure and interference. Thus, since the mid-
1970s and continuing into the early twenty-first century, China has sought
to improve relations with India.

There was, and remains, a contradiction between Beijing's push for rapprochement with India and maintenance of China's entente cordiale with
Pakistan. Given the deep hostility between India and Pakistan, China's close
links with and substantial support for Pakistan could easily become an obstacle to better Sino-Indian relations. New Delhi could demand that Beijing
reduce or suspend support for Pakistan as part of a package improving PRC-
ROI relations. Beijing's strategic dilemma in this regard was how to avoid
being forced to make a choice between rapprochement with India and its
entente cordiale with Pakistan. China's interests were best served by simultaneous achievement of both. Chinese policy served this interest. Beijing has
carefully balanced between these two contradictory objectives.

To some extent the same problem arose with China's relations with other
South Asian countries—Nepal, Burma, Bhutan, Sri Lanka. Yet China's links
with Pakistan outweighed its links with the other countries for several
important reasons. Among the South Asian countries only Pakistan had
national strength adequate to constrain and balance India in any serious way.
Pakistan alone had the will and strength to contemplate war with India.
Pakistan alone was capable of presenting, in combination with China, a serious two-front threat to India. And Pakistan alone was capable of preoccu-
pying India to an extent that hobbled India's rivalry with China for global
status and influence. These fundamental geopolitical realities did not necessarily mean that New Delhi took greater objection to China's links with
Pakistan than it did to China's links with other South Asian countries. This
does not seem to have been the case. As we have seen, New Delhi was
extremely sensitive to China's links with Nepal, Sikkim, and Bhutan, while
(as we will see below) it in fact took a relatively relaxed approach to China's
links with Pakistan. These fundamental geopolitical realities meant, rather,
that because its stakes were higher, Pakistan would be more concerned with
any weakening of Chinese support that accompanied a warming of Sino-
Indian relations. They also meant that China had more to lose if its entente
with Pakistan unraveled. If Sino-Indian rapprochement contributed to an
Indian subordination of Pakistan or to an unraveling of the Sino-Pakistani
entente, the balance between China and India could be fundamentally
shifted to China's disadvantage.

Several broad policies served Beijing's interest in sustaining its entente with Pakistan while engineering rapprochement with India. The most important of these was covert assistance to Pakistan's nuclear weapons program (which will be discussed in chap. 11). Another Chinese policy designed to handle these contradictory PRC interests was to persuade India to delink Sino-Pakistan and Sino-Indian relations. Measures improving PRC-ROI relations, Beijing told New Delhi, should be taken solely on the basis of mutual agreement in those areas. In areas where the two sides disagreed, they should discuss those disagreements, but not let those disputes block progress in other areas. Where agreement was possible, the two sides should move ahead. Improvements in Sino-Indian relations should not be held hostage to intractable issues like the border dispute or Sino-Pakistan relations.

China's policy of delinking emerged clearly during PRC foreign minister Huang Hua's visit to India in June 1981. Indian foreign minister A. B. Vajpayee had established the precedent of formally presenting India's objections about the Sino-Pakistan military link during his visit to Beijing in February 1979.[2] The brief thaw in Sino-Indian relations associated with Vajpayee's visit ended when China attacked Vietnam (while the Indian foreign minister was still in China). China's 1979 "pedagogic war" against Vietnam revived Indian memories of 1962 and seemed to confirm that China was still quite prepared to use force against its neighbors. There were also strong similarities between the Vietnam-China-Cambodia situation and the Pakistan-China-India relationship. Throughout its history China had resorted to force to uphold small, friendly, neighboring states who willingly looked to China for protection against more powerful, aggressive neighbors. A major cause of China's 1979 blow against Vietnam was Hanoi's efforts to establish its "regional hegemony" over a good friend and protégé of China, Cambodia. A common scenario of another Sino-Indian war envisioned Chinese entry into an Indo-Pakistan war to prevent Indian regional hegemonists from vanquishing China's good friend, Pakistan. Vietnam and India also happened to be quite good friends.

Huang's 1981 visit was the first visit to India by a Chinese government leader since Zhou Enlai's visit in 1960, and an attempt to revive movement toward better Sino-Indian relations. At the center of that effort was a proposal to uncouple Sino-Indian and Sino-Pakistan relations. Shortly before Huang's visit, Chinese Premier Zhao Ziyang traveled to Pakistan, Nepal, and Bangladesh to reassure China's friends in those countries that the upcoming push for better relations with India would not be at their expense. In Pakistan, Zhao and Pakistani president Zia ul-Haq had an "extensive exchange of views on international problems and relations between the two countries," according to *Renmin ribao*. The opinions of the two leaders on "many international problems" were "identical." "Both countries are resolved to continue efforts to further strengthen friendship and cooperation in all fields and to preserve peace and stability in South Asia." "All fields" included military and security. "We fully understand," Zhao said, "the effort Pakistan is making to strengthen its national defense to guard against external aggression and expansion, and will actively provide all the support we can." This military assistance was not aimed at India, Zhao insisted, but at the Soviet hegemonists in Afghanistan. Pakistan "has repeatedly stated that the measures it is taking to strengthen national defenses are not aimed at its neighbors. Improved relations between the countries of South Asia benefit the peoples of those countries, not Soviet hegemonism."[3] In his keynote banquet speech in Islamabad Zhao reassured his hosts: "The Chinese Government and people will, as always, firmly support the Pakistan government and people in their just struggle to oppose foreign aggression and interference, and defend their national independence and state sovereignty. Sino-Pakistan friendship has stood the test of time. History will further prove that the Chinese people are reliable friends of the Pakistani people."[4]

In the context of 1981 the Soviet occupation of Afghanistan and Pakistan's role as a front-line state sustaining the Afghan war of resistance was Beijing's foremost concern. Yet the point was: China's military links with Pakistan would not suffer as a result of Sino-Indian rapprochement. China's close, multidimensional ties with Pakistan would be unaffected by improvements in Sino-Indian relations. Speaking at a press conference toward the end of his visit, Zhao indicated that China hoped to "solve certain problems concerning the *bilateral* relations between China and India in a step-by-step fashion via friendly consultations in a spirit of mutual understanding and accommodation."[5] Huang Hua also conveyed to New Delhi the message of delinkage: "Between us there are, of course, still some outstanding issues and divergences of views on certain questions. But we on our part always believe wherever there are disputes, we can discuss them and seek ways to settle them and that we should not allow them to obstruct the development of the bilateral relations between our two countries." China and India should discuss issues like the border or China's links with Pakistan where the two sides disagreed, but if agreement could not be reached in those areas, China and India should nonetheless move ahead in other areas in which they could agree. Regarding China's links to other South Asian countries, Huang said, "We are willing to develop friendly relations and cooperation with all counties, particularly our neighbors in Asia, on the basis of the Five Principles of Peaceful Coexistence."[6] In short, China's ties with other South Asian countries were not on the table. Huang carried the same message to Sri Lanka and the Maldives during his March 1981 South Asian trip.

While insisting on uncoupling China-Pakistan and China-India ties, Beijing did offer New Delhi a different sort of peace offering. China would no longer take sides in intra–South Asian disputes by supporting other South Asian countries that came into conflict with India. During his June 1981 visit to Pakistan, Zhao Ziyang explicitly paired this new Chinese neutrality in intra–South Asian disputes and expansion of China's ties in South Asia: "We desire to develop China's bilateral relations with countries in South Asia. We also desire to see that countries in South Asia will be friendly to each other, and on the basis of the Five Principles of Peaceful Coexistence . . . [will] fight together against outside aggression and intervention."[7] In his banquet speech in Islamabad, Zhao stated: "We sincerely hope that these [South Asian] countries will be able to settle their differences free from outside interference and through consultations on an equal footing, and will treat each other as equals and live in harmony on the basis of the Five Principles of Peaceful Coexistence."[8] The origins of this policy seem primarily linked to Beijing's desire to counter Soviet activities in South Asia. Beijing concluded that conflicts among South Asian nations created opportunities Moscow might exploit. But China's leaders must have understood the utility of this approach in lessening *Indian* opposition to continuing, and expanding, Chinese ties with India's South Asian neighbors.

This new orientation did not take effect overnight. On several occasions during the 1980s China continued to take sides in intra–South Asian disputes (e.g., during the Sri Lankan–Indian confrontation of 1986–87 and in the Kashmir dispute up to 1990). But it did signal an important new direction in China's South Asian policy, a direction very different from the 1960s and early 1970s. India would utilize this Chinese concession to the fullest, insisting that China redeem its promise by adopting a more truly neutral stance on such issues as Kashmir. *China's* links with the South Asian countries remained unaffected.

New Delhi did not accept Beijing's proposal of delinkage until 1987. India's key objection was not, apparently, the continuation of the Sino-Pakistan entente but, rather, the nonsettlement of the territorial issue. Until 1987 India's governments basically continued the policy established by Nehru of insisting on settlement of the boundary question as a condition for normalization of ROI-PRC relations. The failure to achieve a breakthrough on the border issue in talks between 1982 and 1986, combined with the confrontation at Sumdurong Chu in 1986–87, led Rajiv Gandhi's government to drop this policy in mid-1987.[9] While arising out of interactions having to do with the border, New Delhi's acceptance of the principle of delinkage represented de facto Indian acceptance of continuation of the Sino-Pakistan entente parallel to and independent of Sino-Indian rapprochement.

The principle of delinkage was enshrined in the Sino-Indian joint communiqué issued at the conclusion of Premier Li Peng's visit to India in December 1991. After summarizing the measures taken to advance better relations, that document said: "The two sides stated that the improvement and development of Sino-Indian relations was not directed against any third country, *nor would it affect their existing friendly relations and cooperation with other countries.*"[10] The emphasized second phrase meant that China's links with Pakistan need not be curtailed for the sake of better ties with India. Regarding Sino-Pakistan ties, Li Peng told reporters that, while Sino-Indian ties were improving, "China is willing to maintain and develop friendly relations with India, Pakistan, and all countries in South Asia on the basis of the Five Principles of Peaceful Coexistence."[11] In other words, Sino-Pakistan and Sino-Indian relations would develop independently of each other. Implicit in Li's comments was the conclusion that Indian attempts to limit the development of Sino-Pakistan ties by linking them to Sino-Indian ties would violate the Five Principles of Peaceful Coexistence—to which India had agreed.

Indian rapprochement with China proceeded parallel to, and unaffected by, robust Chinese assistance to Pakistan's nuclear weapons, missile, and other military programs. The elements of Chinese support for Pakistan will be discussed in subsequent sections, but a juxtapositioning of key events associated with this support and milestones of Sino-Indian rapprochement, as is done in table 8.1, makes apparent this uncoupling.

As Sino-Indian rapprochement progressed in the years following Rajiv Gandhi's 1988 visit to China, New Delhi downplayed China's assistance to Pakistan's nuclear and missile programs for the sake of not derailing that process. Statements by the Ministry of External Affairs occasionally acknowledged that "We are aware that China has been providing material used by Pakistan in the nuclear field."[12] References in India's annual defense reports to China's assistance to Pakistan's missile and nuclear weapons programs became more direct as the 1990s progressed. The 1993–94 report merely "noted" the "reported proliferation of missiles in our neighborhood such as in Pakistan, Saudi Arabia and Iran" and said that "Pakistan has also reportedly acquired M-11 missiles from China." The 1996–97 report, by contrast, declared

TABLE 8.1 The Delinking of Sino-Pakistani and Sino-Indian Relations

Early 1988	Sino-Pakistani agreement for transfer and indigenous production of M-11 ballistic missiles
December 1988	Prime Minister Rajiv Gandhi's pathbreaking visit to China
October 1990	China undertakes to meet Pakistan's defense requirements in aftermath of U.S. suspension of military assistance to Pakistan over nuclear issue
June 1991	U.S. sanctions PRC for transfer of M-11 technology to Pakistan
December 1991	Premier Li Peng's pathbreaking visit to India
December 1992	PRC shipment of M-11s to Pakistan
August 1993	U.S. sanctions PRC for transfer of M-11 technology and whole missiles to Pakistan
September 1993	Prime Minister P. V. Narasimha Rao visits China; agreement signed on Maintenance of Peace and Tranquility on the Line of Actual Control
1995	China sells several thousand ring magnets to Pakistan for use in uranium enrichment centrifuges
December 1996	President Jiang Zemin visits India; agreement signed on confidence-building measures for border

bluntly: "China has supplied M-11 missiles to Pakistan and is aiding it with technology and man-power as well in the development of its indigenous missile program." "India's concerns regarding China's defense cooperation with Pakistan, its assistance to Pakistan's clandestine nuclear program, and the sale of missiles and sophisticated weapons systems by it to Pakistan were conveyed to the Chinese side."[13] Government spokesmen generally abstained, however, from publicly taking China to task over these issues.[14] Nor did New Delhi attempt to mobilize international pressure on Beijing over its military relation with Pakistan.

Indian concerns were conveyed behind the closed doors of diplomatic discussions.

The Indian attitude, as conveyed to me by a high-level Indian diplomat in Beijing in mid-1990, was that India realized the broad diplomatic value to China of its relation with Pakistan, and did not question that relation. Nor was dilution of China's relation with Pakistan a precondition for improved Sino-Indian relations. India had, however, taken note of the expansion of China's military ties with India's neighbors over the past several years. According to the retired Indian ambassador to China during the early 1990s, C. V. Ranganathan, India frequently raised with China Indian concerns regarding Chinese transfers of military technology to Pakistan. China's response was that China did not, and India should not, believe the U.S. reports upon which these charges were based. The implication was that these charges were lies concocted by the United States to spoil Indian-Chinese relations. When India sometimes relied on its own intelligence assets to raise these issues with China, the stock Chinese reply was that whatever China was doing with Pakistan was entirely for peaceful, nonmilitary, and civilian purposes, and fully in accord with international guidelines.[15]

After a decade of parallel Sino-Indian rapprochement and Chinese assistance to Pakistan's military programs, China's response remained unchanged. In his first major public statement following Indian and Pakistani nuclear tests in May 1998, PRC ambassador to India Zhou Gang addressed the question of China-Pakistan relations. China's ties with Pakistan, Zhou said, were relations between two sovereign countries. (The implication here was that Indian efforts to regulate Sino-Pakistan relations was a violation of the Five Principles of Peaceful Coexistence.) China had not transferred to Pakistan any equipment or technology that could be used for making nuclear weapons, Zhou said. India's concerns over Sino-Pakistan military cooperation were caused by misunderstandings, unnecessary misgivings, and "rumors from the West." China would like, Zhou said, to exchange views on the subject with India through normal diplomatic channels as used to be done in the past.[16] Several years earlier, in 1993, Zhou Gang had served in the same capacity in Islamabad and stated China's position on the other side of the road. China understood, Zhou then said, Pakistan's concerns regarding the development of Indian missile and nuclear programs and arms buildup. China's efforts to normalize relations with India would not hamper China's relations with Pakistan.[17]

The BJP government that came to power in March 1998 attempted to shift away from India's by then traditional policy of delinkage. When PLA Chief of Staff Fu Quanyou visited India in the month after the new government took office, Defense Minister George Fernandes made clear India's concerns and objections to China's transfer of missiles and missile technology to Pakistan. When Fu urged that relations among countries be based on the Five Principles of Peaceful Coexistence as agreed to by China and India, Prime Minister Vajpayee replied that improvements in Sino-Indian relations "should be based on the recognition and respect for each other's concerns."[18] A short while later Prime Minister Vajpayee told the press that he was concerned over China's assistance to Pakistan's military capabilities because the whole thrust of Pakistan's military buildup was Indo-centric.[19] Foreign Secretary K. Raghunath also made condemnation of China's assistance to Pakistan's missile program a major thrust of India's "strategic dialogue" with U.S. National Security Advisor Sandy Berger and Acting Secretary of State Strobe Talbott in the months before India's nuclear tests of May 1998. Raghunath emphasized that Pakistan's missile capability "was not an indigenous one," and had been achieved by "covert means." Pakistan's missile program was part of a "long-standing clandestine program for developing missile capability aimed at primarily one country—India."[20] Defense Minister Fernandes also began to condemn China publicly for its military assistance to Pakistan, warning on television that "China has provided Pakistan with both missile as well as nuclear know-how."[21] The most high-level BJP effort to mobilize international pressure against the Beijing-Islamabad military link was Vajpayee's May 12, 1998, letter to President Clinton. Alluding to China, Vajpayee noted: "To add to [ROI-PRC] distrust, that country [China] has materially helped another neighbor of ours to become a covert nuclear weapons state. At the hands of this bitter neighbor we have suffered three aggressions in the last 50 years. And for the last ten years we have been the victim of unremitting terrorism and militancy sponsored by it."[22]

In the United States the BJP government's newly public criticism of the Sino-Pakistan entente was frequently taken to be a pretext for India's May 1998 nuclearization, the real cause of which was often attributed to the BJP's domestic political needs. In fact, it is more accurate to see both the new approach to the Sino-Pakistan link and the decision to go nuclear as manifestations of the BJP'S apprehension about what Fernandes referred to as China's "strategic encirclement." In its efforts to stem the deterioration of ROI-PRC relations that followed India's nuclear tests in May 1998, the BJP government seemed to move away from this early shift toward linkage. The approach of future Indian governments on this crucial issue will bear close observation.

There seem to be three reasons for India's acceptance of China's proposal of delinkage. One is a sense of powerlessness. This sentiment was expressed to me by several analysts and retired officials during interviews in New Delhi in early 1999. What could India do? they asked. India had no significant leverage with China, they said. If the United States with its vast leverage over China could not succeed in halting China's transfers to Pakistan (as it tried to do in the 1990s), how could India hope to? The second reason seems to be deep mistrust of the United States. The desire to cooperate with China against the

United States and the West was attractive to many "progressive" Indians, leading them to minimize the significance of China's links with Pakistan. Others suspected that some or all of the "western reports" might be, as Beijing charged, deliberate disinformation. The third root was fear of Chinese power. The border confrontation of 1987 had raised anew the prospect of war rising out of the unresolved border issue. It also, apparently, touched Indian nerves still raw from the trauma of 1962. Lessening the prospect of war was of such paramount importance that it required forward progress in bilateral relations, regardless of continuing problems in other areas. China's dramatic 1962 demonstration of its ability and willingness to use military power effectively still echoed at century's end.

CHINESE-INDIAN COOPERATION AGAINST U.S. HEGEMONISM

Another Chinese policy helping to handle properly the contradiction between Sino-Indian rapprochement and Sino-Pakistan entente has been invitation to India to join in common struggle against U.S. hegemonism. Neither side used that phrase and both occasionally declared that their cooperation was not directed against anyone else. That, however, was diplomatic cant. The clear if unstated purpose of these joint efforts was to change the existing international order, which was perceived to be set up and upheld largely by the United States for the benefit of itself and its rich, industrialized allies.

The idea behind such cooperation is that China and India share many important characteristics. They are both large, developing countries which experienced a long period of imperialist aggression in the modern era. Moreover, as ancient civilizations and the world's two most populous countries, China and India bear a responsibility for improving the lot of mankind and especially the Third World. By cooperating on these issues, the two countries will also create an atmosphere conducive to better bilateral relations. This strategy of macro-diplomatic cooperation traces back to Zhou Enlai's very successful diplomacy toward India in the 1950s, when the two countries cooperated on such issues of the day as the Korean War, decolonization, and disarmament.[23]

By the mid-1980s calls for Sino-Indian antihegemony cooperation were a major aspect of Chinese propaganda. Rajiv Gandhi's mid-1987 shift in China policy included a general willingness, in principle, to undertake antihegemony cooperation with China. During his ninety-minute talk with Rajiv Gandhi on December 12, 1988, Deng Xiaoping stressed the prospects for Sino-Indian cooperation on such broad issues as lessening resort to military blocs as a means to security, ameliorating the economic disparities in the world, disarmament, and the "fallacious philosophy" of deterrence. Gandhi later told the press that he was "very impressed" by Deng's comments. Almost everything Deng said was "What we have been working for during these past forty years."[24] India's agreement to undertake anti–U.S. hegemony cooperation with China was embodied in a terse statement in the December 23, 1988, joint communiqué issuing from Gandhi's visit: the two sides had agreed that the Five Principles of Peaceful Coexistence "constitute the basic guidelines for the establishment of a new international political order and the new international economic order."[25] Over the next three years the two sides fleshed out the meaning of this generality. The December 1991 communiqué issued at the conclusion of Premier Li Peng's visit to India contained a full six paragraphs devoted to joint efforts to construct a "new international political and economic order" favoring the developing countries. The two sides declared a set of principles to govern this new international order. Point three conveys well the flavor of those principles:

> Efforts should be made to address the growing economic gap between the North and the South, and achieve the settlement of global economic, social, demographic and environmental problems in a manner which would benefit all members of the world community.... The developed countries are urged to address the questions of the mounting debt burdens of the developing countries, worsening terms of trade, inadequacy of financial flows and obstacles to technology transfers.[26]

An example of Sino-Indian diplomatic cooperation in construction of a new international order came in June 1990 at the international conference in London on depletion of the ozone layer. China and India worked together there to push for the free international transfer of technology necessary for manufacturing chlorofluorocarbon substitutes. When that proposition was rejected because of proprietary rights, the two countries pushed, successfully, for the establishment of an international fund to finance the transfer of necessary technology to developing countries.

While these issues are undoubtedly important, they are far less pressing than national security concerns such as nuclear-armed Pakistani missiles pointed at India. To a considerable degree, cooperation in opposing U.S. hegemony or the existing international order is a substitute for a lack of convergence of interests on security issues and for the paltry results of efforts to increase trade and economic relations between China and India. It also helps cancel, or perhaps obfuscate, the clash of Indian and Chinese interests associated with the Sino-Pakistan entente.

CHINESE DISENGAGEMENT FROM THE KASHMIR QUESTION

Modification of its position on the Kashmir issue was another element of China's effort to balance rapprochement with India and continuing entente with Pakistan. Kashmir has been the crux of Indo-Pakistani conflict since 1947. It was the cause of two wars and the shoal upon which many attempts to improve Indo-Pakistani relations foundered. From Pakistan's perspective, the essence of the problem is that India has denied and continues to deny basic human rights to the largely Muslim people of Indian-occupied Kashmir, including most importantly, the right to self-determination as provided for by United Nations Resolutions of 1948 and 1949. India, on the other hand, contends that Kashmir legally acceded to the Indian union in 1947 and that the people of Kashmir exercised their right of self-determination in 1954 when the constituent assembly of Kashmir voted for accession to India. In any case, India contends, if there remains a problem over Kashmir, according to the Simla agreement of 1972, that dispute should be solved via *bilateral* negotiations. Signed by India and Pakistan in July 1972, six months after Pakistan's defeat by India, the Simla agreement provided that the two countries would "settle their differences by peaceful means through bilateral negotiations." India viewed this as meaning that Pakistan forfeited its standing to raise the Kashmir issue in multilateral fora. In India's view the Simla agreement supersedes earlier United Nations resolutions on Kashmir and precludes efforts by Pakistan to internationalize any disagreements India and Pakistan might have over Kashmir. Pakistan rejects this interpretation of the Simla agreement, and contends that agreement in no way contradicts or supersedes the United Nations resolutions on Kashmir or limits Pakistan's right to avail itself of various international mechanisms to resolve disputes—for example through appeal to the United Nations under the UN Charter and UN resolutions. In this context references to self-determination or to UN resolutions indicate support for Pakistan, while references to strictly bilateral efforts to resolve the Kashmir problem indicate support for India.

The Kashmir issue has long been the touchstone around which the Soviet Union and China have oriented themselves regarding the Indo-Pakistani confrontation. Moscow came down squarely on India's side of the Kashmir issue in 1955, China on Pakistan's side in 1964. The joint communiqué signed during Zhou Enlai's February 1964 visit to Pakistan said that the two sides "expressed the hope that the Kashmir dispute would be resolved in accord with the wishes of the people of Kashmir as pledged to them by the people of India and Pakistan." In February 1979 when Vajpayee visited China, he told Chinese leaders that their attitude regarding Kashmir since 1964 had been "an additional and unnecessary complication to the prospects of Sino-Indian relations."[27] For the sake of better relations with New Delhi, China responded to Vajpayee's suggestion and retreated to a more neutral position on Kashmir in June 1980 when Deng Xiaoping stated that the Kashmir issue was a *bilateral dispute* between India and Pakistan which should be *solved peacefully*. Yet in December of the same year when Pakistani foreign minister Agha Shani visited Beijing, Foreign Minister Huang Hua stated that China "appreciated Pakistan's efforts to seek a just settlement of the Kashmir issue in the spirit of the Simla agreement and in accordance with the *relevant United Nations resolutions*."[28] By mentioning both the Simla agreement and UN resolutions, Beijing straddled the Pakistani and Indian positions. After 1980 Chinese officials no longer spoke about the Kashmiri people's right to self-determination, much less endorsed it, as it had done consistently from 1964 to 1979. Yet such an endorsement was still implicit in Chinese references to "relevant United Nations resolutions." Moreover, by linking the Simla accord with the UN resolutions, China implicitly endorsed Pakistan's contention that these were not mutually exclusive. Thus while China's post-1980 position on Kashmir was substantially more neutral than before, there remained a subtle but perceptible pro-Pakistan slant.

This changed during 1990. The Kashmir issue re-erupted in July 1989 when a series of anti-Indian bombings in Srinagar were followed by vigorous police actions, which were, in turn, followed by demonstrations protesting police brutality. Clashes soon occurred between demonstrators and police. The Indian government attempted to repress the growing resistance movement by massive application of police force, and a cycle of escalating repression and resistance began. The extent of alienation among the Kashmiri population was indicated during India's November 1989 general election when voter turnout in Jammu and Kashmir was perhaps as low as 5 percent. By January 1990 Kashmir was under military control and large numbers of people had been arrested. Yet demonstrations and armed attacks on Indian forces by Kashmiri militants continued. The situation soon escalated to a full-scale confrontation between India and Pakistan.

During the Kashmir crisis of 1990, China's stance on Kashmir underwent further evolution. Initial statements about the Kashmir issue were made by Li Peng during a November 1989 visit to Pakistan, and by a Foreign Ministry spokesman on February 3 and 6, 1990. The relevant words on these occasions are displayed in table 8.2. In none of these early statements was there mention of the United Nations or its resolutions but only of bilateral negotiations leading to a peaceful settlement of the issue. This omission reflected a desire to hew to a more strictly neutral line, thus avoiding antagonizing India.

Pakistan, however, was dissatisfied with Beijing's new formulations since failure to mention the United Nations resolutions contributed to the worldwide impression, which India assiduously attempted to foster, that the United Nations resolutions were obsolete and had been superseded by the Simla agreement. Pakistan's displeasure, along with a plea for a return to mention of the UN resolutions, was conveyed to China's leaders by Prime Minister Benazir Bhutto's foreign policy and national security advisor Iqbal Akhund in February 1990. China responded positively to Islamabad's request, and appropriate statements mentioning the United Nations were made by Li Peng and Qian Qichen during Akhund's visit.

Then New Delhi was unhappy with Beijing's new, revised stance on Kashmir. From India's perspective Beijing was returning to its old line of supporting Pakistan on the Kashmir issue. Talk of UN resolutions was tantamount to raising the plebiscite issue, and both UN resolutions and plebiscite had been rejected by India. The Kashmir issue was entirely India's internal affair, India insisted, in which Pakistan was interfering. As such there was no role for the United Nations, its outdated resolutions, or other variants of Islamabad's efforts to internationalize the issue. The way to solve the Kashmir problem, New Delhi said, was for Pakistan to stop interfering in India's internal affairs, stop supporting and encouraging the extremists in Kashmir. The implicit message was: if China wanted friendly relations with India, it had better stop siding with Pakistan on the Kashmir issue. These views were conveyed to Qian Qichen during his talks with External Affairs Minister I. K. Gujral in New Delhi in March.[29] Qian got the message and complied. His formulations as to how to solve the Kashmir crisis retreated to mutual "consultations." As the president of the Indian Council of World Affairs noted shortly after Qian's visit, this formulation was essentially the same as India's.[30] Qian did, however, find a way to mention the United Nations, noting that the Kashmir issue "has been discussed by the United Nations." This was a small nod to Islamabad. As far as I can determine, it was also the last one. In subsequent Chinese formulations—by Foreign Ministry spokesmen on April 4 and 19, by Wan Li in Pakistan on May 3, and by Li Peng on May 8—there was no reference to the United Nations or its resolutions.

Apparently in response to the insistent Pakistani demands for support on the Kashmir issue, and to avoid misunderstandings with Pakistan over this issue, National People's Congress chairman Wan Li traveled to Islamabad in early May for discussions. The difference between the two sides are clear when their speeches are juxtaposed. At a banquet welcoming Wan, Speaker of the Pakistani National Assembly Mehraj Khalid praised the Pakistan-China bond for upholding the United Nations Charter and referred

TABLE 8.2 Evolution of the PRC Position on Kashmir

November 16, 1989 Li Peng TV interview in Pakistan	Should "resolve on the basis of the Five Principles of Peaceful Coexistence and through friendly consultations."
February 5, 1990 MFA spokesman	Should "settle peacefully through friendly consultations."
February 15, 1990 Li Peng to Akhund	Should "act in accord with relevant UN resolutions and accords reached by both countries, and resolve the dispute on the basis of friendly consultations."
February 16, 1990 Qian Qichen to Akhund	Should "resolve peacefully through friendly negotiations in accord with the relevant decisions of the United Nations and the Simla agreement reached by the two countries."
February 20, 1990 Qin Jiwei to Bhutto	Should "solve the Kashmir issue in accordance with the relevant United Nations resolutions and agreements between the two countries."
March 23, 1990 Qian Qichen in New Delhi	Should "resolve problems through mutual peaceful consultations on the basis of the Five Principles of Peaceful Coexistence." The Kashmir issue "has been discussed by the United Nations."
April 4, 1990 MFA spokesman	Should "sit together soon and seek a peaceful solution through negotiations."
April 19, 1990 MFA spokesman	Should "seek a peaceful solution through negotiations."
May 3, 1990 Wan Li in Pakistan	Should "find a peaceful solution through negotiations."
May 8, 1990 Li Peng to Nusrat Bhutto	Should "seek a peaceful solution through mutual consultation."
May 24, 1990 MFA spokesman	Should "work to ease tension through dialogue."
December 15, 1991 Li Peng during India visit	"As for disputes between India and Pakistan, we hope the two countries will settle them properly through negotiations . . . and will not resort to force."

to Pakistan's support of the struggle of the Kashmiri people for self-determination. Wan merely termed the Sino-Pakistan relation a model of friendly cooperation between countries of different social systems. He made no mention of the United Nations or its resolutions. Instead, he said China "appreciated" Pakistan's willingness to solve the problem through negotiations.[31] Prime Minister Benazir Bhutto later traveled to Beijing to personally lobby for Chinese support for referral of the Kashmir issue to the United Nations. Beijing again declined. China would not become involved in the Kashmir dispute. "The issues existing between Pakistan and India—including the Kashmir dispute—must in the end be resolved properly through patient, bilateral dialogue," a Chinese Foreign Ministry spokesman said.[32]

Beijing declined to support Islamabad's efforts to internationalize the Kashmir issue. By early 1990 Pakistan was considering mobilizing international support for the convocation of a special session of the United Nations on Kashmir. According to Chinese diplomats in Islamabad interviewed by this author in mid-1990, China advised against efforts to bring the Kashmir issue before or to convene a special session of the United Nations. There was simply too little international interest in the issue, they said. India was satisfied with China's position on Kashmir during the 1990 crisis. High-level Indian diplomats in Beijing characterized China's position as relatively balanced. China had not reiterated its old position of support for Pakistan on this issue. Nor had it made any moves to involve the United Nations. China's primary objective was to avoid a conflict between India and Pakistan, they said, and to this end, it had encouraged de-escalation and all trends in that direction.

Six more years of Sino-Indian rapprochement produced further incremental pro-Indian shifts in Beijing's Kashmir policy. Several days before President Jiang Zemin's December 1996 visit to India and Pakistan, China's ambassador to India told the media: "We do not stand for internationalization of the Kashmir question," thereby directly and publicly rejecting Pakistan's approach to the problem. Addressing the Pakistani Senate, Jiang urged resolution of Pakistani-Indian disputes via "consultations and negotiations." Throughout his forty-five-minute speech Jiang did not mention Kashmir, a fact that Indian observers saw as highly significant.[33]

A final aspect of China's policy on the Kashmir issue has to do with the level of China's deterrent support for Pakistan during periods of Indo-Pakistan confrontation over Kashmir. In this area too, China distanced itself from Pakistan during the process of Sino-Indian rapprochement. By deterrent support I mean threats, explicit or implicit, that China might enter a military conflict on the side of Pakistan. Such support was an important component of the Sino-Pakistani relation during the 1960s, 1970s, and 1980s. When Foreign Minister Wu Xueqian visited Pakistan in July 1983, for example, at a time when Moscow was outraged at Pakistan's role in supporting the Afghan mujahideen and was reportedly trying to persuade India to take action against Pakistan, Wu was asked at a press conference what China's position would be if Pakistan suffered foreign armed attack. Wu replied: "First of all, I strongly approve of the Pakistan government's policy of friendly good relations with its neighbors. . . . Pakistan is China's exceptionally friendly neighbor. If there is a war and Pakistan suffers foreign armed attack, the Chinese government and people will, of course, stand on the side of Pakistan."[34]

If we use Wu Xueqian's 1983 statement as a yardstick, it becomes apparent that China's deterrent support during the 1990 Indo-Pakistan confrontation over Kashmir was soft. During his November 1989 visit to Pakistan, Li Peng was presented with an opportunity comparable to Wu Xueqian's earlier one. Li clumsily dodged it. When a Pakistani reporter recalled that China had stood with Pakistan whenever it had faced aggression in the past and asked if China would continue to do so in the future, Li replied that the question seemed to refer to a possible conflict between Pakistan and India. This was a purely hypothetical situation, Li said. China hoped there would be no such conflict.[35] On another occasion Li was briefed by Pakistani officials about the India-Pakistan conflict over the Siachen glacier and about how the agreement to reduce forces in that region had run into snags. When asked if he agreed with the presentation, Li replied that it was not a question of whether he agreed or disagreed but whether Pakistan and China shared common perceptions, which they did.[36]

War clouds thickened over Kashmir in early 1990. New Delhi's strategy apparently was to increase military pressure on Pakistan, forcing it to suspend its (putative) support to the Kashmiri and Punjabi militants.[37] Failing that, New Delhi was preparing the option of striking against the supposed training camps in Pakistan or, in extremis, for a "fourth round" with Pakistan. Pakistan denied supporting the Kashmiri militants and refused to repress demonstrations of sympathy within Pakistan for the Kashmiris. Facing Indian pressure, Islamabad responded with a counter-buildup of its own. In December 1989, Pakistan launched its largest ever peacetime military exercise—a three-week-long operation involving two hundred thousand troops simulating defense against an Indian invasion.[38] As the buildup of Indian forces along Pakistan's borders quickened in early 1990, Indian spokesmen made ominous statements about the danger of war and condemned Pakistani interference in India's internal affairs. Pakistani spokesmen rejected Indian allegations and protests, condemned India's "provocative ultimatums," and called on India to cease its brutal suppression of Kashmiri Muslims. Indian repression in Kashmir stimulated the sympathy of Pakistanis for their Kashmiri brethren, and demonstrations of that sympathy in areas near the border grew. On February 5 thirty thousand Pakistanis demonstrated on the border, with some pushing across the border into Indian territory. When a further border crossing occurred on February 11, Indian troops opened fire. The Indian and Pakistani foreign offices traded protests. The situation was fraught with the danger of miscalculation.

In the midst of these mounting tensions Chinese defense minister Qin Qiwei arrived in Pakistan on February 19 at the head of a ten-man military delegation including the PLA deputy chief of staff, the commander of the Lanzhou military district (which includes China's borders with Pakistan and India's Ladakh), and the deputy commander of the Beijing military region. Given the tense context, the visit by a large PLA delegation itself signaled China's deterrent support for Pakistan. The message was that Sino-Pakistani relations, including military relations, would continue independently of Indian-Pakistani relations. During his speech at a banquet hosted by Pakistan's minister of defense, Qin lauded Sino-Pakistani friendship as solid and having withstood the test of time. He praised Pakistan for supporting the Afghan people's struggle against foreign aggression and for having played an active role in maintaining peace and stability in South Asia. The implicit content of these words was significant: Pakistan was an important strategic partner of China's. Qin continued: "The Chinese government will never change its policy [of] supporting the Pakistan government, people, and armed forces in safeguarding their state sovereignty and territorial integrity, no matter how the international situation changes."[39] These words could be read as a hint that China would support Pakistan if peace failed. This was China's strongest statement of deterrent support for Pakistan during the 1989–90 Kashmir crisis, the language significantly weaker than Wu Xueqian's words had been in 1983.

Most Chinese statements during the 1990 Kashmir crisis simply called for peace. During Iqbal Akhund's February mission to Beijing, for example, Li Peng said that China was "very concerned" about the developing situation in Kashmir and hoped that the situation would soon "calm down." The Chinese government, Li said, expected that Pakistan and India would settle their disputes in line with the Five Principles of Peaceful Coexistence through negotiations and without resorting to force in order to prevent the situation from getting worse. This resolution would be beneficial to stability and peace in the subcontinent and in Asia.[40] China's approach did not change even as tension peaked in April and May with small but lethal clashes between Pakistani and Indian forces and press reports that both sides were readying nuclear weapons for use. During his visit to Pakistan in early May, at the height of the crisis, Wan Li merely said, "We appreciate Pakistan's attitude on opposing the use of military force, trying to stop the escalation of the situation, and resolving the issue through negotiations."[41]

Measured against earlier periods, China's deterrent support for Pakistan has declined under the conditions of Sino-Indian rapprochement. While this is a significant development, one should not conclude from it that Pakistan's leaders were particularly unhappy with China's stance during the 1990 crisis. While they would undoubtedly have liked stronger nuances in China's choice of words, they nonetheless felt that China's pro-peace stance benefited Pakistan. Pakistani officials and specialists whom I talked with in Islamabad during the summer of 1990 were not unhappy with the level of Chinese support during the 1990 crisis. They saw China as a reliable friend that, unlike the United States, could be counted on in emergencies. Subtleties of language were less important to them than underlying perceptions and purposes, and these, they were confident, would lead China to continue to support Pakistan against India. They understood Beijing's need to mince words for the sake of placating India but remained confident that, when push came to shove, China would be there. Pakistani journalists sometimes expected Chinese leaders to speak bluntly, and, when they declined to do so, the journalists misinterpreted China's intentions, according to Chinese diplomatic sources. On these occasions Chinese diplomats sought these reporters out and explained to them that, in view of the long friendship between China and Pakistan, a friendship tested by adversity, China would not abandon Pakistan in the event of a crisis. Most journalists understood and appreciated these comments.

CHINA'S MILITARY AID TO PAKISTAN

Large-scale and sustained assistance to Pakistan's military development has been one of the most important dimensions of the Sino-Pakistani entente. It was unaffected by the Sino-Indian rapprochement. Between 1956, when the PRC began giving aid to noncommunist nations, and the mid-1980s, Pakistan was the top-ranking recipient of Chinese assistance, outranking the next-highest recipient (Sri Lanka) by 500 percent. During that period China extended between $400 million and $1 billion in aid to Pakistan.[42] Much of this aid was military. China has been, along with the United States, Pakistan's major supplier of military equipment. Of Pakistan's two major suppliers, China has been far more understanding of Pakistan's perspectives. Twice when the United States suspended arms aid to Pakistan—in 1965 and in 1990—China stepped in to meet Pakistan's needs. After the United States cut off aid in 1965, China was, for a period, the only nation willing to extend significant military assistance to Pakistan. Again, after a U.S. suspension of military aid in 1990, Chinese equipment substituted for American. China also provided major shipments of military hardware to Pakistan in the run-up to both the 1965 and 1971 wars with India. It also stepped in to make good Pakistan's losses in those contests. Following Pakistan's 1971 defeat, for example, China deferred for twenty years payment on a 1970 loan worth $200 million and wrote off another $110 million in earlier loans. Chinese shipments of tanks, jet fighters, trucks, and small arms helped Pakistan rebuild its shattered armed forces after the 1971 defeat.[43]

China strongly supported Pakistan's military modernization efforts in the mid-1980s. In terms of air force capabilities, between 1986 and 1988 China delivered 90 F-5A fighters and 60 F-7 fighters to Pakistan. In 1987 Pakistan ordered another 150 F-7 fighters from China to be fitted with U.S. General Electric–made F404 engines and U.S.-designed avionics and fire control systems.[44] This hybrid aircraft, designated the F-7P, which Pakistan began to deploy in 1989, is a highly modernized version of the MiG-21, with high engine performance, lethality, and weapons-carrying ability. It is also about one-fifth the cost of a U.S.-made F-16. The F-7P fighters were to replace the F-6 as Pakistan's main ground support aircraft. Some of Pakistan's unneeded F-6s were transferred to Bangladesh. China also helped Pakistan modernize its tank force. Between 1978 and 1988 China supplied Pakistan with 825 T-59 tanks. In the early 1980s it also set up the Heavy Rebuild Factory outside Rawalpindi to overhaul those T-59s and manufacture many parts, including the engines for that tank.[45]

Between 1988 and 1992, a period when Sino-Indian rapprochement was gaining steam, China provided Pakistan with nearly $2 billion in major conventional weapons, which represented about 56 percent of Pakistan's arms purchases during that period.[46] These sales included another ninety-eight F-5As and forty more F-7 fighters.[47] For Pakistan's ground forces China agreed to supply during these years 450 T-69II main battle tanks and another 282 T-85IIAP main battle tanks. China also contracted to supply 200 anti-tank missiles.[48] In June 1990 the North China Industries Corporation (NORINCO) and the Pakistan Defense Ministry signed an agreement regarding the joint design and development of a new tank to be Pakistan's main battle tank in the twenty-first century, expected to be a state-of-the-art weapon with increased mobility, lethality, and survivability. NORINCO was also to provide Pakistan progressively with the technology for the manufacture of T-69 and T-85 tanks.[49] This assistance substituted for Pakistan's lost U.S. cooperation. Abrams main battle tanks were among the U.S. equipment scheduled for transfer to Pakistan but canceled in October 1990. China-Pakistan arms transfers became more intensive as China replaced the United States in the

1990s. China's arms exports to other countries were also falling by the mid-1990s, as customers began turning to higher-quality weapons. China and Pakistan needed each other. Between 1993 and 1997 Pakistan purchased an astonishing 51 percent of China's total conventional arms exports, while China supplied over 60 percent of Pakistan's total conventional arms imports.[50]

During the 1990s China and Pakistan cooperated in joint development of advanced fighter aircraft, thereby partially nullifying U.S. sanctions against both countries. Following the Beijing massacre of June 1989, the United States suspended a U.S. Grumman Corporation program to produce a highly modified MiG-21 fighter for the PLA. The next year the United States suspended the sale of seventy-one F-16 fighters to Pakistan (twenty-eight of which Pakistan had already paid $658 million for) out of opposition to Pakistan's nuclear weapons activities.[51] China and Pakistan responded to American pressure by undertaking joint development of an entirely new fighter, the FC-1. Intended as an equivalent to the F-16, the FC-1 was powered by a Russian-supplied turbojet engine and included other Russian components. It went into service with the Pakistani air force in 1999. An assembly line was set up in Pakistan to put together kits shipped from China, while Pakistan was to play a leading role in exporting the new fighter to developing country clients on behalf of China and Pakistan.[52]

China played a crucial role in Pakistan's guided and ballistic missile programs. In February and May 1989 Pakistan tested 80- and 300-kilometer-range surface-to-surface missiles. New Delhi reacted strongly to both tests. Yet in November of the same year, among four agreements signed during Li Peng's visit to Pakistan was one regarding economic and technological cooperation financed by a Chinese loan of 100 million RMB. According to press reports, one aspect of this agreement dealt with Chinese assistance to Pakistan's rocket program.[53] Two weeks after Li Peng's visit Lieutenant General Ding Henggao, head of China's State Commission for Science, Technology, and Industry for National Defense, signed a memorandum of understanding in Islamabad covering stepped-up joint procurement, research, and development in the national defense industry over a ten-year period. Electronics and computers were two areas highlighted by the agreement. Between 1990 and 1997 China supplied Pakistan with 850 Anza-I portable surface-to-air missiles, 750 anti-tank missiles, and another 275 surface-to-air missiles.[54] It also supplied ninety-six Ly-60N ship-board air defense missiles for use in refitting Pakistan's fleet of British-built 1970s vintage frigates.[55] In addition to whole missiles, China provided technology to facilitate Pakistan's indigenization of these weapons systems.

China also supplied critical assistance to Pakistan's efforts to develop missiles capable of delivering nuclear warheads. In early 1988 Beijing and Islamabad secretly concluded an agreement to cooperate in Pakistan's acquisition of M-11 ballistic missiles. The M-11 is a solid-fuel rocket with a 185-mile (309 km) range carrying a 1,100-pound warhead. It is capable of carrying nuclear warheads. Under the 1988 agreement China agreed to train Pakistanis in the operation of M-11, transfer necessary equipment and technology to Pakistan, transfer thirty or so complete M-11s, and build a factory in Pakistan for indigenous production of the missiles. The deal and subsequent measures implementing it were highly secret, but U.S. intelligence—which had developed wide assets in South Asia to monitor just such matters—soon learned of it. In the early 1990s China transferred M-11-related technology and components to Pakistan. In 1995 complete M-11 missiles arrived in Pakistan, although to avoid U.S. sanctions and under an informal understanding with the United States they were left in their canister containers and stored at a Pakistani air force base. Also in 1995, U.S. surveillance satellites observed construction of an unusual-looking facility north of Islamabad. The buildings were long with very large doors. Outside was a sturdy structure such as is used for testing rocket engines. The whole layout was very similar to an M-11 factory in Hubei province, China. Telephone intercepts and reports from agents on the ground also indicated that a dozen Chinese engineers from the China Precision Machinery Import and Export Corporation, the enterprise responsible for China's exports of M-11s, had visited the site. By October 1996 the CIA and other U.S. intelligence agencies agreed that China was helping Pakistan build an M-11 factory. It was expected to be completed in 1999.[56]

The motivations underlying China's assistance to Pakistan's ballistic missile program were complex. The issue was linked, or at least *became linked,* to the U.S. sale of F-16 fighters to Taiwan in 1992. When U.S. representatives raised with China the M-11 transfers to Pakistan, China's representatives replied by denying it and then raising the issue of the U.S. sale of F-16s to Taiwan. China's M-11 sales were also quite profitable for politically well-connected Chinese enterprises. They also fit with the pattern of Chinese missile sales to other Islamic countries of Southwest Asia such as Saudi Arabia and Iran. But among the important motives for Beijing's assistance to Pakistan's missile program was a desire to strengthen Pakistan against India.

The frequency of high-level military exchanges is a good, if rough, indicator of the intensity of Sino-Pakistan military cooperation. These exchanges were associated with new or ongoing cooperation and were essential for mutual familiarization that is at the core of effective military cooperation. A count of high-level military exchanges between China and Pakistan based

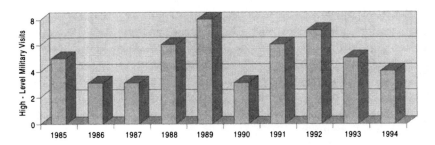

FIGURE 8.1   Sino-Pakistani Military Exchanges, 1985–1994.
SOURCE: Indexes for *Foreign Broadcast Information Service, Daily Report China*
(published by *Newsday*, various years).

on indexes of the Foreign Broadcast Information Service is presented in figure
8.1. It is apparent by this measure, too, that the Sino-Pakistan military relation did not diminish as Sino-Indian rapprochement blossomed after Rajiv
Gandhi's visit. In fact, there was a slight increase in military exchanges in
1988 and 1989 as China maneuvered toward rapprochement with India. This
may have been part of a Chinese effort to prevent China's relation with India
and Pakistan from becoming a zero-sum game. A major purpose behind Li
Peng's November 1989 South Asian tour was to reassure China's friends in
that region that China planned to stay engaged there. Li Peng was accompanied by PLA deputy chief of general staff He Qizhong, who conducted
talks with Pakistan's army chief of staff on "matters of mutual interest."

In sum, while Chinese diplomatic and deterrent support for Pakistan over
Kashmir weakened as a result of Beijing's rapprochement with New Delhi,
its military assistance to Pakistan did not diminish, and that assistance
extended to several crucial areas. Pakistan remained the largest recipient of
Chinese military assistance.

China's assistance to Pakistan's military programs created discomfort in
New Delhi. Beijing has been cognizant of Indian displeasure and tried to address
it. Early in 1990, shortly before Qin Qiwei's visit to Pakistan, for example,
China's Foreign Ministry briefed Indian embassy officials on recent Chinese
exchanges with Pakistan, including exchanges in the military area. The purpose of these briefings was reportedly to develop a mechanism to exchange
information regarding interactions between China and India's South Asian
neighbors in order to minimize misunderstanding.[57] Clearly, Beijing wants to
assure New Delhi of the defensive intent of its military relations with India's
neighbors, thus maximizing the chances that China will be able to improve
relations with India without sacrificing its close relations with Pakistan.

China again carefully balanced between India and Pakistan during the crisis over Kargil in 1999. In April 1999 Pakistani infiltrators occupied strategic mountaintops near Kargil, on the Indian side of the line of control in Kashmir and overlooking a main Indian road to Ladakh. India responded with powerful assaults to retake the heights. A three-month mini-war between India and Pakistan ensued. Pakistan's intention was apparently to raise tensions between recently openly nuclear India and Pakistan to such an extent as to force the international community to place the Kashmir issue on the Security Council agenda. Sino-American relations were then very tense because of Chinese opposition to NATO's war against Yugoslavia and the U.S. bombing of the Chinese embassy in Belgrade. This may have led Islamabad to anticipate China would lend its support to offset American pressure. In any case, as tension over Kargil escalated, Pakistani and Indian leaders traveled to Beijing to lobby for Chinese support. Jaswant Singh made his first visit to China as India's foreign minister in June, followed shortly afterward by Pakistani foreign minister Sartaz Aziz and Prime Minister Mohammad Nawaz Sharif.

China listened to the presentations of both sides regarding the situation in Kashmir and expressed its own, carefully balanced and neutral views regarding the situation there. President Jiang Zemin made publicized remarks about the "all-weather friendship" and "all-round cooperation" of Sino-Pakistani friendship that had "withstood the test of time and has been proven to be vigorous."[58] The Chinese government considered its relationship with Pakistan "very important" and in accord with the "fundamental interests of the two peoples" and "the peace and stability in Asia and the world at large." But Chinese leaders told Sharif and Aziz that China would not support a Pakistani effort to raise the Kashmir issue in the Security Council.[59] Chinese Foreign Ministry statements stressed that the way to solve the Kashmir problem was patient and frank negotiations between India and Pakistan, that is, via bilateral negotiations.[60] *Beijing Review*'s commentary was evenhanded, giving roughly equal coverage to the Pakistani and Indian explanations of events. It also avoided any mention of the UN Kashmir Resolutions of 1948, with their call for a plebiscite.[61] In the midst of the crisis China agreed, in principle, to the initiation of a "security dialogue" between India and China, and Foreign Minister Tang Jiaxuan called for China and India to stop regarding the other as a threat. In all, Indian leaders were quite satisfied that China had not supported Pakistan against India during the 1999 imbroglio. One of the most significant long-range implications of the 1999 Kargil situation may prove to be that China is emerging as a crucial balancer in the Indian-Pakistani relation.

THE FIVE PRINCIPLES OF PEACEFUL COEXISTENCE
AND CHINA IN SOUTH ASIA

Beijing's insistence on the Five Principles of Peaceful Coexistence and its success in persuading India to agree to them as the basis for regulating China's
relations with the South Asian countries have served China's interests well.
The basis for relations among *all* countries of the region, Chinese diplomats
tell their Indian counterparts, should be the Five Principles of Peaceful
Coexistence. In plain speech this means that India cannot expect China to
stunt its relations with Pakistan for India's sake and that, if India does not
attack or threaten Pakistan, Pakistan's China-supplied weapons will not be
directed against India.

Improved Indian-Chinese relations following Rajiv Gandhi's mission to
Beijing have made relations between Beijing and Islamabad more nuanced and
more complex. Beijing has tried to balance its entente cordiale with Pakistan
against its new rapprochement with India. The China-Pakistan-India triangle has not, however, become a zero-sum game. Better relations between India
and China have not led to a weakening of the Sino-Pakistani entente. China
has been fairly effective in pursuing these two relationships simultaneously.

Beijing's policy of carefully balancing continued entente with Pakistan with
an effort to improve relations with India would face the most severe challenges,
and possibly collapse, in the event of a conflict between those two South Asian
powers. This is one reason why Beijing lauds and encourages efforts to improve
Pakistani-Indian relations, for it knows that Indo-Pakistani conflict will present
it with difficult choices between the two contradictory elements of its subcontinental policy. A desire to avoid a choice between Islamabad and New Delhi
was one important reason for China's peace diplomacy during the 1990
Kashmir crisis. A decade later, following the India-Pakistan nuclear tests of 1998,
China again lauded efforts to reduce tensions between those two countries.

In the event of an Indian-Pakistani war, what would China do? The answer
depends on several contingent factors. One would have to do with the causes
of the war, especially the extent to which China's links to South Asian countries were responsible for precipitating India's resort to arms. China would
more forcefully defend its own ties to South Asian countries than it would
other aspects. China's response would also depend on its domestic and international situation at the time. India's objectives and the probable outcome
of the war if China did not intervene would probably be the most important
factor. A limited Indo-Pakistani war would be one matter. A large war in which
New Delhi seemed likely to subordinate Pakistan decisively would be another
matter.

One factor that would probably remain constant is Chinese perceptions of India. There seems to be a consensus among Chinese analysts of Indian affairs that only a firm policy based on a position of strength will compel India to act soberly toward China. One classified and authoritative study that took a relatively optimistic view about Sino-Indian relations concluded that a precondition for the development of Sino-Indian friendship was the maintenance of adequate deterrent force on China's border with India. Even though pro-peace people were currently dominant in India's elite, the article said, many others wanted a test of strength with China to revenge India's defeat in 1962. India was also plagued by many internal contradictions, which could lead to foreign adventures. Moreover, China should recognize the Janus-faced nature of India's leaders—their tendency to speak of peace and rely on force. Therefore, China had to remain vigilant.[62]

For Beijing sustaining a strong Pakistan independent of Indian domination and linked militarily to China is a fundamental element of maintaining a position of strength vis-à-vis India. If India were able to uncouple China and Pakistan, subordinate Pakistan, or destroy its military potential, India would be able to concentrate its forces against China. Another classified Chinese study made this explicit. While there were no indications of a major war between China and India in the immediate future, the study said, under certain circumstances India's leaders might decide on war with China. The main precondition for such a war would be to improve India's relations with Pakistan so that India could avoid a two-front war.[63] In other words, a prudent Chinese policy would sustain Pakistan against India.

Pakistan is in a different category than Sri Lanka or Nepal, which China did, in 1986–87 and 1989–90, respectively, leave to their fates at India's hands. Pakistan is a significant mid-range power that has demonstrated substantial staying power against India over the past forty years, and the substance of Pakistan's national strength puts it in a different category. The Sino-Indian territorial dispute also remains a fundamental source of instability in that relationship, and, given the possibility of war arising out of the territorial conflict, it would not be prudent for China to sacrifice her major subcontinental ally. Moreover, China has aspirations of being an Asian and ultimately a global power. To sacrifice Pakistan would be tantamount to conceding South Asia as India's sphere of influence. This would constitute a devastating blow to China's aspirations of Asian preeminence. A reunited subcontinent, or a subcontinent under effective Indian domination, would also pose a much greater threat to China. The reality of overwhelming Indian power might compel China to accept the situation, but China would resist.

Whatever the validity of these observations, it is clear that Indian security planners believe that, in the event of an all-out Sino-Indian war or a major Indo-Pakistani war, Pakistan or China would enter the conflict against India. Thus, India must keep guard in the west while dealing with any northern challenge. Indian contingency planning for a major war with Pakistan typically assumes Chinese intervention. The scenarios are many. One variant vetted in the early 1990s envisioned a decisive Indian ten-day war against Pakistan in retaliation for the "low-intensity, proxy war" India believes Pakistan has been waging against India since the late 1980s. In response to increasing Pakistani support for terrorists and separatists in Punjab, Kashmir, and other areas of India, India decides to administer a decisive blow to "'break Pakistan's will to support terrorism and insurgency." Indian forces are hypothetically ordered to destroy Pakistan's "war making potential which underpins her confidence in persisting with her destabilization efforts" against India: "You will generate and maintain high levels of psychological shock action [*sic*] to bring the lesson home to the Government of Pakistan and its people that such action of theirs has invited this retaliation." Under such circumstances "it would be sensible to assume that China will also get into the act."[64]

Short of such extreme outcomes, one is left to ponder the balance of gain in the China-Pakistan-India accommodation. India has secured an important shift in China's policy on Kashmir and in Beijing's approach to other intra–South Asian disputes. Beijing also now uses its influence with Islamabad to discourage resort to force to solve or internationalize the Kashmir problem. China would not necessarily like to see a final, definitive resolution of the Kashmir question since that could recast the India-Pakistan relation reducing China's leverage, but neither does it wish to see a major Indo-Pakistani conflict that would force it to choose between the two contradictory strands of its policy. This too would be a major gain for India.

Yet India has also been compelled to acquiesce to a steady increase in Pakistan's military capabilities, with China playing a crucial role in the process. It is probably fair to conclude that, without China's large-scale, sustained, and comprehensive assistance, Pakistan's military capabilities would be far less potent and far less threatening to India than they are today. Nor has India succeeded in weakening the core of the Sino-Pakistani entente. The mutual trust, familiarity, and parallel interests that constitute that core remain unchanged by Sino-Indian rapprochement. This constitutes a major constraint on India's freedom to act.

9 / Burma

The Back Door to China

BURMA'S GEOPOLITICAL ROLE AS THE BACK DOOR TO CHINA

Burma's relations with the world have been deeply influenced by the fact that it has frequently served as a corridor for the movement of goods and armies between East Asia and South Asia. In wartime Burma has been an invasion corridor comparable to the Korean peninsula, the Khyber Pass, or the plains of northern Europe. In times of peace Burma has provided the most convenient access between the high seas and southwestern China over which commerce may flow. Burma has often served, some have said, as the back door to China. The central valley of Burma is formed by the sweep of the Irrawaddy River. On the valley's eastern fringe rises a broad plateau constituting, on the Burma side of the border, the Shan States, and on the Chinese side, the Yunnan plateau. On the Chinese side the elevation rises fairly gradually from Guiyang in Guizhou province up to Kunming, the capital of Yunnan province. From Kunming a westerly route crosses a series of mountain ranges running north to south and between which flow the Mekong, Salween, and Yangtze Rivers, plus many lesser waterways. As these mountain ranges ascend toward the Tibetan plateau in the north, they reach twenty thousand feet. Their elevation falls to half that in their southern reaches, around modern Baoshan. The valley floors between the ranges are at four to five thousand feet, so routes crossing them have only a modest rise. The mountains are steep and the rivers between them swift, especially when the snows melt, but they have been crossed or spanned for commercial purposes for the last two thousand years. In Upper Burma the western edge of this plateau forms the modern Sino-Myanmar border, west of which is what Marco Polo, who traveled this route, described as a "great descent" into the valley of the Irrawaddy River. There land or river travel to the sea is easy.

Building and operating roads over this route to Burma was not easy or cheap in ancient times. Yet by the second century B.C. silk from Sichuan was flowing over this route into India and thence to the West. Indeed, it was probably the most commercially important of the several "silk roads" carrying China's precious products to the world. Securing control over this valuable trade route was a primary factor drawing Chinese armies into the region, and by 105 B.C. China's Han dynasty rulers (206 B.C.–A.D. 220) ordered work to begin on the construction of a road over these ranges. Roads were carved zigzagging up and down mountains. Rope and bamboo bridges were built across some rivers, while ferries served on others. A millennium and a half later, in 1475, during the Ming dynasty, one of the larger of these wooden bridges over the Mekong River was replaced by a 350-foot-long and 13-foot-wide iron-chain bridge, the first of its kind in China (and probably the world) and strong enough to be passable by elephants. This difficult and expensive route was kept open because of the rich trade in Chinese silks which flowed over it into India. Gems, ivory, and rhinoceros horn made up the return cargo.[1]

Han dynasty strategists sought to control this lucrative southwestern route to India via a tributary relation with the local kingdom controlling the area around Dali and Baoshan, plus settlement of Chinese at key points along the route. This system worked for several centuries, but in the mid-seventh century Chinese influence was pushed back by the emergence of a powerful Thai kingdom of Nanzhao in western Yunnan, with its capital at Dali. Nanzhao resisted Chinese advances for the next five centuries, but in 1253 it fell to the Mongol onslaught. With that development the back door to China was finally and fully opened. Yunnan became a part of China, and a centuries-long process of sinicization of that region began.[2]

The Burma back door began to play a strategic military role under the Mongols. The conquest of Nanzhao was linked to the Mongol effort to outflank and finally destroy China's long-resisting Southern Song dynasty (A.D. 1127–1279). Once this was done and the Yuan dynasty was established, Mongol strategists began planning the conquest of Southeast Asia. A pincer campaign along the two flanks of that region was devised. Overland and naval-amphibious offensives were to be launched against Annam (as Vietnam was then known), and through the South China Sea from Guangzhou against Annam and against the Hindu Khmer kingdom of Cham with its capital at Danang. To the west Mongol armies were to sweep down through Burma and then turn southeast to join up with Yuan armies moving west from the South China Sea coast. Continental Southeast Asia would thus be brought into the Mongol imperium. Both elements of this attack eventually failed—largely because of the tenacious resistance of the Vietnamese and the Burmese. The point, however, is that Burma, with its convenient access from southwest China, figured prominently in Mongol strategy.

In 1271 and again in 1273 Kublai Khan, the founder of the Mongol Yuan dynasty, demanded that the kingdom of Pagan in Burma become his vassal. Kublai had adopted traditional Chinese forms of tributary relations with neighboring states but turned them to new expansionist schemes. Pagan was Burma's first unified kingdom, founded in 1044, with its capital southwest of modern Mandalay. By the time of the Yuan ultimatums the kingdom of Pagan encompassed northern and central Burma. In 1277 a Mongol army of sixty thousand invaded Pagan, traveling westward across the Shan plateau. The Yuan army was defeated and thrown back. A larger Yuan army renewed the offensive in 1283. Pagan forces were this time defeated, but a combination of tenacious guerrilla resistance, hot climate, malaria, and monsoon rains halted the Mongol advance. Upper Burma nevertheless became a Chinese province, which then served as the base for renewed Yuan offensives in 1287 and 1301. Pagan was finally taken in 1287. Tropical climates, malaria, and determined Burmese resistance thwarted Yuan imperial designs, and in 1303 Mongol forces withdrew from Upper Burma, and the Chinese province there was abolished. Several of the small states left in the aftermath of the Yuan onslaught, however, became loyal vassals of the Yuan throne.[3] The kingdom of Pagan never recovered, though its myriad magnificent temples remain to this day sprawled across a wide bend of the Irrawaddy River.

Four centuries later, in the interregnum between China's Ming (1368–1644) and Qing (1644–1911) dynasties, Burma's back door again came into play in a less dramatic fashion. The last pretender to the Ming throne fled, first to Yunnan and then into Burma with his defeated armies. Those remnant forces soon became marauders oppressing Burmese villages but were too powerful to be suppressed by the weak Burmese government. Eventually, a strong force of the new Qing dynasty entered Burma (in 1662), apprehended and executed the Ming pretender, and shattered his forces. Fighting was heavy and devastated wide regions of Burma. There were strong echoes of this episode after the collapse of the Republic of China in 1949, when Nationalist Chinese remnants fled into Burma.

The last major Chinese *imperial* thrust into Burma came in the 1760s during Qian Long's long reign. In this case Beijing's objective had to do with maintaining a balance of power in this sensitive region by preventing Burma from becoming too strong. Burma's third great empire had been founded by King Alaungpaya in 1752 and expanded across most of modern Burma into Assam and the Shan states. In the 1760s King Hsinbyushin (r. 1763–76) launched a war of conquest against the Siamese kingdom. Siam's capital of Ayuthia was taken and sacked by Burmese forces in 1766. Siam, a tributary of China, appealed to China's Qing dynasty for help. Beijing, fearful that Burma was becoming too powerful, agreed to help. Between 1765 and 1769 four increasingly powerful Chinese invasions of Burma were launched. Each was defeated with heavy Chinese losses, but ultimately they achieved their purpose.[4] The last Chinese offensive, in 1769, entailed a force of sixty thousand commanded by one of Beijing's top generals. The plan for the invasion called for the advance of two armies down either bank of the Irrawaddy on the Burmese capital at Ava, while a third army seized Bhamo. The Chinese armies were outmaneuvered and outfought and were on the verge of being annihilated when the Burmese commander called a halt and offered the Chinese commander the opportunity to come to terms and withdraw his remaining forces to China. The famous words of the Burmese general are worth quoting, for they convey quite well what became the traditional view of Burmese statesmen toward Burma's large northern neighbor: "Comrades, unless we make peace, yet another invasion will come, and when we have defeated it yet another invasion will come. Our nation cannot go on just repelling invasion after invasion of the Chinese, for we have other things to do. Let us stop this slaughter and let their people and our people live and trade in peace."[5]

Under the agreement ending the 1769 invasion, China agreed to respect Burma's rule over the Shan states that had historically been part of the Burmese kingdom. The emperor of China and the king of Burma also agreed to "resume their previous friendly relations," entailing regularly exchanging embassies conveying goodwill and exchanging presents. From the Chinese perspective this meant that Burma had "resumed" its status as a tributary of China. Twelve Burmese tributary missions subsequently arrived in Beijing between 1776 and 1875.[6] As important, the diversion of Burmese energies to deal with China allowed Siam to recover its independence and begin rebuilding its power after its capital was devastated.

After Qian Long the Qing dynasty began its long slide toward extinction. Not for another 180 years would China reemerge, in 1949, as a major player in this region. Instead, a new imperial power emerged on the scene—Britain. The incorporation of Lower Burma into British India was *not* inspired by a desire to control trade corridors into China. By the time of the third and final Anglo-Burmese war in 1885, however, that objective *did* figure prominently in British calculations. Britain was then rapidly expanding its markets in China's interior. The opening of the Suez Canal in 1869, combined with the development of large, iron-hull, steam powered, propeller- driven commercial ships about the same time, greatly facilitated British exports. Anglo-Burmese trade increased fivefold in the years after the opening of the Suez route. Many of the goods flowed northward into southwest China. British goods also faced (or so it seemed likely at the time) increased competition in southwest China from French goods channeled through Vietnam, where Paris was then consolidating its control. Annexing northern Burma and establishing direct colonial administration there were expected to facilitate the penetration of China's markets by British imperial goods. Those goods would flow from Rangoon to Kunming via increasingly modernized transportation lines and without administrative obstruction.[7]

When Britain annexed Burma and abolished the Burmese monarchy after an eleven-day war in 1885, China protested. Beijing urged London to retain the Burmese monarchy in even a vestigial form so that it could continue its traditional tributary relation with China, but London declined. In July 1886 Britain and China agreed to "settle" their dispute over Burma, with China recognizing Britain's right to "do whatever she deems fit and proper" in Burma, and Britain permitting Burma and China to continue their "traditional practice" of sending decennial Burmese missions to Beijing. From the Chinese perspective this meant that China's suzerainty over Burma would continue. In the 1920s Sun Yat-sen listed Burma as "Chinese territory" that had been "lost" to foreign powers during China's period of weakness.[8]

As the contest between Japan, China, Britain, and the United States intensified in the 1930s and 1940s, Burma's back door to China again played a crucial role in the strategic calculations of all four of those powers. As the Sino-Japanese war slipped into a protracted conflict in late 1937, Chinese supply routes to sympathetic foreign powers became vital. Conversely, sealing those routes became a vital strategic objective for Japan. The USSR provided substantial support via inner-Asian borders, but China desperately needed support from the United States and Britain. In the first year of the Sino-Japanese war quantities of material moved via ports in southern China, but in 1938 Japanese forces seized those harbors. China's government anticipated this move and in December 1937 ordered construction to begin on a motor road linking Dali in Yunnan with Lashio in Burma. The Burma road, as it became known, opened in January 1939.[9] Vital cargoes were unloaded in Rangoon harbor, moved north via rail or barge to Mandalay or Lashio, and then went by truck to Chinese armies in southwest China.

The Burma road figured prominently in British global strategy in 1939–41. Britain was then struggling desperately to cope with the simultaneous challenges posed by Japan in the Far East and Germany in Europe. London concluded that China's continued resistance to Japan improved Britain's global situation by making Japan less likely to challenge Britain's position in the Far East and looked to the Burma road as a conduit for vital assistance to China.[10] In 1938 London agreed to build a rail line from northern Burma into Yunnan and to hard-surface the Burma road. The rail line was not built, but work on turning the Burma road into an all-weather byway rushed forward. London also granted China credits to buy trucks for the road. By the spring of 1939 a thousand tons of supplies per month were transiting the Burma road. Before Japanese occupation of Burma shut it down in January 1942, the maximum monthly flow reached eighteen thousand tons.

Japanese imperial strategists soon concluded that shutting China's international supply lines was vital to forcing China to surrender. By June 1940 there were only two main routes left: the Burma road, carrying 31 percent of all China's foreign supplies, and the road and rail links from Haiphong in French Indochina, carrying 42 percent. In mid-1940 the Haiphong route was shut when Japan occupied Indochina with the approval of France's new Nazi collaborationist Vichy government. After Haiphong was closed, only the Burma road remained.[11] Japanese pressure on British holdings in East Asia succeeded in compelling London to close the road from July to October 1940. Britain was then in a desperate situation, just after the Dunkirk evacuation and with the Battle of Britain beginning. American counter-pressure and guarantees succeeded in persuading London to reopen the road. This action was an important element in the pattern of events that convinced Japan's leaders that they confronted a Chinese-American-British coalition determined to stifle Japan's rise. When Japan decided in late 1941 to "strike south" to destroy that coalition, seizure of Burma and closing the back door to China was a major Japanese strategic objective, ranking in importance only behind securing the "southern resource areas."

One of the first battles of the Great Pacific War, which began on December 7, 1941, was for Burma. Two Japanese divisions invaded Burma from Thailand in late January 1942. Keeping the Burma road in Allied hands was highly important to China and the United States. Chiang Kai-shek's armies desperately needed American supplies, and U.S. strategists thought that keeping China effectively in the war against Japan was vital to the workability of the Europe First strategy. Both Chinese and American strategists wanted to keep Rangoon and the transportation links into Yunnan out of Japanese hands. Chiang Kai-shek therefore ordered nine divisions, totaling some sixty thousand men, from Yunnan into Burma to stop the Japanese. The main line of the Chinese advance was along the Burma road. Two weak British divisions joined the defense of Burma. All to no avail. By May 1942 Burma was in Japanese hands, and the Burma road was closed.

In mid-1944 Japanese planners, confronting the stark prospect of American invasion of the Japanese home islands, turned once again to the problem of knocking China out of the war. This would free Japanese forces to face the Americans, perhaps making the American advance too costly and forcing Washington to accept a compromise peace. Once again Burma's back door played an important role. One element of the Japanese plan called for an offensive against American air bases in south central China. A second element of Japan's strategy was a thrust from Burma to Kunming, where Japanese forces would concentrate for a final push into the Chinese bastion of Sichuan. Two Japanese divisions were to move from Mandalay to seize Baoshan and then push on to Kunming. A detailed operational plan was drawn up, but the operation was shelved when the Americans and Chinese launched an offensive into Burma.[12]

As the correlation of forces in the Pacific began to shift in mid-1943 and U.S. planners began to think about offensive strategies designed to defeat Japan, Burma's back door yet again figured prominently. Until late 1944 American strategy to defeat Japan called for offensives by an American-trained, -armed, and -commanded Chinese army (code-named the X Force) from Assam. There was to be a simultaneous offensive by a large Chinese army (the Y Force) from Yunnan, plus a British amphibious landing in the south. These three assaults would converge to retake Burma. Once the Rangoon-Kunming conduit was reopened, large quantities of U.S. war materiel would flow into China. Approximately thirty Chinese divisions would then be re-equipped and reorganized and proceed to drive to the central China coast, where they would link up with American amphibious forces. The final assault on Japan would then be prepared.[13] This strategy was eventually superseded by the successes of the island-hopping central Pacific campaign and by Britain's inability to allocate sufficient resources for the southern, amphibious portion of the Burma operation. Britain's inability to contribute to the planned campaign meant that the crucial Rangoon anchor of the Burma road would remain in Japanese hands. Nonetheless, the major northern elements of the campaign were carried out as planned. In March 1944 the X Force of 100,000 jumped off from Ledo. By August they had taken Myitkyina. In May the Y Force, also numbering about 100,000, advanced over a front of nearly two hundred miles during the monsoon season against determined Japanese resistance. The Y Force slowly fought its way toward Wanding, where the Burma road crossed the border into Burma. By January 1945 it had linked up with the X Force at Lunze just inside Burma. There were also offensives in 1944–45 by Japanese forces from Burma into Assam and by British Indian forces from Assam into Burma.[14]

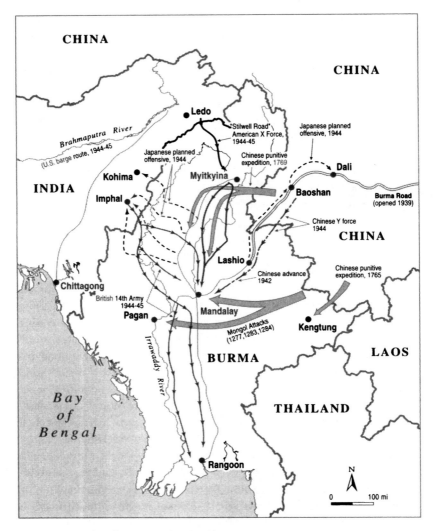

MAP 9.1   Burma's Role as an Invasion Corridor

The routes of various military campaigns in Burma over the centuries are depicted in map 9.1. The geopolitical point to be drawn from these comings and goings is that Burma often became a cockpit of international rivalry because of the relatively easy overland access it provides between South Asia and China's southwest. The ambitions of great powers—Han, Yuan, Qing, or Nationalist China, Britain, Japan, and the United States—have often led them to play out their strategies on Burma's soil. This historical memory is imbued in the awareness of the statesmen of China, Burma, and India.

When Burma won its independence in 1947, its leaders harbored deep apprehensions toward both India and China. There was antipathy toward the large number of Indian citizens (both Hindu and Muslim but more of the latter) who lived in Burma. The British had encouraged Indians to migrate to Burma to provide labor for various industries and staff the colonial administration. After 1885 Burma was ruled from India, first from Calcutta and then from Delhi. Indian troops were also used to maintain colonial authority during the British period. By the time of Burma's independence the Indian population (along with the ethnic Chinese) constituted a commercial elite. Both of those ethnic minorities saw much of their property confiscated and businesses closed by nationalizations during the 1960s, but the Indian minority population remained twice the size of the Chinese (i.e., about 6 percent as opposed to 3 percent of Burma's total population). The comments of Indian leaders before and soon after Indian independence about India's destiny of leading South Asia also roused Burmese apprehensions. Not infrequently, Burma was specified as part of the new Indian sphere of influence or even as a part of an Indian-led South Asian federation. India supplied considerable munitions and money to the embattled Rangoon government in the desperate days of 1948–49, enabling it to hang on in the face of widespread rebellion. This assistance was appreciated, but it also made the Burmese apprehensive about possible Indian domination.[15]

Burmese fears of China were also great. As we have seen, Chinese invasions had ravaged Burma and several times shattered its polity. The entire boundary between China and Burma was undefined in the late 1940s. Since 1885 China's government had claimed Upper Burma (roughly coterminous with Burma's Kachin state). In 1945 China's Nationalist government began pressing that claim, previously dormant since 1885. China also had traditional claims of suzerainty over a number of the Shan states, indeed, over all of Burma itself. Some of the propaganda emanating from the newly established PRC condemned the Burmese government as ripe for revolutionary overthrow. The Communist Party of Burma had been in insurrection since 1948 and by 1950 had established links with the Chinese Communist Party over the Burma-Yunnan border.

To make matters even worse, several thousand defeated Nationalist Chinese soldiers escaped the Chinese Communists by fleeing into the Shan states in 1948–50, and by 1951 those forces were being armed by U.S. clandestine services for commando operations into Yunnan. This gave Beijing good reason and a good pretext for getting more deeply involved in Burma. Burma's central government was itself very weak and was being battered on all sides by insurgencies, mutinies, and crises.

Confronted with this dangerous situation, Rangoon sought to stay away from great-power conflicts, especially those involving India and China. As Burma's Ne Win told Indira Gandhi in March 1969: "In our relations with our neighbors we have assiduously sought to avoid taking sides."[16] Between 1950 and 1988 Burma followed a policy of strict neutralism, trying to avoid involvement in great power rivalries. A key element of Burmese neutralism was friendship with both China and India.[17] Burma was thus one of the first noncommunist countries to recognize the PRC and establish ambassadorial relations with it. Burma also, along with India, became one of the most vigorous advocates of PRC membership in the United Nations. When the Korean War broke out, Burma initially supported UN action there, but once China entered that conflict Rangoon adopted a more equivocal position, abstaining from voting, for example, on the UN resolution condemning China as an aggressor.

In 1953 as Beijing began shedding the ultra-revolutionary line of the early 1950s, Burma was one of the first countries courted by China. Rangoon welcomed the shift, and in the years that followed a solid and impressive edifice of Sino-Burmese friendship was created. Rangoon worked to bring China into the Afro-Asian community. High-level Sino-Burmese exchanges began in June 1954 with a visit by Zhou Enlai which resulted in a statement endorsing the Five Principles of Peaceful Coexistence as the guiding principles of Sino-Burmese relations. China also began providing economic assistance to Burma in 1954, when Beijing agreed to set up a large cotton textile factory at Rangoon. The Chinese technicians involved in that program were strictly professional and carefully abstained from propagandizing among Burmese.[18]

Rangoon consistently sought to avoid offending Beijing. When the Tibetan rebellion erupted in 1959, Rangoon held that it was a purely internal affair of China. As Sino-Indian relations deteriorated, Burma was careful to take a neutral line on those disputes. When conflicts between China-supported North Vietnam and the United States began to rage in Indochina in 1964–66, Rangoon either took no official note of developments there or endorsed innocuous proposals such as reconvening the Geneva Convention. This is not to say that Rangoon slavishly followed Beijing's lead. On key issues in which Rangoon felt its interests were at stake, it differed from Beijing. It did what it could, for example, to strengthen international norms against great-power

interventions in other nations, supporting the move at the Bandung conference to include condemnation of Soviet-style colonialism in the communiqué
and strongly denouncing the Soviet intervention in Hungary in 1956. Rangoon
also endorsed the 1963 partial nuclear test ban treaty and the nonproliferation treaty a few years later, in spite of Chinese protests.

By the early 1960s Beijing was one of the foreign capitals most frequented
by Burma's leaders. Burma also ranked third among noncommunist recipients of Chinese economic aid (after Indonesia and Egypt). Sino-Burma relations became even closer in 1960 with the settlement of the border dispute
and simultaneous conclusion of a nonaggression treaty. The nonaggression
treaty provided that neither country would allow its territory to be used by
a third power for hostile activities directed against the other. On the basis of
this agreement the PLA carried out two large-scale but nonpublicized incursions into Burmese territory in November 1960 and again in February 1961
with the permission of the Burmese government and against the irregular
Nationalist Chinese forces in the Shan state. Simultaneously, the Burmese
army launched offensives against the Nationalists. These joint operations, kept
highly secret at the time, shattered and dispersed the Nationalists but did not
completely eliminate them. Indeed, some identifiable "Nationalist remnants" remain in the Shan states today. The 1960 joint operations were instrumental, however, in persuading the Nationalist remnants to turn from the
dangerous profession of anticommunist guerrilla to the more lucrative and
less dangerous work of smuggling and narcotics trafficking.[19]

Regarding the border issue, negotiations began in December 1954 and
dragged on without much progress until 1959. The onset of the Sino-Indian
border conflict that year led to a softening of China's position on the Sino-
Burmese border, and agreement was quickly reached and formalized in
October 1960. With that agreement China unequivocally relinquished its claim
to Upper Burma (which Chinese governments from 1885 to 1949 had upheld)
and to another disputed area in the Wa state. Minor adjustments were made,
with Burma getting the better deal.[20] During 1960 the border was delimited.
With that development Burma had an agreed-on and delimited border with
China for the first time since pre-British days.

Cordial Indian-Burmese ties paralleled Sino-Burmese amity during the
1950s and 1960s. During the first several years of their common independence
the ROI and the Union of Burma enjoyed parallel foreign policy thinking. Both
were primarily concerned with economic development and looked to cooperation with the West to achieve that objective. Both were also fearful of Soviet-
Chinese-supported communist insurgency. As noted earlier, India provided
Rangoon with important military, financial, and political support during the

powerful Communist Party of Burma (CPB) insurgency of 1948–50.[21] New Delhi watched with some suspicion the growth of Chinese-Burma relations in the mid-1950s, but Nehru chose not to raise those concerns with Zhou Enlai during that period.[22] In the aftermath of the 1962 war India finally roused itself and launched an effort to court Rangoon. Burma's military leader, Ne Win, welcomed India's proffers of friendship, and Indo-Burmese relations began to warm, just as Sino-Burmese ties were starting to cool over the CPB.

CHINA AND THE COMMUNIST PARTY OF BURMA

From 1949 until 1989 Beijing followed a dual-track approach to its relations with Burma. One track was normal state-to-state relations with the government of Burma. A second track was fraternal relations between the Chinese Communist Party (CCP) ruling China and the Communist Party of Burma, which was in insurrection against the government of Burma from 1948 until 1989—a record making it the longest-lived communist insurgency in the world. The particular balance between these two tracks at any point in time was a major characteristic of Chinese policy toward Burma. Following a military takeover in Burma in 1962, the CCP began actively supporting the CPB insurgency, and during the late 1960s and early 1970s its assistance to the CPB became quite substantial. Ultimately, the Burmese revolution would rank only behind the Korean and the Vietnamese revolutions in terms of levels of Chinese assistance. By the 1980s, however, Beijing was trying to shut down the CPB insurgency and ultimately played an important role in that process. By 1990 the insurgency was over, its leaders comfortably retired in China. Considering the scope and underlying logic of China's links with the CPB insurgency is thus essential to understanding Chinese policy toward Burma.

Substantial CCP support for the CPB insurgency did not begin until the 1962 military coup. Although close links between the two parties began in the early 1950s, with most of the top leadership of the CPB living in safe sanctuary in China, it was not until the 1962 coup that the CCP concluded propitious conditions mandated support for the Burmese revolution.[23] Having decided to support the CPB's insurgency, the CCP adopted a multifaceted and long-term plan. In August 1962 the CPB was allowed to begin printing revolutionary propaganda in Beijing for distribution inside Burma. A new CPB leadership group was set up in Beijing at the end of 1963 to provide leadership for the revolutionary offensive. The paramount leader was Thakin Ba Thein Tin, a half-Chinese man who had joined the CPB in 1939, fled to China in 1953, and resided there until 1978. A group was also established to survey possible infiltration routes from Yunnan into northeast Burma. China was then constructing a network of asphalt-surfaced roads into the border regions of Yunnan, and PLA trucks would soon be able to deliver supplies over those roads to forward logistic depots. The CCP also recruited a hardened military core for the new CPB drive, including several hundred Kachin former insurgents who had fled to China in the early 1950s to take up farming in Guizhou province. In early 1963 this group of former peasant soldiers, who were used to the hardships of a guerrilla's life and had practical military skills, was recruited, armed, retrained, and given a political education by CPB cadre. Inside Burma small cells of ethnic Chinese communists were put in touch with the CPB for the first time, further broadening the scope of the CPB organization. During 1967 the CPB army was further strengthened by the assignment of PLA advisors, called "volunteers," to all major CPB units. These advisors served in Burma with CPB forces until 1979. In 1967 several thousand young Chinese Red Guards were also recruited to fight for the CPB. These young Chinese men provided the bulk of the CPB fighting forces from 1968 until about 1973. By the end of 1967 a CPB invasion force was concentrated in southwestern Yunnan, well armed with Chinese weapons and equipment.

Political conditions for the launching of the carefully prepared CPB offensive were created in 1967. In the middle of that year Chinese diplomatic personnel in Rangoon became involved in encouraging Maoist activity among ethnic Chinese students.[24] A backlash soon developed, and Burmese mobs launched pogroms against Burma's ethnic Chinese minority. Beijing reacted strongly, and diplomatic relations ruptured. Beijing began calling openly for the overthrow of the Rangoon government.

The CPB offensive began in January 1968 with a thrust down the Burma road from Yunnan by a powerful, conventionally organized military force. The objective was seizure of Mandalay, which was to serve as the capital of a liberated base area in northern Burma. The CPB invasion army was well armed with modern weapons, including field artillery and antiaircraft guns pulled by tractors, and field communications systems operated by Chinese volunteers. Hospital care for wounded soldiers was provided inside China. The CPB invasion army had initial success. For the first time in Burma's civil wars the Burmese army found itself outgunned and sometimes even outnumbered. The CPB force soon came into conflict, however, with Kachin rebel forces under the command of the Kachin Independence Army (KIA). Heavy fighting developed between the KIA and CPB, which forced the latter to halt its advance on Mandalay. The Burmese army was too weak to push the powerful CPB back into China and adopted a policy of strategic defense along the Salween River.[25]

After five years of heavy fighting (1968–72) the CPB had established a 20,000-square-kilometer base area stretching along the border with China, from the Burmese-Laotian frontier northward to where the Burma road crosses into Burma. The CPB tried again to push west of the Salween in late 1973 but was defeated by Burmese army forces in a pitched battle that raged for forty-two days and in which the CPB employed human wave assaults.[26] Had Mandalay been taken and Chinese arms been provided to new armies raised from the areas between that city and the Chinese border, Rangoon's forces in north Burma would have been isolated. Such a scenario does not account, of course, for the tenacious ethnic insurgencies of that region. Various analysts of the CPB conclude that its leaders did not adequately comprehend the depth of ethnic loyalties in Burma. Presumably, the CPB's CCP comrades shared these misunderstandings. Although it was apparent by the mid-1970s that the CPB was not going to secure control of upper Burma, it remained the most powerful armed challenge to Rangoon into the 1980s. Beijing gave the CPB a monopoly franchise on trade with China and license to purchase weapons in China. It remained the best-armed and -supplied of Burma's insurgencies.[27] During the 1970s some 67 percent of the CPB's annual budget came from its monopoly on border trade with China.[28]

From 1962 through 1989 China pursued a two-track policy toward Burma, except for three years—from mid-1967 through 1970—when it abandoned the government-to-government track. Normal diplomatic relations were restored by mid-1971, however, when Ne Win visited Beijing for talks. Two months later Beijing extended the repayment period for a 1961 loan.

Chinese support for the CPB quickly declined as Deng Xiaoping consolidated power in the late 1970s. Deng had a much more jaundiced view than Mao of the utility of foreign revolutionary movements to China. Deng also placed far greater emphasis on government-to-government cooperation as a way of creating international conditions favorable to China's efforts to enter the world economy. Moreover, during the intense struggle between Maoist radicals and moderates in China in 1976–78, the CPB made the mistake of aligning with the radicals. Once Deng consolidated power in late 1978 the CPB quickly fell silent about developments in China. *Peking Review* also ceased reporting on CPB advances inside Burma. Ne Win was quick to exploit the rift between Beijing and the CPB, twice hosting visits by Deng Xiaoping to Burma in 1978. During the course of that year China shut down the CPB radio station that had been broadcasting from Yunnan since 1971, closed the Beijing office of the CPB, forced the entire leadership of the CPB to move to Panghsang just inside Burma, and recalled the Chinese "volunteers" still serving with the CPB. Ne Win reciprocated Beijing's moves in September 1979, when

Burma withdrew from the nonaligned movement as Vietnam and Cuba began pushing that movement to accept the USSR as the "natural ally" of the developing countries. Burma also voted with Beijing in the United Nations in favor of seating the Pol Pot Khmer Rouge regime of Cambodia and against the Vietnam-installed government of Kampuchea. Of course, this latter move was also a reflection of Rangoon's traditional aversion to stronger nations imposing their will on weaker ones.

What were the broad objectives of the two tracks of China's Burma policy? The key objective of the state-to-state track seems to have been to exclude from Burma the presence of any power hostile to China. The key to this, Beijing concluded, was carefully avoiding any pressure or threat on Rangoon. On issue after issue Beijing carefully demonstrated to Rangoon that China posed no threat to Burma: on the Kuomintang (KMT) remnant issue and CIA covert operations against China from the Shan states; on the overseas Chinese issue; with Beijing's generous approach toward resolution of the border issue; and with China's fairly substantial aid program to Burma. The implicit quid pro quo from Burma for this Chinese friendship was exclusion of a hostile third-power presence from Burma. Rangoon seems to have understood quite well the implicit terms of this relationship and to have respected China's basic security interests with care. Rangoon abstained from actions that might challenge China's security.

Why did CCP leaders decide to support the CPB insurgency? We must view Mao's 1962 decision to support the CPB in the context of intensifying struggle between the Chinese and the Soviet communist parties over the direction of the world communist movement. By supporting the CPB—along with many other revolutionary movements in the early 1960s—Mao was putting into practice his "correct revolutionary line," whose successes, he anticipated, would demonstrate the "incorrectness" of the Soviet "revisionist" line while strengthening the global struggle against U.S. imperialism. Korea, Vietnam, and Burma, the three major recipients of CCP "fraternal support," were all traditional Chinese tributaries that happened to lie on sensitive approaches to China's territory. By rendering strong fraternal support to the revolutionary movements of these three countries, Mao hoped to establish fraternal states in these areas, bound to the PRC by similar political systems and ideologies, grateful to China for its support, and looking to China for protection. Chinese-supported revolutionary movements in Vietnam, Laos, and Cambodia were making substantial advances during the 1960s and early 1970s. Presumably, part or all of Burma was to be added to the belt of communist-ruled, China-friendly states being constructed along China's southern borders.

To come back to Indian-Chinese relations, and assuming that this reconstruction of Mao's objectives is correct, had Mao succeeded and the CPB taken over a large part or all of Burma, that new state might have come into close alignment with China.

THE POST-1989 SINO-MYANMAR STRATEGIC PARTNERSHIP

In 1989 China and Myanmar (as Burma was renamed in 1989) began building a close, cooperative political-military relationship that represented a sharp departure from Burma's carefully balanced policy of neutrality of the previous forty-five years. This partnership derived *not* from a strategic decision by the two governments but from a confluence of expedient considerations. Facing international pressure from the same quarters—the United States and the Western countries, including Japan—Beijing and Yangon (as Rangoon was renamed in 1989) found themselves in need of international support to counter that pressure and welcomed the other's readiness to render such support. Gradually, however, it began to dawn on the two capitals that their new partnership gave them important regional leverage.

India emerged as a major perceived threat to the antidemocratic Myanmar state, and this was a significant factor pushing Myanmar toward alignment with China. Indian leaders understood the contingent factors that were bringing Beijing and Yangon together, and this was somewhat reassuring to them. As the military partnership between China and Myanmar burgeoned, however, and as China began developing a "corridor to the sea" through its historic back door, New Delhi became increasingly apprehensive. Indian security analysts increasingly pondered the possibility that, in the event of a war over Arunachal Pradesh or Pakistan, Chinese armies might outflank Indian forces in the northeast by pushing through Myanmar. The increasingly close ties between Beijing and Yangon made it more likely that Myanmar's government would, perhaps under Chinese pressure, give its consent to such utilization of Myanmar's territory. India's nightmare scenario was that Myanmar might become a close partner of China's comparable to Pakistan. India would then be flanked east and west by two China-allied states, each with easy access to the political and industrial centers of India.

Deep internal crises brought Beijing and Yangon into confrontation with the democratic internationalism of the Western nations at about the same time. In Myanmar popular discontent with political repression and economic stagnation began to erupt into student demonstrations in September 1987. Other sectors of the populace joined in. Myanmar's military rulers met the demonstrations with violence killing thousands, and an escalating cycle of repression and protest unfolded. Finally, in September 1988 a state-managed coup d'état led to abolition of existing state institutions and establishment of a nineteen-member military junta called the State Law and Order Restoration Council (SLORC). After further wide-ranging repression, the new military regime gained control over the situation and consolidated continuing military rule. Misled by its own propaganda and isolation, the SLORC then miscalculated and imagined that it enjoyed strong popular support. In May 1990 it held an election in which the National League for Democracy (NLD), led by Aung San Suu Kyi, won an overwhelming victory. The SLORC invalidated the result and arrested NLD leaders. Suu Kyi is the daughter of the militant nationalist who had led his Japanese-sponsored army into rebellion against the British and then negotiated Burma's independence with London before he was assassinated, in July 1947.

China's internal crisis began building in late 1988 as Beijing began reining in the runaway growth of the previous several years which had generated levels of inflation unprecedented for the PRC. Early in 1989 student protesters began challenging CCP policy. The protests soon escalated into a challenge to the CCP'S monopoly on political power. Initial attempts to overwhelm the protest movement without violent military force failed as street demonstrations, supported by millions of Beijingers, prevented the movement of troops into the city. A second effort in June 1989 employed overwhelming and violent force. Several hundred died in the repression, but the CCP'S monopoly of power was restored.

Western governments and public opinion strongly condemned the crushing of peaceful pro-democracy movements in Yangon and Beijing. In September 1988 the United States suspended its $12 million aid program to Myanmar to protest the military repression. Other Western nations followed suit. China, too, was subject to Western criticism and sanctions following the Beijing massacre.

Yangon and Beijing found cooperation useful in countering international pressure. With Western sources of ammunition and military equipment shut off and facing strong internal opposition, the SLORC needed desperately to find a new source of military supplies. Yangon was also on the brink of insolvency, with its foreign currency reserves virtually exhausted. Beijing was happy to find new customers for its weapons manufacturers and was willing to meet Yangon's military needs on a generous basis. Beijing also had a veto in the UN Security Council and a prominent voice in international affairs which could be used to counter international pressure against Myanmar. Beijing also found it politically useful to have another developing country in a situation similar to China's own, with a government willing to use forceful means to repress domestic challenges to its authority regardless of Western human rights scruples. China rebutted Western criticism of the June 1989 repression in Beijing by asserting that criticism reflected arrogance and ignorance of the situation in developing countries. Being able to defend Myanmar was useful to China, internationally and domestically. With Yangon at its side, Beijing was better able to cast the issue in terms of Western ignorance of the realities of developing countries. Chinese leaders were also concerned that U.S.-led interventionism would become more common in the aftermath of the collapse of communism in Eastern Europe and the decline (and after 1991 the disappearance) of the USSR. Political cooperation between China and Myanmar was a way of thwarting U.S. efforts to establish its "new interventionist" hegemonism.

The convergence of Burmese and Chinese perspectives was exemplified during the August 1991 visit of SLORC chairman Senior General Saw Maung, to China. Upon his arrival Maung declared that "it is necessary at the present time for countries in Asia to preserve their own traditions and customs," even though "some countries regarded and treated them in a wrong opinion." "There are attacks on Myanmar . . . by certain Western nations on human rights. . . . We understand that the People's Republic of China, too, is countering such attacks," Maung said. In reply, Li Peng declared: "I share many of Chairman Senior General Saw Maung's views. . . . The most important [principle of justice] in the field of international relations is non-interference in the internal affairs of one nation by another."[29] Yangon and Beijing agreed that foreign criticism, sanctions, and pressure constituted impermissible foreign interference in the internal affairs of sovereign states and was a violation of the Five Principles of Peaceful Coexistence, and a manifestation of hegemonism.

India condemned the military repression in Myanmar and supported the pro-democratic movement against Myanmar's military dictatorship. India was the only Asian country to criticize SLORC's repression officially and express sympathy for Myanmar's pro-democracy movement in 1988. On September 10, as demonstrations mounted in Rangoon, India announced its support for "the undaunted resolve of the Burmese people to achieve their democracy." Following SLORC's bloody crackdown three days later, India was Myanmar's only neighbor to welcome political refugees, give them some support, and allow them to continue political activities. Pro-democracy activists and students were granted refuge and hospitality in camps set up in Manipur and Mizoram. All India Radio (AIR)—run by India's Ministry of Information and whose broadcasting reflects government policy—also began regular Burmese-language broadcasts into Myanmar conveying news about Myanmar's pro-democracy movement and SLORC repression. AIR employed U Nu's daughter to make some of these broadcasts and became quite popular with audiences in Myanmar. (U Nu was Burma's first prime minister, serving from 1947 to 1958 and again from 1960 to 1962.) Rangoon protested these Indian actions. New Delhi reciprocated by keeping the SLORC regime at arm's length. There were few diplomatic contacts between Yangon and New Delhi.[30]

According to SLORC, Indian diplomats in Yangon (along with those of Europe, the United States, Britain, Australia, and Thailand) met with and encouraged pro-democracy activists. Those activists counted on foreign recognition of the provisional government they were planning to proclaim, and the foreign diplomats gave them encouragement. A counselor from the Indian embassy reportedly provided a substantial amount of money to Myanmar's pro-democracy forces for office supplies, transportation, and financing various political activities. During the single month of January 1989 the Indian counselor purportedly provided the equivalent of U.S.$9,086 to an anti-SLORC activist.[31] The Myanmar democracy movement also drew considerable inspiration from India and from Mahatma Gandhi. One of their main declarations was named the "Gandhi Hall Declaration" after the hall where it was adopted. India also awarded Aung San Suu Kyi the Jawaharlal Nehru Prize in 1993 which carried an award of 1.5 million Indian rupees.

SLORC'S perception of India's support for Myanmar's democratic challengers should perhaps be seen in the context of India's 1987 intervention in Sri Lanka and its economic sanctions against Nepal in 1989–90. India seemed to be pursuing a more forceful approach toward its neighbors. SLORC leaders probably genuinely perceived a potential for Indian military intervention, supported by the Western powers, on the NLD's behalf. SLORC'S perceptions must also be seen in the context of that regime's deep ignorance and isolation. Its leaders did not know much about the outside world and were inclined to reach far-fetched conclusions.

TERMINATION OF THE CPB INSURGENCY
AND THE NEW SINO-MYANMAR ENTENTE

A crucial element of the Sino-Burmese partnership founded in 1989 was Chinese assistance in terminating the CPB insurgency. This CCP-linked and supported insurgency was a major source of distrust in the Beijing-Rangoon relations, and, as Beijing strove to improve state-to-state relations, it downgraded party-to-party ties. That process began in 1981, when Beijing quietly informed CPB leaders that a pension, house, and plot of land in China were available to any veteran cadre of the CPB who wished to retire. Initially, only a few accepted the offer, but the numbers grew as the decade passed. Then in 1986 Beijing revoked the CPB's monopoly on trade with China. By the late 1980s it was pressing the leaders of the CPB to take up comfortable retirement in China. The final act came in March 1989, when the ethnic Wa tribesmen who constituted 80 percent of the CPB's ten- to fifteen-thousand-man army, revolted against the two hundred or so ethnic Burmese who made up the party's leadership. China welcomed the CPB leaders when they fled across the border, provided them accommodations at various places in China, and prohibited them from participating in political activities. By mid-1989 the CPB insurgency—the world's longest-running communist insurgency—was over.[32]

The end of the CPB insurgency had wide-ranging effects on Myanmar's other ethnic insurgencies. Several of those insurgencies had relied on the CPB for ammunition and other types of support. When that support dried up after 1989, it left the rebel groups more vulnerable to governmental pressure. Yangon seized the opportunity to strike deals with various insurgencies. Driven by a need to prevent the ethnic insurgencies from making common cause with the pro-democracy activists of the cities, the SLORC offered the leaders of the insurgencies lucrative business opportunities and (reportedly) the right to engage in any type of business they desired (i.e., teak, gem, and opium and heroin trade), if they would agree not to support urban dissident groups and not to attack government forces. These proposals offered good profits. Yangon also promised development efforts in many long-neglected frontier regions. Negative inducement for the insurgent groups to accept Yangon's offers came from the possibility of government military offensives if those offers were rejected. Those offensives became steadily more effective as Myanmar's army grew larger and better armed, with Chinese assistance. Cumulatively, these methods were fairly effective. By 1998 Yangon had extended its writ across Burma in the widest and most effective fashion of the entire post-1948 period and possibly earlier.

China assisted this assertion of Yangon's authority in several important ways. Beijing's decision to facilitate the closing down of the CPB insurgency considerably strengthened Yangon's hand. Many, though by no means all, of the lucrative business contracts being proffered to rebel leaders by Yangon involved partners in China. Many of the roads being built by and into China also facilitated the reorientation of ethnic minority energies away from insurgency and toward profitable business activities. The roads also facilitated the rapid movement of government military forces into those areas in the event the ethnic insurgencies rejected Yangon's offers. Chinese friendship was thus quite effective in helping Yangon extend its administrative authority across the land.

ECONOMIC AND MILITARY DIMENSIONS
OF THE NEW SINO-MYANMAR ENTENTE

Expanded cooperation in economic, military, and infrastructure development gave substance to the new Sino-Myanmar relation that emerged after
1989. Sino-Myanmar economic relations expanded rapidly. As Burma's crisis deepened, the country's military rulers began to discard the policy of economic isolation followed since 1962. A critical move came in August 1988
with an agreement between Rangoon and Beijing legitimizing cross-border
trade between the two countries. This was Burma's first economic opening
to its neighbors. Chinese goods began to pour into Myanmar. There was a
strong and long-pent-up demand for goods in Myanmar—in part stimulated by the junta's own declaration that various currencies were invalid and
irredeemable. With currency being demonetized, people rushed to spend
what currency they had on goods. Decades of comprehensive state planning
had stunted Myanmar's own industry, rendering it incapable of satisfying
domestic demand. Unless this popular demand for goods could be met,
mounting popular discontent could lead to an uprising. Opening trade with
China offered a quick and effective solution to this problem. By October 1988
trade with China was regularized, taxed, and several border crossings opened
for trade. There was strong demand in Myanmar for low-cost and relatively
fashionable Chinese goods. Burmese wood and gems were also much sought
after by Chinese entrepreneurs. Two-way trade exploded, growing from a
few tens of millions of dollars in the mid-1980s to perhaps $1.5 billion by
1992. By the mid-1990s China had replaced Thailand as the major supplier
of consumer goods to Myanmar. Expanding economic cooperation with
Myanmar, and with other countries through Myanmar, served important
Chinese objectives. In the aftermath of Western sanctions after June 1989,
Beijing sought to diversify exports away from the United States as insurance
against possible American revocation of China's Most Favored Nation trading status.

High-level Sino-Burmese military exchanges also increased. The first
high-level exchanges between the military institutions of the two countries
had been in 1978, as China was moving toward war with Vietnam. Then there
was a lapse in military exchanges until 1989, when, following the June 4 inci-
dent, a large and high-level Myanmar military delegation visited China.
Thereafter, high-ranking military exchanges occurred fairly frequently, as illustrated by table 9.1. One strange thing about these publicly announced
exchanges is that they contained no naval exchanges, even though China was
supplying substantial numbers of naval vessels and was rather heavily involved

TABLE 9.1   Sino-Myanmar Military Exchanges

Year	Exchange
1975	None
1976	None
1977	None
1978	Burma military delegation to PRC; PRC delegation to Burma
1979	None
1980	None
1981	None
1982	None
1983	None
1984	None
1985	None
1986	None
1987	None
1988	None
1989	Commander in chief of Myanmar army and member of State Law and Order Restoration Committee (SLORC) leads twenty-five-member (mostly military) delegation to China
1990	None
1991	PLA deputy chief of general staff leads PLA delegation to Myanmar
1992	None
1993	None
1994	Commander of Chengdu Military Region (MR) visits Myanmar
1995	None
1996	Vice chairman of PRC–Central Military Commission visits Myanmar SLORC chairman and army commander visits China SLORC vice chairman and deputy commander of defense visit China
1997	PLA Lanzhou MR commander on goodwill visit to Myanmar
1998	Commander in chief of Myanmar Air Force to China

SOURCE: *Foreign Broadcast Information Service, Daily Report, China,* indexes, NewsBank (New Canaan, Conn.: NewsBank, various years).

in refurbishing Myanmar's naval base facilities. This suggests that the two sides decided to keep high-level naval exchanges quiet so as not to disquiet Myanmar's neighbors.

China became the major supplier of munitions and training for Myanmar's rapidly expanding armed forces. After the September 1988 coup d'état, Myanmar began expanding its armed forces from around 186,000 to between 350,000 and 400,000, with an eventual objective of a half-million men. This expanded force was armed largely with Chinese weapons. The Western nations had suspended arms sales to Myanmar following the September 1988 coup, so Yangon turned to China. Yugoslavia and Russia also served as arms suppliers to Myanmar, but China was by far the most important. In October 1989 the SLORC concluded the largest arms purchase agreement in Burma's history, purchasing from China jet fighters, patrol boats, armored personnel carriers, tanks, missiles, antiaircraft guns, and trucks as well as small arms and crew-served weapons. A second large deal was concluded in November 1994 involving helicopters, patrol boats, missiles, and armored vehicles. In the decade after 1988 Myanmar acquired from China 180 heavy and light tanks, 250 armored personnel carriers, field and antiaircraft artillery, at least 30 navy vessels including 16 patrol boats, and 4 guided-missile fast-attack craft. For its air force Myanmar acquired 140 Chinese combat aircraft, including 30 F-8 fighters, 24 A-5 ground-attack aircraft, and 46 transport helicopters and helicopter gunships.

Yangon also carried out a wide-ranging reorganization of its military forces in tandem with this rearmament. Command and control systems were renovated with modern equipment. Communications and electronic surveillance capabilities at both strategic and operational levels were modernized. Specialized armor and artillery formations were created. Military bases were modernized and increased in number, with critical maintenance functions, previously performed only in Yangon, decentralized for greater efficiency. Training was also an inevitable part of Chinese arms sales. Chinese personnel trained Burmese in the operation and maintenance of newly supplied Chinese weapons, while Burmese personnel went to China for additional training. China also agreed to set up a small arms factory at Magwe, midway between Mandalay and Yangon on the Irrawaddy. These reforms substantially improved Myanmar's military capabilities for both conventional and counterinsurgency operations. By the late 1990s, for the first time in its modern history, Burma had the means to conduct conventional operations in defense of the country. Burma's soldiers have long been recognized as one of the toughest infantry forces in Asia, hardened by decades of counterinsurgency operations under very harsh conditions. After a decade of Chinese-supported modernization and expansion, Myanmar emerged with significant military capabilities.[33]

A number of factors underlay this military expansion. Most directly, SLORC feared Western and/or Indian military intervention on behalf of Myanmar's democratic movement. Thus, much of the newly acquired sophisticated weaponry was more suited to conventional interstate warfare than to counter-insurgency operations designed to keep SLORC in power against domestic opposition. Of course, an expanded and better-armed military also would be better able to repress internal dissent. The officer corps of Myanmar's military (SLORC's key constituency) was also happier with more modern weapons. From China's perspective arms exports were a high-value-added export which Beijing had long sought to promote. Weapons exports also had the benefit of earning profits for the PLA which were used to finance Chinese weapons development programs. As noted earlier, Beijing also endorsed the major foreign policy objective underlying the expansion of Myanmar's armed forces: deterring or defeating Western and/or Indian pro-democratic intervention.

India was a specific object of Myanmar's China-supported military buildup. India is not the only, or even the major, foreign threat perceived by the SLORC / State Peace and Development Council (SPDC), as the Myanmar military regime renamed itself in 1997. The xenophobic worldview of Myanmar's military rulers sees the United States and its Western allies, along with Myanmar's traditional rival, largely democratic and Western-aligned Thailand, as potentially threatening powers. But India ranks high in the SLORC/SPDC perception of external threats. In the early-1990s words of David Steinberg, "There is little question today that Myanmar regards India as its potential enemy, even if relations are formally appropriate."[34]

SOUTHWEST CHINA'S CORRIDOR TO THE SEA

China's leaders view Myanmar as a market for Chinese goods and as a corridor for Chinese goods to reach large markets in South and Southeast Asia and still larger, more distant markets via the high seas. One of the key elements of China's post-1978 reform process was its embrace of export promotion. Exporting to world markets was seen as a key to capital accumulation, technology acquisition, and increased incomes. China's coastal provinces led the way in this process. Those provinces, of course, had the advantage of ready access to harbors on the oceanic highway of global commerce. As the process of opening and market-oriented reform deepened in the 1980s and 1990s, the coastal provinces developed rapidly. Many areas of those coastal provinces became fairly well-to-do, leaving the poorer, interior regions far behind. Deepening marketization also meant the central government in Beijing had fewer and fewer resources available to invest in pulling up poorer areas. Comprehensive economic planning of the pre-1978 period had given Beijing very effective means of redistributing resources from wealthy to poorer provinces. Redistributive goals had also ranked high during the Maoist era. After 1978 Beijing became increasingly strapped fiscally, while redistribution took second place to growth in terms of policy objectives. In other words, the provinces were increasingly on their own, while the gap between the rich coast and the poorer interior provinces grew rapidly.

The southwestern provinces of Yunnan and Guizhou were among China's poorest. Sichuan, also considered part of China's southwest, ranked only in the mid-level of Chinese development. While poor relative to China's coastal area, the southwestern provinces had a fairly robust industrial base built up during the Maoist decades, when the objective was to develop self-reliant regional economies. Yunnan and Guizhou also had substantial raw materials to export. Transportation was the major bottleneck. Southwestern goods had to travel long distances over crowded rail lines and roads to reach China's east coast ports. Movement was slow and difficult to arrange. East coast provinces also used their powers to move their own products to the head of the queue for haulage, warehousing, and longshoreman service. Access to the Burmese market, and through Myanmar's harbors to global markets, offered a solution to these problems.

In 1985, three years before the Sino-Burma agreement on border trade and while Burma was still mired in economic isolationism, a former PRC vice minister of communications outlined three alternate routes linking China's southwest to the sea. One was construction of a highway west from Tanzhong, Yunnan, to Myitkyina, the northernmost railhead for the line stretching south to Rangoon. A second was improvement of the old Burma road to Lashio and another northern railhead. The third route was construction of a road to Bhamo on the Irrawaddy River.[35] As David Steinberg has pointed out, this vision of Myanmar as corridor for the southward flow of Chinese goods was the reverse of imperial Britain's advance into Burma in the 1880s. Then Britain saw Burma as a corridor for British goods into China.

With the freezing of Japanese and Western aid in 1988, China emerged as the major supplier of development aid to Burma. Not surprisingly, aid served the objectives of the aid giver. China became heavily involved in major transportation development projects. Chinese foreign aid credits were supplied to support construction of many new roads and to renovate others. Many of these roads connected regions of Myanmar with China or tied regions of

MAP 9.2.   Southwest China's Irrawaddy Corridor

Myanmar into the Burma Road trunk line. New bridges were built spanning rivers. A bridge connecting Yangon to outlying districts was built. Hotels and trade centers were constructed at key points. China also provided help for construction of a hydroelectric plant and for the purchase of large numbers of Chinese locomotives and rail wagons, plus trucks.[36]

By the mid-1990s Chinese sources began to speak of an "Irrawaddy corridor" connecting Yunnan with the Bay of Bengal. This road and river corridor had the advantage of avoiding use of the antiquated (1-m gauge), dangerous (frequent derailments), slow (to avoid derailments and damage to the light-gauge rails), and crowded rail line connecting Lashio and Mandalay with Yangon. It also avoided the crowded and outdated Yangon port. New hard-surfaced, widened, and better-bridged roads were to be built connecting Muse, on the China-Myanmar border and astride the old Burma road, with Bhamo, on the upper Irrawaddy. This was a distance of about sixty miles over fairly easy terrain. At Bhamo a new port was to be built where goods would be loaded from trucks onto river barges. Those barges would then proceed downriver to Minbu, where another new port was to be constructed. From there trucks would carry goods westward over the Arakan Yoma Mountains via new hard-surfaced roads. At the coast a causeway was to be built across mudflats and coastal swamps to Ramree Island. There a newly modernized port of Kyaukpyu would load Chinese goods onto seagoing vessels for shipment to markets around the world.[37] This route is illustrated by map 9.2.

A major disadvantage of the Irrawaddy corridor was the continually shifting sandbars that impeded traffic on the upper portions of the river. Constant dredging and marking of navigation channels would be necessary. Dredging and building high-speed roads, bridges, tunnels, and ports are expensive. Several of the regions through which the proposed new roads were to pass were also quite rugged, further raising costs. The monsoon season is also long in this part of the world, and, without hard-surfaced roads and sturdy bridges across flooded rivers, passage slows to a crawl. There is also a basic mismatch deriving from the climatic cycle. During the rainy season, when river draft is deep and passage easy, non-hard-surfaced roads are impassable. During the dry season, when those roads are passable, river draft is shallow. This means that achieving a commercially viable transport system requires a very large up-front investment in both roads and river navigation.

In the mid-1990s it seemed that Chinese parties were willing to undertake financing of these projects almost regardless of commercial viability. Many of the financing offers came from, or at least through, entities affiliated with the Yunnan provincial government. This funding dried up when the Asian economic crisis hit in mid-1997. One of the moves by China's central government in response to that crisis was recentralization of authority to approve major foreign development projects. Moreover, getting central approval of those projects would henceforth require their commercial viability, as demonstrated by stringent feasibility studies. China's provincial governments had been too willing, Beijing concluded, to throw money at grandiose but poorly thought through projects. If China were to undertake overseas projects for noncommercial reasons, that decision would be decided by the central government, not provincial governments. Beijing's move in 1998 to separate the PLA from business activity also had an adverse impact on Chinese funding of projects related to the Irrawaddy corridor. For a combination of strategic and profit-seeking reasons, PLA firms had sometimes been ready to provide financing for Irrawaddy corridor–related projects. Sino-Myanmar talks over financing the Irrawaddy corridor continued in 1999 but were bogged down by disagreement over cost sharing. The virtual suspension of work on the corridor after mid-1997 left the project far from completed.

New Delhi was very concerned with the Irrawaddy corridor project. If completed, it could draw Myanmar further into China's economic order, giving Beijing greater leverage over Yangon. It could accelerate illegal Chinese migration into upper Burma. It would also create larger Chinese interests in Myanmar, possibly leading Beijing to commit more resources there to protect its interests. Most serious of all, a functioning Irrawaddy corridor would have both civilian and potential military uses. Chinese military forces operating in or from Myanmar could be sustained by that logistical line. India was greatly relieved by the virtual suspension of the Irrawaddy corridor project. If that project resumes as the global economy recovers, New Delhi's concerns will again mount.

IMPLICATIONS OF THE SINO-MYANMAR STRATEGIC PARTNERSHIP

By late 1992, after four years of supporting Myanmar's democratic movement, Indian leaders concluded that this approach was pushing Yangon further into alignment with China. Indian policy toward Myanmar began to shift from ostracizing the SLORC regime and supporting the democratic movement toward normalization of state-to-state relations with that country. As J. N. Dixit, India's foreign secretary in 1992–93, put it, Myanmar's geopolitical location made it imperative for India to insure "that Myanmar does not become part of an exclusive area of influence of other great powers." This was to be achieved by "normalizing relations with whatever government is in control of Myanmar and then expanding the range and content of bilateral relations."[38] During a visit to Yangon in March 1993 Dixit discussed with SLORC leaders India's concerns with large purchases of Chinese arms and "information" which indicated that China was "interested in establishing a naval base in the southern and southeastern reaches of Myanmar aimed at obtaining a strategic presence in the Bay of Bengal." Myanmar's leaders acknowledged importing Chinese arms but insisted they were necessary for defense and internal stability. Regarding Chinese naval bases, they "flatly denied any such possibility." Early in 1993 New Delhi ended the AIR broadcasts. Regular visits of diplomatic and military personnel, minimized since 1988, resumed. Agreements on trade and joint suppression of illegal border activity were reached. India also concluded agreements to promote economic development of border areas jointly and to supply Indian electricity to several isolated Burmese villages.[39]

By the late 1990s a fair level of cordiality had been restored in Indo-Burmese ties, yet the basic terms of the Sino-Myanmar-Indian triangle were very different from the pre-1989 period. During the period from 1950 to 1988 Burma was militarily weak and carefully eschewed permanent military ties with either of its giant neighbors. After the decade-long military modernization program that began in 1988, Burma emerged with one of the strongest armies in Southeast Asia. More important was the thick relation between Chinese and Myanmar military institutions. China was Myanmar's major arms supplier and its major backer against foreign pressure.

This outcome was not necessarily what had been intended by the leaders of either Myanmar or China. Burma's SLORC was largely forced into a military relation with China as the Western nations cut arms sales and instituted various sanctions in 1988. Moreover, SLORC was clearly "playing the China card" for diplomatic purposes and understood that moving Myanmar into alignment with China would unnerve the Southeast Asian countries, India, and perhaps the Western nations as well, ultimately causing them to modify their negative policies toward Myanmar. Ultimately, SLORC'S China card worked. India, as noted earlier, reoriented its policy in 1993. The Southeast Asian countries also moved to pull Myanmar out of isolation and away from dependence on China. This was a major factor motivating the Association of Southeast Asian Nations (ASEAN) to grant full membership to Myanmar in June 1997 over American objection.[40] Singapore also undertook clandestine cooperation with the Myanmar military, helping to modernize its communications, meet its munitions needs, and so on, in order (in part) to reduce Yangon's dependence on China.[41] Yangon's link with Beijing in fact gave it significant diplomatic leverage.

There was considerable debate in the late 1990s regarding Chinese motivations behind the intensification of Sino-Myanmar relations. Analysts agree that economic objectives were important: expanding Chinese exports, securing access to Burmese resources, and creating jobs and economic growth for Yunnan province. Beyond that they disagree. Chinese spokesmen deny that there is any strategic or military rationale behind the new Sino-Myanmar relation. In the United States interpretation of Chinese objectives in Myanmar became entangled in the late 1990s with the debate over the "Chinese threat" and whether the United States should "contain" or "engage" China. Perhaps partially because of this, some prominent analysts have insisted that China's actions were *only* inspired by a desire for economic gain. Any attribution of strategic purposes to China's new Myanmar policies was not only wrong but also positively dangerous, since it could lead to a "self-fulfilling prophecy" that China was a threat.[42]

From India's perspective the question of Chinese motives is nearly irrelevant. From New Delhi's perspective what matters is that, for whatever reasons, China has established a close political and military relation on India's eastern flank. The fact of that relationship is, from India's perspective, far more important than the reasons that gave rise to it. India, in other words, focuses on Chinese capabilities rather than intentions. Indian opinion, both specialist and popular, also readily attributes strategic purposes to China's moves in Myanmar. Established beliefs about China make Indians accept nearly any "evidence" regarding China's strategic objectives in Myanmar. While this is not a reason for independent analysts to accept the evidence— indeed, it might be a good reason for them to argue against it—it follows that we must begin with Indian views if we are to understand India's likely reaction to the Sino-Myanmar strategic partnership. As the old saw goes: facts are real in their consequences if they are believed to be true.

Regarding the question of Chinese motivations, different institutions in Chinese society have different interests and view the relation with Myanmar differently. Bureaus of the Yunnan provincial government may be primarily concerned with economic growth. China's politically well-connected arms-exporting firms seek profts primarily. Chinese entrepreneurs who might set up businesses in Mandalay are probably seeking personal fortune and fame. And, when Chinese leaders travel abroad, their Ministry of Foreign Affairs handlers routinely hand them boilerplate speeches about such things as "new stages" of cooperation and expanding friendship. There are many different perspectives and interests in China, but activities related to them take place within the purview of broad policy guidelines that must be approved at a fairly high level. At that level there is a sense that China is and ought to be an emerging regional and global power and that various policies and activities should fit within guidelines designed to achieve that growth. The broad objective is to create an international environment in the South Asian region favorable to the continuing growth of China's power.

In this context China's strategic partnership with Myanmar serves two major purposes. First and foremost, it constrains India, preventing it from becoming a real rival to China. The Sino-Burmese partnership demonstrates quite vividly, and without China needing to say anything, that India is not, whatever its aspirations might be, the master of South Asia. New Delhi might be able to bludgeon little Nepal into submission via a blockade because of favorable terrain, but in a far bigger and more important case, Myanmar, India has been reduced to passivity. Burmese friendship with China, as with Pakistan's friendship with China, demonstrates that South Asia is not an Indian sphere of influence. India is not able to dictate the terms of foreign relations of countries in that region. In other words, and as the Chinese government sees it, India is not able to impose its hegemony on South Asia. And, of course, the creation of a militarily potent Myanmar, confident of defending itself and friendly with China, means that India is in a less favorable military situation, should it ever come to war. A second and related set of Chinese strategic objectives has to do with the Indian Ocean. China aspires eventually to establish a presence in the Indian Ocean (this is discussed in chap. 10). To be effective, those forces must be supported by a forward logistical presence and by timely intelligence. For People's Liberation Army Navy (PLAN) warships to remain deployed in the Indian ocean or to sustain even a moderately intense level of operations there, those warships would need close-by ports to resupply ammunition, fuel, food, water, parts, and replacement personnel and to make repairs.

India will do everything it can to check or undo the Sino-Burmese strategic partnership. Since 1993 it has been courting the SLORC/SPDC regime in order to draw it away from China. If India were to attempt to pressure Myanmar to scale back its economic links with China, it would not work and would probably backfire. A more viable policy would be to offer positive inducements for expanded Burmese cooperation with India. In November 1998 India's Ministry of External Affairs and the Institute of Chinese Studies in New Delhi sponsored a conference exploring the possibility of region-wide development. The focus was on the poverty of India's northeast and the considerable potential for expanding trade between that area, Myanmar, Thailand, Laos, and southwestern China. If transportation were improved by construction of a high-speed roadway or a railway linking India's northeast with Southeast Asia through Myanmar, with spurs into Southwest China and Bangladesh, and if the governments of the respective countries adopted beneficial policies, trade across the region might develop rapidly. Northeast India would be lifted from poverty, while cordial, mutually beneficial, and interdependent ties developed among the countries of the region.[43]

Such an approach may be the most viable strategic direction for India. Expanding India's economic role in Myanmar would counter China's presence and prevent China from economically dominating that country. It would build on Myanmar's deep suspicions of Chinese intentions and ethnic inundation, and on similar apprehensions about future Chinese domination of Myanmar shared by the Southeast Asian countries and Japan. It would also offer opportunities to integrate further the seven northeastern states into the Indian union. Most important, of course, it could improve the lives of the people of India's northeast.

There will be continuing rivalry between China and India as they move down the path of cooperative regional development centered on Myanmar. India will resist Chinese attempts to expand its military role in that country. It will also be suspicious of Chinese attempts to play a more prominent political role in the region—by mediating various conflicts between Myanmar and Bangladesh, for example. China will resist Indian efforts to block or roll back China's military links with and presence in Myanmar. Both New Delhi and Beijing will be sensitive to the political-military implications of each others' road, rail, and trade links with Myanmar and will make counter-moves limiting the adverse effect of those links.

Some analysts have pointed out that overdependence on China is not in Myanmar's national interests and have suggested that at some point Yangon will seek to balance China by improving ties with India and/or other powers. They have also noted that China now has considerable leverage over Yangon and might use this leverage to prevent Myanmar's defection from the partnership.[44] J. Mohan Malik has identified a number of instruments that Beijing might use in this regard. It could threaten to withhold needed military equipment or parts, to restrict the lucrative cross-border trade vital to continuing peace with the ethnic minorities, or to renew support for Myanmar's ethnic insurgencies. It could threaten to cut developmental assistance and other capital flows into Myanmar. Simultaneously, Beijing would appeal to the anti-Western and anti-Indian sentiments of Myanmar's leaders. If China resorted to such coercion, India, Japan, and the Southeast Asian countries could all be expected to counter it through economic, political, and possibly military measures. The great danger in such an eventuality would be that China's leaders might conclude, rather like Japan's leaders in 1941 or Germany's in 1914, that the most forceful measures are necessary to defeat this "encirclement" by hostile powers.

10 / The Indian Ocean in Sino-Indian Relations

In the literature on the evolution of Japanese-American rivalry in the Pacific in the first half of the twentieth century, the overlapping of sea lines of communication in the Pacific Ocean is often identified as a significant factor. After the American acquisition of the Philippines and Guam from Spain in 1898 and Japan's acquisition in 1919 of the former German colonies of the Mariana Islands in the Western Pacific and the Marshall Islands in the Central Pacific, the sea lanes of each power, with its outlying Pacific territories, passed through the territorial security zones of the other. By strengthening the defense of its own territories, each power ipso facto threatened the sea lanes of the other. A similar situation of overlapping and commingled sea lanes, though with a very different historical evolution, exists between China and India today in the Indian Ocean region (IOR). The insecurity inherent in this situation has thus far played a minor but significant role in the international politics of the region. That insecurity may well increase in decades to come, possibly generating considerable mutual suspicion between the two countries.

The essence of the problem is that foreign trade plays a vital and expanding role in both Chinese and Indian economies, that a substantial portion of that trade transits the Indian Ocean, and that the Indian Ocean sea lanes carrying that trade are threatened by the naval activities of the other country. After decades-long experiments with economic autarky, by the 1990s both China and India were moving toward greater integration with the world economy. Foreign trade plays a far more important role in China's economy than

TABLE 10.1   Foreign Trade as a Percentage of Gross Domestic Product

	1993	1988	1983	1978	1973
China	33	26	15	10	8
India	8	5	4	5	4

SOURCE: *International Financial Statistics, Yearbook 1997* (Washington, D.C.: International Monetary Fund, 1997); *China Statistical Yearbook, 1998* (Beijing: China Statistical Publishing House, 1998); *Lishi tongji ziliao huibian (1949–1989)* (*Compilation of Chinese Historical Statistics [1949–1989]*) (Beijing: China Statistical Publishing House, 1990).
NOTE: Total trade / gross domestic product = percentage.

in India's, constituting 33 percent of gross domestic product in 1993 as compared to India's 8 percent. The substantial role of foreign trade in China—85 percent of which is seaborne—means, of course, that China is relatively vulnerable to measures that disrupt it. As table 10.1 indicates, only in the early 1990s did India's foreign trade equal China's trade in the early 1970s, when China was still following policies of Maoist autarky.

At the turn of the twenty-first century about 9 percent of China's foreign trade passes across the Indian Ocean. China's major trading partners lie around the Pacific Ocean littoral: Hong Kong, Japan, Taiwan, the United States, South Korea, Canada, Australia. China's trade with these countries does not normally transit the Indian Ocean. China's Indian Ocean trade includes all Chinese trade with Indian Ocean littoral countries other than Thailand, Malaysia, Indonesia, and Australia whose major ports are east of the Strait of Malacca. Added to this is Chinese trade with African and Middle Eastern states with trade moving via ports on the Mediterranean or Red Seas. This would include China's trade with the petroleum-rich Middle Eastern states. About 67 percent of China's trade with the developed countries of the European Union is also transported by sea, and almost all of that goes via the Malacca Strait, the Indian Ocean, and the Suez Canal.[1] The route between Shanghai and Rotterdam via the Indian Ocean is about fifty-four hundred kilometers (3,350 miles) shorter than a route between the same two cities, following a great arc across the north Pacific, then transiting the Panama Canal. Since China's trade with Europe is substantial, this greatly increases China's trade via the Indian Ocean. China's Indian Ocean commerce includes petroleum imports from the Middle East and its capital goods imports from Europe. Were this massive trade severed or substantially disrupted, it would be a serious but not necessarily devastating blow to China's economy.

The security problem for China in terms of militarily protecting this trade has three dimensions. First, India occupies a very strong naval position in the Indian Ocean. Second, China's own naval position in the Indian Ocean is weak, not so much because of the inadequacy of the country's naval forces—they are actually quite strong in comparison to India's—but because of the distances involved and an absence of forward logistical bases that could sustain PLAN operations in the Indian Ocean. Third, in the event of a PRC-ROI conflict India might be tempted to escalate from the land dimension, where India might suffer reverses, to the maritime dimension, where it enjoys substantial advantages, and employ those advantages to restrict China's vital Indian Ocean trade.

INDIAN POLICY TOWARD THE INDIAN OCEAN

Indian national security thinking minimized the significance of the Indian Ocean for the first several decades of Indian independence. There were several prominent critics of this neglect, but their calls for a more prominent role for the Indian Navy (IN) in the Indian Ocean region were generally rejected as incompatible with Indian ideals. Nehru's policies of nonalignment and antimilitarism led him to oppose continuation of Western military bases in the IOR, but this did not rank high among his priorities. The deterioration of Indian-Chinese relations in the early 1960s led to a certain pro-Western "ambiguity" in Indian policy toward the Indian Ocean, with the Anglo-American naval presence there implicitly (though, of course, not openly) welcomed as useful in countering China. By the late 1960s Indian policy finally began moving toward unambiguous and active opposition to all extraregional military presences from the IOR. A key stimulus for this policy change were Anglo-American preparations (begun in 1965) to establish a U.S. military base in the Chagos Archipelago of the British Indian Ocean Territory. This was finally accomplished in December 1970, when Britain leased Diego Garcia to the United States. Soviet warships had entered the Indian Ocean for the first time in 1968.[2]

India's policy response to the growing superpower presence in the IOR was enunciated at the Lusaka summit of the nonaligned movement in 1970, when Indian leaders secured passage of a declaration calling for establishment of the Indian Ocean as a Zone of Peace. India then engineered passage of a United Nations General Assembly resolution in December 1971 calling for establishment of the Indian Ocean as a Zone of Peace free from all "bases, military installations, logistical supply facilities . . . and any other manifestation of great power presence conceived in the context of great power rivalry." The next year the General Assembly set up an Ad Hoc Committee on the

Indian Ocean to study the implications of the declaration and consider "practical measures" to further it. India used the Ad Hoc Committee to focus attention on extra-regional military activities that it considered antithetical to the Zone of Peace proposal.[3] If India's Zone of Peace plan for the IOR were realized by expulsion of all military facilities "conceived in the context of great power rivalry," India's military presence would remain as the preeminent power in the region. This consideration has led many foreign and some Indian analysts to conclude that the broad and unstated objective of Indian policy in the IOR became the establishment of India as the dominant power in that region. In India a consensus developed within the Indian Navy and among the government that the Indian Ocean was an integral part of India's historical, geographic sphere of influence.[4]

A number of policies served to strengthen India's position in the Indian Ocean. Indian naval forces were expanded. Changes in international law in the 1970s gave India jurisdiction over an extensive "Exclusive Economic Zone," two hundred nautical miles wide. This, combined with the growing superpower naval presence in the Indian Ocean, led to major expansion of the IN.[5] In 1978 a twenty-year naval modernization program was adopted, designed to give India a true blue-water capability—the ability to sustain intense combat operations on the high seas hundreds of miles from a country's coasts. Under this plan the IN acquired long-range guided missile cruisers, antisubmarine warfare (ASW) destroyers, helicopter-carrying frigates, ASW and attack submarines of the Foxtrot, Tango, and Kilo classes, ocean minesweepers, and other warships and auxiliary vessels. In 1986 India purchased from Britain the 24,000-ton aircraft-carrier *Hermes*. Laid down in 1953, the carrier was commissioned by the IN in 1987 as the *Viraat*. This was the IN's second carrier. The other, the *Vikrant*, was decommissioned in 1997. Naval and air bases were built in the mid-1980s on outlying and previously unprotected Indian island territories—the Andaman and Nicobar group southeast of the Bay of Bengal and the Laccadive and Minicoy groups to the southwest of the Indian Peninsula. Port Blair in the Andaman chain was turned into a major air and naval base. Modern communications and surveillance systems were established, including a very-low-frequency network for communication with submerged submarines. A Southern Air Command was established at Trivandrum in 1984 to coordinate air activity over the Indian Ocean. Previously, that had been the responsibility of Central Air Command with headquarters at Allahabad in north India. By the late 1990s the IN clearly constituted the largest, most powerful naval force indigenous to the IOR, although the capabilities of the U.S. Navy dwarfed those of the IN.

Other policies designed to establish India's ascendant position in the IOR have been the promotion of Indian commercial interests there. Trade and investment among India and the IOR countries have been encouraged. New Delhi has drawn on the large Indian diaspora in the IOR to promote such links. That diaspora is vast, including in the mid-1980s well over a million people each in Sri Lanka, Malaysia, and Madagascar, nearly seven hundred thousand ethnic Indians in Mauritius, and over one hundred thousand Indians each in Yemen, the United Arab Emirates, Singapore, Saudi Arabia, Oman, and Myanmar. Tens of thousands of Indians live in over a dozen other IOR countries. Indian policy has also sought to engage IOR military institutions in defense training programs in order to acquaint regional states with the growing effectiveness of India's armed forces. Economic and technical assistance is also provided to IOR countries. Seats in Indian medical, engineering, and other technical institutions are reserved for IOR students, while Indian experts provide in-country technical assistance. Visits by IN warships to IOR ports also promote Indian prestige and influence.

The United States and the Soviet Union were the prime targets of India's efforts to limit and expel extra-regional military presence from the Indian Ocean. Yet China was also targeted. Indian representatives at the United Nations specified that the "great powers" referred to by the December 1971 Zone of Peace General Assembly Resolution included *all* permanent members of the Security Council. China became a member of the Ad Hoc Committee set up to pursue the Zone of Peace proposal, and during the 1970s and early 1980s Beijing occasionally supported Indian criticism of Soviet or American military activities in the Indian Ocean. As India's position in the Indian Ocean grew stronger, China began to show signs of apprehension. An article in the semiofficial journal *Shijie zhishi* in 1989 traced the steady strengthening of India's position in the Indian Ocean and concluded that it "far exceeded" what was necessary for India's own defense but was part of a broader effort to establish India as a "global military power."[6]

CHINA'S FIRST PERIOD OF NAVALISM AND THE INDIAN OCEAN

For centuries China was a major naval power and active in the Indian Ocean. Throughout its long history China was primarily a continental, land power, with little interest in the seas. There have been, however, important exceptions to this rule. The most important exception spanned a period of 306 years, from the collapse of China's Northern Song dynasty in 1127 through the Yuan dynasty of the Mongols and up until 1433, early in the Ming dynasty. Chinese maritime technology had made great strides during the Northern Song, with the imperial government encouraging overseas commerce as a source of imperial revenue. Throughout the Song, Chinese vessels dominated seaborne trade in East and Southeast Asia and played an important role in eastern Indian Ocean trade. The Song also turned Chinese maritime skills and technology to military ends. After the loss of northern China to the non-Chinese Jurchens in 1127, the Song waged a protracted (150-year-long) struggle to defend China south of the Yangtze from the powerful and aggressive Jin dynasty established by the Jurchens in north China. Maritime operations became a major theater of the Southern Song–Jin contest, both on the Yangtze River and along the East China Sea, where the Jin mounted operations designed to outflank the Song. Both Southern Song and Jin states developed substantial naval forces to serve their policies.[7]

Yuan Mongol imperialism was built on Song naval skills. Between 1274 and 1294, with powerful Chinese fleets, the Mongols launched three invasions of Japan, two amphibious assaults against Tonkin, a seaborne invasion of the Cham Kingdom in what later became southern Vietnam, and an invasion of the Majapahit empire in Java. The Majapahit empire was a major maritime empire in its own right. Yuan ships also pushed into the Indian Ocean, calling at Ceylon in 1291. After the restoration of Han rule in China in 1368 in the form of the new Ming dynasty, politically inspired Chinese navalism continued. The early Ming, like the Song and the Yuan, welcomed overseas trade as a way of garnering lucrative taxes. Chinese trading vessels swarmed through the South China Sea, through the Strait of Malacca, and into the Indian Ocean, mingling with Arab and Indian merchants but probably constituting the dominant ethnic group in this trade, at least up to the Strait of Malacca and into the eastern Indian Ocean. Chinese trading vessels plied regular routes between southern Chinese ports and Ceylon, southern India, and Hormuz on the Persian Gulf. The ships of Chinese merchants were the largest and best-equipped ships in the Indian Ocean and, indeed, in the world at that time.

During the early Ming, China became for a period of about four decades a major actor in the international politics of the Indian Ocean region. Between 1405 and 1433 its imperial government dispatched a series of large expeditions into the Indian Ocean under the command of Zheng He, a Chinese Muslim eunuch official. These were impressive expeditions even by modern standards; in medieval terms they were unprecedented. The first expedition in 1405–7 included 317 ships, of which 62 were "treasure vessels" weighing fifteen hundred tons each, or more than three times the combined weight of the three vessels of Columbus's expedition of 1492. The personnel of the first expedition numbered nearly twenty-eight thousand people. A total of seven expeditions passed westward through the Strait of Malacca, calling at ports on the Malay Peninsula, Sumatra, Bengal, Ceylon, southern India, Persia, Arabia, and east Africa. Subsidiary expeditions pushed as far north as Jidda on the Red Sea and the Mozambique channel between Madagascar and the African continent.

The key objectives of these expeditions were political: to persuade rulers of the Indian Ocean region to submit to the suzerainty of China's emperor. Chinese military forces intervened twice in Sumatra. The first time, in 1407, involved destruction of pirate forces led by an émigré Chinese. A very substantial pirate navy was shattered and the pirate chieftain captured and sent to China for execution. Another Chinese émigré who had cooperated with the Chinese expeditionary force was appointed local magistrate to replace the late pirate chieftain. A half-dozen years later Chinese forces intervened successfully in a civil war among contesting Sumatran rulers and on behalf of a ruler who had previously rendered tribute to China's emperor. At Malacca in 1409 the commander of the Chinese expeditionary force conferred tributary status on a Muslim sultan who had previously been a vassal of Siam. The sultan was sent to China to pay personal obeisance to the Son of Heaven, and a Chinese cantonment was established in Malacca. On Ceylon the king was ordered to surrender the holy relic of Lord Buddha's tooth, sought unsuccessfully by Kublai Khan's emissary nearly two centuries earlier. When the Ceylonese king refused to surrender the relic, Chinese forces fought their way to his mountain capital at Kandy, arrested the monarch along with his family and court, and sent the king to Beijing for punishment. He was later allowed to return to Kandy, presumably suitably enlightened and chastened.[8] The sultan of Bengal first sent an envoy to the Chinese imperial court in 1405, thereby becoming, at least in Chinese eyes, a tributary of China. Envoys traveled regularly between Bengal and China for the next three decades. When Bengal was invaded by a neighboring kingdom, Beijing dispatched a special mission to ask the ruler of that kingdom to stop the invasion of China's tributary, Bengal.[9]

So vigorous was Chinese maritime activity in the Indian Ocean in the fifteenth century, so impressive was Chinese maritime technology, and so large in scale the naval operations fielded by the Chinese state that in his 1966 history of the region, for example, Auguste Toussaint, quoting R. Grousset, raises the provocative question: "What would the destiny of Asia have been if European navigators, approaching the Indies and Malaya, had found a Chinese thalassocracy established there?"[10] This, of course, did not happen. In 1433 China's voyages were abruptly terminated by Chinese officials concerned by their great expense and little material return. Official opinion solidified against further maritime ventures. Records of the earlier voyages were actually destroyed, to frustrate any attempt at imitation. By 1525 an imperial edict ordered destruction of all large seagoing vessels along with arrest of their crews. China turned its back on the sea.

THE CONTEMPORARY REEMERGENCE OF CHINESE MARITIME POWER

In contemplating the future of Chinese power in the Indian Ocean region, it is important to understand that China has embarked on another exceptional period of navalism. The PRC's contemporary emphasis on naval power arose out of perceptions deeply rooted in modern China's historical experience. The defining experience for modern China (at least in the CCP view) was its "humiliation" at the hands of foreign barbarian invaders, first European and then Japanese, in the century between 1840 and 1945. The naval dimension of this threat was illustrated by the very names the Chinese used to refer to their barbarian invaders. *Yangren,* "ocean people," described the Europeans and Americans who arrived at China's ports by ship, while *rikou* or *wokou,* "Japanese pirates" or, more pejoratively, "dwarf pirates," referred to Japanese. To a very substantial degree China's strategic failure to deal effectively with these challenges was a failure of naval power. Viewed strategically, China's opponents, moving speedily by sea along China's coasts, enjoyed superior external lines of communication. They could select their point of attack and quickly mobilize local superiority. Moving overland along primitive roads and with, at best, limited warning of the enemy's approach, China's task of defense was nearly impossible. The best way, perhaps the only way, to defend China was by securing the sea approaches to it, though China's leaders did not understand this until late in the nineteenth century.

The leaders of the People's Republic of China recognized very early on that a powerful navy that could, at a minimum, defend the approaches to China's coast was essential to national security Even before the PRC was established, Mao Zedong declared that China needed a strong navy to defend itself against imperialism. Through its alliance with the USSR, the PRC obtained an array of advanced naval weapons and technology. While still far inferior to the American, Soviet, British, or other modern navies, by the end of the 1950s a growing and modernizing Chinese navy had emerged.

The break with the USSR and China's policies of autarky were hard blows to PLAN development. Significant progress resumed in 1969, when China's leaders ordered a major expansion of China's merchant fleet plus modernization of China's outdated harbor facilities. A crash program was launched to build merchant vessels, while even more vessels were purchased abroad. Between 1971 and 1976 China purchased 250 freighters, tankers, and bulk car-

TABLE 10.2 Chinese and Indian Merchant Marine Fleets (in Thousand Gross Registered Tons)

	1995 (in rank order)	1975
Panama	71,922	13,667
Liberia	59,801	65,820
Greece	29,435	22,527
Cyprus	24,653	3,221
Bahamas	23,603	190
Norway	21,551	26,154
Japan	19,913	39,740
Malta	17,678	—
PRC	*16,943*	*2,828*
Russia	15,202	—
Singapore	13,611	3,892
United States	12,761	14,587
Hong Kong	8,795	419
Philippines	8,744	879
India	*7,127*	*3,869*

SOURCE: *United Nations Statistical Yearbook*, 1995 and 1975.
NOTE: Includes oil tankers and ore and bulk carriers.

riers, while it built another 94. Shipbuilding quickly emerged as a major Chinese industry.[11] As table 10.2 indicates, by 1995 China possessed the ninth largest merchant fleet in the world. Many of the countries ranking ahead of China were tiny, and their registries basically offered a flag of convenience. India's fleet was, in 1995, well less than half the size of China's. In the twenty years between 1975 and 1995 China's merchant fleet grew by 600 percent, while India's grew by 180 percent.

The strategic orientation of the PLAN from the onset of the Korean War in June 1950 through the restoration of Sino-Soviet cordiality in the mid-1980s was coastal defense—to meet and undertake active operations to destroy enemy forces as they approached China's coasts. "Active defense, coastal operations" was the strategic guideline.[12] This changed in 1985. China's naval power was henceforth to be used for "active offshore defense." PLAN forces would be configured and trained to meet hostile would-be invaders far out at sea, in the Yellow Sea, the East China Sea, the Taiwan Strait, the South China Sea, and the western Pacific, well away from China's coasts, thereby protecting its land and maritime territories.[13] Since our concern is with the implications of Chinese naval power for India, it is important to note that the key missions defined by the PLAN's post-1985 doctrine did not touch directly on India. Still, the more powerful, long-legged Chinese naval assets developed under the new doctrine were potentially fungible into the Indian Ocean.

Throughout the 1980s and 1990s the PLAN steadily expanded and modernized. In the decade between 1985 and 1995 the PLAN doubled its complement of underway-replenishment ships, thereby substantially enhancing its ability to sustain operations at longer distances from Chinese ports. It refurbished its Soviet-era warships with weapons, electronic communications, and fire-control systems acquired from France, Italy, and other advanced industrial countries, thereby moving substantially beyond technology that was reverse-engineered from earlier Soviet systems. It brought into service new classes of surface combatants and submarines. Critical weaknesses were addressed, if not completely overcome. The anti-submarine warfare (ASW) and air defense capabilities of PLAN warships were substantially strengthened.[14] Chinese intelligence also labored to meet key PLAN needs by covertly acquiring a wide array of U.S. military-related technology, including sensors and other electronics for surveillance, instruments for target detection and target recognition, and other types of sophisticated military information technology.[15]

With the formation of a Chinese-Russian "strategic partnership" in the 1990s, the PLAN gained wide access to state-of-the-art naval technology. Under a five-year cooperation agreement signed in 1993, the PLAN acquired advanced Russian surface-to-air missiles, towed-array anti-submarine sonar, multiple-target torpedo control systems, nuclear submarine propulsion systems, technology improving the range and accuracy of undersea-launched cruise missiles, and much more. The most dramatic PLAN acquisitions from Russia were two Sovremenny-class destroyers armed with extremely lethal SS-N-22 Sunburn anti-ship missiles—a surface-skimming missile traveling at Mach 2.5, with a 90- to 120-kilometer range, and the ability to be programmed to maneuver and select an aircraft carrier target among a fleet of ships. The SS-N-22 was specifically designed to evade and defeat the Aegis-class cruisers that protect U.S. aircraft carriers. Four Russian Kilo-class attack submarines ordered by the PLAN in 1994 are also extremely potent weapons. Being ultra-quiet vessels, these warships are armed with wire-guided acoustic-homing anti-submarine torpedoes and wake-homing anti-surface ship torpedoes, again specifically designed to destroy U.S. aircraft carriers.[16]

Indian naval analysts have followed PLAN development closely and with growing concern. They understand, like students of the PLA around the world, that China has not developed its naval forces primarily with India in mind.

The historical origin of modern Chinese navalism was the seaborne invasions of China by Europeans and Japanese. In the post-1949 period this was reinforced by the maritime threat posed by U.S. and Nationalist Chinese forces on Taiwan. In the 1990s the main Chinese objectives relating to possible application of Chinese naval power had to do with Taiwan and enforcement of China's maritime claims in the Yellow Sea, East China Sea, and the South China Sea. Yet protecting the maritime commerce of the PRC and supporting China's friends and allies in the struggle against "hegemonism" are also PLAN objectives. Naval power is also intrinsically fungible. Under certain conditions and if China's leaders so choose, Chinese naval strength could be applied in the Indian Ocean.

One of the closest Indian studies of this problem, that by Rahul Roy-Choudhury, found that five post-1978 shifts in China's naval policy, when taken together, constituted a mounting challenge to India. They included: the shift in PLAN doctrine away from coastal defense to offensive operations at greater distances from the coast; the construction of modernized principal combatants with deep ocean capabilities; the development of seaborne logistic capabilities; the planned acquisition of aircraft carriers; and construction of facilities in the Indian Ocean region. Roy-Choudhury understood full well that the main objectives of China's growing naval power were in the Western Pacific and had to do with raising China's global influence. Yet he also concluded that, under certain circumstances, China's growing naval power "could constitute a serious threat to India's maritime interests." Such a threat would not necessarily arise out of specific disagreements over seabeds or territorial waters. Rather, "it could simply evolve from a sense of rivalry between two powerful navies over their respective spheres of influence in the Indian Ocean." Roy-Choudhury's concern was not so much with the present naval balance but with existing trends. If those trends continued, he warned, "in the near future, the task forces of the PLAN could be centered around aircraft carriers accompanied by an adequate number of ocean capable surface warships and nuclear powered submarines, to carry out offensive operations in the Indian Ocean. These forces could be used to defend Chinese sea lines of communications in the area or even project power against the Indian mainland and island territories." "[In] the near future, possibly soon after the turn of the decade [i.e., 2000], the maritime dimensions of the Chinese military threat to India will increase in intensity."[17]

While this view probably represents the view of India's military establishment and security analysts, many Indians disagree with it. In fact, as the twenty-first century began, there was considerable debate in India regarding the nature of the maritime challenge from China. Some analysts and politicians are reassured by the fact that China's major naval concerns have to do with Taiwan, the United States, and Japan and maintain that those concerns will preoccupy Beijing for a number of decades ahead. They also point to the very limited capabilities of the PLAN in the IOR at present, plus the absence of evidence that China plans military operations in the IOR. These critics also suspect that the IN inflates the China threat to win support for its growing budget.

In terms of IN missions, countering Pakistan and enforcing India's control over its Exclusive Economic Zones (EEZ) are more pressing concerns in the early years of the twenty-first century than countering a potential Chinese thrust into the Indian Ocean. But, if not the most immediate concern, countering such a PLAN push has been the IN's most important *long-term* concern. Preparing to meet this contingency was a major reason for the decision to establish a new, fourth, operational IN command, the Far Eastern Command based at Port Blair in the Andaman Islands in the mid-1990s. The chief mission of this new command is to watch for and prepare to counter the growing Chinese presence in the Indian Ocean. Its most important, if not immediate, hypothetical mission is to block a possible PLAN movement through the Strait of Malacca. The Far Eastern Command will have upgraded surveillance and monitoring capabilities, plus augmented air and naval forces.[18]

The pattern of PLA activity also indicates a clear interest in the Indian Ocean. That region received the first foreign visits by PLAN warships in November 1985 thru January 1986. Karachi, the main seaport of China's quasi-ally Pakistan, was the PLAN squadron's first stop. After five days the two-ship squadron, made up of a modernized 3,250-ton Luda-class destroyer and a 7,500-ton underway-replenishment ship and headed by the commander of China's Eastern Fleet, headed east for Colombo, Sri Lanka, and then on to Chittagong, Bangladesh.[19] The 1985 cruise demonstrated the PLAN's capability of operating in the IOR, began the process of familiarizing PLAN officers and men with the topography and hydrography of that region, and demonstrated Beijing's refusal to allow New Delhi a veto over China's military relations with countries of the Indian Ocean littoral. Indian analysts saw the 1985–86 visits as displaying China's "interests in the Indian Ocean region."[20]

In November 1993 the 4,500-ton PLAN training ship *Zheng He* carried two hundred cadets to Karachi, Bombay, Chittagong, and Bangkok. Bombay was included as a result of a visit by the Indian defense minister to China in July 1992.[21] From Beijing's perspective including a call at Bombay was an effort to persuade India of the friendly, nonthreatening nature of China's growing naval presence in the IOR. In November 1997 a PLAN squadron again entered the IOR. On this occasion a guided missile destroyer and a guided missile frigate visited Malaysia's Lumut naval base at the northern entrance of the Strait of

Malacca. This was the first visit by PLAN ships to Malaysia. Upon his arrival in Malaysia the commander of the Chinese squadron issued a written statement stressing the need for more exchange visits by warships of the two countries and for stronger friendly ties between the armed forces of the two countries, "especially between the two navies."[22]

THE SINO-INDIAN NAVAL BALANCE

American analysts of China's post-1978 naval modernization effort typically minimize its significance on the basis that the PLAN is still not able to match the U.S. Navy and probably will not be able to do so for at least another two decades. Things look different from an Indian naval perspective. A straightforward comparison of the naval order of battle of the IN and PLAN suggests that, ceteris paribus, China has a substantially more powerful navy in both quantitative and qualitative terms. Table 10.3 depicts the two countries' naval order of battle.

China's naval expansion has been considerably more intense than India's. Between 1976 and 1999 China added an average of 3.04 major warships per year, while India added only 1.26. The addition of major warships is illustrated by table 10.4. In key areas of naval technology the PLAN also holds an advantage over the IN. India recognizes this fact and is currently attempting to overcome its disadvantages vis-à-vis China in such areas as electronic warfare, missiles, air defense, and anti-submarine warfare.

The size and quality of existing naval forces is only one component of naval power. Other key components have to do with geography, including the relative distances between the theater of operations and logistic support bases; the availability of defensible land bases in forward areas for combat and support operations; and the relative capabilities of the combatant forces to use technology to master distance and terrain in the theater of operations. In these areas the IN enjoys crucial advantages over the PLAN in the IOR, and maintaining these geopolitical advantages is absolutely imperative for the IN. To the extent that Chinese diplomacy is able to overcome the geographic disadvantages of the PLAN in the IOR, the quantitative and qualitative superiority of the PLAN can be brought into play against the IN.

The availability of strong logistical support, secure yet fairly close to the forward areas of combat operations, is a key element. PLAN ability to sustain fairly intense combat operations in the Indian Ocean would be dependent on access to logistical support on the littoral of that ocean. Such logistical points would make available replenishment of fuel, ammunition, parts and equipment, personnel, food and water, medical treatment and evacuation,

TABLE 10.3   Comparison of Indian and Chinese Navies in 1999

	India	China
Total naval personnel	45,000	268,000
Naval air force (no. of aircraft)	—	800
Ballistic missile submarine (nuclear powered)	—	1
Ballistic missile submarine (non–nuclear powered)	—	1
Attack submarines	1	9
Patrol submarines	22	65
Cruise missile submarines	—	1
Attack carrier (medium)	1	1
Destroyers	8	20
Frigates	21	37
Corvettes	28	—
Patrol ships	7	15
Fast-attack craft, torpedo	—	17
Fast-attack craft, missile	5	92
Fast-attack craft, gun	—	105
Fast-attack craft, patrol	—	124
Large patrol craft	27	—
Landing ships	11	—
Landing craft, medium and utility	10	130
Landing ships, tank and medium	—	54

and facilities for repair of ships and equipment. Some of these things could be supplied by replenishment ships, but, if those replenishment ships must themselves return to home ports to take on cargoes, the per-period-of-time tonnage they can convey to warships in forward areas of the Indian Ocean would be far less. Replenishment ships operating out of Zhanjiang (in southern Guangdong province and the home port of China's South Sea Fleet) would be far less effective than would identical ships picking up critical supplies at, say, Bangkok or Yangon. The difference could be whether a disabled PLAN warship got needed replacement radar equipment, for example, in several days versus a week or so. Replenishment ships would also themselves constitute valuable and vulnerable targets, the loss of which could severely limit the ability of PLAN warships to operate. There are also some things that cannot be

TABLE 10.3 *(continued)*

	India	China
Troop transports	—	7
Hovercraft	—	10
Mine sweepers, ocean	12	40
Mine sweepers, inshore	6	8
Mine sweepers, drones	—	46
Mine hunters	6	—
Mine layers	—	1
Submarine tenders	1	6
Replenishment and support tankers	10	—
Supply ships	—	22
Water carriers	2	—
Fleet replenishment ships	—	3
Training ships	4	2
Research and survey ships	11	—
Diving support and research ships	1	—
Salvage and repair ships	0	5
Ocean tugs	2	—
Ice breakers	—	4
Merchant marine (no. of vessels)	941	3,175

SOURCE: *Jane's Fighting Ships, 1998–99* (Surrey: Jane's Information Group Ltd., various years), with PLAN figures for submarines, destroyers, frigates, and troop transports adjusted by retired Rear Admiral Eric McVadon.
NOTE: Figures for India include active, building, and projected; those for China include active, reserve, building, and planned.

done at sea—repair of major damage or overhaul of a ship's engine, for example. Nor can supply ships keep on hand the large array of spare parts and replacement equipment which warships may need and which can easily be stockpiled in warehouses on dry land. Again, closer is better. The fact that the U.S. fleet accomplished such repairs at Pearl Harbor in the 1940s rather than on the west coast of North America, for example, contributed substantially to the intensity of U.S. naval operations in the western Pacific during the war against Japan. Bases in Japan and the Philippines served similarly during the Vietnam War.

   The most obvious Indian Ocean logistic point for the PLAN in the event of an India-China war would be Karachi. Pakistan could welcome the opportunity to stand with China against India, hopeful that China's might would

TABLE 10.4   Comparative Rate of Indian
              and Chinese Naval Expansion

| | Number of Submarines, Destroyers, and Frigates Commisioned per Year | |
	India	China
1976	1	1
1977	1	1
1978	0	2
1979	0	2
1980	2	3
1981	1	2
1982	0	3
1983	2	3
1984	0	3
1985	1	3
1986	4	5
1987	2	3
1988	3	3
1989	2	2
1990	1	3
1991	1	5
1992	1	3
1993	0	4
1994	1	4
1995	0	2
1996	0	4
1997	2	2
1998	2	4
1999	2	3
Average	1.26	3.04

SOURCE: *Jane's Fighting Ships* (Surrey: Jane's Information Group Ltd., various years).

limit India's ability to punish Pakistan and inspired by the prospect of decisively humbling India. The material required by PLAN warships could be carried to Pakistani ports prior to the onset of hostilities and stockpiled for future
use. Once hostilities had begun, material could be trucked south over the Sino-
Pakistan Friendship Highway. This logistic trail would be very long: to Kashgar by train and then by truck to Karachi. Overland movement of men and
material is notoriously difficult to interdict completely. Flows may be inter-

rupted or delayed and a portion of forwarded men and materials lost to enemy interdiction, but determined and resourceful commanders can usually find means for moving required materials overland to forward areas. Once stockpiles were accumulated in Karachi, they could sustain a fairly intense level of PLAN operations.

On the other hand, the terrain traversed by the Sino-Pakistan Friendship Highway in Hunza and Gilgit would definitely favor India's efforts at interdiction. After leaving the immediate border region, that highway enters the valley of first the Hunze and then (below Gilgit) the upper Indus River. The mighty Indus River especially has over the millennia carved long, deep, and steep canyons through range after range of rugged mountains. The rock in many areas has also been fractured by the upward thrust that produced the Karakoram Mountains. Even under normal conditions, and especially during the rainy and snow-melt seasons, avalanches and rock slides are common. Traveling over this road in mid-1990, I counted fifty-seven places where the road was blocked by such geological events. Keeping the road open even in normal peacetime requires sustained repair work. Such terrain would be extremely vulnerable to air bombardment. Near-hits by bombs or missiles could easily trigger rock slides, carrying away or burying long stretches of road. Once the side of a sheer mountain has been removed, there may not be many ways of moving trucks past that point.

MYANMAR AS A POSSIBLE BASE FOR PLAN OPERATIONS IN THE IOR

Myanmar would provide far better forward logistical support for PLAN operations in the Indian Ocean. From Kunming, where Chinese railheads presently end, it is a fairly easy 700-kilometer drive to the Sino-Myanmar border and another 900-kilometer drive to Kyaukpyu on the Bay of Bengal. In 1998 plans were announced to extend rail lines to Dali, shortening the driving distance to the border to only 300 kilometers. As noted in the last chapter, plans have also been discussed to link Yunnan's rail system with that of Myanmar. Rail shipment would greatly facilitate concentration of PLAN supplies at forward ports. Most important of all, the terrain traversed by the Burma Road is far less susceptible to air interdiction than is the Sino-Pakistani Friendship Highway. Valleys traversed by the Burma Road are much wider than in Hunza and Gilgit. The Burma Road typically traverses rather than parallels rivers. And the mountains it crosses are far lower and less rugged. Yunnan Province also has a far more developed industrial base than does Xinjiang Province bordering Pakistan. The value of Yunnan's industrial output in 1997 was roughly double Xinjiang's. This means that a larger proportion of naval stores could be locally produced in Yunnan than in Xinjiang. If the PLAN acquired access to forward logistical bases along Burma's coast, Chinese warships could sustain a far more intense and effective pace of operations in the Indian Ocean. It is against this geopolitical background that India's security planners view Chinese involvement in the development and modernization of Burmese port and naval facilities.

The availability of air support would be another pivotal factor in an IN-PLAN contest in the IOR. The Indian Ocean is vast, and the location of enemy ships would be extremely difficult without adequate air search capabilities. And, once enemy targets were spotted, air attack would also be the surest and swiftest means of destroying them. The availability of air forces to help defend ships against air attack would also be extremely important. Here again, the IN currently possesses immense advantages over the PLAN in the IOR.[23] Indian air bases on the Andaman, Nicobar, and Laccadive Islands, and on the Indian subcontinental peninsula itself, give the IN air capabilities in the IOR which are vastly superior to those of the PLAN. So, too, do Indian aircraft carriers. In 1999 the IN operated one carrier, the *Viraat*, with a normal complement of eighteen Sea Harriers and seven Sea King ASW helicopters. In December 1998 India also signed a memorandum of understanding with Russia to purchase 44,500-ton air-capable heavy cruisers. At the turn of the century India is also moving (very slowly) toward funding an already planned light aircraft carrier to serve as an "air defense ship."[24] Taken together, these factors give the IN a very substantial advantage over the PLAN in the IOR. If and when the PLAN acquires aircraft carriers, it could substantially diminish India's advantage in this area. So, too, would the ability of Chinese naval air forces to operate out of bases along Myanmar's coast.

During the 1990s China undertook modernization of a number of commercial harbors and naval facilities in Myanmar. Yangon and Beijing were typically tight-lipped about these projects, which in turn sparked much speculation and inaccurate reportage. After the chaff is winnowed out, however, substantial grain remains.[25] Several of the joint projects were purely commercial. Chinese entities undertook to modernize wharf and cargo handling facilities at Sittwe, Kyaukpyu, Bassein, Mergui, and Yangon. These projects will facilitate China's trade with and through Myanmar, plus, of course, Myanmar's trade with the world. The SLORC regime that came to power in 1988 rejected the economic isolationist, autarkic policies of its predecessor, General Ne Win. Expanding foreign trade made the modernization of Myanmar's antiquated harbors imperative. Old Burmese naval facilities existed in several of the harbors undergoing Chinese-assisted modernization. In several cases the newly modernized facilities could be of dual use. China also undertook to assist in the construction of a new harbor and naval base on Hainggyi Island, south of Bassein at the Mouth of the Pathein River. In early 1999 extensive activity was under way at Hainggyi, including construction of a large casern for Burmese armed forces. Heavy silting in the vicinity of the new harbor, however, raises questions about whether it will be usable by large, oceangoing vessels. It may be used primarily for coastal patrol forces engaged in anti-smuggling, anti-poaching, and internal security activities.[26]

China also helped set up a radar monitoring facility on Cocos Island, just north of India's Andaman archipelago. Currently four to five PLA technicians at a time rotate through the facility, whose purpose is apparently to monitor Myanmar's Exclusive Economic Zone, which suffers heavy encroachment from illegal fishing vessels as well as narcotics and arms smugglers. On Ramree Island, too, China helped establish and operate a similar anti-smuggling, anti-poaching radar station. The most militarily significant facility has been established at Zadetkyi Kyun Island, just off Myanmar's southernmost territory on the Kra isthmus. There China has established an earth satellite station, which Indian officials believe is used to maintain communications with PLAN submarines in the Bay of Bengal. This is apparently the PLA's second land satellite station in southern waters. A similar station was set up in the late 1990s on Tarawa atoll of Kiribati in the South Pacific.[27] Map 10.1 illustrates Chinese involvement in Myanmar's maritime development during the 1990s.

China also became the major supplier of naval vessels to Myanmar in the 1990s. In 1991 and 1993 Myanmar acquired ten coastal patrol craft from China. In 1995, 1996, and 1997 it acquired a total of six fast-attack craft, missile boats from China. There were also repeated rumors in the late 1990s regarding Myanmar's purchase of two Chinese frigates. Earlier Burmese acquisition of foreign naval vessels had all been from countries other than Burma's two big neighbors, China and India.[28] With Chinese equipment came training, and during the 1990s China became the major foreign provider of military training to Myanmar. A military cooperation agreement in late 1996 provided that the PLA would train senior Burmese officers at PLA staff colleges.[29] As we saw in the last chapter, Sino-Burmese military exchanges expanded greatly during the 1990s.

The fundamental question, of course, is what we make of the new Sino-Myanmar military-political relationship. We must approach this at two levels: (1) how Indian analysts see it; and (2) how an independent, nonpartisan analyst sees it.

In terms of Indian views, it is clear that Indian security analysts are deeply concerned with the rapid burgeoning of the Sino-Myanmar military relation. The careful study by Roy-Choudhury in 1995 concluded that India's concern

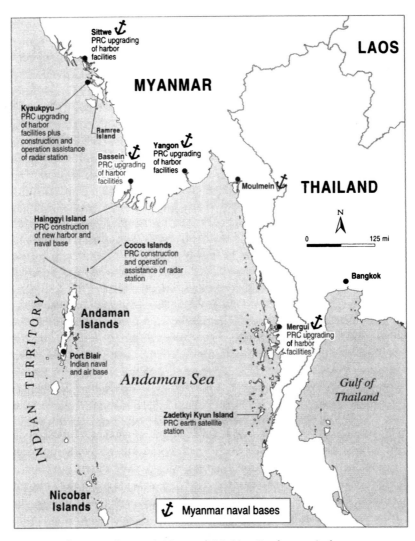

MAP 10.1 Chinese Involvement in Myanmar's Maritime Development in the 1990s

about Chinese acquisition of naval facilities in the Indian Ocean littoral "appears to be well founded" in the case of Myanmar. China's robust activities there at a minimum permit the PLAN to familiarize itself to a far greater extent with conditions in the Indian Ocean. More seriously, because of the growing dependency of the Yangon government on Beijing, Myanmar "may just be willing to grant certain facilities to Chinese warships in order to improve this relation." A "Strategic Defense Review" issued by the IN in 1998 reached similar conclusions. China's activities in the Indian Ocean region, combined with growing PLAN strength, figured prominently in the security environment depicted in the review.[30] The report noted that China was exerting itself "vigorously" to develop political and military links with a number of the IOR countries, including Bangladesh, Myanmar, Pakistan, Sri Lanka, and the Seychelles. Simultaneously, according to the report, China was steadily expanding its navy, and this rapid expansion would cause "great concern" for India in the twenty-first century, with the PLAN becoming the "most powerful [navy] in the region capable of projecting power well beyond its shores." To combat this threat, the report called for India to start building one submarine a year as part of an annual production of six to seven major warships weighing between three thousand and ten thousand tons, development of a submarine-launched land-attack cruise missile, and acquisition of a second aircraft carrier. The report was undoubtedly inspired by considerations of bureaucratic and budgetary politics, yet it simultaneously represented the view of the IN. Such a view may well garner increasing approval in years to come.

In my own view, the China-Myanmar military link constitutes an important part of a pattern of gradually expanding Chinese military activity in the Indian Ocean region. Taken together, this pattern suggests that China's leaders see that region as an area of substantial Chinese interests and that they aspire to *eventual* establishment of a permanent and effective military presence in the Indian Ocean. One of the missions of the PLAN is to protect China's commerce, and China's leaders understand that the vulnerability of China's sea lanes across the Indian Ocean can only be alleviated by securing a forward logistical presence in that region. Without such a presence, the PLAN will not be able to operate effectively there.

But China's military leaders do not have all their desires automatically granted, and there are many reasons why Yangon would not agree to Chinese requests for basing rights. China's leaders also think in very long terms. When the time comes for China to ask for expanded Sino-Myanmar naval cooperation, it will be able to use the goodwill with these countries generated by years of friendly exchanges at least to open official doors to make its pitch.

More broadly, a deeper strategic partnership with Myanmar, founded on mutual trust and common interests, could one day help provide those facilities when they are required. China's efforts to develop a blue-water naval capability are long-term programs that will not come to fruition for a decade or more. When all is said and done, China is not prepared to accept the Indian Ocean as India's ocean.

INDIA AND SINO-BANGLADESHI RELATIONS

China's relations with Bangladesh and with Sri Lanka are especially sensitive in the context of the evolving Sino-Indian naval balance. When Bangladesh was first established, Indian leaders hoped for a close, cooperative relation with it because of India's role in creating that country. This hope was institutionalized in a Treaty of Friendship, Cooperation, and Peace, signed in March 1972. That treaty provided that both countries would not "enter into or participate in any military alliance directed against the other party" and would "not allow the use of its territory for committing any act that may . . . constitute a threat to the security of the other." In the event of an armed attack on either party, each country would "refrain from giving any assistance" to the attacking party and would "immediately enter into mutual consultations in order to take appropriate effective measures to eliminate the threat."[31] The India-Bangladesh partnership did not last long. It began to unravel after the assassination of Sheik Mujibur Rahman in August 1975. *Renmin ribao* then described Mujibur Rahman's replacement by General Zia-Ur Rahman as a "setback" for Soviet hegemonism.[32] China quickly established diplomatic relations with the new Dhaka government.

Zia-Ur Rahman began maneuvering Bangladesh toward greater independence from India and closer friendship with Muslim countries, including Pakistan, and with China. China quickly replaced the Soviet Union as Bangladesh's major weapons supplier. In 1977 China shipped small arms and ammunition plus several squadrons of MiG-21 fighters to Bangladesh.[33] High-level military exchanges began in 1979, when the PLA deputy chief of staff Zhang Caiqian visited Bangladesh. A Bangladeshi military delegation reciprocated later the same year. Then in 1981 two PLA teams visited Bangladesh to discuss arms sales.[34] The Sino-Bangladeshi military relation burgeoned, as is illustrated by table 10.5.

Sino-Bangladeshi naval cooperation began in the early 1980s with the transfer of Chinese warships. Before then Bangladesh's complement of armed vessels (frigates, fast-attack craft, and patrol craft) came exclusively from Britain, India, and Yugoslavia. In 1980 the Bangladeshi navy began acquiring Chinese fast-attack craft. By 1995 it had acquired altogether twenty-six PRC-made fast-attack craft, a Romeo-class submarine, six PRC coastal patrol craft, and four large patrol craft, for a total of thirty-six Chinese-made ships. During the same period Bangladesh acquired a total of three armed vessels from countries other than China (from Singapore in 1984 and South Korea in 1995). Bangladesh's largest, most modern warship is also Chinese, a 1,425-ton frigate built in Shanghai and commissioned into the Bangladeshi navy in November 1989. Bangladesh's other three frigates came from Britain, transferred to Bangladesh in 1976, 1978, and 1982.[35] Chinese T-59 tanks were also supplied in the early 1980s. China built an arsenal near Dhaka to produce ammunition for Bangladesh's China-supplied weapons.[36] Training and advice accompanied Chinese weapons and equipment. In 1987 the Bangladeshi army was substantially reorganized along the lines of the PLA in terms of training and equipment.[37]

Indian leaders tried without much success to arrest the slow evolution of the Chinese-Bangladeshi military relation. Indira Gandhi raised Indian concerns with Bangladeshi president Hussain Muhammad Ershad several months after he took over via a coup in March 1982. During a visit by Ershad to New Delhi, Gandhi conveyed India's concerns about "the introduction of outside arms in our region" and "the growing presence of outside powers" and the "militarization" of the Indian Ocean.[38] In the joint communiqué issuing from his visit, Ershad "reaffirmed" Bangladesh's "consistent commitment to the policy of non-alignment." The development of the Chinese-Bangladeshi military relation did not, however, suffer any apparent adverse effect. Arms transfers and high-level military exchanges continued as before.

Indian concerns with the deepening Sino-Bangladeshi military link were eased by the Awami League's June 1996 return to power for the first time since 1975 under the leadership of Mujibur Rahman's daughter, Sheikh Hasina Wajid. The restored Awami League government placed high priority on improving relations with India. New Delhi responded enthusiastically to this new Bangladeshi orientation, and bilateral relations progressed rapidly. The new government in Dhaka also moved to revise the historiography of the events of 1971, casting India, once again, in a favorable light as a "liberator." Most significantly, the June 1996 election boded well for the consolidation of democratic electoral institutions in Bangladesh, a reassuring development for India. Sheikh Hasina Wajid was careful to maintain good ties with China and to demonstrate that she would not take Bangladesh too far into alignment with India.[39] Accordingly, the Awami League government allowed the 1972 treaty to lapse in 1997, condemning that treaty as "unequal" and an instrument of Indian domination.

TABLE 10.5　Sino-Bangladeshi Military Exchanges

Year	Exchange
1976	None
1977	None
1978	None
1979	PLA deputy chief of staff leads delegation to Bangladesh
	Bangladesh military delegation to China
1980	None
1981	Bangladesh military delegation to China
1982	PLA delegation to Bangladesh
1983	Bangladesh navy chief to China
	PLA navy delegation to Bangladesh
1984	Bangladesh air force chief to China
	PLA air force head visits Bangladesh
1985	Bangladesh army delegation visits China
	PLA navy warships call at Chittagong
1986	Bangladesh intelligence chief visits China
1987	PLA chief of staff visits Bangladesh
	Bangladesh navy chief of staff visits China
	Bangladesh army chief of staff leads delegation to China
1988	Bangladesh army chief of staff visits China
1989	Bangladesh chief of staff visits China
	Bangladesh air force chief of staff visits China
	PLA navy commander visits Bangladesh
1990	PRC minister of defense, deputy chief of staff, and commanders of Beijing and Lanzhou Military Regions visit Bangladesh
	PLA air force chief of staff visits Bangladesh
	Commandant of Bangladesh Defense Services Command and Staff College visits China
1991	Bangladesh army chief of staff visits China
	Bangladesh navy chief of staff visits China
	PLA deputy chief of general staff visits Bangladesh
1992	Bangladesh commanding officer of capital area visits China
	Bangladesh air force chief of staff visits China
1993	PLA air force chief of staff visits Bangladesh
	Bangladesh chief of staff visits China
1994	PLA Chengdu Military Region commander visits Bangladesh

1995	PLA chief of General Logistics Department visits Bangladesh
	Bangladesh chief of staff visits China
1996	Bangladesh secretary of defense visits China
	PLA deputy chief of general staff leads delegation to Bangladesh
	Bangladesh Air Force chief of staff visits China
	Banghadesh army chief of staff visits China
	Bangladesh naval chief of staff visits China
1997	Bangladesh secretary of defense visits China
	Lanzhou Military Region commander leads delegation to Bangladesh
1998	PLA deputy director of General Political Department
	to Bangladesh

SOURCE: NewsBank indexes for *Foreign Broadcast Information Service, Daily Report, China* (New Canaan, Conn.: NewsBank, various years). After July 1996, online search of *FBIS, DRC.*

China worked to insure that the Sino-Bangladeshi military relation was not adversely affected by the Awami League's return to power. Vice chairman of the PRC Central Military Commission, Chi Haotian, visited Dhaka in September 1996 to convey China's desire for continued military cooperation. China attached great importance to ties with Bangladesh, Chi said, seeing them as playing an "active role in maintaining regional peace and stability." To visiting Bangladeshi army chief of staff Mahbubur Rahman two months later, Chi stated that both China and Bangladesh "strongly oppose hegemonism and power politics." During a visit to Bangladesh in November 1997 Lanzhou Military Region commander General Liu Jingsong said that China was gratified that the two countries "always support and sympathize with each other and share identical or similar views on many international and regional issues."[40] Stated plainly, the Sino-Bangladeshi military relation was useful to both because it created a balance of power favorable to constraining India.

In the estimate of veteran Indian diplomat J. N. Dixit, India's approach toward Bangladesh is inspired by "profound political realism." India understands, even if it does not like the fact, that Bangladesh's fear of Indian domination leads it to find diplomatic and other ways of distancing itself from India. Bangladesh's "close relationship with China has been . . . of particular importance to Bangladesh in the subcontinental and the Asian regional context. Linkages with China and Pakistan are of strategic and security interest from Bangladesh's perspective." Yet Bangladesh's governments also understand that they need a normal, nonconfrontational relation with India.

New Delhi understands that to react too negatively to Dhaka's anti-Indian moves would only make matters worse: "It is imperative for India to have a positive attitude and friendly relationships with Bangladesh because an apprehensive and hostile Bangladesh can reach out to other powers for military and security equations which could pose a threat to Indian security."[41]

CEYLON AND INDIA-CHINA RELATIONS

Sri Lanka's geopolitical significance is obvious. As a large island lying a significant distance from the subcontinent, it is defensible by a naval power against a superior infantry force ensconced on the subcontinent. It lies just north of the main sea lanes running between the Strait of Malacca and the Suez Canal, providing an excellent position from which to either defend or disrupt those sea lanes. In relation to India, Sri Lanka provides a platform from which either to mount economic, political, or military operations against the subcontinent or to shield the subcontinent's coasts against hostile operations. The island also has two very good harbors: Colombo and Trincomalee. The latter served as the main British base between Aden and Singapore. Before the British established their thalassocracy over the Indian Ocean, Dutch, Portuguese, Chinese, and Arab maritime empires utilized the island.

India's overriding geopolitical objective vis-à-vis Sri Lanka has consistently been to exclude a hostile third-power presence from the island.[42] Sri Lanka was itself apprehensive of both India and China, having been invaded by both over the centuries. The Chinese invasion of 1409, mentioned earlier, has not been entirely forgotten. Invasions from the powerful kingdoms that occasionally arose in South India were more frequent. The memories of those Indian invasions have commingled with deep ethnic divisions on the island. Seventy-four percent of Sri Lanka's population are Sinhalese-speaking, mostly Buddhists, of Tibeto-Burmese racial stock. Eighteen percent speak Tamil and are mostly Hindus of Dravidian racial stock. In ancient times the Tamils came with invaders from South India and fought against the indigenous Sinhalese. These ancient grievances have not been forgotten. Tension between the two groups has been a constant element of Sri Lanka's politics. The Sinhalese have often suspected that Indian sympathy for Tamil demands extends to providing various forms of support. These suspicions deepened and became more firmly based in reality in the 1960s, when a Tamil separatist movement emerged in South India in the form of the Dravida Munnerta Kazahagam (DMK).

Fear of India was a major factor leading Sri Lanka's first post-independence government to conclude a defense agreement with Britain, under which

Britain maintained its naval base at Trincomalee and an air base at Katunayake. Sri Lanka's government during this period was wary of Nehru's neutralism and generally followed a more pro-Western approach to world politics. Growing Sinhalese nationalism in the mid-1950s led to a more anti-Western and pro-Indian orientation, reflected in the election of Solomon Bandaranaike in 1956. Bandaranaike and his widow, Sirimavo, who succeeded him after his assassination in September 1959, followed India's line in world affairs. Ceylon became a major participant in the India-inspired nonaligned movement. It worked closely with India on such issues as the Hungarian and Suez crises of 1956, the Tibetan uprising of 1959, and the Congo crisis of 1960. One of Bandaranaike's most important gestures toward India was to demand, in 1957, British withdrawal from the bases at Trincomalee and Katunayake. New Delhi greatly appreciated the British withdrawal.

One of the elements of India's mid-1950s political line embraced by the Bandaranaikes was friendship with China. Diplomatic relations with China were established in September 1956, Beijing having responded enthusiastically to Ceylon's overtures of friendship. Trade in Ceylonese rubber for Chinese rice had begun in the early 1950s and continued with increased political coloration. Beijing subsidized Sino-Ceylonese friendship by buying Ceylon's rubber at above–world prices and selling Chinese rice at below–world prices. When China's rice supply proved inadequate to meet its obligations to Ceylon, Beijing purchased Burmese rice for export to Ceylon. China also began an aid program and translated large quantities of Chinese propaganda into Sinhalese. The staff of the Chinese embassy in Colombo grew quite large, with its members paying frequent visits to villages and rubber plantations. In 1961 Beijing returned the Lord Buddha's tooth that had been taken to China in 1409.

With the deterioration of Sino-Indian relations in 1962, Chinese courtship of Sri Lanka intensified and assumed a very different significance for India. Shortly before the 1962 war Beijing made a gift of over two hundred railway wagons to Ceylon. Existing aid agreements were continued on even more generous terms, while new agreements were signed in November 1963 and February 1964. China agreed to redress trade imbalances in Ceylon's favor, and interest was waived on (already low-interest) loans.[43] Following China's 1962 victory, China's prestige was high. As Sino-Ceylonese cordiality and Chinese generosity grew, rumors began to circulate that China was seeking basing rights in Ceylon. Chinese interest in African revolutionary movements was growing in 1963–64, and reports maintained that "bases" in Ceylon would provide a staging port for Chinese shipments to African revolutionary states and movements. One basis for these reports was a November 1962 maritime agreement between China and Ceylon. Under the agreement Chinese ships were empowered to call at Ceylon's ports. Sirimavo Bandaranaike's government decried as completely false and without foundation reports of China's seeking "basing rights." PLAN warships never ventured far from China's coasts in the 1960s, and it is indeed unlikely China's leaders would have wanted to send warships as far forward as Sri Lanka. Midway replenishment of Chinese merchant ships bound for Africa with arms for revolutionary governments (or other cargoes for that matter) is more plausible, though this would seem to have required nothing more than the November 1962 shipping agreement allowing Chinese ships to use Ceylon's ports. There would have been no need, and it would not have made sense, for China to tell Ceylonese leaders that some ships stopping at Ceylon's ports were carrying arms to East Africa.

From another perspective the substantive accuracy of the 1963–64 reports of China's search for naval bunkering rights is secondary. The Indian government was already sufficiently dismayed by the intimate Sino-Ceylonese relations, even without these reports. Within Ceylon the reports were widely credited and, indeed, became the central issue in the March 1965 election that ousted the Bandaranaike government. The opposition charged during that election that the Bandaranaike government was pushing the country too deeply into alignment with China. The Chinese embassy, which had become the largest foreign mission in Ceylon by the time of the 1965 election, mobilized its resources to try to swing the election to Bandaranaike. The effort failed, however, and the government lost the election. New Delhi was much relieved. With a new government in power in Colombo, New Delhi, also under a new government, with Lal Bahadur Shastri succeeding Nehru after his death in May 1964, worked to improve Indo-Ceylonese relations.

The next time India's "Trincomalee raw nerve" was rubbed was in 1971, when a rebellion led by a Trotskyist-Castroite-Maoist group, the Janata Vimukti Peramura (JVP), attempted to seize power in Sri Lanka. Chinese–Sri Lankan relations had collapsed during China's Cultural Revolution, and Beijing's foreign policy was still in its ultra-revolutionary stage of declaring support for the overthrow of most governments around the world. As we saw in earlier chapters, in 1969–71 Beijing stepped up its support for insurgencies in northeastern India and northern Burma. In this context the presence of a Chinese ship in Colombo and carrying arms for Tanzania during the JVP rebellion lent credence to suspicions about Chinese complicity in the revolt.[44] These rumors proved groundless. The only foreign involvement in the revolt was North Korean.[45]

India quickly dispatched military assistance and forces to Sri Lanka, at the request of that country's besieged government.[46] India sent five helicopters and crews, plus an infantry detachment of 150 soldiers to guard an airfield and the Indian embassy. China initially adopted a position of studied silence regarding the JVP revolt. Once it became clear that the revolt would fail and that China risked alienating Sri Lanka, Zhou Enlai sent a letter, in early May, to President Bandaranaike condemning the rebellion. (Mrs. Bandaranaike had returned to power in 1970 and remained in office until 1977.) Beijing followed Zhou's pledge with an offer of a long-term, interest-free loan of 150 million rupees in convertible foreign exchange.[47]

The geopolitical factor in Sri Lanka's situation reemerged in the 1980s. The election victory of Junius Richard Jayewardene in July 1977 had initiated another reorientation of Sri Lanka's domestic and foreign policies. The anti-Western, pro-socialist orientation of the Bandaranaike era gradually gave way to a more pro-Western orientation, albeit still within the framework of non-alignment. In India Morarji Desai was less concerned than Indira Gandhi had been with the adverse implications for India of these new directions in Sri Lankan policy. When Mrs. Gandhi returned to power in January 1980, she was unhappy with numerous aspects of Jayewardene's orientation. She especially resented Sri Lanka's establishment of a military relation with the United States—embodied, for instance, in a visit by U.S. warships to Colombo in 1981 and Washington's extension of $350,000 military assistance in January 1984.[48] Equally objectionable were Jayewardene's policies of friendship with China and Pakistan. Under Sirimavo Bandaranaike's rule, from 1970 to 1977, relations with China had been one component of Sri Lanka's generally "progressive," pro-socialist orientation. There was a certain distance in Sino–Sri Lankan relations during that era, however, due to lingering suspicions regarding China's role in the April 1971 uprising. Close personal friendship between Gandhi and Bandaranaike also mitigated Indo–Sri Lankan differences during the 1970–77 period. The two charismatic female leaders maintained friendly links even after their respective falls from power. Personal relations between Gandhi and Jayewardene were, by contrast, poor, and they deteriorated further after the latter deprived Bandaranaike of civil rights. At the level of high diplomacy the context of Sino–Sri Lankan friendship changed during the 1970s, as China's view of U.S. power in Asia underwent a dramatic transformation. The gradual convergence of U.S. and Chinese global interests, together with the deepening of the Islamabad-Beijing-Washington axis (or so Indira Gandhi saw it) after 1979, placed U.S. and Chinese relations with Sri Lanka in a more sinister light.

Chinese vice premier (and former ambassador to Pakistan) Geng Biao visited Sri Lanka in June 1978 after officiating over the opening of the Sino-Pakistan Friendship Highway. The symbolism was not lost on New Delhi.

Sri Lankan foreign minister A. C. S. Hameel visited China in July 1979, and Prime Minister Ranasinghe Premadasa followed the next month. Premadasa became prime minister only in June 1978, and this was his first foreign trip in that capacity, again a significant symbol.[49] This flurry of diplomatic exchanges was a significant departure from the past. During Mrs. Bandaranaike's 1970–77 rule there had been only one high-level Sino–Sri Lankan exchange—a visit by her to China in June 1972.[50] Sri Lanka under Jayewardene also expanded its military relation with China. In 1980 China gave Sri Lanka two Shanghai-class gunboats.[51] Other arms transfers followed, including small arms and ten Y-12 transport aircraft in 1986. To some extent this increased activity was a result of China's opening to the outside world. Regardless of the cause, this thickening of Sino–Sri Lankan ties caused concern in New Delhi. Jayewardene's Sri Lanka also improved relations with Pakistan.

As troubling to India as the initiation of a Sino–Sri Lankan military relationship, was the parallelism of Sino–Sri Lankan approaches to critical regional problems such as Cambodia and Afghanistan. (Vietnam invaded Cambodia in December 1978, and the USSR invaded Afghanistan in December 1979.) During a nonaligned movement (NAM) coordinating bureau meeting on Cambodia in Colombo in June 1979, for instance, Sri Lanka as the host of the conference played an important role in excluding the foreign minister of the Hanoi-installed Heng Samrim regime. India had not yet recognized the Heng Samrim government, but neither was it enthusiastic about the Sino-U.S. campaign against it. Jayewardene also downgraded the concept of the Indian Ocean Zone of Peace, in line with his more pro-U.S. orientation. Chinese foreign minister Huang Hua visited Sri Lanka in July 1981 after his landmark visit to India. The prime purpose of the visit to Sri Lanka, according to Huang, was to exchange views about Afghanistan and Cambodia. Confronted with the challenge of Soviet and Vietnamese hegemonism, Huang urged the countries of South Asia to unite with China and other like-minded countries to protect the sovereignty and independence of various nations.[52] Colombo did not fully embrace Beijing's antihegemony doctrine, but it did actively support China's positions on Afghanistan, Cambodia, and the Indian Ocean, frequently opposing India's positions in the process. At the NAM summit in New Delhi in March 1983, for example, Jayewardene was responsible for keeping mention of Diego Garcia out of the final declaration.[53]

Indira Gandhi saw Beijing's antihegemony doctrine as a foil for the expansion of China's own influence around India's periphery—as a Chinese attempt to encircle and pressure India. She also feared that Sri Lanka was drifting toward the Beijing-Islamabad axis, perhaps with U.S. encouragement and support. In this situation Gandhi decided to act to force Sri Lanka to abandon its anti-Indian orientation. The instrument she chose was the Sri Lankan Tamil groups seeking to establish a separate Tamil state in that country. Sri Lanka's civil troubles are, of course, rooted deeply in the divisions between the Sinhalese and the Tamils of that island. But it is also clear that Indira Gandhi's government decided to exploit those divisions to enhance India's position in Sri Lanka. By early 1984 dozens of Tamil insurgent camps were operating along the coast of Tamil Nadu, opposite Sri Lanka, with the tacit cooperation of India's central authorities as well as the active support of the Tamil Nadu government.

It is important not to exaggerate China's role in the Indian–Sri Lankan imbroglio of the 1980s. Indian support for Tamil insurgents in Sri Lanka began under the auspices of the state government of Tamil Nadu largely because it was popular with the Tamil voters of that state. The central government under Indira Gandhi took over control of that program in 1983 out of concern for a combination of domestic and international factors. Regarding the international aspect, Gandhi was concerned with Sri Lanka's growing relations with countries she deemed hostile to India. China was one of these countries, but only one and not the most important. New Delhi was at least as concerned with Sri Lanka's links to the United States and Pakistan. Concern with possible U.S. military presence on the island probably topped the list of Indian concerns. Gandhi was deeply fearful of Sri Lanka's increasing pro-Western alignment and feared that country was becoming a "satellite" of the United States.[54]

While providing sanctuary in Tamil Nadu to Sri Lankan rebels, Indira Gandhi also established India as a mediator between the rebels and Colombo. In response to a press report in August 1983 that Colombo had solicited pledges of assistance from the United States, Britain, Pakistan, and Bangladesh in the event of Indian intervention, New Delhi informed those countries that, while India had no intention of intervening in the internal conflicts of any South Asian country, it would not tolerate such intervention by any other country in any situation that had implicit or explicit anti-Indian implications.[55] Following this episode, Jayewardene agreed to Indian mediation of Colombo's conflict with the Tamil separatists. As the civil strife in Sri Lanka escalated over the next four years, New Delhi continued to use the dual instruments (in an off-and-on fashion) of support for the Tamil insurgents and mediation between these groups and the Sri Lankan government to achieve its objectives.

As Sri Lanka grappled with its Indian-supported insurgency, China's support for Colombo was initially fairly firm. When Jayewardene visited China in May 1984, President Li Xiannian made statements supporting Colombo's struggle: "The Chinese government and people very much admire Sri Lanka for the active role it is playing in international affairs and firmly support its just struggle to safeguard its independence, sovereignty, and territorial integrity."[56] Li also stressed the Five Principles of Peaceful Coexistence, asserting that China and Sri Lanka were good friends and neighbors because they abided by these principles. But, he warned, if those principles were violated, "even countries [with] similar social systems may come to confrontation." This was an oblique criticism of India.

The most dramatic Chinese support for Colombo came in November 1985, when a PLAN squadron called at Colombo for a friendship visit. This was the PLAN's second call to a foreign port. It is likely that the connection between this fleet visit and deteriorating Indian–Sri Lankan relations was spurious. Nonetheless, the visit took place in a situation of increasing tensions in the Palk Strait. The Indian coast guard and navy were doing little to intercept the movement of men and arms by sea between Tamil Nadu and Sri Lanka, and the Sri Lankan navy was doing what it could to stanch that flow. There were also incidents involving the Indian and Sri Lankan navies. The previous January, for example, Indian coast guard vessels had seized a Sri Lankan navy patrol boat for interfering in the activities of Indian fishing vessels in the Palk Strait.[57] In such a situation, whatever Beijing's motives, the visit of the PLA squadron heartened the embattled Sri Lankan government.

Chinese President Li Xiannian visited Sri Lanka in March 1986 as part of a five-nation tour. (Bangladesh, Egypt, Somalia, and Madagascar were the other countries.) During the visit Li made public declarations of support similar to those he made in 1984, such as: "The Chinese people treasure the friendship of the Sri Lankan people. It is the unshakable policy of China to continually consolidate and develop Sino–Sri Lankan friendship and cooperation. China will continue, as in the past, to resolutely support Sri Lanka's efforts to uphold national independence, sovereignty, and territorial integrity, and to strengthen national unity."[58]

In private Li had a different message. He conveyed to Jayewardene China's preference for a political solution to the island's problems and told him that China would supply no more arms to the Sri Lankan government.[59] In about 1986, according to Sri Lankan diplomats, China indicated to Sri Lanka that it should handle its internal affairs with the help of India. The Sri Lankan government interpreted this as an indication that the PRC did not want to antagonize India by intervening. Thereafter, Colombo noted that China pulled back from events in Sri Lanka. Another indication of China's reduced involvement was the suspension of high-level military interactions between China and Sri Lanka. This is illustrated by table 10.6.

It is perhaps not surprising that China decided to disengage militarily from

TABLE 10.6   Sino–Sri Lankan Military Exchanges

Year	Exchange
1975	Sri Lankan army commander to PRC
1976	Sri Lankan navy commander to PRC
1977	PLA friendship delegation to Sri Lanka
1978	None
1979	None
1980	None
1981	Sri Lankan army commander to PRC
1982	Sri Lankan air force commander to PRC
1983	Sri Lankan navy commander to PRC
1984	PLA air force commander to Sri Lanka
1985	Sri Lankan armed forces commander to PRC
	PLA naval squadron to Sri Lanka
1986–95	None

SOURCE: Foreign Broadcast Information Services (FBIS), Daily Report, China (DRC) indexes published by NewsBank (New Canaan, Conn.: NewsBank, various years).

the Sri Lankan conflict at this juncture. By this point it was clear that the United States had accepted India's leadership role in the Sri Lankan situation. Acting by itself, there was not much China could do. Its naval power could hardly begin to compare with India's in this region of the world. Not only was continued military involvement likely to fail; it would probably be counterproductive, antagonizing India and inciting it to an even more interventionist approach. Beijing may also have had in mind events in East Pakistan in 1970–71, when Islamabad's quest for a military solution to its ethnic problems laid the groundwork for India's intervention in December 1971.

Developments reached the stage of open, direct conflict between the Indian and Sri Lankan governments in the spring of 1987. Following the collapse of Indian-mediated talks, Jayewardene rejected Indian advice and warnings and opted, in May 1987, for a military solution. New Delhi reacted strongly to this move, and for a period of about three months there was a sharp and increasingly militarized confrontation between New Delhi and Colombo. India began concentrating military forces in Tamil Nadu, raising the possibility of a 1971-style invasion. Then it dispatched a flotilla of twenty unarmed civilian boats to carry relief supplies to the besieged Tamil areas on the Jaffna Peninsula. The boats were repulsed on June 3 by the Sri Lankan navy. India then dispatched military cargo planes escorted by Mirage jet fighters to air-drop supplies to the rebels. Colombo was outraged by what it termed a naked violation of its independence and a rehearsal for invasion, lodged a formal protest with the United Nations Security Council, and appealed to its foreign friends for help. Such help was not forthcoming, and Jayewardene capitulated, signing an agreement with Gandhi on July 29, 1987. Following his signature of the agreement, Jayewardene summed up China's role as follows: "They are good friends and gave us military equipment, guns, etc. at reasonable terms. But what could they do? I could not ask them to start a border war in the north to keep the Indians busy. Even if I had, I doubt they would have done it."[60]

China's response as the confrontation intensified during the May–July 1987 was low key. *Renmin ribao*'s coverage of events was factual, but between the lines one could detect sympathy for Colombo. On June 3, for example, the newspaper reported that the Sri Lankan government had ordered its armed forces to prepare to repulse Indian ships and that it had taken this action "after India ignored strong Sri Lankan protests and declared its intentions of continuing interfering in Sri Lanka's internal politics." The next day the paper reported that the Sri Lankan navy had repulsed Indian boats "within Sri Lankan territorial waters."[61] When Zhao Ziyang was in Pakistan in June, just as the Indo–Sri Lankan confrontation was reaching its peak, he made no reference to Sri Lanka. Nor was the Indo–Sri Lankan confrontation listed among the international and regional issues discussed by Zhao and Pakistan's leaders. During his banquet speech on June 22, however, Zhao said that, as a close neighbor and friend of the South Asian countries, China sincerely hoped that those countries would "treat each other as equals, live in amity and act according to the spirit of mutual understanding and accommodation, [and] resolve their differences through consultations on an equal footing."[62] These words implicitly criticized India. It was, however, extremely oblique criticism.

China's acquiescence to Indian coercion of Sri Lanka did not signify its approval. Privately, China's leaders were angry about Indian actions. A 1988 internal study of the Sri Lankan–Indian agreement of July 1987 by the Chinese Academy of Social Sciences, for example, was extremely critical of India's actions. New Delhi's aim in intervening in Sri Lanka's internal affairs and forcing Colombo to sign the July 1987 agreement was to "control" Sri Lanka and realize its dream of achieving "regional hegemony" in South Asia. According to the study: "India has continually dreamed of establishing its regional hegemony. It carved up Pakistan and created Bangladesh. It annexed Sikkim. It has purchased aircraft carriers. It has done everything to accomplish this objective."[63]

Another authoritative Chinese analysis of the Indian intervention in Sri Lanka concluded that India sought, inter alia, to "expel the influence of other countries, strengthen control over Sri Lanka, increase influence over neighboring countries in order to strengthen India's position as a regional big power." India had "aggressed against the territory and sovereignty of a neighboring country," the article said. It quoted Jayewardene to the effect that "Sri Lanka cannot but accept India's position of regional leadership for no other country is able to match the great pressure of India." The result was that, "internationally, India's actions create unease and fear among the small countries of South Asia. They fear that if India can intervene in Sri Lanka, it can also intervene in other neighboring countries."[64] Virtually all Chinese specialists with whom, three years later, I discussed the 1987 Indo–Sri Lankan imbroglio expressed similar sentiments, though not in as strident or polemical a fashion as in the passages quoted here. These views were not, to repeat, expressed openly or in unclassified materials.

The letters exchanged between Rajiv Gandhi and Jayewardene at the time of the Indo–Sri Lankan settlement of July 29, 1987, were a major advance for Indian's dominance over Sri Lanka. In the letters Sri Lanka agreed to respect Indian security concerns. Specifically, these letters provided that neither party would allow its territory to be used for activities threatening the security of the other. The two sides would reach an understanding regarding foreign military and intelligence personnel in Sri Lanka and guarantee that such personnel would not injure Indo–Sri Lankan relations. Sri Lanka guaranteed that it would not make Trincomalee available to any foreign navy for purposes that would injure India's interests; the refurbishing of the Trincomalee tank farm would be conducted jointly by Sri Lanka and India. And an agreement would be reached regarding foreign broadcasting operations in Sri Lanka, under which Sri Lanka would guarantee that the broadcasts would not be used for any military or intelligence purposes.[65] Indian diplomats and strategists viewed the exchange of the Indo–Sri Lankan letters as a major gain for India. One Indian analyst compared the imposition of a "partial Monroe doctrine" on Sri Lanka as the second decisive turning point in India's march to hegemony in South Asia. The first was the dismemberment of Pakistan in 1971.[66] India's gain was China's loss—at least in terms of its ability to develop relations with Sri Lanka as the governments of China and Sri Lanka deemed appropriate.

THE INDIAN OCEAN AS AN ARENA OF INDIA-CHINA RIVALRY

Sri Lanka or Bangladesh would serve the PLAN far less well than Myanmar as a base for operations in the IOR. Both Sri Lanka and Bangladesh would be vulnerable to an Indian economic blockade similar to that employed by New Delhi against Nepal in 1989–90. Both are too distant from China and separated from it either by Indian territory or large tracts of sea, and both are too close to Indian centers of power. Myanmar is equidistant from China and India, with overland transportation with China being somewhat easier than with India. Such calculations entirely set aside the likes and dislikes of Myanmar's government. A chief objective of Indian diplomacy is to see to it that Yangon does not, ever, allow such a development.

China's security dilemma in the Indian Ocean is that a large and ever-increasing volume of Chinese trade, especially Middle Eastern oil, transits that ocean, where the Indian Navy enjoys an overwhelmingly superior position because of its geographic advantages. The key instability-producing factors in Indo-Chinese relations lie elsewhere: in the Sino-Pakistan entente cordiale, in the Himalayan Mountains, and in the status of Tibet. But Chinese security planners must consider the possibility that, in the event of a Sino-Indian war arising out of conflicts in one of these other areas, India might decide to escalate the war horizontally, into the naval dimension. Perhaps in response to the defeat of Indian land forces in the Himalayan region, Indian leaders would opt to utilize their power in the area where it had a substantial superiority and where it could inflict crippling damage on China—by severing Chinese commerce in the Indian Ocean.[67] A Sino-Indian maritime confrontation could also arise out of a fourth Indian-Pakistani war. Chinese material support for Pakistan could move most cheaply, swiftly, and effectively via sea. The IN would probably blockade Pakistan ports—as it did in both the 1965 and 1971 wars. But, if Iran opted to support Pakistan, Chinese ships might enter port at Iran's Bandar Beheshti, with unloaded supplies being shipped eastward overland to Pakistan. Indian efforts to stem this flow would thus entail interference in trade between two neutral countries. There would be multiple possibilities for escalation to a Sino-Indian naval clash.

China's crucial weakness in dealing with this threat is geographical; without bases in the IOR the PLAN could not sustain intense and effective operations there to protect Chinese commerce. Yet, if China openly seeks to remedy this weakness, by seeking out bunkering options in Burma or Pakistan, for instance, it will rouse Indian suspicions, thereby making even more likely the very unpleasant situation Beijing seeks to avoid.

India's security dilemma in the Indian Ocean is that establishing and maintaining the naval supremacy it feels it needs to be secure necessitates excluding any extra-regional military presence—in the case at hand, Chinese military presence. Yet Indian actions denying or limiting China's military presence in the Indian Ocean convinces China of India's anti-China hegemony and leads to Chinese resentment of Indian actions—although that resentment might not be manifest in Chinese foreign policy at the time. That reservoir of Chinese resentment makes it even more necessary for India to maintain a strong position of superiority in the Indian Ocean to protect against possible Chinese hostility. Beijing insists that, for the sake of Sino-Indian friendship, New Delhi not seek to block the growth of China's military links in the Indian Ocean region. Yet, to the extent that India does not act to block China's gradually expanding military position in the Indian Ocean region, it allows China to wear away the geographical advantages India has heretofore enjoyed. If the PLAN were able to sufficiently overcome its geographic handicaps, it might introduce into and effectively sustain a large portion of its superior naval power in the Indian Ocean. PLAN forces might then undertake classic naval diplomacy, dispatching squadrons to the vicinity of such confrontations as that between India and Sri Lanka in 1987.

Preventing this possibility requires sustained Indian vigilance regarding PLAN activities in the IOR. Chinese tactics of incrementalism, obfuscation, and denial will only go so far. At some point, at some level of Chinese presence, India will intervene, and has, to close the IOR door to the PLAN. If India failed to do this, the naval balance in the IOR could be radically altered in favor of the PLAN. Of course, by keeping PLAN bunkering operations out of the Indian Ocean, India also keeps Chinese commerce vulnerable. What exists in the Indian Ocean is a classic security dilemma in naval guise. Each side acts to defend itself but, in doing so, threatens the other.

Several factors may lead to increased Indian-Chinese rivalry in the IOR in the future. One factor may be China's fulfillment of other objectives currently at or near the top of China's foreign policy agenda. Coercing Taiwan into a "reunification" arrangement acceptable to Beijing and establishing China's control over the major islets in the South China Sea (currently in Taiwanese and Vietnamese hands) are objectives involving the utilization of Chinese naval power which are currently higher on Beijing's agenda than strengthening China's position in the IOR. To a substantial degree China's drive to develop a modern, powerful naval force is targeted at Taiwan and the South China Sea. Once Beijing secures its objectives in those two areas, the PLAN will by then probably be a very potent modern force, including aircraft carriers, stealthy submarines, and substantial amphibious capabilities. Achieving reunification with Taiwan and PLA occupation of Taiping and Spratly Islands in the South China Sea would free up powerful naval assets for use elsewhere. It would also secure the movement of Chinese vessels southward to the eastern entrance of the Malacca Strait.

The recession of Soviet and American naval power from the Indian Ocean would be another factor exacerbating Indian-Chinese rivalry in that region. The Russian naval presence in the IOR had evaporated by the mid-1990s. The

American naval presence declined after the Gulf War of 1991 but stabilized thereafter. Should the United States draw down or eliminate its presence in the Indian Ocean region, it would throw onto China's navy the full responsibility for securing China's sea lanes across the Indian Ocean. Given generally cordial Sino-American relations and the "strategic partnership" proclaimed in 1997, and given America's traditional commitment to the freedom of the seas, a viable American presence in the Indian Ocean is reassuring to Beijing. Without it Chinese leaders may well conclude that they must be more prepared to defend China's interests in the region themselves.

A final factor that may generate increased Sino-Indian tension in the IOR is the very growth of the naval capabilities of the two sides. With more powerful and long-legged naval forces, the leaders who have paid the bills to acquire those forces will probably want to use them to show the flag. China has many friends around the Indian Ocean littoral who may welcome visits by Chinese ships. Indian security planners will no doubt watch such visits with dismay.

11 / Nuclear Weapons and
the Sino-Indian Relationship

Since 1962 nuclear weapons have played a significant role in Sino-Indian relations. Sino-Indian nuclear interactions have been different from nuclear interactions along the three legs of the better-understood Sino-Soviet-American "strategic triangle" in which each actor perceived clear and direct nuclear threats, from time to time, from the other two actors. In Soviet-American-Chinese nuclear interactions the perceived threat from each was direct and concrete, if not always imminent. Each saw the other two as posing a threat of nuclear attack under certain circumstances and worried about how to deter such a resort to nuclear weapons. The Sino-Indian nuclear relation has been more subtle and complex, less symmetrical, and less direct. But it has not been less substantial.

There have been three central characteristics of the Indian-Chinese nuclear relationship: asymmetry, indirection, and status enhancement. By *asymmetry* I mean that Indian and Chinese threat perceptions have *not* been mirror images. Chinese and Indian perceptions of the origin and nature of nuclear threats, and of the role of the other in those threats, have been very different. China perceived the nuclear threat as coming from the United States and the USSR and simply did not believe that India posed a potential nuclear threat. There is no evidence that such a threat perception ever entered the consciousness of Chinese leaders and considerable evidence that Chinese leaders gave India little thought when they considered how China might use its own nuclear weapons or when they thought about possible threats of nuclear attack on China. Indian leaders, on the other hand, have perceived a clear nuclear threat from China since 1964, when China exploded its first atomic bomb, and have continually debated about how to deal with that threat.

There are two aspects of "indirectness" in the Sino-Indian nuclear dyad. First, the nuclear threat from China perceived by India came not primarily from fear of a direct Chinese nuclear attack on India. Ever since 1964 there have been a few Indian analysts and leaders who believed that the threat from China was substantial and immediate enough as to require that India acquire nuclear weapons. But this has been a distinctly minority view and was not manifest in government policy until 1998. The mainstream Indian point of view worried not so much about another Chinese attack on India but about China's links with India's neighbors, *especially Pakistan,* which might require India to act to defend its national security, with China supporting, say, Pakistan. In the event of another Indian-Pakistan conflict or of Indian measures to prevent the establishment of a Sino-Nepali military relationship or the establishment of a Chinese naval presence in Myanmar ports on the Bay of Bengal, an India without nuclear weapons might come into confrontation with a nuclear-armed China. China's nuclear threats might be subtle enough so that Beijing would not have to bother denying their existence. Nonetheless, from the Indian perspective they could be quite real. India could then either run the risks of such a situation and pursue its chosen path of action against Pakistan without deterrent protection against China's threat, or it could back down before Chinese nuclear might. When Indian analysts concluded by the 1980s that China was assisting Pakistan's nuclear weapons program, the Pakistani nuclear threat became linked, cognitively, to the Chinese threat. It was almost as though China were transferring a portion of its nuclear arsenal to Pakistan, allowing that country to threaten India. Thus, the China threat grew with the progress of Pakistan's nuclear program.

The second aspect of indirectness is that China's strategy for dealing with the perceived threat of Indian "hegemony" over South Asia was not to challenge Indian actions directly but to support the antihegemony resistance of South Asian countries, again first and foremost Pakistan. Crudely stated, China has sought to thwart Indian hegemony over South Asia by strengthening Pakistan. An implicit nuclear component to this dual indirect relationship appeared in 1965, when China threatened to intervene in the Indo-Pakistan war on Pakistan's side, a year after testing its first atomic bomb. The nuclear component of the China-Pakistan-India relation grew steadily over the next thirty-three years.

A third characteristic of the Indian-Chinese nuclear dyad has been the role of nuclear weapons in enhancing international status. The ROI and the PRC have been rivals for status among the Asian and the developing countries since the establishment of those regimes. The status derived in the post-1945 world from possession of nuclear weapons became linked to Sino-Indian rivalry for status among these international constituencies. But in this area, too, the Chinese-Indian nuclear dyad was extremely complex and asymmetrical. China's leaders ardently and early on embraced the pursuit of international status via nuclear weapons. Their nuclear thinking concerned mainly the American and Soviet superpowers, but they also had a very clear awareness of how enhanced Chinese leverage with the two superpowers, and the status deriving from possession of nuclear weapons, related to China's rivalry with India. India, on the other hand, attempted to found its leadership of the Asian and developing countries on a moral revolt against the established international regime in which military power, including nuclear weapons capability, determined international status. Once again, India's target in doing this was not the other power in the dyad of concern to us here, China, but primarily the Western alliance and especially the United States. But India's effort to lead a revolt against the nuclear terror–based international order also had China very much in mind and greatly exacerbated India's conflict with China. Between 1962 and 1974 India incrementally modified its moral rejection of the military power–based international status quo but more or less continued this line throughout the Cold War. When it became apparent in the aftermath of the Cold War that China had been right all along and that its steady development of a nuclear arsenal was rewarded by inclusion in the top tier of world powers, India moved belatedly to rectify its mistake.

In terms of nuclear weapons and enhancing international status, we again find a curious asymmetry in the Indo-Chinese nuclear dyad. For China strengthening its international status was an important but clearly secondary objective in acquiring nuclear weapons; countering clear and present threats of nuclear attack was primary. India, on the other hand, seems to have been concerned primarily with enhancing its international status and only secondarily with countering possible Chinese nuclear coercion.

CHINA IN INDIA'S PROCESS OF NUCLEARIZATION

China developed nuclear forces largely (though not entirely) to deal with American and Soviet threats. (The caveat has to do with China's awareness of the role of nuclear weapons in determining international status in the post-1945 world, a problem dealt with in chap. 12.) China experienced repeated explicit and implicit American threats of use of nuclear weapons against it, starting with its entry into the Korean War in late 1950 and continuing through the Taiwan Strait crisis of 1958. Possible American resort to nuclear attack was also very much on Chinese minds in 1965–66 as the nation moved to support North Vietnam in its war against the United States. By 1967 Chinese leaders were worried about possible Soviet intervention in China and the unforeseeable consequences that might ensue therefrom. Then, following the clashes on the Ussuri River in early 1969, Soviet leaders seriously considered using nuclear weapons against China and signaled their deliberations to both China and the United States. Such Soviet threats and deliberations continued for several years.[1]

In the 1980s, as China improved relations with both superpowers and began to leave behind fears of a possible superpower invasion or nuclear attack, its thinking about the possible use of nuclear weapons nonetheless still focused on deterring the two superpowers. By 1985 China envisioned conventional, high-intensity wars of short duration for limited means—"partial wars," they were called—with several of its neighbors. Those potentially hostile neighbors were nonnuclear (Vietnam, India, and Taiwan topped the list), but they were aligned with one or the other nuclear superpower. In the event that China's leaders decided that the nation's vital interests mandated resort to military means against one of China's recalcitrant neighbors, that neighbor's superpower supporter might rely on its nuclear weapons to attempt to alter China's chosen course of action. China's own nuclear weapons would then counter and nullify this superpower threat. China would thus not be prevented by U.S. or Soviet nuclear weapons from pursuing a course of military action its leaders deemed essential to upholding China's vital interests.[2]

Indian thinking about the need for and possible acquisition of nuclear weapons focused on China. From 1962 through 1998 there was periodic debate within India about the threat posed by China and about whether India needed nuclear weapons to deal with this threat. Nehru outlined what became India's traditional approach to nuclear weapons even before Indian independence. Speaking to the Constituent Assembly as prime minister of India's interim government in January 1947, he condemned nuclear weapons as contrary to the "human spirit" and called for a struggle against such inhumane arms. Nehru believed that arms buildups and the formation of alliances led to war and that introducing nuclear weapons into those alliances and buildups further increased tensions, making war virtually certain. Moreover, when war came, it would be nuclear war, and this, Nehru explained, would be the greatest disaster: "For war today means total destruction of humanity, without victory or profit to any nation or bloc of nations."[3] Based on these premises, by the early 1950s Indian policy was directed toward the eventual abolition of all nuclear weapons as part of a program of general disarmament.[4] This philosophy of complete and universal disarmament as the route to peace had strong roots in Mahatma Gandhi's pacifism and appealed greatly to India's early sense of national identity.

The 1962 war with China fundamentally altered the Indian discourse over nuclear weapons. In a very real sense this war began the process that culminated in the Indian nuclear tests of 1998. The 1962 war was a searing experience for India, undermining the country's sense of national identity and competency as a nation. Nehru's foreign policy had built on and reflected a Gandhian identity stressing nonviolence and prevention of war via moral sentiment and public opinion. China's decision in 1962 to employ overwhelming military force against India, and India's complete unpreparedness for what followed, led India to deep soul-searching and a reappraisal of its approach to the world, especially to China. India's leaders rejected their earlier anti-military ethos and began paying far more attention to strengthening India's military capabilities.

The 1962 war also shaped an enduring Indian perception that China could not be trusted because it had "betrayed" Indian friendship. Nehru had befriended China, but China responded with war. China was not a nation interested in living as a friendly and peaceful neighbor with India but was ready to resort to superior military force whenever it found that advantageous. This profound shift in the Indian perception of China was one of the most important results of the 1962 war. The emergence of India as a nuclear weapons power stems from this change in perception.

China's testing of an atomic bomb on October 16, 1964, precipitated a national debate in India over the acquisition of nuclear weapons. U.S. Secretary of State Dean Rusk had given the world a warning (on September 29) about China's upcoming test, and Nehru tried to rally the nonaligned movement to thwart it. At a nonaligned conference in Cairo on October 7 Nehru proposed the conference send a delegation to Beijing to persuade China to desist from making nuclear weapons. India also sent a memorandum to the UN secretary-general on October 10 calling for effective action to prevent the proliferation of nuclear weapons. The recently concluded Partial Test Ban Treaty had been a good first step, the Indian statement said, but the "next logical step" was a nonproliferation treaty prohibiting the manufacture, acquisition, receipt, or transfer of these weapons.[5] Implicit in India's memorandum was concern about China's imminent nuclearization, along with the possibility that China might share its nuclear weapons technology with Pakistan. Beijing replied on October 9 with a blistering attack on Nehru's "slanders and distortions" about China at the Cairo conference. Beijing's statement spoke exclusively of the boundary issue and India's refusal to negotiate a settlement of that dispute, completely ignoring Nehru's protest of China's

imminent development of nuclear weapons. By doing this, Beijing's statement implicitly denied any link between the Sino-Indian boundary conflict
and China's development of nuclear weapons.[6]

China's test sparked a tremendous wave of indignation in India. There
was strong sentiment in the media and across virtually the entire political spectrum, and among the public, for India to match China's nuclear capability
as quickly as possible. Media commentary pointed to China's 1962 attack and
warned that China could now repeat that performance using nuclear weapons.
The events of 1962 had proved that India could not count on gestures of friendship to deter China from territorial claims. They also testified to India's
deplorable military unpreparedness. India had to build an independent
nuclear capability of its own, Indian journalists asserted. The Congress Party
split over the issue. Although a desire for a public united front led to unan-
imous votes in favor of what became the official policy eschewing nuclear
weapons, there was strong sentiment within Congress in favor of the bomb.
At the first Congress Conference after the Chinese test, speaker after speaker
demanded an Indian bomb. One member of parliament insisted the issue
not be left to the cabinet or to the top leaders of Congress but be submitted
to a plebiscite. "Go to the people and get the verdict," he insisted. "You will
find that they want the bomb." In parliament, members of Congress openly
criticized government policy. At a meeting of the Congress Working Committee in January 1965 there was strong push to reconsider the earlier government decision not to make a Indian bomb.

Aside from the Communist Party most of India's parties favored a strong
Indian response to China's nuclear test. The Central Working Committee of
the Jan Sangh demanded a crash nuclear program and production of an Indian
bomb as quickly as possible. "No price is too high where the country's defense
is involved," the Jan Sangh committee stated. The Samyuktha Socialist Party
also favored an Indian bomb. The largest opposition party, the Swatantra Party,
stopped short of calling for immediate nuclearization, asking instead that India
abandon its policy of nonalignment—only a slightly less radical solution. The
leader of the Swatantra Party, C. Rajagopalachari, called for India to abandon nonalignment and enter into firm defensive alliances with the "Western
nuclear powers." That party's parliamentary leader called on the government
to reach an agreement with the United States and the USSR about their
response to a Chinese nuclear threat to a nonnuclear power. The Chinese, he
said, had demonstrated that they did not care about world opinion.[7]

Prime Minister Lal Bahadur Shastri and Minister of External Affairs
Swaran Singh rallied forces to stand against this highly emotional pro-bomb
groundswell. Shastri and Singh were worried enough by China's nuclear threat

that they approached Britain and the United States about the possibility of some sort of extension of a "nuclear umbrella" to India in the event of Chinese threat or attack. According to Itty Abraham, Shastri used these overtures to London and Washington as a way of countering strong pro-bomb forces in the Indian government. The head of India's Atomic Energy Commission, Homi Bhabha, was lobbying the United States for American assistance to Indian nuclear weaponization, and talk of an Anglo-American guarantee was a way of sidetracking those talks. The British and American embargo of India and Pakistan, imposed in April 1965 as the second Indo-Pakistan war began to unfold, eliminated support among the Indian elite for reliance on Washington for protection.[8] Although discussion of an American nuclear guarantee was suspended, Shastri's government nonetheless decided not to move forward, then, with the manufacture of an Indian bomb.

There were several elements of the official Indian policy which emerged under the leadership of Shastri and Singh in the aftermath of the Chinese test of October 1964. India shifted from Nehru's policy line that India would never make nuclear weapons to a policy of not making them now but keeping open the option of doing so later if international developments made it necessary.[9] The essence of this policy was "don't build the bomb now, but prepare the political and technological ground for doing so if developments unfavorable to India require it." More simply, it meant keeping India's nuclear option open. India would not manufacture a nuclear weapon "at present," Shastri said. When pressed about how long a period "at present" implied, he responded: "It is a very long period. It is not going to be a short one. . . . I cannot say anything as to what might happen in the distant future. So long as we are here, our policy is clear—we do not want the atomic bomb to be manufactured in India."[10]

The key condition determining how long India would continue to renounce development of nuclear weapons was effective action by the international community, first and foremost by the United States and the Soviet Union, to halt and roll back the spread of nuclear weapons. The nuclear superpowers, working together and via their unilateral policy, within and outside of the United Nations, should stop the dissemination of nuclear weapons and related technology. They should also undertake serious, long-term disarmament programs that would move humanity toward an era without nuclear weapons. In the words of M. J. Desai during the 1964–65 bomb debate in India:

> The refusal to have nuclear weapons has been deeply ingrained in Indian politics since before Independence. But the hostility of China, especially since 1962 and the Chinese nuclear tests, makes it possible this refusal may not last for

long. To make sure of perpetuating it, the major powers must eliminate underground weapons tests, progressively reduce their armaments, including nuclear armaments, and eventually eliminate the latter. "The choice is for the nuclear superpowers to make."[11]

While renouncing development of a nuclear weapon at present, the official policy set by the Shastri government accelerated India's research and development into the peaceful uses of atomic energy. It also initiated an Indian space program to research rockets and satellites. It was understood that much of the basic knowledge and human talent was fungible from civilian to military purposes, if and when the government decided. As for dealing with the China threat, Shastri specified that India would continue to enhance its conventional military forces. Chinese nuclear weapons could never intimidate or defeat India, he asserted, and it would be "childish" for China's leaders to imagine otherwise.

China had issued a statement at the time of its first nuclear test, in October 1964, "solemnly declaring" that China "will never at any time or under any circumstances be the first to use nuclear weapons." This statement apparently had a modest impact on India's 1964–65 bomb debate. Those Indians favoring Indian nuclearization spoke as though China's nuclear weapons were directed at India, regardless of Beijing's declaration. Yet, in line with China's declaration, comments by Shastri and others opposed to immediate Indian nuclearization argued that China's nuclear weapons were directed toward the United States and other "white powers," not toward India. Interestingly, even though Shastri and Singh noted and apparently credited China's nonuse pledge, they still insisted on preparing for certain eventualities. The classic problem was unavoidable: Chinese intentions might change very quickly, while Indian capabilities might take much longer to develop. Prudent Indian leaders such as Shastri and Singh accelerated India's nuclear research and development efforts so as to insure that the acquisition of the requisite Indian nuclear capabilities would not take too long, should India's leaders ever decide that Chinese activities made such a move prudent.

Both sides of the 1964–65 bomb debate in India argued from the premise that India was locked in rivalry with China. Advocates of nuclear weapons generally argued that China's bomb, like its 1962 attack on India, was part of an effort by that nation to reduce India's prestige and influence among developing countries. To thwart this effort, India had to build its own bomb. Opponents of an Indian bomb, on the other hand, generally argued that Indian nuclearization would actually reduce India's stature among the developing countries by demonstrating that India had abandoned the nonviolent idealism that it had heretofore represented. The immense costs of nuclear weapons would also hobble India's economic development, which was the most critical factor in India's standing among the developing countries. The two sides of the bomb debate differed regarding the impact of nuclear weapons on India's rivalry with China for international stature. But they shared the premise that China sought to diminish India's stature and that India had to foil this Chinese effort.

INDIA'S 1974 NUCLEAR TEST

China's nuclear development program continued unabated despite Indian protests and concerns. Between 1965 and 1973 China conducted fourteen additional tests. The country's first thermonuclear weapon was tested in 1967. As Indira Gandhi consolidated her power within the Congress Party in the late 1960s, she began to shift India's nuclear policy. From her perspective nuclear capability was one criterion of power in the modern world, and demonstrating this capability would help establish India as an independent center of power in a multipolar world.[12] Thus, in 1969 she accepted a ten-year nuclear energy plan designed to strengthen India's capabilities in nuclear science and energy; it included development of gas centrifuge technology for uranium enrichment and accelerated development of a fast breeder reactor. Another component of the plan was to move toward testing a "peaceful nuclear explosive." This decision to test a nuclear explosive was reinforced and given a new strategic coloration by the 1971 war between India and Pakistan.

As Indira Gandhi led her nation toward war with Pakistan in 1971, she had to consider the possibility that China might enter the conflict or otherwise pressure India in support of Pakistan. For a decade, by 1971, Beijing had supported Pakistan as a way of balancing India. Gandhi was now contemplating a bold strike against Pakistan to dismember that nation, fundamentally altering the balance of power between it and India. Although, as we saw earlier, China informed Pakistan as early as April 1971 that it would not militarily enter an India-Pakistan war over East Pakistan, that policy could still change as circumstances developed. China's military position was weaker in 1971 than it had been in 1965. On the other hand, China had by 1971 a fairly substantial arsenal of nuclear weapons. While the danger of Chinese entry into the 1971 war was never great—and was not perceived to be by Indian leaders—as Gandhi maneuvered her nation toward war, she nonetheless sought further insurance against Chinese entry or nuclear coercion.

Gandhi initially hoped to secure joint Soviet and American support to keep China out of the upcoming war—as had been the case in 1965.[13] It soon became apparent, however, that Washington was more interested in improving relations with Beijing than in confronting it, so Indian diplomacy moved ahead with the Soviet Union alone. Moscow was very receptive. Since the clashes of early 1969 Moscow had become increasingly interested in India as a counterweight to China. The Sino-American rapprochement increased India's need to avoid international isolation in its upcoming war against Pakistan. China now had a great-power friend—one, moreover, that gave increasing signs of being willing to align with China in support of Pakistan and against India. Even if Sino-American cooperation against India did not reach that extent (which would have been hard to imagine in mid-1971), Beijing could have been encouraged to weigh in militarily on Pakistan's side, knowing that it would have American support. Thus, on August 9 the Indian-Soviet Treaty of Friendship, Peace, and Cooperation was signed. Article 9 provided for immediate consultations "in the event of either party's being subjected to an attack or a threat thereof" in order to "remove such threat and to take appropriate effective measures to insure . . . the security of their countries." India now had guarantees against Chinese entry and against possible Chinese "nuclear blackmail."

It is necessary to repeat that our concern here regarding the 1971 war is the degree to which nuclear weapons played a role and the implications thereof on Indian policy. As is well known, President Richard Nixon and his national security advisor, Henry Kissinger, concluded in the middle of the war that Indira Gandhi had decided to eviscerate West Pakistan once Pakistani forces in the east were defeated. They also believed that China was preparing to enter the conflict in support of Pakistan once India struck in the west. Nixon's solution was to pressure Moscow, causing the USSR in turn to pressure India to suspend its putative offensive in the west. Otherwise, a chain of events might touch off a war that could very easily become nuclear. If India attacked West Pakistan, China would attack India, which would obligate the Soviet Union to strike against China on India's behalf, and this could bring the United States into the fray in support of China. To underline this danger and the consequent need for Soviet assistance in securing suspension of the putative planned Indian offensive in the west, Nixon ordered the aircraft carrier U.S.S. *Enterprise* into the Bay of Bengal.

In this high-stakes card game India was the only player without nuclear weapons. This fact that does not seem to have hampered India's achievement of its posited objectives during the 1971 war but did pose some potential dangers.[14] What if the triangular interests of the three nuclear powers toward one another superseded the interests of those powers toward India? What if, for example, Moscow retreated in order to avoid a war with the

United States and China? What recourse would India have? Would it stand vulnerable and without protection before the nuclear weapons of one of the other two nuclear powers? These were primarily political, not military, threats, though they were linked in a very complex way to nuclear diplomacy. India's response was also political as well as nuclear. In May 1974 India exploded an atomic device. New Delhi insisted this was not a "weapon" but, rather, a "peaceful nuclear explosion" intended to advance India's overall nuclear science capabilities. In spite of such disclaimers, the 1974 test was a potent statement by India to the nuclear powers that India would not tolerate disregard of its basic national interests—that is, the nuclear powers could not impose their fiat on India. The fact that India did not proceed to develop a nuclear arsenal following the 1974 test, in spite of a decade-long Chinese nuclear program, demonstrates that enhanced political stature and leverage, not countering a military threat from China, was the primary rationale behind the 1974 test.

Beijing did not protest or even comment on India's 1974 nuclear test until several months had passed. Although it is difficult to demonstrate exactly why the Chinese government did not act sooner, this kind of near-silence became a major and long-term characteristic of China's policy toward India's nuclear program. When hard-pressed by foreign journalists following India's 1974 test, Chinese leaders would resort to bland formulations, such as an observation by Deng Xiaoping that India's nuclear program would have an adverse impact on its economic development or that by another Chinese official that India had the "right" to pursue its own nuclear path.[15] When toward the end of the year China began to comment on the May 1974 test, it explained the event in terms of India's drive for hegemony in South Asia. Why did Chinese leaders choose not to make this point earlier and more prominently?

The first and most important point regarding Beijing's low-key response to the May 1974 test is that it seems to confirm, yet again, that Beijing perceived Indian nuclear weapons as constituting a threat not to China but to India's weaker neighbors. K. N. Ramachandran has suggested two further reasons for China's studied silence. First, to question openly India's intentions in the nuclear sphere might confirm Indian suspicions about China, thereby pushing India more quickly down the nuclear path. Second, Chinese protests and condemnations might help justify India's actions before foreign audiences. China clearly believed that India was vulnerable to Soviet and American pressure, far more vulnerable than China, and pressure from the United States, the USSR, and other countries might block India's advance toward the genuine acquisition of nuclear weapons. Indian nonnuclearization would serve China's interests. Loud Chinese condemnations of India's moves toward nuclearization might diminish foreign nonproliferation pressure on India, thereby working against China's interests. A low-profile Chinese approach would better allow third-country pressure to keep India non-nuclear.

Beijing's low-profile approach to India's nuclear efforts was paralleled by an even lower-profile, covert effort to assist Pakistan's efforts to match India's moves toward nuclearization. Chinese spokesmen have repeatedly and consistently denied that China has assisted Pakistan's nuclear weapons program. In June 1998, to cite an example following the Pakistan tests that May, President Jiang Zemin was asked flatly by a foreign reporter: "Has China helped Pakistan make its nuclear bomb?" to which he replied as flatly, "No, China has not helped Pakistan."[16] Such denials can be traced back to a 1984 statement by Premier Zhao Ziyang. There is substantial evidence from a range of sources, however, suggesting that we must treat such disclaimers as political camouflage for a more subtle policy.

In January 1972 Pakistan, then headed by Zulfikar Ali Bhutto, reportedly made a top-secret decision to acquire nuclear weapons.[17] India was then flush with pride and confidence, while Pakistan was grappling with the catastrophe of partition. India also had access to top-of-the-line Soviet military equipment, while Pakistan had lost its access to U.S. equipment with the 1971 war and could not hope that weapons it might obtain from China would enable it to match India's Soviet-supplied hardware. Under such circumstances nuclear weapons seemed to offer the best, perhaps the only, guarantee of continuing independence from Indian domination. As Pakistan's former air chief marshal, Zulfiqar Ali Khan, declared shortly after Pakistan acquired nuclear weapons capability in 1987: Pakistan had "no reasonable choice for its very survival other than to achieve the so-called balance of terror. It is time to cease being apologetic about it and adopt necessary measures to acquire this necessary deterrent. For us, this appears to be the only feasible insurance and the sooner we obtain the coverage, no matter how high the premium, the better for us."[18] Nuclear weapons were the "great equalizer" through which Pakistan could foil Indian coercion.

Pakistan had begun following India's nuclear activities closely in 1965, when India intensified its nuclear research and development programs. India's large industrial base and pool of scientific talent meant that its nuclear program could and would be largely self-reliant. Pakistan's weaknesses in these areas made it far more dependent on foreign assistance. Thus, shortly after Pakistan's decision to begin a crash, covert nuclear program, Prime

Minister Bhutto visited a number of countries, where he attempted to rally support for that effort. From wealthy Islamic countries he attempted, apparently with some success, to get funding. The last country on Bhutto's early 1972 itinerary was China, which he visited from January 31 through February 2. According to the joint communiqué signed at the conclusion of his visit, Bhutto and Premier Zhou Enlai "had a detailed exchange of views . . . on the Indo-Pakistan conflict and its aftermath, major international issues and the further consolidation of friendly relations and cooperation between China and Pakistan."[19] In his speech welcoming Bhutto, Zhou rejected the idea that India's December 1971 victory marked a triumph for an "imperialist and expansionist policy of aggression." Rather, he argued,

> the fall of Dacca was definitely not a "milestone" on the road toward victory for the Indian aggressors, but the starting point toward their own defeat. By pushing power politics and an expansionist policy, the Indian government has . . . intensified its contradictions with its neighboring countries. . . . We can say with certainty that by its doings the Indian Government is lifting a rock only to drop it on its own feet and will eventually eat the bitter fruit of its own making.[20]

Bhutto probably asked for Chinese help in 1972, but evidence suggests that Chinese assistance to Pakistan's nuclear program began only after India's nuclear test of May 1974. India's demonstration of a nuclear explosion capability, coming seventeen months after Pakistan's dismemberment, underscored the possibility that India could dominate Pakistan. The tenor of India-Pakistan-China relations at the time was illustrated during a visit by Bhutto to Beijing about a week prior to the May 1974 Indian test. In a talk with Mao, Bhutto "reviewed the international situation—in particular . . . the situation prevailing in the subcontinent and in our region." In talks with Mao, Zhou, and Deng Xiaoping (then vice premier, who was being groomed as Zhou's successor) Bhutto stressed Pakistan's readiness to live in peace and equality with India but also the obstacles his country faced in doing so. In his formal banquet speech toward the conclusion of Bhutto's visit, Deng ended with the words: "Our Pakistan friends may rest assured that, come what may, the Chinese Government and people will, as always, firmly support Pakistan in her struggle in defense of national independence, state sovereignty and territorial integrity and against hegemonism and expansionism, and firmly support the people of Kashmir in their struggle for the right to self-determination." Deng's declaration of support for Pakistan caused the Indian representative at the banquet to walk out, an act of protest which in turn prompted Bhutto, in his speech, to reflect on India's more sinister motives. "Distinguished guests," Bhutto said, "are we to conclude that India wants the further dismemberment of Pakistan and that because the Chinese vice premier said that China will support the territorial integrity of Pakistan that he chose to leave the banquet hall? . . . What troubles us," Bhutto continued, "is that while Pakistan and China were promoting good relations, friendship, and an end to conflict among the countries of South Asia, India apparently had other objectives. . . . Does India want conflict and confrontation instead of cooperation and friendly relations? . . . If India wants that, then I can tell you that Pakistan is prepared for it." Pakistan would never, according to Bhutto, accept India as its "big brother."[21]

In early June 1974, shortly after India's nuclear test, Pakistan's foreign minister visited Beijing to secure Chinese support in the face of India's new nuclear might. Subsequently, the Pakistan Foreign Ministry, but not China, released a statement in which China pledged "full and resolute support [to Pakistan] in its just struggle in defense of its national independence and sovereignty and against foreign aggression and interference including that against nuclear threat and nuclear blackmail."[22]

By late 1974, as India's push to annex Sikkim accelerated, China began to comment on India's new nuclear explosion capability, describing it as an instrument of India's drive for hegemony in South Asia. India's May 1974 test, according to Beijing, was an integral part of New Delhi's expansionist drive for hegemony in South Asia. By conducting the May explosion, India was "carrying out nuclear blackmail and nuclear threat to South Asia." Shortly after the test, Chinese commentary now pointed out, India had moved toward annexation of Sikkim and promulgated the idea of a plan for a "South Asian countries bloc." It was pursuing this expansionist policy with Soviet "social imperialist" support and encouragement and in service to Soviet purposes. India's nuclear test "was condemned by public opinion all over the world" except for the Soviet social imperialists, who "alone were beside [themselves] with joy."[23]

If we put China's stated views about India's May 1974 test together with its stated views about the peace-upholding effects of destroying "nuclear monopoly," we may deduce the rationale for China's support for Pakistan's nuclear weapons program: India, with Soviet support, was pushing for hegemony over South Asia. Its 1971 dismemberment of Pakistan, its 1974 nuclear explosion, and its annexation of Sikkim were all steps in that direction. If India succeeded, China's relations with the South Asian countries would be restricted and China's security diminished by Soviet-Indian encirclement. Pakistan was determined to resist Indian expansionism and decided that the acquisition of nuclear weapons was necessary to do this. Pakistan asked for

China's help in this effort. By helping Pakistan develop nuclear weapons, China was satisfying the wishes of a close ally on an extremely important issue while forcing India to live with a fully sovereign and independent Pakistan. Stated differently, China was helping Pakistan thwart Indian expansionist aspirations in South Asia. By helping Pakistan acquire nuclear weapons, China was righting the balance of power in South Asia, which seemed to be developing dangerously to China's disadvantage.

A nuclearized Pakistan might also reduce the danger that China itself would have to choose between going to war with India to uphold Pakistan's independence or watching passively while Pakistan was subordinated by India. In 1965 and in 1971 China had faced such unpleasant choices. Given the greater disparity in Indian and Pakistani power after 1971, a "fourth round" with India using its overwhelming power to subordinate Pakistan decisively may have seemed more likely. In such an eventuality Beijing would face the unpleasant choice of intervening to save Pakistan, thereby assuming the costs of another war with India, or doing nothing while its key South Asian ally was reduced to impotence. Support for Pakistan's nuclear program averted such a choice by diminishing the likelihood that India would opt for a decisive war against Pakistan. Once this policy had been set, about 1974, it would continue by inertia for fifteen years. Not until the early 1990s would it be discarded.

Covert Chinese assistance to Pakistan's nuclear program apparently began after India's May 1974 test. According to a report by the U.S. Defense Intelligence Agency, sometime before October 1974 China assigned twelve scientists to assist Pakistan's nuclear energy program.[24] Such preliminary measures were apparently consolidated in 1976. A top-level Pakistani scientific-military delegation headed by Bhutto visited China between May 26 and 30, 1976. It included Pakistan's Nobel Prize–winning nuclear physicist Dr. Abdus Sala, who was then Bhutto's scientific advisor. Two public agreements resulted from the visit—one on military cooperation, the other on scientific cooperation. Soon after this, in the first week of June, a high-level Chinese scientific team visited Islamabad.[25] According to Indian sources, in June 1976 a secret nuclear technology cooperation agreement was signed between China and Pakistan.[26]

Bhutto himself confirms the existence of a mysterious agreement concluded in June 1976, which he felt was of paramount importance for Pakistan's continued national independence. In his death cell testament Bhutto refers cryptically to "the agreement of mine concluded in June 1976," which, in his words, was his "single most important achievement which I believe will dominate the portrait of my public life" and which "will perhaps be my greatest achievement and contribution to the survival of our people and nation." Bhutto did not specify the content or even the parties of this momentous agreement, but he did say that negotiation of the agreement took "eleven years," thus tracing back to 1965, the year after China tested its first atom bomb. Bhutto's last testament is a rambling document, as befits a manifesto written in a "tiny death cell" by a man facing imminent execution. But the reference to the June 1976 agreement comes in a chapter denouncing India's desire to establish itself as Pakistan's "senior partner" and thus exercise hegemony over it. Bhutto argues in his testament that the vigorous nuclear energy program he pursued was the reason for his overthrow, which he implies was inspired by the United States: "I have been actively associated with the nuclear program of Pakistan from October 1958 to July 1977 [when Bhutto was overthrown by a military coup] . . . When I took charge of Pakistan's Atomic Energy Commission [in the 1950s] it was no more than a signboard of an office. It was only a name. Assiduously and with granite determination, I put my entire vitality behind the task of acquiring nuclear capability for my country."[27]

Bhutto insisted that the nuclear capability he sought for Pakistan was "peaceful," but at the same time he asked: "What difference does my life make now when I can imagine eighty million of my countrymen standing under the nuclear cloud of a defenseless sky?" It is clear that what Bhutto meant by "peaceful" was that the nuclear capability he sought was meant to deter India from launching a war against Pakistan. It is also clear that the mysterious June 1976 agreement played a central role in that process.

While China was providing important assistance to Pakistan's nuclear program, Pakistan's efforts to acquire nuclear technology and know-how focused during the 1970s not on China but on Western Europe and North America. Pakistani agencies running the covert nuclear program set up a series of dummy companies in the West and went shopping for various components in West Germany, the Netherlands, France, Switzerland, Britain, and the United States. These efforts soon came to the attention of U.S. authorities, and U.S. and allied intelligence, police, and legal agencies began cooperating to detect and thwart Pakistan's efforts.[28] Beginning in 1974 the United States started using its influence to persuade and pressure Western countries to withhold nuclear-related technology from both Pakistan and India. Since Pakistan was more dependent on foreign assistance, U.S. nonproliferation vigilance fell mainly on Pakistan. In the words of one United States Senate study, "The United States led an international effort to block export of nuclear-related materials to Pakistan."[29] U.S.-led nonproliferation efforts were not completely effective, but increased vigilance and enforcement created serious difficulties for Pakistan's program.

Chinese assistance helped Pakistan foil U.S.-led Western efforts to deny Pakistan nuclear weapons. Thwarted by U.S. efforts in its quest for a reprocessing capability to extract plutonium from spent reactor fuel, Pakistan turned to uranium enrichment via gaseous diffusion at a facility at Kahuta, east of Islamabad. By the fall of 1979 critical centrifuge equipment at the enrichment plant was ready to be tested. China reportedly supplied uranium hexafluoride for these tests.[30] Chinese personnel also reportedly helped Pakistan master the technical difficulties associated with the production of highly enriched uranium at the Kahuta plant.[31] About 1983, it was reported, China supplied Pakistan with the design of a nuclear weapon—specifically, of the fourth weapon tested by China, in October 1966, a 25-kiloton fission implosion device.[32] U.S. spies reportedly went through the luggage of a Pakistani nuclear scientist, Abdul Qadeer Khan, when he made a trip abroad in the early 1980s and found the plan for this Hiroshima-size bomb. The plan bore Chinese characters and other indications that it had come from China.[33]

In 1984 U.S. officials were still concerned that China was helping Pakistan solve problems related to the centrifuges used in the enrichment process. Chinese scientists were seen at Kahuta working in the uranium enrichment area. Chinese technical personnel were also observed working in the weapons research section of Pakistan's key nuclear research facility, in an area restricted to personnel with special clearances. In the words of a U.S. Joint Chiefs of Staff report, China was providing "considerable assistance" to Pakistan in the area of nuclear weapons as well as "in the development of rockets and satellites." U.S. officials later told *Washington Post* reporters that about 1983 China gave Pakistan enough weapons-grade enriched uranium to fuel two bombs of China's fourth-test type. China also reportedly sold tritium—used to enhance fission explosions and to produce fusion explosions—to Pakistan via a private German company, which served as the intermediary for a number of China's questionable transfers of nuclear materials and technology.[34] By November 1986 Pakistan was reportedly enriching uranium to 93.5 percent and was testing high-explosive triggering devices.[35]

China's Institute of Atomic Energy reportedly designed for Pakistan a research reactor (Paar-2), which used highly enriched uranium as fuel and was completed in 1989.[36] In November of that year China also agreed to build a 300-megawatt nuclear power plant at Chashma. The contract for the project was signed on December 31, 1991. Premier Li Peng assured the world at that time that the project was "totally for peaceful purposes" and that the plant would be under International Atomic Energy Agency (IAEA) safeguards.[37] As part of the Chashma project, China trained eighty-three Pakistani nuclear technicians.[38] Work on the Chashma reactor was scheduled to continue to the end of the century. There was widespread concern among Western officials that the project would provide cover for covert Chinese assistance to Pakistan's weapons programs.[39] Chinese scientists and engineers traveling to Pakistan or Pakistani personnel traveling to China as part of the Chashma project could easily arrange to consult quietly during their stay on weapons-related problems.

Top-level U.S. officials gave credence to these reports of Chinese assistance to Pakistan's nuclear weapons effort. CIA director James Woolsey testified to the Senate in 1993 that "Beijing, prior to joining the Non-Proliferation Treaty in 1992, probably provided some nuclear weapons related assistance to Islamabad." Woolsey declined to discuss in open session the details of China's assistance.[40] Throughout the 1980s the United States sought to persuade China to stop aiding Pakistan's nuclear program. According to later testimony by Deputy Assistant Secretary of State for Non-Proliferation Robert Einhorn, U.S. concerns were then "particularly acute" over "China's assistance to Pakistan's efforts to produce unsafeguarded fissile materials and to Pakistan's program to develop nuclear explosives." There was "very strong evidence," Einhorn said, that prior to 1992 China "had engaged in assistance to a non-nuclear weapons state's unsafeguarded nuclear program."[41]

Beijing resisted American pressure to suspend its assistance to Pakistan's nuclear program. China's civil nuclear power technology was embryonic in the early 1980s, and it desired access to U.S. technology in this area. Washington was willing and welcomed this as an opportunity to begin a "dialogue on non-proliferation issues" with China. The crux of U.S. concerns in this regard was China's assistance to Pakistan's nuclear program. Five rounds of negotiations between July 1983 and April 1984 produced the text of a proposed U.S.-PRC Agreement for Cooperation in Peaceful Uses of Nuclear Energy. Throughout the discussions "the U.S. side made clear to the Chinese . . . that shared non-proliferation principles were an essential ingredient for bringing [the agreement] into force." China joined the IAEA in January 1984 and shortly thereafter pledged to "request the recipient countries [importing Chinese nuclear material and equipment] to accept the safeguards in line with the principles established by the Agency's statute." This promise was inadequate from the U.S. perspective. Washington believed that China should require Pakistan to place *all* of its nuclear facilities under IAEA safeguards as a condition for China's assistance in the nuclear area. Further bilateral discussions followed "to ensure that the United States and China had a full mutual understanding of our respective non-proliferation policies and practices." The agreement was signed during Reagan's mid-1985 visit to China and approved by the

Congress at the end of that year. The Reagan Administration decided not to implement the agreement, however, "because of continuing questions about contacts between Chinese entities and elements associated with the Pakistani nuclear weapons program."[42] Stated in plain language, information collected by U.S. intelligence agencies about China's continuing assistance to Pakistan's nuclear weapons program convinced U.S. leaders that China was still giving covert assistance to Pakistan in spite of whatever understanding might be in place with Washington. Beijing, for its part, was unwilling to accede to U.S. pressure to suspend support for Pakistan's nuclear program in spite of China's need for U.S. civil nuclear technology.

By 1987 Pakistan had assembled a uranium-enrichment facility at Kahuta using plans stolen from the Netherlands and critical components acquired from Switzerland, Britain, the Netherlands, West Germany, and the United States. By this point the Kahuta plant was only partially complete but was producing enough weapons-grade uranium for one to three nuclear explosive devices annually. Pakistan had also completed and tested the various components of a bomb and had conducted tests of the integrated system. In January 1987 the head of Pakistan's nuclear program, Dr. Abdul Qadar Khan, in an apparently calculated interview with an Indian journalist, tacitly admitted Pakistan possessed nuclear weapons. The Indian government saw Dr. Khan's revelation as a warning to Washington that Pakistan's bomb was a fait accompli that would have to be accepted if the United States wanted continued Pakistani cooperation on such issues as Afghanistan. A month after Khan's "nuclear bombshell" the U.S. ambassador to Pakistan, Dean Hinton, delivered the first public warning to Pakistan since 1979 that development of nuclear weapons would lead to a cut-off of U.S. aid to Pakistan.[43]

Under strong American pressure, early in 1989 Pakistan's leaders decided to cap uranium enrichment at 3 percent, a level of richness adequate only for civil purposes. But, as Pakistan-Indian tensions escalated in the spring of 1990 over unrest in Kashmir and Punjab, Pakistan's leaders decided to resume enriching weapons-grade uranium.[44] Pakistan's decision to do so led to the suspension of all U.S. military and economic aid to Pakistan in October 1990.

In 1989 China's policy toward the international nonproliferation regime began to change. In that year China concluded a voluntary safeguards agreement with the IAEA to apply IAEA safeguards inside China. The next year China attended for the first time one of the review conferences of the Non-Proliferation Treaty (NPT) held every five years since the treaty's implementation in 1970. Early in 1992 China signed the NPT. A number of other steps soon followed. China thereby formally joined the nuclear nonproliferation regime.[45]

EXPLAINING THE EARLY-1990 SHIFT IN CHINESE POLICY

Did China defer entry into the nonproliferation regime until Pakistan had acquired, with substantial Chinese assistance, an independent nuclear weapons capability? If one sets aside the question of Chinese intentions—that is, if one does not infer that the pace of development of Pakistan's nuclear weapons effort was significant in China's decision to begin participating in the nonproliferation regime—then the answer must be yes. The chronology of events outlined here indicates that China's policy toward nonproliferation changed shortly after Pakistan effectively acquired a nuclear weapons capability. *After* China helped Pakistan develop nuclear weapons, *then* it joined the established nonproliferation regime. Such an approach, of course, sets aside the whole question of Chinese intentions and deals with China as a unitary national actor. It focuses primarily on capabilities and largely ignores the internal decision-making processes of China. Considering Chinese intentions and the question "Did Chinese leaders join the nonproliferation regime in the early 1990s because Pakistan had by then acquired a nuclear weapons capability?" it is helpful to remember the logical maxim *post hoc ergo propter hoc*—that is, sequence cannot be used to infer causation.

There are two major alternative hypotheses to explain why China delayed entry into the nonproliferation regime until Pakistan had acquired a nuclear weapons capability. One is the commercial hypothesis. According to this view, China's arms sales of all sorts have largely been inspired by the desire of various well-connected firms for profits, plus the desire of China's top leaders for robust foreign currency earnings.[46] From this perspective it is wrong to infer any grand strategic purpose behind China's assistance to Pakistan's various programs in the 1980s, including its nuclear program. What inspired these transfers was profit. It follows that changes in China's nonproliferation policies circa 1990 could not have been inspired by Pakistan's achievement of certain defense capabilities postulated by Chinese leaders in the 1970s and 1980s.

There are several problems with the commercial explanation of China's assistance to Pakistan's nuclear effort. First, as we have seen, the roots of China's assistance to Pakistan's nuclear weapons program trace back to the mid-1970s, to the Maoist, not the Dengist, era. (This is not the case with other nuclear-suspect countries that became importers of Chinese nuclear supplies in the 1980s, such as Brazil, Algeria, Argentina, and India.) When China began supporting Pakistan's nuclear weapons program, there were no autonomous, profit-seeking enterprises in China, and there were no economic incentives to export nuclear technology. Such incentives emerged only with Deng Xiaoping's post-1978 reforms. Moreover, in the mid-1970s control over

China's foreign relations was highly centralized, and prudent Chinese decision makers kicked responsibility to a higher level.

What probably happened with Chinese policy is that the fundamental rationale for the 1974 decision to support clandestinely Pakistan's top-priority, top-secret nuclear weapons program was to keep Pakistan strong and independent of Indian domination, thereby constraining India and enhancing China's own security. Profits or export earnings did not enter into consideration. Indeed, Chinese assistance then must have entailed a burden on China's treasury. As China's economy was marketized and decentralized in the 1980s, however, commercially inspired and politically influential enterprises emerged, and they found that the established policies regarding assistance to Pakistan's nuclear program served their interests very well. Under these policies they profited by participating in Pakistan's programs. There was policy inertia. The old, established policy continued with new justifications and rationale. The original rationale did not disappear, but powerful new interest groups now found it in their interests to demand that the old policy continue.

A second conceptual alternative to the hypothesis that China delayed acceptance of nonproliferation until Pakistan had an essentially self-reliant nuclear weapons capability can be termed the "learning process." According to this hypothesis, China simply did not know much about the nonproliferation regime in the 1970s and early 1980s, and what it did know led it to mistrust the regime as a mechanism of superpower hegemony. It was only gradually, in the mid- and late 1980s, that China became familiar with the norms and mechanisms of the international nonproliferation regime and began reaching new policy conclusions about it.[47] It follows from this paradigm that the temporal correlation between Pakistan's nuclear weapons program and China's embrace of nonproliferation was spurious.

As with the commercial hypothesis, there is much substance in the learning paradigm. During the 1980s the United States and other Western governments frequently raised with PRC officials issues related to nonproliferation. These "dialogues" undoubtedly caused Chinese leaders to rethink long-established doctrines. China began to train a cohort of specialists in the esoterica of nonproliferation; they wrote articles and briefing papers for higher officials and sometimes participated in discussions of policy issues. Yet the learning hypothesis provides only a partial explanation of China's shifting policy toward Pakistan's nuclear weapons program. If we postulate a process of Chinese rethinking in the late 1980s and early 1990s, we must ask how achieving the goal of a nuclearly self-reliant Pakistan influenced that rethinking. By 1990 the aim of helping Pakistan acquire the nuclear "great equalizer," thus insuring Pakistan against Indian domination, had been achieved. Pakistan had the bomb and was able to produce nuclear weapons on its own. The central goal of China's original policy had been achieved, and maintaining the policy would no longer serve its original purpose; it was no longer needed. Against this situation weighed the increasing costs of continuing that policy. As evidence accumulated that China was assisting Pakistan's clandestine nuclear weapons program, the costs of extending that policy increased. The United States, Japan, West European countries, and, by no means least, India raised the matter of Chinese support for Pakistan's nuclear weapons program with greater frequency and force. The repeated Chinese denials were increasingly unbelievable and were generating bad faith. As China began to signal its acceptance of certain elements of the nonproliferation regime in the mid-1980s (e.g., by joining the IAEA in 1984), Western expectations about China's conformity to nonproliferation norms increased, as did, consequently, the negative costs of being caught violating those norms.

Powerful institutional interests probably pushed for greater Chinese compliance with international nonproliferation norms. One of Deng Xiaoping's reforms was to encourage military industry of all sorts to move into production of civilian goods. China had poured tremendous resources into nuclear energy during the Mao years, but all of it had gone toward developing and manufacturing bombs. Virtually none had gone into civilian uses such as producing electricity. In the early 1980s China did not have a single nuclear power plant (it began construction of its first in 1983). Electricity was then a major bottleneck in China's economic development; it was in very short supply, and demand was growing rapidly as marketization took hold. Through its investments in the Mao years China had a strong ability to produce nuclear fuel. If it could use the fuel to produce electricity, it would be extremely helpful—and profitable. The problem was that China did not have the requisite nuclear electrical technology. It had not concerned itself with this technology during the Mao years and now had to acquire it from abroad. To facilitate its smooth transfer, China would have to cooperate with international nuclear nonproliferation norms, at least to some extent.[48]

In 1982 the Ministry of Second Machine Building, in charge of nuclear weapons production, was restructured into a Ministry of Nuclear Industry. Shortly afterward the China National Nuclear Corporation (CNNC) was set up and charged with putting China's large nuclear fuel industry to use in making electricity. The CNNC stood to profit by doing so and understood the need to acquire foreign technology to do it swiftly. In the process of building a liaison with U.S. and other foreign nuclear suppliers and governmental agencies, the CNNC became aware of the established international norms and regulations governing nuclear transfers and of the reality that China would have to comply with these norms, again to some extent, if it desired broad access to the technology of the advanced Western countries. In 1984 China received from the U.S. Department of Energy twelve hundred documents about nuclear safeguard regulations. The CNNC began the process of translating and assimilating the documents and, eventually, injecting proposals derived from them into China's decision-making process.

The CNNC's pro-nonproliferation battle was not easy. There were strong and long-established beliefs among China's elite about the hegemonist nature of superpower-inspired nuclear nonproliferation. Those Maoist-era beliefs were probably especially strong among China's conservative elder leaders, who also happened to be fearful of foreign penetration of China. By the mid-1980s politically powerful enterprises, often linked to the military, had also discovered the profits to be made by supplying hard-to-get nuclear materials to foreign entities. These enterprises, and the military, who took a large share of their earnings, had no interest in changing long-established policies. The CNNC itself may have had an ambivalent approach. While it needed access to foreign nuclear technology, it also stood to profit handsomely by nuclear exports. This may have led it to advocate merely those concessions absolutely essential to securing access to Western nuclear technology while not accepting terms that would substantially restrict China's nuclear exports. Beginning in 1987, China began to require that countries importing Chinese nuclear materials accept IAEA safeguards regarding the use of those imports. This was not a crippling limitation on Chinese assistance to Pakistan, since know-how acquired at one facility could easily be used at another non-safeguarded facility. The U.S. wanted China to insist that nuclear-suspect countries, such as Pakistan, importing Chinese nuclear materials place *all* of their nuclear facilities under IAEA safeguards and inspection. China refused.

According to Weixing Hu, the tectonic shifts associated with the end of the Cold War finally secured China's participation in the international nonproliferation regime. Western reactions to the Beijing massacre of June 1989 left China isolated and feeling vulnerable to international pressure, and escaping that isolation became a major objective. In the area of nonproliferation there had been informal consultations between France and China for many years, but in 1991 France suddenly announced it would accede to the Non-Proliferation Treaty. This meant that China was the only nuclear weapons state outside the NPT. China's top leaders concluded that China should not suffer such isolation and moved to bring the nation within the NPT regime. Meanwhile, academic nonproliferation specialists pointed out that China's national interests were not served by having nuclear weapons states as neighbors. Finally (and this point is mine, not Hu's), the old policies had already achieved their purpose in the key case of Pakistan.

CHINA AND INDIA'S DECLARATION OF NUCLEAR WEAPONS STATE STATUS

In May 1998 India conducted a series of five nuclear tests in quick succession. India was led at the time by a shaky fourteen-party coalition with a very narrow parliamentary majority and headed by the Bharatiya Janata Party (BJP). The BJP had long called for India to exercise its nuclear option and reiterated those calls in the program on which it fought the March 1998 election. There is a danger of overexplaining India's nuclear decision of early 1998. The main reason seems to be relatively straightforward: new leaders with new views who were committed to establishing India as a nuclear weapons state were elected to power and did what they had pledged to do. But those men perceived a clear Chinese threat to India, and to understand their actions we must understand their perceptions.

George Fernandes, the defense minister of the BJP-led government, aired his views on China during a news interview on May 3. Chinese activities and links with Pakistan, Burma, and Tibet had, according to Fernandes, begun to "encircle" India. "China has provided Pakistan with both missile as well as nuclear know-how." "It [China] has its nuclear weapons stockpiled in Tibet right along our borders." Because of these and other similar activities, China was India's "potential threat number one." India should face up to this fact, Fernandes said, and abandon the "careless and casual attitude" that had characterized the Indian approach to national security in recent decades. India should be prepared to make "real economic sacrifices" (presumably in the form of higher taxes for increased defense spending) to counter the Chinese military threat.[49] Fernandes has a reputation of being something of a loose cannon. It seems that in this case, however, what separated him from others in his coalition government, and even from leaders of the Congress Party, was not the substance of what he said but the directness and openness with which he said it.

Prime Minister Atal Bihari Vajpayee reiterated Fernandes's views in a less direct fashion in his May 12, 1998, letter to President Clinton following the first Indian tests. India had faced "for some years past" a "deteriorating security environment, especially the nuclear environment," Vajpayee told Clinton, referring to China without naming it. He continued: "We have an overt nuclear weapon state on our borders, a state which committed armed aggression against India in 1962. Although our relations have improved in the last decade or so, an atmosphere of distrust persists mainly due to the unresolved border problem." Referring cryptically to Pakistan, Vajpayee asserted that India's "overtly nuclear neighbor" (China) had also "helped another neighbor of ours to become a covert nuclear weapons state," which had "attacked India three times in the last fifty years." Moreover, according to Vajpayee, "for the last ten years we have been the victims of unremitting terrorism and militancy sponsored by it" in Punjab and Kashmir.[50] During the Lok Sabha debates that followed India's tests, some members of parliament suggested that Vajpayee's letter to Clinton had been intended to remain confidential.

China responded strongly to India's use of a China threat to justify its nuclear tests. Responding in early May to Fernandes's comments, a Chinese Foreign Ministry spokesman termed the remarks "ridiculous and not worth refuting." Moreover, he said, "[Fernandes's] criticism of China's relations with other countries is also a groundless fabrication. These remarks have seriously destroyed the good atmosphere of improved relations between the two countries. The Chinese side has to express extreme regret and indignation over this."[51]

A Chinese Foreign Ministry statement issued on May 15, two days after India's second round of tests, rejected India's "slander [of] China as constituting a nuclear threat to it," saying it was "completely groundless." Ever since 1964 China had "unilaterally promised unconditionally not to use nuclear weapons against any non-nuclear country or area."[52] A commentary accompanying the Foreign Ministry statement said that "even more depraved than India's going against the international community's efforts to ban testing of nuclear weapons, was India's suddenly blaming its immoral development of nuclear forces on China." India's "propagation of the China threat theory" was "an attempt to turn international criticism from India to China." "China has never threatened any other country," the commentary proclaimed, and India's statement to the contrary "gravely injures the feelings of the Chinese people and injures the development of cordial Sino-Indian relations."[53] Another *Renmin ribao* commentary several days later reiterated that "no one will believe the absurd logic of these lies about the so-called China threat." It cited U.S. leaders to the effect that "domestic factors were the reason for India's test." "U.S. leaders," the commentary declared, "absolutely did not agree that China constitutes a threat to India."[54] China's first-ever White Paper on defense, issued in July 1998, asserted that India's tests had "produced grave consequences on peace and stability in the South Asian region and the rest of the world."[55] As in 1974, there was no suggestion that Indian nuclear weapons constituted a direct threat to China.

Shortly after China's top leaders drew conclusions about India's nuclear tests, mid-level cadre convened study meetings to learn the new line, which they could then convey to foreigners whom they encountered. The central idea was that internal factors within India were the cause of India's tests. The proof was that Sino-Indian relations had in fact improved in the several years prior to India's test. The two sides had reached an agreement in September 1993 to respect the existing line of actual control in disputed territories and in December 1996 had agreed to an elaborate set of confidence-building measures to reduce tensions along the border further. President Jiang Zemin's visit to India in December 1996 had gone well, and Sino-Indian relations had become quite cordial. Since Sino-Indian tensions were low and declining, they did not provide an explanation for India's tests. On the other hand, the needs of the BJP government to rally domestic support were clear.[56]

The stridency with which Beijing condemned India's May 1998 tests was in sharp contrast to China's low-key approach in May 1974. On the other hand, since New Delhi had chosen to justify its nuclear tests by referencing China, Beijing had little choice but to reply. Failure to rebut New Delhi's arguments forcefully might lend credence to those arguments, which in turn might place China in the middle of South Asian nuclearization. China's interest was to stay uninvolved, thereby keeping international focus clearly on the India-Pakistan dyad. In this sense Beijing's policies of 1998 served the same interest as its 1974 policies.

In the aftermath of the 1998 tests Beijing worked to increase international pressure on India. It moved quickly to encourage the strongest possible U.S. reaction to India's moves and lobbied other, less enthusiastic members of the Perm Five (France and Russia) to give their full support to American-proposed sanctions against India. Chinese representatives avoided linkages between South Asia and Taiwan which they had frequently raised in other, earlier contexts.

Under the hot breath of strident Chinese criticism and implicit threats to retaliate for India's talk of the China threat, India retreated. Its parliament sharply criticized the BJP's open justification of India's nuclearization by reference to the China threat. Official Indian spokesmen soon began to speak more diplomatically, yet they still continued to insist on the reality of the Chinese threat to India. During talks between Minister of External Affairs Jaswant Singh and U.S. representative Strobe Talbott in mid-1998, for example, the Indian side made clear that it would insist on a "minimum nuclear deterrent against China." In Singh's own words: "Our problem is China. We are not seeking parity with China. We don't have the resources, and we don't have the will. What we are seeking is a minimum deterrent."[57]

BJP spokesmen in the Lok Sabha also stood by the government's reference to the China threat. Defending government policy in the Lok Sabha on

May 27, 1998, Jag Mohan was fairly specific about the Pakistan threat. Referring to Pakistani president Zia-ul-Haq's purported consideration of an attack on India in 1988, he asked his colleagues, "Do you want something like Pearl Harbor to happen?" Pakistan's leaders were "saying all types of things," Mohan said, and "we want to be prepared." Regarding China, Mohan saw a less immediate threat but was concerned about possibilities. "We do not have any grievance or any intentions against China. We only . . . want to remain prepared. Time, tide, and events change suddenly and we must be prepared for all eventualities. This is the basic issue." With both Pakistan and China, India should negotiate from a position of strength: "We only want that when we sit at the negotiating table they should not get the impression that we are a weak nation and we can be pushed around."[58]

A close reading of opposition commentary during the Lok Sabha debates also indicates that, while highly critical of the rushed and apparently undeliberate process leading up to the May tests and, while highly critical of the open reference to a China threat to justify those tests, the opposition typically did not deny that the threat was real. Natwar Singh, speaking for the Congress Party during the May 27 debate, for example, charged that Fernandes's reckless words had "thrown into the dustbin ten years of hard diplomatic work," had "helped to produce a Pakistan, Washington, China axis," and "create[d] the impression of growing aggressitivity and . . . that we are on the brink of military confrontation with our neighbors." But Singh did not deny, even by insinuation, the proposition that India faced significant security challenges from China. His point, rather, was that India's leaders ought not to talk openly and recklessly about such challenges.

What, then, was the role of the China threat in India's May 1998 decision? Once again, we must answer this question at two levels: in terms of Indian perceptions and in terms of this independent observer's assessment about the accuracy of those perceptions. The evidence leaves little doubt that the leaders of the BJP government do, in fact, perceive a genuine Chinese challenge to Indian security. Are these perceptions accurate? It seems to me that Indian perceptions are fairly well grounded. We can identify several areas that constitute a serious possibility for military conflict between India and China: the status of the Himalayan kingdoms; the Sino-Pakistan entente cordiale; a possible Chinese military presence in Myanmar; and, of course, the unresolved territorial dispute.

Regarding the territorial issue in the Himalayan region, in spite of the success of diplomatic efforts to reduce Indo-Chinese tension over the past decade, the underlying problem remains unsolved. China still claims ninety thousand square kilometers administered by India, and India still claims fifteen thousand square kilometers administered by China. The two sides also fundamentally disagree about the status of Sikkim, Bhutan, Nepal, and Kashmir. Taking these regions together and speaking broadly, Beijing and New Delhi are at odds about the political-military regime regulating the Himalayan massif. Moreover, there has been chronic policy conflict, occasional militarized confrontations (the last of which was in 1986–87), and one major war between China and India over the various components of this regime. A second level of the Chinese threat involves the Sino-Pakistan entente cordiale. Because of the depth of conflicts between India and Pakistan, Indian leaders and defense planners cannot rule out the possibility of another war between India and Pakistan. In such an eventuality the role of China would be a major Indian concern.

China has, of course, said it would not be the first to use nuclear weapons in a war and that it would not use nuclear weapons against a nonnuclear state. Reiterating these statements, however, does not end analysis. One can imagine all sorts of ambiguities that would leave room for Chinese atomic diplomacy against India without violating China's no-first-use pledge. Carefully calculated words or subtle actions designed to signal possible use of nuclear weapons—such as those used by Beijing during its confrontation with the United States over Taiwan in 1996—could make the point clear to New Delhi without breaking Beijing's nonuse pledges.[59] We must also ask what the status of China's pledges would be in the midst of a Indo-Pakistani war in which nuclear weapons had been used. Would Chinese use then be "first use"? Most fundamentally, would China's nonuse pledges continue to stand in the midst of the intense hatreds and confusion inherent in war? Would they stand in the aftermath of Indian defeats of China's conventional forces? What if continuation of China's nonuse policies risked other very important Chinese interests—insuring the flow of Chinese commerce across the Indian Ocean in the context of overwhelming Indian naval superiority there, preventing definitive Indian subordination of Pakistan, or insuring continued Chinese control over Tibet? What means would India have to insure that China's policies did not change under such conditions? Minimum nuclear deterrence is a sensible answer.

PLUMBING CHINA'S POLICY TOWARD SOUTH ASIAN NUCLEARIZATION

A critical starting point for analysis is whether one accepts or sets aside China's denials of assistance to Pakistan's nuclear program. The range of evidence from the diverse sources reviewed here leads me to conclude that we should set aside these denials. We are then left with two identifiable elements of

Chinese policy: (1) a studied low-profile approach to India's nuclear activities; and (2) covert assistance to Pakistan's nuclear program. I believe we can also posit the broad objective of Chinese policy: preventing Indian hegemony over South Asia. The question then becomes: how do these two policies relate to the posited objective?

Bhabani Sen Gupta in the early 1980s wrote that the risk of nuclear weapons for India was that it would get locked into a nuclear rivalry with Pakistan which would chain it to a position of parity with that country and permanent relegation to the status of a merely regional power.[60] As discussed in an earlier chapter, since the Bandung conference of April 1955 China's leaders have had good reason to understand the utility of the deep Pakistan-Indian enmity in hobbling India's efforts at international leadership. Chinese leaders certainly understood that by helping Pakistan acquire nuclear weapons they were encouraging Indian moves in the same direction. Of course, if China did not help Pakistan, India might acquire nuclear weapons while Pakistan remained without them. Were this to happen, Pakistan might, finally, be subordinated by India. Apparently, the risks derived from Indian domination of Pakistan outweighed the risks associated with its acquisition of nuclear weapons. A nuclear-armed Pakistan, matched by a nuclear-armed India, would insure continued Pakistani independence—and Indian-Pakistani hostility.

But why the studied low-profile approach to India's nuclear efforts? And why the insistence on hiding and denying Chinese assistance to Pakistan's nuclear efforts? Both policies seem to be designed to focus international attention and pressure—first and foremost, pressure from the United States and the USSR but also from the international community more broadly—on India and Pakistan and away from China. Perhaps Beijing concluded that either of the two likely outcomes would serve its interests. If international pressure were successful in rolling back Indian and Pakistani nuclearization and in subordinating both countries to denuclearization via the nonproliferation regime, China would remain as the only recognized, legitimate nuclear power in Asia. If international pressure failed to denuclearize Pakistan and India, those two now-nuclear-armed states would be locked in an even more deadly rivalry. The world would live in fear of another Indo-Pakistan war, fought this time with nuclear weapons, while China wielded its prestige as a nuclear power on a higher, calmer, plain.

We can explain China's strategy in terms of exploitation of contradictions. From Beijing's perspective, before the end of the Cold War the two superpowers were China's rivals. Seeking to exercise global hegemony either in collusion or in contention with each other, they violated China's rights in various ways. India was a client of the two hegemonist superpowers and served their hegemonist plots in various ways through its anti-China and expansionist policies. But, as a client of the superpowers, India was vulnerable to superpower pressure. Since 1963 the two superpowers had agreed to uphold global nonproliferation in order to strengthen their hegemony. India would probably not be able to resist joint superpower pressure, or so China's leaders may have concluded. China certainly could and would reject superpower efforts to deny it nuclear weapons. The end result would be that China would become a nuclear power, while India remained nonnuclear.

12 / Nuclear Weapons and the International
Status of China and India

During the 1990s Indian-Chinese rivalry for status was manifested in two ways. First, in India's effort to become a permanent member of the United Nations Security Council and China's cold reaction to that effort. Second, in conflicting Indian and Chinese positions toward the global nuclear nonproliferation regime.

The global nonproliferation regime is an evolving set of rules and norms agreed to by the international community beginning in the late 1940s and continuing through the 1990s. For our purposes the central objective of this regime is limiting the spread of nuclear weapons and nuclear weapons technology. The most significant mileposts of the regime were the Partial Test Ban Treat (PTBT) of 1963 prohibiting above-ground testing of nuclear weapons, the 1968 Non-Proliferation Treaty (NPT) aimed at preventing the spread of nuclear weapons and related technology, and the Comprehensive Test Ban Treaty (CTBT) of 1996 prohibiting all explosive nuclear tests. The policies of China and India toward the global nonproliferation regime reflected their quests for international status, though their approaches differed greatly.

China decided in the mid-1950s that it should acquire nuclear weapons as quickly and as completely as possible, and this determination strongly influenced China's foreign relations. Once the Soviet Union and the United States began working together to create the nonproliferation regime, Beijing condemned their efforts as attempts to stifle China's emergence as a great power. India, in contrast, initially and for a long time sought international recognition by rallying a global movement in favor of an alternative to the current order—which was based on competitive alliances, arms races, and nuclear balances of terror and which emerged after 1945. Indian leaders saw the existing Cold War order as fundamentally irrational and inhumane, and envisioned India's mission as providing a counter to it. India's rejection of the Cold War nuclear order was without doubt genuinely felt and can be traced to the pacifist teachings of Mahatma Gandhi. But, simultaneously, by rallying the world's forces to push for a fundamental change in the existing nuclear order, by prevailing against what Indians perceived as the perverse views of the superpowers, or even by taking a principled stand against the nuclear madness of those superpowers, India's leaders would demonstrate their country's leading role in world affairs. In the words of Itty Abraham:

> No one was more seduced by the flights of Indian [antinuclear] rhetoric than Indians themselves, which is why Indian elites have never quite fully understood why their country is not given the importance it naturally deserves in the world. Hence, to continue to hold a number of important positions in international meetings, not the least of which was the U.N. Conference on Disarmament, was very important both for the self-image of the Indian foreign policy elite as well as for the country that traditionally told itself that it was held in the highest esteem internationally.[1]

India's efforts to move the world in a new direction were not highly successful—though this lack of success did not necessarily make the views underlying those efforts less satisfying to Indians. The failure of their country's efforts to alter the global nuclear order fundamentally did not become unacceptable to Indians until the 1990s. Or, perhaps, it was not until the 1990s that this failure became clear.

It is an unpleasant but important fact that the possession of nuclear weapons has been a significant determinant of status in the international system throughout the second half of the twentieth century. Both the Chinese and Indian cases testify to this fact. China's relatively high status is, as we shall see in this chapter, partially a function of its nuclear arsenal. India's attempt to acquire high status by rejecting nuclear weapons did not work, and the country's explicit embrace of nuclear weapons in 1998 may be regarded as socialization to the dominant norms of the late-twentieth-century international system.

Heightening their international status was an important determinant in the nuclear weapons decisions of China in 1955 and of India in 1998. The leaders of the People's Republic of China embraced early and with clarity the status-enhancing effects of nuclear weapons. In 1955 they decided to launch a nuclear weapons program with the goal of producing atomic bombs as quickly as possible. The status-enhancing effect of nuclear weapons was explained by Marshal Nie Rongzhen when he recorded in his memoir why he had agreed in 1956 to Mao Zedong's request that he assume overall command of China's newly inaugurated nuclear weapons program:

After the founding of the nation [in 1949], while we were still healing the wounds of war, several other big countries [da guo, which could also be translated as "great powers"] had already achieved modernization, entering the so-called "atomic age" and "jet age." Even more important, we had already had the experience of the War to Resist America and Aid Korea [the Korean War] in which backward technology caused us to suffer much bitterness. We also faced a new threat of aggressive war, a war which would be a test of steel and technology. Imperialism dared to bully us because we were backward.

When I was young I saw with my own eyes the poverty and backwardness of old China, and encountered situations of humiliation. This left a deep impression on me. . . . The Chinese people under the leadership of the Chinese Communist Party . . . can certainly . . . catch up with and overtake the advanced industrial countries of the world, establishing the Chinese nation as one of the powerful nations of the world.[2]

Two sentiments can be distinguished in Marshal Nie's words. One is a desire to acquire nuclear weapons to prevent or defeat foreign attack. The second is a drive to acquire nuclear weapons so that China will stand among the ranks of the "powerful nations of the world."

China's rivalry with India for status in Asia and among the developing countries became entangled with nuclear weapons when the Sino-Soviet alliance collapsed. Up to 1959 Soviet support for China's economic and military modernization had generally satisfied Beijing. In spite of differences over de-Stalinization and the general line of the international communist movement, China found Soviet policy broadly satisfactory. In 1959, however, Moscow took two moves that Beijing believed signaled a fundamental shift in Soviet policy away from support for China, toward collaboration with the United States to stifle China's rise. First, Moscow terminated support for China's nuclear weapons program. Second, it supported India in its dispute against China (at least this is how Beijing viewed Soviet policy toward the Sino-Indian dispute in 1959). In 1957 the USSR had agreed to assist China's development of nuclear weapons, yet in June 1959 Moscow "unilaterally tore up the agreement on new technology and refused to provide China with a sample of an atomic bomb and technical data concerning its manufacture." Then in September of the same year Moscow, "ignoring China's repeated objections," issued a statement on the Sino-Indian border dispute disassociating the USSR from it. In Beijing's eyes this statement "brought the differences between China and the Soviet Union right into the open before the whole world" for the first time. Moscow's statement also deprived China of support by its putative Soviet ally in its conflict with India. Both moves were intended, Beijing believed, as "gifts to Eisenhower so as to curry favor with the U.S. imperialists" as part of a broader strategy of cooperating with U.S. imperialism against revolutionary China.[3] Moscow's de facto support for India against China was intended to form a "joint-stock company" with the U.S. imperialists with the corporate aim of "aiding India and opposing China."[4] Moscow's suspension of aid to China's nuclear weapons program was one of the early pivotal events in the evolution of the nonproliferation regime.

Confronted with this new American-Soviet-Indian combination to stifle China's emergence, Mao ordered a series of key countermoves. One was to push forward with the development of nuclear weapons without Soviet support and in spite of the fact that China's economy was collapsing and a devastating famine was sweeping the land.[5] Another countermove was to intensify the polemical struggle against Soviet revisionism's efforts to misdirect the world communist movement. As we saw in chapter 4, refuting India's advocacy of a "third way," together with Khrushchev's putative advocacy of a "peaceful transition to socialism" à la India's way, figured prominently in Chinese efforts to educate the world revolutionary movement in the early 1960s. As Moscow moved toward signing the PTBT, Beijing tried to dissuade it, arguing, in effect, that Moscow could choose between continuing its alliance with China or signing the nonproliferation agreement with the United States. A Chinese memorandum of September 1962, for example, said it was "a matter for the Soviet government whether it committed itself to refrain from transferring nuclear weapons and technical information concerning their manufacture to China; but ... the Chinese government hoped the Soviet government would not infringe on China's sovereign rights and act for China in assuming an obligation to refrain from manufacturing nuclear weapons."[6] Moscow chose Washington over Beijing. Moscow's signature of the PTBT over China's objections led Mao to conclude that Moscow was set on a course of anti-China collaboration with the United States. India and nuclear weapons were the key instruments of this superpower anti-China collusion. Soviet-

American efforts to develop a global nonproliferation regime (embodied in the partial test ban treaty of that year) *and* joint Soviet-American support for India were ways in which the two superpowers were trying to keep China weak. Acquiring nuclear weapons became, for Mao, a way of defeating this anti-China superpower "collusion." China's rivalry with India thereby became indirectly linked to its acquisition of nuclear weapons. Over the next fifteen or so years Beijing vehemently denounced Soviet- and American-sponsored international efforts to regulate or limit nuclear weapons.

Regarding India, from its earliest days the Republic of India was an active and important proponent of complete nuclear disarmament. In 1948, as the United Nations was establishing the International Atomic Energy Agency, India called for limiting the use of atomic energy to exclusively peaceful, non-military, purposes. Repeated Indian proposals along these lines followed in the 1950s. One of the more important of these was a call by Nehru in 1954 for a complete halt to all nuclear testing pending agreement on complete nuclear disarmament. This made India one of the earliest proponents of a comprehensive test ban treaty. This was one year before China decided to produce nuclear weapons. India also welcomed and was one of the first signatories of the 1963 Partial Test Ban Treaty. Following the signing of the PTBT, India continued to work to put nuclear nonproliferation on the UN agenda. In a memorandum to the secretary-general shortly after the PTBT was signed, India called for a comprehensive and effective nonproliferation treaty embodying an acceptable balance of mutual responsibilities and obligations between nuclear have and have-not powers. It would also be a step toward general and complete disarmament—"more particularly, nuclear disarmament."[7]

Following the Partial Test Ban Treaty, India pushed for China's inclusion in the disarmament process. India's representative at the United Nations Conference on Disarmament in Geneva asked repeatedly that China be included in the nuclear arms limitation and disarmament process. Speaking at a special session of the conference in August 1973, for example, India's representative, P. K. Banerjee, lamented that the "great hope of having achieved a breakthrough in disarmament negotiations" raised by the 1963 treaty had not been realized. One major shortcoming, Banerjee said, was that "adherence to the PTBT, though wide, is not universal. A few militarily important countries, such as Argentina and Pakistan, and especially China and France, are still missing from the list of parties." Nuclear testing continued unabated, Banerjee noted. Indeed, "almost one half of the total of 924 announced and presumed nuclear explosions conducted since 1945" had been conducted since the signing of the Partial Test Ban Treaty. "We have always emphasized,"

Banerjee continued, that "those nuclear weapons states which have not yet adhered to that treaty should do so without any further excuse or delay."[8]

The NPT, signed in July 1968 by the United States, the Soviet Union, and Britain, would ultimately prove decisive by establishing two categories, nuclear weapons states and non–nuclear weapons states, with differing responsibilities and rights under the treaty. The treaty defined a nuclear weapons state as one that had manufactured and exploded a nuclear device prior to January 1, 1967. Since China had begun atomic testing in 1964 and India's first test was not until 1974, under the NPT China enjoyed the status of a nuclear weapons state, while India was consigned to non–nuclear weapons state status. Nuclear weapons states were forbidden to assist any non–nuclear weapons state in acquiring nuclear weapons while themselves enjoying the right to acquire nuclear weapons–related technology freely. Non–nuclear weapons states were forbidden to acquire nuclear weapons or sensitive nuclear weapons–related technology. At the time it was not this disparity that India objected to. Rather, India's chief concerns had to do with the fact that the treaty was not linked to a program of general nuclear disarmament and lacked limitations on the quantitative or qualitative development of the arsenals of nuclear weapons states. While the non–nuclear weapons states were denied the right to acquire nuclear weapons, the nuclear weapons states enjoyed the right to expand and improve their nuclear arsenals without limit. Regarding China, New Delhi's main concern was that signing the NPT would make it more difficult for India to exercise the option of developing nuclear weapons if and when China's behavior toward India necessitated it. Entry into the NPT regime contradicted the country's policy of "keeping the option open," set by the Shastri government in 1964.

There were strong parallels between China's and India's rejection of the NPT. Beijing denounced the treaty as "superpower collusion" to uphold their "nuclear monopoly," so as to be able to exercise "nuclear blackmail" against the non-nuclear countries of the Third World. New Delhi denounced the treaty as discriminatory and as obstructing movement toward general nuclear disarmament. But, because China was classified as a nuclear weapons state under the NPT, it enjoyed the option of joining the regime as one of only five, recognized (i.e., implicitly legitimate) nuclear weapons states in the world. These five states also happened to be the permanent members of the Security Council. The NPT, together with the UN Charter, institutionalized the status of these five states as the five leading powers of the world. China's willingness to play the role of rebel and pariah during the 1960s and 1970s probably encouraged India's leaders to minimize the challenge to India deriving from its implicitly inferior ranking relative to China under the NPT. China's willingness to play a pariah role reduced the costs to India of its remaining outside the NPT regime. In the 1990s, when China finally decided to exercise its option under the NPT, India found the result completely unacceptable.

INDIAN DENUCLEARIZATION VIA A SOUTH ASIAN
NUCLEAR WEAPONS–FREE ZONE

The previous chapter explored the origins in the mid-1970s of China's support of Pakistan's nuclear weapons program. Significantly, China's covert support for Pakistan's nuclear program was paralleled by its public endorsement of the establishment of a nuclear weapons–free zone (NWFZ) in South Asia. China first endorsed the concept of an NWFZ in various regions of the world in the 1950s, apparently because this suited its security needs by expelling American weapons from those regions.[9] Ironically, China took its first stance on this issue in February 1958, when it endorsed a proposal by none other than Indian prime minister Nehru to establish and expand an area "free from weapons of mass destruction." In 1960 Zhou Enlai proposed establishment of a nuclear weapons–free zone in Asia and the Pacific, including the United States, the Soviet Union, China, and Japan. During Zhou's trip to Africa in December 1963–January 1964 he endorsed a NWFZ for that region—a concept that had earlier been proposed by a conference of African states.

China's endorsement of a South Asian NWFZ was in line with this earlier policy. Pakistan first proposed the idea of a South Asian NWFZ in the aftermath of India's 1974 nuclear test. It also succeeded, with China's help, in having the issue placed on the UN General Assembly agenda. Beijing endorsed the idea of a South Asian NWFZ during the August 1974 General Assembly debate and called on the South Asian states to begin the necessary negotiations toward that end. Beijing periodically reiterated this position over the next twenty-five years. While Mao lived, Beijing linked the denial of nuclear weapons to India à la a South Asian NWFZ with the limitation of India's tendencies toward regional hegemony. In the General Assembly debate of November 1974, for example, China's representative argued that, "if the desire for the establishment of a nuclear free–zone in South Asia is to be realized, it is imperative to guard against and oppose superpower hegemonism and intervention and the expansionist acts of any country."[10]

India rejected the concept of a South Asian NWFZ—or, more precisely, of an *exclusively* South Asian NWFZ—on the basis that South Asia was part of a larger region of Asia and that it was unrealistic to view it in isolation as regards the threat posed by nuclear weapons. The proposal, if adopted, might place some states, including India, at a disadvantage.[11] In plain speech, a South

Asian NWFZ would leave a nonnuclear India vulnerable to a nuclear-armed China. Establishing such a zone would institutionalize India's status as a non–nuclear weapons state while leaving China with nuclear weapons. Indian acceptance of a South Asian NWFZ in tandem with Pakistan would leave China as a recognized nuclear power, free to develop its nuclear arsenal without restriction, and as the only recognized, legitimate Asian nuclear power. While legitimizing China's nuclear arsenal, a South Asian NWFZ would also create barriers to India's future acquisition of nuclear weapons. While India remained nonnuclear, China's nuclear arsenal would be open to steady qualitative and quantitative improvement.

In the view of one authoritative Indian analyst, K. N. Ramachandran, China's endorsement of Pakistan's calls for a South Asian NWFZ was "not too subtle an effort by Beijing to foreclose the possibility of India going nuclear."[12] It would mean that the gap between the military capabilities of China and India in the nuclear area would increase, while Indian-Pakistani differences remained unresolved and the Sino-Pakistan entente cordiale remained firm. Under such circumstances India would be increasingly vulnerable to Chinese nuclear blackmail if and when Chinese leaders ever decided that would best serve Chinese interests. In such an eventuality India would also remain dependent on powers such as the United States and the USSR / Russian Federation for whatever deterrent support they might decide to give India. Such a course would entail a high degree of uncertainty, a high degree of dependence, and a high degree of reliance on Chinese and/or American goodwill. In the event that these costs became too great and Indian leaders decided to acquire a nuclear deterrent, the costs of violating the terms of a South Asian NWFZ agreement could be substantial—heavier than if India had not agreed to abide by such terms in the first place.

The second set of unacceptable consequences of a South Asian NWFZ for India had to do with the broad international status of India vis-à-vis the five recognized nuclear weapons states, especially China. By agreeing to a South Asian NWFZ, India would be permanently and by its own admission paired with Pakistan in a category inferior to that of China. India would thereby implicitly recognize its equivalency with Pakistan as a merely local power, and China would consolidate its position as Asia's only recognized and legitimate nuclear power. India would thereby implicitly recognize China as the preeminent Asian power and itself as inferior, at least in this crucial area.

Pakistan over the years presented India with a series of proposals designed to prevent or limit the introduction of nuclear weapons in South Asia. These included simultaneous accession to the Non-Proliferation Treaty, placing the nuclear facilities of both countries under the full scope of International Atomic

Energy Agency safeguards, and establishing a regime for mutual inspection of each other's nuclear facilities. India refused to discuss nuclear issues on a purely bilateral basis with Pakistan and called, instead, for total nuclear disarmament achieved via *multilateral* negotiations. Multilateral talks would, of course, involve China—and the United States. India also advanced nuclear disarmament proposals that embraced a universal, multilateral approach. One of the most elaborate was a three-tier system broached during Rajiv Gandhi's 1987 visit to Washington. According to this proposal, nuclear nations would be divided into three categories with separate obligations: (1) the United States and the USSR, (2) second-rank nuclear nations such as China, France, and the United Kingdom, and (3) "near nuclear" states such as India, Pakistan, Israel, South Africa, Brazil, and Argentina. Each tier would assume different obligations under Gandhi's plan. The nonnuclear states would agree to remain nonnuclear. Second-rank powers would freeze their arsenals at current levels. The United States and the USSR would undertake deep cuts in their nuclear arsenals.[13] China did not publicly respond to Gandhi's three-tier proposal, although Beijing did continue to call for universal, complete nuclear disarmament. Instead, Beijing continued steadily to modernize its nuclear arsenal while endorsing Pakistan's nuclear arms control proposals limited to South Asia.

THE GROWING COSTS AND DANGERS FOR INDIA OF "KEEPING THE OPTION OPEN"

The relationship between India, China, and the evolving structure of international nonproliferation regimes is paradoxical. India began as an early and ardent supporter of international efforts to develop such a regime. Its views about the regime differed in important ways from those of the United States and the Soviet Union. India favored more rapid movement toward complete nuclear disarmament. Yet it participated in the regime and, indeed, played an important role in its early development. China, on the other hand, fundamentally rejected such agreements, and this rejection exercised a deep influence on China's foreign relations. It was, as we have seen, one of the major reasons for China's rupture with its Soviet ally in 1960. Over the next two decades China was a strident critic of the international nuclear weapons regime. Then, curiously, China and India switched positions at just about the same time, in the 1990s. China became supportive of the international nuclear nonproliferation regime, apparently as a result of a top-level decision that the regime now served China's interests. India, about the same time, concluded that the regime no longer served its interests and, indeed, threatened them in important ways. Both countries then shifted long-established policies. Why did this simultaneous switch occur? One likely cause was the shifting international status of India and China, especially in relation to each other, along with India's desire for greater security against possible future Chinese nuclear intimidation during disputes between the two countries over the balance of power in South Asia.

During the early 1990s China moved toward supporting the nonproliferation regime and started working with the United States to uphold it. At bottom this shift reflected China's awareness that its interests were well served by capping at five the number of legitimate nuclear weapons states, with itself as one of that elite club and Japan and India not. China's shift toward participation in the nonproliferation regime presented India with a dangerous situation. New Delhi increasingly found itself confronted with Sino-American cooperation against India in the nuclear area. It increasingly seemed to Indian leaders that China and the United States were working together to lock India into permanent status as a non–nuclear weapons state. China was establishing itself as a partner and equal of the United States, as a legitimate nuclear weapons state with all the attendant political benefits of that status, while India was being boxed into a lesser status as a permanent, legitimately non–nuclear weapons state. The differing treatment accorded India and China in this regard during the mid-1990s appeared to Indians as tantamount to crowning China as the new number two power in the world and consigning India to a distinctly second-tier status. Growing numbers of Indians concluded that China's rising international status was due to its nuclear arsenal. If India wanted comparable status, they reasoned, it would have to follow China's lead.

Interactions between India and China over nuclear weapons during the 1990s were, as in earlier periods, characterized by asymmetry and indirection. The shifts in China's policies toward the nuclear nonproliferation regime were linked primarily to considerations having to do with China's relations with the United States. China's leaders were concerned with the steady deterioration of Sino-American relations during the 1990s and looked for areas of possible cooperation which might stanch those declining relations. Shifts in China's policies on nonproliferation offered first and foremost a way to safeguard an international environment conducive to China's drive for economic development by forging a workable relationship with the United States. For India, on the other hand, concerns having to do with China ranked much higher. While New Delhi was fully cognizant of Washington's immense influence on the situation, what troubled Indian leaders most was the fact that the United States seemed to be moving toward acceptance of China as a leading global power while consigning India to permanent status as a second-tier power. New Delhi was reacting to China's apparent rise to global power status, and Beijing was struggling to prevent that rise from leading to a confrontation with the United States. Neither Beijing nor New Delhi framed the nuclear nonproliferation issue in terms of their standing vis-à-vis the other. Both preferred, instead, to frame the issue in terms of either global principles or their relation to the United States. It is likely, however, that Indian and Chinese decision makers were well aware of the implications of nuclear weapon state versus non–nuclear weapons state status for the international standing of the two states vis-à-vis each other. Academic honesty requires frank recognition, however, that this is a *hypothesis,* which the following analysis attempts to substantiate.

The 1990s was a period of what came to be called "unipolar" dominance over the global system. The industrial, technological, financial, cultural, and military power of the states making up the Western alliance was huge. Moreover, that alliance system remained coherent, with the United States as its recognized leader. Chinese and Indian rivalry for status in the post–Cold War era took place in the shadow of Western unipolar dominance. Neither China nor India liked the fact of unipolarity. Both resented it and felt it was unjust both in terms of its origins and its consequences. Both resented their inferiority to the power of the Western alliance, and in a fundamental sense their struggle for international status was a struggle to achieve equal status with the West. But both China and India realized that equality with the Western "pole" was a very long-term goal. Western preeminence was an unchangeable fact of life and would remain so for some time to come. The relative status of China and India, however, was a different matter. Here the outcome was far more open, more subject to the exercise of Indian and Chinese diplomatic influence. Would China be accorded de facto status as the number two power in the post-Soviet world? Would India be consigned to the status of a purely regional power, somewhere below the leading world powers? These were questions that *could* be influenced by Chinese and Indian actions in the 1990s. It is not necessarily that Indians chafed more at a national status subordinate to China than they did at a status below the United States. Rather, India could do more about its status relative to China than it could about its status relative to the United States.

India's concern for international status was paralleled by its concern for national security. A large and growing disparity between the nuclear weapon capabilities of China and India had existed since the early 1960s, but in the 1990s it became increasingly unacceptable to India. One reason for this was the fruition of Pakistan's China-linked nuclear weapons programs about 1988–90. The military confrontation with China over Sumdurong Chu in

1986–87 also led to renewed awareness that war over the border remained a possibility. China's thrusts toward Nepal in 1988–89 and the consequent Indian reaction underlined the fact that China and India had fundamentally different approaches toward that state. The burgeoning of the new Sino-Myanmar strategic partnership raised the specter that the Sino-Pakistan entente to India's west might be coupled with a comparable entente on India's east. These developments combined with an awareness of China's growing national power to stimulate Indian fears of a further shift, against India, in the balance of power in the South Asian region. India recognized that it might need to undertake major exertions of national power to prevent such shifts, and that in such an eventuality it might find itself confronting China. Stated differently, there was a growing belief that the nuclear balance was linked, in a complex and subtle fashion, to the overall balance of power in South Asia.

For India the end of the Cold War brought deeply troubling trends. The USSR, which since 1971 had been India's major nuclear weapons state provider of a security guarantee against China, disappeared, and its Russian Federation successor slid into a steadily deeper crisis. Sino-Soviet rapprochement in the late 1980s had already sapped much of the credibility from Soviet extended deterrence, but it disappeared entirely with the demise of the USSR and the forging of a Sino-Russian "strategic partnership" in the early post–Cold War era. Large cuts in Soviet/Russian and American nuclear arsenals also began. These cuts had been long sought by India, but the United States and Russia refused to link the cuts to an ultimate goal of universal and complete nuclear disarmament, as India insisted. Major efforts were also undertaken to enlarge and strengthen the global nonproliferation regime by bringing India and Pakistan into it. New Delhi was dismayed by this growing international pressure and especially a trend toward American-Chinese cooperation. Washington seemed to be treating China as the new number two power in the world, with the new Sino-American "partnership" being manifest in joint efforts to force India to accept status as a non–nuclear weapons state. It became increasingly clear that India's traditional strategy of rallying the world's forces to create an alternative to the superpower-sponsored nuclear order offered few payoffs and entailed growing risks.

With the Soviet withdrawal from Afghanistan in early 1989 and the suspension of U.S. aid to Pakistan in late 1990 over Islamabad's resumption of enrichment of weapons-grade uranium, the Bush Administration concluded that the time was right for a push to solve the increasingly dangerous South Asian nuclear issue. During the Indian-Pakistan confrontation of 1990 both countries had readied their "basement bombs," moving a substantial increment closer to outright weaponization. Washington's solution, proposed in the spring of 1992, was to convene a conference of India, Pakistan, Russia, China, and the United States to establish and guarantee a nuclear weapons–free zone in South Asia. Pakistan and China welcomed the proposal. India rejected it. From New Delhi's perspective the proposal meant that India would accept permanent nuclear inferiority to China and assume a status equivalent to Pakistan, with peace between India and Pakistan being guaranteed by Washington, Beijing, and Moscow. New Delhi countered the U.S. proposal with a call for *global* efforts to restrict nuclear weapons.[14]

Renewed movement toward a comprehensive test ban treaty also became linked to pressure on India to accept non–nuclear weapons state status. A CTBT had been under discussion since the mid-1950s but with little chance of success during the Cold War. Then in 1991 USSR president Mikhail Gorbachev announced a one-year moratorium on all explosive nuclear testing and called on other powers to join in. The United States and France followed suit the next year (though France later resumed testing) and Britain in 1993. In August 1993 the Conference on Disarmament gave its Ad Hoc Committee on a Nuclear Test Ban authority to negotiate a CTBT.[15] Both China and India participated actively in the CTBT negotiations at Geneva. China had begun participating in the Conference on Disarmament in 1990 as one aspect of its growing acceptance of the international nuclear nonproliferation regime.

As for India, according to the head of India's mission to the Committee on Disarmament, Ambassador Arundhati Ghose, India's orientation toward the CTBT negotiations can be divided into two stages, demarcated by the NPT Review and Extension Conference that met in New York City in April and May 1995. Prior to the NPT conference India believed its concerns with embedding the CTBT into a context of comprehensive and time-limited nuclear disarmament would be incorporated into the emerging test ban treaty. India envisioned the CTBT as not only preventing the emergence of new nuclear weapons states but limiting as well the quantitative and qualitative development of the nuclear arsenals of the existing nuclear weapons states. After witnessing the proceedings of the NPT Extension and Review Conference, however, India began to doubt that its concerns would be incorporated into the emerging CTBT.[16]

When the NPT came into force in 1970, its terms provided for a duration of twenty-five years, with conferences to review the treaty's performance to be convened every five years. Review conferences were duly held in 1975, 1980, 1985, and 1990. The NPT also provided that, when the twenty-five-year term expired, the scheduled conference should consider renewing it and making emendations. The NPT Review and Extension Conference was scheduled for

1995. As the conference approached, India faced growing pressure to join the NPT as a non–nuclear weapons state. On April 5, 1995, after prodding by the United States, China issued a "National Statement on Security Assurances" with India and the upcoming NPT extension conference in mind. China's standing policy on the possible use of nuclear weapons then traced back to an April 1982 declaration that China "undertakes unconditionally not to use or threaten to use nuclear weapons against non-nuclear countries and nuclear-free zones." Beijing's April 1995 Security Assurances reiterated this phraseology but dropped the word *unconditionally*, replacing it with the phrase "at any time or under any circumstances." Beijing's Security Assurances also added the phrase "This commitment naturally applies to non–nuclear weapons state parties to the Treaty on the Non-proliferation of Nuclear Weapons or non–nuclear weapons states that have undertaken any comparable internationally binding commitments not to manufacture or acquire nuclear explosive devices."[17] Some Indian analysts saw a new conditionality in China's April 1995 declaration. Whereas China's previous pledge had been "unconditional," its new formulation could be construed as applying only to parties to the NPT—a construction vehemently denied by the Chinese embassy in New Delhi.[18] More indisputable, and more significant, was China's shift from opposing the NPT regime to its growing cooperation with the U.S. to uphold that regime. New Delhi now faced joint Sino-American pressure to accept non–nuclear weapons state status.

Once China issued its Security Assurances, the five permanent members of the Security Council—the Perm Five—issued a multilateral assurance. On April 11, 1995, six days before the NPT extension conference opened, the UN Security Council passed Resolution 984, extending direct and indirect security guarantees to non–nuclear weapon states that were parties to the NPT and which encountered threats of the use of force by a nuclear weapons state. Resolution 984 recognized "the legitimate interest of non–nuclear weapons states as Parties to the Treaty on the Non-proliferation of Nuclear Weapons to receive security assurances" against the use or threatened use of nuclear weapons. In the event of such use or threatened use of nuclear weapons against "non–nuclear weapons states who are party to the Non-proliferation Treaty," the Security Council, "and above all its nuclear weapons states permanent members, will act immediately in accordance with the relevant provisions of the Charter of the United Nations."[19] In line with the purpose of pressuring nonparty states to join the NPT, the Security Council guarantees contained in Resolution 984 were made clearly contingent upon a non–nuclear weapons state being a party to that treaty. Of course, for states that chose to remain outside the NPT, Resolution 984 could be construed as diminishing their security against nuclear threat or attack. Indian critics of Resolution 984 pointed this out and also the fact that all Resolution 984 really required was for the Security Council to meet. Any action that resulted from such a meeting could be blocked by a veto by any one of the Permanent Five.[20] Beyond that was the more fundamental question of all collective security efforts: is it prudent for a nation to rest its security on the willingness of other, nonallied nations to bear the costs of war on its behalf?

As the duly scheduled NPT Extension and Review conference convened, most states favored extension of the NPT without condition and for an indefinite period.[21] Since India was not a party to the NPT, it did not participate in the conference. It could have participated as an observer but decided against this, probably because it feared the conference would become a forum for pressuring India to join the NPT. In response to mounting pressure to join the treaty, New Delhi outlined its reasons for refusing do so. Its core objections had not changed since 1970: by creating two classes of countries, the treaty was discriminatory; an acceptable solution would be based on the principle of equality and move the nuclear powers toward complete nuclear disarmament. The NPT as it stood was not a step toward general nuclear disarmament. Extending the treaty indefinitely, New Delhi believed, signified acceptance of the existing unequal, nuclear status quo. Why else should it be perpetuated indefinitely? By requiring nuclear disarmament only of specified non–nuclear weapon states, the NPT in effect legitimized the continuing nuclear weaponization and nuclear superiority of the five specified nuclear weapons states.

Once the NPT extension conference opened, achievement of "universality" by securing the participation of all countries, especially of countries that operated non-safeguarded nuclear facilities—such as India and Pakistan—dominated the agenda. One of the early decisions of the conference was to term this an "urgent priority." Eventually, the treaty was extended indefinitely and without conditions. The 1995 Extension and Review Conference also provided for continuing five-year review conferences, one of whose purposes would be to "address specifically" what might be done to achieve universality. The conference also affirmed regional nuclear weapon-free zones.[22]

As Ambassador Arundhati Ghose indicated, the outcome of the 1995 NPT Extension and Review Conference had a strong impact on India. In the face of mounting international pressure on India to accept permanent consignment to a nonnuclear, second-tier international position—combined with the U.S. decision to ease restrictions on military assistance to Pakistan in place since 1990—India's government, then led by a Congress Party–dominated coalition headed by Prime Minister P. V. Narasimha Rao, moved toward creation of a nuclear fait accompli to reject that pressure.[23] A tentative decision was made to conduct a nuclear test. Preparations were under way at the Rajasthan desert test site, when their detection led to heavy international pressure. Eventually, the test was canceled.[24] This near-test of late 1995 is important because it indicates that the impulse toward open declaration of India's nuclear weapon status covered a wide range of the political spectrum and was not confined to such groups as the BJP. Domestic factors played a role in stimulating the emphasis on India's international status. Rao's government was strongly attacked for its handling of the NPT Extension and Review Conference. The BJP's "Foreign Policy Agenda for the Future," issued in October 1995 in the midst of a year of intense electoral campaigning, began: "India today bears the appearance of a nation which can be managed and maneuvered. Its voice can be ignored without consideration. Its sovereignty can be questioned without hesitation. Its security can be threatened without trepidation. Never during the last fifty years did the nation reach such a low level of respectability in the comity of nations."[25]

After the indefinite and unconditional extension of the NPT, the CTBT talks moved into high gear. China's cooperation with the United States over NPT extension boded well for the CTBT. On the other hand, China alone among the nuclear weapons states declared itself in favor of the "total destruction" of all nuclear weapons.[26] This stance pointed toward possible Indian-Chinese cooperation. India and China both called at the CTBT talks for complete nuclear disarmament, but their efforts did not greatly influence the course of the negotiations. Most other participants wanted a comprehensive test ban and did not want to make achievement of that end dependent on a far more complex and difficult agreement on comprehensive nuclear disarmament.

As the CTBT and NPT negotiations progressed, China pushed forward with a program of intensive nuclear testing. It test-exploded nuclear weapons in June and October 1994, in May and August 1995, and in June and July 1996. These tests were accompanied by statements that China favored complete and universal nuclear disarmament, supported a CTBT, and developed nuclear weapons only for reasons of self-defense. These professions did not mollify international critics. Japan, South Korea, and Germany, along with many other countries, condemned the tests. Japan suspended its grant aid to China in protest. While grant aid constituted only a small portion of Japan's total economic aid to China, it was highly significant. This was the first time that Japan had used economic sanctions to express displeasure about Chinese actions. India was among the countries that condemned China's nuclear tests.

Confronting such strong international pressure, Beijing began shifting positions in the CTBT negotiations. Prior to June 1996 China had insisted that nuclear weapons states be allowed to conduct peaceful nuclear explosions under the treaty for such possible uses as civil engineering or deflection of an asteroid that might be discovered careening toward earth. Of course, since there were only minor technical differences between a "peaceful" and a "military" nuclear explosion, such caveats would have allowed China and other nuclear weapons states to continue testing their nuclear devices whenever they deemed it necessary. China objected to the use of national detection systems of individual states to monitor compliance with the treaty. It also continued to insist on inclusion of no-first-use pledges in the proposed CTBT. Then in June 1996 Beijing dropped these demands and announced it would suspend nuclear testing by September, when the CTBT was scheduled to take effect.[27] These moves signaled that China's leaders had concluded that their nation's interests were best served by joining the new, emerging nuclear regime as one of its elite members. Beijing had decided that China's interests were best served by strengthening the international consensus in which it was one of only five recognized nuclear weapons states and the only nuclear weapons state in Asia.

In May 1996 the chair of the CTBT ad hoc negotiating committee submitted a "clean text" produced after extensive consultations. India discovered to its dismay, and contrary to its expectations, that this text did not incorporate its major concerns. On June 20 Ghose declared that India would not sign the draft treaty as it stood. Referring elliptically to China and Pakistan, she said:

> This cannot be the CTBT that India can be expected to accept. . . . Countries around us continue their weapons programmes, either openly or in a clandestine manner. In such an environment, India cannot accept any restraints on its capabilities, if other countries remain unwilling to accept the obligation to eliminate their nuclear weapons . . . such a treaty is not conceived as a measure towards universal nuclear disarmament and is not in India's national security interest. India, therefore, cannot subscribe to it in its present form.[28]

India would not sign a CTBT, Ambassador Ghose said, unless that agreement required the complete destruction of existing nuclear weapons within a prescribed period, imposed limitations on all countries, and prohibited nonexplosive, computer simulation–based development of nuclear arsenals. India could not "accept any restraints on its [nuclear weapons] capability if other countries remain unwilling to accept the obligation to eliminate nuclear weapons," Ghose said.[29] By signing the CTBT and renouncing the option of displaying or confirming the reliability of its nuclear weapons, while allowing China and other powers to maintain indefinitely and improve their nuclear arsenals via nonexplosive computer testing, India would permanently consign itself to a second-tier status and weaken its national security. This Indian declaration came about two weeks *after* Beijing's crucial shift at the CTBT negotiations. The same international pressure worked on both India and China. But China had an acceptable option of entry into the evolving nuclear regime as one of the recognized elite counties under that regime. India had no such option.

After India's declaration that it would not sign the CTBT as it stood, stringent Entry into Force provisions were introduced to compel India's accession. The Entry into Force provisions were an ominous manifestation of the position of isolation and vulnerability into which India was sinking. Article 14 of the treaty contained the Entry into Force provisions; it specified that the treaty would enter into force "after the date of deposit of the instrument of ratification by all the states listed in Annex 2." Annex 2 listed forty-four states with nuclear reactors, including India, Pakistan, Israel, and Iran. If the treaty had not entered into force—that is, if all the enumerated forty-four states had not ratified the treaty within three years after it was opened for signature in December 1996—then states that had already ratified the treaty were to meet and "shall consider and decide by consensus what measures consistent with international law may be taken to accelerate the ratification process in order to facilitate the early entry into force of this treaty." Such conferences would then be held annually to consider additional measures.[30] This arrangement was designed to mobilize pressure from the international community on countries like India, Pakistan, and Israel in order to persuade them to join the CTBT regime. Israel had already declared it was prepared to sign the emerging treaty. Pakistan had also said that it would sign if India did. That left India. From the Indian perspective, India was the primary target of Article 14's Entry into Force provisions.[31]

The United States initially favored less stringent requirements to insure that the treaty would take effect, but eventually modified its stance and agreed to the more stringent provisions.[32] In the Indian view Britain had originally been the key proponent of these tough Entry into Force provisions. After India's declaration that it would not sign the treaty, China became a vigorous advocate of the stringent Entry into Force provisions. According to Ghose, Chinese and Russian lobbying was decisive in securing American assent and pushing through adoption of the stringent, anti-Indian Entry into Force provisions. The United States was flexible in this regard and did not favor endangering the whole instrument by making its implementation contingent on fulfillment of perhaps unattainable elements like Indian, Pakistani, and

Israeli accession. Washington was primarily concerned with securing participation by China and Russia. Russia felt that, unless India were in the CTBT, China would not sign, and without China's participation the treaty could seriously affect Russia's security. China also insisted on the Entry into Force provisions. Its position was "noted with interest, not least by India," according to Ambassador Ghose.[33]

India saw the provisions of Article 14 as a violation of principles of national sovereignty and of the 1969 Geneva Convention on the Law of Treaties. According to that convention, a treaty could not bind nations that were not party to it. Nor could nations be coerced to sign a treaty against their will. Ghose condemned the Entry into Force provisions as "adopted at the insistence of a small number of countries with the clear aim of imposing obligations on India and also placing it in a position in which it did not wish to be." Such an attempt to deny a sovereign country its "right of voluntary consent in adherence to an international treaty" was without parallel and "has been perceived very negatively in our capital," Ghose complained.[34] India announced it would vote against the draft treaty in the Committee on Disarmament. Since that body had previously functioned by consensus, this approach prevented it from taking formal action on the CTBT text. India insisted that this made impossible any submission of a treaty text to the General Assembly. China and the United States ignored India's objections and overrode its attempts to block action on the CTBT by jointly conveying the CTBT text to the General Assembly together with their endorsement of it. The General Assembly functions by majority vote, and India was thus unable to block that body's adoption of the treaty. The CTBT was approved by the General Assembly on September 11, 1996, by a vote of 158 to 3. Only India, Bhutan, and Libya voted against it. Pakistan voted for the agreement and stated it would sign the treaty when India did so.[35] This vote was indicative of the international isolation into which India was sliding. While China increasingly worked with the United States as a partner, India stood with the support of only tiny Bhutan and the pariah state Libya. At the time of the General Assembly vote, China's UN ambassador, Sha Zukang, called on India to join the treaty.

An especially ominous aspect of the developing situation from India's point of view was that China and the United States were increasingly working together as partners in the development of the nonproliferation regime—particularly in trying to compel India to accept non–nuclear weapons state status. Beijing offered benign explanations of this. When Ambassador Ghose asked her Chinese counterpart to explain the mid-June shift in China's approach from opposition to the CTBT draft favored by the majority to coop-

eration with the United States in pushing through that draft, the Chinese representative intimated that China feared United States pressure and harassment via on-site verification inspections. If China were alone in the CTBT,
it would be the sole target of U.S. pressure and harassment. If India were also
part of the nonproliferation regime, however, U.S. attention would be diluted
and China would not stand alone in opposing U.S. harassment. A while later
the Chinese delegation leader told Ghose that whatever came out of the
Conference on Disarmament now would not be in the interest of either China
or India. The proper response, however, was not to disengage from the process
but to engage and struggle to limit the damage to their interests. In the 1990s
"a strong wind was blowing" adverse to the interests of both China and India.
In fifteen years or so a different situation would prevail, with the wind blowing in a different direction.[36] Once again, Beijing's message was that India
should cooperate with China to thwart U.S. hegemony.

India did not feel its interests were best served by joining with China in
its struggle against U.S. harassment and pressure within the CTBT regime.
It understood that pursuing such a course would institutionalize India in a
nuclear and political status inferior to China in a situation, moreover, in which
India would have less U.S. sympathy. Another high-ranking Indian diplomat felt that China shifted positions on the CTBT once it learned of an Indian-
U.S. understanding to the effect that India would not sign but would also not
block the CTBT in the Committee on Disarmament.[37] Confronted by an
apparent U.S.-Indian understanding that, Beijing probably felt, boded ill for
Chinese interests, China played the American card, in effect outbidding India
for U.S. support. If New Delhi would not work with China against Western
unipolarity and toyed with the idea of cooperating with the United States
against China, Beijing would trump New Delhi by aligning with the United
States against India. Beijing's role in mobilizing international pressure on India
in 1996 was a demonstration that China could outbid India in a competition
for United States support if New Delhi chose to play that game.

The outcome of the CTBT talks reinforced the NPT Extension and Review
Conference in strengthening Indian support for outright nuclear weaponization. A *Times of India* editorial of July 1997 expressed the growing Indian concern for international disregard of India's voice and policies. It also traced
India's declining international influence to its non–nuclear weapons status.
The editorial spoke in almost laudatory terms of China's earlier refusal to go
along with U.S. wishes on nuclear and nonproliferation issues. China's ability to do so was the result of its "breaking of the U.S. nuclear monopoly and
opposing its blackmail." Because China had a mere "seventeen intercontinental missiles which can reach U.S. targets," Washington no longer dared

to threaten China but felt compelled to find ways of cooperating with it. "China has sent out a clear message to the world that nuclear weapons are needed in today's world if hegemony is to be restricted and nuclear blackmail is to be opposed."[38] The clear implication was that India should be more like China and acquire the great equalizer, nuclear weapons.

While still chafing at U.S.-Chinese outflanking of India's efforts to block action in the Conference on Disarmament, New Delhi watched Beijing and Washington move further along the road toward a joint approach to South Asian nuclear problems. President Jiang Zemin's state visit to the United States in October–November 1997 was the first state visit by a top-level Chinese leader since 1985. It was part of an effort by Washington and Beijing to rebuild their relationship after the serious deterioration of 1995–96. Leaders in both capitals felt that the direction of the Sino-American relation had to be shifted from confrontation and multiplication of tensions toward a new direction stressing cooperation. The two sides sought to do this by taking a "strategic," "long-term" perspective in which the two countries identified areas of common interest and built a "constructive strategic partnership" to deal with those areas while setting aside areas of disagreement. As the U.S.-China joint statement of October 29, 1997, said: "The United States and China have major differences on the question of human rights. At the same time, they also have great potential for cooperation in maintaining global and regional peace and stability."[39]

South Asia was specified by the joint statement as one area in which the two countries shared a common interest in maintaining "peace and stability." The two countries "agreed to work to bring the Comprehensive Test Ban Treaty into force at the earliest possible date." They also reiterated "their commitment not to provide any assistance to unsafeguarded nuclear facilities and nuclear explosion programs." The latter statement represented a significant U.S. concession to Beijing on Chinese nuclear links with Pakistan. Earlier the United States had insisted that China cease *all* assistance to Pakistan's nuclear programs, since nuclear technology was highly fungible and Pakistan obviously was conducting covert nuclear weapons programs. Now Washington agreed that China could continue assistance to "safeguarded" nuclear facilities in Pakistan.

Washington had long argued to New Delhi that U.S. efforts to bring China into the nonproliferation regime accorded with India's interests, since they would limit or end Chinese assistance to Pakistan's nuclear weapons programs. China's "commitment" to nonproliferation in South Asia via the October 29 Sino-American statement accorded with Indian interests, or so U.S. representatives argued. The mainstream Indian view, however, was that China's commitment to nonproliferation in South Asia, along with American efforts to enforce that commitment, had both already proved to be specious. Through a combination of covert operations, hard bargaining, and legalistic technicalities about agreements reached with Washington, China had been able to assist Pakistan's nuclear programs in any way it deemed necessary. The United States, in the Indian view, had not placed a high priority on ending Chinese assistance to Pakistan's nuclear program in the 1980s because it needed Pakistan and Chinese cooperation in confronting the Soviets in Afghanistan. Washington had deemed driving the Soviets out of Afghanistan more important than ending Chinese aid to Pakistan's nuclear program and either turned a blind eye or accepted legalistic and ultimately meaningless "caps" on Chinese assistance to Pakistan's nuclear effort.

This pattern continued during the 1990s following the Soviet withdrawal from Afghanistan and the end of the Cold War. When confronted with instances of Chinese assistance to Pakistan's nuclear or missile programs, Washington downplayed the matter, again in the Indian view. On several occasions when evidence of Beijing's covert assistance came to light, Washington protested ineffectually while adopting very limited and short-lived sanctions. It seemed clear, in India's view, that the United States valued good relations with China far more than it did strict enforcement of nonproliferation norms in South Asia. In this context Beijing's "reiteration" of its commitment to nonproliferation in the October U.S.-China joint statement was meaningless.[40]

A more significant aspect of the October 1997 Sino-American statement, in India's eyes, was the implicit declaration of a common intention to pressure India to accept status as a non–nuclear weapons state under the NPT. This was not explicit in the words of the October 1997 statement, but was, as India saw it, the clear implication of that document, especially against the background of the NPT and CTBT interactions of 1995–96. India's nuclear decision of 1998 arose out of this context. From this perspective India's tests are perhaps best seen as rejection of a perceived Chinese-American attempt to coerce India into a second-tier status in which Indian security would ultimately be dependent upon Chinese and American nuclear might and goodwill.

INDIA'S REJECTION OF PERMANENT NONNUCLEAR STATUS

In the context of the evolution of the international nuclear weapons regime during the 1990s, it is clear that several concerns underlay India's May 1998 nuclear weapons test and declaration of nuclear weapons state status. One was a growing international consensus that India should accept permanent status as a non–nuclear weapons state. Such an outcome would overturn the policy of "keeping the nuclear option open" which had defined Indian nuclear doctrine since 1964. It would also make it more costly if India decided at some future date to develop nuclear weapons openly. A second major Indian concern had to do with enhancing its international status. India was being locked into a status inferior not only to that of the United States and Russia but also of China. India's voice in the international system, its status, was increasingly being ignored. In a parliamentary defense of the May 1998 tests, BJP spokesman Jag Mohan dwelt at considerable length on the status-enhancing aspect of India's tests. According to Mohan, the tests had

> put India on the map of the world. Now the world cannot take us for granted. Earlier what was being done was just that . . . one-sixth of the human race was being ignored by the nuclear club and we were just being dictated [to]. They were saying: "This is good for us and not good for you." What is this? This great civilization and this great culture could be dictated [to] by the nuclear club. Are we living in a democratic world or not? . . . [The tests are] our assertion against the undemocratic behavior of this nuclear club or this power cartel. It is an assertion of our self-respect.

According to Mohan, "A Directorate headed by the United States" dominated the world. Mohan quoted approvingly Samuel Huntington's words that "the West in effect is using these international institutions, its military power and economic resources to run the world that will maintain Western predominance, protect Western interests, and promote Western political and economic values." India's tests were a way of saying, "You have dominated for quite long, but by this self-assertion, we have said that this power cartel is not acceptable to us." Mohan adduced a number of ways in which India's nuclear weaponization would enhance its international influence: it would revive the nonaligned movement; it would help bring about a new international economic order in which wealth was redistributed from the wealthy to the developing countries; and it would help bring about complete disarmament. Whether these beliefs were well founded is beside the point. The point is that these desirable consequences were to flow from India's enhanced status deriving from the country's nuclear weapons status. Bolstering India's status in the world was a major motivation, just as it had been with China's nuclear decision forty-three years earlier.

India's traditional approach to the international nuclear weapons regime—its efforts to establish India's stature as a global leader of the counterculture to the superpower-inspired nuclear balance of terror—became increasingly irrelevant as the 1990s progressed. India's advocacy of complete disarmament, including nuclear disarmament over several decades, had not moved the world noticeably closer to that goal. The established nuclear powers instead moved toward more effective cooperation to perpetuate their nuclear monopoly. Nor had the nonproliferation regime prevented the development of nuclear weapons by India's rivals, China and Pakistan. The nuclear program of both countries may have been delayed by obstacles imposed by nonproliferation, but both had surmounted those obstacles and achieved a nuclear weapons capability. By 1997 India faced strong and mounting international pressure to trust its security to the nonproliferation regime and to the willingness of one or several of the Permanent Five nuclear powers to bear costs, should it come to that, on India's behalf. If it did this, India would permanently renounce its quest for parity with the first-rank nations of the world.

In terms of security, dependence on the guarantees of the Perm Five nuclear weapons states led to political and military vulnerability. Of the Permanent Five only the United States was realistically in a position to extend a nuclear umbrella over India. But other countries that enjoyed U.S. nuclear protection were allies of the United States—including Germany, Japan, South Korea, Australia. Alliance is a relation of mutual support and close partnership. The mutually supportive relations signified by alliance gave great powers real, substantial interests in fighting to protect their allies. By protecting allies, powers protect themselves. But India was not and did not wish to become an American ally. Could a nonallied India realistically expect U.S. nuclear protection? Could India realistically expect the United States to run the risks and bear the potentially heavy costs of using nuclear weapons on behalf of a nonallied India? Would other powers hostile to India, perhaps China, find such a U.S. pledge credible? This, of course, was the classic problem of all collective security arrangements. States, in fact, are willing to assume the heavy costs of war only for their own vital interests. When the vital interests of *other* states are at stake and only second-order interests of their own, the tendency of states will be to equivocate, to find ways of dealing with the challenge which do not entail first-order costs for second-order interests. Stated most bluntly, India could not expect the United States to run the risk of nuclear war with China for the sake of Indian interests.

If India chose to rely on U.S. guarantees for its nuclear security, would India be expected to modify its policies toward the United States to secure that protection—to adopt more friendly and supportive approaches toward the United States? Would not this be a natural quid pro quo? Could the United States be expected, realistically, to bear the risks and costs of protecting a country that was critical of it and perhaps even unfriendly toward it? Was not friendship toward the United States a necessary correlate of depending on the United

States for protection? Allies of the United States from Berlin to Canberra to Tokyo might have no difficulties with such necessary friendship, but India's very conception of its role in the world required it to keep its distance from the United States. India, like China, envisioned an independent role for itself in the world.

In many ways India's response to the developing nonproliferation regime in the 1990s was similar to China's response thirty years earlier. In the early 1960s, when China was confronted by strong pressure from the USSR, the United States, the United Nations, India, and the nonaligned movement to forgo possession of nuclear weapons, Beijing refused. China persisted in developing nuclear weapons in the face of strong international pressure and paid a very high price for doing so. Domestically, resources were channeled into strategic weapons programs during the early 1960s, while several million Chinese died of famine. Internationally, China accepted confrontation with both the USSR and the United States, and yet it persisted with its nuclear weapons program. The payoff for this sacrifice came in 1968, when the fait accompli created by China was recognized and January 1, 1967, was accepted as the cut-off date for qualifying as a nuclear weapons state under the Non-Proliferation Treaty. China's determination and sacrifice in the early 1960s created the basis on which China finally and fully claimed in 1995–96 the status as one of only five nuclear weapons states. In order to establish itself as a nuclear weapons state India may well have to pay a similar price in order to establish its own nuclear fait accompli. If it is unable or unwilling to bear the necessary costs, its long-term prospects for parity with China are not good.

13 / Prospects for a Qualitative Change
in PRC-ROI Relations

If, as this book has argued, the last fifty-some years have seen protracted geopolitical conflict between the foreign policies of China and India across the South Asian region, it seems appropriate to conclude by thinking about how this conflict might be brought to an end. How might this constant pulling and tugging between Beijing and New Delhi end, thereby ushering in a new era of predominantly cooperative, nonconflictual Sino-Indian relations? Conceptually, there are two ways in which this might happen. One, China could agree that South Asia is India's security zone and sphere of influence and desist from actions there which are objectionable to New Delhi. Two, India could accommodate itself to a seemingly inexorable growth of China's political-military role in South Asia. This second course might involve an Indian-Chinese partnership in dealing with security problems in the South Asian region and could possibly evolve toward Indian acceptance of Chinese preeminence in that region. While it is possible to imagine any number of future paths that do not conform to either of these two polar possibilities, it is analytically useful to organize an investigation around these two polar outcomes. This the chapter at hand will do.

Historically, rival powers desirous of finding a way of managing their rivalry have often resorted to sphere of influence agreements. Steven I. Levine has suggested that by the late 1980s there existed an understanding between Beijing and New Delhi tantamount to a de facto sphere of influence arrangement.[1] For the sake of reducing tension with India and bringing about better PRC-ROI relations beneficial to Chinese economic development and diplomatic objectives in other areas, Beijing supposedly signaled New Delhi that it would respect India's preeminent role in South Asia. The doyen of American study of South Asia's relations with China, Leo E. Rose, has argued along similar lines. Pakistan in 1965 and 1971 and Nepal in 1988 decided to challenge India partly on the basis of anticipated Chinese support. That support was far less than they had anticipated, leaving them to confront Indian power alone. When India confronted various China-supported South Asian countries with over-whelmingly superior power, China carefully limited its support to avoid being drawn into intense conflict with India. According to Rose:

> Beijing's objectives in South Asia have been directed at enhancing the auton-omy of the smaller states in the Subcontinent, but without really challenging, other than vocally, India's status in the region. Thus, the Chinese accepted in essence the reality of power politics in the Subcontinent. While most South Asian states interpreted Chinese policy south of the Himalayas as directed at limiting New Delhi's hegemonistic role in the region, in reality Beijing accepted this as the status quo. Thus, China was never an effective counter-balance to Indian hegemony in South Asia and it carefully avoided assuming such a role even in those instances in which it was vocally critical of Indian policies towards its neighbors in the Subcontinent. . . . China's policy in the Subcontinent was, in fact if not in form, Indo-centric.[2]

Rose does not use the term *sphere of influence,* but his argument points in that direction. Greater clarity all around would open the way to a "new rela-tionship" between China and India in South Asia, he proposes. India should realize that China in fact respects and will not challenge India's hegemonic position in South Asia, which in turn should lead New Delhi to be less para-noid about China's ties to the region. The smaller South Asian countries should forget about "playing the China card" and come to terms with India with-out such illusions. China should perhaps bring its rhetoric into greater cor-respondence with its practice of deferring to Indian dominance in South Asia. If, Rose argues, all parties recognized the fact that China's overriding inter-est in South Asia has been avoiding confrontation with India, everyone would act more soberly, opening the door to a new type of Sino-Indian relation in the subcontinent.

Because China has declined to enter into very high-cost confrontations with India over New Delhi's exertions of power in South Asia, does it nec-essarily follow that China accepts Indian hegemony in South Asia, or, to use our terms, that it accepts South Asia as an Indian sphere of influence? Part of the problem here is definitional: what do we mean by *acceptance?* It seems to me that the term implies at least two things. First, it means that the "accepting" country does not oppose or try to alter the situation being created by the country granted the sphere of influence. Second, *acceptance* implies that the accepting country not view the situation being created as adverse to its interests and/or nurture a sense of grievance at the new situation resulting from force majeure.

The history of international relations is replete with instances of powers limiting their responses to adverse situations created by other powers but in which it is clear that this self-limitation should not be construed as acceptance. Two well-known examples are U.S. "nonrecognition" of Japan's creation of Manchukuo in 1932 and the PRC's nonrecognition of the de facto independence of Taiwan created by the application of U.S. power in 1950. In 1931–32 the Hoover Administration objected strongly to Japan's efforts to detach Manchuria from China. Washington declined, however, to implement economic sanctions or naval demonstrations to counter Japan's actions. Its priorities were on easing its domestic economic crisis and avoiding confrontation with Japan. Yet Washington stubbornly refused to recognize Japan's fait accompli and nurtured a sense of grievance against its actions. A decade later Japan's attempted detachment of Manchuria from China was a significant element in the complex of events that led to the Japan-U.S. war. The situation with Beijing and Taiwan is similar. Beijing has over the years carefully limited its application of power toward Taiwan in order to avoid a confrontation with the United States, which Beijing believed would carry seriously adverse consequences for China's economic and security interests. Yet few analysts of the Beijing-Taipei-Washington relationship would argue that the carefully limited application of Chinese power toward Taiwan should be construed as Chinese acceptance of the situation created by the application of superior U.S. power regarding Taiwan. Chinese resentment of the situation created by American force majeure simmers just below the surface.

Acceptance by one country of another's sphere of influence implies a self-limitation by the accepting power. One power deliberately abstains from actions in another region which it knows will be offensive to another power. This does not seem to be the case with China in South Asia. This book has chronicled China's sustained disregard for Indian sensitivities and claims to a special status in South Asia. During the post-Mao era the roster includes China's support for Pakistan's nuclear and missile programs; the effort to establish a military relation with Nepal; the development of a dense military-logistic relation with Myanmar; the robust Sino-Pakistan and Sino-Bangladesh military relations; PLAN activities in the Indian Ocean; and Beijing's insistence on treating Bhutan as any other sovereign, independent country.

Even in the instances cited by Rose one finds Chinese actions, and not merely words, opposing Indian policies. It is still impossible to say how far Mao Zedong was willing to go in 1965 to support Pakistan—had Pakistan's leaders called for such support and decided to protract the war with India. When China's foreign policy records are finally opened, we may find that Mao was prepared in September 1965 to order limited military actions in the Himalayas to help Pakistan. Even without this information, it is clear that in the aftermath of both the 1965 and 1971 wars China helped Pakistan rebuild its shattered military forces. It is significant that Pakistan's leaders emerged from both the 1965 and 1971–72 crises generally satisfied with the level of China's support. China also supplied substantial amounts of economic aid to Pakistan and gave critical assistance to its nuclear weapons and missile programs. Pakistanis look upon China's record during the two crises as proof of China's standing as a true and reliable friend. In the case of Nepal, China built expensive and provocative roads through the Himalayas, gave substantial economic aid to Nepal, and attempted to end Nepal's dependence on India for weapons purchases. Even during Nepal's 1989–90 confrontation with India, when China was in a dire domestic and international situation, China gave Nepal some, though not very much, support. The point is that China *did oppose,* in substantive and not merely rhetorical ways, India's efforts to establish its preeminence in South Asia. Nor did Beijing passively, without protest or counteraction, accept the situation being created by Indian power. China's opposition was not open-ended, and Beijing did refuse to trump India. But China's support was repeated, frequently went beyond mere words, and was sometimes significant.

The fact that China has carefully limited its assistance to South Asian nations so as to avoid confrontation with India is more economically explained in terms of competing policy objectives in a world of scarce resources than by postulating Chinese acceptance of an Indian sphere of influence. China's objectives in South Asian rank below objectives in other areas and could easily divert resources essential to pursuing those more important objectives. China's limitation of support has also been deeply influenced by hard realities about power. Nepal is a landlocked country, and 99 percent of its trade is with or through India, trade that China could replace only at astronomical costs. Sri Lanka is an island deep in the midst of an Indian sea, while China has only a brown-water navy. Myanmar and Pakistan, however, are far more accessible to Chinese power, and there Beijing has not bowed out in deference to Indian wishes. The situation is more akin to a general's careful selection of the battlefield on which to fight, of careful weighing of anticipated costs and prospects for ultimate success, than to concession of the war to the enemy.

As noted earlier, there was an important shift in Chinese policy in the 1990s, when Beijing signaled that it would no longer take sides in intramural South Asian disputes, that is, disputes between India and other South Asian countries. The most important manifestation of this new Chinese neutrality came on the Kashmir issue, in which, as we have seen, Beijing adopted a neutral position. On lesser issues as well—for example, disputes over use of river waters between Nepal, Bangladesh, and India—China hewed to a similar approach during the 1990s. After 1990 there is no instance of Chinese intervention against India in an intramural South Asian dispute. The shift in China's South Asian policy in the early 1990s was significant but, again, did not constitute a tacit, self-denying sphere of influence arrangement. It appears, rather, that Beijing recognized that its core interests had to do with the expansion of *PRC links* with the countries of South Asia.

China's overriding interest is in the steady expansion of its political, economic, cultural, and military and security ties with its neighbors in South Asia. It has not, and probably will not, countenance the creation of barriers to that expansion. Repeated Chinese intervention in disputes between India and other South Asian countries on the side of India's opponents did not serve China's own major long-term interests. Its siding with other South Asian countries against India encouraged India to view China as hostile. This perception then led India to try to limit the expansion of China's links in South Asia. The growth of Chinese ties in South Asia would be facilitated by convincing New Delhi of China's friendly intentions—as in the 1950s.

When one searches for broad principles that guide China's South Asian policies, one is drawn not to a concept of a sphere of influence but to the Five Principles of Peaceful Coexistence. According to Beijing's interpretation of this doctrine, China and the sovereign nations of South Asia have the right to establish whatever sort of relations they deem appropriate. The relations between China and its sovereign neighbors are justly limited only by the wishes of the governments of those sovereign states. The application of this broad principle is, of course, regulated by the realities of power, the cost of pursuing various policies, and competing policy objectives. But it is the broad Five Principles of Peaceful Coexistence, not agreement to an Indian sphere of influence in South Asia, which guides Chinese behavior in the South Asian region.

A major problem with a sphere of influence arrangement, from China's perspective, is that it could become a factor limiting the expansion of China's South Asian influence. The availability and willingness of China to serve as a counterweight to India is, in fact, a major source of the attractiveness of links with China to South Asian governments concerned with

India's overwhelming presence in the region. One important reason why those governments want to establish or expand ties with China is, in fact, because they hope these ties will offset Indian domination. Links with other countries may, of course, serve the same purpose: with Japan, the United States, Germany, France, Britain, Australia, and so on. But those countries may not be willing to stand up to Indian pressure and continue the relationship in the face of possible Indian objection and hostility. The fact that Beijing is not willing to grant New Delhi such a veto is a major factor making links with China attractive to South Asian governments. At a psychological level of national identity South Asian nations apprehensive about assimilation by an economically and culturally dynamic India may find an association with China more satisfying than links with, say, Japan or Britain, which are less likely to "say no" to India even if doing so creates some tension in its relation with India.

Implicit in all of this is the unspoken awareness that China maintains a large and powerful military presence on India's northern border and has fought one war against India plus several other wars on behalf of smaller, neighboring ally states (Korea in 1950, Vietnam in 1965–67, and Kampuchea in 1979). These military factors need not be spoken about; they loom in the background, unmentioned but understood by everyone. There are no comparable associations and psychological incentives in the case of Japan, Britain, or France, though the United States *may* be an exception. Were Beijing to signal that it was no longer willing to anger New Delhi because of China's links in South Asia, it would forfeit a large amount of political capital in South Asia. If Beijing agreed to abstain from various South Asian links for the sake of respecting India's South Asian security zone, the attractiveness of links with China to South Asian countries apprehensive about Indian domination would diminish. China would recede to a par with Japan or Britain in South Asia.

Chinese acceptance of an Indian sphere of influence in South Asia would limit the growth of Chinese ties there in a more direct way as well: to be meaningful and effectively obviate Indian suspicions, such a sphere would require granting New Delhi the power to approve or reject (or at least to claim a prior consultation with Beijing regarding) China's links with the region. There is a wide range of Chinese activities that India might find objectionable: weapons sales; transfer of military-related or dual-use technologies, especially advanced technologies; probably all cooperation in the nuclear area; construction and/or military utilization of roads, airports, harbors, railways, and telecommunications systems; military training programs; intelligence cooperation; fleet visits; too frequent or otherwise suspicious military exchanges; activities in border, coastal, or other sensitive areas; and so on. Were Beijing to signal its acceptance of New Delhi's right to consultation about such links, it would substantially restrict the development of a wide range of relations with a large swath of Asia. Abstaining from involvement in intramural South Asian disputes and limiting Chinese support to South Asian countries confronting Indian pressure over issues unrelated to ties with China is one thing. Recognizing South Asia as India's security zone, which China has an obligation to respect, is quite another.

Accepting South Asia as an Indian sphere of influence could also encourage greater Indian assertiveness in the region, at least this is how Chinese realists might see it. Being less fearful about negative responses from China, India could become more inclined to use its superior power against other countries there—or so Chinese strategists would probably conclude. Expressions of Chinese anger, combined with even modest negative Chinese demonstrations, focus India's attention and cause it to act with greater circumspection. India also moves more cautiously in South Asia out of a fear that heavy-handedness may push countries there further into alignment with China. If China signals beforehand that it will refuse such alignment, this concern would be lifted from the minds of Indian decision makers, allowing them to act more freely. Behind everything, once again, stands the unspoken but clearly understood reality of Chinese military power. The broader China's security and military links in South Asia—precisely the sort of links India is most likely to object to—the more likely that India will act with caution in the region. South Asian politicians are also encouraged to resist Indian assertions of power because they believe that Chinese power is available and might, under certain circumstances, support them against India. Without such checks New Delhi might well be able to bring a large part of South Asia into some sort of Indian-led bloc. This development could easily hinder the growth of China's links with members of that bloc. It could also signal a shift in the broader balance of power to India's advantage and China's disadvantage.

A top-ranking Chinese objective is to prevent the emergence in Asia of barriers to the gradual, long-term growth of China's presence and role—that is, to the spread of Chinese influence. In the South China Sea, for example, Beijing adamantly opposes multilateral approaches to the disputed ownership of the islets and waters of that region. Regarding the Japan-U.S. alliance, it watches carefully for signs that this relationship is becoming a mechanism for containing China and protests vigorously when such signs are discovered. It uses strong means to block efforts to increase Taiwan's international standing. In South Asia, too, Beijing has no interest in the formation of barriers to the growth of PRC power. Recognizing an Indian sphere of influence would be such a barrier.

PROSPECTS FOR INDIAN ACCOMMODATION
TO A GROWING CHINESE ROLE IN SOUTH ASIA

What, then, of the second possible resolution of Sino-Indian rivalry—that India will accommodate itself to China's gradual but steady expansion in South Asia? Will India conclude that accepting and accommodating China's slowly but inexorably expanding presence in South Asia is imperative? Will India conclude that the costs and dangers of trying to block the expansion of China's South Asian role and position are simply too great? Might India conclude that China is too strong, and India too weak, and thus to be realistic India must accommodate China's steadily growing national power? Having started down this road, would India be willing or able to reverse course? If China expanded its political, military, and economic position in South Asia into the second and third decades of the twenty-first century and India awoke to the reality that China was becoming not simply a major power but perhaps the preeminent power in South Asia, would Indians not conclude that the same arguments that had previously pointed toward accommodation to China's expanding power now make even more sense?

The psychological milieu of such an Indian accommodation to the emergence of China as a major power in South Asia could be either sullen, reluctant acceptance, on the one hand, or a warm, friendly embrace, on the other. In the first case Indians might recognize that it was their own county's weakness and fear of China's superior power which required them to abandon long-cherished dreams of Indian regional preeminence and a global role. Alongside such conclusions might coexist deep resentment of China. In the second case Indians might begin to perceive China as a friendly power, perhaps even as a partner of India in the South Asian region. Indians might come to believe that China was willing and able to work with India to protect India's security and development interests. India would probably be required to renounce its rivalry with China for global status, implicitly acknowledging China as Asia's greatest power and as the primary voice of the non-Western world. In exchange India would receive from China friendship and respect. India would become China's regional partner, working with China to maintain peace and stability in South Asia.

The growing disparity between the national capabilities of China and India, combined with China's growing ability to project its national power into the South Asian region, would probably be key factors impelling India toward accommodation. Comparisons drawn from a data set prepared by the World Bank make clear the extent to which India has fallen behind China over the past two decades.[3] In 1980 India's gross national product at market prices was

133 percent of China's; by 1995 it had fallen to 70 percent of China's. In terms of value added by the manufacturing sector, India stood at 52 percent of China in 1980 but fell to 28 percent by 1995. The comparison for total industrial value added saw roughly the same shift. In terms of gross national savings, India's level in 1980 was 47 percent of China's; by 1995 the figure was 27 percent. In terms of international economic relations, the shifts in China's favor are even more dramatic. In 1980 India had about $79 million in foreign direct investment, while China had none. By 1995 foreign investment in India had increased over twenty-five times, to over $2 billion, but that represented only about 6 percent of China's $35.8 billion foreign investment in that year. In terms of exports, in 1980 India exported 75 percent of what China did. By 1995 it exported 40 percent as much. In terms of imports, India equaled 82 percent of China's 1980 level. By 1995 India imported 46 percent as much as China did. In sum, in terms of the crucial economic base of national power, China is rapidly pulling ahead of India.

India's aggregate military capabilities are also far inferior to those of China, though this deficit has been largely offset by geographic factors. Yet India's traditional geographic advantages are rapidly being diminished by the expansion of Chinese transportation links to South Asia. Finally, India is deeply fearful of China's power. The "lesson" taught by Mao Zedong in 1962 was learned quite well and proved very lasting—just as the lesson learned by the Americans in Korea subsequently led to the United States using far greater caution in dealing with PRC power. And the United States is far more powerful than India.

India is hobbled by its chronic confrontation with Pakistan. At international events Pakistan can be relied on to counter Indian proposals and arguments. India believes itself confronted with a Pakistan-inspired low-cost proxy war waged by terrorists in a half-dozen Indian states. And the most immediate threat to Indian security, and since Pakistan's acquisition of nuclear weapons perhaps the *greatest* threat as well, comes from Pakistan. China, in contrast, has forged predominantly nonconflictual relations with Russia, Japan, and Vietnam. This gives Beijing a far greater degree of confidence and flexibility in dealing with challenges.

India also has few close supporters among the major powers—since the demise of the USSR, really none. The reasons for this are extremely complex. Suffice it to say that India has been unwilling and unable to forge a strategic partnership with the United States or China or even with major second-tier powers like Japan, Germany, or Britain. Beijing, in contrast, has forged a viable strategic partnership with Russia and has undertaken quite effective diplomacy designed to persuade the United States to "engage" rather than "contain"

China. While India has prided itself on nonalignment, China has been a master of maneuvers among the major powers. In the contest for power among nations, diplomatic skill is an important ingredient, and here, too, China seems to have the advantage over India. India also seems to be handicapped by a dearth of strategic thinking. China, by contrast, has a tradition of strategic thought that is second to none in the world. It is arguably the major power best able to think strategically for long periods of time and mobilize the national resources and will needed to attain its postulated strategic objectives.

Finally, India has been unable to formulate a morally appealing rationale for a preeminent Indian role in South Asia: effective power is morally justified power. Yet, in the ROI-PRC rivalry in South Asia, China has captured the moral high ground. The Five Principles of Peaceful Coexistence, with its moral defense of the weak against the strong, is an appealing doctrine to South Asia's smaller states. India has not found an effective counter to China's justification. This is in spite of the distinguishable ideological element of the Sino-Indian rivalry. Indian influence has broadly supported democratic institutions and values. Frequently, those democratic impulses have inspired Indian policies that clash with those of China: in Nepal in 1960–62 and again in 1989–90; in Myanmar in the early 1990s; in Bangladesh in 1971–72; in Sikkim; and in Tibet. While a preference for nondemocratic institutions does not seem to have inspired Chinese policy—except in Tibet—Beijing has often found its closest friends in South Asia among antidemocratic regimes suspicious of Indian influence. Yet India has not been able to capitalize on this ideological dimension to garner support for its international role in South Asia.

These Indian disabilities are severe. They could move India toward accommodation to a growing Chinese presence and ultimately Chinese preeminence in South Asia. This is Beijing's preferred outcome and, I believe, the broad objective of China's diplomacy toward India. Such an outcome also looks rather more likely than that China would accept Indian leadership of the South Asian region. The future is hard to predict, especially when dealing with the diplomatic alignments of complex countries like India and China. Yet, from the perspective of the early twenty-first century, it seems rather more likely that India will accommodate itself to a steadily expanding Chinese presence and role in South Asia than it is that China will accept South Asia as an Indian sphere of influence.

BEIJING'S MANAGEMENT OF CONTRADICTORY POLICY OBJECTIVES

During the post-Mao era Beijing has pursued two broad objectives in South Asia. There is a significant degree of tension between these two policy objectives, and "correct handling of contradictions" between them has required considerable attention and skill. On the one hand, Beijing has sought improved relations with India so as to produce an international environment conducive to China's long-term modernization and security. On the other hand, Beijing has sought to build close, multifaceted relations with *all* the countries of South Asia. India has objected to many of these relationships, especially in the security and military areas, and Beijing's furtherance of these relationships has worked contrary to Sino-Indian amity.

One of the main ways in which Deng Xiaoping reoriented China's foreign policies after Mao's death was by seeking, ceteris paribus, to reduce the conflictual element in China's relations with other countries. Mao had frequently welcomed higher levels of political and even military conflict as useful to achieving his revolutionary objectives. Deng saw such conflict as contrary to the goal of securing the foreign capital, technology, education, and export markets essential for China's modernization. He felt that involvement in avoidable international disputes diverted vital resources that could be going toward the country's pressing development needs. This development-oriented logic pointed first and foremost toward rapprochement with the developed countries, which alone could provide the economic inputs China needed. In the case of Tibet, trade with India (even though it was not a developed country) would clearly play an important role in lifting that region out if its abject poverty. Deng's perspective also pointed toward seeking less conflictual relations with China's neighbors that China might, or might not if China's diplomacy were skillful, have to confront in war. When fundamentally conflicting security or political objectives between China and one of the superpowers made such a development-oriented relationship impossible, China's interests were best served, Deng concluded, by persuading all possible countries, and especially the major countries among China's neighbors, to disassociate themselves from that "anti-China superpower." This, too, pointed toward rapprochement with India. During the 1980s Beijing sought better relations with India as a way of persuading India to disassociate itself from Soviet actions hostile to China. During the 1990s the United States replaced the former USSR as Beijing's major perceived threat, but the same logic impelled Beijing to seek to persuade New Delhi to disassociate itself from the "anti-Chinese policies" of the United States and its Western allies. Beijing's development and security objectives thus converged to propel China toward improving relations with India. In short, Dengist and post-Deng China have desired better relations with India.

There seem to have been two bases for China's drive for expanded ties with India's South Asian neighbors. The first is an amorphous but deeply rooted desire to establish China as a great power in Asia and the world. To be a great power China must have robust, influential relations with the widest possible range of countries. To the extent that China's foreign ties are stunted by foreign powers, it will not be a great power. South Asia is an especially attractive region for establishing robust, multidimensional, influential Chinese links with Asian countries.

In considering the various regions in which China might seek to realize its ambitions of international preeminence, South Asia offers certain distinct opportunities. China's major interests and ambitions lie in East Asia and the West Pacific. But in those regions China comes directly into conflict with Japan and the United States, whose combined power far exceeds China's and will continue to do so for the foreseeable future. In East Asia there are also few opportunities for Chinese exploitation and advance without risk of war or major setbacks to economic growth. In Siberia and (Outer) Mongolia, China confronts a Russian Federation still armed to the teeth with nuclear weapons, which could easily be pushed into alignment with the West, and determined to prevent the undoing of Russia's epic seventeenth-century march to the Pacific Ocean. When approaching Russia, China walks cautiously to avoid pushing that country into alignment with the West and so that "post-Weimar" Russia, if and when that day arrives, does not direct its anger eastward. Southeast Asia probably ranks only below East Asia in terms of the gravity of Chinese interests. But in Southeast Asia China faces deep suspicions among the indigenous nations: Vietnam, Indonesia, the Philippines, Malaysia, among others. The local powers in Southeast Asia could easily unite to block Chinese advances. Japan, the United States, Australia, and Europe are also deeply engaged in Southeast Asia, balancing, diluting, and possibly checking Chinese advances. Central Asia, with its newly independent states, post-communist and secular governments, and extremely rich energy resources, is an area of growing Chinese interest and involvement. But it is also an area very remote from the urban centers of Chinese power, with only embryonic overland transportation links with China and very far from the seas across which the growing PLA might project Chinese power.

South Asia offers China some distinct advantages. Most important, China enjoys the opportunity of playing a liberating, or antihegemonist, role in South Asia. While few countries in Northeast, East, or Southeast Asia would welcome a significantly greater Chinese role, that is not the case in South Asia. In that region there are a dozen smaller countries that chafe to greater or lesser degrees at India's overwhelming presence, perhaps domination, and are happy to see an extra-regional power like China willing to "say no" to India.

A second major motive behind the expansion of China's ties with the South

Asian countries has been to create a balance of power favorable to constraining India. The operative Chinese assumption has been that India has a tendency toward regional hegemonism but can be prevented from acting in a hegemonic way toward its neighbors—including "China's Tibet"—by a balance of power constraining it. Thus, China has fortified its military position on India's northern borders and has demonstrated an ability and willingness to use force in response to unacceptable Indian actions. Beijing has tried to guide developments in the Himalayan kingdoms along lines conducive to a balance of power favorable to the antihegemony forces—building roads that made possible the projection of Chinese military power; drawing Nepal into a military-security relationship with China; dissolving India's "special relations" with Nepal, Bhutan, and Sikkim; developing military relations with Bangladesh and Myanmar; and constructing a potentially dual-use logistic system through Myanmar to the Bay of Bengal. Most important of all was fostering a strong, self-confident Pakistan on India's western flank. American observers are often baffled by China's willingness to foster the emergence of nuclear powers on its own southern borders through its assistance to Pakistan's nuclear program. This is an ethnocentric view. When looked at from China's perspective of constraining India, the nuclearization of Pakistan has worked quite well. The more India is constrained, the less it will be willing and able to act in a hegemonistic fashion. China's sovereignty over Tibet plus the sovereignty of the smaller nations of South Asia would be more secure from Indian interference.

The essence of Beijing's strategic problem in South Asia is how to minimize the contradiction between the push for improved Sino-Indian relations and continual, unlimited expansion of China's ties to other countries of the region. Several Chinese policies help manage this contradiction. One policy might fairly be called "plausible denial." Chinese links to South Asian countries which might be construed as threatening to India are kept covert, thereby rendering them deniable. Chinese representatives thus have a ready, reasonable reply to Indian queries. Some portion of the Indian public will accept China's denial. Indian rejection of China's denial can be blamed on anti-Chinese Western influences, thereby generating pressure on India to prove that it has not been swayed by these Western influences. And the activity can continue without negating the push for better Sino-Indian relations because "it does not exist." Thus, the existence of Chinese assistance to Pakistan's nuclear weapons and missile programs or the intelligence cooperation arrangement with Nepal or PLA involvement with Myanmar's marine telecommunications facilities were denied. With activities that cannot be kept covert, such as arms sales to Nepal or the construction of roads, bridges, and harbors in Myanmar, Beijing categorically denies that these activities have any strategic purpose or significance. Assertions to the contrary are condemned as anti-China or as inspired by sinister Western influences, creating pressure on those raising these objections to prove their friendship toward China and their independence from Western influences.

Probably the most important Chinese policy means for handling this contradiction is incrementalism. The great danger to the expansion of PRC links with South Asian countries is overassertion of Chinese power. By going too far, too fast, China has repeatedly precipitated vigorous Indian countermeasures resulting in major setbacks for China. The two clearest examples of this are East Pakistan in 1970–71 and Nepal in 1988–90. As we have seen, in the late 1960s Beijing and Rawalpindi (then Pakistan's capital) began using East Pakistan as a base of operations for support of insurgencies in India's northeast. The scope of Chinese support to those insurgencies expanded significantly, as did CCP support to the Communist Party of Burma, then engaged in its effort to carve out a people's republic in Upper Burma. In the background was China's ultimatum in support of Pakistan during the 1965 war. These assertions of Chinese power contributed significantly to India's decision to intervene to partition Pakistan, easing the threat to India's northeast presented by the "Beijing-Islamabad axis." The result was a major setback for China. Again in 1988, China moved to inaugurate military links with Nepal via the intelligence cooperation agreement and arms sales, which would have created a very significant beachhead for China in the central Himalayas. India reacted strongly, and again China suffered a major setback.

India's geopolitical advantages over China in South Asia are so great that vigorous assertions of Indian power can be countered by China only at great cost. The one case in which China did override a vigorous Indian assertion of power was in 1962. Had China tried to override India's 1971 and 1990 assertions of countervailing power, the fiscal, human, and political costs would have been at least as great as in 1962, and this was unacceptable. It makes sense that, until China's leaders are willing, or feel compelled, to pay such costs, China's interests are best served by moving slowly and incrementally and under cover of adequate political camouflage, so as not to rouse India to action.

An incremental approach fits well with the mid-level ranking of South Asia in Beijing's global scale of priorities. At the top of China's post–Cold War concerns are relations with the United States. Closely related to this are China's concerns about Japan and Taiwan. Not too far down the ladder are interests relating to the Korean peninsula, Russia, and Southeast Asia. Then come South Asia and the Indian Ocean region. This is not an insignificant ranking. There are several areas of the world weighing *less* heavily on Chinese policy concerns than South Asia: Latin America, Africa, the Middle East, and even Europe. The point, however, is that, since South Asia is not among Beijing's highest priorities, large commitments of resources to that region could interfere with its ability to achieve its interests in higher-priority areas. This suggests that China should move slowly and deliberately. It also means that what happens in other higher-priority areas will affect Beijing's policies in South Asia.

A final diplomatic tactic used by China to reconcile the contradiction between its South Asian objectives is to propose Indian-Chinese partnership against the West. In the 1980s the West took the name of the "wealthy, developed countries." In the post–Cold War era countries of the West were known by such euphemisms as "unipolar bully." The collection of countries referred to in both cases was the alliance of rich, democratic capitalist nations currently headed by the United States.

Beijing stumbled upon this approach in the mid-1950s, when Nehru was enthralled by the idea of Indian-Chinese cooperation in building a new world order and took the initiative in proposing such cooperation. By 1954 Beijing succeeded in persuading New Delhi that the expansion of China's ties with India's South Asian neighbors did not constitute a threat to Indian security— or at least that India should not block the expansion of China's South Asian links. For several years China's ties with South Asian nations grew rapidly (with Nepal, Burma, Pakistan, and Sri Lanka) without Indian opposition. Indian policy shifted in 1959, with the deterioration of PRC-ROI relations, and India became far more vigilant. For the next forty years there was a chronic contradiction between movement toward Sino-Indian rapprochement and the expansion of China's links to South Asia.

As China pushed for rapprochement with India in the late 1980s, Beijing began trying to re-create the "broad cooperation on global issues" which had laid the basis for ROI-PRC alignment in the mid-1950s—and for Indian acceptance of growing Chinese ties to India's neighbors. In the 1950s the burning issues on which the two powers cooperated were peace, nuclear disarmament, and decolonization. In the 1980s comparable issues identified by Chinese analysts included international environmental, trade, and technology transfer issues; increased levels of aid to developing countries; and a restructuring of the international economic order to the benefit of the developing countries. With the international realignments that constituted the end of the Cold War, China began stressing the potential for anti-unipolarity cooperation between China and India.

A high-level Sino-Indian conference in June 1994 provides a good example of this stratagem. Attended by representatives of seven of the PRC's top foreign policy research centers, a central theme of virtually all the Chinese participants was the need, and good prospects, for Indian-Chinese cooperation in creating a new international order. The deputy director general of the China Center for International Studies, Qian Jiadong, for example, maintained that the current system of international law was "formulated in the days of bourgeois revolution" and reflected "the political will of the rich and powerful [countries]." The "old international order" was set up and run by "major western powers," based on "complete disregard of the interests of the broad ranks of colonial and semi-colonial countries," and was a system in which the strong nations "impose their will on weaker nations." What was needed, Qian maintained, was a "new, just and reasonable international order." "Western major powers are now drumming up their assertions that the notion of sovereign rights has become 'obsolete' and that 'human rights should take precedence over sovereign rights, for pursuit of their 'neo-interventionism' in a bid to damage the sovereign rights of small and middle countries and interfere in the internal affairs of developing nations." China and India should work together to produce a new international order targeting such things as terms of trade, debt, "rampant protectionism," and so on.[4] The same theme appeared in virtually all of the Chinese presentations at the conference. Clearly, this was a calculated pitch.

The Indian response to the Chinese invitation to anti-Western cooperation at the June 1994 conference was very instructive. Authoritative Indian representatives said, in effect: Yes, we are aware of the interesting possibilities of Indian-Chinese cooperation and generally agree with what you say about the need to counter Western domination, but let's talk first about issues of concern to India in PRC-ROI relations. Jasjit Singh, the director of the Institute for Defense Studies and Analysis, maintained in his introduction that "the real test of Panchsheel lies in the way India and China structure their bilateral relationship." India, for example, had accepted that Taiwan and Tibet were both parts of China, but China was "yet to fully reconcile to the fact that Sikkim is an integral part of India." The doyen of Indian strategic studies, K. Subrahmanyam, made the same point about Sikkim. He went on to subtly link genuine Chinese acceptance of the principle of equality and mutual benefit as a basis for China's and India's relationship with China's status as a nuclear weapons power and permanent member of the Security Council. Subrahmanyam was implicitly saying that, if China really wanted to base ROI-PRC relations on "Panchsheel" and cooperate against Western hegemonism, it should first demonstrate its good faith by satisfying India on these two critical issues.[5]

INDIA ACCOMMODATES CHINA'S RISE

China's preferred resolution of the ROI-PRC rivalry is that it gradually mutate into a cooperative relationship in the context of steady, unlimited growth of China's links with other countries in the region. Gradually, over a period of decades, China's regional ties will expand greatly. There will be robust transportation links—by air, sea, road, and railway—capable of swiftly carrying large quantities of materiel and men between China and South Asia. Thick cooperative ties will develop between China and countries of South Asia in a wide range of areas. In the security area there will be ties between the PLA and many armed forces of the region. China will be a major supplier of arms, high-tech and otherwise. The PLA will also become more long legged, more capable of sustaining operations in the South Asian region. Naturally, it will engage in friendly exchanges and cooperative activities with the military institutions of South Asian countries. With its considerable economic, political, and military resources and its presence in South Asia, China will be viewed as an important partner in dealing with the security problems of the countries of the region. Politically, China will be an important voice in the region and will use this role to insure that PRC interests are not ignored and to uphold the just interests of its friendly South Asian neighbors. India will become a partner in this arena, working *with China* to uphold peace, justice, and stability in the South Asian–Indian Ocean region.

It is not clear whether India, given its national psychology and character, will accept such an arrangement. Observations based on India's response to date are more feasible. While the outcome of over fifty years of policy conflict between the PRC and the ROI shows gains and setbacks for both sides, broadly speaking, India *has* progressively accommodated itself to the growth of PRC power in the South Asian region. As we have seen, Indian policy was not without successes. India imposed and upheld prophylactic treaties/relationships on Nepal, Bhutan, and Sikkim. In those three Himalayan regions India successfully resisted Chinese advances, although in the case of Bhutan one gets the sense that the development of China-Bhutan relations proceeded faster than New Delhi would have liked. New Delhi also dealt successfully with Chinese-backed insurgencies in its northeast. It intervened decisively to partition Pakistan in 1971, easing the Pakistani-Chinese threat to northeastern India. Indian actions in the late 1980s aborted the emergence of an incipient Chinese–Sri Lankan military relationship, yet, in Bangladesh, India watched helplessly as a robust Sino-Bangladeshi military relationship burgeoned in the late 1970s and waxed throughout the 1980s. After the Bangladesh election of 1996, Dhaka moved to restore more cordial ties with India. It is difficult to conclude that this was a result of Indian diplomatic efforts, how-ever, and seems to have been more a fortuitous gift of fortune to India.

In the larger, more crucial arenas of Tibet, Pakistan, and Myanmar, Indian policies ultimately failed to check Chinese advances. Instead, India progressively accommodated itself to the growth of a dense Chinese security presence. As our earlier review of Indian policy toward Tibet showed, Indian policy sought to uphold the integrity of Tibet's Indian-influenced civiliza-tion and limit the degree to which Tibet would become a platform for China's military power. Both elements of this policy failed. India responded to that failure, very broadly speaking, by gradually accepting the reality of Chinese control of Tibet. Tibet has been transformed into a military bastion ever more closely tied to the military infrastructure of China proper. The road, rail, air, and telecommunication links between Tibet and China proper have become steadily more dense, and Han settlement is rapidly changing the character of that region irrevocably. Tibetan civilization is rapidly disappearing and will probably exist in several decades primarily in books, tourist centers, and a few remote pockets. Tibet will truly become an "integral part of China" with a largely Han population engaged in lifestyles not very different from those in the heartland of China. India has been unable to alter this development and seems generally inclined to adjust to it.

On India's western flank New Delhi was unable to prevent, and learned to live with, the quasi-alliance between China and Pakistan. After 1965 and again after 1971, India watched passively as China helped rebuild Pakistan's shattered military power and morale, helping Pakistan become, once again, India's nemesis in a variety of deadly ways. After 1974 India again watched impotently as evidence mounted of covert Chinese assistance to Pakistan's nuclear weapons and missile programs. Again, after a long period of inef-fectual protest, India chose to accommodate a nuclear-armed and China-aligned Pakistan. In spite of the modifications in Sino-Pakistan relations in the 1990s, the Sino-Pakistan military link remains deep and strong. India has been unable to find a solution to this two-front threat. Instead, it has cho-sen to live with it.

On India's geopolitically sensitive eastern flank, in Myanmar, again India watched with dismay but without an effective response during the 1990s as Myanmar abandoned the traditional Burmese policy of strict neutrality between China and India and, instead, engaged in a close military-political relation with China. Under that new relation China has built a strong mili-tary and logistical presence in Myanmar. India could not find an effective policy to counter these PRC thrusts. Indian concern was eased by the fiscal difficulties encountered by Beijing in the late 1990s—but, as in the case of

Bangladesh's reorientation at about the same time, this was a fortuitous gain for India and not due to India's own efforts. India responded to the Sino-Myanmar entente by shifting policy to woo Yangon. It also responded to the growing Chinese involvement in Burma's maritime sector by strengthening its naval presence in the Andaman Islands. Again, the pattern seems to be one of India responding to, accommodating, the expansion of the Chinese presence, rather than of finding an effective way to thwart the growth of that presence.

The contrast between New Delhi's handling of its rapprochement with Beijing and Beijing's earlier handling of its rapprochements with Washington in the 1970s and with Moscow in the 1980s is very instructive. In dealing with Washington, Beijing set out a list of demands regarding the core issue of Taiwan and refused to move forward with normalization until Washington more or less conceded those demands.[6] In moving toward normalization with the USSR in the 1980s, Beijing once again demanded Soviet satisfaction on core security issues having to do with Soviet support for Vietnam's occupa-tion of Kampuchea, Soviet occupation of Afghanistan, and the Soviet mili-tary presence on China's northern borders, including Mongolia. Eventually, Gorbachev met these demands, and Sino-Soviet normalization moved for-ward. Prior to the mid-1980s India's approach to normalizing relations with China was somewhat similar, with New Delhi insisting that China satisfy Indian demands regarding the boundary as a precondition for full normal-ization. Given the mounting evidence of Chinese assistance to Pakistan's nuclear program during this period, the focus on the boundary was narrow. Even these narrow demands were dropped after the mid-1980s, and New Delhi unconditionally moved forward with Sino-Indian rapprochement. New Delhi periodically protested Chinese assistance to Pakistan's nuclear programs but apparently laid out no clear demands to China in this regard as related to progress in Sino-Indian rapprochement. Ultimately, New Delhi was satis-fied by modest shifts in China's formal stance on the Kashmir issue. Chinese assistance to Pakistan's strategic weapons programs continued unimpaired by Sino-Indian rapprochement (though it was conducted covertly). By the time of the Kashmir crisis of 1999, India had even begun to look to Beijing as a part-ner in dealing with an adventurous and now nuclear-armed Pakistan. Having found itself incapable of preventing Beijing from creating a balance of power in South Asia designed to constrain India, India began inviting China to play a role in achieving India's objectives within that balance.

A sense of strength and confidence underlay Beijing's handling of rap-prochement with Washington and Moscow. The overriding Chinese senti-ment in dealing with both superpowers seems to have been that China could afford to wait until the superpowers accepted China's terms. Sooner or later the superpowers' need for China would bring them to accede to China's core demands. Until then China could afford to wait. New Delhi's handling of rapprochement with Beijing, in contrast, seems to have been underlaid by a sense of weakness and helplessness. The dominant Indian sentiment seems to have been that India did not really have very much leverage vis-à-vis China, and thus there was really not much reason to expect China to feel compelled to accede to Indian demands. Moreover, the costs and risks of continuing tense relations with China were simply too great for India to bear. Thus, while Beijing secured from both superpowers its core demands, India normalized relations with China without receiving anything in return on the border, Tibet, or Myanmar and only minor shifts in Chinese policy toward Kashmir. There was chronic conflict between Indian and Chinese policy in Tibet, Pakistan, and Myanmar, but in the end, when China persisted, India acquiesced or protested ineffectually. If the trends of the latter half of the twentieth century continue into the first decades of the new century, China's presence will continue to grow in South Asia. As China's political influence and military presence expands, the nations of South Asia will increasingly look to China to help mediate disputes and solve problems. India itself may begin to look on China as a security partner in South Asia.

One critical variable influencing the future development of the ROI-PRC relationship will be shifts in Indian thinking. A number of Indian analysts perceive significant changes in Indian thinking during the 1990s about India's approach to foreign affairs. The traditional Indian approach stressed idealism and morality grounded in Mahatma Gandhi's powerful spiritual message. This idealistic approach, put into practice by Nehru, stressed the paramount role of public opinion and principle in constraining the exercise of power and viewed foreign policy as essentially a quest to build a more just world. Nehruvianism, as it came to be called, also had a strong sympathy for the world's "progressive" forces, including the USSR, and a visceral suspicion of the Western nations that had long exercised imperial dominion over the nonwhite world. Toward the United States Nehru combined the ideological prejudices of the British Labor Party with the cultural distaste for American vulgarity of the English aristocracy. This approach was shaken by the 1962 war and was often paralleled by hardheaded practical policies, but until the 1990s it was never reevaluated at a fundamental—that is, philosophical—level.[7]

The outcome of the Cold War was not what Indian idealists had expected. The "progressive" ideas dear to much of the Indian intelligentsia were dramatically rejected by those who were actually subjected to those ideas. India

lost its major backer when the USSR disappeared. It found itself in a paradoxical situation of being "the world's largest democracy" yet feeling pecu-
liarly uncomfortable about the dramatic victory of the alliance of democratic
countries in the protracted global struggle that dominated the post-1945 world.
There were probably few celebrations in India when the Berlin Wall fell. The
end of the East-West Cold War polarity, plus the immense economic and
ideological appeal of the victorious Western alliance to many developing countries, also raised questions about the continuing relevance and effectiveness
of "nonalignment." China's rapid rise in economic and military power and
in international status raised further questions. It gradually became apparent that China was the new number 2 power in the post–Cold War world and
seemed to be on a trajectory for even greater things. This steadily more powerful China also showed every intention of expanding its links in South Asia
and the Indian Ocean.

As these trends unfolded, realistic voices became more prominent in India's
debate about its role in the world. These people argued, of course, that the
essence of foreign policy should be the promotion of a nation's own interests through the most efficacious means available. They looked back on the
track record of Indian idealism and found it gravely inadequate by this standard. They called for increased attention to the instruments of Indian
national power and far greater thought about how these instruments could
be used effectively to serve Indian interests.

There is not a simple correlation between Indian realism and the perceived
threat from China and Indian idealism and antipathy to the West. The situation is far more complex than that. Some of India's most prominent realists stress the threat to India from the United States. The late chief of staff K.
Sunderji, for example, advocated Indian nuclearization as necessary to deter
a U.S. attack on India.[8] On the idealist side there are many individuals whose
great concern for Tibet leads them to a deeply skeptical view of China. In
spite of these qualifications, however, it is fair to say that, by and large, Indian
realists are more concerned with China's "strategic encirclement" and advocate more vigorous Indian countermeasures. Idealists tend to be concerned
with Western domination and exploitation and to be sympathetic to Chinese
calls for Indian-Chinese cooperation to counter these evils. As of the turn of
the century, realists still hold a minority point of view among India's elite.
Throughout the 1990s, however, they became more articulate and influential. Realism also dominated in certain centers of military and civilian decision making and therefore had a disproportionate influence on Indian policy.
The evolution of this debate in the years ahead will deeply influence the course
of PRC-ROI relations. The debate between Indian idealism and realism will

also be deeply influenced by the policy behavior of China toward India and South Asia.

The evolution of Sino-Indian relations will also be deeply influenced by China's relations with the United States and Japan. Chinese concerns regarding those two countries rank far higher than any Chinese concerns in South Asia. At the top of China's foreign policy agenda in the late 1990s was managing the contradictory objectives of avoiding military-political confrontation with the United States while preventing "Taiwan independence." Just below that objective was preventing the reemergence of Japan as a major military and political power in Asia. Continuing difficulties in these areas could well lead China to be more solicitous of India in its concerns about Chinese moves in South Asia. Even then, it remains an open question whether India will have the skill and confidence to utilize this leverage effectively vis-à-vis China. If China is successful in accomplishing its objectives regarding Taiwan and the South China Sea, it might increase its activity in the Indian Ocean region. If Taiwan were under PRC control, the Chinese could turn their attention and resources from the western Pacific to other areas. In the South China Sea, if Beijing secures control of Spratly Island from Vietnam and Taiping Island from Taiwan—the two islands in the Spratly archipelago large enough for airfields for fixed-wing aircraft—the PLAN will have substantially enhanced capabilities. A new era of Chinese maritime activity in the Indian Ocean region could well follow.

More broadly, if China is able to sustain into the first quarter of the new century rates of growth approximating those of the last two decades of the twentieth century, India will feel the heat of growing Chinese national capabilities. Unless India is able to alter its lackluster development record and to work out a skilled and confident program employing Indian national capabilities in the South Asian region, India could well conclude that the prudent way to enhance its security is to assume a role as junior partner to an emerging Chinese superpower.

Notes

1 / SINO-INDIAN RELATIONS

1. See John W. Garver, "The Indian Factor in Recent Sino-Soviet Relations," *China Quarterly*, no. 125 (summer 1991): 55–85. Surjit Mansingh and Steven I. Levine, "China and India: Moving beyond Confrontation," *Problems of Communism* 38 (May–June 1989), 30–49.

2. Wang Hongwei, "Gong jian mian xiang 21 shiji jianshexing hezuo huoban guanxi" (Jointly build relations of constructive cooperative partnership facing the 21st century), *Waiguo wenti yanjiu* (International studies), no. 1 (gen. issue no. 46) (1997): 37–41. Regarding the attribution of India's fears of China to the views of Western elements "hostile to China," which I expect to be a common reaction to this book among Chinese readers, I might as well address the matter here. There may in fact be a tendency for Indian (or Chinese) scholars to pay attention to the conclusions of American scholars for a combination of valid and ill-founded reasons. In my own experience, however, this tendency is more than offset by a deep suspicion among Indians that the United States wants to exacerbate Indian-Chinese tensions to serve the purposes of U.S. global strategy. Indian analysts are quite independent minded and very critical.

3. Ministry of Defence, Government of India, *Annual Report 1997–98* (New Delhi: Government of India, 1997), 2.

4. M. D. Nalapath, "China Confident of Positive Ties with India," *Times of India*, September 10, 1998.

5. See *Beijing Review*, July 5, 1999, 15.

6. George Tanham, "Indian Strategic Culture," *Washington Quarterly* (winter 1992): 129–42.

7. *Asian Relations, Being a Report of the Proceedings and Documentation of the First Asian Relations Conference*, New Delhi, March–April 1947 (New Delhi: Asian Relations Organization, 1948), 302–10.

8. Central Intelligence Agency, *People's Republic of China: Atlas* (Washington, D.C.: Government Printing Office, 1971), 75.

9. Raju G. C. Thomas, *Indian Security Policy* (Princeton: Princeton University Press, 1986), 14. See also Surjit Mansingh, *India's Search for Power: Indira Gandhi's Foreign Policy, 1966–1982* (New Delhi: Sage, 1984). Tanham, "Indian Strategic Culture."

10. Devin T. Hagerty, "India's Regional Security Doctrine," *Asian Survey* (April 1991): 351–63.

11. Tanham, "Indian Strategic Culture," 133.

12. Jaswant Singh, *Defending India* (London: Macmillan, 1999).

13. James Clad, "A Calming Influence," *Far Eastern Economic Review* (March 15, 1990): 29. Shakhar Gupta, *India Redefines Its Role* (London: Institute of International and Strategic Studies, 1995), 52–56.

14. I. K. Gujral, *The Progressive Prime Minister* (New Delhi: Kanishka Publishers, 1997). For a critical view, see J. N. Dixit, *Across Borders: Fifty Years of India's Foreign Policy* (New Delhi: Picus Books, 1998), 217–22.

15. *Zhong Yin bianjiang ziwei fanji zuozhanshi* (History of the Sino-Indian war of self-defensive counter-attack) (Beijing: Junshi kexue chubanshe, 1994), 37–41.

16. Xu Yan, *Zhong Yin bianjie zhi zhan lishi zhenxiang* (True history of the Sino-Indian border war) (Hong Kong: Cosmos, 1993), 28–30. The author, one of China's foremost military historians, is a professor at China's National Defense University.

17. Speech by President Jiang Zemin, December 2, 1996, in *Strategic Digest* 27, no. 1 (January 1997): 17–20.

18. *Area Handbook for the People's Republic of China* (Washington, D.C.: Government Printing Office, 1972), 15–16.

19. For biographies of Patel and other Indian leaders mentioned, see Surjit Mansingh, *Historical Dictionary of India* (London: Scarecrow Press, 1996), 317–19.

20. Patel's letter is reproduced in L. L. Mehrotra, *India's Tibet Policy* (New Delhi: Tibetan Parliamentary and Policy Research Centre, 1998), 44–48.

21. Sujit Dutta, "China's Emerging Power and Military Role: Implications for South Asia," in *In China's Shadow: Regional Perspectives on Chinese Foreign Policy and Military Development,* ed. Jonathan D. Pollack and Richard H. Yang (Santa Monica: RAND, 1998), 91–114.

22. Colonel Gurmeet Kanwal, "China's Long March to World Power Status: Strategic Challenge for India," *Strategic Analysis* (New Delhi) 22, no. 11 (February 1999): 1713–28.

2 / THE TIBETAN FACTOR IN SINO-INDIAN RELATIONS

1. Regarding the contours of Tibetan civilization, see R. A. Stein, *Tibetan Civilization* (London: Faber, 1971); originally published in French in 1961.

2. Morris Rossabi, *Khubilai Khan: His Life and Times* (Berkeley: University of California Press, 1988), 143–45. Melvyn C. Goldstein, *The Snow Lion and the Dragon: China, Tibet, and the Dalai Lama* (Berkeley: University of California Press, 1997), 1–29. Hugh E. Richardson, *A Short History of Tibet* (New York: H. P. Dutton, 1962), 32–36.

3. John F. Avedon, *In Exile from the Land of Snows* (New York: Knopf, 1984), 41.

4. Mao Zedong, "On the Ten Great Relationships," April 25, 1956, in *Chairman Mao Talks to the People; Talks and Letters: 1956–1971,* ed. Stuart Schram (New York: Pantheon Books, 1974), 74.

5. "Adhere to the Four Basic Principles," in *Deng Xiaoping wenxuan* (Selected works of Deng Xiaoping), *China Report: Political, Sociological, and Military Affairs, Joint Publication Research Service* (hereafter JPRS), no. 84651, October 31, 1983, 127; emphasis added.

6. *World Development Report: Knowledge for Development, 1998–99* (Washington, D.C.: World Bank, 1998), 204–5.

7. *The Europa World Year Book, 1998* (London: Europa Publishers Limited, 1998), 1:896–99.

8. Tsering Shakya, *The Dragon in the Land of Snows: A History of Modern Tibet since 1947* (London: Pimlico, 1999), 518 n. 72.

9. "Tibet Vice Chairman on Development Plans," *Beijing Review,* no. 30 (July 27–August 2, 1998): 11–14. See also Chinese Academy of Social Sciences, *Information China* (Oxford: Pergamon Press, 1989), 1:37.

10. Pui-kwan Tse, "The Mineral Industry of China," in *Mineral Yearbook,* Mineral Industries of Asia and the Pacific (Washington, D.C.: U.S. Department of the Interior, Bureau of Mines, 1989), 3:67–90.

11. "Resource Prospecting in Tibet Stepped Up," *China Daily,* May 9, 1992, 2. Regarding uranium mining in Tibet, see *Nuclear Tibet: Nuclear Weapons and Nuclear Waste on the Tibetan Plateau* (Washington, D.C.: International Campaign for Tibet, 1993), 40–42.

12. L. L. Mehrotra, *India's Tibet Policy* (New Delhi: Tibetan Parliamentary and Policy Research Centre, 1998), 1–4. Mehrotra served from 1961 to 1976 in the Indian foreign service, much of that time dealing with Tibetan and Chinese affairs.

13. Tsepon W. D. Shakabpa, *Tibet: A Political History* (New Haven: Yale University Press, 1967), 303; emphasis added.

14. *Dalai Lama and India* (New Delhi: Hind Book House, 1959), 77–78, 107–8. The first quote is from March 30, 1959 , the second from April 5, 1959.

15. Luciano Petech, *China and Tibet in the Early XVIIIth Century: History of the Establishment of the Chinese Protectorate in Tibet* (Leiden, Netherlands: Brill, 1972), 67–74.

16. Goldstein, *Snow Lion and Dragon,* 26–29. Shakabpa, *Tibet,* 216–45.

17. *Tibet: Proving Truth from Facts* (Dharmsala: Department of Information and International Relations, 1996), 99. This is Dharmsala's response to *Tibet: Its Ownership and Human Rights Situations* (Beijing: State Council Information Office, 1992).

18. Melvyn C. Goldstein, *A History of Modern Tibet, 1913–1951: The Demise of the Lamaist State* (Berkeley: University of California Press, 1989), 564–65; emphasis added. Goldstein uses this quote to argue that India broke decisively in 1947 with the British policy. It seems to me, however, that considerable evidence, including this very quote, suggests that Nehru continued the policy of upholding Tibetan autonomy, albeit not at the cost of relations with China.

19. K. P. S. Menon, *Many Worlds: An Autobiography* (London: Oxford University Press, 1965), 270. Quoted in Yun-yuan Yang, "Controversies over Tibet: China versus India, 1947–49," *China Quarterly*, no. 111 (September 1987): 407–20.

20. Shakya, *Dragon in Land of Snows*, 12–13.

21. Goldstein, *History of Modern Tibet*, 564.

22. Ibid., 562.

23. *Tibet since the Asian Relations Conference* (New Delhi: Tibetan Parliamentary and Policy Research Centre, 1998), 1. This publication shows the objectionable map, a list of participants, and coverage and commentary by the Indian press at the time of the conference.

24. Shakya, *Dragon in Land of Snows*, 12–13. Goldstein stresses the small amounts of these arms deliveries plus their complete inadequacy for the needs of Tibet as demonstrating India's abandonment of the British policy of support for Tibet's autonomy.

25. Yang Gongsu, *Xin Zhongguo dui wai zhengce yu waijiao shilu (1949–1982)* (Foreign relations and diplomatic practice of new China [1949–1982]), MS, 44. Yang Gongsu was foreign affairs assistant to General Zhang Jingwu when the latter was dispatched to Lhasa as the representative of the central government in 1951. He later helped negotiate the 1954 Sino-Indian agreement on Tibet. Still later he served as China's ambassador to Nepal.

26. Shakya, *Dragon in Land of Snows*, 24–25.

27. Mao Zedong, *Jianguo yilai Mao Zedong wengao* (Documents of Mao Zedong since the founding of the country) (Beijing: Zhongyang wenxian chubanshe, 1987), 1:208–9.

28. *Liushi nian da shiji (1927–1987)* (Major developments over sixty years [1927–1987]) (Beijing: Junshi kexue chubanshe, 1988), 495. Yang Yizhen, "Jin jun Xizang jishi" (Record of the military movement into Tibet), *Zhonggong dangshi wengao nian kan* (Yearbook of materials on CCP history) (Beijing: Renmin chubanshe, 1985), 399–400.

29. B. N. Mullik, *My Years with Nehru: The Chinese Betrayal* (Bombay, London, and New York: Allied Publishers, 1971), 63.

30. *Jianguo yilai Mao Zedong wengao*, 1:627–28.

31. The text of the Indian notes and China's response is in R. K. Jain, *China South Asian Relations, 1947–1980* (New Delhi and Brighton: Harvester Press, 1981), 1:23–47.

32. I have written about this in *The Sino-American Alliance: Nationalist China and U.S. Cold War Strategy in Asia* (Armonk, N.Y.: M. E. Sharpe, 1997).

33. Shakya, *Dragon in Land of Snows*, 22–24.

34. Jain, *China South Asian Relations*, 1:41–47.

35. Mullik, *My Years with Nehru*, 80–81.

36. Dalai Lama, *My Land, My People* (New York: McGraw Hill, 1962), 85–86.

37. Shakabpa, *Tibet*, 302–4.

38. The text of the agreement is in Shakya, *Dragon in Land of Snows*, 449–52.

39. On these and other issues related to Indian-U.S. relations during the Korean War, see Dennis Kux, *India and the United States: Estranged Democracies* (Washington, D.C.: National Defense University Press, 1992), 72–78.

40. John Rowland, *A History of Sino-Indian Relations: Hostile Coexistence* (Princeton, N.J.: Van Nostrand, 1967), 76–84.

41. Yang Gongsu, *Xin Zhongguo dui wai zhengce*, 56–57.

42. Mullik, *My Years with Nehru*, 157.

43. For the text of the agreement, see Jain, *China South Asian Relations*, 61–67.

44. J. N. Dixit, *Across Borders: 50 Years of India's Foreign Policy* (New Delhi: Picus, 1998), 354.

45. R. K. Karanjia, *The Mind of Mr. Nehru* (London: George Allen and Unwin, 1960), 83.

46. Mullik, *My Years with Nehru*, 181–83.

47. Yang Gongsu, *Xin Zhongguo dui wai zhengce*, 65–66.

48. John K. Knaus, *Orphans of the Cold War: America and the Tibetan Struggle for Survival* (New York: Public Affairs, 1999), 138–55.

49. Regarding the brutal means used in this counterinsurgency program, see *Tibet and the Chinese People's Republic: A Report to the International Commission of Jurists by Its Legal Inquiry Committee on Tibet* (Geneva: International Commission of Jurists, 1960).

50. Girilal Jain, *Panchsheel and After: A Reappraisal of Sino-Indian Relations in the Context of the Tibetan Insurrection* (Bombay: Asia Publishing House, 1960). See also Frank Moraes, *The Revolt in Tibet* (Calcutta: Srishti Publications, 1998).

51. "The Truth about How the Leaders of the CPSU Have Allied Themselves with India against China," *Peking Review*, no. 45 (November 8, 1965).

52. Steven A. Hoffman, *India and the China Crisis* (Berkeley: University of California Press, 1990), 37–38.

53. Knaus, *Orphans of the Cold War*, 248–58.

54. Leo E. Rose, *Nepal: Strategy for Survival* (Berkeley: University of California Press, 1971), 94.

55. *Mao Zedong sixiang wansui* (Long live Mao Zedong thought), in "Miscellany of Mao Tse-dong Thought (1949–1968)," pt. 2, no. 61269 (February 20, 1974), *Joint Publication Research Service*, 573.

56. Wang Hongwei, "Zhong Yin bianjie wenti lishi beijing yu 1962 nian Zhong Yin bianjie zhanzheng" (Background history of the Sino-Indian border and 1962 border war), *Ya Tai ziliao* (Asia-Pacific materials), no. 1 (March 18, 1989): 1–13.

57. *Zhong Yin bianjing ziwei fanji zuozhan shi* (China's war of self-defense counter attack with India) (Beijing: Academy of Military Sciences, 1994), 37–41.

58. Xu Yan, *Zhong Yin bianjie zhi zhan lishi zhenxiang* (True history of the Sino-Indian border war) (Hong Kong: Cosmos Books, 1993), 27–28.

59. The Indian view is very different. Nehru rebutted Chinese accusations during his Lok Sabah testimony in March–April 1959. See *Dalai Lama and India.*

60. Yang Gongsu, *Xin Zhongguo dui wai zhengce*, 68–69. The events described by Yang cannot be confirmed, and Yang is certainly not an impartial source. We can, however, take Yang's account as describing the *Chinese view* of Indian policy.

61. Yang Gongsu, *Xin Zhongguo dui wai zhengce*, 71–74.

62. *Zhou Enlai waijiao wenxuan* (Collection of Zhou Enlai's diplomatic documents) (Beijing: Zhongyang wenxian chubanshe, 1990), 268–76.

63. Knaus, *Orphans of the Cold War*, 287.

64. Avedon, *Exile*, 121–22.

65. Satyanarayan Sinha, *Operation Himalaya: To Defend Indian Sovereignty* (New Delhi: S. Chand, 1975).

66. Mullik, *Chinese Betrayal*, 571.

67. Knaus, *Orphans of the Cold War*, 271–73.

68. *Almanac of World Military Power*, ed. T. N. Dupuy and Wendell Blanchard (New York: Bowker, 1972), 317–21. *World Armies*, ed. John Keegan (New York: Facts on File, 1979), 313–14.

69. Avedon, *Exile*, 129–30.

70. Thomas J. Wersto, "Tibet in Sino-Soviet Relations," *Asian Affairs* 10, no. 3 (fall 1983): 70–85.

71. *Peking Review*, no. 50 (December 10, 1971): 7–8.

72. Hollis S. Liao, "Communist China's Policy toward Tibet," *Issues and Studies* 17, no. 1 (January 1981): 26.

73. Victor Louis, *The Coming Decline of the Chinese Empire*, with a dissenting introduction by Harrison Salisbury (New York: Time Books, 1979), v, xv, xvii.

74. IDR research team, "Studies in Low-Intensity Conflict: The Tibetan Rebellion," *Indian Defense Review* (New Delhi) (July 1988): 67–75.

75. Regarding the changes of the Deng era, see Goldstein, *Snow Lion and Dragon*,

61–99; Shakya, *Dragon in Land of Snows*, 374–411; Dawa Norba, *Red Star over Tibet* (New York: Envoy Press, 1987), 253–66, 285.

76. *International Resolutions and Recognitions on Tibet (1959 to 1997)* (Dharmsala, India: Department of Information and International Relations, 1997).

77. The classic study of this process is C. P. Fitzgerald, *The Southern Expansion of the Chinese People* (Canberra: Australian National University, 1972).

78. *Tibet—Its Ownership and Human Rights Situation*, 39.

79. President Jimmy Carter, personal communication with the author, May 11, 1999. See also Xinhua, June 29, 1987, in *Foreign Broadcast Information Service, Daily Report, China* (hereafter *FBIS, DRC*), June 30, 1987, B3–5.

80. Tibet Support Group, U.K., *New Majority: Chinese Population Transfers into Tibet* (London: Tibet Support Group, 1995).

81. "Tibet's Today and Tomorrow," *Beijing Review*, no. 20 (July 27–August 2, 1998): 11–14.

82. *FBIS, DRC*, December 23, 1988, 12; emphasis added.

83. Ibid., December 16, 1991, 21.

84. Discussions in New Delhi, February–April 1999.

85. An organizational chart of the Tibetan exile government is in *Tibet's Parliament in Exile* (New Delhi: Tibetan Parliamentary and Policy Research Center, 1996), 32–33.

86. Interview with former Chinese consul to India from 1984–87, Foreign Affairs College, Beijing, April 1990.

87. Sujit Dutta, "Sino-Indian Relations: Some Issues," *Strategic Analysis* 11, no. 11 (February 1988): 1261.

88. E.g., see Brahma Chellaney, "The Dragon Next Door," *Hindustan Times* (New Delhi), April 3, 1998; "The Politics of Flattery," *Jansatta*, Nov. 20, 1996, in *Foreign Broadcast Information Service—Near East South Asia (FBIS-NESA)*, 96–226; Rakshat Puri, "Perspective on Tibet," *Hindustan Times*, Nov. 27, 1996, in *FBIS-NESA*, no. 96-231.

89. Rajinder Puri, "The Great Leap Forward," *Illustrated Weekly of India*, November 17, 1985, 57.

90. Shubha Singh, "Strengthening Bilateral Ties," *Pioneer*, November 21, 1996, 9, in *FBIS-NESA*, no. 96-226.

91. "Tibet Policy Ignored to Allow Hunger Strike," *Asian Age*, April 28, 1998. See also Seema Mustafa, "Effect of Tibet Issue on India Ties Noted," *Asian Age*, April 30, 1998, in *FBIS-NESA*, no. 98-120.

92. AFP, Hong Kong, October 22, 1998, in *FBIS, DRC*, no. 98-295.

93. Personal communication from Tibetan Parliamentary and Policy Research Centre, New Dehli, June 9, 1999.

94. "India for China Dalai Talks," *Hindustan Times* (Patna), October 29, 1998.

95. Xinhua, December 25, 1998, *FBIS, DRC*, no. 98-360.

96. Zhang Wenmu, "Issue of South Asia in Major Power Politics," *Ta kung pao,* September 23, 1998, in *FBIS, DRC,* no. 98-293.

3 / THE TERRITORIAL DISPUTE

1. Other scholars have made this point and noted the special significance of the Aksai Chin road in this regard. See Allen S. Whiting, *The Chinese Calculus of Deterrence: India and Indochina* (Ann Arbor: University of Michigan Press, 1975); Neville Maxwell, *India's China War* (Garden City, N.Y.: Anchor Books, 1972).

2. A good topographical map of the Aksai China road is available in *Zhonghua Renmin Gongheguo guojia putong dituji* (Compilation of ordinary maps of the People's Republic of China) (Beijing: Zhongguo ditu chubanshe, 1995), 176–77.

3. *World Atlas of Agriculture,* Asia and Oceania (Rome: Committee for World Atlas of Agriculture, 1973), 2:82–83; *The Times Atlas of China* (New York: Time Newspapers Ltd., 1974), xx–xxi.

4. Yang Gongsu, *Xin Zhongguo dui wai zhengce yu waijiao shilu (1949–1982)* (Foreign relatons and diplomatic practice of new China, 1949–1982), MS. For Yang's background, see chap. 2, n. 25.

5. *Liushi nian dashiji (1927–1987)* (Major developments of sixty years, 1927–1987) (Beijing: Junshi kexue chubanshe, 1988), 542–43; hereafter cited as *Liushi nian dashiji.*

6. Yang Gongsu, *Xin Zhongguo dui wai zhengce.*

7. Tom Grunfeld, *The Making of Modern Tibet* (Armonk, N.Y.: M. E. Sharpe, 1987), 110–11, 118.

8. *Shi nian minzu gongzuo chengjiu, 1949–1959* (Ten years of achievement in nationalities work, 1949–1959) (Beijing: Minzu chubanshe, 1959), 860.

9. *Dangdai Xizang* (Contemporary Tibet) (Beijing: Dangdai Zhongguo chubanshe, 1991), 1:132.

10. Yang Gongsu, *Xin Zhongguo dui wai zhengce.*

11. *Liushi nian dashiji,* 542–43, 656–57, 678–79.

12. *China Daily,* May 2, 1992, 3.

13. *Jiefangjun bao,* October 11, 1994, *FBIS, DRC,* November 1, 1994, 41.

14. Steven A. Hoffmann, *India and the China Crisis* (Berkeley: University of California Press, 1990), 13–28, 35–36.

15. See sources cited in chap. 2, nn. 55–56.

16. *Documents on the Sino-Indian Boundary Question* (Beijing: Foreign Languages Press, 1960), 1–13.

17. "Arunachal Pradesh," http://www.indiagov.org. See also J. N. Chowdhury, *Arunachal Pradesh: From Frontier Tract to Union Territory* (New Delhi: Cosmo Books, 1983), 43–45.

18. *South Asian Mineral Yearbook: 1988* (Washington, D.C.: U.S. Department of Interior, Bureau of Mines, 1988), 352.

19. P. S. Dutta, "Flaming Frontiers and Burning Peripheries: Understanding Insurgency in the North-East," in *The Turbulent North-East,* ed. Prosenjit Chowdhury and Metabuddin Ahmed (New Delhi: Aksan Publishers, 1996), 85–120; Subhir Bhaumik, *Insurgent Crossfire: North East India* (New Delhi: Lancers, 1996).

20. Bertil Lintner, "The Long Fight for Freedom," *Far Eastern Economic Review* (hereafter cited as *FEER*), August 21, 1986, 24–25.

21. Bertil Lintner, "The Turbulent Tribes," *FEER*, August 21, 1986, 22–23.

22. Unless otherwise indicated, the discussion of Chinese links to Indian insurgencies comes from Subir Bhaumik, "The External Linkages in Insurgency in India's Northeast," in *Insurgency in North-East India,* ed. P. Pakem (New Delhi: Omeons Publications, 1997), 89–100; Bertil Lintner, "Appendix: Missions to China by Insurgents from India's North-East," in Surjit Mansingh, *Indian and Chinese Foreign Policy in Comparative Perspective* (New Delhi: Radiant Publishers, 1998), 433–38. Bhaumik's study is based on extensive interviews with former rebel leaders, military and intelligence reports, and interrogation reports.

23. Jaswant Singh, *Defending India* (London: Macmillan Press, 1999), 142.

24. *Keesings Contemporary Archive* 27, no. 43 (1981): 31153.

25. See "Yindu assamu bang weihe dongluan?" (What accounts for the instability in India's Assam state?), *Renmin ribao,* June 5, 1980, 7.

26. Bhaumik, "External Linkages."

27. *Renmin ribao,* April 23, 1987, 1, and April 26, 1987, 6.

28. Regarding the 1987 crisis, see Manoj Joshi, "Situation on the Sino-Indian Border," *Mainstream,* May 30, 1987, 4; Jari Lindholm, "The Dragon's Teeth," *India Today,* August 15, 1987, 82–84; "No Passage," *Far Eastern Economic Review,* July 23, 1987, 7.

29. B. Sarkar, *Pakistan Seeks Revenge and God Saves India: A Study of Indo-Pak Conflicts* (New Delhi: Batra Book Service, 1997).

30. Administrative Reform Commission, *Report of Study Team on Administration of Union Territories and North East Frontier Agency* (New Delhi) 1 (n.d.): 42.

31. Detailed coverage of Zhou's press conference and the implicit proposal of an East-West swap is in Maxwell, *India's China War,* 161–69.

32. Hoffmann, *India and the China Crisis,* 86–87.

33. *Foreign Broadcast Information Service, Daily Report, China* (hereafter *FBIS, DRC*), June 25, 1980, F1.

34. *FBIS, DRC,* June 25, 1980, F1–2.

35. Xu Yan, *Zhong Yin bianjie zhi zhan lishi zhenxiang* (True history of the Sino-Indian border war) (Hong Kong: Cosmos Books, 1993), 54.

36. Cited in Nevil Maxwell, *India's China War,* 164.

37. Hoffmann, *India and the China Crisis*, 80–81, 86–87.

38. *Keesings Contemporary Archive* 27, no. 43 (1981): 31153.

39. A. G. Nooroni, personal communication with the author, Bombay, 1986.

40. Author's discussions of Sino-Indian relations with Chinese analysts, officials, and retired diplomats, Beijing, April–May 1990.

41. Shen Chun-ch'uan, "Peking–New Delhi Relations in Recent Years," *Issues and Studies* 22, no. 3 (March 1986): 141–52.

42. Chandan Mitra, "Chinese Position Seems to Have Hardened," *Statesman Weekly*, June 7, 1986, 2.

43. Jing Wei, "You guan Zhong Yin bianjie zhengduan de yi xie qingkuang he beijing" (Some background and situations regarding the Sino-Indian border conflict), *Guoji wenti yanjiu* (International studies), no. 2 (April 1986): 1–8. This article was probably the talking paper used by the Chinese side in the sixth round of talks.

44. Mitra, "Chinese Position Seems to Have Hardened."

45. Author's discussion with high-ranking Indian official in Beijing, May 1990.

46. Chamdrika Singh, *Emergence of Arunachal Pradesh as a State* (New Delhi: Mittal Publishers, 1989), 126–56.

47. *Renmin ribao*, December 12, 1986, 1.

48. Ibid., February 22, 1987, 1.

49. *Wen wei bao, FBIS, DRC*, December 15, 1986, F1.

50. Wang Hongwei, "Yindu dui Hua zhengce de tiaozheng yu wofang duice de jianyi" (Adjustments in India's policy toward China and proposals regarding China's response), *Ya Tai ziliao* (Materials on Asia and the Pacific) (Beijing: Chinese Academy of Social Sciences, 1989).

51. The English translation is from the text of Zhou's letter printed in *Documents on the Sino-Indian Boundary Question* (Beijing: Foreign Languages Press, 1960, 7).

52. Yang Gongsu, *Xin Zhongguo dui wai zhengce*, 119–23, 128.

4 / SINO-INDIAN RIVALRY FOR INFLUENCE AND STATUS AMONG DEVELOPING COUNTRIES

1. Quoted in Nicolas Mansergh, *The Commonwealth and the Nations* (London: Royal Institute of International Affairs, 1948), 100, 110–16.

2. Chen Jian, *China's Road to the Korean War: The Making of the Sino-American Confrontation* (New York: Columbia University Press, 1994); Shu Guang Zhang, *Mao's Military Romanticism: China and the Korean War, 1950–1953* (Lawrence: University of Kansas Press, 1995).

3. R. K. Karanjia, *The Mind of Mr. Nehru* (London: George Allen and Unwin, 1960), 91.

4. Carlos P. Romulo, "Nationalism, Non-Alignment, and World Order," *Indian and Foreign Review* (New Delhi) 1 (April 15, 1964): 10–12.

5. "Mao Tse-tung's 'Trimetrical Classic,'" *Chinese Law and Government* 9, nos. 1–2 (spring–summer 1976): 7–11.

6. Miloslav Krassa, "The Idea of Pan-Asianism and the Nationalist Movement in India," *Archiv Orientalni* (Prague) 40 (1972): 238–60.

7. Surjit Mansingh, *Historical Dictionary of India* (London: Scarecrow Press, 1996), 414–15.

8. "Asian Conference and Asia's Future," *China Digest* (Hong Kong) 5, no. 8 (February 8, 1949): 13.

9. Ibid.

10. Sergei N. Gancharov, John W. Lewis, and Xue Litai, *Uncertain Partners: Stalin, Mao, and the Korean War* (Stanford, Calif.: Stanford University Press, 1993), 65, 71–72, 108.

11. Zhai Qiang, "Transplanting the Chinese Model: Chinese Military Advisors and the First Vietnam War, 1950–1954," *Journal of Military History*, no. 57 (October 1993): 692–99.

12. Kuo-kang Shao, "Chou En-lai's Diplomatic Approach to Non-aligned States in Asia: 1953–60," *China Quarterly*, no. 78 (June 1979): 324–38.

13. Mohammed Yunus, *Reflections on China: An Ambassador's View from Beijing* (Lahore: Wajidalis Ltd., 1986), 102.

14. Miloslav Krasa, "Three Main Stages in the Development of Sino-Indian Contacts during the Indian Freedom Movement," *Archiv Orientalni* 49, no. 3 (1981): 240–44.

15. Regarding India's objections to the treaty, see *Foreign Relations of the United States* 6 (1950): 1379–83; and 11 (1952–54): pt. 2, 1115.

16. George M. Kahin, *The Asian-African Conference, Bandung, Indonesia, April 1955* (Ithaca, N.Y.: Cornell University Press, 1956), 6.

17. Unless otherwise indicated, this discussion of Bandung is drawn from Kahin's study. Kahin personally observed the conference and spent several months interviewing delegates and governmental officials about it.

18. Carlos P. Romulo, *The Meaning of Bandung* (Chapel Hill: University of North Carolina Press, 1956), 10–21.

19. Kahin, *Asian-African Conference*, 29, 25.

20. Peter Willetts, *The Non-Aligned Movement: The Origin of a Third World Alliance* (London: Frances Pinter, 1978), 5–7.

21. Regarding the radical shift in Chinese foreign line and policy in the late 1950s, see John W. Garver, *Foreign Relations of the People's Republic of China* (Englewood Cliffs, N.J.: Prentice Hall, 1993), 127–41.

22. For an authoritative example of this analysis, see He Fang, "You guan dang-

qian minzu duli yundong de jige wenti" (On several problems facing the nationalist independence movement), *Guoji wenti yanjiu,* no. 3 (July 3, 1959): 10–19.

23. B. D. Arora, *Indian-Indonesian Relations, 1961–1980* (New Delhi: Asian Educational Service, 1981), 209.

24. "Make the Anti-Imperialist, Anti-Colonialist United Front Still Stronger," *Peking Review,* September 15, 1961, 5–7.

25. J. Nehru, "Changing India," *Foreign Affairs* 41, no. 3 (April 1963): 453–65.

26. "Sino-Indonesian Joint Statement," *Peking Review,* April 26, 1963, 11–12.

27. "India's 'Non-Alignment': What Does It All Add Up To?" *Peking Review,* December 28, 1962, 8–10.

28. Unless otherwise indicated, the following discussion of Chinese-Indonesian-Indian interactions is from Arora, *Indian-Indonesian Relations.*

29. *Afro-Asian Solidarity against Imperialism—A Collection of Documents, Speeches, and Press Interviews for the Visit of Chinese Leaders to Thirteen African and Asian Countries* (Beijing: Foreign Languages Press, 1964), 439.

30. *Proceedings of the Meeting of Ministers in Preparation of the Second African-Asian Conference, Djakarta, Indonesia, 10–15 April 1964,* Organizing Committee. Djakarta: Organizing Committee of the Conference, 1964.

31. Arora, *Indian-Indonesian Relations,* 175–77.

32. Sukarno, "Address to the Second Conference of Non-Aligned Countries, Cairo, October 6, 1964 (full text)," *The Era of Confrontation* (Djakarta: Department of Foreign Affairs of the Government of the Republic of Indonesia, n.d.), cited in Arora, *Indian-Indonesian Relations,* 175.

33. "Sheep's Head and Dog's Meat," *Peking Review,* October 16, 1964, 16.

34. "World Opinion on Non-Aligned Conference," *Peking Review,* October 23, 1964, 14–15.

35. Guy J. Pauker, "The Rise and Fall of Afro-Asian Solidarity," *Asian Survey* 5, no. 19 (September 1965): 425–32.

36. Kapileshwar Labh, "Intra-Non-Aligned Discords and India," *India Quarterly* 38, no. 1 (January–March 1982): 64–77.

37. "Chairman of Delegation of the People's Republic of China Teng Hsiao-ping's Speech at the Special Session of the United Nations General Assembly," *Peking Review,* supplement to no. 15 (April 12, 1974): i–iv.

38. Jayantanuja Bandyopadyaya, "The Non-Aligned Movement and International Relations," *India Quarterly* 33, no. 2 (April–June 1977): 137–64.

39. *FBIS, DRC,* August 16, 1976, A2–3.

40. Ibid., August 16, 1976, A3–5.

41. "Conference of Foreign Ministers of Non-Aligned Countries: An Important Session," *Peking Review,* no. 32 (August 11, 1978): 20–22.

42. "A Critical Test for the Non-Aligned Movement," *Beijing Review,* no. 25 (June

22, 1979): 19–20; see also "What Should the Non-Aligned Movement Do?" *Beijing Review,* no. 30 (July 28, 1980): 12–13.

43. "Foreign Minister's Address to Non-Aligned Coordinating Bureau," *Foreign Affairs Record* (May 1976): 142–46.

44. Samuel S. Kim, "China and the United Nations," in *China Joins the World: Progress and Prospects,* ed. Elizabeth Economy and Michel Oksenberg, 48–49 (New York: Council on Foreign Relations Press, 1999).

45. David Malone, "The UN Security Council in the Post–Cold War World: 1987–97," *Security Dialogue* 28, no. 4 (1997): 393–408.

46. M. H. Ansari, "Democratizing the Security Council," in *The United Nations at Fifty: An Indian View,* ed. Satish Kumar, 205–22 (New Delhi: UBS Publisher, 1995).

47. Prime Minister I. K. Gujral's Address to the 52d sess. of the UN General Assembly, September 24, 1997; "Discover India," http://www.meadev.m/un; see also Statement by Kamalesh Sharma of India, December 4, 1997, in General Assembly Press Release GA/9372.

48. Interview with author, T. P. Sreenivasan, deputy chief of mission, Indian Embassy, Washington, D.C., November 17, 1998. Sreenivasan was head of India's delegation to the OEWG.

49. Statement by H. E. Shri Pranab Mukherjee, 49th sess. of UN General Assembly, New York, 3 October 1994.

50. Barbara Crossette, "U.S. Bending a Bit, Will Offer Wider Role for 3rd World at U.N.," *New York Times,* July 17, 1997, 14.

51. Statement by Kamalesh Sharma of India, December 4, 1997, UN General Assembly press release.

52. General Assembly press release, GA/9509, November 20, 1998.

53. "Statement by External Affairs Minister in Both Houses of Parliament on 5 December 1996 on the Visit of the President of the People's Republic of China to India," *China Report* 33, no. 2 (April–June 1997): 238–40.

54. Kim, "China and the United Nations."

55. "Tang Reviewing Change in Current International Situation," *Beijing Review,* October 12–18, 1998, 6–8.

56. Foreign Minister Tang Jiaxuan in his September 23, 1998, speech, for instance, says that Security Council reforms should be based on "considerations of history." This is probably an allusion to Japan's aggression in the 1930s and 1940s. There were no such allusions to India in Tang's speech, made five months after India's nuclear tests.

5 / INDIAN-CHINESE RIVALRY IN NEPAL

1. Leo E. Rose, *Nepal: Strategy for Survival* (Berkeley: University of California Press, 1971).

2. See the maps showing the scope of the Yuan realm in Tan Qixiang, *Jianming Zhongguo lishi dituji* (Concise historical atlas of China) (Beijing: Zhongguo ditu chubanshe, 1996), 57–58, 59–60.

3. Leo E. Rose, personal communication with author, April 5, 1999.

4. T. R. Ghoble, *China-Nepal Relations and India: New Delhi* (New Delhi: Deep and Deep, 1991), 19–33; Leo E. Rose, "Sino-Indian Rivalry and the Himalayan Border States," *Orbis* 5 (1961): 198–215; Rose, *Strategy for Survival*, 52–65.

5. The text of the treaty and ancillary letters is in Raj Kumar Jha, *The Himalayan Kingdoms in Indian Foreign Policy* (Ranchi, Bihar: Maitryee Publications, 1986), 347–50.

6. B. L. Sukhwal, *Modern Political Geography of India* (New Delhi: Sterling, 1985), 349.

7. Jawaharlal Nehru, *India's Foreign Policy: Selected Speeches, September 1946–April 1961* (New Delhi: Publications Division, 1971), 436.

8. A list of these concessions is in *India News*, Embassy of India, Beijing, May 2, 1989.

9. M. D. Dharamdasani, "Zone of Peace: Nepal's Quest for Identity," *China Report* 15, no. 5 (October 1979): 12–19.

10. *India News*, May 2, 1989.

11. Ghoble, *China-Nepal Relations and India*. For a Chinese view that is essentially similar, see Wang Hongwei, "Sino-Nepal Relations in the 1980s," *Asian Survey* 25, no. 5 (May 1985): 512–20.

12. Unless otherwise indicated, the following analysis of Chinese-Nepali-Indian relations through 1978 is drawn from Ghoble, *China-Nepal Relations and India*.

13. Quoted in Rose, *Strategy for Survival*, 206.

14. Yang Gongsu, "Xin Zhongguo duiwai zhengce yu waijiao shilu (1949–1982)" (New China's foreign policy and diplomatic practice [1949–1982]), MS; see also interviews with both Yang Gongsu and Zhang Wenjin, Beijing, May 1990.

15. Alexander Eckstein, *Communist China's Economic Growth and Foreign Trade* (New York: McGraw-Hill, 1966), app. E, 501.

16. Rose, *Strategy for Survival*, 212–14.

17. "High Himalayans: A Computer Generated Landscape Portrait," map, National Geographic Society, November 1988.

18. Rama Swarup, "Red China Builds a Bridge to Nepal," *Issues and Studies* (Taipei) 4, no. 1 (October 1967): 15–18.

19. Meeting between Mao Zedong and Nepali delegation, August 29, 1964, *Mao Zedong sixiang wansui* (Long live Mao Zedong thought) (August 1969): 573; published in *Miscellany of Mao Tse-tung Thought (1949–1968)*, 2 pts. (Arlington, Va.: Joint Publications Research Service, 1974).

20. Yang Gongsu, *Xin Zhongguo duiwui zhengce*.

21. *Survey of China Mainland Press*, no. 2835, 34.

22. Swarup, "Red China Builds a Bridge," 15.

23. Regarding the 1965 letters, see *Asian Recorder*, August 27–September 2, 1989, no. 20740-42.

24. S. D. Mundi, "India and Nepal: Erosion of a Relationship," *Strategic Analysis* 12, no. 4 (July 1989): 341–64.

25. Bishwa Pradham, *Nepal: A Peace Zone* (Kathmandu: Durga Devi Pradhan Publishers, 1982); M. D. Dharamdasani, "Zone of Peace: Nepal's Quest for Identity," *China Report* 15, no. 5 (October 1979): 12–19.

26. John F. Copper, "China's Foreign Aid in 1978," University of Maryland Law School, Occasional Papers in Contemporary Asian Studies 29, no. 8 (1979): 20.

27. From *Statesman* (New Delhi), reported in *Asian Recorder*, May 21–27, 1981, 16039.

28. Leo E. Rose, "India's Foreign Relations: Reassessing Basic Policies," in *India Briefing*, ed. Marshall Bouton, 51–75 (Boulder: Westview Press, 1990), 63.

29. Muni, "Erosion of a Relationship," 348.

30. S. D. Muni, "Chinese Arms Pour into Nepal," *Times of India*, September 1, 1988.

31. *Renmin ribao*, March 18 and 19, 1988.

32. *South China Morning Post*, May 26, 1990, 10; *Times of India*, September 1, 1988, May 31, 1989; *Organizer* (New Delhi), August 21, 1988.

33. *India Today* (Bombay), December 15, 1987, 83.

34. *Pakistan Times* (Karachi), April 15, 1989; *Hindustan Times*, July 29, 1988.

35. *Organizer*, August 21, 1988.

36. *Hindu* (Madras), September 24, 1988.

37. *Telegraph* (Calcutta), May 3, 1990; Far Eastern Economic Review, *Asia Yearbook, 1990*, 186–87.

38. Leo E. Rose, personal communication with author, April 5, 1999.

39. *India News*, Embassy of India, Beijing, March 27, 1989, no. 7/89.

40. Regarding the evolution of Indo-Nepali trade and transit arrangements, see Martin Ira Glassner, "Transit Problems of Three Asian Land-Locked Countries: Afghanistan, Nepal, and Laos," Occasional Papers / Reprint Series in Contemporary Asian Studies, School of Law, University of Maryland, 1983, 4, no. 57, 19–34.

41. *India News*, Embassy of India, Beijing, May 2, 1989, no. 12/89.

42. *Gulf News* (Dubai), March 28, 1989.

43. See Abdul Majid Khan, "The Indo-Nepal Dispute," *Regional Studies* (Islamabad) 8, no. 2 (spring 1990): 87; Khalid Mahood Malik, "Indo-Nepal Relations since 1962," *Regional Studies* 7, no. 4 (fall 1989): 65–97; *Asian Recorder*, June 25–July 1, 1989, 20644–45; Far Eastern Economic Review, *Asia Yearbook, 1990*, 187.

44. *Gulf News*, May 11, 1989; *Pakistan Times*, April 17, 1989; *Muslim* (Islamabad), April 19, 1990.

45. Ren Yujun, "Will Nepal-Indian Relations Improve?" *Beijing Review*, July 24–30, 1989, 15–16.

46. *FBIS, DRC,* October 16, 1989, 7.

47. Ibid., November 20, 1989, 20–21.

48. United Nations General Assembly, provisional verbatim record of the twenty-first meeting, 44th sess., October 12, 1989, 97–98.

49. Ibid., provisional verbatim record of the twelfth meeting, 44th sess., 38–53.

50. *FBIS, DRC,* November 21, 1989, 12.

51. Ibid., November 20, 1989, 20–21.

52. Ibid., November 16, 1989, 8–9.

53. Ibid., May 31, 1989, 23.

54. For examples of this argument, see Amar Zutshi, "Nepal Alienating India to Preserve Monarchy?" *Times of India,* May 31, 1989, 3; Lok Raj Baral, "Triangular Relations," *Seminar* (Bombay), no. 274 (June 1982): 20–26; Parminder S. Bhogal, "Indian Security Environment in the 1990s: The South Asian Factor," *Strategic Analysis* (New Delhi) 12, no. 7 (October 1989): 772; Mundi, "India and Nepal," 361.

55. *Zheng ming,* no. 151 (May 1990): 18.

56. *Renmin ribao,* April 13, 1990, 4.

57. Ibid., May 3, 1990.

58. *South China Morning Post* (Hong Kong), May 26, 1990, 10.

59. *Link* (New Delhi), June 24, 1990, 6; *Telegraph* (Calcutta), June 11, 1990.

60. *Link,* June 24, 1990, 6.

61. *FBIS, DRC,* April 17, 1989, 22.

62. *Statesman* (New Delhi), June 11, 1990.

63. Leo E. Rose, "Nepal and Bhutan in 1998," *Asian Survey* 39, no. 1 (January–February 1999): 155–62.

6 / SIKKIM AND BHUTAN

1. Tan Qixiang, *Jianming Zhongguo lishi dituji* (Concise historical atlas of China), sponsored by the Chinese Academy of Social Sciences (Beijing: China Cartographic Publishing House, 1991). This atlas is based on a longer, eight-volume series.

2. Leo E. Rose, personal communication with author, August 12, 1999.

3. Regarding the evolution of Sikkim's government, see Leo E. Rose, "Modernizing a Traditional Administrative System, 1890–1973," *Himalayan Anthropology: The Indo-Tibetan Interface,* ed. James Fisher, 205–26 (The Hague: Mouton, 1978).

4. B. S. Das, *The Sikkim Saga* (New Delhi: Vikas, 1983), Das was the Indian political officer in Sikkim at the time of its incorporation into India in 1974–75.

5. Satyendra R. Shukla, *Sikkim: The Story of Integration* (New Delhi: S. Chand and Co., 1976), 246–49.

6. George McTurnan Kahin, *The Asian-African Conference, Bundung, Indonesia, April 1955* (Ithaca: Cornell University Press, 1956), 7.

7. Das, *Sikkim Saga,* 23; Surjit Mansingh, *India's Search for Power,* 76.

8. "China Letter to Sikkim Improper," *Patriot* (New Delhi), March 4, 1964.

9. A detailed account of the fighting is in G. S. Bajpai, *China's Shadow over Sikkim: The Politics of Intimidation* (New Delhi: Lancer Publishers, 1999).

10. *Facts on File, 1967* (New York: Facts on File, Inc. 1967), 432; Suresh Chopra, "Battle of the Barbed Wire," *Patriot,* September 13, 1987.

11. Shulka, *Story of Integration,* viii, 206.

12. Leo E. Rose, "Sino-Indian Rivalry and the Himalayan Border States," *Orbis* 5 (1961): 198–215.

13. Hem Lall Bhandari, "Sikkim: The Sore Still Festers," *Lex Et Juris* 1, no. 4 (August 26, 1986), special supplement, n.p.

14. Das, *Sikkim Saga,* vi, 13–19, 30, 46–48.

15. Statement of the Ministry of Foreign Affairs of the People's Republic of China, September 11, 1974, *Peking Review,* September 20, 1974, 14.

16. Das, *Sikkim Saga,* 61; Shukla, *Story of Integration,* 207.

17. Wang Wenjing, "1641–1793 nian Zhongguo Xizang yu Zemengxiong (Xijin) de guanxi," (Relations between China's Tibet and Sikkim, 1641–1793), *Zhongguo Zangxue* (Chinese Tibetology) 7, no. 3 (1989): 118–28.

18. Premier Zhou Enlai's letter to Prime Minister Nehru, September 8, 1959, in *Documents on the Sino-Indian Boundary Question* (Beijing: Foreign Languages Press, 1960), 7.

19. *Zhongguo waijiao gaijian* (Chinese diplomatic almanac) (Beijing: Shijie zhishi chubanshe), 1988, 1989, 1991, and 1994. (This is the publishing house affiliated with the Ministry of Foreign Affairs.)

20. *The Statesman, Asian Recorder,* May 21–27, 1981, 16036.

21. *China Report* 33, no. 2 (April–June 1997): 238–39.

22. Jasjit Singh, ed., *India, China and Panchsheel* (New Delhi: Sanchar Publishing House, 1996), 8. The conference was held in June 1994 with the Inaugural Address given by Prime Minister P. V. Narasimha Rao.

23. The text of the treaty and ancillary notes is in Manorama Kohli, *From Dependency to Interdependency: A Study in Indo-Bhutan Relations* (New Delhi: Vikas, 1993), 231–35.

24. Leo E. Rose, personal communication with author, April 5, 1999.

25. B. S. Das, *Mission to Bhutan: A Nation in Transition* (New Delhi: Vikas Publications, 1995), 12. Das was India's "special officer" in Bhutan from 1968 to 1972. After his assignment to Bhutan he served in Sikkim. Das observed this was India's first official reference to Bhutan's "independence."

26. Nari Rustomji, *Bhutan: The Dragon Kingdom in Crisis* (New Delhi: Oxford University Press, 1978).

27. S. D. Muni, "Sino-Bhutanese Boundary Talks," *Indian Express* (New Delhi), June 12, 1984.

28. Meenakshi Misra and R. C. Misra, "Bhutan's Foreign Policy in the New Context," in *Bhutan, Society and Polity*, ed. Ramakant and R. C. Misra (New Delhi: Indus, 1996), 274–84.

29. Lal Babu Yadov, *Indo-Bhutan Relations and China Interventions* (New Delhi: Anmol Publications, 1996), 60.

30. Das, *Mission to Bhutan*, 40.

31. Rose, "Sino-Indian Rivalry and the Himalayan States," 199.

32. Rustomji, *Dragon Kingdom*, 77, 137.

33. Das, *Mission to Bhutan*, 44–45, 50, 63–64, 89.

34. Rustomji, *Dragon Kingdom*, 27–28, 103–4; statement by Shri Samar Sen, February 10, 1971, *Foreign Affairs Record* 17, no. 2 (February 1971): 29–30.

35. Das, *Mission to Bhutan*, 86.

36. Rahimullah Yusafzai, "Indo-Bhutanese Relations: Bhutan's Quest for an International Role," *Regional Studies* (Islamabad) 3, no. 1 (winter 1984): 11–49.

37. Li Liaowen and Li Dechang, "Lun Budan zhengqu guojia zhuquan de duozheng" (On Bhutan's struggle for national sovereignty), *Nan Ya janjiu ziliao* (Materials on South Asia research) 5, no. 5 (1979): 11–15; Yusafzai, "Bhutan's Quest," 26.

38. Xinhua, June 7, 1974, in *Survey of People's Republic of China Press* (hereafter cited as *SPRCP*), June 17–21, 1974, nos. 74-25, 75-76.

39. Sujrit Mansingh, "China-Bhutan Relations," *China Report* 30, no. 2 (1994): 179.

40. Meenakshi Misra and R. C. Misra, "Bhutan's Foreign Policy in the New Context," 281; Yusafzai, "Bhutan's Quest," 26–27.

41. *Far Eastern Economic Review 1981 Yearbook*, 110.

42. Kohli, *From Dependence to Interdependency*, 157.

43. S. D. Muni, "Sino-Bhutanese Boundary and Implications for India," *Mainstream*, June 14, 1986, 18–20; Kohli, *From Dependency to Interdependency*, 159, 162–65.

44. *Renmin ribao*, April 4, 1982, 6.

45. *Asian Recorder* 21, no. 9, 18213-14; and 21, no. 28 (9–15 July 1985): 18388.

46. Sino-Bhutan interactions are chronicled annually in the almanac published by China's Ministry of Foreign Affairs, *Zhongguo waijiao gaijian* (Almanac of China's diplomacy) (Beijing: Shijie zhishi chubanshe).

47. Parmanand, "China and Bhutan, Border Dispute Unresolved Yet," *Statesman*, August 2, 1997.

48. Surjit Mansingh, "China-Bhutan Relations," 177. The quote is from a February 1993 speech by Cheng Ruisheng, China's ambassador to India. For other expressions of Indian apprehensions regarding China's intentions in Bhutan, see Parmanand,

"Bhutan Today—II"; Kohli, *From Dependency to Interdependency*, 165; Syed Sikander Mehdi, "Bhutan and Its Strategic Environment," *Strategic Analysis 7*, no. 2 (winter 1998): 72–87.

7 / THE SINO-PAKISTANI ENTENTE CORDIALE

1. J. P. Jain, *China, Pakistan and Bangladesh* (New Delhi: Radiant, 1974); Anwar H. Syed, *China and Pakistan: Diplomacy of an Entente Cordiale* (Amherst: University of Massachusetts Press, 1974); Yaacov Vertzberger, *The Enduring Entente: Sino-Pakistani Relations, 1960–1980* (New York: Praeger, 1982).

2. S. M. Burke, *Pakistan's Foreign Policy* (London: Oxford University Press, 1973), 213.

3. I owe this point to Stephen P. Cohen, "Geostrategic Factors in India-Pakistan Relations," *Asian Affairs* 10, no. 3 (fall 1983): 24–31, 28.

4. *Almanac of China's Foreign Economic Relations and Trade, 1997–98* (Beijing: China National Economy Publishing House, 1997), 461–69.

5. William J. Barnds, "China's Relations with Pakistan: Durability amidst Discontinuity," *China Quarterly*, no. 63 (September 1975): 463–89.

6. Syed, *China and Pakistan*, 55.

7. George McTurnan Kahin, *The Asian-African Conference, Bandung, Indonesia, April 1955* (Ithaca: Cornell University Press, 1956), 57–58; Jain, *China, Pakistan and Bangladesh*, 25; Syed, *China and Pakistan*, 55–62.

8. Burke, *Pakistan's Foreign Policy*, 215.

9. Geng Biao, "Tuidong Zhongguo he Bajisitan guanxi chuan xiang youhao fazhan de jice zhongyao waijiao xingdong" (Several major activities promoting the development of Chinese-Pakistani friendship), *Xin Zhongguo waijiao fengyun* (Diplomatic currents of new China) (Beijing: Shijie zhishi chubanshe, 1991), 2:57–63.

10. Haider Khan, "Pak-China Relations, 1959–1966," *Central Asia* (Peshawar) 10 (summer 1982): 171–98; Barnds, "China's Relations with Pakistan," 471.

11. W. M. Dobell, "Ramifications of the China-Pakistan Border Treaty," *Pacific Affairs* (Vancouver, B.C.) 37 (fall 1964): 284.

12. Russell Brines, *The Indo-Pakistani Conflict, 1965* (London: Pall Mall, 1968); see also Burke, *Pakistan's Foreign Policy*, 275–357. Much of the following discussion of the 1965 war is from Brines and Burke.

13. Brines, *Indo-Pakistan Conflict*, 211.

14. Burke, *Pakistan's Foreign Policy*, 293.

15. George McTurnan Kahin, *The Asian-African Conference, Bandung*, 57–58; Jain, *China, Pakistan and Bangladesh*, 25; Syed, *China and Pakistan*, 55–62.

16. G. W. Choudhury, *India, Pakistan, Bangladesh, and the Major Powers* (New York: Free Press, 1975), 183–85.

17. Regarding the Kashmir issue, see Sumit Ganguly, *The Origins of War in South Asia: Indo-Pakistan Conflicts since 1947* (Boulder: Westview Press, 1986).

18. Mohammed Musa, *My Version: India-Pakistan War, 1965* (Lahore: Wajidalis, 1983), 2–6. Musa was commander of the Pakistan army in 1965. He says that the army, and he personally, argued against the plan on the basis that successful conduct of guerrilla war takes elaborate and careful preparation and that India was likely to respond with a general, conventional attack on Pakistan, which, of course, turned out to be the case. See also, Brines, *Indo-Pakistan Conflict*, 301–3; Burke, *Pakistan's Foreign Policy*, 326–28.

19. Burke, *Pakistan's Foreign Policy*, 297.

20. Intelligence Information Cable, May 14, 1965, Central Intelligence Agency, IDCS-314/06391-65. Obtained by author via Freedom of Information Act (FOIA) request.

21. Choudhury, *India, Pakistan, Bangladesh*, 184.

22. Xinhua, June 2, 1965, in *Survey of the China Mainland Press* (hereafter *SCMP*), no. 3472, 33; Xinhua, 28 March 28, 1965, in no. 3429, 39–40.

23. Musa, *My Version*, 27.

24. Brines, *Indo-Pakistan Conflict*, 302, 306.

25. *Dangdai Zhongguo waijiao* (Contemporary Chinese diplomacy) (Beijing: Dangdai Zhongguo chubanshe, 1987), 151–53, 173–86.

26. Xu Yan, *Zhong Yin bianjie zhi zhan lishi zhenxiang* (True history of the Sino-Indian border war) (Hong Kong: Cosmos Books, 1993), 215–16.

27. Indonesia, where China clandestinely supplied weapons to radical military elements in early 1965 to arm the Communist-led militia, may have been still another. See U.S. Central Intelligence Agency, *Indonesia: 1965, the Coup That Backfired*, research study (Washington, D.C.: Central Intelligence Agency, 1968), 130, 173–74. It was against this background of Chinese support for revolutionary wars in Vietnam, Kashmir, and Indonesia that Mao ordered the all-out effort to prepare China for war with the Third Front movement in mid-1965.

28. *Renmin ribao*, June 3, 1965, in *SCMP*, no. 3473, 27–29.

29. Xinhua, June 3, 1965, in *SCMP*, no. 3473, 29–30.

30. *SCMP*, no. 3535, 37–38; *SCMP*, no. 3535, 33–34.

31. *SCMP*, no. 3536, 31–32.

32. *SCMP*, no. 3536, 42.

33. Choudhury, *India, Pakistan, Bangladesh*, 189.

34. *SCMP*, no. 3537, 30–31.

35. *SCMP*, no. 3539, 29–30.

36. CIA, Intelligence memorandum, October 14, 1965, SC 10519/65. Obtained by author via FOIA request.

37. CIA, Intelligence memorandum, "Growing Chinese Communist Deterrent Pressure on India," September 8, 1965, SC 08115/65. Obtained by author via FOIA request.

38. Special National Intelligence Estimate, "Prospects of Chinese Involvement in the Indo-Pakistan War," September 16, 1965, SNIE 13-10-65. Obtained by author via FOIA request.

39. *Foreign Relations of the United States, 1964–1968,* vol. 3: *China* (Washington, D.C.: U.S. Government Printing Office, 1989), 203.

40. *SCMP,* no. 3541, 30–32. The note was delivered by the deputy director of the Asian Affairs Department of the MFA, Yang Gongsu.

41. CIA, Intelligence memorandum, September 15, 1965, SC 10509/65. Obtained by author via FOIA request.

42. *Jianguo yilai Mao Zedong wengao* (Correspondence of Mao Zedong since the founding of the nation) (Beijing: Zhongyang wenxian chubanshe, 1996), 11:461–62.

43. *SCMP,* no. 3543, 29–32.

44. Xu Yan, *Zhong Yin bianjie zhi zhan,* 215.

45. Ibid.

46. Brines, *Indo-Pakistan Conflict,* 373–75.

47. Choudhury, *India, Pakistan, Bangladesh,* 190–91. Choudhury describes his research into China's diplomacy during the 1965 war: "In preparing this account, I read, most carefully, minutes of the wartime discussions between Ayub and Bhutto and the Chinese Ambassador to Pakistan, between Chou [Enlai] and Liu [Shaoqi] and the Pakistani ambassador to China; between Ashgar Khan and Chinese leaders; and between Ayub—who like Ashgar, flew to Peking in the heat of crisis—and Mao, Chou, and Liu, and Chinese military chiefs. After his retirement in 1969, I questioned Ayub at length about his secret mission to China. I read the diplomatic cipher messages exchanged daily between Peking and Rawalpindi during the war. As a member of the Cabinet . . . I conducted lengthy interviews with the top Pakistani military and civilian leaders who made the war's crucial decisions" (197–98).

William Barnds, based largely on Choudhury's testimony, agrees with the conclusion that China was ready to enter the 1965 conflict. An older view, presented by W. F. Griffith shortly after the war, maintained that China's actions of September 17–22 were largely a bluff. China was determined not to become involved in the conflict out of fear that it would lead to war with the United States. Yet Beijing felt it needed to do something to demonstrate support for Pakistan and therefore created the "crisis" over Sikkim. China never intended to enter the war. W. F. Griffith, "Sino-Soviet Relations, 1964–65," *China Quarterly,* no. 25 (January–March 1966): 3–143. Brines's account, published in 1968, is based on Griffith's analysis. While it might be possible to reconcile Griffith's and Choudhury's account through the calculated ambiguity of Chinese phraseology, such an approach does not seem justifiable to me in this case. Pending further declassification of Chinese and/or Pakistani archives, I believe we must accept Choudhury's account as the most authoritative.

48. Brines, *Indo-Pakistan Conflict,* 379.

49. Syed, *China and Pakistan*, 109, 127, 247.

50. Ibid., 121; Vertzberger, *Enduring Entente*, 21–22.

51. Burke, *Pakistan's Foreign Policy*, 361–64; Syed, *China and Pakistan*, 125–26; Choudhury, *India, Pakistan, Bangladesh*, 192–93.

52. R. Rama Rao, "Pakistan Re-Arms," *India Quarterly* (April–June 1971): 140–48.

53. Barnds, "China's Relations with Pakistan," 479. The absence of Red Guards in the Islamabad embassy was conveyed to me by Zhang Wenjin in an interview in May 1990.

54. The authoritative study of the Karakoram Highway is Mahnaz Z. Ispahani, *Roads and Rivals: The Political Uses of Access in the Borderlands of Asia* (Ithaca: Cornell University Press, 1989), 145–213.

55. *Foreign Affairs Record* 15, no. 7 (July 1969): 142.

56. The most authoritative study of Indian and Pakistan decision making in the 1971 war is Richard Sisson and Leo E. Rose, *War and Secession: Pakistan, India and the Creation of Bangladesh* (Berkeley: University of California Press, 1990).

57. Choudhury, *India, Pakistan, Bangladesh*, 211.

58. "Bangladesh and India's Security," *Foreign News and Features*, April 3, 1971, in K. Subrahmanyam, *Bangladesh and Indian Security* (Dehra Dun: Palit and Dutt, 1972), 39–41.

59. Sisson and Rose, *War and Secession*, 249–50.

60. Mehrunnisa Ali, "China's Diplomacy during the Indo-Pakistan War, 1971," *Pakistan Horizon* (Karachi) (1972): 53–62.

61. Sultan M. Khan, *Memories and Reflections of a Pakistani Diplomat* (London: Centre for Pakistan Studies, 1997), 304–7. Khan was Pakistan's "additional foreign secretary" at the time and participated in the special mission to Beijing in April 1971. See also Choudhury, *India, Pakistan, Bangladesh*, 21.

62. Syed, *China and Pakistan*, 149.

63. Choudhury, *India, Pakistan, Bangladesh*, 211.

64. T. J. S. George, "Peking's Pre-War Message to Pakistan," *Far Eastern Economic Review*, February 5, 1972, 8.

65. Sisson and Rose, *War and Secession*, 250–51.

66. Khan, *Memories*, 304–7.

67. Mizanur Rahman, *Emergence of a New Nation in a Multi-Polar World* (Seattle: University of Washington Press, 1978), 97–102. The chapter dealing with China in Rahman's insightful book is entitled, for instance, "China: On the Horns of a Dilemma—To Help an Ally or Support a People's War?"

68. Sisson and Rose, *War and Secession*, 250–51; Choudhury, *India, Pakistan, Bangladesh*, 213.

69. "Pakistan Delegation in China," *Peking Review*, November 12, 1971, 5, 23.

70. Mira Sinha, "A Comparison and Assessment of China's Attitudes and Comments

in 1965 and 1971," and S. K. Gosh, "Chinese Reactions to Bangla Desh Developments," both prepared for a July 1971 seminar held under the auspices of the Indian Council of World Affairs, in K. Subrahmanyam, *Bangla Desh and India's Security*, 113–28, 128–34.

71. Dennis Kux, *India and the United States: Estranged Democracies, 1941–1991* (Washington, D.C.: National Defense University Press, 1993), 303.

72. Sisson and Rose, *War and Secession*, 251–52. For the contrary view, see Choudhury, *India, Pakistan, Bangladesh*, 212–13, 217 n. 39; see also Ali, "China's Diplomacy during the Indo-Pakistan War," 55.

73. "Government of 'Bangla Desh'—A 'Manchukuo' and Quisling Government," Huang Hua to UN Security Council, December 6, 1971, in *Peking Review*, December 17, 1971, 15–16.

74. "The Chinese Strategy toward the Subcontinent," September 4, 1971, in Subrahmanyam, *Bangladesh and India's Security*, 167–70.

75. Syed, *China and Pakistan*, 150.

76. Henry A. Kissinger, *White House Years* (Boston: Little, Brown, 1979), 906.

77. Among the analysts that make this point are Rahman, *Emergence of a New Nation*, 106; and John F. Copper, "China's Policy toward Bangladesh," *China Report* (May–June 1973): 11–17.

78. Chiao Kuan-hua, "Condemning Soviet-Supported Indian Aggression against Pakistan," *Peking Review*, December 17, 1971, 11–12.

8 / MANAGING THE CONTRADICTION

1. Regarding this shift in China's orientation and its impact on policy toward India, see John W. Garver, "The Indian Factor in Recent Sino-Soviet Relations," *China Quarterly*, no. 125 (summer 1991): 55–85.

2. Swaran Singh, "Vajpayee's China Policy," *Pioneer* (New Delhi), July 14, 1999, 10.

3. In *Foreign Broadcast Information Service, Daily Report China* (hereafter *FBIS, DRC*), June 9, 1981, F1–2.

4. *FBIS, DRC*, June 2, 1981, F2.

5. Ibid., June 3, 1981, F3–4; emphasis added.

6. Ibid., June 29, 1981, F2–3.

7. Ibid., June 3, 1981, F3–4.

8. Ibid., June 2, 1981, F2.

9. Garver, "Indian Factor in Recent Sino-Soviet Relations," 81.

10. *FBIS, DRC*, December 16, 1991, 20–22; emphasis added.

11. Ibid., December 16, 1991, 18–20.

12. *Foreign Affairs Record* 35, no. 1 (January 1989): 18–19.

13. *Ministry of Defence, Government of India, Annual Report*, 1993–94, 2, 3; 1996–97, 2, 6.

14. Seema Guha, "Ghauri Plays Spoil-Sport in Sino-Indian Relationship," *Times of India*, April 9, 1998.

15. Interview with Ambassador Ranganathan, New Delhi, February 25, 1999. Ranganathan served in Beijing from 1987 to 1991. Also "Chinese Hand Seen in Ghaui Development," *Hindu*, April 7, 1998.

16. *Indian Recorder* (New Delhi) 5, no. 32 (August 6–12, 1998): 3833–34.

17. *Foreign Broadcast Information Service, Middle East, South Asia*, February 11, 1993.

18. "Missile Issue Dominates Sino-Indian Talks," *Hindu* (Madras), April 28, 1998, 38.

19. "Vajpayee Expresses Concern over Sino-Pak Nexus," *Hindu*, May 14, 1998.

20. Ramesh Chandran, "U.S. Told of Chinese Aid to Pakistan," *Times of India*, May 4, 1998.

21. John Burns, "India's New Defense Chief Sees Chinese Military Threat," *New York Times*, May 5, 1998, A6.

22. *New York Times*, May 13, 1998, A12.

23. See Bei Mouyi, "Song 50 niandai de Zhong Yin guanxi kan Zhou Enlai zongli dui jianli zhanhou guoji zhengzhi xin zhixu de lishixing gongxian" (Viewing Premier Zhou Enlai's historic contributions to the establishment of a postwar new international political order from the standpoint of Sino-Indian relations in the 1950s), *Waijiao xueyuan xuebao* (Diplomatic college journal) 1, no. 15 (1990): 6–12.

24. *Asian Recorder* (New Delhi), February 12–18, 1989, 20431–24331; see also *Renmin ribao*, December 22, 1988, 1.

25. The communiqué is in *FBIS, DRC*, December 23, 1988, 111–12.

26. *FBIS, DRC*, December 16, 1991, 20–22.

27. Report of February 21, 1979, to Lok Sabha, in *Keesings Contemporary Archive* 27, no. 43 (1981): 31153.

28. Naveed Ahmad, "Sino-Pakistan Relations, 1971–1981," *Pakistan Horizon* (Karachi) 34, no. 3 (1981): 73.

29. *Times of India* (New Delhi), March 22, 1990.

30. "Forty Years of Indian-Chinese Relationship" (on the fortieth anniversary of the establishment of Indian-Chinese diplomatic relations), *Foreign Affairs Reports* 29, no. 4 (April 1990): 52.

31. *Renmin ribao*, May 5, 1990, 1; Xinhua (Islamabad), May 3, 1990.

32. *Arms Control Record, A Chronicle of Treaties, Negotiation, Proposals, Weapons, and Policy* (Cambridge, Mass.: Institute for Defense and Disarmament Studies, 1993), 454.3.190.

33. *Hindu*, January 2, 1997.

34. *Renmin ribao*, July 30, 1983, 6.

35. *Frontier Post* (Rawalpindi), November 17, 1989.

36. *Pakistan Times*, November 15, 1989.

37. "Gujral Talks about Aspects of Kashmir Conflict" (interview with Indian minister of external affairs I. K. Gujral), *Frontier Post,* June 9, 1990, 1, 3.

38. *Asian Recorder,* January 29–February 4, 1990, 20987; and March 26–April 1, 1990, 21069–70.

39. *FBIS, DRC,* February 22, 1990, 11; emphasis added.

40. Ibid., February 15, 1990, 6. Qian Qichen's comments to Akhund were similar but less elaborate than Li's. So too were MFA statements on February 8, April 4, and April 19.

41. Xinhua (Islamabad), May 3, 1990.

42. John F. Copper, "China's Foreign Aid Program: An Analysis and Update," *China's Economy Looks toward the Year 2000,* vol. 2, "Economic Openness in Modernizing China," selected papers, Joint Economic Committee, U.S. Congress, May 21, 1986, 506–7.

43. John F. Copper, "China's Military Assistance," in *Communist Nation's Military Assistance,* ed. John F. Copper and Daniel S. Papp (Boulder: Westview Press, 1983), 108–9.

44. *Stockholm International Peace Research Institute (SIPRI) Yearbook,* 1989, 259.

45. *Asian Recorder,* December 24–31, 1989, 20934; Altaf A. Shaikh, "China—A Friend Indeed," *Nation* (Lahore), November 24, 1989; *India Express,* February 4, 1990; Aabha Dixit, "Enduring Sino-Pak Relations: The Military Dimension," *Strategic Analysis* 12, no. 9 (December 1989): 981–90.

46. *SIPRI Yearbook, 1993: World Armaments and Disarmament* (London: Oxford University Press, 1993), 481.

47. *SIPRI Yearbook, 1994,* 535–36.

48. Ibid., *1996,* 514–15; *1994,* 535–36.

49. *Frontier Post,* June 10, 1990, 1.

50. *SIPRI Yearbook, 1998,* 294, 300.

51. Barbara L. LePoer, *Pakistan-U.S. Relations,* CRS Issue Brief, August 3, 1998, IB 94041, 6.

52. Man Mohan, "China Helps Pak Get over F-16 Setback," *Hindustan Times* (New Delhi), June 27, 1995; "China, Pak, to Collaborate on Fighter Aircraft," *Pioneer,* June 16, 1995.

53. *Frontier Post,* May 1, 1990.

54. *SIPRI Yearbook, 1998,* 350.

55. *Jane's Fighting Ships, 1997–98,* 485–89.

56. Douglas Waller, "The Secret Missile Deal," *Time,* June 30, 1997, 29; Robert Greenberger and Mat Forney, "China-Pakistan Missile Pact Shows Calculated Strategy," *Wall Street Journal,* December 15, 1998, A14; "India-Pakistan Nuclear and Missile Proliferation: Background, Status and Issues for U.S. Policy," December 16, 1996, FAND, Library of Congress, 97-23F.

57. *Frontier Post,* February 7, 1990.

58. *Renmin ribao* coverage of Kargil developments is available at http://www. peoplesdaily.com. Jiang Zemin's comments were carried on June 30. Li Peng's are on June 12 and Zhu Rongji's on June 29. Relevant Indian coverage from the *Times of India* for June 15 and 30 is available at http://www.timesofindia.com.

59. Sadanand Dhume, "On Higher Ground," *Far Eastern Economic Review* (hereafter *FEER*), July 8, 1999, 10–11.

60. Foreign Ministry statements are in *Beijing Review*, June 14, 1999, 15; July 5, 1999, 15; July 19, 1999, 11; and August 2, 1999, 11.

61. Li Bian, "Settlement of the India-Pakistan Conflict Calls for Dialogue," *Beijing Review*, July 19, 1999, 9.

62. Wang Hongwei, "Yindu dui Hua zhengce de diaozheng yu wofang duice de jianyi" (Adjustments in India's policy toward China and proposals regarding China's response), *Ya Tai ziliao* (Materials on Asia and the Pacific), no. 2 (March 3, 1989): 1–18.

63. Fan Mingxing, "Qian tan Yindu de dui Hua zhanlüe" (India's strategy toward China), MS, n.d. (but apparently written in 1989).

64. "Operational Scenario Alpha: The Run Up to Conflict," *Indian Defense Review* (July 1992): 18–22.

9 / BURMA

1. Sun Yifu, *The Silk Road on Land and Sea* (Beijing: China Pictorial Publishing Company, 1989), 60–62.

2. C. P. Fitzgerald, *The Southern Expansion of the Chinese People: Southern Fields and Southern Oceans* (Canberra: Australian National University Press, 1972), 60–66.

3. Maung Htin Aung, *A History of Burma* (New York: Columbia University Press, 1967), 67–81, 149–50.

4. For an account of Qian Long's campaigns and for an account of the evolution of the China-Burma tributary relation, including a full translation of an 1875 letter by Burma's king to China's emperor, see Robert K. Douglas, "China and Burmah," *Asiatic Quarterly Review* (London), no. 1 (January–April 1886): 141–64.

5. Aung, *History of Burma*, 181.

6. John K. Fairbank and S. Y. Teng, *Ch'ing Administration: Three Studies* (Cambridge: Harvard University Press, 1960), 194–97.

7. Frank N. Trager, *Burma, From Kingdom to Republic: A Historical and Political Analysis* (London: Pall Mall, 1966), 239; Aung, *History of Burma*, 247–56.

8. Sun Yat-sen, *San Min Chu I: The Three Principles of the People*, trans. Frank W. Price (Taipei: China Cultural Service, 1953), 9.

9. "Dian Mian gonglu zai kangri zhanzheng zhong de lishi zuoyong" (Historic role of the Burma road in the anti-Japanese war), *Zhonggong dangshi wengao niankan*,

1986 (Almanac of materials from the Chinese Communist Party archives) (Beijing: Zhonggong dangshi ziliao chubanshe, 1988), 384–50.

10. Bradford A. Lee, *Britain and the Sino-Japanese War, 1937–1939: A Study in the Dilemmas of British Decline* (Stanford, Calif.: Stanford University Press, 1973).

11. Hata Ikuhiko, "The Army's Move into Northern Indochina," in *The Fateful Choice: Japan's Advance into Southeast Asia, 1939–1941* (New York: Columbia University Press, 1980), 155–208.

12. Military History Section, Headquarters, Army Forces Far East, *Burma Operations Record: Outline of Burma Area Line of Communications,* Japanese Monograph, no. 133.

13. Barbara W. Tuchman, *Stilwell and the American Experience in China, 1911–1945* (New York: Macmillan, 1971); Michael Schaller, *The United States Crusade in China, 1938–1945* (New York: Columbia University Press, 1979).

14. F. F. Liu, *A Military History of Modern China, 1924–1949* (Princeton, N.J.: Princeton University Press, 1956), 209–16; Charles F. Romanus, Riley Sunderland, *China-Burma-India Theater: Time Runs Out in CBI, United States Army in World War II,* Office of the Chief of Military History, U.S. Army, Washington, D.C., 1959; Field Marshal Viscount Slim, *Defeat into Victory* (London: Macmillan, 1956), 275–77.

15. B. Pakem, *India Burma Relations* (New Delhi: Omsons Publishing, 1992), 31–33.

16. Ibid., 195.

17. Unless otherwise indicated, this discussion of Burmese neutralism in the 1950s and 1960s is drawn from Trager, *Burma;* and John H. Badgley, "Burma and China: Policy of a Small Neighbor," *Policies toward China: Views from Six Continents* (New York: McGraw-Hill, 1965), 203–38.

18. Alexander Eckstein, *Communist China's Economic Growth and Foreign Trade* (New York: McGraw-Hill, 1966), 500.

19. Regarding the Chinese incursions, see *Zhongguo 9 ci da fabing* (Nine cases of China's dispatch of troops) (Chengdu: Sichuan wenyi chubanshe, 1992), 138–41.

20. Daphne Whitam, "The Sino-Burmese Boundary Treaty," *Pacific Affairs* 34, no. 2 (summer 1961): 174–83.

21. Pakem, *India Burma Relations,* 25–36, 187, 193–94; Uma Shankar Singh, *Burma and India, 1948–1962* (New Delhi: Oxford and IBH Publishing Co., 1979), 52–61.

22. J. N. Dixit, *Across Borders: Fifty Years of India's Foreign Policy* (New Delhi: Thomson Press, 1998), 62.

23. Bertil Lintner, *The Rise and Fall of the Communist Party of Burma (CPB)* (Ithaca: Cornell University Press, 1990), 22–57.

24. Peter Van Ness, *Revolution and Chinese Foreign Policy: Peking's Support for Wars of National Liberation* (Berkeley: University of California Press, 1971), 97–98.

25. Tin Maung Haung Than, "Burma's National Security and Defense Posture," *Contemporary Southeast Asia* 11, no. 1 (June 1989): 40–60.

26. Lintner, *Rise and Fall of the CPB*, 25.

27. Michael Fredholm, *Burma: Ethnicity and Insurgency* (Westport, Conn.: Praeger, 1973), 208–29.

28. P. Stobdan, "China's Forray's into Burma—Implications for India," *Strategic Analysis* 16, no. 1 (April 1993): 21–37.

29. *China-Myanmar Goodwill Visits of Great Historic Significance* (Yangon: Ministry of Communications, Posts, and Telegraphs, November 1991), 160, 175, 176.

30. Balados Ghoshal, "Trends in China-Burma Relations," *China Report* 30, no. 2 (1994): 201; Bertil Lintner, "Different Strokes," *Far Eastern Economic Review* (hereafter *FEER*), February 23, 1989, 12–13; David I. Steinberg, "Myanmar as Nexus: Sino-Indian Rivalries on the Frontier," *Terrorism* 16 (1993): 1–8; Donald M. Seekins, "Burma-China Relations: Playing with Fire," *Asian Survey* 37, no. 6 (June 1997): 525–39.

31. *Web of Conspiracy Complicated Stories of Treacherous Machinations and Intrigue of BCP UG, DAB, and Some NLD Leaders to Seize State Power* (Yangon: Ministry of Information, Government of Union of Myanmar, June 1991). This pamphlet offers an itemized "disbursement account for the Indian Counselor's payment for January 1989" (unnumbered p. 86). The monetary units used in the ledger are not identified. I've assumed they refer to Burmese kyats. If, however, they refer to Indian rupees, the equivalent in U.S. dollars at the 1989 market exchange rate would be $3,904.

32. Regarding the end of the CPB insurgency, see "Infirm Revolutionaries," *FEER*, November 15, 1990, 8; Bertil Lintner, "Spiking the Guns," *FEER*, May 23, 1991, 12–13; Bertil Lintner, "Triangular Ties," *FEER*, March 28, 1991, 22–26; Seekins, "Playing with Fire," 528.

33. Seekins, "Playing with Fire," 534–35; Andrew Selth, "The Burmese Armed Forces: Toward the 21st Century" (paper prepared for conference on "Toward a 21st Century Burma," Washington, D.C., May 28, 1998).

34. Steinberg, "Myanmar Nexus," 3–4.

35. Pan Qi, "Opening to the Southwest: An Expert Opinion," *Beijing Review*, September 2, 1985, 22–23.

36. Mya Maung, "On the Road to Mandalay: A Case Study of the Sinonization of Upper Burma," *Asian Survey* 34, no. 5 (May 1994): 447–59; see also Seekins, "Playing with Fire."

37. Author's discussions in Yangon, Myanmar, March 1999, with U.S. and Indian officials charged with monitoring China's "Irrawaddy corridor"–related activities.

38. J. N. Dixit, *My South Block Years: Memoirs of a Foreign Secretary* (New Delhi: UBS Publishers, 1996), 167–71.

39. J. Mohan Malik, "Myanmar's Role in Regional Security: Pawn or Pivot?" *Contemporary Southeast Asia* (Singapore) 19, no. 1 (June 1997): 52–73.

40. Sheldon W. Simon, "Burma's International Environment: The ASEAN Relationship" (paper prepared for conference on "Toward a 21st Century Burma,"

May 28, 1998). Burma first attended an ASEAN summit in December 1995. Six months later it became an "observer" in ASEAN and joined the ASEAN Regional Forum.

41. William Ashton, "Burma Receives Advice from Its Silent Suitors in Singapore," *Asia* 10, no. 3 (1998): 32; cited in *Jane's Intelligence Review*, March 1, 1998, at http://web.lexis-nexis.com.

42. I was invited to review Chinese policies for a U.S. State Department conference on Burma in May 1998. I began my presentation with a review of the long history of strategic use of Burma by various powers and asserted that China's Burma hands were certainly familiar with this history. This drew a heated rebuttal from one of the U.S. diplomatic corps' top-ranking China hands (then retired) to the effect that whatever China was doing in Burma was inspired entirely and solely by the desire to make money.

43. Conference on Regional Development in India and China, November 19–20, 1998, *India's North East: Exploring New Possibilities in Trade and Communication with Special Reference to China,* report prepared by Udayon Misra and Jayanta K. Gogoi, Dibrugarh University, Dibrugarh, India.

44. Malik, "Myanmar's Role," 68–69.

10 / THE INDIAN OCEAN IN SINO-INDIAN RELATIONS

1. James Heyman, Eurostat, personal communication with author, February 2, 1997.

2. Devendra Kaushik, *Perspectives on Security in the Indian Ocean Region* (New Delhi: Allied Publishers, 1987), 110–19.

3. C. S. R. Murthy, *India's Diplomacy at the United Nations: Problems and Perspectives* (New Delhi: Lancers, 1993), 79–105.

4. Jerrold F. Elkin and Andrew Ritezel, "New Delhi's Indian Ocean Policy," *Naval War College Review* (August 1987): 50–63; Onkar Marwah, "India's Strategic Perspectives on the Indian Ocean," *The Indian Ocean: Perspectives on a Strategic Area* (Durham: Duke University Press, 1985), 301–17; Gary L. Sojka, "The Mission of the Indian Navy," *Naval War College Review* 36, no. 1 (January–February 1983): 2–15.

5. Rahul Roy-Choudhury, *Sea Power and Indian Security* (London: Brasseys, 1995), 175–76.

6. Min Zhu, "Yindu de junli he zhanlüe mubiao" (India's military strength and strategic objectives), *Shijie zhishi* (World knowledge), no. 9 (May 1, 1989): 11–12.

7. Jung-pang Lo, "The Emergence of China as a Sea Power during the Late Song and Early Yuan Periods," *Far Eastern Quarterly* 14 (1954–55): 489–503; Auguste Toussaint, *History of the Indian Ocean* (Chicago: University of Chicago Press, 1966), originally published in French in 1961.

8. Louise Levathes, *When China Ruled the Seas* (New York: Simon and Schuster, 1994); Philip Snow, *The Star Raft: China's Encounter with Africa* (Ithaca: Cornell University Press, 1988).

9. Tatsuro Yamamoto, "International Relations between China and the Countries along the Ganga in the Early Ming Period," *Indian Historical Review* 4, no. 11 (July 1977): 13–19.

10. Tousssaint, *History of the Indian Ocean*, 79.

11. Regarding PRC naval development, see David Muller, *China's Emergence as a Maritime Power* (Boulder: Westview Press, 1983); Bruce Swanson, *Eighth Voyage of the Dragon: A History of China's Quest for Seapower* (Annapolis, Md.: Naval Institute Press, 1982).

12. Wen-Chung Liao, *China's Blue Water Strategy in the 21st Century: From the First Island Chain toward the Second Island Chain* (Occasional Papers Series, Chinese Council of Advanced Policy Studies, Taipei, Taiwan, September 1995).

13. Liao, *China's Blue Water Strategy;* see also Alexander Chien-cheng Huang, "The Chinese Navy's Offshore Active Defense Strategy," *Naval War College Review* 47, no. 3 (summer 1994): 7–23.

14. Christopher D. Yong, *People's War at Sea: Chinese Naval Power in the Twenty-First Century,* Center for Naval Analyses, CRM 95-214, March 1996.

15. *Report of the Select Committee on U.S. National Security and Military/Commercial Concerns with the People's Republic of China, Submitted by Mr. Cox of California, Chairman,* 105th Congress, 2d sess., declassified May 25, 1999.

16. Richard D. Fisher, *How America's Friends Are Building China's Military Power,* Heritage Foundation Backgrounder no. 1146, November 5, 1997; Gary Klintworth, "Expanded Horizons," *Free China Review* (October 1998): 50–53.

17. Roy-Choudhury, *Sea Power and Indian Security*, 105–6.

18. Ken Gause, *India Profile* (Alexandria, Va.: Project Asia, Center for Naval Analyses, 1999).

19. Regarding the 1985 fleet visit, see *Liaowang* (Outlook), no. 11, March 17, 1986, 26–27; see also *Foreign Broadcast Information Service, Daily Report, China* (hereafter *FBIS, DRC*), December 9, 1985, f1.

20. Chintamani Mahapatra, "Chinese Navy: Development and Diplomacy," *Strategic Analysis* 12, no. 8 (November 1988): 865–78.

21. Roy-Choudhury, *Sea Power and Indian Security*, 103.

22. Xinhua, *FBIS, DRC,* March 18, 1997.

23. Rear Admirals (Ret.) Eric McVadon of the United States Navy and Sumihiko Kamura of the Japanese Maritime Self-Defense Force helped me understand the intricacies of the naval balance in the Indian Ocean Region.

24. Gause, *India Profile.*

25. In March 1999 I reviewed case-by-case reports of Chinese-involved projects with officials in the United States and Indian missions in Yangon, Myanmar. These officials had professional responsibility for following such activity, traveled widely in-country, and had good contacts with the Burmese military. Officials in both missions

were not alarmed by Chinese activities, discounting a number of press reports. The views of the two missions generally converged.

26. Regarding the topography of Hainggyi, see William Ashton, "Chinese Bases in Burma—Fact or Fiction?" *Jane's Intelligence Review* 7, no. 2 (February 1, 1995): 84–87.

27. "Pacific Outpost," *Far Eastern Economic Review* (hereafter cited as *FEER*), April 30, 1998, 26–27.

28. *Jane's Fighting Ships, 1998–99*, 79–84.

29. *FEER*, reported by Agency France Press, January 22, 1997, in *FBIS, DRC*, January 22, 1997, at http://wnc.fedworld.gov.

30. Rahul Beki, "China's Modernization Is a 'Great Concern' for India," *Jane's Defense Weekly*, October 14, 1998, at http://web.lexis-nexis.com.

31. J. N. Dixit, *Liberation and Beyond: Indo-Bangladesh Relations* (New Delhi: Konark, 1999), 294–97.

32. R. Chakrabarti, "China and Bangladesh," *China Report* 30, no. 2 (1994): 149–59.

33. Cited in Mizanur Rahman, *Emergence of a New Nation in a Multi-Polar World* (Seattle: University of Washington Press, 1978), 97–102.

34. Suchita Ghosh, *China-Bangladesh-India Triangle Today: Towards a Solution?* (New Delhi: Sterling Publishers, 1995), 81–82.

35. *Jane's Fighting Ships, 1998–99*, 41–46.

36. *Stockholm International Peace Research Institute (SIPRI) Yearbook, 1984*, 232; *SIPRI Yearbook, 1986*, 324.

37. Ghosh, *China-Bangladesh-India Triangle Today*, 16.

38. Speech by the prime minister of India, October 6, 1982, in *India-Bangladesh Relations, 1971–1993: Documents*, vols. 1–2, ed. Autar Singh Bhasin (New Delhi: Siba Exim Private Ltd., 1996), 196–98.

39. Stanley A. Kochanek, "Bangladesh in 1996: The 25th Year of Independence," *Asian Survey* 37, no. 2 (February 1997): 136–42.

40. Xinhua, September 13, 1996, October 9, 1996, November 8, 1996, and November 2, 1997, in *FBIS, DRC*, at http://wnc.fedworld.gov.

41. Dixit, *Liberation and Beyond*, 270–83.

42. Dhirendra Mohan Prasad, *Ceylon's Foreign Policy under the Bandaranaikes (1956–65): A Political Analysis* (New Delhi: S. Chand, 1973), 304–88. The following account draws heavily on Prasad.

43. Prasad, *Ceylon's Foreign Policy*, 368–79.

44. V. Suryanarayan, "Sri Lanka's Policy towards China: Legacy of the Past and Prospects for the Future," *China Report* 30, no. 2 (1994): 203–14.

45. Politicus, "The April Revolt in Ceylon," *Asian Survey* 12, no. 3 (March 1972): 259–74.

46. Jaswant Singh lists this as one instance of Indian use of military force in the form of bilateral peacekeeping (*Defending India*, 143).

47. A. Jeyaratuam Wilson, "Ceylon: A Time of Troubles," *Asian Survey* 12, no. 2 (February 1972): 109–15.

48. Regarding Indian apprehensions, see Sreedhar, "An Anatomy of the Trincomalee Deal," *Strategic Analysis* (New Delhi) 8, no. 3 (June 1984): 234–42. Regarding Indian–Sri Lankan relations more generally, see Ravi Kant Dubey, *Indo–Sri Lankan Relations* (New Delhi: Deep and Deep, 1989); Shelton V. Kodikara, *Foreign Policy of Sri Lanka: A Third World Perspective* (Delhi: Chanakya Publishers, 1982).

49. Vijay Kumar, *India and Sri Lanka–China Relation (1948–84)* (New Delhi: Uppal Publishing House, 1986), 160.

50. *China's Foreign Relations: A Chronology of Events (1949–1988)* (Beijing: Foreign Languages Press, 1989), 241–42.

51. *SIPRI Yearbook, 1981* 239. *SIPRI Yearbook, 1987*, 263–64.

52. *Renmin ribao,* July 4, 1981; see also Xinhua (Colombo), June 30, 1981.

53. Kumar, *India and Sri Lanka–China Relation,* 166; Kodikara, *Foreign Policy of Sri Lanka,* 140–41.

54. Rohan Ganaratna, *Indian Intervention in Sri Lanka: The Role of India's Intelligence Agencies* (Colombo: South Asian Network on Conflict Research, 1993), 1–12; see also Shekhar Gupta, "Ominous Presence in Tamil Nadu," *India Today,* March 31, 1984.

55. See *Hindu* (Madras), August 3, 1983; *Hindustan Times* (New Delhi), August 2, 1983. For an analysis of the episode and the consequent doctrine, see Bhabani Sen Gupta, "The Indian Doctrine," *India Today,* August 31, 1983.

56. *FBIS, DRC,* May 23, 1984, F5.

57. Ibid., January 18, 1985, F1–2.

58. *Renmin ribao,* March 14, 1986, 6.

59. *FEER,* April 17, 1986; see also Subramanyam Swamy, "Superpower Game in Sri Lanka," *Outlook,* June 16–30, 1986, 48. One bit of contrary evidence is that in 1987 China apparently agreed to sell more Y-12 transport planes to Sri Lanka (*SIPRI Yearbook, 1988,* 243).

60. Suryanarayan, "Sri Lankan Policy towards China," 212.

61. *Renmin ribao* carried articles on Indo–Sri Lankan developments on May 6; June 3, 4, 5, 6, 15; and July 31, 1987.

62. *FBIS, DRC,* June 23, 1987, F3.

63. Zhen Ru, "Si Yin hexieyi yi qi yingxiang" (The Sri Lankan–Indian peace agreement and its influence), *Nanya yu Dongnanya ziliao* (Materials on South and Southeast Asia), Chinese Academy of Social Sciences, no. 28 (1989): 87–96.

64. Ma Jiali, "Yin Si heping xieyi de qianqian houhou" (Circumstances surrounding the Indian-Sri Lankan peace agreement), *Nan Ya janjiu jikan* (Journal of South Asia research) (Chengdu) 3, no. 52 (September 30, 1988): 57–60.

65. The text of the agreement and letters is in Gunaratna, *Indian Intervention in Sri Lanka,* 489–93.

66. Achin Vanaik, "IPKF in Sri Lanka: For Whose Sake?" *Illustrated Weekly of India* (Bombay), December 6, 1988; see also Dilip Bobb, "High Stakes Gamble," *India Today,* December 15, 1987, 81–84.

67. This concern was first pointed out to me by a retired PLA general.

11 / NUCLEAR WEAPONS AND THE SINO-INDIAN RELATIONSHIP

1. Regarding China's confrontation with and reaction to U.S. nuclear might, see Gordon H. Chang, *Friends and Enemies: The United States, China, and the Soviet Union, 1948–1972* (Stanford, Calif.: Stanford University Press, 1990); John W. Lewis and Xue Litai, *China Builds the Bomb* (Stanford, Calif.: Stanford University Press, 1988). Regarding similar experiences with the Soviet Union, see John W. Garver, *Foreign Relations of the People's Republic of China* (Englewood Cliffs, N.J.: Prentice Hall, 1993), 308–10.

2. Paul H. B. Godwin, "Chinese Military Strategy Revisited: Local and Limited War," *The Annals of the American Academy of Political and Social Science* 519 (January 1992): 191–201, special issue on China's foreign relations.

3. R. K. Karanjia, *The Mind of Mr. Nehru* (London: George Allen and Unwin, 1960), 87.

4. Manilal Jagdish Desai, "India and Nuclear Weapons," *Disarmament and Arms Control,* no. 3 (Autumn 1965): 135–42.

5. *Disarmament: India's Initiatives* (New Delhi: External Publicity Division, Ministry of External Affairs, Government of India, 1988), 26–28.

6. *Survey of the China Mainland Press,* no. 3317, 24–25.

7. Regarding India's 1964–65 bomb debate, see A. C. C. Unni, "Indian Reactions to the Chinese Bomb," pts. 1–2, in *Parliamentary Studies,* no. 9 (January–February 1965): 19–22; no. 10 (March–April 1965): 12–21; "India and the Chinese Bomb," *Gandhi Marg* (New Delhi), no. 9 (January 1965): 1–12; R. K. Nehru, "The Challenge of the Chinese Bomb—I," *Indian Quarterly,* no. 21 (January 1965): 3–14; M. R. Masani, "The Challenge of the Chinese Bomb—II," *India Quarterly,* no. 21 (January 1965): 15–28; Raj Krishna, "India and the Bomb," *India Quarterly,* no. 21 (April–June 1965): 119–37.

8. Itty Abraham, *Making of the Indian Bomb: Science, Secrecy and the Post-Colonial State* (Hyderabad: Orient Longman, 1998), 125–29. Some American deliberations in reaction to these Indian probes are presented in *Foreign Relations of the United States, 1964–68,* vol. 11: *Arms Control and Disarmament* (Washington, D.C.: Government Printing Office, 1997).

9. Kripaasagar, "Indo-U.S. Talks on Nuclear Issue," *Foreign Broadcast Information Service, Near East Africa,* November 6, 1992, 56.

10. Desai, "India and Nuclear Weapons," 135–47.

11. Ibid., 142.

12. Surjit Mansingh, *India's Search for Power: Indira Gandhi's Foreign Policy, 1966–1982* (New Delhi: Sage Publications, 1984), 98.

13. Mansingh, *India's Search for Power*, 143; Abraham, *Making the Indian Bomb*, 133, 141–45.

14. This assumes, of course, that Nixon and Kissinger were wrong about Gandhi's having decided to attack West Pakistan. If we assume they were correct, India's actions may have been altered very substantially by its lack of a nuclear deterrent.

15. K. N. Ramachandran, "China and Nuclear Non-Proliferation Issue," *IDSA Journal* 13, no. 1 (July–September 1980): 94–105.

16. Hong Kong, Agency France Press, June 3, 1998.

17. Stated by Bhutto's press secretary, Khalid Hassan, in BBC Panorama Programme, June 16, 1990; cited in Sumita Kumar, "Pakistan's Nuclear Weapons Program," *Nuclear India*, ed. Jasjit Singh (New Delhi: Knowledge World, 1998), 173. An article in *Der Spiegel*, June 16, 1980, also drew on Khalid Hassan and an unnamed scientist to make the same point. The young scientist had been recruited to participate in the bomb project but declined because he feared the heavy economic consequences for the country. The *Der Spiegel* article is translated in Sreedhar, *Pakistan's Bomb: A Documentary Study* (New Delhi: ABC Publishing House, 1986), 115–27.

18. *Muslim*, March 31, 1988, cited in Kumar, "Pakistan's Nuclear Weapons Program," 175.

19. Joint communiqué, *Peking Review*, no. 5, February 4, 1972, 7–8.

20. "President Bhutto Visits China," *Peking Review*, no. 5, February 4, 1972, 5.

21. Deng's speech, Bhutto's speech, and the joint communiqué are in *Peking Review*, no. 20, May 17, 1974, 4–11.

22. Cited in *China Quarterly*, Quarterly Chronicle and Documentation, no. 59 (July–September 1974): 653–54.

23. "It's Not 'Good Neighborliness' but Aggression and Expansion," *Peking Review*, November 22, 1974, 16–18.

24. The report was obtained under a Freedom of Information Act request and conveyed by Kyodo news agency (*Asian Recorder*, September 17–23, 1995, 25081).

25. B. K. Kumar, "Nuclear Nexus between Peking and Islamabad: An Overview of Some Significant Developments," *Issues and Studies* (August 1985): 140–50. Kumar also discusses reports from Arab-language newspapers that China tested a Pakistani A-bomb in the early 1980s.

26. Cited in Kumar, "Pakistan's Nuclear Weapons Program," 173.

27. Zulfikar Ali Bhutto, *If I Am Assassinated* (New Delhi: Vikas Publishing House, 1979). The reference to the June 1976 agreement is on page 221 in the final chapter of Bhutto's testament. He develops his anti-nuclear coup conspiracy hypothesis on pages 107, 137–38, and 168–69.

28. *Nuclear Proliferation: The Situation in Pakistan and India*, Hearings before

Subcommittee on Energy, Nuclear Proliferation, and Federal Services of the Committee on Government Affairs, United States Senate, 96th Cong., 1st sess., May 1, 1979, 10, 14–15.

29. *Nuclear Proliferation in South Asia: Countering the Threat,* Staff Report to the Committee on Foreign Relations, United States Senate, August 1988, 3–5.

30. The Pakistani journalist Mohammed Beg reportedly learned this from a Pakistani official who had been personally involved in the test. Steve Weissman and Herbert Krosney, *The Islamic Bomb: The Nuclear Threat to Israel and the Middle East* (New York: Time Books, 1981), 218.

31. Judith Miller, "U.S. Is Holding Up Peking Atom Talks," *New York Times,* September 19, 1982, 11.

32. *Financial Times,* August 14, 1984; "Despite U.S. Pressure over Algeria, Europeans Won't Blacklist China," *Nucleonics Week,* May 23, 1991, 1.

33. Reuters, March 31, 1996, c-reuters@clari.net.

34. Gary Milhollin and Gerard White, "A New China Syndrome: China's Arms Bazaar," *Washington Post,* May 12, 1991, C1, C4.

35. *Washington Post,* November 4, 1986.

36. Rauf Siddiqu, "With China's Aid, Pakistan Has New Research Reactor in Pinstech," *Nucleonics Week,* August 9, 1990, 4.

37. *Foreign Broadcast Information Service, Daily Report China* (hereafter *FBIS, DRC*), December 31, 1991, 11–12.

38. *Arms Control Record,* 1995, 454.B.213.

39. Shirley A. Kan, *Chinese Proliferation of Weapons of Mass Destruction: Background and Analysis,* CRS Report for Congress, September 13, 1996, 96-767F, 29.

40. Testimony of R. James Woolsey, director of the Central Intelligence Agency, in *Proliferation Threats of the 1990s: Hearings before the Committee on Government Affairs, U.S. Senate,* 103d Cong., 1st sess., February 24, 1993, 19.

41. *Proliferation: Chinese Case Studies,* Hearings before the Subcommittee on International Security, Proliferation, and Federal Services of the Committee on Governmental Affairs, United States Senate, 105th Cong., 1st sess., April 10, 1997, 8, 12.

42. *Agreement for Nuclear Cooperation between the United States and China: Communication from the President of the United States,* February 3, 1998, Report Relating to the Approval and Implementation of the Agreement for Nuclear Cooperation between the United States and the PRC Pursuant to 42 U.S.C. 2153Cd., 9–10.

43. *Nuclear Proliferation in South Asia: Countering the Threat,* 5; Dilip Bobb and Ramindar Singh, "Pakistan's Nuclear Bombshell," *India Today,* March 31, 1987, 72–80; General Aslam Beg, *Pakistan,* December 15, 1993, cited in Kumar, "Pakistan's Nuclear Weapons Program," 181.

44. These disclosures came from army chief of staff General Aslam Beg. The principals in the January 1989 meeting were President Gulam Ishaq Khan and Prime

Minister Benazir Bhutto. Cited in Savita Pande, "Pakistan's Nuclear Strategy," in *Asian Strategy Review, 1993–94*, ed. Jasjit Singh (New Delhi: IDSA, 1994), 331, 336.

45. China's moves embracing nonproliferation are enumerated in *Communication from the President of the United States*, 10–11; see also "Prepared Statement of Mr. Einhorn," in *Proliferation: Chinese Case Studies*, 60–67.

46. The classic presentation of this case is John W. Lewis, Hua Di, and Xue Litai, "Beijing's Defence Establishment: Solving the Arms-Export Enigma," *International Security* 15, no. 4 (spring 1991): 87–109.

47. Dingli Shen, "China and Nuclear Proliferation: General Policy with Application to South Asia" (paper presented to Summer School on Security, Technology, and Arms Control in South Asia, Bhurban, Pakistan, May 20–30, 1993).

48. Weixing Hu, "China and Nuclear Nonproliferation," in *In the Dragon's Eyes: China Views the World and Sino-American Relations*, ed. Fei-ling Wang and Yong Deng (New York: Rowman and Littlefield, 1999), 119–40.

49. "India's New Defense Chief Sees Chinese Military Threat," *New York Times*, May 5, 1998, A6.

50. The text of the letter is in *New York Times*, May 13, 1998, A12.

51. Foreign Ministry News Briefing, *Beijing Review*, May 25–31, 1998, 7.

52. *Renmin ribao*, May 15, 1998, 1.

53. Ibid., May 15, 1992, 2.

54. Ibid., May 19, 1998, 1.

55. *FBIS, DRC*, July 28, 1998; http://wnc.fedworld.gov.

56. Author's interviews in Beijing, June–July 1998.

57. John Burns, "India's Line in the Sand: 'Minimum' Nuclear Deterrent against China," *International Herald Tribune*, July 8, 1998.

58. Lok Sabha Debates, May 27, 1998, sess. 2 (Budget).

59. Regarding Beijing's 1996 "nuclear coercion with Chinese characteristics," see John W. Garver, *Face Off: China, the United States, and the Democratization of Taiwan* (Seattle: University of Washington Press, 1997).

60. Bhabani Sen Gupta, *Nuclear Weapons? Policy Options for India* (New Delhi: Sage Publications, 1983), 42.

12 / NUCLEAR WEAPONS AND THE INTERNATIONAL STATUS OF CHINA AND INDIA

1. Itty Abraham, *The Making of the Indian Atomic Bomb: Science, Secrecy, and the Postcolonial State* (Hyderabad: Orient Longman, 1998), 147.

2. Nie Rongzhen, *Nie Rongzhen huiyilu* (Memoir of Nie Rongzhen) (Beijing: Jiefangjun chubanshe, 1984), 764–68.

3. "The Origins and Development of the Differences between the Leadership of

the CPSU and Ourselves," September 6, 1963, in *The Polemic on the General Line of the International Communist Movement* (Beijing: Foreign Languages Press, 1963), 55–104, 77.

4. *The Truth about How the Leaders of the CPSU Have Allied Themselves with India against China* (Beijing: Foreign Languages Press, 1963), 27.

5. Regarding this and other milestones in China's nuclear weapons program, see John W. Lewis and Xue Litai, *China Builds the Bomb* (Stanford, Calif.: Stanford University Press, 1988), 35–72.

6. Statement of the Chinese Government, in *Peking Review*, August 15, 1963, 3. For an analysis of China's reaction to the 1963 treaty, see Walter Clements, *The Arms Race and Sino-Soviet Relations* (Stanford, Calif.: Hoover Institution Press, 1968).

7. *Disarmament: India's Initiatives* (New Delhi: External Publicity Division, Ministry of External Affairs, 1988), i–iv.

8. Sri R. K. Banerjee's Statement at UN Conference of Committee on Disarmament, *Foreign Affairs Record* 19 (August 1973): 302–3.

9. K. N. Ramachandran, "China and Nuclear Non-proliferation Issue," *IDSA Journal* 13, no. 1 (July–September 1980): 94–105.

10. Ramachandran, "China and Nuclear Non-proliferation," 102.

11. C. S. R. Murty, *India's Diplomacy in the United Nations: Problems and Perspectives* (New Delhi: Lancers Books, 1993), 106–17.

12. Murty, *India's Diplomacy in the United Nations.*

13. *Nuclear Proliferation in South Asia: Containing the Threat*, Staff Report to the Committee on Foreign Relations, United States Senate, August 1988, 20–21.

14. David Albright and Mark Hibbs, "India's Silent Bomb," *Bulletin of Atomic Scientists* (September 1992): 27–31.

15. *Arms Control Record*, 1996, 608.A.1–6.

16. Arundhati Ghose, "Negotiating the CTBT: India's Security Concerns and Nuclear Disarmament," *Journal of International Affairs* (New York) 51, no. 1 (summer 1997): 239–61.

17. "China's National Statement on Security Assurances," *Beijing Review*, April 24–30, 1996, 20.

18. Brahma Chellaney, "Chinese N-Policy Shift May Pose a Threat to India," *Indian Express*, April 15, 1995.

19. United Nations web site, http://www.un.org.

20. Chellaney, "Chinese N-Policy Shift."

21. *Arms Control Record*, 1995, 602.A.1–6.

22. U.S. Department of State home page, January 23, 1999; Arms Control and Disarmament Agency, Non-Proliferation Treaty, Review and Extension Conference, Text of Treaty and Decisions of Conference, http://www.state.gov.

23. Sumit Ganguly, "India in 1996," *Asian Survey* 37, no. 2 (February 1997): 126–35.

24. *Strategic Survey 1996–97* (London: International Institute for Strategic Studies, 1997), 202–3. This near-test was confirmed to me by several analysts and former officials in New Delhi during my February 1999 visit.

25. Walter Anderson, "India in 1995: Year of the Long Campaign," *Asian Survey* 36, no. 2 (February 1996): 165–77.

26. Ghose, "Negotiating the CTBT," 255.

27. Barbara Crossette, "In Concession, China Is Ready to Ban A-Tests," *New York Times*, June 7, 1996, A1, A4.

28. Ghose, "Negotiating the CTBT," 255. This had also been part of China's "National Statement on Security Assurances."

29. Barbara Crossette, "India Warns It Won't Sign Test Ban Pact as It Stands," *New York Times*, June 21, 1996, 5.

30. U.S. Arms Control and Disarmament Agency, *Comprehensive Nuclear Test Ban Treaty* (Washington, D.C.: Government Printing Office, n.d. [1996?]).

31. Ghose, "Negotiating the CTBT," 257.

32. Crossette, "India Warns It Won't Sign."

33. Ghose, "Negotiating the CTBT," 258.

34. Statement by Indian Ambassador Arundhati Ghose, Conference on Disarmament, August 20, 1996, http://www.indianembassy.org.

35. Barbara LePoer, *India-U.S. Relations*, CRS brief, November 2, 1998, IB93097, 5–6.

36. Arundhati Ghose, interview with author, New Delhi, March 31, 1999.

37. Joint Secretary of Ministry of External Affairs, interview with author, New Delhi, March 30, 1999.

38. "Great Equalizer," *Times of India*, July 24, 1997.

39. "Joint U.S.-China Statement," October 29, 1997, released by the White House, http://www.state.gov

40. Author's discussions in New Delhi, February–March 1999.

13 / PROSPECTS FOR A QUALITATIVE CHANGE IN PRC-ROI RELATIONS

1. Steven I. Levine, "China and South Asia," *Strategic Analysis* 12, no. 10 (January 1989): 1107–26.

2. Leo E. Rose, "India and China: Forging a New Relationship in the Subcontinent," *Asia Pacific in the New Millennium: Geopolitics, Security and Foreign Policy*, ed. Shalendra D. Sharma (Berkeley: Institute of East Asian Studies, 1999).

3. *World Development Indicators, 1998*, CD-ROM, World Bank, Washington, D.C. I selected 1995 for comparison rather than 1998 because the data for the earlier year was much more complete. There is often a lag of several years with data from China

and India. I believe, however, that the trend between 1998 and 1995 is the same as that over the previous several years.

4. Qian Jiadong, "Upholding Panchsheel: Call of the Hour," in Jasjit Singh, *India-China and Panchsheel* (New Delhi: Sanchar Publishing House, 1996), 35–42.

5. Jasjit Singh, "Introduction," 5–11; and K. Subrahmanyam, "Panchsheel and the Twenty-first Century," 62–67, both in Singh, *India-China and Panchsheel*.

6. Beijing's three demands were abrogation of the 1954 security treaty with Taiwan, severance of U.S. diplomatic ties with Taiwan, and withdrawal of all U.S. military forces from Taiwan.

7. Jaswant Singh's *Defending India* (London: Macmillan, 1999) is probably the most prominent expression of this debate. Singh was minister of external affairs in the BJP government of 1998–99. His book traces the roots of Indian moralism in the nation's historical experience and philosophical traditions. For an overview of the Indian debate, see Sujit Dutta, "China's Emerging Power and Military Role: Implications for South Asia," in *In China's Shadow: Regional Perspectives on Chinese Foreign Policy and Military Development,* ed. Jonathan D. Pollack and Richard H. Yang, 91–114 (Santa Monica: RAND, 1998).

8. K. Sundarji, "External Security Environment: India's Threat Perception," in *India and Chinese Foreign Policy in Comparative Perspective,* ed. Surjit Mansingh, 89–107 (New Delhi: Radiant Publishers, 1998).

Index

CPSIA information can be obtained at www.ICGtesting.com
Printed in the USA
BVOW02s2046240716

456470BV00002B/8/P

9 780295 980744